DRAGON A[N]

Philip Short has been a foreign correspondent since 1967 and is well known for his radio and television broadcasts. He worked in Malawi and Uganda before becoming the BBC's man in Moscow from 1974 to 1976, and their first Peking correspondent from 1977 to 1981. He currently heads the BBC's Paris Bureau.

Philip Short

THE DRAGON AND THE BEAR

Inside China and Russia Today

First published in Abacus by
Sphere Books Ltd
30–32 Gray's Inn Road, London WC1X 8JL

Copyright © Philip Short 1982

First published in Great Britain by
Hodder & Stoughton Ltd, 1982

Printed and bound in Great Britain by
Cox & Wyman Ltd, Reading

To my friends,

Anatoly Scharansky (Chistopol Prison),
Vladimir Klebanov (Dnepropetrovsk
  Special Psychiatric Hospital)
and Ren Wanding (Peking Prison No 1)

and to Leonid Brezhnev and
Deng Xiaoping, who put them there,
in the hope that they will let them out.

Contents

Author's Note

Chinese names drive all who are unfamiliar with them to despair. Yet it is impossible to write about China and its politics without identifying the protagonists. The task is made more difficult by the existence of two separate systems for transliterating Chinese characters.

This book uses the *pinyin* system, which, since its adoption in 1979 as the official transcription within China, has gradually become accepted in the West as the standard form, displacing the older Wade-Giles method. Some names in *pinyin* may appear unfamiliar: Mao Tsetung becomes Mao Zedong and Chou En-lai, Zhou Enlai; but in most cases the spelling approximates better to the standard Chinese pronunciation. Only the place names Amoy, Canton, Inner Mongolia, Peking and Tibet, and the personal names of Chiang Kai-shek, the pianist Fou Tsong and Soong Chingling, the widow of China's first President, have been retained in the old form since the new spellings are so different as to be unrecognisable. Non-Chinese names, such as that of the Politburo member, Ulanfu, have also been left in the traditional form.

Pinyin uses three letters in the alphabet to represent Chinese sounds which have no precise English equivalent: *C* is pronounced roughly like *Ts*; *Q* like *Ch*; and *X* like *Sh* (*Hs* in the Wade-Giles system).

Vowels are also full of traps for the unwary: Deng (Xiaoping) rhymes with dung (as in manure); so do all other Chinese words ending in -eng.

Wang and Huang rhyme with song, but other words ending in -ang rhyme with sang.

Hua rhymes with car; Ye (Jianying) is pronounced like the American, yeah; (Wu) De like the French particle, de; and terminal -i rhymes with see (as in Li) or with sir (as in Chi). Further refinements are there many, but these basic rules should permit most names to be pronounced without serious error.

Acknowledgments

Many people, Chinese and Soviet as well as colleagues in the West, have helped to make this book what it is; the credit for whatever insights it offers is in large part theirs. To all of them go my thanks. But since not all can safely be named, I shall name none – except the two who bore the brunt of the actual writing: my wife, Chris, who transformed my drafts into legible typescript, and my ten-year-old son, Sengan, whose forebearance at two years of lost weekends, which should have been spent flying kites at the Ming tombs or climbing the Great Wall, was the price of its completion. This is their book, as well as mine.

Paris, February 18th, 1982

Illustrations

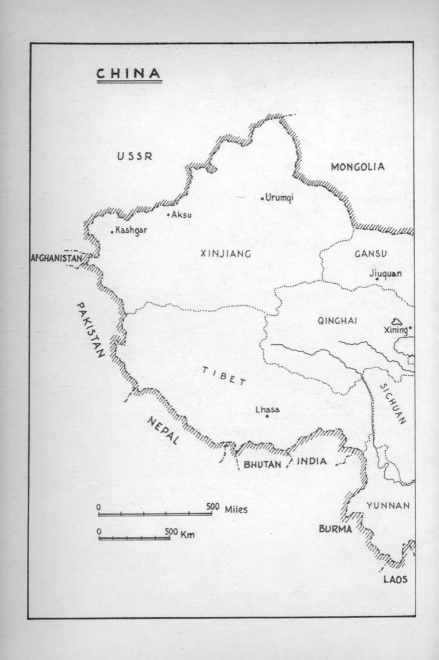

CHINA

USSR

MONGOLIA

Urumqi

Aksu

Kashgar

AFGHANISTAN

XINJIANG

GANSU

Jiuquan

PAKISTAN

QINGHAI

Xining

TIBET

SICHUAN

Lhasa

NEPAL

BHUTAN   INDIA

0   500 Miles

0   500 Km

YUNNAN

BURMA

LAOS

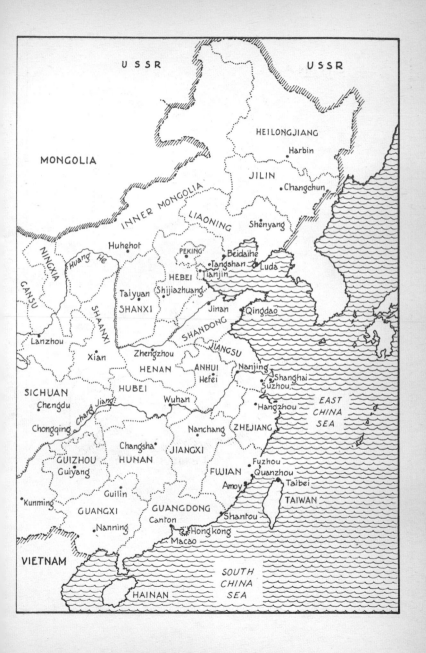

THE DRAGON AND THE BEAR

Introduction

In the centre of Peking, on the crimson gate that leads to the Forbidden City, the face of Mao stares sightlessly down across the vast, empty field of paving stones that is Tian An Men Square. Opposite stood thirty-foot-high portraits of Marx, Engels, Lenin and Stalin. Between these symbols of communism, one bleak January afternoon, a procession of ragged men and women, holding banners made from old newspapers stuck together and calling on China's leaders to help them, moved painfully along against a wind that froze the bones, like medieval Russian peasants following the cross. 'Oppose oppression, oppose hunger', they chanted – slogans which the communists themselves used against Chiang Kai-shek's nationalists in the 1940s. One man carried his crippled wife on his back. Several others had home-made crutches. These were the wretched of China – the human detritus of the Cultural Revolution and the Maoist political movements that preceded it, victims of persecution by petty officials – who had come to the capital to seek redress. Some were from Manchuria and the hard, bare villages of North China. An old man who said he had been a worker, one of tens of millions sent to the countryside in the near-famine years of the early 1960s, told me he had come on foot all the way from Jiangxi, 800 miles to the south. He took off his jacket, exposing his bare, bony chest, and weeping, tore at the material to show how it was rotten and came apart in his hands. He had no money, he said, and nothing to eat.

Behind them a huge traffic jam built up. But the police made no attempt to intervene. Nor did they try to move the demonstrators when they halted, a mile further on, at the gate of Zhongnanhai, the heavily-guarded walled park which contains the chief government offices and is to Peking what the Kremlin is to Moscow. Not till the following afternoon did the last of them disperse.

That demonstration took place in 1979. In Moscow I have watched many attempts at public protest. It is usually only a matter of seconds, and never more than a few minutes, before they are broken up and the participants arrested. Yet, in Moscow, there are no portraits of Stalin: they were all taken down by Khrushchev. In China, Mao's ideas are being overturned, but Mao himself is still praised for 'immortal contributions'. In the Soviet Union Stalin has been repudiated, but the basic structure erected by Stalinism is largely intact.

That is not to say that life has not changed for the Soviet people in the three decades since Stalin's death: it has – out of all recognition. A few months before Mao's successors decided that their own key priority was to raise living standards, a Chinese commentator fulminated: 'Privately owned cars move about the streets of Moscow, the capital of the Soviet Union where capitalism has already been restored, in an endless stream. The Soviet revisionists boast about it: our wealth, you see, is increasing from year to year and private car ownership is nothing remarkable!' To an American or a Briton, the daily business of living in a big Soviet city is colourless, inefficient, and shoddy to the point of despair. But to the average Muscovite, with his television set and washing machine, it is a lifestyle which in Stalin's time was only to be dreamt of (and which most Chinese can only dream of today). He looks on a man such as the Nobel Peace Prize winner, Dr Andrei Sakharov, as a traitor to his country, and the KGB, when he thinks of it at all, as a frightening but remote organisation which has no bearing on his own life. More than most Westerners, his concern is with material living standards and with the gap between his expectations and his ability to fulfil them.

But these advances have been achieved on the basis of a system of management and distribution so arthritic that were it not for agricultural produce from private plots and the activities of factory 'fixers', wheeling and dealing behind the planners' backs, it would by now have seized up altogether. Indeed, unless Brezhnev's successors introduce some of the reforms announced in 1965 but never put into effect, it may yet do so, producing economic stagnation by the mid- or late-1980s.

The system of political controls, although altered a good deal in appearance, is likewise in all its essentials unchanged. Political prisoners are no longer shot, but they are incarcerated in mental hospitals. The studied arbitrariness which was at the core of the Great Terror in the 1930s is used now against Jewish refuseniks, against Soviet artists and musicians who want to travel abroad, and against the dissident movement. The parameters of control have changed, but the instrument and the technique remain the same.

In the opening chapter of *The Gulag Archipelago* Alexander Solzhenitsyn describes how, under Stalin, the GPU and the NKVD (the forerunners of the KGB) would construct with theatrical precision the arrest or incrimination of a victim. Decades later, under Brezhnev, the telephone rang in my Moscow apartment one day in July 1975, and a voice at the other end identified itself in faultless English as John G---k, a schoolmaster who was trying to emigrate to Australia. He had called several times before from Karaganda, in Soviet Central Asia, where he taught. This time, however, he was in Moscow and wanted to know if we could meet. An hour later I found him waiting in front of the Obraztsov Puppet Theatre on the Moscow ring road, a stocky, well-built man with a briefcase. He had finally got his exit visa, he said, but before he left there were some books he wanted to give me. 'What kind of books?' I asked. After a long pause, he replied, 'Books with military secrets, for the British Embassy.' Ten yards away, across the wide pavement, a man was standing at the entrance to a subway, with a camera, disguised as a transistor radio, hanging from his shoulder. I declined the offer and walked home. I discovered later that the story about the exit visa had been true. The provocation had been the payment for it.

In China the police are used less as an instrument of political control, but when they take on that role they behave in much the same way. In March 1979, a few weeks after the peasant demonstrations at Zhongnanhai, I was sitting late one evening in a diplomat's flat at Qi Jia Yuan, one of the big complexes of apartment buildings where the Chinese authorities, like the Soviets, make foreigners live apart from the rest of the population. Suddenly a Canadian journalist, John Fraser of the *Toronto Globe and Mail*, burst in with a terrified young Chinese behind him. He had been trying to drop the young man near his home, he explained, but had been ostentatiously tailed from one side of Peking to the other by a succession of police cars. Being unable to shake them off, he had returned to the sanctuary of the diplomatic 'ghetto', where the police could not follow. The young Chinese seemed numbed, and kept saying dully, 'I want to die'.

What followed was pure farce. While the Chinese was disguised in Western clothes and smuggled into another diplomat's flat to spend the night, Fraser and two friends roared off in their cars, with much hooting and screeching of tyres, to draw off the waiting police – only to discover that they had given up and gone home. Next morning the young man was driven home without difficulty. But his fears proved justified. Soon afterwards he was arrested.

The similarity of the Chinese and Soviet organs of repression was shown dramatically later that year by the trial of Wei Jingsheng, a twenty-nine-year-old dissenter sentenced to fifteen years' imprisonment on charges of counter-revolutionary agitation and passing military secrets to a foreigner. It was a Stalinist show trial, staged for the education of the Chinese people, and next day the *People's Daily* said defiantly: 'The sovereignty of our country brooks no interference. No matter what banner of "human rights" the criminal Wei waves, and no matter who speaks out publicly to defend him . . . the people will not allow anyone to carry out counter-revolutionary activities under the signboard of "democracy".'

The following week in Prague six members of Czechoslovakia's 'Charter 77' group were sentenced to up to five years' imprisonment on charges of subversion and accepting money from foreign agents. The Party newspaper, *Rude Pravo*, commented: 'The West thought Czechoslovakia would not act against these "dissidents" because of the Helsinki Agreement, but we will not free the hands of counter-revolutionary elements who wish to disrupt our state.'

The language is slightly different. The charges are slightly different. The sentiments are the same.

Wei's trial took place towards the end of a year of extraordinary freedom, from mid-November 1978 to December 1979, which became known as the Peking Spring. It signalled the limits beyond which China's leaders would not tolerate a challenge to their monopoly of power. But the Peking Spring marked the beginning of a process of profound change in China which has not yet ended.

How deep-rooted is it? How far will it go? There is no precise answer. Yet these are questions on which all our futures may one day partly depend. And one way of looking for an answer is through the parallels and differences between China after Mao and the Soviet Union after Stalin.

At first it is the differences between the two countries which are more striking. Russia in 1890 was already among the world's ten leading industrial powers; today it is second only to America. China, as one of the victors of the last war, may have warranted one of the five perma-nent seats on the Security Council, but it was then and remains now backward and poor. Yet the historical processes each has undergone show remarkable similarities. At the turn of the century, Russia and China were the two great decaying empires of the Eurasian land mass. Within six years of each other, the two dynasties collapsed. A period of chaos followed, lasting several months in Russia and several decades in China, and then communists came to power. Stalin in Moscow and Mao in Peking each ruled his country for nearly thirty years.

Both regimes began with bloodshed: in the Soviet Union, collectivisa-tion took the lives of fifteen million people; in China, the expropriation of the landlords cost at least one million lives. Later, each unleashed its period of terror: the great purges under Stalin, and the Cultural Revolution under Mao, which his successors now acknowledge was marked by 'white terror' and fascist dictatorship. Then came a brief respite of opening up to the West, due to the wartime alliance against Germany in Stalin's case, and to fear of the Soviet Union in Mao's. And finally, in the last years of each man's rule, both countries endured periods of national conservatism and extreme cultural sterility.

In the Soviet Union, the late 1940s were marked by the *Zhdanov-shchina*, a campaign against 'cosmopolitanism' and 'the worship of foreign things'. The writers Zoshchenko and Akhmatova were publicly humiliated. The composers Shostakovich and Prokofiev were accused of formalism and lack of Party spirit. 'Kowtowing before the West' became a crime; cultural and scientific contacts and even football matches with bourgeois countries were stopped; and a law was passed prohibiting any Soviet citizen from marrying a foreigner. In China, in the mid-1970s, Mao's followers not only enforced similar policies but in some cases used the same words. They, too, accused their opponents of 'worshipping foreign things'. Foreign marriages were also banned; Beethoven was denounced instead of Shostakovich; and the Ministry of Foreign Trade was called the Ministry of National Betrayal. There was even an upsurge of political repression, though only a faint echo of the murderous scheming that marked Stalin's final days.

Yet when they died, Stalin on March 5th, 1953, and Mao on September 9th, 1976, each country indulged in an outpouring of grief. In Moscow, hundreds were trampled to death in the hysteria of Stalin's funeral. In Peking, the old army chief of staff, Luo Ruiqing, who had both his legs broken by Mao's supporters during the Cultural Revolution, recalled how, having been refused permission to attend the memorial meeting for Mao in Tian An Men Square, he made his own way there and sat for an hour in his wheelchair after the crowds had gone, crying like a child. Ordinary people in both countries felt suddenly at a loss and fearful of the future: all the old certainties were gone, and no one knew what would come in their place.

Within a month Mao's closest followers, his widow Jiang Qing and her radical group, the so-called 'Gang of Four', were overthrown and denounced as renegades, traitors and agents of the Chinese Nationalists. In Moscow it took three and a half months before Beria, the security chief and long Stalin's closest confidant, was arrested and denounced, equally improbably, as a British spy. The way was then clear for the gradual emergence of Khrushchev and Deng Xiaoping as the dominant forces in the new regimes, and for de-Stalinisation and de-Maoisation.

Mao and Stalin created their systems of rule not in a vacuum but on the basis of what preceded them: in China the mandarinate; in Russia, the tsarist autocracy. Moreover each man reflected – no matter with what distortions – the character and civilisation of his people.

Stalin ruled in the boorish, brutal tradition of Ivan the Terrible and Peter the Great. Like them, his overriding concern was to make his country strong, and to a great extent he succeeded. Stalin aspired to be regarded as a philosopher-king: his eulogists let it be known that he had written 'very good poetry'; he was celebrated in the Soviet press as a critic of Hegel and Kant; his was the only permitted interpretation of Marxist-Leninist theory. When he wanted to impress a visitor to his Kremlin office, he would have his secretary, Poskrebyshev, bring in a pile of books on some abstruse topic, so that the man would go away thinking 'What doesn't Comrade Stalin find time to study?' One of his last works was on linguistics, a subject in which, at his suggestion, researchers spent fifteen years trying to find a non-existent connection between Azerbaijani and the language of the ancient Medes. But for all his cunning and devious acuity, he was no intellectual: his achievements were the result of single-minded and total ruthlessness.

Where sheer willpower was concerned, Mao was no laggard either. He inspired a movement which in twenty years dragged nearly a quarter of mankind from feudalism to the verge of statehood. When, after another twenty years, as an old man in his seventies, he decided he did not like the results, he launched 800 million people into a cataclysmic wave of destruction unparalleled in modern times, overthrowing the colleagues of decades and obliterating their policies in a last, ultimately unsuccessful attempt to impose his vision on China through political violence.

Unlike Stalin, however, Mao's ruthlessness was complemented by a formidable intellect. Few rulers in history have combined as he did the Renaissance ideal of poet, thinker, soldier and statesman. Like Lenin, Mao was concerned with ideas, which in China have always been the key to power. Where Stalin physically annihilated his enemies and even his friends, Mao stripped them of power and sent them for thought reform. In the late 1940s, when the Soviet economist Professor Kubanin suggested in the journal *Voprosi Ekonomii* that the Soviet Union was lagging behind the United States in agricultural productivity, Stalin had him shot and the journal closed down. In 1957 when the Chinese economist Ma Yinchu called for efforts to control population growth, Mao – with equal arbitrariness – had him accused of Malthusianism and purged. But three years after Mao's death, Ma was rehabilitated and, at the age of ninety-eight, reinstated in his old post as honorary President of Peking University. In Kubanin's case, Khrushchev did not have that option.

Mao had no qualms about the brutality of revolution. The upheaval he unleashed in the 1960s caused suffering on a scale which has only begun to become apparent since his death. It wrecked the lives of tens of millions, and another million died. But Mao did not cold-bloodedly read through lists of hundreds of thousands of political prisoners and order their judicial murder, as Stalin and his subordinates did. In China political executions were the sometimes frequent exception but never the rule. The distinction may be academic to those who perished, but its bearing on the nature of the two regimes, and on those which succeeded them, was immense. Within the Stalinist monolith it was simply inconceivable for a purged leader to return to power; and none did. In Mao's system a plurality of views and policies was tolerated, even encouraged. He never commanded absolute obedience as Stalin did, and he had to manoeuvre to get the rest of the leadership behind him. After Mao's death, the Chinese politburo included six former purge victims, most of whom had been rehabilitated while he was still alive.

Where Stalin sacrificed the welfare of the Soviet people on the altar of state ambition, Mao, in the last twenty years of his life, subordinated the material interests of the Chinese people to the working out of his ideas. The dichotomy between ends and means, results and ideas, appearance and essence, goes to the core of the difference between the Soviet and Chinese systems. The Soviets are concerned with results. Ideology is significant only as a barrier to change. The people, apart from a small minority of dissidents, are politically passive. The Soviet Party as a vehicle for political debate has been destroyed. Even in closed Party meetings, issues of real importance, such as strategic arms limitation, are simply not discussed, because only the highest leadership is permitted to express an opinion on them.

In the China of Deng Xiaoping, people are expected not only to produce results, but also to think and to understand. The main stress in the propaganda campaign to promote China's modernisation programme is not on increasing production, but on the need to clear up ideological confusion and straighten out people's thoughts. The Chinese are not politically passive. After ten years or more of the most intensive political indoctrination, those who gathered to read the wall-posters and to discuss human rights and democracy in the first, hectic days of the Peking Spring were still able to produce lucid, original arguments against Maoism and all its works. They were still able to think for themselves, and were encouraged to do so by almost daily editorials in the Chinese press. The Party newspaper, the *People's Daily*, wrote: 'Let people say what they wish, the heavens will not fall! If a person is to be punished for saying the wrong thing, no one will say what he thinks.' Contrast that with Khrushchev's words, at the end of his secret speech in 1956, three years after Stalin's death: 'We cannot let this matter get out of the Party, especially not to the press. We should know the limit. We should not give ammunition to the enemy.'

Admittedly a few months later the *People's Daily* ate its words, and confessed to having been imprudent. And Khrushchev's speech was a far more devastating indictment of Stalin than anything that has been said about Mao. Even now, after a quarter of a century has elapsed, and allowing for all that Khrushchev left out, it makes compelling reading. He spoke of Stalin's capricious and despotic nature, his sickly, suspicious mind, his persecution mania. Stalin, he said, sanctioned torture and oppression; he used mass terror and surrounded himself with loathsome adulation. The war made him nervous and hysterical, and his so-called military genius cost the Soviet people hundreds of thousands of lives.

Yet in practice most of Khrushchev's prescriptions for eliminating the consequences of Stalin's abuses – more democracy, criticism and self-criticism – remained on paper. Appearances changed: Stalin's statues were demolished; the names of towns were altered; in the end, even his body was removed from the Red Square mausoleum. But Khrushchev, although sincere in wanting to have done with Stalinism, never really intended to go back even to the relative freedom which existed under Lenin in the 1920s. The Stalinist monolith was too rigid and too strong. Khrushchev is sometimes criticised today for not adequately preparing the Soviet people for de-Stalinisation, but he was unable to do so. For him, the option of the gradual approach which the Chinese used towards Mao simply did not exist. It was either the shock tactic of the Secret Speech or nothing. To have gone further, and to have effected basic changes, would have required the monolith to be overturned. That was something which no one in the Soviet leadership wanted, for fear of that current of blind anarchism which runs beneath the surface of the Russian character. In the end, even Khrushchev's modest efforts at reform were defeated, and he was replaced by the *apparatchiki* who rule the Soviet Union now.

Will the same thing, or something analogous, eventually happen in Deng Xiaoping's China? He and Khrushchev have much in common, in character as well as in their historical roles. Take this extract from a typical Khrushchev speech: 'Some of you may say, "What's this! Has Khrushchev come to criticise and tell us off?" What did you think I'd come for, to read you poems? I've come to show up defects, to blow some wind of change at some of the directing cadres.' The words could be Deng's. He once advised Party bureaucrats: 'Don't sit on the privy if you can't move your bowels, make room for those who can!'

Both men were impatient. Both came slowly to dominate their

regimes. Both inherited very similar practical problems: communist parties ridden with privilege and careerism; low living standards; weak agricultural sectors; over-centralised economies; and outdated foreign policy positions that had become untenable. But the parallels go only so far. Unlike Khrushchev under Stalin, Deng was not a party to Mao's policies in the Cultural Revolution, but a victim. Again unlike Khrushchev, he has the backing of thousands of other rehabilitated veteran officials. As an agent of change, therefore, his position is more solid than Khrushchev's, and he is operating in a country which is much better able to deal with change than was the Soviet Union after Stalin. Yet in the end Khrushchev fell, not merely because he was rocking the boat and upsetting the bureaucrats, but because the Cuban missile crisis of 1962 and a disastrous harvest failure the following year showed that both at home and abroad his policies were not succeeding. Taking a long view, will Deng's policies succeed any better?

These are not idle questions. China today is a poor underdeveloped country. Yet because of its policies and its sheer size, it has a disproportionate weight in world affairs. With the Soviet Union (and its Warsaw Pact allies) and the United States (and its allies in NATO), China is already one of only three nations powerful enough and sufficiently motivated to act independently in a global, as distinct from a local, conflict. By the end of the 1980s, if the goals of its modernisation programme are even halfway achieved, China's emergent status as one of the three world powers will be assured.

This portends a profound change in the geopolitical balance. But it will not happen in isolation. The dominant strand in world politics in the decade ahead will be the continuing struggle between the Soviet Union and the United States, not so much in the first instance for world hegemony, as the Chinese argue, but for world leadership. It is a struggle which began in earnest in the mid-1970s, based on the gradual build-up of Soviet military power and on the political understandings implicit in detente. In the 1980s it will be complicated by a transitional period in the Soviet Union, perhaps lasting several years, when the leaders of Brezhnev's generation are replaced by younger men; by shortages of energy and of labour, aggravating the weakness of the Soviet economy; and by asymmetries in the nuclear balance, which are already reflected in a Soviet advantage of more than three to one in long-range theatre nuclear weapons in Europe and may, in the second half of the decade, bring Moscow closer to a second-strike capability – the ability to devastate American population centres after an initial nuclear exchange limited to military targets. In a crisis in which Soviet leaders might be tempted to take that step, their estimation of China's intentions will be one of the determining factors permitting or preventing war. The stronger China becomes, the more important that factor will be.

In most of Western Europe, throughout the 1970s, it was heresy to speak of global war as a realistic possibility. To a lesser extent the same was true of the United States. But it was never true of the Soviet Union or China. And today, after two decades of detente, nuclear war is more, not less, likely than it was in the 1960s.

Washington and Moscow then espoused the comforting doctrine of Mutual Assured Destruction (MAD), which made nuclear war unthinkable because no sane leader would embark on it if it meant the certain destruction of his own people. But by the 1970s, the two superpowers were searching for ways in which a nuclear war could be fought and won. MAD was formally abandoned by the American Defence Secretary, James Schlesinger, in 1974, when the increased accuracy of strategic missiles made it possible to use them against military targets, and so raised the spectre of one side attempting a pre-emptive strike against the missile silos of the other. At the same time, a range of tactical nuclear weapons was developed, including nuclear mines and artillery shells, and a range of doctrines devised for their use. The 1980s will see this taken a stage further with the deployment of the neutron bomb and the expansion of chemical weapon stockpiles. Nuclear war today has become so routinely thinkable that current NATO planning provides for tactical nuclear weapons to be used virtually from the start against a conventional Soviet thrust into Western Europe. In any future European war the use of nuclear arms is almost inevitable.

Until President Reagan took office at the beginning of 1981, Western governments avoided spelling out these changes and what they entailed. Talk of war made war more likely, it was argued, and detente had to be preserved. The same reasoning led the West throughout the 1970s not to identify the Soviet Union by name as the potential enemy.

Even Mrs Thatcher in Britain, the 'iron lady' of Soviet cartoons, has made no serious effort to prepare the British people for what a future war would involve, be it at so basic a level as civil defence. The Soviet Union and China both have elaborate civil defence systems, but the only Western country so equipped is Switzerland. Britain, unlike most of Western Europe, does not even have any system of compulsory military training, on the grounds that a future war will require an elite, professional army, and if larger forces are needed they can be trained after mobilisation – a recipe which is popular with the electorate, but has not commended itself to any of the other potential combatants; even the United States, since the Soviet invasion of Afghanistan, has restored the mechanism for the draft.

10

Talk of war does not win votes. But the reluctance of Western politicians to acknowledge the realities underlying detente has left public opinion unprepared for the idea that war may come, and we may, once again, have to fight for our homes and beliefs: the very notion sounds quaint and old-fashioned. We are at the stage of which George Orwell once wrote, 'The re-statement of the obvious is the first duty of intelligent men'. Man has fought wars since the beginning of recorded history, using all the weapons at his disposal. Viewed dispassionately, it is unlikely he will suddenly stop now.

The Soviet leaders have been less inhibited about denouncing 'the aggressive circles of imperialism', and their charges have been orchestrated by a ramified apparatus of official propaganda. Compare *Pravda* with *The Times*, *Le Monde* or the *Washington Post*, and you are left in no doubt on which side cold war attitudes are being maintained.

Pravda, 1979

If Western correspondents in Moscow used the same terms to describe Soviet life as Soviet correspondents use in the West, they would very quickly find themselves being expelled. The Soviet press today, no less than in Stalin's time, depicts Western society and governments in unvarying tones of black; detente, even at its high point in the mid-1970s, merely added a few patches of grey.

Similarly the Chinese leaders speak bluntly of the threat from 'Soviet social-imperialism'. In Peking, as in Moscow, the source of war is clearly labelled: Russians and Chinese are left in no doubt who their potential enemies are. And for historical reasons, Russians and Chinese are psychologically much better able than most Westerners to reconcile the possibility of future war and the memory of past war with the routine cares of daily life. In China, until 1949, war was as normal a hazard as famine, flood, earthquake and disease: for a hundred years the country had been continuously wracked by foreign war, civil war, warlordism, banditry and peasant uprisings. In the Soviet Union, the short-lived Western attempts at a blockade after the Bolshevik revolution were used by Stalin to foster a siege mentality: rooted in a historical ambivalence towards the West which stretches back through tsarist times, and reinforced by the atrocious suffering of the 1941–45 war – a memory which, for political reasons, is deliberately kept alive – the sense of being surrounded by antipathetic forces continues to exert a profound influence on Soviet attitudes.

In Detskii Mir, the huge children's store opposite the Lubyanka prison in central Moscow, a third of the toys on display are war toys. A young Soviet couple on their wedding day go, not to pray before an icon as their grandparents would have done, but to lay wreaths before a statue of Lenin and at a war memorial which bears the epitaph: 'No one has been forgotten, nothing will be forgotten!' The tales of sacrifice and of horror which have come down from the war years, one Soviet writer has explained, are 'chains binding the past to the present, and the present to the future'. Each year there is a new crop of war films and war novels; each year wartime collaborators are tried and executed. The constant reminders of war are both a call to vigilance, and an exculpation for the failings of the regime. *Pravda* blamed the disastrous harvest failure in 1975, thirty years after the war ended, on 'war damage to Soviet farms'. I have heard Russians explain away everything from the housing shortage and alcoholism to the malfunctioning of hotel lifts as the result of war losses. When a Russian says – and it is something that Russians say often – 'We don't want another war, but . . .' and his voice trails away with a shrug that means no one can be sure of the future, he speaks with greater conviction than a Briton or an American, because he is more conscious of what his words mean. To him the possibility of war is real, and its memory undimmed.

The absence in the West of any such sense of menace has helped make all our lives easier over the last fifteen years. It is also the reason why the military balance has shifted so strongly in the Soviet Union's favour. In a political climate conditioned by detente, there has been no public support for defence expenditure, either to match Soviet conventional arms levels in Europe, or to ensure American superiority over the Soviet strategic nuclear arsenal. It is not that in the late 1970s the Russians suddenly broke faith and leapt ahead. For fifteen years they have chosen to spend more money on arms, while we have chosen to spend less.

This does not mean that war will come within the next decade. But peace is more fragile than most of us like to believe. As long as the United States and the Soviet Union compete for leadership and influence in the world, the risk of crises such as those over Korea, Berlin and Cuba will continue. To the extent that the Soviet Union, over the next few years, perceives itself as having even a limited military advantage, that risk will increase. Every power in history has tried to translate military strength into political gains. In the last great crisis, over Cuba in 1962, President Kennedy used the assurance of America's overwhelming military superiority to inflict a humiliating political defeat on the Soviet Union. But if such a crisis were to occur now, in conditions of approximate nuclear parity, the results would be far harder to predict.

For the West, it is in these broad, strategic terms of war and peace that the Soviet Union and China assume their true importance. Our economic, cultural and scientific exchanges with both countries are relatively small and likely to remain so: trade with all the Soviet-bloc states and China taken together accounts for less than five per cent of most Western countries' turnover. Except in the field of defence spending, even the indirect effects of Soviet and Chinese policy on Western economies are negligible. War apart, the quality of our lives in the coming decade will depend far more on developments within and among the Western countries, and between them and the developing nations, than on anything the Soviets or the Chinese are likely to do. Yet should war come, it would obliterate all other concerns.

The 1980s will be a critical decade for the future of the West – the most crucial, perhaps, for almost half a century. The decisions taken in Washington and the other NATO capitals, in Peking and in Moscow, during these ten years will either lay the basis of a triangular understanding permitting a more stable peace than any achieved so far; or they will begin a slide towards war, as in the 1930s.

It is in this context that what happens in China, what kind of a country it becomes, and what happens in the Soviet Union after Brezhnev dies, will affect all our lives. From our standpoint in the West, the key indicator of internal change in both countries is how they compare with our notions of democracy; how they come to terms with dissent; how far their values are antagonistic to ours, and how far they coincide. But if that is not to produce a one-sided and superficial picture of the likely evolution of Chinese and Soviet society, it must be set within the broader perspective of how these one and a quarter billion people think and live.

Part I

The Chinese and the Russians

There are more misconceptions about China than any other country on earth. It is not so much that they have been fostered deliberately by misleading propaganda, but rather that China is so different from anything in Western, or even Soviet experience, that there is a tendency to abandon the normal criteria of judgment and to forget that Chinese, no less than Russians or Americans, have the same concerns and motivations, the same needs and passions, as people anywhere else. Throughout the 1960s and early 1970s, a procession of Western travellers came back from Peking declaring, like Lincoln Steffens returning from the Soviet Union in the 1930s, 'I have seen the future and it works.' Even those who were more sceptical about Mao's attempts to transform the Chinese people held that his system had redeeming features and a sincerity that the Russians lacked. Yet the differences between Chinese and Soviet communism have less to do with differing interpretations of Marx than with the differing civilisations which underlie them. The difficulty for the West in coming to terms with China is not of ideology, but of culture.

For six thousand years, China has been the centre of an autochthonous world, developing and stagnating without significant external influence until the middle of the last century. While our ancestors, in Europe, were painting themselves blue with woad, China's scholar gentry were painting scrolls and writing poems whose beauty has not faded through the intervening millennia. Chinese craftsmen discovered the secrets of gunpowder and porcelain, printing and paper-making, and Chinese administrators devised the world's first civil service examinations, a thousand years or more before they were thought of in Europe.

But the cultural compactness and feudal isolation which permitted the Chinese genius to develop so distinctively, later became a suffocating blanket, protecting the outworn, old ways, and keeping out new ideas. China today may stand alone with the two superpowers in having the ability to launch and recover satellites, in having built and deployed independently its own nuclear weapons, and in having inter-continental missiles capable of delivering them to Moscow or Washington. Yet it is still a country more profoundly conservative than the most dyed-in-the-wool Western traditionalist could conceive of; a country where peasants still drown girl-children at birth, where a hundred million people are short of food, and hundreds of millions more spend their lives in a brutish struggle to exist.

17

Mao's revolution pierced the cocoon of feudalism and cultural exclusiveness, but did not destroy it. The main challenges for China in the 1980s are still, as they have been for the last century, to come to terms with the outside world and to free itself from the weight of its own past.

The combination of emergent superpower and backward developing country, ancient civilisation and feudal peasantry makes China unlike anywhere else. Other countries, including the Soviet Union, embody similar contradictions between new and old, urban and rural, but they are less dominant and less sharply drawn. China is not one but two nations – a sophisticated, educated elite, numbering 60 to 80 million people, which, given the right conditions, could become the equal of Japan; and an undifferentiated, mainly rural mass of 900 million peasants and unskilled labourers, whose lives have changed hardly at all in two thousand years.

The gulf between these two nations survived almost unaltered the great social upheaval of the Cultural Revolution, and Mao's emphasis on 'learning from the masses'. A middle-aged Chinese intellectual told me in 1979, 'You cannot conceive how the people live in the countryside. Even we don't understand.' The so-called 'educated youths', the urban secondary school leavers who, from the late 1950s onward, were sent in their millions to work on communes and state farms, found a world for which they were totally unprepared. 'Thanks to that experience,' one Chinese youth wrote later, 'I finally learnt what Chinese society really was: a mainly peasant population more backward than I could have dreamed . . . If China is truly to progress, the first step must be to raise the level of the peasantry.'[1]

That was one of Mao's aims in launching the down-to-the-countryside movement, and to a limited extent it succeeded. 'To them we were like a radio, or a television set,' another young man recalled. 'They were made to understand that there were other things besides their immediate surroundings, another world.'[2] Above all, to the young people in the villages, the girls and youths from the cities were a window on to the unknown. They aped their manners and language, and hung around their houses to learn more. For some it was the first time they had seen people brushing their teeth, or heard that water could come from a tap, and not just from a bucket in a well.

But while the educated youths broadened the peasants' horizons, they were in most cases a burden to the villages, extra mouths eating into the harvest, unable to earn their own keep. And to them, in turn, life in the countryside was a kind of internal exile, from which there was no legal escape apart from a transfer back to the city, in practice obtainable only by great good luck or official connections.

18

Thousands returned clandestinely. No longer being registered as city residents, however, they have not been able to obtain work or ration tickets for grain. So they form a semi-criminal sub-culture, living on their wits, supported by their families or supporting themselves by petty theft. Others try to make their way to the border, and cross illegally to Hong Kong or Macao, risking drowning or a grisly death from sharks. Four out of five illegal emigrants are rusticated city dwellers, and in the summer of 1979, when border patrols were particularly slack, over a thousand a day were finding refuge in Hong Kong. Nor is illegal emigration limited to Southern China. Further west, educated youths cross into Burma, where they join the communist insurgents fighting the government in Rangoon. In the north, some even make their way to the Soviet Union, and to North Korea – a country so regimented that China is liberal by comparison; one of those who went there, and returned, was the young man John Fraser had such difficulty taking home the night the police were chasing him.

The desperation of the young city dwellers who flee their farms, many of them at the risk of their lives, is one measure of the divide between town and country in China. Another is the overriding importance Chinese attach to possession of an urban residence registration, as highly prized in a small country town as in the biggest cities such as Peking and Shanghai. When in 1979 the boundaries of Yingxian, a county seat in Shansi province, were extended, the *People's Daily* reported 'a huge influx of rural residents' into the newly-formed urban area, with members of the county Party committee taking the lead in bringing in their own relatives to be registered as town dwellers; one new street was so full of local officials' relations that the townsfolk called it 'Authority Row'.[3]

Residence restrictions also prevent marriage between city dwellers and peasants. If an educated youth marries a villager, he gives up all hope of being allowed to return to the city. Girls sometimes do so for love, or because they have slept with a village official in the hope of being given easier work, become pregnant and feel they have no choice but to marry; but even in these cases, their families often try to dissuade them.[4] Young men, being more self-centred, almost never voluntarily tie themselves through marriage to the lifetime of stupefying monotony which is a Chinese peasant's lot.

The barrier is so absolute than even between a small town and an adjacent commune marriage is often impossible. When a girl named Lu Yuhong, in a county town in Jiangsu province, in South-Eastern China, fell in love with a peasant from a nearby village, her father, a pillar of the local community, violently objected 'because the young man is a

19

commune member, working in the countryside'. At first Lu was beaten to try to make her sever the relationship. Then, one day in June 1979, her father and brother saw them talking outside their house, and, in broad daylight, beat the young man to death before Lu's eyes. Afterwards they said in court: 'We accept the responsibility for what we have done. We beat him to death. We are ready to go to prison and to pay with our lives.' The father was shot; the brother was given ten years in a labour camp.[5]

Such an extreme case is uncommon, but not unique. Even marriages between people living in different towns are rare and face extraordinary strains, because it is so difficult for either partner to change job and residence so that they may live together. The bigger the city, the higher the standard of living and the better the cultural facilities, the harder it is to obtain registration. Peking, Shanghai and Tianjin are the most difficult of all – although such is the pressure of people trying to get in that even with all the restrictions that officialdom has created, almost a quarter of a million persons managed by hook or by crook, and in many cases by crook, to register in Peking in 1979.[6]

In the Soviet Union, where a similar system is used, Moscow, Leningrad and Kiev are subject to special restrictions. But under Soviet regulations, marriage does provide grounds for obtaining a city residence permit. Every year there are thousands of cases of ambitious young women (and sometimes men) from the provinces, contracting marriages of convenience with the sole aim of gaining admission to one of the big cities: Maria Sychova, attractive and well-educated, married a chronic alcoholic because he had a Moscow apartment, and then had him imprisoned for hooliganism; Kirill Aleksanyants, a male nurse from Kharkov, married a woman old enough to be his grandmother for her Moscow registration; one man I came across, who without any ulterior motive divorced his wife in the provinces and married a Muscovite, but then decided he wanted his first wife back and divorced again and remarried her, was deprived of his Moscow registration because the judge refused to believe that it was not a deliberate ploy to obtain residence permits for his family. Deceptions are that common.

Registration can be used as an administrative weapon to limit the movements of Soviet dissidents, as in the exiling of Sakharov to Gorky in January 1980. But apart from the three largest Soviet cities – and even there, hundreds of thousands of Russians manage to live illegally, without registration – the Soviet Union has far fewer restrictions on residence than China. The average Soviet town dweller can move from one part of the country to another with relative ease, impeded only by the shortage of accommodation, and the bureaucratic frustrations which are the daily fare of Soviet life. However, that is true only of a town dweller. Although the gulf between town and country in the Soviet Union is small by comparison with China – when viewed from the standpoint of a Western country, the Soviet people, also, are two nations, living in two different worlds. The Russian peasant, though far from the millennial servitude of his Asian cousin, is still the last true peasant of the old world, representing a way of life which has all but vanished elsewhere.

On the outskirts of Moscow, scarcely a dozen miles from the Kremlin, are villages which tourists do not see, consisting of a couple of rows of idyllically picturesque, rickety wooden houses with elaborately carved window-frames, as crazily askew as in a Chagall painting, and a single unpaved road which turns to mud in the thaw. There is electricity ('Communism equals Soviet power plus the electrification of the whole country', proclaims a huge Lenin slogan on one bank of the Moscow river), but no telephone and no shop. Even on the coldest days, when the temperature falls to −40°C, water has to be drawn from a well, and if you want to take a bath, you begin by chopping wood for the stove. Yet it is a way of life which in Russia, too, is slowly dying. In such a village near Moscow one autumn, I met an old man ploughing, who told me that before collectivisation fifty years earlier, it had numbered 200 souls, and that every family had its own plough-horse. Now the young men had all left, and his horse was one of only six which remained. Further north, around Yaroslavl and Suzdal, in the old heartland of Russia, among birch forests and rolling green hills, villages lie deserted where the peasants have quit the land.

In the Soviet Union, such migration has been permitted, although with strict controls, because it conforms to economic needs. In most of European Russia, the population is no longer increasing: nearly two-thirds of all families have no child or one, and only six per cent have more than two.[7] As a result, despite the third largest population in the world (260 million), there is a growing shortage of labour. Ninety per cent of Soviet women of working age either study or have a full-time job, and in European Russia the figure is still higher – which, in a classic vicious circle, has accelerated the decline of the birthrate. Two-thirds of all retired people also work at least part-time – due as much to the inadequacy of Soviet pensions, particularly for the lower-paid, and to the erosion of the traditional large Russian family, which provided a home in which to grow old, as to a conscious effort to make people work longer. Being a member of a working collective, 'a second family', as the Soviet press likes to call it, helps to fill the gap that the weakening of family bonds has left.

Despite official claims to the contrary and the labour shortage, the Soviet Union also has unemployment – notwithstanding a law against parasitism, which makes it an offence punishable by imprisonment for a man not to have a job for more than five months at a stretch. But it is mainly limited to the workshy and the drifters, rather than to people who cannot find work. True unemployment, in the Western sense, is counted in the tens of thousands, and is found principally in the Soviet Central Asian Republics, which are among the least industrialised in the country, and where the birthrate, in contrast to European Russia, has been consistently high.

Sixteen million Soviet peasants left the villages to provide labour for Soviet industry in the decade up to 1975. In May of that year the second-class status imposed on the peasantry by Stalin, binding them to the land in a modern form of serfdom, was finally ended by the announcement of a five-year programme to issue internal passports – a form of identity card. These enabled them to travel freely for the first time outside their home districts like any other Soviet citizen. It was conceived as an economic measure, to ease the flow of labour to the cities, but a peasant still needs authorisation and a job to go to, before he can actually leave. And by no means all who wish to can do so. A survey in the mid-1970s found that one person in five wanted to leave the land; among young people the figure probably reached one in two. Nonetheless, the barriers between town and country have been lowered, and since the Soviet Union's workforce is expected to contract for the next decade, restrictions on residence may be further eased.

China has the opposite problem: a super-abundance of labour for which there is not enough work. In April 1979, Vice-Premier Li Xiannian told a Central Committee work conference that among an urban workforce of 110 million some 20 million were unemployed, including more than 12 million young people.[8] Part of this reservoir has since been absorbed through a dramatic expansion of small, collectively-owned enterprises and more liberal regulations governing service trades and individual businesses. Yet, at the beginning of 1980, the urban unemployment rate among the young was still almost thirty per cent, and for the rest of this decade the pressure of population growth on employment will increase, as the baby boom of the 1960s produces more and more teenagers needing jobs – three million a year in the cities, and 20 million in the countryside.[9] Not for another two decades, and then only if industry develops satisfactorily and the present efforts to limit the growth of the population succeed, will any significant relaxation of residence restrictions become possible.

Had China's population continued to grow at the rate of the mid-

1970s, in a hundred years' time it would have reached 4.26 billion, roughly the present population of the world; but mass starvation, and a breakdown of government, would occur first. At the present rate of increase, a modest 1.17 per cent, which most developing countries would be only too proud to have achieved, the figure in 2080 would be 2.1 billion – still half the world's present population – to be fed from only seven per cent of the world's arable land. Early in 1979 China's leaders set a target of stabilising the population at about 1,200 million by the end of the century, which will require the growth rate to fall to 0.5 per cent (the present Soviet level) by 1985, and each couple of child-bearing age to have no more than one, or at most, two children; in 1980 a revised plan proposed that 90 per cent of families should be limited to one child.

To accomplish this in a country of ill-educated, deeply conservative peasants will be no mean feat, and a draconian system of enforcement has been devised to try to make it possible. Where in the Soviet Union, there is talk of granting two years' maternity leave and increasing child allowances, and a woman who has ten children receives a state award as a 'mother-heroine', in China a woman waits her turn to have a child, and if she fails to conceive in the time allotted, it will be another three or four years before her turn comes round again. The Chinese award a 'planned parenthood glory coupon' to every couple who pledge not to have a second child. It carries with it a five per cent bonus on annual earnings (six per cent if their one child is a daughter, reflecting the authorities' recognition that more encouragement is then needed to dissuade them from trying again for a son), an extra grain allowance, free health care, education and other benefits, payable until the child is fourteen, and priority in housing and employment. If they default and have a second child, it all has to be paid back. For all parents, a third child brings a fine of between five and ten per cent of annual earnings for fourteen years, usually increased by a further five per cent for each additional child.

The regulations vary from province to province, but in most parts of China a woman who becomes pregnant out of turn, or who conceives a third child, faces strong pressure to have an abortion. In some provinces, this extends even to those who wish to have a second child. But it has had little effect on the peasants' primordial desire for sons. In 1978, when social pressure was the only deterrent, one in three of the 17 million babies born were third or subsequent children.[10] Nor is it only peasants who want large families: Xu Zhenxiang, a deputy director of a factory in Huanren, in North-East China, refused to allow his wife to have an abortion when she became pregnant with their ninth

23

child – and was sacked as a result.[11] His case is by no means unique.

Since the introduction of the new system, extra-legal measures have been widely used to back up economic sanctions. Some provinces have simply announced that third children 'will not be permitted',[12] and instituted mandatory annual quotas for the number of abortions to be carried out.[13] Quasi-compulsory sterilisation is also practised. By liberal, Western standards, or even those of the Soviet Union, such measures would be intolerable – and they are certainly not welcome in China. Warnings have been issued in several provinces against those who 'spread rumours, deal blows at and frame planned parenthood work personnel' in order to sabotage the birth control programme.[14] But the alternative to a single-child family, procured by coercion, is that the country will remain locked into poverty.

According to one Vice-Premier, Chen Muhua, 1,000 billion yuan (£300 billion), representing thirty per cent of China's national income from 1949 to 1979, has been spent by the state, by collectives and individual families, on raising the 600 million children born since the communists gained power.[15] If the birthrate had been halved, £150 billion more would have been available for economic development and raising the standard of living; China would have 700 million people, instead of an officially estimated 980 million, and they would be far better off than they are now. 'We should have started twenty years ago,' another Vice-Premier, Wang Renzhong, told me in the summer of 1980. But twenty years ago Mao was arguing that 'the more people China has, the more quickly she will develop', and those who disagreed, such as Professor Ma Yinchu, were condemned and disgraced. China's huge population is the gravest burden Mao left behind, and one for which he bears a heavy responsibility, as the *People's Daily* acknowledged, when it asked in July 1979, 'Does a person have genuine feeling for his fellow-countrymen when he preaches "the more people, the better", so that they are always toiling just to make ends meet?'[16]

Although grain production was doubled in China in thirty years of communist rule, the per capita increase was only twenty per cent. In the cities, housing conditions are now more cramped than in 1949, floor space per person having decreased by twenty per cent.[17] According to an official Chinese account, 'similar problems have occurred in health care, culture and education'.[18]

Whereas in the United States and Western Europe about four per cent of the population works on the land, in the Soviet Union the figure is about twenty per cent, and in China, forty per cent. That is one measure of the economic backwardness of the Soviet and Chinese peoples. But as the Soviet Union and China are divided into two nations, urban and rural, in a way that Western countries are not, the comparison, on its own, is misleading. In some fields, including certain areas of science and technology, Soviet and Chinese achievements outstrip those of any country.

Chinese chemists were the first to synthesise insulin; China leads the world in earthquake prediction; a Chinese mathematician is the foremost authority on an abstruse problem of number theory known as the Goldbach conjecture. Soviet welding technology and ultra-high voltage power transmission are the most advanced in the world, and Soviet military equipment is on a par with that in the West (Chinese weaponry, by contrast, is generally twenty-five to thirty years behind). But while Soviet weapons are in many cases as effective as their Western equivalents, they are usually less sophisticated, whether in terms of guidance systems for missiles or crew quarters in submarines. This is partly because of a deliberate no-frills approach on the part of Soviet military planners, and partly because of a technology gap: the Soviet Union does not possess the cruise missile and the neutron bomb because it has not yet been able to develop them.

The size of this technology gap is easier to particularise than to quantify overall. In 1980 China had 2,400 computers; the Soviet Union, an estimated 40,000; the United States, 130,000, plus half a million mini-computers. The Soviet TU144 supersonic airliner, visually and in most other respects a straight copy of the Anglo-French Concorde, began scheduled passenger service within the Soviet Union in 1977, three years later than planned. Services were soon discontinued, because Soviet engineers were unable to replicate the technology that went into the Concorde; to all intents and purposes, the project has now been abandoned. In the late 1970s, Chinese aircraft designers in Shanghai tried to make a copy of the Boeing 707, of which China has a fleet of ten, purchased some years earlier. In the Chinese version, however, the centre of gravity was displaced, and the plane never flew. The Soviet space programme, despite successes such as the sending back of the first photographs from the surface of another planet, Venus, in 1976, is generally seven or eight years behind the Americans, and has had a far higher failure rate. China's space programme is at the level of the late 1950s: it has, or will have in the first half of this decade, the ability to put a man into orbit, though it may well not choose to do so.

Any broad judgment about the relative development of the Soviet Union and China is necessarily subjective: even if all the relevant information were available, which it is not, like and unlike cannot be directly compared. In civilisation, aims, priorities and economic conditions, the Soviet Union and China are unlike, both from each other and from Western countries. But with those caveats, Soviet technology can be thought of as five to ten years behind the West, and Chinese technology as twenty to thirty years behind.

If the gap often seems larger it is because of the difficulty each country has in absorbing and applying the technology it possesses. To take an extreme case, a 16,000-foot oil well takes just under five months to drill in the United States and five years in the Soviet Union. The main reason is the poor quality of Soviet drill bits. This is partly a matter of technology, now remedied through the completion, in 1980, of a £60 million American drill-bit plant, sold to Moscow by a Texas firm before President Carter's embargo; and partly because the Soviet armaments industry gets first call on high-grade steel. That the Soviet Union, like China, makes too little special-purpose steel, and too much that is low grade, has nothing to do with technology, however; it is a matter of poor economic management. Similarly, large Soviet computers are mainly copied from the IBM 360 and 370, introduced in the United States ten to fifteen years ago. So faithful is the replication that even the colour coding is the same. But since Soviet industry is unable to produce precision parts on a large scale, due to the primitiveness of its machine tools, the Soviet copies cannot be mass produced. And inadequate programming means that such large computers as the Soviet Union does possess are used at only a fraction of their capacity.

The technology gap, compounded by problems of management, is reflected in low productivity. Even by the Soviet Union's own figures, the average Soviet industrial worker produces barely half as much as his American counterpart, and the Soviet peasant one-fifth as much as an American agricultural labourer. The productivity level of Chinese industry is ten times below that of America, and Chinese agriculture is fifty times less efficient. American gross national product (GNP) in 1980 was US $2,626 billion; Soviet GNP was estimated at US $1,170 billion; Chinese GNP, by Peking's own figures, was US $245 billion, for four times the American population.

The Soviets themselves measure their progress against American development. It was the United States, not Western Europe, which Khrushchev said the Soviet Union would catch up and surpass by 1970 in its advance towards full communism, to be attained a decade later. Although that boast is now quietly forgotten, Soviet commentators, throughout the 1970s, reassured Soviet television viewers that the willingness of the 'imperialist states' to develop trade and economic cooperation with Moscow was because, 'faced with our country's growing economic might, they realise they no longer have any choice'.[19] Each year Soviet successes in surpassing America in coal extraction, fertiliser manufacture, the production of oil and pig iron, are enumerated by the media. Even Mao, during the Great Leap Forward in 1958, spoke of overtaking Britain in fifteen years and America in fifty.

National income is no more foolproof a measure of development than any other: if it were, Kuwait would be at the top of the list, with US $17,100 per person. It does, however, provide an index of relative prosperity, which is one measure of development, and the one which China's leaders have chosen to set a target for the country's development over the next twenty years.

In 1980, national income per person in the United States was US $10,630. In the Soviet Union, which ranked thirty-seventh in the listing, behind all the West European countries and East Germany and Czechoslovakia as well, it was estimated at US $3,800. In China, in 138th place, it was US $250. Deng Xiaoping, speaking in January of that year about China's objectives for the coming decade, said that if national income could be raised to US $1,000 by the end of the century, 'we would be reckoned a comfortably well-off society'; subsequently, a figure of $800 was cited.[20]

Compared with the grandiose targets set by Mao and Khrushchev, US $800-1,000 per person is a modest enough goal, and the realism with which it has been set provides the strongest ground for thinking that it may be attained, unlike the targets of Mao and Khrushchev. It is equivalent to the present level of prosperity of the Chinese nationalist-ruled island of Taiwan, or one-third that of Singapore – although Deng was careful to add that, given such a level of income, 'our life will be much better than theirs, because we have no exploiting class system'. Moreover, it should be attainable: Japan, in 1949, had a national income of about US $200 per person a year, and by 1969 had raised it to more than US $1,500. China itself, despite the near doubling of its population, has increased its national income nine-fold from US $28 per person in 1949.

If Deng's goal is reached, China in the year 2000 will enjoy the general prosperity and living standards of Western Europe in the 1950s. It would then still be half a century behind. But even that would be a phenomenal achievement.

Anarchy and Conformism:
Soviet and Chinese minds – and bodies

'The Russian always feels the urge to overdo it, to go to the brink of the precipice, and even to throw himself madly over. Under the influence of anger, of drink, of love, of eroticism, of pride, of jealousy, he shows himself ready to smash up everything: family, tradition, beliefs. The best of men may become criminals. Nihilism arose among us because at heart we are all nihilists.' Thus Dostoyevsky, in *The Devils*, on the blind, destructive violence which is one trait of the Russian character.

Today it shows most clearly in alcoholism: Soviet Russians drink not for conviviality but for oblivion – to annihilate themselves. In part this is because there is so little else on which to spend money; in part it is due to the climate. In winter, vodka is used as human anti-freeze, and it is then that the sobering-up stations are at their busiest. The climax comes on New Year's morning, when that half of the population which has spent the night out drinking in the flats of the other half tries to make its way home. In a good winter, the sky is a brilliant blue, the snow is crisp and glints like diamonds: here and there groups of two or three lurch uncertainly in a collective, funambulistic caricature of revelry, before sagging irrevocably on to the frozen ground. It is a tragi-comedy Russians have been playing out for centuries. Nowadays bodies stretched out on the pavement are less common than they used to be; living standards have risen. But an elderly person who slips and falls on a winter's day may well find that passers-by ignore his entreaties to be helped up. To a Russian, anyone on the ground in winter is automatically assumed to be drunk.

Yet it is not just the climate, the penury of consumer goods or the other frustrations of Soviet life which drive Russians to drink, for alcoholism is less of a problem among other Soviet nationalities.* 'So

* The Soviet Union comprises more than a hundred nationalities, of whom the Russians are the most numerous. Strictly speaking, to apply the term 'Russian' to other Soviet nationalities is as wrong, and in many cases as offensive, as to call a Welshman English. Confusion arises, however, because before 1917 the entire country was known as Russia and its people described accordingly, and in discussing the relationship between the

28

you come from Moscow, where they teach fourteen-year-olds to take vodka and play with women!' snorted an Azerbaijani taxi driver, on one occasion when I was in Baku. 'They are boors up there. We don't bring up our children like that.' It is in Russia, Byelorussia and the Ukraine that men congregate most thickly outside liquor stores, holding out one, two or three fingers to show how many others they are looking for to share the price of a bottle of vodka, which will then be gulped down, hastily and without pleasure, in a nearby doorway. I watched a Russian, in an Avar restaurant in a remote Caucasian town, sitting beneath a sign which warned sternly, 'Citizens are forbidden to bring their own drink', surreptitiously extract a bottle of cognac from his briefcase and drink it down in three straight tumblerfuls before eating lunch. Drink, the 'green serpent', as Russians call it, is part of every child's education; five per cent, according to one survey, begin at the age of seven. To Russian parents, mothers as well as fathers, for a young man to get drunk is normal; not to do so is unmanly.

The state revenue from alcohol sales is far outweighed by the losses they cause: half of all crime (and ninety per cent of juvenile delinquency); a third of all car accidents; and economic damage estimated at one-tenth of gross national product. Yet the Soviet authorities have never made a serious effort to curb alcoholic abuse, mainly because there is no other leisure activity as innocuous politically as drinking to put in its place. To paraphrase Marx, vodka, not religion, is the opium of the Russian people.

A Soviet radio commentator in 1979 argued defensively that 'it would be naive to expect tremendous results in only sixty-two years', the time that had then elapsed since the Bolshevik Revolution.[1] In fact, the problem is getting worse. According to a Soviet specialist, Dr Emiljans Brokans, alcoholic patients have become younger and younger, and many have developed 'harmful personalities' or become 'psychologically so unstable that they can be of no appreciable benefit to either society or the family'.[2]

Dostoyevsky's works are rarely found in Soviet bookshops. Ideologically they raise too many questions. Moreover the Soviet Union, despite having some of the world's greatest forests, suffers from a chronic shortage of paper. Collections of Brezhnev's speeches have priority;

Russian past and the Soviet present, it is impossible to avoid using the word in a broader sense than it properly now has. With that caveat, I have used the term, Soviet, to pertain to the whole country and its peoples, and Russian to describe that which is ethnically Russian, or whose essential quality lies in its Russianness.

nineteenth-century classics come near the bottom of the list. Even when a new edition does appear, it is sold off, under the counter, to favoured customers, without ever reaching the shelves. Yet it is in the men and women who people Dostoyevsky's novels, more than those of any other great Russian writer, that young Russians today find a reflection of themselves. He chronicled the extremism which mixes uneasily with conformity in the Russian soul. To a Russian, you are a friend or an enemy; for or against. There is no middle course, no possibility of compromise. Love and hatred, truth and falsehood, are absolute. There are no shades of grey.

In China, compromise is the very stuff of life. During the Cultural Revolution, the wife of an elderly professor in Shanghai decided she could no longer endure the persecution of the Red Guards, and urged her husband to commit suicide with her. He tried to persuade her to change her mind. But, as he told friends later, 'Neither of us could persuade the other, so she hanged herself, and I lived.' Or, to take another example, in 1640 a great famine occurred in Shandong, in Eastern China. A local historian, Pu Songling, recorded how a young couple decided that since they could not both survive together, the man would sell his wife and use the proceeds to try to leave the famine-stricken region; in that way they could at least survive separately. Three hundred years later, an educated youth in a village near Canton tried to persuade another young man and his wife, both also educated youths, to join him in an attempt to flee to Hong Kong. 'I remember,' he wrote afterwards, 'that she exhorted her husband to go with me. She would stay behind and bring up their children.'

Except in times of great tension, the Chinese abhor extremes and absolutes. Where the mental world of a Russian divides into black and white, good and evil, and his mood swings violently from one to the other, a Chinese sees both good and evil in all things. His ideals are harmony and stability.

Under the tsars, under Stalin, even now, though more mildly, under Brezhnev, the Russian people have been subdued by the knout. Mao, like his imperial predecessors, tried to rule by precept. Confucius said: 'If the people are led by laws, and uniformity is sought in giving them punishment, they will try to avoid the punishment but will have no sense of shame. If they are led by virtue, and uniformity is sought in ruling them by propriety, they will have a sense of shame and moreover will become good.' Mao, like Confucius, was concerned not with the appearance of obedience, but with its substance, the 'goodness', the inner nature of man.

In the Soviet Union, the purpose of prison is punishment; in China it is thought reform. In Russia, over the centuries, extremism, on the part of rulers and ruled alike, has fostered repression; anarchism is complemented and controlled by strong central government. Russian stubbornness is legendary. Chinese are pliant. For all Mao's affirmations of the primacy of the people, life is still lived by the Confucian prescription, 'The relation between the ruler and the ruled is like that between the wind and the grass. When the wind blows, the grass must bend.'

These differences colour life at every level. Soviet motorists spend their time overtaking on the inside, speeding, driving with unsafe loads – particularly lorries, which invariably spill a good part of their cargo en route, be it bricks or cabbages, to the peril of anyone driving too close behind – in short, trying in every way to sneak out of the strait-jacket of traffic regulations, while 300,000 Soviet traffic police (roughly one for every fifty vehicles) spend their time trying to stop them. In the cities, a police post is sited at every major cross-roads, the largest of which are also monitored by television. On main roads, there are police posts every twenty miles, linked by radio, at which motorists are required to slow down to a crawl. On some inter-city highways police use helicopters, as well as radar traps, to spot 'failures of road discipline'. Those who are caught are given on-the-spot fines, and after three or more offences their driving licences are suspended.

China has nothing comparable to this apparatus of control: traffic police, in the view of Chinese road-users, are part of the grass, not the wind, and neither they nor the rules they are supposed to enforce are paid the least attention.

During the Cultural Revolution, groups of Red Guards in some parts of Peking decided that traffic lights would be more revolutionary if red meant 'go' and green meant 'stop'. Some lights were altered, others were left as they were – an action which in most cities would cause chaos. In Peking, it made hardly any difference.

Ignoring traffic lights is only one peculiarity of Chinese traffic. Drivers turning on to a main road from a side-street neither slow down nor look to see if anything is coming. Pedestrians walk straight out into a stream of cars without lifting their heads. Cyclists shoot blindly across busy main roads, laughing to cover their embarrassment if a screech of brakes tells them they were almost killed. One result is that Peking, with fewer motor vehicles than any other major capital, has as many road deaths each year as London or New York. Another is that all Chinese drivers keep one hand permanently on the horn. Peking is also therefore one of the noisiest cities in the world. At the end of 1979, an international conference there on environmental problems had to move to another building after traffic and factory noise made the original venue unusable.

The lack of traffic sense among Chinese affects city dwellers and peasants, old and young alike. It is not so much a sign of recklessness or ignorance, as it would be in the Soviet Union, but of fatalism. 'They know it is dangerous,' a Chinese friend said, 'but they just don't care.'

The Russian character owes much to the vastness of the country. Even near Moscow, you can walk all day through birch forests and across fields and see not a single soul. In summer the ground is carpeted with tiny wild strawberries and a teeming profusion of wild flowers, and in the distance you see the glint of the onion domes of a village church – a landscape unchanged since the days of Tolstoy. In winter, you travel on cross-country skis across a patchwork of white fields, through dark brown and silver woods, where the ice is packed like grey scrambled egg at the sides of frozen rivers, waiting for the thaw. It is a landscape of the same brooding strength as is written in the faces of the Russian people.

For centuries, they have lived in tiny communities, many days' journey apart, dwarfed by the immensity of the steppe, the forests, the tundra and the desert, lashed by bitter cold and scorching heat. Those are the extremes reflected in the Russian spirit. A similar sense of space, of huge skies and immense plains, has made individualism an American virtue.

The Chinese have none of this. Their countryside is among the most densely populated in the world. The grandeur of Tibet, where the mountains rear up to 20,000 feet from wide, desolate, boulder-strewn valleys, or the bleak emptiness of northern Heilongjiang, near the border with Soviet Siberia, the Great Northern Wilderness, as Chinese call it, are lost on them. Those who are sent to live there often cannot adjust to the loneliness of a land with few people.

Individualism and anarchism are not the same thing; the differences between Soviet Russia and capitalist America do not need to be spelt out. Yet Americans and Russians have more in common than is generally acknowledged. As superpower adversaries, they are well matched. Each sees in the other's views a mirror image of its own – the truth, stood on its head. There is the same unwillingness to compromise, the same absolute conviction in the correctness of one's own position, the same naive, dogmatic moralism. Americans and Russians delight in building taller sky-scrapers, bigger aircraft, in jumping higher, running faster, speaking longer than other nations. Even in opposites there are similarities. In the Soviet Union, censorship is total; in the United States, the absence of censorship is total. In pre-revolutionary Russia, it was only by an accident that translations of Marx's works were published, the censor regarding them as too dull to do harm. Americans make public things which their own interests require them to keep secret. Russians keep secret even those things which are already public. The same extremism which guides the Russian temperament has made America a country where the best co-exists with the worst, the super-rich with the very poor, absolute probity with absolute corruption. Americans are brash, Russians heavy-handed. In both countries life is raw, utilitarian.

Chinese and Europeans are more pragmatic and cynical. In politics they share a polished wiliness, a sense of having seen it all before, that is absent in the more recently emerged superpowers. 'Empires wax and wane; states cleave asunder and coalesce' – begins one of China's greatest novels, the fourteenth-century *Romance of the Three Kingdoms*. Despite twenty years of Maoist turbulence, the Chinese character, like the European, has an essential moderation, a willingness to bend or modify convictions that in a Russian or an American would be seen as weakness.

Russians are immoderate. A Russian wallows in human relationships, and regards Europeans as cold and superficial in their feelings. He is intolerant, self-righteous, patriotic to the point of chauvinism, the most generous and the most maddening of men. The Russian soul is a cross which all who deal with Russians have to bear. A Chinese is at the opposite pole of reserve. His loyalty and obligations lie first to his immediate family, then to relatives and friends, next to his home district, and lastly to anyone else. Friendship and trust are built up slowly. To outsiders, he conceals his feelings behind forms and conventions, and if he has something to say he approaches it with caution, elliptically not directly.

The emotionalism of Russians, the yearning for perfection that has produced some of the world's great literature and music, the repudiation of individual values in favour of a universal truth, the duality of anarchy and conformism, make them the hardest people for Westerners to come to terms with. They, in turn, find it equally hard to come to terms with us.

'We may draw near to Westerners, be more or less in agreement with them,' wrote Dmitri Mereshkov, 'but sooner or later there comes a moment when they cease to understand us, and regard us as inhabitants of another planet.'[3] Those words were published in a Russian newspaper in 1908, but they have not lost a jot of truth. Exactly seventy years later, a Soviet official in the Central Committee *apparat* told an American journalist:

33

You cannot understand us because you have not suffered and survived what we have. You have not been under the Tartar yoke, you have not lived under a Stalin – and God keep you from ever having to. You are from a different world. You are like Martians to us. And I suppose we are like Martians to you.[4]

Mereshkov explained this gulf of incomprehension as that between sceptics and mystics, individuals and an unformed collective mass. The Soviet Party official hinted at another element, the ambiguity of Russians towards their own identity. They are in Europe but not of it, living on the borderline between East and West. 'We are the Scythians,' wrote the Russian poet, Alexander Blok. 'Yes, Asians, a slant-eyed greedy tribe.'

Ever since the humane, liberal tradition of Yaroslav the Wise was swept away by the Mongol hordes in the thirteenth century and replaced by weapons of terror and the lash, oriental despotism has coloured Russian rule. Moscow and the older Russian cities have an Asiatic quality not found further west. The debate between Eastern slavophiles and liberal Westernisers, which once pitted Dostoyevsky against Turgenev, carries on today among Soviet dissidents, and within the Soviet Politburo: the KGB chief, Yuri Andropov, is said to be the leading slavophile; Brezhnev, the leading Westerniser.

Solzhenitsyn was not the first to believe that 'the West is on the road to ruin . . . We Russians, on the other hand, are young and vigorous; we shall inscribe our spirit in the history of the human mind.' Those were the words of Prince Odoyevski, 150 years ago. When, in 1974, Solzhenitsyn put forward a set of authoritarian, nationalist prescriptions for Russia's salvation, it was his friend, the mild-mannered liberal, Andrei Sakharov, who issued a statement from the cluttered, ever-welcoming flat on Chkalov Street, where he then lived, warning Russians to be on their guard against what he saw as dangerous parallels with some of Stalin's policies. Yet the slavophile, Solzhenitsyn, rather than the Westerniser, Sakharov, was closer in that debate to the thinking of the majority of ordinary people.

To a Soviet citizen, for whom the very notion of pluralism is wholly alien, Western-style democracy is incomprehensible, unattractive and chaotic. The dictatorship under which he lives is not merely imposed from above, but also answers an almost pathological need from below for guidance and order.

The uncertainty of Russians over where they really belong and the division of the world into conflicting absolutes are a form of national paranoia. The same attributes which have created the Russian genius for chess, have also produced mistrust, suspicion, and a pervasive insecurity which must constantly be reassured. Soviet cities are festooned with placards and slogans, sometimes so gigantic that they cover an entire side of a nine-storey building, declaring: 'Glory to the Soviet People!' and 'Glory to the Heroic Leninist Communist Youth League!' To comprehend the mental gulf between such a nation and the people of a Western country, imagine the response if, say, the English Midlands were littered with slogans proclaiming, 'Glory to the people of Birmingham!' Even in China, where very different values obtain, no placards praise the people of Peking.

The Chinese have no such doubts about their identity; for millennia they lived at the centre of a cultural world of their own making, secure in the belief that all without were barbarians. China's problems in coming to terms with the West stem not from present insecurity, but from the feudal isolation of the past.

If I have dwelt on the timeless aspects of the Russian and the Chinese mind, rather than the qualities of the new Soviet man and his erstwhile Maoist equivalent, it is because, in the Soviet Union and, above all, in China, communism is skin deep, a new veneer (actually, on closer examination, not even so new) beneath which the essential forms of Russian and Chinese life have survived unchanged. Apart from periods of extreme dogmatism, such as the great purges of the 1930s and the last years of Stalin's life, or the Cultural Revolution in China, the communist element in Russian and Chinese behaviour, whether as individuals or nations, is far outweighed by what went before.

Nonetheless, communism has been a modifier, and, in some respects, a great leveller of behaviour, particularly under Stalin and Mao. While theoretically in both the Soviet Union and China innovation is encouraged, in practice, outside research laboratories and the defence industry, it is obstructed. Soviet and Chinese bureaucrats value security above success. An untested new process which, to a Western factory manager, offers the possibility of profit, is viewed by a communist functionary in terms of the risk of failure.

Not only inventiveness but initiative of all kinds is repressed. Here communism has reinforced a collectivist ethic which, in both countries, was already firmly entrenched. In Confucian China, the individual was subordinate both to the family and the state; the Chinese word for 'everyone' is *da jia*, 'big family'. Mao's short-lived appeals to China's youth in the 1960s and 70s to 'dare to rebel', and to 'go against the tide' were not a call for individualism – merely a demand for a new tide, running in the contrary direction to the one that had prevailed before. In Russia, the word used to describe the traditional village community (and by extension, the world), *mir*, also means 'peace'. To this the communist system has added a centralised decision-making process and a blanket of personal security that have smothered initiative, by obviating both choice and responsibility. A Soviet citizen is in practice guaranteed the basic, and bare, necessities of life: work, food, shelter, free health care and education. His ingenuity is expended in finding loopholes in the system through which that bareness can be made a little more comfortable. In China, a much poorer country, the security blanket is thin and full of holes. But the provision of housing, however primitive, of food and other essentials is accepted as a social responsibility, and individual choice is even more limited than in the Soviet Union when it comes to such matters as employment and where to live.

After sixty years of communism, Russians who emigrate to the West or Israel find extraordinary difficulty in adjusting to their new surroundings. It is not just their inflexible nationalism, the longing for the birch forests and the steppes, that eats away their souls. What floors the Soviet emigrant is the sheer difficulty of coping with a society where each man is an island, where he has to fend for himself, where at every turn, at work and in the home, he has to make independent decisions and choices which before, in the Soviet Union, were always made for him.

Chinese, being less dogmatic in their attitudes and less marked by a communist system that has been in existence only half as long, adjust more easily to societies, such as Hong Kong and Singapore, where survival depends on individual initiative. Yet a Chinese Communist Youth League delegation, visiting the United States in 1979, was astonished to discover that most young Americans are self-supporting from the age of eighteen, living independent lives and frequently working their own way through college. Chinese youth, it commented on its return, would do well to learn more of the same spirit of self-reliance.

Communist rule has also affected behaviour in more specific ways. Among the quarter of a million people killed by the Tangshan earthquake, in July 1976, several thousand died in the city of Tianjin, sixty miles from the epicentre. Most of them were women. The quake struck at night in the full heat of summer when many Chinese sleep naked. At first people rushed into the street straight from their beds, but as soon as the initial terror subsided, the women, in great embarrassment, ran back indoors to get their clothes. They were caught by a violent after-shock, which brought down many of the buildings that had withstood the first tremor.

After a similar earthquake in 1668, an eyewitness reported: 'After an hour or so, calm began to return; and then one could see, out in the streets, undressed men and women standing in groups, excitedly telling of their own experiences, having quite forgotten that they were wearing no clothes.'[5]

Sexual puritanism characterises the doctrines of both the Soviet and the Chinese parties, and both countries present a prudish exterior. The change has been most dramatic in China, which until 1949 was renowned for its singing girls and brothels and sexual licence of every kind. In Shanghai, a fourteen-year-old prostitute had an average life expectancy of two years. But since the communist takeover, even talk of sex has been largely taboo. When in 1979 the *China Youth News* published a letter from a young man asking how to stop compulsive masturbation (he was advised to go for a run and take a cold bath before bed),[6] several foreign correspondents found their Chinese interpreters refused point blank to make a translation; the subject was simply too shameful. In summer, in many Chinese towns, people take to their bathing costumes and flock to the rivers, crowding the banks as densely as a Western seaside resort in August. But all are men: there is not a woman to be seen.

In the Soviet Union, the Party also insists that sex is not a subject for public discussion. Nudity on stage or on the screen is generally banned (Tarkovsky's great film about the life of the medieval icon painter, *Andrei Rublev*, is one of the few exceptions, but even that was held up by the censor for four years). As in China, there is no sex education in schools. The first-ever Soviet sex manual was published in 1974 – in a small edition which sold out within days and has not been reprinted.

This policy is based on Lenin's dictum, 'The Revolution demands concentration . . . It cannot tolerate orgiastic conditions. Dissoluteness in sexual life is bourgeois . . . Self-control, self-discipline is not slavery, not even in love.'[7]

But beneath the prim and proper façade, the reality in both countries is rather different. Russian women have never been unduly retiring. Tolstoy, in *War and Peace*, has Natasha, on her first visit to the opera, gazing wide-eyed at 'the half-naked women in the boxes, especially at Helene, in the next box . . . her whole bosom completely exposed'. Half a century later, when Tsar Nicholas II's strait-laced German Empress, Alexandra, expressed disapproval of the court ladies' décolleté, she was told rudely that that was how Russians liked it. In the Soviet Union, girls took to the mini-skirt as nowhere else, and mountainous women, well past middle age, regularly appear on the beach bulging grotesquely in bras and pants. On summer evenings, in Moscow, half the young couples are locked in unrestrained public embrace, lost to the world. The most ardent and abandoned partings I have ever witnessed, on the screen or off, have been played out in Soviet railway stations.

In the towns, young Russians are quite as promiscuous as their contemporaries in the West. As early as 1966, a survey of university students in Leningrad, admittedly the most sophisticated of Soviet cities, showed that half the men had had sexual relations before the age of eighteen. By twenty-one the figure rose to eighty-five per cent, and seventy per cent of the women. Another survey found that half of all young married women in Leningrad approved of extra-marital affairs. In the 1970s, venereal disease, which had been decreasing, started to rise again, particularly among the young. According to a specialist in Soviet Latvia, the main cause was 'casual sexual intercourse with unknown or little known persons'.[8]

Even in China, the official puritanism is being eroded. Indeed, at one level it has always been hypocritical. Mao married four times – on the last occasion summarily divorcing his faithful companion of the Long March, He Zizhen, to make way for Jiang Qing, then a seductive young film actress from Shanghai. The State Chairman, Liu Shaoqi, married six times. To young Chinese, urged to practise total abstinence, such inconsistency rankles, and scurrilous stories continually circulate about the alleged sexual prowess of their leaders, most commonly and most improbably, the venerable eighty-four-year-old Vice-Chairman Ye Jianying.

By 1980, attitudes among the young had evolved to a point where an enraged official in Hangzhou was moved to complain in the press that in one of the city's parks, 'young men and women were kissing against trees along the lake, and others were embracing and necking on benches . . . Their conduct was so mean and disgusting as to spoil other people's fun.'[9] In Wenzhou, a large city on the East China coast, so many unmarried women were becoming pregnant and resisting abortions that the municipal population control programme was undermined. Further south, in Guangdong province, regulations were issued declaring illegitimate births illegal, and levying a fine of ten per cent of the mother's wages 'until nine months after a marriage licence has been obtained'.[10]

Official concern showed most clearly in an article in *China Youth*, which, after recounting a salutary tale of a Shanghai girl who had been made pregnant and then abandoned, declared that love was 'absolutely not a solely private affair', but affected the whole of society. It went on to call for a strict dividing line between courtship and marriage, in order to prevent pre-marital sex.[11]

> Certain young people . . . guided by . . . confused ideas, have an extremely casual attitude towards sexual relations. For young women this brings all kinds of disastrous consequences. Some fall pregnant while not being married and must seek abortions, which affect their reputation quite as much as their health. Others, having had sexual relations, discover that they don't like their partners after all, and the best thing is to part. Still others, while discontented with their partners, feel that since 'the rice is already cooked', there is nothing for it but to marry against their will . . .
>
> This is a problem to which we must attach the greatest importance . . . It is better to take preventive measures than to shut the stable door after the horse has bolted. Therefore we solemnly exhort young women during their courtship: '*Do not lightly give your body to anyone, no matter whom it may be!*'

Permissiveness is most marked among intellectual families, who will sometimes set aside a room for a young unmarried couple to sleep together, or at least, as many families have only one room, arrange for them to spend some time alone there. Even in the countryside it is not uncommon for unmarried girls to become pregnant. A schoolteacher who taught in a remote rural area for three years in the early 70s said fifty per cent of the seventeen- and eighteen-year-olds, while still at school, had babies which they drowned in the river at birth. However there are enormous variations from one village to another, from one neighbourhood to the next, depending on the extent to which the official puritanism is enforced or ignored by the local Party committee.

In some districts, even in Peking, a girl who sleeps around is liable to be sent to a reform school. Adultery is regarded as a crime against the family, and a man who has an affair with the wife of a serving soldier risks a three-year prison term. Cases involving soldiers' wives are treated with particular severity to protect army morale. For the same reason a woman is forbidden to seek a divorce from a soldier without his consent. Divorce has always been discouraged in China as contrary to the Confucian ethic of family and social harmony, and even in ordinary cases, communist courts have seen it as their task to reconcile warring couples rather than to approve their separation. One result of this is that bigamy, although illegal, is widespread, especially in the countryside. In January 1981, a new more liberal marriage law was introduced, authorising divorce on the grounds of 'a complete breakdown of mutual affection'. The special provisions for soldiers' wives, however, were retained unchanged.

Soviet courts, by contrast, grant divorce virtually on demand. Since 1965 the divorce rate has tripled, becoming an important factor in the declining birth rate. One in three Soviet marriages breaks up, and in the Baltic Republics it is two in five, the same level as in the United States. In Britain, one marriage in five fails; in Peking, about one in fifty. A quarter of Soviet divorces are caused by alcoholism, which in China is almost non-existent; in four years, I have only once seen a Chinese drunk in public, a middle-aged man weaving his way through Peking on a bicycle, singing.

Crimes with a sexual element are never reported in the Soviet press, but in China, especially since Mao's death, certain types of offences have been publicised. In 1978, the director of a district housing bureau in Shanghai was imprisoned for obtaining sexual favours from local women in exchange for putting them at the head of the queue for flats.[12] And in Amoy, two years later, I came across a series of cases, described in official proclamations posted outside the municipal courthouse, which showed a ferocity echoing the fantastic cruelty of the Cultural Revolution. Among the least violent was a case of incest.

A commune member, Lin Jianxi, aged 22, and his sister, Lin Qiuhua, aged 26, began having sexual relations in January 1979. The girl's husband, Lin Mushan, tried to intervene, but she refused to mend her ways. On the night of November 23, Lin Jianxi, although he knew that the husband was at home in bed, entered the house and had intercourse with his sister. The husband awoke and caught them in the act. But instead of admitting his error, the criminal Lin Jianxi picked up a wooden club and beat Lin Mushan crazily about the head. He then used a chopper to hack him to death. His sister did not try to stop him. After this, they fled to the mountains to hide.

He was executed. She was sentenced to ten years' imprisonment.

The violence of that murder is typical. A Russian is capable of great rage and brutality – and great tenderness, but not, in ordinary circumstances, of such abandonment in fury. Chinese give the appearance of being much more restrained. But should the normal restraints on behaviour be lifted, few limits remain. The same is true of Japanese and Koreans, and many South-East Asians.

Incest is one of the commoner forms of deviance among Chinese. Homosexuality, though a criminal offence in both the Soviet Union and China, also occurs: in Shanghai, in 1979, the press complained of young men who 'flirt and walk in an effeminate manner . . . and regard peculiar, abnormal, vulgar and disgusting things as beautiful'.[13] Sex crimes against children appear rare in both countries but are not unknown. One ghastly case, in which an eight-year-old boy was tortured and killed, was described in harrowing detail in wallposters put up in

January 1980 outside a housing estate in Northern Peking, where the child had lived.

China also suffers from an unusually high incidence of rape and gang rape, particularly by groups of youths, and of indecent exposure, reflecting the frustration and tensions generated by the Maoist taboo against pre-marital sex combined with a policy of late marriage. By law Chinese women may marry at twenty, and men at twenty-two, but in practice, to reduce population growth, permission to marry is often withheld until several years later. In 1980, signs appeared that this policy might be starting to change. The *People's Daily* said late birth was preferable to late marriage so as 'not to suppress a human being's biological needs', and quoted Mencius as saying, 'to like sex is human nature'.[14] There have also been calls for better-quality condoms. As in the Soviet Union, where the domestic product is known colloquially as *kaloshi*, 'galoshes' – and it is a very fair description – Chinese-made sheaths are a positive deterrent to birth control, thick, clumsy and designed to be washed and re-used. One proposal was for the import of Japanese technology to upgrade them.

Chinese, and Russians, draw a clear distinction between sex, as an instrument of love and pleasure, which is hemmed about with embarrassment, and other bodily functions, which are treated with complete openness. In the British public-school tradition, Chinese and Soviet public lavatories usually have no doors, and a Chinese woman finds nothing strange in standing talking to her friend, who is emptying her bowels. In small towns, forty years ago, people squatted in the open each morning at street corners, their faeces being collected and spread, raw, on the fields as fertiliser. Today settlements exist in Soviet Siberia where conditions are little better: the lavatory is an outhouse, knee-deep in frozen excrement. Even in Peking, most houses have no sewage system – any more than they do in Tokyo, superficially one of the most modern of cities. In both capitals the average family relies on the daily collection of slops by what is euphemistically called a 'honey cart'.

Defecation in China has always been a matter of public rather than private concern, because intensive farming and the pressure of population mean that the soil must be constantly replenished and enriched. The main sources of organic fertiliser are still humans and animals. On country roads you see children and old men armed with scrapers and baskets, collecting dung that has missed the bags normally hung beneath horses' tails.

This view of excrement, as a commodity in daily use, is unique to China, and has led to it becoming an established means of humiliating enemies. The Qing dynasty legal code prescribed a punishment of twenty blows for striking another person; eighty blows for throwing excrement at him; and a hundred blows for stuffing it into his mouth. During the Cultural Revolution, victims of struggle sessions were frequently smeared with it, and in December 1979, the *People's Daily* reported a case in Xuzhou, north-west of Shanghai, in which a woman, aggrieved by the authorities' refusal to reinstate her husband in his job, 'threw excrement at the responsible official and then emptied a bucket of urine over another functionary who came to stop her'. For her pains she was sentenced to two years' 're-education through labour'.[15]

Imperial Shadows

The changelessness of China has its roots in feudalism, and to a lesser extent, the same is true of Russia. Westerners who live in Moscow find it a standing source of amazement that Lenin was ever able to push a people as stubborn, long-suffering and rooted in their own ways as the Russians into making a revolution; it is a fair certainty that no one will succeed in doing so again. But in China, the weight of the past has an altogether different quality.

Chinese have a sense of historical continuity, of the irrelevance of the passage of time, which is unique. In the Soviet Union, the memory of the Second World War is deliberately kept actual for political reasons. In China, the events of 2,000 years ago *are* actual, to be discussed in the same breath as the doings of yesterday and tomorrow. The event is primary; when it happens is much less important. In 1975, Deng Xiaoping told Cyrus Vance, 'We can wait five years, ten years or a hundred years, but reunification with Taiwan will finally be realised'; and, on East and West Germany, 'This will be a problem until they are reunified, if not in a hundred or two hundred years, then in a thousand years.'[1] The figures are arbitrary; the principle is not. Deng could say, in an interview in 1979, that the Chinese people 'have accomplished not a few things in 2,000 years, but in the last four or five hundred years we have fallen behind'.[2] It is rather as though an Italian prime minister, appearing on a television current affairs programme, were to evoke the glories of Ancient Rome and then admit that, since the Renaissance, things had not been going too well. Yet in China, the perspective of history is that long.

This shows most clearly in the press. The *People's Daily*, for example, begins an article on official corruption with the words:[3]

> In the Song dynasty, Bao Gong, an upright magistrate, threw an intricately carved ink slab into the river as soon as he found out that his servant had secretly accepted it as a gift on his behalf. Are cadres of the Communist Party no match for an upright magistrate?

The Song dynasty ended 700 years ago.

More often the parallel with the present is left to be inferred. The national newspapers regularly carry long disquisitions with titles such as, 'A Tentative Discourse on the Resurgence during the Zhao and Xuan reigns', which ostensibly discuss political intrigues in the Western Han dynasty, a century before Christ, but are in fact veiled commentaries on present-day politics. An article may say[4]

> The Wu Emperor craved for greatness and success and was arrogant and imperious. Especially during his later years he divorced himself from his ministers . . . Crafty sycophants took this opportunity to seize high posts. This deepened the split inside the ruling group. In 91 BC troubles arose within the imperial family, a case of witchcraft was concocted and the Crown Prince died uncleared of false charges, thus shaking the foundation of the country. In 88 BC Ma Heluo and his brother launched a coup d'état in which the Wu Emperor almost lost his life

but what it is actually talking about is Mao (the Wu Emperor), the Cultural Revolution ('troubles'), the purge of Liu Shaoqi (the Crown Prince) and Lin Biao (Ma Heluo) and his abortive coup. To write an 'objective' account of the past in China is all but impossible. History is written, and read, as allegory, and always has been. Ever since the days of Confucius, scholars have used historical articles about previous dynasties to say what could not be said openly about their own time.

Language has also fostered continuity. Chinese records go back nearly 4,000 years in the world's oldest writing system still in general use. Classical phrases such as, 'the jade-like firmament is cleared of dust and a long-standing grievance has been redressed', still sometimes shine out from slabs of communist jargon.[5]

But the most important factor is a mentality which continues to view the present as co-existent with the remote past. An American academic, visiting the home village of his Chinese wife, asked local people whether he was the first foreigner to set foot there. No, he was told, he wasn't. When he enquired further, an old man explained that the Mongol army had passed that way, going to Kaifeng. That was Kublai Khan's army, in the thirteenth century.

'Beneath our accomplishments,' wrote the Chinese philosophical journal, *Zhexue Yanjiu*, in 1979, 'there still exists the basis of the feudal society and traditional consciousness. The dead still maintain their hold on the living.'[6] An unofficial journal, *Hailanghua*, put the same thought more tersely: 'The cloak of Marxism covers the soul of feudalism.'[7] Even the Party press has acknowledged that feudal ideas are 'deep-rooted and firmly implanted',[8] and have 'extensive influence on every aspect of society and on the Party as well'.[9]

The Soviet system, propped up by the KGB, mirrors the feudal system of the tsars, maintained by their secret police the *Okhrana*, quite as faithfully as communist China reflects the institutions of the Empire. With China and Vietnam, it is one of the only three countries in modern times, all communist, to embalm and display as a holy relic the body of a dead leader. But no Soviet leader, no Soviet newspaper ever admits any resemblance to the past. The Soviet system is depicted as 'the most progressive social system in human history'; its shortcomings are attributed never to the system itself, but to the inadequacies of the officials who operate it. Even Soviet dissidents rarely look for the source of the regime's repressiveness in the legacy of the past, Sakharov and the independent Marxist, Roy Medvedev, being among the very few exceptions. Most are like Solzhenitsyn, blaming all on the communist present as though it had no connection with what went before.

In this, as in much else, Solzhenitsyn puts himself on a par with the very men he condemns. His system would be no more liberal than theirs. The same Russian qualities that have made him a great writer have also made him a zealot, whose mind is as impervious to contrary views as the most dogmatic Soviet official. This inflexibility, this lack of pragmatism in the Russian character, led to the execution of the Tsar and his family at Ekaterinburg. Communism was good; tsarism must be expunged. China's last emperor, Pu Yi, was treated very differently. Even though he committed treason, heading the Japanese puppet empire in Manchuria during the Sino-Japanese war, he was imprisoned for only nine years, and spent the last part of his life in a large mansion north of the Forbidden City, with a maid provided by the government and the use of an official car, until dying of cancer in 1967.

The same contrast is found in the two countries' attitudes to religion. Both insist that church be subservient to state; both guarantee in their constitutions 'the freedom to believe and not to believe and to propagate atheism'. Dissident priests who refuse to accept these limits are as likely to finish up in a labour camp in China as they are in the Soviet Union. But the public propagation of atheism, which forms the core of Soviet religious policy, is largely absent in China. The stream of anti-religious articles which floods the Soviet press has no parallel in Chinese newspapers. There is nothing comparable to the Soviet *Znaniye* (Knowledge) Society, which claims a membership of two million atheist militants. There are no atheist museums, such as the one at the Pechersky Monastery in Kiev, where the walls are covered with ancient frescoes of Christ and his disciples, and the display cases contain photographs of atrocities, to show the support Ukrainian churchmen gave the Nazis during the war, and old cartoons of priests with hideously distorted faces standing at church doors like spiders luring the faithful into their webs. In China, religious policy is based on the proposition that 'religion will die out only . . . when social productive forces and science and technology are highly developed and the people's material and cultural lives are greatly improved,'[10] efforts to suppress it prematurely being therefore pointless.

In the Soviet Union, at Easter, women wait in line outside the painted Orthodox churches for black-garbed, bearded priests to sprinkle holy water on the *kulich*, the traditional Easter cake, and hand-coloured eggs they have brought for blessing. At midnight, the bells ring out, tinny and jangling, and the clergy, wearing white and silver robes, followed by the choir, also in white, walk round the church in a candlelight procession carrying an icon, before proclaiming the joyous message, '*Khristos Voskres!*' – 'Christ Is Risen!' It is perhaps the most beautiful sight the Soviet Union has to offer, profoundly Russian, attracting card-carrying communists as well as the faithful, atheists and believers, young and old. But the young never get closer than the churchyard railings before being stopped by police and *druzhinniki*, volunteer militia. Easter, according to the Moscow youth newspaper, *Moskovsky Komsomolyets*, is 'a harmful survival from the past' which must be combated by militant atheism. 'We cannot remain indifferent,' it said, 'when children and teenagers appear at church festivals. This first step towards religion may prove fatal, leading them to choose a false path in life.' In fact the Soviet authorities are so far from being indifferent to the religious upbringing of the young that it is a wonder that there are any believers left. A Soviet child, born into a religious family, is under relentless pressure from his peers, teachers, social and youth organisations, to abjure his family's faith from the moment he enters primary school until he completes his military service. But while old people are the mainstay of the Orthodox Church, when they die new old people always emerge to take their place.

In China there are also restrictions on religious instruction for the young. However, in 1980 teenage acolytes were being admitted to Buddhist monasteries, twelve-year-old boys took part in Friday prayers in the mosques, and in Tibet, where children accompanied their parents to the temples, I watched a group of nomad youths from Qinghai, prostrating themselves in the unmade streets of the old quarter of Lhasa, as they measured out with their bodies the four sides of the Jokhang, the holiest place of Tibetan Buddhism.

Nevertheless it would be misleading to give the impression that China has greater religious freedom than the Soviet Union. For almost twenty years, starting in 1958, the country was caught up in an accelerating campaign of destruction of all old things, which at its height, during the Cultural Revolution, halted religious activity with a brutality and completeness far exceeding any Soviet atheist campaign. The Soviet Union, with an estimated 25 million believers, has 20,000 churches, mosques and synagogues nominally open for worship. In China, with four times the population and probably 200 million people with elements of Buddhist or Taoist belief, the number of places open for worship is far smaller. The Soviet Union ordains nearly 150 priests each year. That may be few, relative to the number of churches, but China has ordained only one priest since 1965; in 1980 its seminaries and Koranic schools were just beginning to re-open.

Yet since Mao's death, and earlier, in the 1950s, China has shown a willingness to permit religion and communism to co-exist which finds no place in Soviet policy. In the Soviet Union atheism and belief are in perpetual conflict; the churches are circumscribed and undermined by legal chicanery and crude oppression. For a Soviet leader to describe religious faith as a 'fine' thing, as Hu Yaobang, when General Secretary of the Chinese Party, said of Buddhism in Tibet, would be inconceivable, no matter what his motives.[11]

In China, people have always assimilated elements of different faiths. Buddhism, Taoism, even – to the horror of the missionaries – Christianity have not been mutually exclusive. In Russia, such pluralist tendencies are totally denied. Orthodoxy was ever the one, true faith. So, today, is Soviet communism.

Religion may be one of the most visible elements of each country's feudal inheritance, but others are far more important. 'Feudal things,' said the *People's Daily*, 'include the practice of officials holding their posts for life, patriarchal behaviour, the cult of the individual, bureaucracy, factionalism, love of privilege and nepotism.'[12] That is a fair summary of the most glaring faults of the Chinese and Soviet systems, but it omits one problem which is at least as important as all the others. 'Feudalism and anti-foreignism are twins,' wrote a Chinese communist historian. 'The feudal closed-door mentality and anti-foreignism linger on like ghosts.'[13]

Throughout their history, Chinese have held foreigners and foreign countries at arm's length. In the Tang dynasty, 1,000 years ago, when Arab merchants started trading in Quanzhou and Canton, special districts were set up for them where no Chinese was permitted to live. They were allowed to build mosques there, to live under Islamic law and to administer their own affairs. But they were not permitted to live elsewhere. China tried to apply the same principle in the nineteenth-century foreign concessions, and it applies today in the diplomatic ghettos which house foreigners in Peking. Green-uniformed soldiers of the People's Liberation Army mount a round-the-clock guard at the gates, and no Chinese is allowed to enter without a special pass. On one occasion even a fire engine was held up until clearance was given. Nor will the Chinese police investigate crimes committed by foreigners within the ghettos, stating that unless Chinese are involved they have no jurisdiction.

In the Soviet Union, the element of extra-territoriality is absent, and the guards are police, not military, but otherwise the system is the same. It was Ivan the Terrible, in the sixteenth century, who first herded foreign merchants into enclaves such as *Kitaigorod* (literally, 'China-town'), just outside the Kremlin wall, where they had little contact with the ordinary townsfolk. The motive, as in China, then and now, was to control the influx of foreign culture and ideas.

Visiting ambassadors fared little better. In Tang dynasty China, according to Arthur Waley, they spent

> the whole time of their stay under the charge of a Chinese official specially appointed to keep an eye on them . . . They were shepherded to the Capital, had a formal interview with the Emperor, deposited their 'tribute' and were then taken back to the coast, escorted in some cases (nominally as a mark of high consideration, but no doubt also as an additional precaution) by a senior Palace eunuch. They had no opportunity of mixing with the general public or finding out anything that they had better not know.[14]

When I arrived in Peking in 1977, a year after Mao's death, the approach was not significantly different. Nor was it in nineteenth-century Russia. 'The Russians . . . accompany you everywhere,' wrote the Marquis de Custine. 'Courtesy becomes a means of surveillance here . . . The Russians are still convinced of the efficaciousness of the lie. In Russia, secrecy presides over everything.'

That, too, holds true today. The only change is that the restrictions on travel have become still tighter. Apart from day trips to a few nearby towns, foreigners may travel freely only within a radius of twenty-five miles of the Kremlin (and even there some parts are closed), and in narrower areas of open cities. The overwhelming majority of Soviet towns and cities are closed to foreigners altogether, as are huge areas of the countryside, under regulations promulgated by Stalin in 1947. Even areas which are nominally open may be declared temporarily closed. In 1975, Yerevan was closed for one day on the sixtieth anniversary of the Armenian massacre by the Turks, because the authorities were afraid nationalist demonstrations might occur. A more typical ploy was that of the Soviet Foreign Ministry when I asked to visit Troitsko-Pechorsk, a small logging town in Northern Russia. Situated in the middle of an open area, it has both an airport and an hotel, so there is no practical obstacle to going there. Yet for months I was told, whenever I put forward a fresh travel proposal, that on the dates I wanted to go there it would be 'temporarily closed'. Finally, I asked how long its closure could be expected to last. 'Mr Short,' said the voice at the other end of the telephone, with the candour of extreme weariness, 'it will remain temporarily closed for as long as you want to go there.'

In practice, more than ninety-eight per cent of the Soviet Union is closed to foreigners, not just Westerners, but East Europeans as well. The remaining two per cent consists of fewer than 200 open cities, mainly accessible by air or rail, though in European Russia also in some cases by road. To visit them, a special permit is required, issued by the Interior Ministry or by Intourist. A foreigner travelling by road must follow a predetermined route, and is clocked through by each police post he passes. If he is overdue, a police motorcyclist is despatched to look for him.

The system is not completely foolproof, however. I once drove, with my wife and son, 250 miles across the Southern Ukraine, along an unmarked by-road well away from the authorised route. Having, by chance, slipped through the network of controls, we found ourselves free, for the first and only time in the Soviet Union, to drive anywhere we wanted. Since foreigners were never intended to get into that area, the local police had not been told what to do if a foreigner appeared, and so did nothing. There was much head-scratching the next morning, when the authorities discovered that we were in Rostov-on-the-Don, instead of Zaporozhe, without apparently having passed through any of the checkpoints between. We did not enlighten them.

In China, similar regulations apply. They originated in the days when foreigners living in the coastal settlements were permitted to journey inland only as far as they could return the same day. In 1981, only one road was open to foreign motorists, the sixty-mile stretch from Peking to Tianjin. Three of China's twenty-nine provinces were completely closed. Elsewhere, as in the Soviet Union, foreigners were restricted to about a hundred and fifty open cities and their immediate surroundings.

Foreign students escape some of the restrictions. So, in the Soviet Union, do comrades from fraternal parties. Their counterparts, in old China, were the foreign monks who had access to the political gossip of the monasteries and could visit the homes of ordinary people to beg alms. But the only foreigners who have ever been completely accepted in China are those who have, in effect, 'become Chinese'. Marco Polo did so, when he served at the court of Kublai Khan. So did men such as

George Hatem, an American doctor who joined Mao's forces in the 1930s, and is now a member of the Standing Committee of the Chinese Parliament, the National People's Congress. They have no real Soviet counterpart. The small group of defectors who live in Moscow lead a twilight existence, Soviet citizens on the fringe of Soviet society. Donald Maclean, whom I visited for afternoon tea in his flat on the embankment of the Moscow River, acts as an adviser to the Soviet Government on British affairs. Philby has a job with the Soviet Press Agency, Novosti, the disinformation arm of the KGB.

The Chinese position was explained to Lord Macartney by the Emperor Qian Long, when he came to try to set up a British embassy in Peking in 1793. Foreigners might live in the Chinese capital if they pledged loyalty to the throne, and adopted the dress and habits of mandarins, he was told, but otherwise their presence would 'not be appropriate'; the most that could be permitted would be for them to make periodic visits to bring tribute.

It was Qian Long who rejected George III's overtures for trade with the immortal words, 'We have never valued ingenious articles, nor do we have the slightest need of your country's manufactures.' Half a century later, the development of naval forces, which for the first time meant Europe could project its military power to the Far East, coupled with the greed and aggressiveness of first, British, and then other European trading houses, made such views no longer tenable. By the 1860s, a Westernisation movement had been launched, one of whose leaders wrote, 'Perpetual benefit can be expected when we learn to adopt the barbarians' expertise in producing our own cannons and vessels.'[15] But to others, the feudal diehards, increased contact with foreigners simply strengthened the urge for isolation. In 1900, at the time of the Boxer Rebellion, the Empress Ci Xi said:

> We never asked the foreigners to come here. They are here on sufferance . . . Our country was a civilised country while the people in so-called civilised countries were swinging from their tails from trees; yet those same countries have the audacity to send missionaries to us, to teach *us* religion and civilisation . . . What have they to offer that is better than we have? Nothing at all! . . . The foreigners are the curse of China today . . . The foreign ways are not our ways, and I am bitterly opposed to making them our ways.[16]

Sixty years later Chinese xenophobia exploded again in the Cultural Revolution. In the altered political climate of 1980, Chinese were warned in the press and elsewhere not to show 'blind hostility' to foreigners,[17] or to 'think that all foreigners are bad people'.[18]

The Westernisation movement did not advocate the wholesale adoption of foreign ways. Its slogan was: 'Chinese learning for substance, Western learning for practical use.' It failed because, in the words of a communist historian, 'the flower of the West's modern production technology, grafted onto the tree of Chinese feudal society, proved fundamentally incapable of fruition'.[19] China's leaders today say they want 'advanced science and technology and the management experience of foreign countries, not the bourgeois, decadent way of life'.[20] But technology cannot be excluded from the social and cultural context in which it is created. China's success in absorbing the one depends on its willingness to come to terms with the other.

Mao recognised the problem. In 1956 he said that, in 'grafting foreign things on to the basic Chinese stock', they must be 'cross-bred and combined organically' as a horse combines with an ass to produce a mule.[21] But to produce a mule requires intercourse. The barriers have to come down, and horse and ass have to recognise that they are essentially the same kind of beast. That has not happened.

Barriers to normal contact, political as well as physical, exist in both the Soviet Union and China. Like the nineteenth-century Chinese reformers, who hoped that Western cannons would enable the dynasty to survive without structural change, Brezhnev has imported Western technology to put off the day when the Soviet Union must undergo structural economic change. In so doing, he has followed a precedent that goes back five centuries. Ivan the Great, Prince of Muscovy, brought in Italian architects to build the Kremlin towers and walls, and two of its ornate, onion-domed cathedrals. Ivan the Terrible employed English printers and German military engineers. Peter the Great spent three years touring Europe, and brought back thousands of foreign artisans and administrators to spur Russia to modernise. Yet all ruled with a rod of iron, and rigorously excluded the infection of foreign liberalism.

That, today, is the task of the KGB, and one carried out with deliberate heavy-handedness. Subtlety is not the hallmark of Soviet dealings with foreigners. In 1974, when detente was at its height, Senator Kennedy came to Moscow and was permitted to address a hand-picked audience of students and teachers at Moscow University. Parts of his speech were deliberately not translated, and, at the end, when he asked whether they thought the Soviet Union was spending too much or too little on defence, one elderly professor shook his fist and shouted out that such a question was a provocation. After a few more attempts at discussion, the Soviet interpreter announced that the senator was feeling unwell and the meeting would have to close. Senator

Kennedy said he was not feeling unwell at all; nonetheless, the meeting ended. When in 1975, shortly after the European Security Conference in Helsinki, President Scheel of West Germany reminded the Soviet leaders, at a Kremlin banquet, of the commitments they had made to facilitate emigration, that sentence was missing from the verbatim text of his speech published, as is usual in the Soviet Union, in *Pravda* next morning. Nor has the Helsinki Agreement made much difference to Western television networks which try to satellite film from Moscow; in 1980, at the Olympic Games, as in 1974, during President Nixon's last visit, if the authorities did not like what they saw, the technicians pulled out the plug. But the heavy-handedness of the KGB goes beyond such reflex actions: it is used consciously, artfully, to sow uncertainty and distrust. Since telephones are known to be tapped and rooms are known to be bugged, a foreign diplomat or businessman in the Soviet Union has to proceed on the assumption that every telephone is tapped, every room bugged. Most, of course, are not; not even the KGB has infinite resources. But there is no way of telling which are listened to and which not. Since the KGB makes frequent use of provocations, any unusual approach from a Russian becomes suspect. He may be a spiv, offering to sell you icons, or to change money on the black market at five times the official rate; she may be an old lady, with a letter to be taken abroad, or a young woman who knows the friend of a friend and must see you alone. Most are what they say. A few are not. In this scheme of things, the objective is less to entrap than to intimidate and deter, to create a climate of suspicion and fear in which Russians and foreigners alike conclude that unofficial contacts are better avoided. A similar approach is adopted towards Soviet dissidents, among whom distrust is sown by the use of informers. No one can ever be completely sure who is an informer and who is not under a system where a fourteen-year-old peasant, Pavel Morozov, who reported his own father for keeping back grain in 1932, and was killed by other peasants as a result, is eulogised as a national hero for all Soviet children to emulate.

If people do not trust each other and are afraid to speak openly, the mechanism of control is already largely in place. In the Soviet Union it is backed up by arrests of dissidents, the refusal of exit visas to would-be emigrants, the refusal of marriage licences – the Helsinki Agreement notwithstanding – to Russians who want to marry foreigners, and other forms of harassment. Not all dissidents are arrested, not all exit visas and marriage licences are refused. But arrests and refusals are sufficiently frequent to silence the most outspoken and to convince the uncommitted that deviance is dangerous.

That, at least, is the theory. In practice, Russians being the indisciplined, wilful people they are, the controls are often disregarded. Any foreign car driving from the Finnish border to Leningrad will be flagged down by small children standing in the middle of the empty road, who ask for chewing gum, or by young women wanting to buy cosmetics or clothes. Even Soviet policemen have been known, on occasion, to ask Westerners for sex magazines. Until jamming resumed in 1980 millions of Soviet citizens listened to Western radio stations, despite constant denunciations of them as 'centres of ideological subversion'. One of my favourite letters in Moscow came from an old couple on a collective farm near Krasnodar, asking the BBC to broadcast more church services. They were hard of hearing, they added, so please could the announcers speak a little louder? Others, no less ordinary, sought help directly. A Georgian from Batumi said the local authorities had wrongly turned him out of his apartment. If the BBC broadcast his story, perhaps the ensuing scandal would make them give it back. In general, the further away you are from Moscow, above all in non-Russian Republics, the more willing people are to invite you into their homes and to ignore official warnings that all foreigners, even those from other communist countries, are potential spies.[22]

КУКРЫНИКСЫ-79

Pravda, 1979

Such casual contacts are countered half-heartedly where ordinary people are involved. The KGB's objective is not to prevent contact for its own sake, but to stop foreigners, and Russians, obtaining ideas and information the authorities do not want them to have. In Stalin's time no such distinction was made. Any unauthorised contact was treated as a violation of State security. But today, a Russian girl who meets a Westerner at a dance and spends the night with him risks no more than the disapproving chatter of the old women, the *babushki*.

At higher levels the controls are stricter. A probationary member of the Soviet Party is told to stop seeing a family of French communists he has befriended in Moscow, otherwise his Party membership may not be confirmed. Another man is refused Party membership because he once had too close a friendship with an American student.

The key to the Soviet system is surveillance. In Moscow, twenty-five years after the abolition of Stalin's terror, George Orwell's words in *1984* still ring true: 'All that was your own was the few cubic centimetres inside your skull.'

In Mao's China, not even that could be said; there conformity was required, not only in action but in thought as well. Political control is the key to the Chinese system. Police surveillance is secondary and usually discreet; many foreigners spend years in Peking without ever being aware of it. Only when deliberate warning is being given does it become obtrusive. A Western journalist may find, like my colleague, Francis Deron of *Agence France Presse*, one June evening in 1980, that the Chinese friend he goes to pick up in his car is seized by plain-clothes thugs as he is about to get in and dragged off to a waiting police jeep; after that, all friendships with Chinese must be broken for fear of exposing others to similar reprisals. A Chinese soldier, overheard talking too freely to a foreigner, is ostentatiously hauled off and interrogated just as surely as a Soviet soldier would be in similar circumstances. But such shows of force are not the rule. Control is omnipresent and inescapable, but it takes other forms.

A waiter at the Peking Hotel whose quick service and cheerfulness win frequent commendations from foreign guests, is abruptly transferred to work as a cleaner. The stream of praise from foreigners, one of his friends explains later, excited the suspicion of the hotel's management. Chinese students are briefed on how to keep contacts with foreign students to a minimum without seeming rude. All Chinese, except those whose work is dealing with foreigners, must obtain clearance before meeting them.

These are not examples of Chinese behaviour in the Cultural Revolution. They are from the 1980s. So is the saga of the foreign beer bottle label collector who wrote to a brewery in Xian requesting a specimen for his collection. The manager passed the letter on to his superiors, who passed it on to their superiors until eventually it reached the provincial trade department. No label was ever sent, because, even at that high level, no one would take the responsibility and risk later being accused of 'unauthorised foreign dealings'.[23]

As in the Soviet Union, some have the courage, the foolhardiness or the independence of mind to evade or ignore the controls. But for most practical purposes, outside the narrow limits of what is officially approved, Chinese and foreigners are separated by an *apartheid* as complete, and as racial, as in South Africa.

A Chinese girl who sleeps with a foreigner and is caught is accused of damaging national dignity and 'making the Chinese people lose face'.[24] She is not put on trial, because she has broken no law; China has no equivalent of South Africa's Immorality Act. Instead she is sent, under extra-judicial regulations, for three years' re-education in a labour camp.

Even the suspicion of improper behaviour with a foreigner risks ruining a person's career. An Australian student in Peking spent a summer afternoon walking with a Chinese girl in the former Imperial Hunting Park, in the Fragrant Hills, west of the city. The park closed earlier than they thought, and they found themselves locked in. The park attendants called the police, who immediately jumped to the conclusion that they had been making love. At the police station to which they were taken, the girl was treated extremely roughly. When the Australian protested, one of the policemen told him: 'This girl is Chinese. We can do with her whatever we want. You foreigners come to China, you should obey our laws and customs.' He was released after five hours. She was forced to take a virginity test, and freed only two days later, after it had shown that no intercourse had taken place. Despite that, the incident remains recorded in her dossier, and will mark her for the rest of her life.

As in South Africa, the *apartheid* has two sides. Foreigners are not permitted to stay in Chinese hotels. Chinese may not enter foreigners' hotels without special authorisation. In restaurants, foreigners eat in cleaner, more spacious rooms, from which ordinary people are excluded. If a lone foreigner insists on sitting among the masses, he risks ruining a meal that the Chinese around him may have been looking forward to for weeks: I have seen waitresses shout abuse at Chinese families whom a foreigner has ignorantly joined, ordering them to move or to finish their meal quickly and leave, so that the 'foreign guest' can have the table to himself.

On trains, foreigners eating in the restaurant car are given white tablecloths; Overseas Chinese get plastic covers; ordinary Chinese are served their food in metal lunch-boxes to take back and eat in their compartments.

At most airports and stations, there are separate waiting rooms. The best plane, train and theatre tickets go to foreigners. Often, in provincial towns, the start of a concert will be delayed if foreign tourists are late in arriving. There are special shops for foreigners, the so-called 'Friendship Stores', where antiques and imported goods can be bought with foreign currency certificates. Partitioned-off sections of ordinary shops, marked, 'Foreign Guests Only', offer a better selection of goods than is found in Chinese stores. Even some beaches at seaside resorts carry signs reading, 'Foreigners Only beyond this point'.

Such forms of discrimination, by Chinese against Chinese in their own country, are endless. It is as though there is an unwritten rule that foreigners are served first and given the best, while Chinese are served last and given what is left. It applies not just to government guests; any and every foreigner automatically gets special treatment; anyone with Chinese features does not, unless he can produce a passport to prove that he, too, has foreign citizenship.

'People are very angry. They say, "Why do you build new apartment blocks for foreigners and do nothing for us, when our housing conditions are so poor?" They are boiling, like a kettle with the lid about to blow off,' a Foreign Ministry official said in 1979. That winter, for the first time, the issue was raised publicly when the *People's Daily* printed a letter from a Chinese American complaining that in a queue for taxis, Europeans behind her were taken first. In other countries, she wrote, discrimination on the basis of colour was prohibited by law. 'In front of foreigners,' the paper commented later, 'some Chinese treat their fellow-countrymen as slaves . . . This is not friendship, it is a decadent, feudal way.'[25]

The problem was aired again in the Chinese parliament, the National People's Congress (NPC), in September 1980. Hao Deqing, President of the People's Institute for Foreign Affairs, complained, 'It's got to the point where Chinese aren't even allowed to use lavatories reserved for foreigners.' Other deputies spoke of scenic sites, museums and department stores being closed to Chinese when foreign tourists visited, and of segregated swimming pools. 'Chinese people are not discriminated against abroad,' lamented one elderly scientist. 'It is in China that they are insulted.'[26]

Many of the barriers have been erected deliberately by the Chinese Party. As in the Soviet Union, abstract affirmations of 'friendship between peoples', buttressed by an apparatus of officially controlled friendship associations and politically useful slogans about international solidarity, have been substituted for genuine friendship between individuals. In China this process has been taken to such an extreme as to make normal social contact all but impossible. In part, the barriers, the special treatment and the contempt for the rights of the mass of the Chinese people, reflect the feudal elitism which colours all aspects of the Chinese system. The parallel between current practices and the sign in a Shanghai park at the time of the foreign concessions, which supposedly stated, 'Chinese and Dogs not allowed', has been noted even in the *People's Daily*.[27]

But the biggest barrier, and the one hardest to dismantle, which makes the Chinese attitude to foreigners quite different from that of Russians, lies in the minds of ordinary people. To most Chinese, a foreigner is not an equal and cannot be treated as an equal: he is a foreigner, and therefore not in the same scale of things as a Chinese. He may be treated with hostility – as during the Cultural Revolution – or a deference bordering on servility, as in the years after Mao's death, 'ostracised or fawned on', in the words of one NPC deputy.[28] But, except among intellectuals who have travelled abroad and among the young, what he will not be treated as is just another human being.

This, in turn, relates to a much larger question: how do you open the minds of a thousand million people who, for most of their recorded history, have been closed in on themselves in the absolute certitude of their own superiority? For the Japanese, another inward-looking nation-race, who faced, on a lesser scale, similar problems, the solution emerged from war, specifically the American occupation in 1945. China, in the 1980s, must try to achieve the same modernisation, not just of the economy but of outlook, by peaceable means.

When I arrived in Peking in 1977, I was told of an African student visiting a remote provincial town whom a man approached and put out a finger to rub his arm, to find out whether the black came off. I did not believe it, until, three years later, the same thing happened to the wife of a senior African diplomat in Peking itself. On another occasion, the same woman, who speaks Chinese, having earlier been in China as a student, found herself being stared at particularly intently by a middle-aged man. As she tells the story, when she asked him what he was looking at, he replied, in genuine amazement, 'You have a nose and two eyes, like us. You have hands and fingers, as we do. But you are black.'

An African is stared at in China for his colour. I, as a European, am stared at for my big nose and curly hair. Old people refer to us both as *guai lou*, 'foreign devils', not with malice but as a simple statement of fact. Outside the big cities, a foreigner is a curiosity, a freak for small boys to run after, for grandparents to show to toddlers, for grown-ups to point out to each other with as much excited astonishment as though a circus were passing by. It is an attitude one encounters nowhere else in the world. I have been in small towns in South-West China where, within minutes, the mere rumour that a foreigner had arrived produced a crowd of several thousand people and brought every other activity to a halt. Even in the suburbs of Peking, if you stop and ask a peasant the way, the chances are he will stare back with blank incomprehension. It is not that he cannot understand you, but that, being convinced that no one looking so strange could speak Chinese, he closes his ears and will not listen to what you are saying.

For any foreigner, constant staring is trying. But for a black person, highly conspicuous and temperamentally and culturally quite out of tune with Chinese ways, the strain can be intolerable, particularly when backed up by other forms of discrimination. And in both China and the Soviet Union, black people are discriminated against.

In Kiev, in November 1976, 500 African students demonstrated against attempts by the authorities to separate a Czechoslovak girl from a Nigerian student she had married. A few weeks later, African students in Lvov petitioned their embassies for protection against attacks by local people. In Shanghai, at a textile engineering college in July 1979, three days of race riots left nineteen foreigners, twenty-four Chinese students and an unknown number of police and college officials injured, some of them with stab wounds which kept them in hospital for a month. The fighting started when Chinese complained that African students were playing their radios too loudly, and quickly escalated after wallposters appeared taunting them as 'black devils'. The root cause however was the friendships certain students had established with Chinese girls. In Peking, a year later, another such incident led the African diplomatic corps to cancel its annual Liberation Day reception, normally attended by a Chinese Politburo member. The Foreign Ministry was informed that the decision had been taken because of the risk of hostile demonstrations by African students, enraged by the arrest of a Sierra Leonean at Qinghua University, who had been found with a Chinese girl in his room. The girl disappeared into a labour camp. The student was jailed for six days, and released only after the intervention of the wife of Sierra Leone's President, Mrs Siaka Stevens, who happened to be visiting China at the time.

Chinese racism shows up particularly clearly against Africans, but it remains part of a generalised pattern of discrimination, in which one billion Chinese maladjust to three and a half billion 'others'. Soviet racism, like that in the West, is specific to particular groups. A Soviet actor I knew, himself Jewish, once tried to convince me that syphilis was unknown in the Soviet Union until Khrushchev permitted Africans to come to the country as students, and was genuinely astonished when I declined to believe him. Russians assured me, with equal conviction, that 'the Jews' were the cause of all the Soviet Union's problems.

Anti-Semitism runs deep in Russia. Until the Revolution, Jews were made to live within the so-called Pale of Settlement, where they were the victims of pogroms fuelled by the same hatred as inspired the Nazi extermination camps. In a village near Moscow, in 1974, when KGB officers prevented a group of Soviet and American Jews from holding a picnic, local people who gathered to watch shouted, 'Hitler should have killed the lot of you!' Such sentiments do not appear in the pages of the Soviet press; anti-Semitism in the Soviet Union is a criminal offence. But anti-Zionism is state policy, and the dividing line between the two is frequently blurred.

For many years one of the most prolific authors of officially-sponsored anti-Zionist propaganda has been Dr Valery Yemelyanov, who believes that 'the Jews are a stable criminal genotype of a hybrid character, created . . . on a basis of cross-breeding of ancient professional dynasties of the criminal world of the black, yellow and white races'.[29] In 1980, Yemelyanov fell foul of the authorities after having a book published abroad, without official approval, by a Palestinian front organisation. But his Nazi beliefs which, although he could not state them directly, coloured all his writing, have never been repudiated. Moreover others, such as the Byelorussian poet Maxim Luzhanin, have openly published work which is only marginally less extreme. In an anthology called *Through the War*, published in Minsk, Luzhanin wrote of Soviet Jews in these terms:

> Just look! This is their breed:
> A pure ferret in his manner and in his ugly snout!
> You can spit in his face, he's not proud, just wipes it away.
> Spit again, and he'll push his face at you for more.
> But if you give him what he asks for,
> He runs off and begins to curse you.

Not only did the Soviet censor approve these lines, but attempts by a group of Jews to take Luzhanin to court were rejected out of hand.

Anti-Semitism in the Soviet Union is the obverse of Russian nationalism. Even in the labour camps, dissidents say, Jews and Russian nationalists split into two irreconcilable groups.

Under Brezhnev, Russian nationalism has shown a marked resurgence. Correspondingly, the Jewish sense of identity has been strengthened, as has nationalistic feeling among other Soviet peoples, particularly in Armenia, Georgia, the Ukraine, Estonia and Lithuania. Unless Brezhnev's successors act to reverse this trend, which means actively discouraging Russian ethnic dominance, it must eventually create serious strains in the Soviet system. This is a long-term rather than an immediate prospect. In the 1970s, attempts in Armenia and Estonia to set up underground organisations to agitate for secession were discovered and smashed with little difficulty by the KGB; and Moscow has been able to keep so-called 'nationalist deviations' in republican governments and Party Committees within narrow bounds. Soviet Moslems in Central Asia, potentially the biggest source of national discontent, have remained passive, tightly controlled by a colonial regime in which Russians hold most of the positions of power. Despite the rise of Islamic fundamentalism across the border in Iran and Turkey, Moslems in the Soviet Union, at least through the 1970s, seemed to give more weight to the dramatic rise in living standards that the Russian presence had brought than to the religious and cultural restrictions which accompanied it.

Yet the Soviet Union is the last of the world's great nineteenth-century colonial empires and is not invulnerable to the pressures which, historically, have caused all other empires to fail. The geographical contiguity of its possessions, which has enabled it to outlive the far-flung empires of the West, will become less of an advantage as the political consciousness of the colonised peoples, particularly in Central Asia, grows, and the proportion of 'European' Russians in the population declines. The 1979 census found that out of 262 million Soviet citizens, 137 million were Russians, 43 million Ukrainians and 40 million Moslems. If present growth rates are maintained, in thirty years' time there will be 160 million Russians to 100 million Moslems.

China has a very different ethnic balance. All but six per cent of its people are Hans. In Tibet and Xinjiang strong nationalist feeling exists, partly as a reaction against the blatantly colonial policies followed there when Mao was alive, and China's leaders plainly cannot expect them to remain for ever under alien rule without allowing much greater autonomy than has yet been suggested. But that is a long way off. The numbers involved are small, and at worst pose a problem of border security, not a serious threat to the central power.

In China the most important differences are regional. A Russian in Vladivostok speaks the same language as a Russian in Leningrad. A Chinese in Canton may find that a Chinese in a village thirty miles away speaks a language which, to him, is completely unintelligible. Written Chinese, historically the preserve of scholars, is the same throughout the country. The spoken language, however, is fragmented into innumerable dialects, a Babel which testifies to the immobilism and isolation of the Chinese peasantry. It will be at least another two generations before all Chinese can express themselves in standardised speech, based on the Peking dialect, and until then no attempt can be made to change to a phonetic script, which is the long-term plan. Because of the complexity of the ideograms, Chinese children take twice as long as their Western counterparts to learn to read and write, and the lack of an alphabet makes many aspects of modern life, from telecommunications to information storage and retrieval, infinitely more difficult.

In language, and in temperament, the great divide is between the north and south. Ever since the Three Kingdoms, in the third century, China has periodically split between rival southern and northern governments, the last time in the 1920s, before the ascendancy of Chiang Kai-shek.

The south is noisy, gregarious. Its cities have a seedy run-down air, tempered by sleazy charm. Life spills out on to the streets from restaurants and shops. Tinsmiths hammer at pots and pans. A portrait-painter sketches his subjects from passport photographs. Street stalls stay open late at night, selling bowls of noodles and sweetmeats by the flickering light of acetylene lamps. A dentist stands in a doorway, exchanging pleasantries with passers-by as he drills a woman's tooth, and at the corners of alleys mobile libraries set up shop, often no more than a suitcase full of battered picture books and a couple of low benches for the customers, mainly children, to sit on, as they read about PLA heroes, Lenin, and the Sherlock Holmes mystery called, in the Chinese transliteration, 'The Dog of the Ba-Si-Ke-Wei-Li'.

In the north the stuff of daily life is hidden behind high walls. Northern China itself lives behind a Great Wall. Raiding barbarians and foul weather are only part of the explanation. It is the closed, inward-looking mentality of northerners which makes them shut out the world. All over Northern China stand empty brick enclosures crumbling away in the middle of fields. The outer wall is always built first, and plans often change before anything can be put inside.

Southerners look on the north as a source of alien rule, and only a wily northerner manages to get through a visit to Canton without being cheated somewhere along the line. Where Southern Italy has its mafia, Southern China has its triads. It was from the south that the Overseas Chinese set out to make new homes in South-East Asia, Europe and

America. Today, Chinese businessmen dominate the commerce of Singapore, Malaysia, Thailand and much of Burma, Indonesia and the Philippines. Certain well-to-do Overseas Chinese families send their children to universities in China, just as British families in the colonies used to pack off their offspring to a public school. Their success in the cut and thrust of the capitalist market contrasts dramatically with the inefficiency and incompetence of economic management inside China, and Overseas Chinese students are often astounded by the lack of drive and initiative in Chinese communist society. 'We notice,' said a Hong Kong youth at university in Fujian, 'that Chinese people here don't seem to know what they are doing.'

This once again is a case of the Chinese grass bending with the wind. In South-East Asia, virtually unrestricted economic competition has spurred on native Chinese acumen, while within China, feudal attitudes, the dead hand of bureaucratism and two decades of Maoist egalitarianism have had the opposite effect. Unlike the Germans, who have worked to make their countries' economies respectively the most efficient in capitalist and in communist Europe, the Chinese have responded to each system in kind – meeting inefficiency with inefficiency. Their ability to fit in with prevailing circumstances, not to fight against the system but to go with it, to compromise and to live with unresolved contradictions, enables capitalist Chinese businessmen to send their children to communist universities, and communist China to co-exist and cooperate with capitalist Hong Kong and Macao.

The Soviet Union has no capitalist enclaves, no 'Overseas Russians', nor would it tolerate any such arrangement. Since the place of all loyal Russians is at home, working for the motherland, émigrés are *ipso facto* disloyal, and no contact is possible with them. But exceptions are made for Ukrainians and Armenians, which helps to make the Armenian capital, Yerevan, politically one of the freest Soviet cities. There is a constant traffic with the West and formerly with Beirut; returnees who have come back to settle drive flashy American cars with Soviet number plates, like those which wealthy Overseas Chinese drive in Peking; and visitors bring in the latest foreign ideas and fashions. Ukrainians, when they come back to visit relatives, are kept on a shorter leash. The only other part of the Soviet Union with a comparable contact with the outside world is Estonia, on the Baltic Sea coast opposite Finland. Its capital, Tallinn, a city of steepled, Lutheran churches and cobbled streets, belongs not on the rim of Russia but in Central Europe. With Helsinki so close, and the languages being so similar, Estonians can watch Finnish television, which gives them a window on to the West denied other Soviet citizens. In summer, a ferry service across the gulf brings thousands of Finnish tourists. The window of a dress shop contains a huge blow-up of a French model. There is even a modest cabaret, staged in the Soviet Union's only nightclub.

Yet these are only small gaps in a heavy curtain, compared with the welter of connections which exist between China and its overseas communities. Despite China's isolation from the West in Mao's lifetime and before, most urban Chinese, especially in the south, understand far more of life in the Asian countries across their borders than do Soviet citizens about their European neighbours. Russia has no 'Taiwan' or 'Singapore' to act as a living model of how Russians might manage their country under a capitalist system. For China, the model exists, and the comparison is made.

Soviet ignorance, even among those who should be well-informed, about the most straightforward aspects of Western life, can hardly be exaggerated. An Intourist guide, whom I started baiting about the restrictions on foreigners' travel, told me with complete assurance that it was the same everywhere in Europe. A group of railway workers, on a train in Daghestan, laughed in disbelief when I explained that in Britain, the unemployed were paid a weekly allowance by the state until they found jobs. 'That,' said one sceptically, 'would be communism.' Nor were they any more impressed by my account of Western press freedom. 'We know it's not your fault what the BBC says,' they said kindly when I had finished. 'Everything you write is dictated by your bosses in London.'

Since the Soviet news media operate in this way, the same must be true of news media in the West. As Soviet elections are charades, so all elections must be charades. As Soviet justice is political, so all justice must be political.

This tendency to see the West in the Soviet Union's own image is reinforced by the press:

> The activity of the political secret police in Britain has assumed really threatening proportions . . . The British authorities have virtually set up a regime of total surveillance in the country . . . Files compiled by British counter-intelligence and the so-called Scotland Yard Special Branch . . . even now contain the names of over 1,000,000 Britons whom the British authorities have classed as 'suspicious elements' in need of 'scrupulous attention'.[30]

Tass, reporting from London on civil liberties in Britain in 1979.

As journalism, this mirror-image approach is a conscious propaganda ploy. But the attitude that underlies it goes much deeper, and is not confined to one side alone. Many of the difficulties of understanding between the Soviet Union and the West are caused by each side attributing to the other patterns of behaviour appropriate to its own society, and then being surprised when its expectations are not met.

Pravda, 1980

Andrei Sinyavsky has described how, like virtually all Soviet exiles, his initial reaction to the disarray and confusion, the din of conflicting ideas, the multiplicity of voices and the endless arguments that characterise Western democracy, was that any system so weak and disorganised would be helpless before a Soviet onslaught. Only after a visit to Rome, beset by strikes and protest marches, did he understand that a society in which such disruption could be tolerated as a normal occurrence must have great inner strength. Soviet society, he wrote, was like a bag of sand, hard and tightly packed. But unless the bag were kept securely fastened, the sand would lose its shape and collapse.

Western radio broadcasts have had some effect in modifying the Soviet view of the West. So have the influx of foreign tourists since the 1960s and occasional exhibitions about the American way of life, reluctantly admitted under cultural exchange programmes. But the effect has not been large. Foreign travel is still the perquisite of the favoured: in 1980, it was harder for a Soviet citizen to go to Poland or Hungary than for a Pole or a Hungarian to visit the West. Nonetheless, Eastern Europe is the least difficult area for a Soviet tourist to visit –

since the mid-1970s about 1.5 million have been going there each year – and the revelation of the dramatically higher living standards of East Europeans (the reason for making it hard for Russians to visit in the first place) has probably been the biggest single foreign factor in changing Soviet ideas.

To Russians, strength is synonymous with strong controls. Along the whole length of the Soviet border are watchtowers and barbed wire, and in some places minefields and ploughed strips of bare earth, not so much to keep others out as to keep Soviet citizens in. One of the saddest visitors I had in Moscow was a father seeking news of his son, who had set off some months before in a small boat across the Black Sea, heading for Turkey, and from whom nothing had been heard since. In the Soviet Union such attempts are rare, and few succeed. Even at official checkpoints, the searches and formalities are exhaustive, and to enter the country overland often takes several hours. Rigid border controls are not new. They were the same in tsarist times. But to fly into Moscow's Sheremetyevo airport, heavily guarded by KGB border troops, and to have one's face and visa scrutinised mistrustfully for minutes on end by a young man, also in KGB uniform, whose demeanour proclaims that his purpose in life is vigilance against subversion, is to be reminded in no uncertain terms that one has made a transition from one world to another, whose values are profoundly alien to those of the West.

Chinese airport security, on the other hand, is so lax that cyclists take short cuts across the runways: one Swissair pilot, after a close encounter with a peasant who wobbled across his path as he was about to land, vowed never to fly to Peking again. Chinese immigration officers take the view that if the government has given you a visa, your presence must be beneficial and you should be treated accordingly. Among Chinese, not only is illegal emigration widespread, but hundreds of people leave legally every day to join relatives abroad. The obstacles to lifting emigration restrictions altogether lie as much with the recipient countries as with China itself. The story is told of how President Carter advocated free emigration when he met Deng Xiaoping in Washington in 1979. 'How many hundred million Chinese immigrants would you like?' Deng replied. Mr Carter blanched, and changed the subject. The story may be apocryphal, but the problem is real.

To the Soviet authorities, emigration is morally akin to treason, and politically unacceptable because it shows dissatisfaction with the Soviet system. To maintain the fiction that no true Soviet citizen wishes to leave, but only disloyal Jews (and ethnic Germans, who are allowed to rejoin relatives in West Germany), most emigrants, even, occasionally, those who are Moslems, are told that they may only apply for exit visas to Israel. No other destination is permitted. All who apply are immediately dismissed from their jobs, with no way of telling whether they will wait weeks or years for their visas to be granted. As a further deterrent, Soviet newspapers regularly carry long accounts of the plight of emigrants who fail to adapt to life in the West. They do so not from compassion. In Vienna, there is always a queue of former Soviet citizens, pleading to be allowed to return. In some cases they, too, are made to wait for years. 'People must be made to understand,' a Soviet journalist told me approvingly, 'that Soviet citizenship is not something to be discarded lightly.'

The Soviet Union's refusal to treat the right to travel abroad, to emigrate and return, as basic freedoms to which its citizens, like those of other countries, are entitled, is indispensable so long as the regime remains determined to prevent all internal political change. It has not been without cost, however. Many of the most talented Soviet artists and writers, faced with an absolute choice between permanent exile and permanent isolation from foreign cultural life, with no middle course permitted, have chosen exile. Had the policy been more flexible, they would still be living in the Soviet Union today.

The ballet dancer, Valery Panov, whom I drove to Leningrad airport one June day in 1974, with a one-way ticket to Vienna, spoke of arbitrary, unexplained decisions to prevent him going on foreign tours, and artistic restraints which made it impossible to try anything new. The cellist, Mstislav Rostropovich, whom, a month earlier, I had seen off from Sheremetyevo airport as he departed for Britain, complained of being put in 'cultural quarantine'. Mikhail Baryshnikov has said, 'If I had had the opportunity to leave Russia for one month, two months at a time, to work with different choreographers and return home to the Kirov, I would never have left. My homeland, my theatre, my friends mean more to me than anything. But the time came for a choice: my art or my peaceful contentment.'[31] The writers Nekrassov, Galich and Maximov; the sculptor, Neizvestny; the Bolshoi star, Alexander Godunov, could all tell similar tales.

But while Soviet cultural life has been greatly weakened by this constant bleeding into the West, it has retained more vigour and originality than most Western critics give it credit for. The great mass of socialist realist works being churned out is as appalling as ever. But novels such as those of Vasily Belov and Valentin Rasputin, and the poems of Voznesensky and Akhmadulina, rank with the best being written anywhere in the world. Nor is it surprising that a people who, under the tsarist autocracy, produced Tchaikovsky and Tolstoy – who, under Lenin, produced Mayakovsky and Mandelshtam and, under

Stalin, Pasternak and Shostakovitch – should, under Brezhnev, still be producing men and women of creative brilliance.

Chinese culture has been in steady decline since the end of the Ming dynasty, 400 years ago. It is not that nothing of value has been produced since then, but individuals of real stature, such as the writer Lu Xun, who was active in the 1920s, have been increasingly few and far between. Although, today, China has writers and painters with no lack of ability or political courage, no great art has been produced since the communists came to power. In part, this is due to the devastation wrought by the Cultural Revolution and Mao's earlier political campaigns. But the deeper cause lies in the way art in China over the centuries has been diluted by politics until it no longer has any independent life of its own.

Unlike Russia, where artists have kept the creative spark alive, under tsarism and under communism, by kicking against authority and being kicked by it, in China far-reaching political democratisation is the precondition for a true cultural renaissance.

At a less elevated level, both China and the Soviet Union have failed dismally to develop popular culture to anything like the extent that is needed. China has its acrobats and the Soviet Union its circuses. In practice, though, in both countries, in most small towns and many larger ones, there is little or nothing for people to do after they finish work. At the end of 1981, Canton was the only city in China with an amusement park where young people could go in the evenings. Shanghai had a roller-skating rink, and in a few other towns there were improvised shooting galleries, set up on the pavements by enterprising young men who charged a penny a time for potshots with an airgun at a home-made tin target. The only other opportunities for outside entertainment were provided by the cinema, which Chinese visit, on average, once a fortnight, and, in the bigger cities, occasional trips to the theatre. In the Soviet Union the penury of leisure activities is less acute, but the difference is not great. *Pravda*, like the *People's Daily*, writes of towns where there is no entertainment at all.[32]

In the Soviet Union, boredom leads to drunkenness and so to crime. In China, the drunkenness is usually dispensed with; boredom leads to crime directly. Soviet crime statistics are secret, but East Germany in 1978 had 75.6 offences per 10,000 population (compared with 490 in Britain and more than 2,000 in the United States). The Soviet rate, though below those of the Western countries, is almost certainly higher than the East German figure and there is strong circumstantial evidence that it is increasing. In China, the crime rate in 1977–79 was given officially as 6.5 per 10,000 population, compared with 4.5 in the early

1960s.[33] But that appears to exclude many offences considered as crimes in the West, and in the cities it probably approaches the East German rate.

The Soviet Union has a particularly high incidence of homicide, rape, robbery with violence and arson (nearly fifteen per cent of all offences, compared with seven per cent in China and one per cent in Britain), and a strong professional criminal element (twenty-five per cent of Soviet offenders are recidivists, compared with ten per cent of Chinese). Bank robberies and hold-ups by armed gangs are no longer unknown even in Moscow, where security is tightest, and in Rostov, in the mid-1970s, one gang was operating with submachine-guns and hand-grenades. In China, too, bank raids have been reported from many different areas, and cases have occurred of robbers breaking into military armouries to obtain weapons.

In both countries, however, the 'outstanding social problem', as the *Peking Daily* described it, is crime by young people. Two drunken teenagers break into the Moscow zoo, where they batter and stab to death two rare kangaroos, one carrying a baby in its pouch. In Leningrad, vandals systematically destroy twenty-nine historic statues in a city park. In Grozny, a provincial capital in the North Caucasus, parents form vigilante groups to protect their children from gangs of thugs who set on them after school. At Povarova, in Central Russia, a drunken sixteen-year-old kills an engine driver by throwing a rock at an oncoming train one evening when he has 'nothing better to do'.

Such behaviour has no single cause. The Soviet press cites alcoholism and the lack of leisure facilities to make it appear that delinquency, like emigration, is the result of 'objective' factors, unrelated to the social system. For the same reason, Soviet sociologists maintain that crime is a survival from pre-revolutionary times, kept alive by bourgeois influences coming in from abroad, and Soviet scientists try to show that criminality is a genetic defect caused by an extra chromosome. Such thinking underlies Dr Yemelyanov's belief that the Jews are 'a stable criminal genotype'. The Western view that delinquency, like alcoholism itself, stems from social alienation is politically unacceptable and therefore rejected. Yet alienation is precisely what the profile of a typical Soviet delinquent shows. He is ill-educated (five times more likely than the average to have left school early); workshy (half of all those without jobs have criminal records); never takes part in community activities, does not read newspapers and rarely listens to the radio.[34]

In China, these problems are compounded by unemployment and the presence in the cities of 'educated youths' who have returned illegally from the countryside. If more than half of all Soviet crime is committed by the young, in Chinese cities the figure is closer to seventy per cent. One study in 1979 found that juvenile delinquency had increased ten times since the early 1960s.

Young Chinese criminals operate in gangs, bound by codes of loyalty similar to the feudal outlaw brotherhoods. Leadership goes to the most fearless. A man named Fang Wenxin established his position at the head of a gang in Tianjin by lying across the rails in front of an express train and having a friend pull him away a split second before it passed. On another occasion, he picked up a red-hot poker with his bare hands without uttering a sound. Fang's gang showed its disrespect of authority by snatching the hats off people's heads in the street; he himself was caught doing it 170 times. By the time he was thirty, he had a record of 200 street fights, sixty arrests and four years of re-education in a labour camp. Fang is unusual because he reformed – which is why so much detail about his case has become known.[35] Others have not. A typical incident was described by the newspaper, *Tianjin Ribao*, in October 1979:

> In broad daylight, hooligan Li Guodong and 30 confederates . . . carrying choppers, bayonets, triangular files, firearms and other lethal weapons, went to Tonglou in Hexi district to have a gang fight with another mob of hooligans. As they did not find the other mob, they harassed the neighbourhood . . . [and] using knives, robbed passers-by of army caps, army jackets and sunglasses and injured four people.[36]

Similar cases of gangs turning on bystanders when rival mobs have failed to show up for battle have been reported in Shanghai.[37] In Tianjin, there have been shoot-outs between the police and hooligans armed with home-made pistols, and in 1979 one gang tried unsuccessfully to hold up a police van and free the prisoners it was transporting. Elsewhere gangs of youths have held up buses to rob passengers, and in schools pupils have beaten up teachers. In Peking, one summer evening, 140 young men fought a pitched battle, after an argument between rival gang-leaders, using knives, spades and guns, only a few hundred yards from my apartment. One was killed and an unknown number injured.[38]

Youths at a reform school in Peking told me they had fought over girls, over territory, to revenge insults by other gang members, or simply because they got a kick out of fighting. Tempers flare easily in China, and even when no gang is involved, street-corner quarrels often erupt into blows.

The increase in the crime rate is blamed mainly on the Cultural Revolution, which, as one newspaper put it, left many young people 'with no sense of law and discipline whatsoever'. But, unlike the Soviet Union, China also acknowledges the general proposition that 'problems among young people and teenagers are a comprehensive reflection of the social situation', whose roots must therefore be sought within society itself.

Cai Yuanzhen was born in a small town in Guizhou, one of the poorest provinces in China. When she was six months old, her father was arrested for causing an accident at his factory and sent to do forced labour. Her mother remarried, and when the second husband died, remarried again:

> At that time, I was about 11 years old. Mother supported the family by taking in sewing, while I and my elder brother begged in the streets and picked up what we could from rubbish tips. Our home conditions were not good. Mother often lost her temper and beat me . . . Step-father did not like me and hit me when he was drunk. When I could stand it no longer, I ran away. At first I did not want to steal, but I could not keep myself alive on leftovers and what I could get from begging. When I saw how others stole and were able to eat good meals, I admired them very much. Slowly, I learned to steal.[39]

For ten years, starting at the age of twelve, she was a professional thief, living rough, sleeping in the open, summer and winter. She never went to school, and no one would give her a job. It is a story as old as China itself. Yet Cai Yuanzhen was born in 1957, eight years after the communists came to power, and it was not until 1979 that an official finally took pity on her and found her work on a state farm.

The Soviet authorities deny that they have any problem of child abuse or wife-beating. In China, there is greater candour. 'Some parents are callous and cruel and treat their children (particularly foster-children) heartlessly,' said the *People's Daily*. 'Some look upon their wives as playthings or slaves, saying, "I have taken a wife and bought a horse, I beat them and ride them for I am the boss."'[40] In 1980, there were cities in Northern China where little bands of homeless children roamed the streets.[41] At a reform school in Peking, twenty per cent of the youngsters had been maltreated by step-parents.[42]

Yet appearances can be misleading. In the Soviet Union, the problem of violence in the home, especially towards women, is actually more serious, because of the prevalence of alcoholism. It is concealed by being treated as just another element of drunken behaviour rather than a separate social issue. 'Throughout history,' said a Soviet Supreme Court judge, 'the Russian woman has had a hard life, dragging her husband out of the tavern.' However the effects of domestic violence are limited, because in Russia brutalised families can usually find refuge and support within the community. Even in the bleak new multi-storey housing estates, where more and more town dwellers live, the *babushki* still regard themselves as the moral arbiters of society, and little escapes their notice. A Russian grandmother has no more compunction about going up to a young woman who is a perfect stranger and telling her that she is not dressed warmly enough, or her skirt is too short, than she would about telling off her own family. Where children are concerned, this solicitude is overwhelming. From birth to the early teens, a Russian child is generally over-swaddled, over-indulged and over-protected. The day after our arrival in Moscow, in 1974, my wife and I went for a walk along Gorky Street with our son, then aged three, to be stopped constantly by elderly women, and men, who admonished us that the ice cream he was eating would make him ill, that he ought to have warmer gloves, and why didn't he have his hat on? This pattern was repeated on many subsequent excursions. Such communal vigilance cannot rule out child abuse completely, but it means that when it occurs it is quickly discovered.

Chinese society is not self-policing to anything like the same extent. One autumn, in a park on the outskirts of Peking, I saw an old man brandishing a staff and shouting at a boy aged eight or nine, who walked, sobbing, beside him. The child's face was swollen and bruised, apparently from beatings. But no one attempted to intervene. Had that happened in the Soviet Union, the man would very quickly have been surrounded by angry citizens, telling him to stop.

In China, mutual responsibility has well-defined limits. I once spent an evening in a small back street in Fuzhou, watching a group of retired bus company workers entertaining themselves and their neighbours on the pavement outside their hostel, a rude barn of a place with a line of worn bamboo beds. Three old men with bald heads and beatific faces, evidently the street committee, sat like Buddhas, surveying the proceedings. The band played – gongs and cymbals, drums and flutes – and a six-year-old boy sang arias from local operas, taught him by his mother. Virtually the whole street turned out to watch, and the sense of communal belonging was palpable, as though it were a huge, extended family, in which everyone knew and felt responsible for everyone else's children, and each person, from the smallest to the eldest, even the street idiot, had his place. But where the street ended, there also the sense of responsibility stopped.

Throughout their history, Chinese have been required to watch over each other by political pressure from above. The imperial system of *bao-jia*, whereby in each group of ten households, one was designated to be responsible for the others, appears in communist clothes as a network of neighbourhood security committees. But this mutual surveillance, mainly for political purposes, is not generally backed up by independent moral initiatives from below. China has no equivalent of the *babushka* or of the attitude she represents.

In Russia, the harshness of the climate and the difficulty of winning a living from the earth meant that people had to band together if they were to survive. From the *mir*, the village assembly, grew Soviet collectivism. In China, collective life has the family as its foundation. Five, or more commonly, four generations under one roof was the Confucian ideal, and, despite twenty years of Maoism, for many families it remains so. Under the emperors and under Mao, Chinese feudalism mirrored this patriarchal family structure. But outside the family, the community has had little role. Through the ages, Chinese peasant households have laboured as isolated small producers, cooperating among themselves only when the authorities made them. In essence, that is still true in the 1980s.

Half Stalinist, Half Victorian

Henry Kissinger, musing aloud during a visit to Peking in 1979, observed that when Britain underwent its industrial revolution, it had a population of fewer than 15 million; at the time of the Meiji restoration, which marked the beginning of Japan's modernisation, the Japanese numbered 30 million; when Russia and the United States laid the foundations of their industry at the end of the nineteenth century, their populations were 60 to 70 million; but China was trying to do what no other country had ever remotely attempted, to carry out an industrial revolution among a thousand million people, almost a quarter of mankind.

Chinese industry is an untidy amalgam of the sweatshops of Victorian Britain and Russian factories of the 1930s, with the odd, ultra-modern plant from Japan or West Germany thrown in. In every small Chinese town, and in the *hutungs*, the backstreet lanes which riddle the big cities, there is a world of cramped, ill-lit workshops, where men and women labour amid the din of ancient machinery in conditions of Dickensian squalor and grime. Minimum standards of health and safety are often not observed, and apart from six public holidays a year, Chinese workers are not ordinarily entitled to any paid leave. By contrast, Soviet workers, whose conditions under Khrushchev and Brezhnev have improved enormously since Stalin's time, can look forward to four weeks' annual holiday by the sea or in the mountains.

Yet one factor distinguishes China's industrial revolution from all others before it. Chinese officials habitually list among the country's strengths its '900 million industrious and hard-working people'. Hard though it may be to reconcile with that conventional image, the truth is very different. 'Our industry has complex problems,' said Deng Xiaoping, in an interview with a Japanese newspaper. 'The people are many, but they just do not work.'[1] That also applies in the Soviet Union and in a number of Western countries. But there low work efficiency became a problem only after a measure of prosperity had already been achieved. In China, it presents an obstacle which has to be overcome first.

Like much else in the China of the 1980s, this is in part a consequence of the Cultural Revolution. For more than a decade, Chinese workers

spent most of their time disregarding the instructions of factory committees, playing cards instead of attending their machines or sneaking out
for games of basketball, and criticising those who wanted to work for
'following the capitalist road'. The worst year was 1976, when, in the
political tension and uncertainty generated by the struggle for succession to the dying Mao, some factories halted production completely for
nine months. Even after Hua had been in power for two years, Western
companies erecting plants in China still found that Chinese workers
would refuse to follow directions they did not like, necessitating weari-
some negotiations to find a face-saving compromise. In 1980, a deputy
to the Chinese parliament, the National People's Congress, complained
that 'the slovenliness of the workers' had consequences 'even worse
than foreigners' strikes'.[2] The problem is compounded by a policy of
deliberate overstaffing – 'employing five people for the wages of
three' – begun in the 1950s to try to cut urban unemployment. In
consequence, throughout Chinese industry, for every three people who
work, two others sit and watch.

In the Soviet Union absenteeism and high labour turnover cause
losses comparable to those from strikes in the United States. Even when
Soviet workers do go to their workplaces, according to one study, they
spend on average only fifty to seventy per cent of their shifts actually
working. The rest of the time they are out shopping, or queueing for
cinema tickets. Set against timewasting of that order, even the British
teabreak pales into insignificance. Moreover, for the first ten days of
each month, the *spyachka* – the 'time for sleeping' – as Russians call it,
there is often no work to be done, because other factories have not yet
delivered the raw materials for the monthly plan. In the second ten days,
the *goryachka* – the 'time of haste' – work begins, but most of the plan
has to be accomplished in the last few days of the month, because only
then have all the necessary supplies arrived. Chinese industry experiences similar difficulties. A boiler-making factory I visited in Harbin in
1977 had completed its year's plan in three months. The other nine
months were one long *spyachka*: there was no steel to make anything
more.

However the main cause of low work efficiency is the lack of power
in the hands of management. In a workers' state, for a state-
owned enterprise to fire a worker is all but impossible. 'This is a
socialist country,' a Chinese manager replied indignantly when I
raised the question of dismissals. 'To sack a man would deprive him of
the means of supporting himself. We have never sacked anyone for
not working hard enough.' The result is exactly what one would expect.
'You must understand,' explained a harassed Chinese official, when two

repairmen refused to service my telex machine, 'we cannot make them do it.'

If Chinese and Soviet workers cannot be compelled to work, they in turn cannot compel the state to improve their working conditions. The right to strike is partly honoured in Yugoslavia, but elsewhere it exists only on paper, on the disingenuous argument that workers striking in a socialist state would be striking against themselves.

When, in Shanghai, in May 1980, the cooks in a dumpling restaurant downed tools in a dispute over bonuses, their action was condemned in the newspapers as a manifestation of 'the pernicious influence of ultra-individualism'. The three ringleaders were made to repay from their own pockets the entire value of the day's lost business, and all the workers who took part were fined a day's pay. In the Soviet Union the last serious strike, in Novocherkassk in 1962, was put down by troops. Since then other rumblings of discontent have occurred, including a two-day stoppage by car workers at Tolyatti in 1980. The authorities have generally responded with concessions, to avoid a confrontation, followed by selective repression against those judged to be trouble-makers.

Even when conditions are acknowledged to be bad, strikes are not admitted to be legitimate. Wuhan is known as one of the furnaces of China, an old, sprawling city on the Yangtse River, fiercely hot in summer and freezing in winter, whose narrow streets of rickety two-storey wooden houses have not seen a coat of paint in decades. But when a Japanese correspondent told officials at the city's steel mill that workers in Japan would strike if asked to work in such a dirty and unhealthy environment, he was given the bureaucratic reply, 'Yes, but our workers have high socialist consciousness.' A Soviet official, whose attention was drawn by a Western reporter to a particularly monotonous task in a factory in Alma-Ata, produced exactly the same response. 'In our country,' he said, 'a worker has a different attitude from in your country, regardless of what conditions he works in.'

To the bureaucracy in China and the Soviet Union, the theoretical superiority of socialism outweighs its practical faults, particularly when those faults are mainly felt by others. Strikes are unacceptable in both countries, because they represent a political challenge to the regime's monopoly of power, which shirking, idling, and even go-slows, do not.

In the interests of the bureaucracy, Chinese workers are also deprived of a still more basic freedom, the freedom to choose their jobs. As in the Soviet Union until 1956, when Khrushchev introduced sweeping re-forms, they are assigned jobs when they leave school and must remain in them until they retire, or until the higher leadership decides to transfer them elsewhere. The only influence they themselves can bring to bear on their careers is by courting favour with the bureaucrats who make such decisions. Otherwise personal preference is wholly ignored. An eighteen-year-old leaving school in China has no way of knowing whether he will spend his life as a steelworker, an office messenger, a cook – or whether he will spend his first years of adult life unemployed; he may not even be permitted to stay in the city at all, but be sent to the countryside as an 'educated youth'. Young Chinese who reply to foreigners' questions about their future ambitions with the words, 'I will go wherever the Party needs me,' are not being selfless, but merely stating the plain truth. They are not given any choice. In the last years of Mao's life, even professional qualifications were often disregarded. In a country where it costs more to produce a graduate than a peasant earns in his lifetime, and where there is a chronic shortage of trained personnel, hundreds of thousands of men and women emerged from the universities to be assigned to jobs totally unrelated to everything they had learnt.

It was precisely to avoid that kind of waste and to make the best use of the qualified manpower available that the communists introduced the system of job assignment when they came to power. Instead it became an instrument of bureaucratic convenience, used with callous indifference to the suffering of the very people the Maoist regime was supposed to serve.

Millions of Chinese, particularly intellectuals, spend years and sometimes decades living in enforced separation from their families, because the political bureaucracy has assigned a man to one part of the country and his wife to another, or because residence restrictions prevent her going with him. Their lives are blighted. Their marriage is soured. Their children grow up with half a home. But they can do nothing about it unless they know someone with influence who will intervene on their behalf. In Canton, I know a young interpreter who was abruptly transferred to Dalian, in North-East China, for three years, leaving his new wife behind to carry on with her job as a teacher. There was no element of choice; he was simply ordered to go. It was his good fortune that when the three years were up he was transferred back to Canton and not to some other city. Others are less lucky. Two engineering students fell in love while at university in Shanghai. After graduating, the girl was assigned to a factory in the city, but the boy was sent to a commune in Guangdong, 700 miles to the south. They married nonetheless and had a baby son. But seven years later, after all his appeals to join her had been rejected, he gave up hope and went illegally to Hong Kong.

While Mao was alive, husbands and wives who were forced to live apart were given just twelve days' leave a year to see each other. Yet little though that was, they were, and remain, the only people in China to have any paid holiday, apart from schoolteachers and high officials – and young workers in the bigger cities, who may, if they are lucky, get three or four days off for a honeymoon when they marry.

Since 1978 many of these practices have begun to be questioned, on both humanitarian and economic grounds. To force scientists and teachers needlessly to live apart from their families for years on end is not only a violation of one of the most basic human rights, it also prevents them working properly.[3] To assign workers without regard to their aptitudes and talents, and, still more, to assign graduates without regard to their fields of specialisation, is the most profligate misuse of human resources, guaranteed to kill enthusiasm and depress working efficiency.

Efforts at reform have been strongly resisted by the bureaucracy, which saw in them, correctly, a threat to its own entrenched power. In 1980, urban factories were still recruiting out-of-town workers on condition that they did not bring their families with them, and a Central Committee directive on family separation urged only that the problem 'gradually be solved, if conditions permit'.[4]

Nonetheless, by 1981 more than 100,000 families had been reunited; the annual leave granted those still apart was increased from twelve days to four weeks; and the beginnings of a network of labour exchanges were being put in place. Young people were encouraged to go out and look for work, instead of waiting for work to be assigned to them, and in Peking a system of competitive recruitment was tried out in which, for the first time, personal preference was taken into account. The *Peking Daily* said workers should have the right to quit their jobs, either for personal reasons or to seek work they liked better, and factories should have the right to hire and fire workers, depending on the needs of production.[5] Such radical proposals, in communist terms, remained deeply controversial, but in a more limited sphere, in 1980, scientists were given the right to choose their own research assistants. To mark the change, Chinese newspapers described how one young researcher 'with a deep bow presented a gift to his new teacher as a sign of respect', a conscious evocation of the Confucian tradition of the pupil kowtowing to the master which would have been anathema in Mao's day.[6] That the restoration of so modest a freedom should be presented as a break-through showed the extent to which choice had been eroded.

In industry a campaign was launched to remove two of the chief causes of nineteenth-century factory conditions by improving labour safety and reducing pollution. But this, too, promised to be a long haul. The trade union newspaper, *Gongren Ribao*, complained in June 1980:

> At present some leading cadres really do not care at all about the workers' safety and health . . . 'Production is like war,' they say, 'to be wounded or die is unavoidable' . . . Some leading cadres know that safety cannot be ensured but break rules and regulations and force workers to work at risk. Many occupational diseases have become prevalent as a result of not taking measures against dust and poisonous fumes.[7]

'The leaders have the money to buy coffins, but no money to cure illnesses,' was the sour comment of Chinese chemical workers, quoted at the NPC three months later.[8]

In one incident, fifty-two miners were killed in a gas explosion at a coalmine in North-East China, after being ordered to work in a shaft known not to be properly ventilated, to make up a shortfall in production. In the Bohai Gulf, seventy-two workers died when an oil rig capsized after bureaucrats in the Petroleum Ministry ignored storm warnings – a disaster which became grist to the political manoeuvring among China's leaders and eventually cost the minister his job. At steel mills molten metal is poured through open runnels in the floor, and men work stripped to the waist, without goggles or protective headgear, in cascades of sparks from huge oxygen-blown steel converters. Chinese surgeons have been able to develop some of the world's most advanced techniques for treating serious burn cases and rejoining severed limbs because they have had so much practice on the victims of industrial accidents.

In many cases the blame lies with the workers themselves. Safety covers are removed to make machinery easier to work with. In textile mills, where the noise level is often over a hundred decibels, ten times louder than the statutory maximum, workers refuse to use earplugs because they are too much trouble. In some factories, ninety per cent of the workforce have health problems due to excessive noise. It is the same attitude that leads Chinese cyclists to career unhesitatingly across busy main roads. The one causes deafness, the other traffic accidents.

Pollution of all kinds in China has attained staggering proportions. Each year, 25 million tons of soot and sulphur dioxide are pumped into the atmosphere, a quarter of a ton for every urban inhabitant. In Peking, on a windless day in winter, it is often difficult to see from one end of Tian An Men Square to the other, a distance of a quarter of a mile. The air is white with a dry fog of smoke particles from factory chimneys and the half-million households in the city which use briquettes of coal dust as fuel. Even on a clear winter's day the concentration of pollutants in the atmosphere is six times the level considered safe. In most cities, the water supply is contaminated, and Chinese town dwellers are careful to boil any water that they drink. In communes outside Peking whose fields have been polluted by factory effluents, fruit trees no longer bear fruit and oil-bearing crops flower but yield no seed. Near Baodou, in Inner Mongolia, fields poisoned by waste have had to be abandoned altogether. Where there is direct economic damage of this kind, fines are levied. But it is much harder to persuade factories to install purification equipment – even in Western Europe, let alone in a country as poor as China – when there is no readily identifiable economic effect.

Throughout the 1970s, the model for Chinese industry was the Daqing oilfield, which lies in a desolate wasteland of marsh and plain, 100 miles north-west of Harbin. China has used models since the time of the Sui dynasty, 1,400 years ago, when the Emperor commended exemplars for the instruction of the people. By the time of the Qing, in the eighteenth century, a model worker was appointed in each province, with the rights and privileges of a mandarin of the eighth rank. Under the communist regime, model workers and peasants are members of the Party Central Committee and even of the Politburo – a much higher status than they are given in the Soviet Union. Models usually have both the best and the worst points of the system they represent. Daqing is no exception.

Lines of single-storey barrack huts, built of sun-dried mud bricks, sprawl across the plain with all the impermanence and squalor of a huge refugee camp. The open drains are surrounded by heaps of rubble and garbage. Apart from elms and poplars planted along the roadsides and the occasional splash of colour from a political slogan board, nothing has been done to relieve its ugliness. Mosquito-infested in summer, in winter the ice forms half an inch thick inside the windows of the dormitories where workers live, five to a room, seeing their families – who work on nearby agricultural settlements – only at weekends. Despite an abundance of natural gas, their homes are heated by peat fires, because the authorities have refused to spend the money to lay gas-pipes; water has to be carried in buckets from the pump; and there are hayricks among the well-heads, because even in this pace-setter of Chinese industry, the commonest form of transport is the humble horse and cart.

Under Mao, Daqing's message was inspirational. It was an example of how men could overcome the harshest conditions in the service of communist ideals. A museum was built there to celebrate the feats of a labour hero named Iron-man Wang, who once, to stop a blow-out, leapt into a pool of liquid concrete to mix it with his body. For years, two to three thousand visitors a day went there from factories all over China, like pilgrims to a shrine. But as Maoism gave way to a more pragmatic approach, the usefulness of a girl storekeeper who memorised the serial number and location of every spare part in the oilfield, or of a telephone operator who knew by heart the number of every subscriber, became secondary to the absence of proper inventories and telephone books. (What happened, for example, when the omniscient storekeeper was ill, or when the operator was off duty?) By 1980, Daqing was having to eat humble pie. Officials confessed that by laying undue stress on 'revolutionary enthusiasm and death-defying spirit' they had caused numerous accidents. The workers' wretched living conditions were no longer a source of pride.

Throughout industry, one Chinese economist wrote that year, the lack of attention paid to social welfare had resulted in

> poor food, poor clothing and poor living quarters for everyone. But . . . the heaviest penalty is the low degree of labour enthusiasm. The basic reason . . . for the lack of a positive attitude on the part of the workers is that their lives have not been improved for a long time.[9]

Most Chinese workers not only have no control over what job they do and where they live, they often have no choice of housing and sometimes not even of food. Under Mao, communist paternalism was amalgamated with the company store philosophy of nineteenth-century American capitalism. Government and economic management were confounded to a greater extent than in any other communist state except North Korea, where clothing and other consumer goods are distributed by the Party to fuel the 'Big Brother' cult of Kim Il Sung, and Kampuchea, where the social fascist regime of Pol Pot abolished money, distributed all goods and abrogated all choice.

A worker at Daqing cannot go out and buy meat. There are no food shops. Each settlement of five to ten thousand people has just one general store, one canteen and one filmshow a week. Everything else required by Daqing's half-million people is provided directly by the oilfield's administration which, until March 1980, when a separate municipal government was established, was also responsible for education, health services, transport and all the other tasks normally undertaken by a local authority.

Under such a system, even if the management has the power and the will to dismiss a worker, it cannot do so unless it is also prepared to turn his family out of their home and his children out of the factory-run school. In 1982 that was essentially the position all over China.

Going south from Daqing in winter, you travel by train, pulled by an old-fashioned black steam engine with bright red wheels and polished brass piping, across a dead white landscape, past poor villages, marooned in frozen mud, and country stations whose platforms are piled high with tyres, bricks, bags of fertiliser splitting open and pieces of rusting machinery. The railway was built by the Russians in the 1880s. In Harbin, their influence lingers on in the onion domes of abandoned Orthodox churches, the yellow and white façades of European-style buildings and a theatre modelled on the Bolshoi in Moscow. The Japanese were there too. The war memorial they built is now a training tower for parachutists. Still further south, in what was once their puppet empire of Manchuguo, the city of Changchun has become one of the country's biggest industrial centres. In that metropolis of 2.4 million people, Alain Jacob of *Le Monde* was astonished one winter to discover cabbages piled six feet high between the assembly lines of China's largest truck plant. Factory officials agreed that it was neither their job nor that of their workers to provide warehousing for cabbages. But if they did not, they said, they would have no vegetables to eat.

Cases like Daqing and Changchun apart, food is normally regarded as a matter for the individual. Housing is not. In Peking, half of all accommodation is enterprise-owned.

The average Chinese city dweller in 1979 had 3.6 square metres of living space, down from 4.5 square metres when the communists came to power, thirty years before.[10] In Peking, a quarter of a million people had less than two square metres, roughly the area of a single bed. That compares with fifteen to twenty square metres in most Western cities.

The Soviet average is about eight square metres, up from five square metres in 1913. While better than China's performance under Mao, the entire increase has been achieved since Stalin's death, and has to be set against an increase in industrial production in the same period of 223 times. The Soviet Union has still not met the norm, set in the 1920s, of nine square metres per person. Nor has Brezhnev's target that by 1980 every family should have its own flat been reached. Nearly a quarter of Soviet town dwellers (and well over half of Chinese) still live in communal apartments, in which several families each have one room and share the kitchen and lavatory.

In both the Soviet Union and China, raising living standards has had a very low priority for most of the time the communists have been in power. The newspaper *Guangming Ribao* said at the end of 1979 that

38.5 million people, a third of the urban population, were inadequately housed, and six million had no proper homes at all.[11] The latter were mainly married couples unable to live together. Their plight was described by the unofficial magazine, *Peking Spring*, in an account of conditions at a Peking textile mill:

> More than 500 married couples do not have even a single room to live in. After marrying, they go on living in male and female dormitories. When the women have children, they have to stay in so-called 'mothers' quarters', where each room is occupied by two women with two children each or by three women with one child each.[12]

Some women live like this for ten years. If they want their husbands to spend a night with them, which depends on the goodwill of the other women in the room, their only privacy is from a sheet hung round the bed. Even when they do get a room of their own, in one family in four it is shared with grown-up children, and in one family in forty with both children and grandparents, three generations living together in one cramped cubicle:

> Every family has trunks, furniture and other household articles piled high. Things which cannot be piled, like bicycles, are hung on the walls . . . Some workers add a piece of board to a double bed, so that four or five people can sleep on it crossways; others make a double bed lower by shortening its legs, and then put a single bed on top of it. There will then be three levels of sleeping space, which the workers call jokingly air, land and sea . . .

Squalor and overcrowding cause a third of the mill's workforce to be permanently sick, and lead to incest, infidelity and juvenile delinquency:

> A student returning home cannot study. If the parents are strict enough, or if the student himself is diligent, he has to wait until his younger brothers and sisters are asleep before he can begin his homework. Many young people cannot stay at home. They go out and form gangs . . . They fight, exchange vulgar literature, gamble and get drunk . . .

The problem is not confined to industry. All organisations, from mines to newspaper offices, have a responsibility to house at least part of their workforce. Chinese scientists complain of having to compete with their children's homework, writers of having to negotiate with their families for the use of the only desk.[13] Municipal housing is no better.

Since 1978, an immense new building programme has been under way. In three years, an extra one square metre of living space was built for every city resident. If that rate is maintained, urban living standards in China will change dramatically by the late 1980s. Harbin, which had 2.8 square metres of housing per person in 1979, aims to have five square metres by 1985. But judging by the experience of the Soviet Union and Eastern Europe, where in most of the bigger cities there is a queue of several years for state-built flats, that may only increase demand. In the late 1970s the pressure on housing in Prague forced the Czechoslovak authorities to become the first in Eastern Europe to introduce residence restrictions like those in Chinese and Soviet cities. In Warsaw and Cracow, builders deliver apartment blocks with bare concrete outer walls. 'Painted façades are a luxury we cannot afford,' a Polish planner explained.

In Soviet cities, many of the old districts have been torn down to make way for the new construction. In Moscow, in 1976, I saw entire, quiet streets of old wooden houses – the Moscow of Dostoyevsky and Tolstoy – being burnt to the ground by demolition squads. But by the end of the decade, the revival of Russian nationalism brought a growing nostalgia for the past. Conservation societies were formed to do battle with the planners. Exhibitions of paintings of old Russia drew huge crowds. Samovars, icons, and old heavy furniture enjoyed a new vogue.

Peking is also falling victim to the relentless advance of high-rise buildings, though it has managed to retain some of its traditional character as a huge, sprawling village of ancient one-storey dwellings, built around what were once family courtyards. The buildings are grey, the streets are grey, even the earth is yellowish-grey. Old ladies with tiny bound feet, no bigger than a man's fist, hobble along, wearing velveteen jackets and baggy, black quilted trousers against the winter cold. The courtyard houses are heated by small, round iron stoves, and some still have the traditional paper windows instead of glass. In winter, old newspapers are pasted on the walls for insulation. Water comes from a communal tap, and light from a single forty-watt bulb.

Rent, however, is extremely low. In the Soviet Union it rarely accounts for more than four per cent of a family's budget, and in China often as little as two per cent, eighty-five pence a month for a couple with two children.

To avoid the waiting list for rented accommodation, it is possible in Soviet cities, and in China since 1980, to buy a flat outright. Three rooms in Moscow cost the equivalent of £6,000, four years' wages for a Soviet worker; four rooms in Nanning, in South-West China, cost £2,400, twelve years of a Chinese worker's wages. In both countries the payment period is up to fifteen years, at an interest rate of one or two per cent. The flats, which in the Soviet Union are in theory cooperatively owned, can be bequeathed or sold back to the cooperative or the state, but not put on the open market. The same applies to privately-owned town houses, which in both countries still account for a substantial proportion of urban dwellings. Only the Russian *dacha*, the country home which is one of the most coveted possessions of Russian town dwellers, can be freely bought and sold. It can be anything from a ramshackle log cabin, lost in the middle of the forest, miles from the nearest town, to a gabled villa with wood-panelled rooms in a village of exclusive weekend homes outside Moscow or Leningrad, or on the Black Sea coast. The price varies accordingly, from a few hundred to tens of thousands of pounds. China has no equivalent of the *dacha*. No one outside the elite has the use of a second home.

For rented accommodation, both countries operate housing exchanges in the bigger cities where a couple getting a divorce can parley a two-roomed flat into two separate single rooms, or a family can exchange their home for one in another area that suits them better. But in practice it is often an immensely complicated procedure, involving not just a straight swap but a round robin with as many as ten families taking part, any of which can wreck the arrangement by deciding to pull out.

The chronic shortage of living space contributes to many of the idiosyncrasies of Chinese city life. In Peking, each morning at dawn, the population pours out into the streets and parks to perform the slow, balletic motions of *taiqichuan*, shadow boxing, in a surrealistic ritual of awakening. Men stand flexing their muscles and singing at the tops of their voices. Students practise violins, trombones, French horns, quite oblivious of the cacophony around them. It is as though the city is clearing its lungs and tuning up for the day ahead. On summer evenings, they are all back again, sitting under the streetlamps talking, reading or playing cards. In southern cities, throughout the year, the pavement becomes an extension of the home. It is there that the family squats to breakfast on rice porridge or noodles, the women clean vegetables and protesting children have their hair washed in wooden tubs. Hot red peppers are strung from the windows and washing hangs overhead from wooden poles. Peasant instincts die hard: chickens peck in the doorways, and in the north and west, people keep calves in their courtyards. In Harbin in 1979, lost property reclaimed included 542 wristwatches and twenty-one cows.

Chinese wage-earners, in 1979, were paid an average of fifty-four yuan (£16) a month. At a state-owned enterprise such as the Daqing oilfield, a trainee earns from eighteen to twenty-six yuan (£5.25 to £7.50) a month for three years, before graduating to an eight-grade wage scale which varies slightly from province to province but is generally in the range of thirty-four to 110 yuan (£10 to £32.50). Technical personnel, from draughtsmen to computer scientists, have a thirteen-grade scale, from forty-six to 340 yuan (£13.50 to £100), and cadres, from the humblest clerk to Premier Zhao Ziyang, a twenty-five-grade scale from thirty-four to 450 yuan (£10 to £132.50). The starting rate for a university graduate is about fifty yuan (£15) a month.

Soviet wages are in most cases five to eight times higher. In 1979 the average was £120 and the minimum £48 a month. A university professor, a senior judge, a coalmine manager all earn about £350 a month, President Brezhnev reputedly £700 and a top-ranking ballet dancer about £800. The highest salaries of all go to Red Army marshals, who take home, including fringe benefits, about £1,500 a month. In the army, too, the lowest wages are found. A Soviet conscript is paid £4.60 a month, a Chinese conscript £1.75. At the end of 1980, only twenty individuals, mostly artists or stage performers, out of China's one billion people, earned more than £270 a month. In both countries, the state claws back a large slice of foreign-derived income, either directly or through taxation. A Chinese interpreter paid £200 a month by a foreign embassy is lucky to be able to keep £20.

In the Soviet Union, doctors and teachers, who generally earn less than the average wage, can triple their income by giving private treatment or tuition. In China, that is permitted only after retirement. But, unlike the Soviet Union, where all workers are paid by the state, in China almost a quarter of the non-agricultural labour force, some 23 million people, work in collectively-owned enterprises or individually as cobblers, tailors, pedlars or petty traders.

The main difference between the two types of employment is in the social security benefits they confer. Chinese state employees with twenty years' service receive a pension of seventy-five per cent of their wages when they retire, and their children are given preference in filling the jobs they vacate, no small benefit in a country with China's unemployment problems. Outside the state sector, no pensions are paid, nor is there any minimum wage. Even in the Soviet Union, to qualify for a pension you must have worked: there is no old age pension as such. As a result elderly Russians, particularly women, are sometimes left destitute when the former breadwinner in the family dies. One such old lady in Moscow regularly lay in wait to beg from foreigners near the apartment block where I lived.

In the Soviet Union, education and health care are free. But standards are often low and sometimes appalling, particularly in provincial cities. In a *samizdat* journal, *Almanack of Woman and Russia*, in September 1979, Vera Golubeva described conditions at an abortion clinic in Archangelsk, on the White Sea coast:

> The clinic is in an enormous building on Lermontov Street. Women call it 'the meat-mincer'. It has a turnover of 200 to 300 patients a day . . .
>
> The women wait in line outside the operating theatre. Abortions are induced by twos, and inside there are six women at any one time. The operating chairs are placed facing each other, so that each woman sees the bloody pulp being removed from the insides of the woman opposite her. There are two doctors and a nurse . . . One of the doctors shows the woman how to sit astride the chair . . . and the operation begins. Sometimes he gives an injection, but it does not stop the pain because very little novocaine is used and they do not wait for it to take effect. Without anaesthesia, the woman suffers atrociously. Some pass out altogether. The nurse, who must serve two doctors at once, has no time to help the patient. When she has aborted, she is revived and led out.
>
> It is left to the other women waiting their turn outside to help her back to the ward. For another hour and a half she writhes in nausea and pain. Next day she is sent home, regardless of what state she is in.[14]

Such experiences, together with dirty wards, poor food and widespread septicaemia after operations, explain why, despite enormous investment in the Soviet health service and more doctors per head of population than any other country in the world, many Soviet citizens prefer to pay and be treated privately.

The Chinese health service, operating in a far poorer country, experiences similar problems on a much bigger scale. For every 10,000 people, China has fewer than four doctors and twenty hospital beds; the Soviet Union has thirty-five doctors and 115 beds. Where Chinese sanatoria can accommodate 100,000 patients a year, the Soviet Union, with a quarter of China's population, sends 40 million of its citizens for a subsidised annual rest-cure. Both countries have immense medical expertise, which when applied to a narrow field – cancer research in China, or eye surgery in the Soviet Union – produces outstanding achievements. But neither has been able to make adequate general medical care available.

Chinese newspapers write of 'very bad conditions' even in hospitals in Peking, as well as overcrowded out-patient clinics and a chronic shortage of beds for mental patients – only enough for five per cent of those who need treatment.[15] In the provinces, the situation is worse. In Guangdong, in 1980, the only specialist cancer hospital for 50 million people was so crowded that patients slept in the corridors and out in the road. 'We hope the leading comrades of the relevant departments will step out of their offices and seriously listen to the cries of cancer patients,' said the local paper, *Guangzhou Ribao*. Chinese complain of incompetence among younger doctors trained during the Cultural Revolution, and of a general indifference among medical staff which is dissipated only by the promise of a bribe. One elderly Chinese lady I know, too honest to resort to such practices, found that the only alternative was to get up at four am, wait for three hours outside the clinic before it opened so as to be at the head of the queue, and keep coming back until she got the treatment she wanted.

Expectations have risen. A health service which would have been thought remarkable in the Soviet Union in the 1940s or in China in the 1960s is no longer enough. Moreover, in China there is a real problem of poverty of resources. In 1980, government spending on health, education and culture was 14.8 yuan (£4.30) for each member of the population, compared with £340 in Britain. While Chinese doctors often over-prescribe, particularly Chinese traditional medicines, which are generally preferred to the faster-acting Western drugs, painkilling injections are rarely used. Abortions are induced and teeth drilled without novocaine, and acupuncture anaesthesia, used in many operations, is not always effective.

Chinese have to pay for their own health care, except workers in state-owned enterprises, who are treated free, and their families, who pay half the cost. State sector employees are also entitled to up to six months' sick leave on full pay, and thereafter at sixty per cent of their salary – a system which leads to widespread skiving and bribery of doctors to issue sickness certificates. For other workers there is no social insurance, and a child who spends two weeks in hospital can cost his family fifty yuan (£15), the equivalent of a month's wages.

In the countryside, basic medical care is provided by a cooperative health scheme, for which each family pays ten yuan (£3) a year. But this does not cover operations and the treatment of serious illnesses. A bed in a commune hospital costs £1 a week; an appendectomy is £2.50. More complicated operations cost upwards of £30, which often has to be borrowed from a credit cooperative and leaves the family heavily in debt. That even a rudimentary health service should be available throughout rural China, where none existed before 1949, is among the communists' greatest achievements. But rudimentary it is. Thirty per cent of Chinese children under three years of age suffer from rickets due to dietary deficiencies, and in some provinces the figure is above eighty per cent.[16] In the low, stone hill villages of North China you see grimy, unwashed youngsters, their hands covered with sores. In Tibet, the poorest region of the country, every other person has a skin disease. There, in the 1950s, six children out of ten died in infancy. By 1980 it was two in ten, still twenty times more than in a city like Peking.

The level of hygiene throughout China is low, not only because of unsanitary living conditions, but also because of the prevalence of unhygienic practices. Like nineteenth-century Europeans and Americans, Chinese expectorate and blow their noses in the gutter rather than using handkerchiefs. No official meeting room is complete without a spittoon, and among China's leaders Deng Xiaoping, in particular, uses it with great panache and accuracy. Not even the theatre is exempt. Derek Jacobi, in Shanghai to play Hamlet, found his soliloquies had to compete with a barrage of hawking and spitting which would have done credit to the Elizabethan playgoers for whom Shakespeare wrote them. A campaign against spitting was launched tentatively in 1980, but, as in other countries, such habits will disappear only after a substantial rise in living standards. That is also true of the practice of clothing children, up to the age of four or five, in trousers with an open crotch. Even in winter, when the temperature is far below freezing, you see toddlers sitting astride their grandfathers' laps, their exposed parts blue with cold, as though that were the most normal way in the world to go about in icy weather. It avoids the need for nappies, but displays a very casual attitude to sanitation.

This cavalier approach notwithstanding, the Soviet Union rather than China has been having the greatest problems with child care. In the 1970s the Soviet infant mortality rate steadily rose, reaching 35.6 per thousand, more than twice the American figure, by 1976, the latest year for which statistics are available. It is the only developed country in the world where this has happened, and one of the causes is thought to be increased alcoholism among pregnant women.

Education, like health care, is not free in China. In contrast to the Soviet Union, where Khrushchev abolished tuition fees in 1955, everyone, including state employees, has to pay part of the cost of their children's schooling. University students receive grants, but only one Chinese in 200 has a higher education, compared with one Soviet citizen in twenty. At secondary and primary levels, many schools in Peking are so crowded that pupils can attend only half-days. Throughout the country, in 1978, more than a sixth of the school buildings were found to be in danger of collapse. There are shortages of desks and chairs, let alone books and laboratory equipment, and teachers are paid on average twenty per cent less than people in other professions.

The problem has been recognised. China is among the twenty countries which spend least on education relative to gross national product. In 1980 Deng Xiaoping said that unless the proportion were increased substantially within the next two years, China's modernisation could not be accomplished.[17]

But Deng also acknowledged that to make China a welfare state at its present stage of poverty was impracticable. 'Developing production without improving the people's livelihood is not right,' he said. But 'calling for an improved livelihood without developing production is not right either, and it cannot be attained'.

The lack of social security for all except state employees is one of the biggest obstacles to lowering the birth rate. Not only in the countryside, but in the towns as well, people want children in order to have someone to look after them in their old age. As single-child families become more general, Chinese couples will increasingly find themselves the sole support of two sets of grandparents, and more and more old people will be left with no one to support them at all. This will be tolerable only if, as in the Soviet Union, pensions are paid to the peasants and to all, not just some, workers, and if social welfare and commercial services are greatly expanded. In 1980 that was accepted in principle by the Party Central Committee, but putting it into practice will be something else again. Many urban services which are taken for granted elsewhere – laundry, home delivery services, health visitors, 'meals on wheels' – scarcely exist, and other, still more basic, facilities have actually declined. Over three decades, while China's urban population quadrupled, the number of shops decreased seven times, to one for every 500 people in the large cities and fewer than one per thousand in smaller towns. Peking, in 1950, had one restaurant or foodstall for every 200 people. By 1980, through constant amalgamation, the number had fallen to fewer than one for every 3,000 people.[18]

Of all the elements that constitute security in China, one is dominant: food is a national obsession. The colloquial greeting, the equivalent of 'How are you?', is *Ni chi fan le ma?*, 'Have you eaten?' The newspapers write of the 'seven basic necessities' of life – rice, cooking oil, salt, soy-sauce, vinegar, tea and firewood.[19] Office workers and shop assistants spend the morning talking about lunch, the afternoon sleeping it off and the evening making and eating dinner. It is an attitude born of generations of hunger. The infinite variety of Chinese cooking stems from the scarcity of food as much as a desire for the exotic. In a country where every year one region or another experiences famine, nothing is wasted – camel pads, shark's fin, snakemeat, bear's paws, chicken blood and fish lips all were made palatable and now are regarded as delicacies.

The average family in Peking spends nineteen yuan (£5.50) a head, half its monthly income, on food.[20] Cooking oil is rationed, and because production has not kept pace with the growth of population, supplies have been cut from 330 grams a month in 1956 to 250 grams in 1979.[21] Grain rationing is more liberal, and most city dwellers receive more than they can eat; a student or worker gets fourteen to seventeen kilograms a month, which rises to thirty kilograms for a man doing heavy manual labour.

The system is as much a means of controlling movement as conserving food. Grain coupons are issued only to registered town dwellers, which makes it harder to survive clandestinely in the cities, and they are valid only in the province of issue, which imposes strong constraints on individual travel. Special coupons exist for inter-provincial use, but they are generally issued only to those on official business. Tourism for Chinese is still in its infancy, and although the first package tours started in 1980, offering five days by the sea or at a scenic resort for about £15, they were mainly for teachers, students and retired people. Others, even if they have the money, have no time, and are limited to day-trips at weekends.

In most parts of China, rationing of pork and eggs ended in 1980. Beef is rarely available, except at butcheries for Chinese Moslems, and poultry is too expensive for most people to buy regularly. A chicken, at six yuan (£1.75), costs more than two days' wages. Nonetheless, according to official statistics, meat consumption in Chinese cities has trebled since the 1950s, to reach nineteen kilograms per person in 1979.[22] In the Soviet Union, the figure is a little over fifty kilograms, and in the United States, 120 kilograms. Vegetables are unrationed, but, as in the Soviet Union, often limited to cabbage in winter. Fruit (less than two kilograms a year) and dairy products (less than fifty grams a year) are so scarce that in many small towns, even in summer they are unobtainable.[23]

In short, Chinese town dwellers in the 1980s eat as badly as Soviet town dwellers did in the 1950s. The lack of vitamins and protein is the prime cause of lassitude and low output in China. A young taxi-driver in Canton told me he was able to make 120 yuan (£35) a month, more than twice the national average, by working overtime shifts. He was little better off, however, because in order to be able to work twelve hours a day, seven days a week, he was spending most of it on extra food. Similarly a group of peasants in South-East China who changed from growing two rice crops a year to three found they were eating the equivalent of the extra crop in order to have the strength to do the extra work involved.

The Soviet Union does not admit to any formal rationing. But outside

Moscow, Leningrad and a few other big cities, fruit, meat and dairy products are often in chronically short supply. After the disastrous grain harvest of 1975, each Thursday was declared a 'meatless day' throughout the Soviet Union, and restaurants and canteens were made to serve fish. In Cheboksary, 400 miles east of Moscow, and perhaps in other closed cities, in the late 1970s, 'temporary' meat rationing was reported to have been introduced, with adults limited to one kilogram a month. In many smaller towns in 1976 and again in 1980, no fresh meat at all was available for months at a time. At the Tyumen oilfields in Western Siberia, the Soviet equivalent of Daqing, it was officially confirmed that there were shortages even of bread, potatoes and cabbage.[24]

Soviet families spend on average almost half as much on clothing as they do on food. In China the proportion is less than a third. Cotton is rationed to seven metres per person a year, and even in Peking, most people's clothes budgets are only five yuan (£1.50) a month – which explains why they dress so drably. Only those with above-average incomes, and the young who have no financial dependants, can afford to think of fashion.

Cats and dogs, though illegal in Chinese cities because of the risk of rabies and liable to be killed on the spot by municipal inspection teams, are a source of food as well as companionship. A cat may earn his keep catching mice, but the fat puppies with appealing eyes which appear at market just before the Spring Festival are destined for the pot.

In Russia that would be as unthinkable as it is in Britain. Moscow, like London, has its annual dog-show, and the country's first canine beauty parlour, where well-heeled Muscovites can get their poodles clipped for ten roubles (£8) a time, has been open since 1975. In post-Mao China, such frivolities are still a long way off. But then, Moscow has a cosmetic surgery clinic where Soviet women can have their noses remodelled or their stomachs taken in, a notion beyond the wildest imaginings of most women in China. They may, in Mao's phrase, 'hold up half the sky', but they are even further away than Soviet women from having half the rewards and half the freedoms. Chinese life is more spartan and makes fewer concessions to femininity. As in the Soviet Union, women are predominantly in the lower-paid jobs and are expected, in addition, to do most of the work in the home.

'Socially productive labour,' a Chinese women's congress was told in 1977, 'is the fundamental condition for women's liberation.' But it was also 'the unshirkable duty of every woman' to bring up the next generation.

Housekeeping in the Soviet Union and China takes four to six hours a day. One survey found that in six out of ten Soviet families, women do all the shopping, cooking, washing and ironing. In only one family in eight does the husband help at home in the evenings after work.[25] And in only one family in twenty-five is there a real division of labour, with the husband taking over one of the main household chores. A woman engineer at Kishinyov, mother of two children, complained in the press in 1980:

> I get back from work at about 7 o'clock in the evening and leave in the morning, so that I am away from home practically all day, except for days off. There's no time or strength for a smile or a kind word. You get to bed after half the night and your head doesn't even touch the pillow before you're asleep. You get up in the morning a little bit earlier just so as to be able to look at yourself for a moment in the mirror before hurrying off to work.[26]

Those problems are not unique to the Soviet Union, but their connection with the falling Soviet birthrate, the high level of divorce and juvenile delinquency, is plain. Soviet women simply do not have time to look after their children properly.

In China, cooking alone takes three hours a day. In 1978 a campaign was launched to popularise instant rice and factory-baked bread instead of home-made noodles and steamed bread. But Chinese are conservative eaters and do not take easily to such new-fangled ideas.

In both countries thrift is a way of life. Not because Russians are naturally thrifty – far from it – but because, compared with America or Western Europe, where fashions change by the day, obsolescence is built-in and goods are junked before they are half-used, thrift is dictated by scarcity. Drive to Helsinki after living for a few months in Moscow, and the sheer abundance, the prodigality of Western life is overpowering, almost obscene in its immoderation. The shops – ordinary shops as in any Western city – seem to bulge with goods. Where in Moscow, at night, even the main streets are badly lit, in Finland every small town, every store and hotel, is a blaze of lights. There is a colour, a variety, a quality, a wealth and glitter which make Russians look on Westerners with the eyes of deprived orphans. In Moscow hotels, even the paper serviettes on the tables have been cut by hand into quarters to make them go further.

Yet in the hierarchy of parsimony, Russians are outdone by the Chinese. In Peking, a man will wear the same shirt day after day, for months if not years, until the collar is worn through. Families strain off tealeaves and dry them for re-use. Old women pick over garbage heaps at street corners looking for fragments of wood for fuel, and men scavenge for cigarette ends.

In the United States eighty per cent of housework is mechanised, in the Soviet Union, fifteen per cent, and in China, less than one per cent. Until 1980, it was impossible for a Chinese even to have a private telephone. That year, one family in three in Peking had a television – and hoped to have a washing machine by 1985.[27] But Peking is exceptional. In the whole of China, only one family in seventy has a television set, compared with two families in three in the Soviet Union and almost every family in Britain. Private car ownership in China is restricted to a few hundred former capitalists and returned Overseas Chinese. In the Soviet Union in 1980 there were 6 million private cars, against 100 million in the United States, and 14 million motorcycles. The Chinese can also buy light motorcycles, and since 1980 these have been available in a choice of colours, not just black as in the past. However, production is only a few thousand a year and they cost £150 (nine months' wages) each.

In town and country alike, the main means of individual transport in China is the humble bicycle. The cheapest model costs £50 and, for many Chinese, is the biggest purchase of their lives. It has no lights and often no brakes and causes more than half of all traffic accidents. Peasants use it to transport live pigs and sheep to market, tying them to a board, strapped on crossways behind the saddle. Chickens and vegetables are carried in huge wickerwork paniers, on either side of the back wheel. Bicycles are used to carry gas cylinders, brushwood, armchairs, even trees. In the countryside whole families travel on them, the father pedalling, one child sitting on the crossbar, and his wife, carrying a second child, perched behind. There are bicycles with side-cars for children, pedicabs and tricycle carts for short-distance goods haulage. In a country where the few ambulances are reserved for the elite, the bicycle is often the only means of bringing the sick to hospital. Peasants cycle in from outlying communes with a relative, wrapped in a quilt, prostrate in the cart behind them.

Prices in the Soviet Union and China for all but the most basic consumer goods are kept higher than in Western countries, relative to earnings, as a matter of deliberate policy, to depress demand and sop up excess liquidity. For, despite the modest spending power of Russians and the poverty of Chinese, the shortage of goods in both countries is more acute than the shortage of money. The average savings of an urban Chinese family in 1979 were £190, almost twelve months' wages, twenty-eight per cent more than a year earlier. For a Soviet family it was £1,700, fourteen months' wages, up thirty-seven per cent over the previous three years. The reason was in each case the same: there was nothing to spend it on.

In China, consumer demand is contained by rationing as well as price. Television sets, the cheaper brands of bicycle, in some cities even furniture, can only be bought with special vouchers, issued through places of work on the basis of one for every so many employees. The Soviet Union limits demand through the waiting list and the queue. As a result the Soviet, even more than the Chinese, economy is locked into an unending cycle of shortages and hoarding. Deficit goods, as they are called, range from horseshoes to detergent by way of secateurs, toothpaste, Christmas trees and women's tights. Tights were unfindable when I left Moscow in 1976, and still unfindable in 1980. *Literaturnaya Gazeta* explained why: 'If your wife sees them in stock somewhere, she won't buy the three pairs she needs, she'll buy eighteen. Hoarding is a natural and justifiable reaction when goods are scarce.'

Spare parts are hardest of all to find. It is so well understood among Soviet motorists that the only way to obtain windscreen wipers is to steal someone else's that no car is ever parked without its wipers being removed and locked safely inside. To obtain a set of pistons or an accelerator cable can take six months, and then a garage still has to be persuaded to fit them. If you break down on the open road, the best you can hope for is to be near a *smotrovoi*, a 'looking place', which consists of a concrete ramp in a lay-by on to which the car can be driven so that you can get underneath and mend it yourself.

The tribulations of Soviet car-owners deserve a volume on their own, but they are not the only Soviet consumers to suffer. A tape recorder or a washing machine, no matter how laboriously acquired, often has to be abandoned when it goes wrong because there are simply no parts available to repair it.

Many of these deficiencies are intrinsic to the system. Motor spares are unobtainable because it is unprofitable for factories to make them. Spectacles in the Soviet Union are in short supply because most of the frames are so ugly that people refuse to buy them; the resultant glut of unsaleable pairs convinced the State Planning Commission in 1979 that production should be reduced, thereby rendering the shortage even more acute. 'While none or very few of the products the masses want are produced,' one newspaper lamented, 'unwanted products are turned out in large quantities.'[28] That was *Nanfang Ribao* in Canton, and it was talking not about Soviet spectacles but problems closer to home. In China, electric light bulbs for household use are so scarce that a person buying one must first produce the broken bulb to show that he really needs it and is not just adding an extra light. Yet there is chronic overproduction of 1,000-watt bulbs, because the factories make a profit on big bulbs but barely break even on small ones.

Chinese go short of many things. But rationing, poverty and lack of choice mean that queues are not ubiquitous as in the Soviet Union. Russians carry everywhere a string bag which they call an *avoska*, a 'just in case' bag, on the off-chance that they will see something unusual for sale. Chinese rarely bother as the chance of finding anything is so small. Chinese men, like the group signing themselves 'We who are fat and over-40' who complained to the *People's Daily* of the lack of long johns for the well-rounded male – an essential undergarment in the Peking winter, usually worn in several layers – buy the wool themselves and get a workshop to make it up. Chinese children who have no toys salvage an iron hoop from a scrapyard or make a kite from newspaper, or in summer, catch a dragonfly and tie a piece of thread round its body. There is little hoarding, and because Chinese consumers are less demanding than Russians, the accumulation of unsold goods, while not small, is far from attaining the size it has in the Soviet Union, where clearance sales of unwanted items lose over £1 billion a year.

In most respects the living standards of Chinese town dwellers in the 1980s are at the level the Russians reached two or three decades before – in some areas, like television ownership, a little ahead, in others, like housing, a bit further behind. But that applies only to town dwellers: the Chinese countryside remains a world apart. The gulf between rural China and the advanced countries is measured not in tens but in hundreds of years.

The Idiocy of Rural Life

The phrase is from Engels. He and Marx regarded the peasantry as backward and conservative, an obstacle to change. To their nineteenth-century minds, the newly emerging urban proletariat was the class to push the wheel of history forward. For Stalin, too, this was an article of faith. In 1927, his advice to the infant Chinese Communist Party to win power first in the cities almost encompassed its destruction. While Stalin lived, Russian peasants were crushed under an iron heel. Only by ruthlessly exploiting them could the money be obtained to finance Soviet industrialisation and feed the new aristocracy of labour, the industrial workers, who carried it out. Even in China, where Mao rejected conventional Marxist wisdom and based his revolution on the long tradition of the peasant uprising, the Party is called the 'party of the proletariat' and its method of rule, 'proletarian dictatorship'. In China, too, the peasants are paying for industrialisation. Engels's cruel and bigoted judgment has been self-perpetuating: the peasants have been communism's fools.

In China, in 1978, the output of each peasant was valued at 364.3 yuan (£107). The output of each industrial worker in the state sector was nearly £3,000, and in industry as a whole, £825. Since peasants work harder than industrial workers, their labour is being undervalued by at least eight times.

Feudalism and exploitation by the state mirror the relations in the family and the village. In 1980 a commune official in Guizhou, in South-Western China, was expelled from the Party for taking a concubine. Cases are reported of girls from poverty-stricken villages selling themselves, or being kidnapped and sold by others, into marriage with cripples or men with deformities who would not otherwise be able to find wives.[1] Even in ordinary circumstances, most peasant marriages are still arranged between families by a go-between, usually an elderly woman, who often pays little attention to the wishes of the couple themselves.

In a village in Anhui, in Eastern China, a girl named Guo Dexiu fell in love with a young man named Wei in a village nearby. Both were members of the Communist Youth League, and both their fathers were

Party members. But each had been committed while still a child to an arranged marriage with a neighbour, and local opinion was so strongly in favour of these traditional matches that even Party officials in the district insisted that they must take place. In March 1977, Guo was married against her will to the man her family had chosen. When, a year later, all her efforts to have the marriage annulled had failed, she hanged herself. Wei committed suicide six weeks afterwards.[2]

Such cases are less common than in the past. In 1951, in Southern and Central China alone, 10,000 women were said to have died in marriage disputes. Since 1980, interference in the freedom of marriage has been punishable by up to seven years' imprisonment. But Chinese newspapers say the problem is 'still very serious'.[3] A survey that year found that in a commune in Shanxi, forty-three per cent of the children under five had been betrothed by their parents, and eighty per cent of those under ten. In another small village, in Hunan, there were more than fifty child-brides, many of whom had been seduced before puberty; their parents were so poor that girl-children were given away to the first male who presented himself.[4]

Even when a couple do choose each other freely, the central element of a rural marriage is money. 'Selling a girl for a high price to another family . . . violates the law,' warned the *China Youth News*.[5] Yet in 1978 a young man from Zhejiang province could still report:

> When I got engaged to a girl from a neighbouring village, four years ago, her family imposed many demands on me: First, betrothal money calculated according to the girl's age, at 12 yuan a year . . . Second, six jars of wine to show respect for her parents. Third, eight garments, three made of wool or flannel, and three catties [1.5kgs] of woollen yarn. Fourth, 12 yuan placed on a platter as an offering to her grandmother. Fifth, one gold ring and one set of gold earrings. Sixth, a grand betrothal feast.

In all he paid more than 500 yuan, and afterwards the girl's family demanded a suite of furniture and a wedding banquet costing more than 1,000 yuan, altogether equivalent to seven years of a rural labourer's income. The biblical Jacob toiled for seven years to win Rachel, but for the young man in Zhejiang, it was too much. When he said he could not pay, the family forced him to break off the engagement.[6]

One thousand yuan is the going rate for a marriage in many parts of China, in town as well as country. Graham Earnshaw of the *Daily Telegraph* recalls meeting a young man in Canton in 1979, who told him that he had saved 500 yuan 'but you can't get much for that'. Often it takes the whole of a family's savings to marry off a son, and even then he and his bride start their new life four or five hundred yuan in debt. 'The bad old habits of lavish marriage celebrations still exist in a serious way,' grumbled the Peking Youth League. 'Music is played and drums are beaten loudly and the streets are crowded with wedding guests. Sometimes, even if the bride and groom live nearby, they have to circle around the town in a car just to show that a wedding is taking place.'' At one wedding in 1980, bickering over the gifts culminated in a pitched battle between the two families, in which tables spread with the marriage feast were overturned and windows and furniture smashed. The bridegroom was knocked unconscious by a flying brick, while others were taken to hospital with injuries from staves and shovels. When it was all over, the wretched bride was left to contemplate the ruins of what should have been the happiest day of her life.

Although arranged marriages are discouraged, go-betweens are not. After the devastating earthquake which destroyed the town of Tangshan in 1976, Party officials drew up lists of widowed men and women and 'helped them to find suitable partners'. Trade union officials and Youth League organisations often play a similar role, to the extent, at some factories, of going out and recruiting unmarried girl workers to balance the number of young unmarried men. When in 1980 the Peking Youth League set up China's first marriage bureau, the press said it would be 'a good go-between among young people'.

As with marriages, so with funerals, the old customs endure. In the cities, cremation is obligatory but in the countryside the fields are dotted with small conical gravemounds. Each year, at Qing Ming, the Festival of Souls, they are scattered with brightly-coloured paper flowers, and, in place of traditional stone ancestor tablets, reverence is done to photographs of the dead.

Party satraps in rural China, despite condemnation from the press, are often buried with great pomp and ceremony. When Wang Kuike, chairman of a county revolutionary committee in Shanxi, died in March 1980,

large sheets of white paper were pasted on to the walls and door of the mourning hall, and pieces of charcoal were placed at either side of the entrance to prevent devils from entering. Oil lamps and sticks of incense burnt on a low table, set beside the lacquered coffin. In front stood a memorial tablet, and boxes for paper money and paper gold and silver . . . Wang's body was laid in the coffin with 'cloud-stepping shoes' on his feet, a gold and silver funeral pillow beneath his head and a red cloth over his face. His children wore [white] mourning clothes and hats, and . . . when the coffin was placed in the hearse, a cockerel, known as a 'soul-guiding cockerel' was tied on top. The procession was accompanied by fireworks and firecrackers, and two bands – one with Chinese and one with Western instruments – played a funeral dirge . . . After the burial, a stele was erected bearing the words, 'Wang Kuike's Tomb'.[8]

Almost every village has a former Taoist monk, who clandestinely carries out funeral rites. It is he who sets up the memorial tablet, calms the spirit of the dead and calculates the most auspicious hour and date for the interment, while a geomancer chooses a burial site where the *fengshui*, the combination of wind and water, is favourable. The dead man's relatives distribute alms, and burn paper money to accompany his soul to heaven.

Funerals, like marriages, have a strong commercial element, and those who wish to ingratiate themselves with the dead person's family give generously. When the wife of a district Party secretary in Shangdong died,

he received 740 catties of wheat, 750 yuan in cash, six planks, 1,000 bricks, 400 catties of cabbage, more than 10 catties of oil, 30 catties of wheat bran, 18 mourning scrolls and more than 40 wreaths.[9]

Geomancy is not restricted to the grave site. In Southern China, in 1980, peasants attacked an oil drilling team, stole survey instruments and destroyed core samples obtained at a cost of nearly half a million yuan (£150,000) because, they said, the drillers were interfering with the geomantic aspect of the coastline. In the north-west young children sometimes have a protective red mark painted on their foreheads or a charm in the shape of a lock around their necks to 'lock' them to life. Before a solar eclipse, rumours circulate for months that the sky will go dark and calamity will come, and on the day itself, villagers beat gongs and drums and let off firecrackers to stop the Hound of Heaven swallowing the sun. Each time they succeed, they strengthen their belief.

Wizards and fake divines feed on such superstitions, tricking the gullible. In Shandong, a man whose wife was mentally ill was told, for a large fee, that she would be cured if he moved to a new house in a more favourable position. On the chosen day, the firecrackers which were supposed to drive out evil spirits before the family moved in failed to go off because of heavy rain. To make sure that no demon took advantage of the bad weather, he borrowed three hand-grenades from the local construction bureau's explosives' store. The first two went off successfully. The third blew him to pieces. Near Peking, a young peasant was arrested for having seduced seven village girls on the pretence that he was a Living Buddha and could win them favour in heaven. Another man, pretending to be an Immortal, swindled a peasant family out of their savings by telling them he could make money grow by sealing it in a box for twenty days. While they were kowtowing as he had instructed, he exchanged it for pieces of coloured paper.

Communism has not only failed to eradicate such beliefs, but in some cases has itself been assimilated to them. A group of peasants in Shanxi who told fortunes by reading the cracks in oracle bones also prayed to portraits of Mao, Zhou Enlai and the late Red Army commander, Zhu De. Party officials at a commune in Hainan, believing devils to be responsible for a number of recent deaths, decided to rebuild the village temple. Guards were posted at the gates to keep away outsiders, and for several days all farmwork stopped as the entire village took part in exorcism rites.

That exorcism was non-violent. Others frequently end in death. In one atrocious case near Shanghai in 1978, a witch murdered two six-year-old boys in front of a large crowd in the village square. The children were first beaten with branches, then boiling water was poured over them, and finally one was strangled and the other burnt to death, all supposedly to rid a paralysed woman of a spirit which was haunting her.[10] In Guizhou, a year later, a twenty-four-year-old labourer convinced the Party Secretary of his commune and another worker that he was Kui Xing, the God of Literature, and often went up to heaven to discuss with the other gods the vices and virtues of mortal man. On this basis he obtained from his two followers more than 1,600 yuan, the equivalent of eight years' wages. But in February 1980, fearing discovery, he told them that the time had come for them and their families to go to heaven and become immortals too. First, he took eight of the Party Secretary's nine children to a cave, where he helped the Secretary to kill them. Then, on his instructions, the two men and their wives, with two more children tied to their backs, weighted themselves down with rocks and threw themselves into a river. The killings were discovered because the worker, when he hit the water and sank, realised that the 'God' had tricked them, and managed to break loose and reach the bank.[11]

Life in rural China is hard, rough and simple. In the south battles take place between rival clans, often with loss of life. At home, peasant fathers rule their families like patriarchs. By the age of four, children are expected to help in the house and at six or seven they are set a daily task, collecting manure or cutting grass for fodder. Discipline is strict; fathers beat both boys and girls with bamboo switches.

One child in twenty does not go to school at all, and rather more, particularly girls, drop out after only a year or two of primary education in order to help their parents in the fields. Adult literacy campaigns in the 1950s taught 120 million peasants to read and write, but at the end of 1979 the Education Ministry estimated that there were still 250 million illiterates, including a high proportion of young people. 'Primary education has still not truly been introduced everywhere,' said the *Peking Daily*. 'In reality it is constantly turning out new illiterates and semi-illiterates.' In developed provinces, one teenager in four cannot read or write; in remote areas, more than half are illiterate.[12] In the Soviet Ukraine, three agricultural labourers out of four have a secondary education. In a typical Chinese county, it is nearer one in ten. In the country as a whole, the proportion of secondary school teachers with university degrees has dropped from seventy to thirty per cent since 1965, and in rural areas many secondary schools have no graduate teachers at all.[13] In 1979 plans for universal secondary education were abandoned in favour of developing vocational and technical training.

How desperately this was needed was shown by a report from Guangxi:

A production team bought a hand-guided tractor and sent a youth to the county seat for a few days to learn how to operate it. On the day he was to return, all the men, women, old and young people gathered in the village and beat drums and gongs to welcome the 'little iron ox'. The youth and the tractor failed to arrive. This was because he and the tractor had fallen into a ditch.

One team laboriously manhandled a tractor into the mountains. After a few days it stopped working. No one knew how to repair it, so it was carried back down the mountain to the nearest town. There it was discovered that it had run out of petrol. Another village had precisely the opposite problem. No one knew how to turn off a new generator. In desperation, the villagers tried beating it with clubs; when that failed, they pushed it into a pond. In China in 1978, fewer than one rural labourer in fifteen could operate machinery of any kind.

Women do much of the heavy work. Often they outnumber men in gangs breaking rock to build terraces, or digging irrigation canals. However, Chinese officials admit that 'their pay is always lower than that of men of equal strength', usually by thirty to forty per cent, and that 'proper allowance is never made for their biological characteristics'.[14] In Southern China I have watched middle-aged women tethered to carts, hauling loads of bricks uphill along muddy

101

roads, where every step was a brutish struggle not to slither back. Yet at least there were roads. In 1978, one commune in ten in China had no road at all. In poor, mountainous provinces, such as Guizhou, it rose to one commune in five and one village in two. And in Sichuan – not to speak of Tibet and Qinghai – in 1980 a whole county was still inaccessible by motor vehicle. Similarly, fewer than half of China's villages have electricity, and in remote areas, only one quarter.[15]

As in most poor societies, animals are routinely maltreated. So are people. A peasant near Peking was executed in 1980 after punching his fifteen-year-old daughter, who was pregnant with his child, in the stomach to induce a miscarriage, hiding the dead baby in a cave, and then drowing the girl in a vat of water when he feared that she would talk. In Shaanxi I have seen a man working in harness beside a mule, and in Hunan men, instead of oxen, pulling ploughs.

Superstition offers one escape from the appalling harshness of rural life. Gambling is another. From peasants to ministers, Chinese have an almost pathological compulsion to gamble. Moscow and other Soviet cities have racecourses where Russians can go for a mild flutter on a Sunday afternoon. In China, all gambling – and horseracing – was banned in 1949. Yet three decades later the first thing any Chinese official wants to see when he visits Hong Kong is the island's racecourse. In Anhui, a man whose relatives I knew lost 400 yuan (£120) in one night at cards, as much, in his desperately poor village, as a family could save in five years. When he went home his young wife, faced with the impossibility of repaying such a sum, hanged herself, the recourse of Chinese women through the centuries when life has become too awful to continue. Near Shanghai, in May 1980, gambling reached such a pitch in one village that half the adult male population was arrested. In the south, peasants rustled cattle and chopped down communal rubber trees to pay off gambling debts. The *People's Daily* complained that it was causing murder, robbery and divorce.

Soviet farmworkers seek refuge from rural drudgery in drink and religion, sometimes both at once:

There are the 'big' holidays like Easter and Christmas, and there are the holidays of the local patron saints. All too often, no sooner have they [the villagers] finished celebrating a 'big' holiday than along comes a 'Yegor's Day', which has to be celebrated too, and then the day of some other patron 'saint' . . . In the Rameshkov district of Kalinin region alone, about 70 local saints' days are celebrated every year . . . The peasants and their brigadier 'bless' cows, pigs and sheep. The next day they get drunk. The best time for sowing is missed.[16]

That account is from a Soviet atheist pamphlet in the late 1950s. Ten years later, three peasants out of five still possessed an icon, and after another decade had passed, in 1979, *Pravda* still wrote of farms where the cattle were starving, the grass unmown and the fields untilled because the workers would not work.[17]

Within a hundred miles of Moscow lie villages forty miles from any tarred road, which in spring are cut off completely for weeks at a time by the thaw that turns the earth into a bog. On the great festivals, if no longer on every local saint's day, the men go off on a drunken rampage, and, as often as not, someone's head is broken. But if the police try to intervene, the whole village rallies to the culprits' defence: 'What have they done wrong?' they say. 'They're only following the custom.' Yet even in such a place, no more than a cluster of twenty or thirty wooden *izbas*, the 1970s brought electricity. Old people get a pension of £12 a month. In each home logs are piled high round the fireplace that takes up more than half of the one big room. Each village usually has a lorry, and a few families own motorcycles and television sets.

A Soviet farmworker earns on average about £90 a month, which, when augmented by income from the private plot, is not much less than an industrial worker. In China the average in 1980 was about £6. Unlike Russians, Chinese peasants are not paid wages but awarded work-points. At the end of each year the production team, the village under a new name, distributes its profits on the basis of the number of work-points each family has amassed. Throughout the country, the teams are grouped into brigades and the brigades into 53,000 communes. Peasant incomes, including earnings from private plots, and grain rations, seventy per cent of which are distributed on a per capita basis, regardless of workpoints, average about half an industrial worker's earnings. However, if the gap between town and country is to close, they will have to grow twice as fast as urban wages. In 1980 the gap was becoming wider.

Six pounds a month for a rural labourer with a family to support does not go far. In a village in Yunnan, in South-West China, each peasant was allowed only thirteen square metres of land to farm on his own account, and prosperity was defined as every rural inhabitant having one pig and producing half a ton of grain a year, and every labourer achieving a monthly income of £7.40. It was to be attained by 1985. In that village, a huddle of ochre mud-brick dwellings, roofed with round grey tiles with ornamented ends, set amid the brilliant green of rice seedlings, the peasants cut winter wheat by hand with sickles. From the fields it was carried on the bent backs of women to be threshed by a line of girls with bamboo flails, rising and falling in unison. Children played in the hay beside the village square, and a horse walked in a circle, turning a millstone.

The temple, with slender upward-curving eaves and glazed green diamond-shaped tiles, had been turned into a school, where the pupils sat bolt upright on ancient gnarled benches, learning to write characters. The priest's house had become the clinic, in which a 'barefoot doctor' with a few months' paramedical training dispensed traditional medicines and contraceptive pills.

Other villages offer different images of poverty: in Hainan, an idiot, dressed in rags, hobbled by a rope round his legs to prevent him wandering; in Fujian, groups of youths working on treadmills in the fields, pumping water for irrigation.

In the far west, tea-sellers sit by the roadside beneath huge, square umbrellas of tattered sun-bleached canvas. The local dentist stands behind a stool on which rest the tools of his trade, a small hammer and chisel, and a pink mould of grinning teeth. A group of wandering musicians – a blind girl, a man with one eye and a cripple – who travel from settlement to settlement, begging for their food, sit at a street corner playing two-stringed fiddles, black with age, and singing old ballads. Nearby a ragged woman lies asleep in the dust, a small naked child playing by her side: a cardboard notice propped in front of a mug says that she is destitute.

Those scenes are from Gansu, in North-West China, in 1980. Even a Chinese official with whom I travelled from Peking was shaken by its poverty. The hills are like wrinkled folds of sandy velvet, parched and dead. Much of the population lives in caves, cut into loess cliffs. In the desert, there are clusters of rude mud and stone huts, half buried in the sand and covered with brushwood for insulation, where peasants scrape a living cutting stunted thorns for fuel. The harvest in some communes fails in nine years out of ten. Chinese newspapers quoted a farm director as saying: 'The peasants here are poverty-stricken . . . Since 1959, one political movement after another was launched in our villages, and with each, the peasants' lives became a little more intolerable.'[18]

Yet over vast areas of China, these conditions are the norm. According to the *People's Daily*, in a quarter of the country's villages, containing 200 million people, production in 1980 was 'extremely difficult' and each rural labourer earned less than £4 a month. A hundred million peasants, it said, had 'drawn no benefit from collectivisation' and were still as poor as in 1949, needing state assistance to survive; in the worst-off areas, living standards had actually declined. One Chinese peasant in eight, in 1980, was permanently hungry, and throughout the country the supply of grain and cotton cloth for each rural inhabitant had not increased since 1957.[19] 'We have been building socialism for thirty years,' a county Party secretary in Anhui lamented, 'but still many people in the rural areas do not have enough to eat and are poorly clothed.'[20]

In the most wretchedly poor communes, a peasant is paid only eight fen (two pence) a day, representing an annual income of £7. In some areas relief grain is provided, but usually within a daily limit of 400 grams.[21] Where there is no relief, the peasants abandon their villages.[22] Internal Party documents, circulating among high-level officials in January 1980, contained photographs from Shaanxi of children with distended bellies suffering from severe malnutrition. Pockets of starvation were reported unofficially in the 1970s from several other areas, including Anhui, Fujian and Sichuan.

Even in areas of average income, the material gap between town and country is immense. One Chinese in two in Peking has a watch, and one in three a bicycle; in rural areas, the figure for both is closer to one in twenty. Sewing machines and radio sets, which complete the quartet of basic consumer durables that Chinese call 'the three things that go round and one that stands up', are five times commoner in the towns than in the countryside. And of the two million television sets manufactured in 1980, ninety-five per cent were sold to the ten per cent of the population which lives in the cities.

By the 1990s it is planned that television will be available throughout the countryside. If that can be achieved it will revolutionise rural attitudes, opening the minds of the peasantry to new ideas as nothing else could. But, at best, it is more than a decade away.

In the 1980s it is not a shortage of television sets that bothers China's peasants but shortages of the most basic daily necessities – soap, iron wire, nails and cotton thread. In the countryside, as in the towns, the lack of goods to buy is even more acute than the lack of money: peasant savings in 1979 grew on average three times faster than peasant incomes. Families in richer areas often have silver and pieces of gold stashed away from pre-communist days, and occasionally silver dollars bearing the effigy of the warlord, Yuan Shikai, are still seen at rural markets.

Poverty and shortages are compounded by the tyranny of local officials. When vouchers for the purchase of bicycles and sewing machines arrive at a production brigade, the Party secretary distributes them among his cronies. An ordinary peasant may have the money to buy a bicycle, but without the influence to obtain a voucher he will have a five-year wait.

Commune and county leaders embezzle relief supplies – ranging from a few bags of grain diverted from illiterate villagers in Guizhou and Tibet to a £50 million scandal in Henan after a flood disaster in 1975. Out of state aid to the stricken area totalling £110 million, nearly half was spent on luxurious villas for local Party bosses, guest houses, office blocks, and 'prodigious lavish parties'. Two years later, one million peasants were still homeless, living in temporary shelters.

Under the emperors, the *yamen* magistrate imposed a corvée for maintaining roads and dikes, building canals, and furnishing timber for palace construction. The same system was used under Mao: the communes provided unpaid labour for irrigation schemes, and had to maintain roads and railway lines traversing their land. In Guangdong, villages were forced to sell their buffaloes and seed grain to finance a canal-building project. In Shanxi, in Northern China, from 1974 to 1978 a prefecture levied £400,000 in cash, 5,500 tons of grain and 15 million man-days of labour for projects which were of no benefit to the villagers made to carry them out.[23]

Some projects were of no use to anyone at all, yet staggering sums were exacted from the peasants to pay for them before the waste was discovered. In a notorious case in Shanxi, for which responsibility was eventually traced up into the Politburo itself, 5,000 peasants worked every day for five years on a water diversion scheme. By 1980, £15 million had been expended, but the project was still only a third complete. It was cancelled when the leader promoting it lost power; only then was it admitted that it would have taken all the water from another, larger irrigation scheme which already existed nearby. Engineers had warned as much before the project began, but for political reasons had been overruled.[24]

The petty tyrants of the Chinese countryside grow their little finger-nails an inch long, to show that they do no manual labour. Like the *baozhang*, the district officials in Chiang Kai-shek's day, the peasants give feasts for them at each Spring Festival, they take bribes and grant favours, and in their own small kingdoms, as the newspaper *Guangming Ribao* complained at the end of 1979, they are constrained neither by Party policy nor the law of the land:

> In some communes and brigades, the people are terrified of the Party secretaries, for they control the politics, economy and life of the people, call black white according to their will and commit all kinds of outrages . . . You may publish what you want but they will do as they like. Words can do nothing to these local despots.[25]

Near Shijiazhuang, 200 miles south of Peking, a Party secretary had a peasant imprisoned and tortured and made him pay a fine of £90, because the man had killed his dog. In Guangdong, at the end of 1980, the provincial radio station reported that cases were occurring 'all the time' of local Party officials 'detaining people illegally, setting up clandestine tribunals, interrogating people, tying them up and parading them round to be struggled against, and extorting confessions by torture'. One Party secretary arrested two youths for stealing trees from a farm, and kept them bound and confined for so long that one died and the other was crippled. An official of the Supreme Procuratorate said similar problems existed in other parts of the country.[26]

In Hubei, in Central China, a commune Party secretary ordered that seventy-five peasants' homes be demolished in mid-winter to make way for a dam, without preparing anywhere else for them to live. The team leader of another village, given a similar order, resisted as long as he could and then committed suicide. The money intended for new housing had been diverted to build an office block, the most splendid in the county.

In that commune two-thirds of the members of the Party committee and one in four of the brigade and team leaders maintained their authority by beating up anyone who disagreed with them. In Shanghai, a brigade Party branch hired a thug to do its beatings for it. Chinese newspapers in other provinces reported cases of Party secretaries personally beating peasants to death.[27] In Peking, in 1978, the parents of a twenty-one-year-old labourer named Sun Qingji put up a wall-poster on the main street containing photographs of his battered body, after he had been killed during a struggle meeting at a prosperous suburban commune. 'Incidents of illegally beating and persecuting people to death occur constantly,' said a procuratorate report in Guangdong.[28]

The callousness and brutality of the unjust official in China through the ages were summed up in a tragedy which befell a family in Sichuan. In March 1976, fifty kilograms of fresh ginger were stolen from a village in Hexi commune. Two peasants confessed, but were not dealt with until September, when the Party secretary decided to make an example of the case. First they were tortured until they signed statements implicating others, including Zhang Baiyu, the wife of a demobilised soldier named Xiong Yifu. Then Zhang and five others were arrested and taken to the brigade, where they were subjected to beatings, hung up by their hands, and made to kneel in stocks. After three months of this, 'they had no choice but to confess whatever the leaders wanted them to' – which was that they had stolen not fifty kilograms but nearly two tons of ginger, and that Zhang had poisoned two pigs belonging to a neighbour. Her share of the compensation was assessed at more than

£140, the equivalent of three years' income. To pay it she and her husband surrendered their savings of £18, sold their sewing machine and other possessions and dismantled their house to sell the beams and tiles. Left destitute, they spent the next two years petitioning the county and the prefecture for redress, 'but they were denied at every stage and not one unit sent anyone to investigate'. In April 1979, Xiong Yifu despaired, and hanged himself in the county courthouse. Only then did higher officials begin to take an interest. They found that the entire case was a fabrication from beginning to end.[29]

'How could this tragedy have occurred,' asked the *People's Daily*, 'if even one of his appeals had been handled conscientiously?'

At this point I shall digress.

Most reportage, whether by journalists for newspapers, writers for books or diplomats for governments, has an in-built tendency to overlook the obvious. When I was a correspondent in Uganda, in the first years of Amin's rule, almost every week someone I knew was taken away and killed. Yet while the outside world spoke, not without reason, of a reign of terror, those of us who lived there went about our daily business as we had always done; most foreigners never saw a roadblock, still less a dead body. Both sides of the story were true: the killings, and the relative normalcy for those whom they did not touch.

Most Soviet Jews do not want to emigrate. Most Russians are not dissidents. Nine out of ten Chinese are adequately fed. In the commune in Hubei, three team leaders out of four did not brutalise the peasants; in many communes maltreatment is unknown. This is not to diminish the importance of emigration and dissent in Russia or of poverty and petty despotism in China. But it must be seen in perspective.

Western tourists frequently return from the Soviet Union impressed because it seems so much less bad than they have been led to expect. The package holiday is not just a source of foreign exchange, but a propaganda instrument which is played with skill. The tourist is insulated from the frustrations of Soviet life, kept busy with visits to the Bolshoi, troika rides, museum tours, shown what he ought to see and shielded from what he should not. Much of what he sees is what Russians call *pokazukha*, 'for show', from the eight-page menus provided at Soviet restaurants where in practice only half-a-dozen dishes are ever available, to the elegant clothes and video recorders in the windows of GUM, which can never be found at the counters inside. Moscow itself is such a shop window, unrepresentative of the emporium behind.

The greatest exponent of *pokazukha* was Count Potemkin, who had the façades of non-existent villages built to impress Catherine the Great with the wealth of his lands. Brezhnev did the same when Nixon came to Moscow in 1972: streets were widened, wasteland cleared, buildings repainted, flowerbeds installed. It happened again on an even bigger scale for the Olympic Games in 1980. Old churches, which for decades had been crumbling into decay, were suddenly refurbished to beautify the scenery on the main tourist routes. Communist slogans were removed, and in one place an apartment block built only five years before was demolished because it obstructed a picturesque view.

Even at ordinary times, in China and the Soviet Union, the preparations made for visiting foreigners often transgress the dividing line between self-promotion and deceit. At the end of 1980, Chinese doctors admitted that operations performed in front of foreign surgeons in the 1970s, supposedly under acupuncture anaesthesia, were often fraudulent: some patients were given conventional local anaesthetics beforehand, others were forced to endure in silence atrocious pain to give fake glory to Chinese medicine.

In Lhasa, in 1979, I was among a group of Western journalists taken to visit the Norbulingka, the Dalai Lama's former summer residence, now a park. We were shown groups of clean, rather well-dressed Tibetans, drinking large quantities of *chang*, the local barley beer, singing at the tops of their voices, and playing *karom*, a form of billiards using draughts instead of balls. They were all locals, we were told, enjoying their day off. In fact, we learnt later, the park had been closed to local people that day and junior officials were instructed to go there instead with their families to provide 'healthy' local colour.

No independent foreign observer has ever been allowed to visit a poor commune in China. Even visits to communes of average income are rarely permitted. Every television film about rural life that has appeared abroad has been shot in model villages, mainly on the outskirts of big cities, where the average income for a labourer, £10 a month, is almost twice the norm. In 1980 only one production brigade in forty in China had that level of income. It is to these prosperous, atypical communes that foreign tourists are taken. But even there they are given only a glimpse of what life is really like. The Evergreen commune, outside Peking, is one of the most advanced in China, and has a steady stream of foreign visitors, including heads of state. Yet it was there, in 1978, that Sun Qingji, the young man whose broken remains were shown in a Peking wallposter, was beaten to death. No foreign visitor, escorted from briefing room to school, from kindergarten to 'typical' peasant's home, heard or could have heard any whisper of it.

The model communes, exceptional – and sometimes flawed – though they are, nonetheless represent a genuine achievement. Like the model factories and collective farms to which foreigners are taken in the Soviet Union, they, too, are part of the truth.

Gansu, in the 1980s, may be wretchedly poor. But in Gansu, in the 1930s, eight million people died of starvation. 'What good has Marxism-Leninism done you?' an old peasant from Shanxi was asked by a Chinese youth in 1979. 'Look at yourself – see what state you're in, thirty years after the revolution!' 'Yes,' came the reply, 'but you don't know what I was like before.'[30] Pockets of starvation are to China what aberrant cases of witchcraft are to Europe. In January 1980 the *People's Daily* reported the arrest of a witch who killed a woman by beating her stomach to exorcise a water-monkey spirit that had taken up residence there. Eight months later *The Times* reported the trial of two British Christians who killed a woman by beating her stomach to drive out the devils which they believed were possessing her. One of them said in court that he had seen a devil above her body. An old lady I know in Peking assures me that she once saw a dragon. The 'God of Literature' in Guizhou killed thirteen people; the Reverend Jones, in Guyana, killed 900.

Systems, like people, are both good and bad. None succeeds or fails completely. Average life expectancy in Shanghai is as high as in London; Britain has more than a million illiterates. That does not absolve each individual from making a judgment about the system he lives under and the alternatives to it. But when we condemn the communist dictatorships in China and the Soviet Union for abuses of power and the denial of basic freedoms, we may spare a backward glance at the plank in our own eye. In just one city, New York, in 1980, there were 20,000 child prostitutes, the youngest of them ten years old; Western pornographic magazines show children being sexually abused with animals. In many American prisons, homosexual rape and the torture of inmates is commonplace. In France, a young man can be given a three-year jail term simply for being in an area through which a demonstration passed – as happened to nineteen-year-old Philippe Duval in Paris in 1979. In Britain, under the 'sus' law, until its repeal in 1981, a person could spend three months in prison if the police suspected intent to commit a crime; forty per cent of those jailed were black.

Inside the System

An old Uighur peasant in Khotan, Southern Xinjiang, compared the policies of the Chinese Communist Party to the waters of the Tarim River. When they reached the county, they were as wide and strong as a trunk canal. When they reached the commune, they were more like a branch canal. But by the time they reached each individual peasant, they were just a faint trickle.

When Richard Nixon came to China in 1972, he spoke of Mao as a man whose writings had 'moved a nation and changed the world'. 'I have not changed it,' Mao replied. 'I have only been able to change a few places in the vicinity of Peking.'[1] *Tian Gao, Huang di Yuan* – 'Emperor Far, Heaven High' – say the classics, meaning that the further away a place is from the capital, the more scope there is for local officials to do as they will. But distance is not the only factor. In September 1978 the Chinese government and the Party's Military Commission ordered the army and local authorities to vacate school buildings which had been converted into barracks and factories during the Cultural Revolution. Two years later, only sixteen per cent had been handed back. Some provinces had not returned any at all, and even in Peking, army units, flouting official directives, stayed put in their comfortable college quarters and made clear they had no intention of leaving.[2]

This was not just foot-dragging, though China has its fair share of that, as does the Soviet Union. It was rather a reflection of the way the Chinese political system operates. In the Soviet Union, communism is enforced by command; in China, by manipulating a consensus.

In a leafy, sunlit lane, near a muddy village south of Kiev, where I had stopped with my family for a picnic on the way to Budapest, an old man came up, and we fell into conversation about the history of the place. First, he said, there was the Great War. Then, after the revolution, the civil war. In 1931 came collectivisation: Stalin deported the rich peasants beyond the Urals, to Siberia; for the poor, who remained, the quota of grain deliveries set by the state was increased year by year – and he quoted me the figures from forty years before. Then came the great famine, when his village, and thousands of others like it, starved. The country lay under three feet of snow, he said, with temperatures of

111

−40°C, and men's bodies lay where they had fallen until the spring. And then, again war, and the Germans occupied the village. 'Up there,' he said, pointing to a telegraph pole halfway up a grassy hillside, 'they shot a group of partisans, and over there' – pointing again – 'a young girl.' He started to hobble off to look for his ancient cow, and then paused and asked: 'Do you have Soviet power in England yet?'

Power is the essence of the Soviet system, permeating everyday life as well as politics. My successor in Moscow, Kevin Ruane, recalls being at a party in a Russian friend's flat late one night when a neighbour came banging at the door to complain about the loud Western records being played. Eventually she called the police. 'I stand for Soviet power,' she told the party-goers triumphantly. Russians describe the divide between tsarism and communism not in terms of ideology or social structure, but as 'the establishment of Soviet power' – the replacement of one power system by another. Except in transitional periods, when the central leadership is weak, power in the Soviet Union flows only downwards: it may be used or abused, but only to the extent that it is received from above.

In China power is dispersed throughout the system, and ideological as well as organisational means are used to direct it towards specific political objectives. In the Soviet Union ideological levers are scarcely used at all. Russians are told what to do. To Chinese it is explained what they should do.

When Soviet troops invaded Czechoslovakia in 1968, ordinary soldiers were given no information about the purpose of their mission, and some actually believed they were in West Germany. When Soviet troops were sent to Afghanistan in 1980, they were told they were going on manoeuvres. But when Chinese soldiers attacked Vietnam, the operation was preceded by months of ideological preparation. They knew not only where they were going, but why. The Soviet army is a professional force which puts a premium on rigid discipline and blind obedience. While it exerts political influence in its own narrow field, its job, like that of a Western army, is to carry out the orders of its civilian masters. The Chinese army is a political force, deeply enmeshed in every aspect of the country's political life. 'Political power,' Mao wrote, 'grows out of the barrel of a gun.' Military leaders in China have political power, and political leaders have military positions; from county level up, Party secretaries are concurrently army political commissars. Army units, like civilians, have to be mobilised behind the political line, motivated and convinced.

But ideological pressure and political trade-offs alone would be insufficient to obtain a consensus if they were not backed up by the threat of the police. In the Soviet Union, the KGB is the prime instrument of political control. The Chinese police play a subsidiary role. Yet China, even after the emptying of the prisons that occurred after Mao's death, still has many times more political prisoners than the Soviet Union. Dr Andrei Sakharov told me in 1975 he estimated that between two and ten thousand Soviet citizens were being held for political reasons. Amnesty International five years later, also put the figure at 10,000. The number of Chinese political prisoners in 1980 was probably well over 100,000.*

The seeming paradox underscores the disparity between the two systems. Marxism in China has been superimposed on a pantheistic tradition utterly different from the militant, dogmatic exclusiveness of Christendom. No Soviet leader would wonder aloud whether Marx and Lenin will still be remembered in a thousand years' time – as Mao did, talking to Edgar Snow in 1970. No Soviet leader would talk of the possibility of the Party being overthrown in an anti-communist revolution if it did not reform itself – as Vice-Chairman Chen Yun did in 1979. But in China to speak in those terms is merely to re-state the Mencian principle that when a ruler loses virtue, the people have the right to rebel.

Soviet communism is monolithic, a faith dressed up as a science which admits no questioning. Chinese communism has a philosophical basis which acknowledges the world to be mutable and values relative. In the Soviet Union, all that is required of a citizen politically is not to oppose the monolith; and since it is a monolith, opposition offers little reward.

A Soviet citizen who deviates from the official line risks immediate, crude pressure from the KGB. For an artist or a scholar, it may be the withdrawal of the right to travel abroad, expulsion from his union or dismissal from his job. His telephone may be disconnected, his mail cut off and his family threatened. In 1975, KGB agents warned Dr Sakharov that if he continued to speak out, an accident might befall his fifteen-month-old grandson, Matvei. In a letter to the KGB chief, Yuri Andropov, he wrote: 'Don't shame your department by threatening children, as was the practice in Stalinist times.' A year later, when his

---

*According to China's Procurator-General, Huang Huoqing, 84,000 people were committed for trial on criminal charges in the first half of 1980, half of them for 'grave offences'. Ninety-five per cent of such cases normally result in convictions. At an average sentence of eight years, that represents a prison population of 1.2 million. Several hundred thousand people, not tried by the courts, are also held in 're-education through labour' camps. In 1979 and 1980, counter-revolutionaries were said to account for upwards of seven per cent of the total, compared with twenty per cent in 1977.

wife Yelena was given permission to travel to Italy for eye surgery, he found among his mail an envelope containing Western horror film advertisements: one showed a skull with daggers poked through the eye-sockets; another an eye, with a skull reflected in the pupil; and the third, the tortured remains of a naked woman. When Lev Kopelev published his memoirs in the West, he had a spate of telephone callers claiming to have seen an advertisement for his flat, and anonymous threats that 'your wife will soon be a widow'. Even foreigners are not exempt. Late one night I picked up the telephone to hear a Russian voice say melodramatically, 'Mr Short, we advise you to be careful. Moscow can be like a jungle.' Others had calls from heavy breathers. American diplomats were especially vulnerable as a result of attacks by Jewish militants against the Soviet mission in New York. In 1971 US embassy cars were damaged and diplomats manhandled in the street; five years later there were bomb hoaxes and threatening telephone calls to diplomats and their families in the small hours of the morning. Even at less dramatic times, a diplomat or journalist who parks his car too often near a dissident's flat may find his tyres slashed or a window broken.

If harassment is not enough, a Russian can be banished from Moscow, as happened to Dostoyevsky, Lenin and Stalin in tsarist times, and to Sakharov in the present day; or, like Solzhenitsyn, he may be banished altogether – a punishment which, outside the Soviet bloc, is used only by South Africa. Alternatively, he may be declared mad and put with genuinely mad people in a psychiatric hospital, or charged with a political crime and sent to a labour camp. In the history of the Soviet legal system, no one accused of a political crime has ever been acquitted.

In such unpromising circumstances it is surprising not that there are so few dissenters, but that they are as numerous as they are. The number of political prisoners is correspondingly small.

In China, where policy and power are not monolithic, this year's orthodoxy may be next year's dissent. Political differences are not the exception but the rule. Officials play off one power centre against another, and every citizen has to declare a political position. But the dividing line between political *differences* – 'contradictions among the people', in the Maoist jargon – which must be resolved by political argument, and political *opposition* – 'contradictions between the enemy and ourselves' – which are a matter for the secret police, is fuzzy, and shifts with the political climate. Dossiers are kept on all Chinese, containing details of their class status, political behaviour and work record, with cross-references to their relatives, both within China and overseas. A statement treated as a difference of opinion one month may become opposition the next. China's political prisoners are those who by conviction, miscalculation or chance have found themselves on the wrong side of the divide, or who have been treated as such by local officials seeking scapegoats for political errors or 'negative examples' to dramatise a shift in political line. In a country where politics permeate every aspect of life, their number is correspondingly large.

Every county and town has forced labour brigades, every province, prison farms and factories. Vast labour camp complexes have been built in the 'Great Northern Wilderness' in Heilongjiang, and in Qinghai, on the borders of Tibet. As in the Soviet Union, under Stalin, prison labour plays a significant economic role. One prison in Peking produces enough socks and sandals to keep the population of the capital in footwear. In Hebei, prison-made centrifuges and long-distance buses have won industrial good-quality awards.

Soviet prisoners are paid wages, and, provided they fulfil their tasks, the prison authorities have little interest in what goes on inside their heads. Chinese prisoners are unpaid, and their productivity is treated as an index of political attitude. A man who consistently overfulfils his quota may have his sentence cut; a man who consistently underfulfils it will be judged to have a bad attitude and may have his sentence increased. Even when the sentence is completed, an ex-prisoner often has difficulty finding a job and the police may refuse to re-register him in the area where he used to live, forcing him to stay on at his labour camp as a so-called 'free-worker'.[3]

Each cell in a Chinese prison holds a daily study session, at which the prisoners make self-criticisms and assess each other's 'political progress'. In 1980, prison regulations stated:

> Prisoners must seriously study the works of Marx, Lenin and Chairman Mao, combine theory with practice, persistently criticise the bourgeoisie and all kinds of reactionary ideologies, analyse seriously the roots of their crimes, reform their bourgeois world outlook and strive to reform themselves . . . Prisoners . . . must make a clean breast of their crimes, expose and denounce the crimes of other convicts and report what they know to the authorities.

Conditions are spartan. The inmates sleep, ten or twelve to a cell, lying side by side on a wooden platform which runs down the length of each wall, packed in so close together that there is hardly space to turn over. They bath twice a month. Visits are in theory permitted every two months, but often in practice forbidden. Long-term prisoners may be deprived of all contact with their families – to the extent of forcing their spouses to divorce them – to make them more amenable to 're-moulding'.

Except in the model prisons which foreigners are taken to visit, violence to prisoners is much more widespread than in the Soviet labour camp system. In Changchun, in August 1980, a prisoner who tried to escape from a forced labour brigade was beaten to death by a group of trusties; two weeks later, at a detention centre in the same city, another prisoner was beaten to death 'because he did not promptly confess his crimes'.[4]

The unofficial magazine, *Tansuo (Exploration)*, cited the experiences of Yuan Guoru, a railway worker from Lanzhou, who was detained in 1978 at Gongdelin ('Virtuous Forest') detention centre near the Desheng Gate in Northern Peking:

> During his confinement, he was brutally and callously tortured. They burned him with a poker, punished him with electric current and hung and beat him for as long as five hours. They beat him many times until he was unconscious.[5]

Similar abuses have been reported from commune prisons,[6] and from the labour camp complex in Qinghai. Conditions there were said to have improved after riots which were put down by troops at the end of 1979.

Chinese wallposters have also recounted cases of political offenders being confined in psychiatric hospitals, but the practice does not seem to be systematic as it is in the Soviet Union.

The KGB keeps a high profile, using its visibility as a deterrent. At Red Square, for the May Day parade, the dignitaries on the tribunes are separated from the workers' procession by a line of green-uniformed KGB troops, and between each column of marchers stands a line of plainclothesmen. Sharpshooters are positioned on the rooftops, and to reach the square at all you need a special pass, written out by hand in copperplate cyrillic script, which must be shown at fourteen separate checkpoints, some only a few yards apart. Near Vladivostok in 1975, when Brezhnev and President Ford travelled by train to hold talks at a remote coastal resort, the only living things in the snowbound wilderness through which they passed were KGB guards, posted every hundred yards along the track.

In China, the secret police are not conspicuous. Their role expands or contracts with changes in the political climate, but they remain the last resort, used only when political controls fail.

Yet the secret police in China are hated more than the KGB – for the same reason that China has more political prisoners than Russia. A normally prudent Soviet citizen can feel confident that the political police will never bother him. That was not so in the 1950s, immediately after Stalin's death – and is not so in China in the 1980s. In a country where political struggles have pitted children against parents, husbands against wives, brothers against brothers, people will not discuss politics in front of their neighbours or even their families; no one can ever be certain where the consequences of a political error will end.

The police, in both countries, are the ultimate enforcers of orthodoxy. But it is the task of the press to expound what that orthodoxy is. Soviet newspapers are, in Lenin's phrase, 'a collective organiser, agitator and propagandist'. Their role is not to inform, but to advocate, to crusade and convince. They project an image of monolithic unity, befitting the system they represent. In three years of daily scrutiny of the main Soviet papers, in Moscow from 1974–76, I found only one case where significant differences of view, indicating a high-level debate on a question of political theory, were given clear public expression, and that was over the attitude the Soviet Union should take to Eurocommunism.

Clues to the manoeuvring for power among the Soviet leaders are even rarer. In 1976, a Ukrainian newspaper published a speech by an obscure local functionary which included one passing critical reference to the Agriculture Minister, Dmitri Polyansky. Three weeks later it was announced that Polyansky had been dismissed from the Politburo. In 1979 *Moskovskaya Pravda* hinted at the ambitions of the Moscow Party Secretary, Viktor Grishin, by doctoring a photograph of the May Day parade to make it appear that he was standing closer to Brezhnev than in fact was the case. But these are the exceptions that prove the rule. Even in Khrushchev's time, Kremlinology was an inexact science, more useful to the historian after the event than to the diplomat before it. Its heyday was in the early 1950s, during the power struggle after Stalin's death. By the time Khrushchev had consolidated his position, the press was already becoming duller; no observer was able to predict the rise to power of Brezhnev and Kosygin in 1964. Since then the traditional tools of Kremlinology, name lists, rank orders, variations in the treatment of policy themes in different provincial newspapers, have lost much of their value. The leadership has become still more secretive, the Central Committee more oligarchical, its in-fighting hidden from view by a mantle as impenetrable as the windowless walls of the assembly building, a few blocks from the Kremlin, where it meets to decide on policy.

The Chinese press, like the Chinese system, is not monolithic. Where *Pravda* sets out 'the Party line', the *People's Daily* reflects the contradictory views of individual leaders or groups of leaders. Other Chinese newspapers do the same. Officials lower down watch to see which leaders appear strongest and which are unable to prevent criticism of their policies appearing. The press is not merely a barometer of struggle but a weapon used by rival groups to erode each other's support until one is able to build up enough strength to overwhelm the rest.

This is not journalism for the masses. It is aimed at the Party elite. Liu Shaoqui's articles, in the 1940s, were studded with classical aphorisms and quotations from Confucius and Mencius. So was much of what Mao wrote. In 1979, Marshal Ye Jianying used a couplet from the Song dynasty poet, Lo Yu, as a commentary on the state of the Party. Like the Latin tags which used to grace the editorials of *The Times*, old intellectuals grasp the references, but most ordinary readers do not.

The use of the press in this way makes the control of it a key objective for contending leadership groups, and the posts of Director of the Propaganda Department and of the General Political Department of the People's Liberation Army (PLA) are subject to intense bargaining as each side tries to get its candidate preferred. No comparable mechanism exists in the Soviet Union because there power is centralised and policy is not the subject of public debate. It is the dispersal of power in China that enables the press to play the role it does. The same is true of another key facet of the Chinese system, the prevalence of factionalism.

Factions in China are the dominant force in political life. An area or unit which falls wholly under factional control becomes an 'independent kingdom', where the writ of the higher leadership does not run except with the faction's consent. In 1954, in the first great political feud after the communists came to power, Mao purged Gao Gang, the Party chief of Manchuria, for allegedly turning that region into an 'independent kingdom'. Two decades later, first Mao and then his successors ordered reshuffles of military region commanders to prevent them establishing 'independent kingdoms' in the warlord tradition. Factories and government ministries may also become factional strongholds.

If no faction is able to win control, a unit remains permanently split into rival alliances which engage in ceaseless jockeying for power.

In 1972, a seventeen-year-old girl named Jiang Aizhen was given a job as a nurse in a military hospital in Xinjiang. Her elder brother asked the hospital's deputy Party secretary, a middle-aged doctor named Zhang, to keep a fatherly eye on her. Six years later, the hospital vice-president and two other doctors, who bore a grudge against Zhang, decided to make use of this relationship to undermine his position. Several of their factional supporters lay in wait outside the girl's room one night, and next morning spread the story that she and the doctor had slept together, potentially a very serious charge. Both denied it, but the strain of the accusation was such that Jiang became mentally unbalanced; the diagnosis was incipient schizophrenia.

After two weeks, the regimental Party Committee sent a work team to the hospital. Its leader, Deputy Chief of Staff Yang, had factional ties with Zhang's opponents. Wallposters and scurrilous cartoons were posted all over the hospital, vilifying Zhang and the girl, and those who tried to defend them were forced to make public self-criticisms. Jiang herself, when she recovered, was kept under permanent surveillance:

> [Her] private letters were opened. She was under constant pressure from the work team. Nobody in the hospital dared to talk to her, or to speak out on her behalf . . . At a meeting of the hospital on August 5th, the work team read out its report, which concluded that illicit relations probably had taken place . . .

The report was discussed again at a meeting of the hospital Party branch on September 26th, at which the doctors who had instigated the case demanded that she take a virginity test, and Deputy Chief of Staff Yang warned her that the incident was not closed. Three days later, she took a rifle and shot dead three of her tormentors before being overpowered and disarmed.

The three who died were eulogised as 'martyrs' by the regimental Party Committee, and Jiang was condemned to death. On review, the Xinjiang Supreme Court recommended that the sentence be commuted to life imprisonment, and called for the punishment of those who had persecuted her. But the faction looks after its own. Deputy Chief of Staff Yang was transferred to another province before any action could be taken against him, and others, who had played lesser roles, far from being punished were rewarded with promotion.[7]

Factionalism exists in most Chinese organisations. Its main concern is not with policy, but with the protection of personal power by establishing ties of mutual dependence. 'What the rules of propriety value is . . . reciprocity,' said the Book of Rites, 2,000 years ago. 'If I give a gift and nothing comes in return, that is contrary to propriety; if the thing comes to me and I give nothing in return, that also is contrary to propriety.' In such a system, loyalties and debts are personalised, and override abstract moral principles. A son may tell lies to protect a father. An examiner who passes a student must be repaid. An official who promotes a subordinate must be supported.

Nepotism and favouritism flourish in all communist states. Brezhnev's son and son-in-law are vice-ministers; Kosygin's son-in-law has similar rank; Khrushchev's son-in-law was the Editor of *Izvestia*. President Ceausescu's wife, Elena, is second in the Rumanian hierarchy, and eleven other relatives also hold positions of power. President Zhivkov's daughter, Lyudmila, was Minister of Culture and the second most powerful person in Bulgaria. President Kim Il Sung of North Korea is grooming his son, King Chong Il, for the communist world's first hereditary succession. Mao's wife, Jiang Qing, was a Politburo member, his nephew a senior army commissar, and his niece a vice-minister.

But in China, nepotism is merely one facet of factional behaviour that is endemic and solidly based in Confucian tradition. In the 1960s factions fought pitched battles in the streets with rifles and handgrenades. In the 1970s factory workers belonging to one faction refused to take orders from foremen belonging to another. At the end of that decade, as stability was restored, factions became 'submerged reefs and hidden shoals', obstructing policies which threatened their interests. But their underlying purpose, as 'joint stock companies organised to scramble for profit and power', in the phrase of one Chinese newspaper, did not alter.[8] Even in the relative calm of 1979, villagers in Hainan were caught buying stolen rifles and sub-machine-guns 'for the purpose of factional fighting', and the *People's Daily* complained that 'stubborn factionalists'

> praise cadres who favour their factional interests and oppose . . . [those] who act according to Party principles . . . They dismiss all accusations against people in their own factions and give them every consideration. They deliberately delay solving the problems of those not in their factions and make things difficult for them. They . . . proceed from factionalism in making appointments, inducting new Party members, holding elections, recruiting workers, deciding on awards, giving promotions, readjusting wages, allocating housing and alloting allowances . . . They follow their factions rather than the Party.[9]

In such circumstances, 'hanging around leading comrades and acting as trumpeters and sedan chair carriers', as the *People's Daily* put it, is an industry in itself.[10] In 1979 these practices were satirised by the unofficial magazine, *Peking Spring*, in a sketch entitled, 'The Awkward Predicament of a Flatterer'.[11]

According to the need of the Revolution, I was assigned to serve under Section Chief Tang as a worker. In other words, I put my fate in his hands. My political life, grade, raises in salary, promotion, dwelling and furniture, everything, even love and marriage, are all in his keeping. He can make arbitrary decisions, issue orders, eat and drink the blood and sweat of the workers and plot against them – and all those around him keep saying, 'Section Chief Tang, good, good!' Do I dare to say, 'Not good, not good'?

I hope my comrades will understand my predicament. The path of life is like navigating the ocean. In a force-10 typhoon, even ships of 10,000 tons have to take shelter, let alone an insignificant little boat like me. In China to get a transfer in one's work is harder than flying an airship. Above, I have parents of advanced years. Below, I have yet to find a wife and have children. Whether he is right or wrong, I have to follow suit and flatter. Only thus will I get promoted.

I dream of becoming an official, because in China it is not money that is everything, but power. I want to become an official. I want to become an official regardless of the means.

Some comrades may ask: 'If you do so, will the masses not oppose you?' What can the masses do to me? As long as I flatter my superiors successfully, their words can do nothing. They have not the power to dismiss me. At worst I shall be transferred to be an official somewhere else. Furthermore, when I become an official, others will have to flatter me. The smiling face I show my superiors I will wipe into a glare for my subordinates.

Probably my comrades feel concerned for me: 'Maybe you will come to a bad end?' No! As proved by practice, such concern is unnecessary. To tell the truth will earn a beating. I do not want to take a beating and I also want to eat good food. Therefore I must learn how to flatter.

Some comrades may ask: 'After flattering Section Chief Tang for such a long time, what will you do if he is dismissed?' It doesn't matter. One can then flatter Section Chief Hou and Section Chief Gao.

The comrades may ask: 'When will you stop flattering?' As for that, probably one has to do it all one's life. Let me propose the slogan, 'Long live flattery!' Most likely the comrades will oppose it. If I shout it out everyone will join in to give me a beating. But it is no more than the truth. It is false to say 'Long live you!' or 'Long live me!' – but flattery will live for ever. Long live flattery!

In China, factionalism reinforces bureaucracy, officially described as the biggest single obstacle to the country's plans to modernise. In the Soviet Union, bureaucracy feeds on the networks of personal relationships and special interest groups – the military, the planners, the heavy industrial ministries – which regulate Soviet internal political dynamics. In both systems, bureaucracy is dominant, and in both systems for the same reason: they are, in effect, the world's largest state companies, huge, unwieldy, over-centralised, hidebound by regulations and reluctant to delegate authority.

'Our government organs are improperly managing almost every aspect of society's life,' Chairman Hua acknowledged candidly in 1980.

121

'By [using] administrative methods, [they are] . . . burdening themselves with a complex, back-breaking and unparalleled task.'[12]

The result, in both the Soviet Union and China, is an avalanche of paper and meetings. 'Meetings have become a disaster,' wailed the *People's Daily*. The Shanghai newspaper, *Jiefang Ribao*, said Party branch secretaries were so inundated with conflicting instructions from higher authorities that even if they were superhuman, they could not handle them all. 'The biggest headache is that some leading organs and cadres issue orders compulsively,' it added. 'They often issue orders in the morning only to change them in the evening.'[13] In China the problem is compounded by too many Chiefs and too few Indians. Some provincial offices have a director, several deputy directors and one worker, whose task is to make tea. To justify their existence, each feels called upon to generate a quota of instructions and memoranda, regardless of relevance or need.

One small rural county in Sichuan in 1978 issued more than a million pages of documents; China has more than 2,000 counties. A factory manager in Shenyang, who wanted to build a new dormitory for his workers, had to negotiate with eleven separate departments. An Overseas Chinese refrigeration expert, who came to offer his knowledge to help the country develop, was shuffled from one department to another for ten years without being given a job, until eventually, in despair he applied for an exit visa and left.

Departmental rivalries outdo the worst restrictive practices in the West. An oil pipeline to a port in Southern China, completed in 1978, was prevented from opening for two years because the oil company and the port administration were wrangling over ownership of a pump. In 1979, it was discovered that deposits of pyrite ore were being mined by the Metallurgy Ministry, which extracted the metal and left the sulphur as waste, and by the Chemical Industry Ministry, which extracted the sulphur and left the metal as waste. However the ore was at least being used. Not so in the case of stainless steel pipes for the oil industry. The metallurgical industry said their manufacture was the task of the machine building industry; the machine builders said it was the metallurgists' job. Neither would back down, and in the end they had to be imported.

A particularly graphic illustration of bureaucratic rivalry was provided in 1979 by the Soviet railway system. In that year it was decided that responsibility for the line from Odessa, in the Ukraine, to Kishinyov, in Moldavia, should be divided between two different railway administrations. Afterwards the Moldavians discovered that none of their trains which set out for Odessa ever returned. The Odessans, it transpired, no longer having any interest in the Moldavian half of the line, had commandeered them to work on their own network and help overfulfil their plan. The fact that the Moldavian fruit harvest was rotting for lack of transport was of so little consequence in Odessa that when the Moldavians placed an emergency order for three new locomotives, the Odessans seized them en route and hid them away working on branchlines. Only after Moscow intervened, and threatened that heads would roll, were the engines reluctantly freed.

Pravda, in 1980, commenting on the state of Soviet railways: 'Now they've bloomed, next year we shall have the fruits.'

Bureaucracy in the West is tempered by humanism. Bureaucracy in the Soviet Union is limited by the fear of wrath from above. But the bureaucrat in China, supreme in his own small world, is amenable neither to reason nor morality. He is arrogant, pompous, petty-minded and ferocious in defence of his self-interest; if he digs his heels in, all the power of the Party and state is hard put to make him withdraw.

Combined with factionalism and incompetence, Chinese bureaucracy causes appalling waste. In 1973, the Kellogg Company of Houston, Texas, contracted to build eight fertiliser plants in China, making ammonia from natural gas. When construction was already well advanced, it was found that two of the plants had been sited in areas without natural gas supplies. In Qinghai, a province without iron ore or coal, £20 million was spent building a steelworks, which lost £1 million a year using raw materials brought in from outside to make unusable pig iron. Thirty million pounds was thrown away on a similar steelworks in Xinjiang. In 1980 a huge political row developed after it was admitted that an £800 million steelworks being built by Nippon Steel of Japan, under the biggest foreign contract ever awarded, as part of a £10,000 million iron and steel complex at Baoshan, near Shanghai, had been sited on marshland because no proper preparatory study had been made.

Some factories are never completed at all, or if they are, never start production. A tractor factory in Canton was closed in 1978 after it was found that in twelve years it had not produced one tractor that worked properly. Yet even that pales before the achievement of a tractor repair works near Leningrad. After being formally handed over by the builders, it began its first year's production plan in 1979. Its returns showed from the start that its repair work was not very satisfactory, but it was not until the beginning of 1980 that the reason was discovered: the factory did not exist. Where it should have stood were only foundation trenches and the shells of a few half-finished buildings. The project had become so far behind schedule that the construction trust had decided the only way to get rid of it was to certify that it was finished; thereafter the paperwork had taken on a life of its own.

No one who has not lived in a communist country knows what inefficiency really is. In Peking, it means telephoning the state airline to ask the price of a ticket to Paris, and being told they will let you know next week. In Moscow, it means sitting in a crowded restaurant and waiting an hour to order lunch while a steady succession of dishes is carried through to a side room, only to discover behind its door the reason for the delay: it is lunchtime, so all the waiters are having *their* lunch.

There are many reasons for this difference of attitude – the lack of incentives under socialism, the state monopoly, the absence of competition, the knowledge among workers and managers that, however little work they do, they can only be dismissed for political or criminal offences – but perhaps the most important is the absence of any sense of ownership, and of the personal responsibility that goes with it.

In theory, what belongs to the state belongs to the whole people, and everybody should look after it. In practice it belongs to nobody, and no one looks after it. 'See this car?' said a Soviet taxi-driver when I reproached him for furious driving. 'It's not mine, it belongs to the state. So I drive it as hard as I like. If it was mine I'd take care of it. But it isn't. So why should I?' The Soviet press qualifies that attitude as 'the psychology of a philistine'. In China, officials complain of factory managers who leave raw materials to spoil and machinery to rust. 'They'd never do that if it were theirs,' one young functionary grumbled, 'but under our system, they just don't care.'

In capitalist countries, indifference to publicly-owned funds is reflected in income-tax evasion; in communist countries, in endemic pilfering and theft. The Soviet Union has a special police force, the *OBKhSS* – 'Organ for the Security and Protection of Socialist Property' – whose sole task is to prevent fraud, embezzlement and petty thieving. Yet economic crime is so widespread that it is estimated to account for ten per cent of Soviet national income. In China, in 1980, when a steelworks in Henan closed, local people looted it so thoroughly that even the doors and window frames were taken; it was state property, therefore no one would miss it. 'State property is a "supermarket",' wrote the magazine, *China Youth*. 'You can help yourself to whatever you like there. All you need is a job which lets you enter and leave.'[14]

The absence of responsibility produces an all-pervading shoddiness. In many small Soviet towns, and even in parts of Moscow, it is impossible to tell whether a building is going up or coming down, such is the general air of dilapidation. At the Institute of Computer Studies in Peking, 2,000 scientists and staff members work in a seven-storey office block, where the one lift broke down years ago and has never been repaired; broken windows are boarded up to stop the wind coming through; the main doors hang off their hinges; the walls are scuffed and shabby, and the floors are thick with grime. It is one of China's most renowned research bodies, and given a few coats of paint and reasonable care and maintenance, the building could be perfectly decent; instead, it is a squalid hole.

At a new housing scheme in Nanjing in 1980, it was found that only fifteen per cent of the doors and thirty per cent of the windows were up to specification. In a typical apartment

the entrance door is out of true, so that it can neither be closed nor bolted. None of the six inside doors close properly; either the doorframe is not properly set, or the door itself is cracked. The floor is uneven . . . Some of the rooms are uninhabitable; on many of the walls there are yellow or grey spots. Most of the door handles and light switches are not properly fixed; they are neither secure nor safe.[15]

Nor is the problem limited to housing. 'Some Chinese-made TV sets have to be fanned while in use,' reported the *People's Daily*. 'Some have to take a rest from time to time. Some need to be knocked constantly, and some give neither sound nor picture but burn and smoke.'[16]

Many of the ills of communist systems are due to the way they are structured: all the lines of command are vertical, from higher authorities to lower ones; horizontal lines, between different units at the same level, are missing. When a television tube factory in Peking discovers quality problems in the glass tube casings it is using, it must make contact with the Peking Broadcasting and Television Company, which contacts the Municipal Electronic Instruments Bureau, which contacts the Municipal Light Industry Bureau, which contacts the Peking General Glass Factory, which contacts the glass casing works and asks it to improve product quality. The system simply does not permit the tube factory to phone up the casing works and the problem to be sorted out on the spot. 'The result,' according to the Peking journal *Jingji Guanli* (*Economic Management*), 'is that whenever a quality problem crops up, the factory stops production for several months.'

The only way round such problems is to go outside the system. Were it not for the *tolkachi*, the 'fixers' employed by Soviet factories to side-step the planning regulations and illegally obtain needed materials direct from the suppliers, Soviet industry would come to a complete halt. Were it not for *blat* and the black market, Soviet consumers would have to make do without most of their creature comforts. Were it not for the *hou men*, the 'back door', privilege and factional power in China would confer no material benefit.

Corruption in communist states is not a passing aberration, but is intrinsic to the way the system is ordered. When politics outweigh merit and patronage is more important than ability, when power is un-trammelled by democracy and the exchange of favours is more useful than money, corruption becomes part of the currency of daily life, a lubricant that must be constantly applied just to get anything done.

If in Moscow you need building materials to put up a garage or repair your dacha, there is no way that, as a private citizen, you can obtain them legally. So you go to the outer ring road and hitch a lift in a concrete-mixing truck. For a few roubles the driver will deliver as much as you like; the state will never miss it. In China, in 1980, so much material was misappropriated by individuals and organisations from one fifteen-mile-long highway project that three months after its completion the road surface began to break up. An investigation disclosed that 1,200 tons of cement, 500 tons of asphalt and 137 tons of steel had gone astray. Part of it was found metamorphosed into three new apartment blocks, inhabited by local officials and their families.[17]

In both China and the Soviet Union, skimping on materials and embezzling what has been saved are among the commonest forms of corruption. Of 1,500 enterprises in Soviet Azerbaijan investigated in 1975, one-third were found to be cheating their customers by adulterating their products. Chinese peasants put sand in the grain they sell and water in the milk. Soviet train crews on the trans-Siberian sell off restaurant car supplies. One of the reasons why the food in Soviet hotels is so abysmal is that the best ingredients, the choicest cuts of meat, even fruit and vegetables, are kept back by the kitchen staff to sell or exchange. In the Caucasus whole factories have been set up using misappropriated machinery and embezzled raw materials; one such scheme, making textiles in Armenia, earned its organisers £250,000 in four years until it was exposed in 1975. Other variants on the misappropriation theme include factory managers entering wages for non-existent workers and pocketing the money themselves (known in Soviet newspapers as the 'Dead Souls' racket, after Gogol's novel of that name), and schoolteachers claiming subsidies for classes which have no students.

If embezzled goods are to be sold, they must pass through the black market. This ranges from groups of youths hanging about at street corners, to a ramified network of under-the-counter sales outlets in Soviet department stores. At the bottom of the scale, the *Peking Daily* in 1980 agonised over 'gangs [of young people who] whisper to each other, chatter away, gesticulate and behave in a generally shady manner. What are they up to? Many are engaged in the illegal practice of buying things and selling them at a profit . . . It really is a dreadful scene with all kinds of weirdness.'[18] At the top of the market a deal organised by the head of the republican textile trade bureau in Soviet Tadjikistan used state shops all over the Soviet Union to sell millions of pounds' worth of black market silk. It ended in 1976 when, after a six-month trial, twenty-eight republican officials were sentenced to long prison terms.

The black market is only the small, visible tip of the iceberg of corruption. Money itself does not provide a desirable lifestyle in communist states, but having the connections to obtain what money cannot buy. *Blat* and 'going through the *hou men*' are what keep the wheels of Chinese and Soviet society turning.

How *blat* works was explained satirically in a Soviet newspaper series which detailed the machinations of a Georgian, the archetype of all Soviet wheeler-dealers:

Supposing you want tickets to the ice-hockey final. What would you do? Go and buy a red fox fur hat for the cashier at the ticket office? No, that's not the best way. Ask Volodya? I prefer to keep him in reserve for the time I need airline tickets.

No, first go round to my cousin who works in the bakery where you can get fresh Georgian bread. Come round after hours and he'll give you all you need for just a few roubles extra for 'service'. Take the bread across the road to the council offices. There's a man there who adores our bread, and he has a wife who works in the stores taking orders for spare parts for cars. She'll get you an accelerator pedal. I know that the husband of the woman who runs the hairdressers' has been searching for one everywhere. You can get a voucher for a magnificent hair-do in return. Take that along to the shop, exchange it for the red fox and then off you go to the ticket office at the rink to get some choice seats.[19]

It does not have to be so complicated. *Blat* covers anything from a straightforward, but unspoken, bribe – a bottle of vodka for the mechanic who is going to repair your car, or some lipstick for his wife – to participation in a labyrinthine network of contacts, favours and services rendered, which can provide Western designer jeans, copies of *Playboy* ('enough to make a telegraph pole blush', blurted out one official), a place at the head of the queue for new cars, or even an acquittal for drunken driving. Almost nothing in the Soviet Union is immune from *blat*. 'If you have it,' wrote Michael Binyon in *The Times*, 'you can get along nicely. If you do not, you are for ever walking away disappointed as that last pair of imported shoes is sold, there are no tickets left for the theatre, the aircraft is fully booked and the surly old man at the restaurant door insists there are no free tables.'[20]

The linchpins on which the system depends are the personnel who control the distribution of scarce goods – shop assistants who put things aside for their favoured customers, storekeepers and cashiers at ticket offices. *Sovietskaya Rossiya* in 1980 described how a woman worker who was promoted to become director of a wholesale foodstuffs distribution department was so disorientated by the flood of bribes and gifts from the managers of the shops she supplied that her health collapsed and her marriage broke up. She worked late into the night, preparing deliveries for 'her' shops, the newspaper said, but those who brought no gifts went away empty-handed. In one campaign against such practices, in Soviet Azerbaijan in the early 1970s, 12,000 people – one in four of the republic's employees in state trading organisations – were sacked in the space of two years for bribe-taking and embezzlement.

China, too, is plagued by officials for whom 'everything will be all right so long as they are given gifts, but anyone who fails to do so will encounter difficulties in whatever he does', as the newspaper, *Jilin Ribao*, put it. Factories making consumer goods routinely send specimens of their latest products to local leaders for so-called 'trial use'. Department stores reserve television sets and other rationed items for Party officials and their friends. A factory in Changchun exchanges supply vouchers for bicycles against flour and vegetables for its staff;[21] a film studio canteen in Peking gets better meat in return for free cinema tickets.

Even at the level of the village, tractor drivers refuse to plough fields without presents of cigarettes and rice wine; lorry drivers refuse to make deliveries; building foremen say: 'Give us wine and meat and we'll do the job fast. Without wine and meat, we work slowly.'[22]

In Mao's day, foreigners living in China saw none of this, and returned home brimming with enthusiasm for the incorruptible Chinese whose honesty was displayed in 'lost and found' cabinets in hotel foyers, full of rusty razor-blades, broken shoelaces and other detritus which 'foreign friends' had managed to leave behind. Since then, as the political climate has eased, the taboo on accepting gifts from foreigners has diminished. But it still carries a political risk which many Chinese prefer to avoid. For the foreigner, this brings mixed results. When I needed a plumber in Moscow, it cost me a bottle of vodka but at least the plumbing was done. In Peking such blandishments were rejected, and for four years every cistern in my apartment ran, the taps dripped, the radiators leaked and the drains were regularly blocked.

Among Chinese themselves, however, it is quite a different story. The *People's Daily* complained at the end of 1980 that

> in many spheres of economic work, entertainment and gifts have become indispensable to get anything done. Such unhealthy tendencies are very serious. For example, without entertaining and sending gifts, it is impossible for any organisation to ask a construction company to put up a building. After a building has been completed, the power and water companies will not connect their services until a few apartments have been allocated to them. Even police sub-stations may refuse to accept residence applications until they have had their demands met.[23]

In China, corruption and political factionalism usually go hand in hand, especially among higher officials. How this works was described in a sensational documentary story, entitled 'Between Man and Devil', by the writer Liu Binyan, recounting the rise and fall of a woman named Wang Shouxin, executed in 1980 for embezzling 500,000 yuan

(£150,000) from a county coal company, of which she was Party secretary and general manager:[24]

The courtyard of the Party Committee of Bin county in Heilongjiang province used to be a centre of attraction for the people of the whole county. But as time wore on the wall around the courtyard seemed to grow higher and thicker until it took on a secretive, awe-inspiring look. In the famine years in the early 1960s, people smelt the sweet smell of meat, oil and steamed bread, coming from the Party cadres' messroom whenever they walked by. They felt bad, and some of them would smile bitterly. 'They're doing all right for themselves, this bunch of officials,' they said.

When the people had to live on ersatz food made from the crushed leaves and cobs of maize, the children of the county Party secretary threw steamed bread stuffed with meat to the dogs for fun. In regions that were poor and backward, political power was most enticing.

When Wang Shouxin took office as manager and concurrently Party branch secretary of the coal company, the first thing she did by way of reform was to sell coal according to the customer's importance. Coal of the best quality was selected and packed in straw flood-control bags to be delivered to the houses of the county Party secretary and all the members of the Standing Committee. What about payment? No hurry!

As for the People's Military Department, that went without saying: the army men were at the top of the list. Then came the Party's Organisation Department. No one who was useful to her needed to open his mouth. She would approach them of her own accord. 'Hard up for money?' she would ask. Even if they repaid the 'loan' they would still feel under obligation to her, so the best way of making recompense was to provide reciprocal favours by abusing their own power. In the course of these interchanges of power, Party and government officials degenerated into worms, eating into the fruits of the people's labour.

Language is a strange thing. When Political Commissar Yang referred to Wang Shouxin's family as a 'red' family, he meant it as a commendation. But when the people mouthed the phrase, they meant it as a curse. Everybody in her family had either joined the Party or won promotion or both, and in the people's eyes they had all done so by crooked means.

At times, when Wang Shouxin thought of the 40,000 crisp new 10 yuan [£3] banknotes in her black treasury [embezzled by fraudulently passing off one type of coal as another], she could not help feeling a little scared. But then an image always came to mind to comfort her. 'Aren't the leading provincial cadres also grabbing their share?' In 1978, when she travelled to Guangzhou, as many as three department heads from the provincial government drove her to the airport and saw her off.

One winter, Inspector Yang Qing from the county Party Committee's Discipline Inspecting Committee came to warn her that a member of the Standing Committee had received an anonymous letter accusing her of corruption and illegal activities. 'It's in my hands now,' he said. It was a hint, a promise. He could turn to good account his power to shield a criminal. As a seller he was offering that power for sale in the market. He had found his buyer. When she would pay did not matter. Yang Qing kept the promise. The letter vanished into thin air.

Nine out of the eleven Standing Committee members accepted gifts from Wang Shouxin, as did more than 200 other officials [at county, prefectural and provincial levels, and even in the central government in Peking]. 'If not oiled, the machine won't run', was a universal truth. Lorry loads of foodstuffs, sent with the compliments of the coal company, cars laden with crates of Binzhou wine from the brewery, and boxes of apples from the fruit company, all sped along the Bin county-Harbin highway, heading for government departments. Even within Bin county itself, different economic departments found it necessary to pay 'tribute' to each other. Almost every one had its own guesthouse and its own special supplies. Extravagant wining and dining was commonplace. Wang Shouxin was the coal queen of Bin county, but she was not alone. There was an electricity king, who was nick-named 'the Millionaire'. His annual outlay for parties, bribes and feasting amounted to 20,000 yuan [£6,000]. Like Wang Shouxin's coal company, the electricity department also paid regular 'tribute' to higher-ups. Feasting alone was not enough to satisfy their greed; they grabbed. Not only they grabbed, but their dependants also grabbed.

A net with small meshes was woven from the strings of inter-connecting, overlapping human relationships. Whether a thing had to do with Marxist-Leninist principles or general or specific policies, once it became entangled in that net it was trapped. When an enterprise fell into that net, its system was perverted. When a court case fell into that net, the law was abused. Right and wrong were confounded; rewards and punishments were reversed; truth yielded to falsehood; kindness bowed before wickedness.

Wang Shouxin's case was eventually broken. But the social conditions favouring the growth and emergence of Wang Shouxin – how much have they changed? Is it not true that countless Wang Shouxins, big and small, are still nibbling the foundation of socialism and corroding the organism of the Party without being penalised?

Liu Binyan did not pull his punches, and even in the more tolerant political climate after Mao's death, the story caused a furore. Yet no one suggested the case was untypical. A year earlier, a PLA general, Liu Decai, who was a deputy commander of the strategic Shenyang Military Region, bordering the Soviet Union, and also Mayor of Luda, was stripped of all his posts for diverting £17.5 million from the city's budget to build luxurious private mansions for himself and his friends, and clubs for officers and cadres. He was said to have connived at the activities of five 'corruption syndicates' operating in the city's factories, and to have extorted 'contributions' for his pet schemes from the populace, under threat from the police of having their ration tickets withdrawn if they did not pay up. The *People's Daily* acknowledged that similar cases existed elsewhere, and after Liu Binyan's story was published, *Guangming Ribao* commented: 'Wang Shouxin misappropriated 500,000 yuan in cash. This was a big sum. But it is insignificant compared to the amounts of money which some big-shots have taken.'[25]

Fraud at this level, in both China and the Soviet Union, is inseparable from politics. Wang Shouxin rose to power on the wave of leftist policies that broke over China in the Cultural Revolution. She fell, not because some intrepid policeman had sniffed out her crime – the police are the last people to become involved in such cases – but because the political tide had changed. In Moscow in 1974, when the Minister of Culture, Yekaterina Furtseva, was reprimanded by the Party for corruptly obtaining building materials for a £110,000 dacha, it did not signify the beginning of a clean-up campaign; it was merely an outward sign that her political career was at an end. A month later she lost her seat in parliament and had she not died soon afterwards of a heart attack she would no doubt have lost her ministry as well. Similarly, in Peking in 1979, when Vice-Chairman Wang Dongxing, then a member of the Politburo Standing Committee, was accused of misappropriating £2 million to build himself a palatial residence with its own cinema and gymnasium at Zhongnanhai, in the centre of the city, details of his alleged offence – which may or may not have been true – were deliberately leaked by supporters of Deng Xiaoping to hasten his political demise. Yet even though the sum involved was ten times greater than that for which Wang Shouxin was executed, there was never any suggestion that he should bear criminal responsibility. Analogous considerations shielded the Georgian leader, Vasily Mzhavanadze, who reputedly embezzled some £20 million in his long Party career. After his forced retirement from alternate membership of the Politburo for political reasons in 1973, a huge clean-up began in Georgia in which several hundred senior officials were purged for corruption. But, according to Roy Medvedev, the Georgian Attorney-General's request for authority to investigate the affairs of Mzhavanadze himself was never granted. To use allegations of corruption as a political weapon is one thing; to treat a former Politburo member as a common criminal is quite another. Pyotr Shelest, who was sacked from the Politburo a year earlier after a policy dispute with Brezhnev, was likewise protected from prosecution when his corrupt dealings were exposed.

The biggest scandal of all in the Soviet Union since the Second World War surfaced in 1980. For the previous ten years, Fisheries Ministry officials had been smuggling caviare to Western Europe in tins marked as herring. The proceeds were banked in Switzerland. Whenever the officials travelled abroad they were able to live in luxury and return home laden with expensive Western consumer goods for their families and friends. Altogether, tens of millions of pounds were said to be involved. Occasionally, mislabelled tins found their way into Soviet shops, and in 1975 I heard stories from Russian friends about lucky people who brought home what they thought was tinned herring only to find five kilograms of top-grade caviare glistening inside. Yet it was not until four years later that an investigation was launched, more than 200 senior officials arrested and the minister and several of his deputies forced to resign. The cause of the arrests and resignations was never officially acknowledged.

If I, as a Western journalist, got wind of these activities, it is inconceivable that they were unknown to the KGB. That the investigation was so long delayed indicates that, in this case too, there was protection from the highest level – almost certainly from Prime Minister Kosygin himself. It cannot have been chance that the deposed minister was one of Kosygin's trusted supporters, and that the scandal broke when the Prime Minister was seriously ill and Brezhnev was preparing to bring the government apparatus under his personal control as soon as Kosygin died, which happened within the year.

All through the system, people who possess power, even to the most miniscule degree, abuse it for their own benefit. Position confers privilege, and rank affords protection. In Cheboksary, 400 miles east of Moscow, in 1975, thirteen officials and workers of an agricultural machinery trust stood trial for operating a house of debauchery – complete with sauna, compliant young 'hostesses' and a private beach – entered in the books as a workers' convalescent home. The eleven junior defendants were given sentences of up to fifteen years' imprisonment: the trust's director and his deputy got off with fines.

But, more commonly, abuses of power occur in the margin of the law. A Chinese Party official does not need to give bribes to get his children admitted to university or placed in city jobs instead of being sent to the countryside: these things are done for him automatically by others who want to gain his favour. An army medical school in North-East China in 1980 was found to have places reserved 'exclusively for the sons and daughters of leading cadres'.[26] Chinese students awarded grants to study abroad included not only Deng Xiaoping's physicist son but no less than five close relatives of the Politburo member in charge of education, Fang Yi. 'Some leading cadres have become big mandarins,' the *People's Daily* complained. 'They have power in their hands, and when relatives make all sorts of unreasonable demands on them they . . . help them by improper means to get into colleges, study abroad, enter the Party, get promotion, find jobs and undertake foreign travel.'[27] In 1979, when a 600-member friendship delegation went by ship to Japan, so many places were taken up by the families of high officials that eleven maids were needed to look after the children; one Japanese newspaper named it scornfully 'the pleasure boat'.

Many of those sent abroad are unqualified. The pro-communist Hong Kong magazine, *Qishi Niandai*, reported that an engineering delegation which visited the United States included not one engineer; all the places had been grabbed by Party officials. In another case, Culture Ministry officials spent so long wrangling over which of them should be included in a film group going to America that 'the US side thought China had declined and withdrew the invitation. On hearing this, the officials who were so anxious to go abroad could only gaze at one another in speechless despair.'[28]

Among the common people – *lao bai xing*, 'old hundred names', as they are called – the folk saying, 'When a man becomes an official, even his dogs and chickens go to heaven', has re-surfaced in a new form: 'Better to be an official's son than to be brilliant at maths.' Shanghai university students, in a 1979 opinion poll, rated the feudal, privileged mentality of Chinese officials as the country's biggest social problem, more serious than unemployment and crime.

Yet privilege, like bureaucracy, in both the Soviet Union and China, is intrinsic to the system: it cannot be rooted out until the system itself changes.

Where formerly the nine ranks of the mandarinate set out the perquisites and prerogatives of imperial officials, nowadays the twenty-five grades into which communist Chinese officialdom is divided regulate no less comprehensively the lives of their successors. The First Secretary and the Governor of a province each have an official limousine reserved for their personal use, a fulltime personal chauffeur, a personal cook and valet. Secretaries of provincial Party committees can call up a car and driver from the pool, and have a personal cook *or* valet. Deputy secretaries share one servant between two.[29] An official's grade determines his class of train travel – 'soft sleeping', 'hard sleeping' or 'hard sitting'; what quality of cloth is used for his suits; what standard of food and accommodation he is given.

In theory these gradations of emolument set limits to the affluence of officials; in practice, at all levels, they are treated as a minimum to be exceeded. A prefectural Party secretary in Shanxi, instead of using the car pool, designates a jeep and a Shanghai saloon to be kept exclusively for his own use, and has part of the Committee offices re-modelled as a 300 square metre 'official residence' for himself and his wife. In Anhui, a city Party official lives with his family in a hotel for four years, at a cost to the state of 23,000 yuan (£7,000), because it is more convenient than the house that has been provided for him. A senior army officer in Peking occupies a twenty-three-room mansion belonging to a disgraced opera singer, and, when the man is rehabilitated, adamantly refuses to move out. The Minister of the First Machine Building Ministry, Zhou Zijian, spends £50,000 of state funds refurbishing his house immediately after his appointment; for his six-member family, he wants five bedrooms with bathrooms en suite. 'The fine tradition of plain living,' commented the *People's Daily*, 'has faded among some of our comrades, and faded to an astonishing degree.'[30]

The problem is not new. In Ding Ling's novel, *Sun over the Sangkan River*, published in 1948, even before the communists won power, one character, a landlord in a 'liberated area' tells his friend: 'The communists always say they're working for the poor . . . But that's just so much fine talk. In Kalgan, who lives in the best houses? Who rides in cars? Who're always in and out of fine restaurants? Aren't they the ones who have grown fat?' His companion answers: 'A new dynasty needs new ministers.'

Mao called it 'the sugar-coated bullets of the bourgeoisie'. George Orwell satirised it in *Animal Farm*. Mao's followers, the 'Gang of Four', asked: 'When a leading cadre earns 200 or 300 yuan a month, and has a Western-style house, a car, and servants provided by the state, he appropriates the fruits of the labour of the working people. Does this not constitute exploitation?'[31]

But for all their vaunted egalitarianism, Mao and the 'Gang of Four' were no better than the reformers who succeeded them at eliminating the inequalities between leaders and led. Jiang Qing used an imported Hasselblad camera to indulge her fondness for photography. Deng Xiaoping lives in a large, rambling house, hidden behind high walls in a tree-shaded street just north of the Forbidden City. Rong Yiren, a former millionaire capitalist, has a traditional Chinese-style courtyard house, with a rose garden, in Peking, and a Western-style villa in

Shanghai; in Peking, he uses a Hongqi limousine, hand-made for the top leaders at a rate of one a week, and in Shanghai, a Mercedes. Vice-ministers occupy flats of five or six rooms, plainly but solidly furnished, in high-rise buildings with sentries outside. They have paintings on the walls, heavy old-fashioned sofas, and armchairs with loose covers and antimacassars; the floors are carpeted, the kitchen is equipped with a refrigerator and a washing machine, the rooms are clean and well-painted, with none of the grime and shabbiness found in ordinary homes. 'In China,' said the pianist, Fou Tsong, after visiting the flats of fellow musicians during a tour in 1980, 'even cleanliness is a luxury.'

In the Soviet Union and Eastern Europe, leaders develop eclectic tastes. Brezhnev collects luxury cars; he owns a Rolls-Royce, a Cadillac, a Lincoln Continental, a Chevrolet, a Citroën-Maserati, among others. The wives of Soviet Politburo members, ample, matronly ladies, will only use French perfume. The former Polish leader, Bierut, was re-nowned for his knowledge of French wines (another connoisseur of good living, the Khmer Rouge Foreign Minister, Ieng Sary, at a time when hundreds of thousands of Kampucheans were dying each year of starvation, would specify the year when ordering vintage champagne). A more recent Polish Central Committee member, Maciej Szczepanski, collected houses; he was found to have acquired no fewer than ten, including a forty-two room palace in Warsaw, a villa on a Greek island and a country house with a glass-bottomed swimming pool and four prostitutes in attendance. In Peking, ambitions are more modest: the elite status symbol is not a Western car, but a Western colour television, and the children of high officials earnestly debate the merits of Grundig and Sony.

A few remain defiantly untouched. One old general refuses to use the new-fangled flush lavatories in his fine villa in Peking, and goes out to an earth latrine in the garden, because 'that's the way we did it in Yenan', the old revolutionary base area. But even he, with his peasant ways, lives in an ambiance of comfort and space as remote from the masses as the town-houses of the Inner Party leaders in Orwell's *1984* were from the proles in their 'decaying, dingy cities, where underfed people shuffled to and fro in leaky shoes, in patched-up nineteenth-century houses'.

In Peking, where a quarter of a million people each have two square metres of living space, eighty-nine-year-old Mme Soong Chingling, the widow of China's first president, Sun Yatsen, occupied a sixty-room mansion until her death in 1981. In a country where the dying are carried to hospital on bicycle carts, the elite, their children and grandchildren pile into official limousines at weekends for excursions to the Great Wall or the Miyun reservoir.

Such disparities are not to be wondered at; they exist in all countries. But neither can they be denied. And in both China and the Soviet Union, they take peculiarly perverse forms.

At the end of 1980, China's Commerce Minister, Wang Lei, was publicly censured for eating in Peking's best restaurants and never paying the bills. By coincidence, shortly afterwards the Soviet press revealed that the Mayor of Sochi, Vyacheslav Aleksandrovich Voronkov, had been doing exactly the same. In each case all doors were opened and all payments automatically waived solely because of their rank.

Above a certain level, money actually becomes irrelevant. In the Soviet Union there are people, including the writer, Mikhail Sholokhov, who have so-called 'open bank accounts'; they are not paid any formal salary, but can draw as much as they need, *with no limit*, because it is calculated that 'in the conditions of Soviet reality' they cannot possibly spend all that they earn.

The Soviet elite is based on the *nomenklatura*, which derives from the fourteen official ranks, or *chins*, known as the *chinovnichestvo*, laid down by Peter the Great. The highest *nomenklatura* posts, comparable with the top eight grades in the Chinese system, the so-called *gaoji ganbu*, or 'high cadres' (vice-ministers and above), are controlled by the Party Organs Department of the Central Committee. But *nomenklatura* listings at lower levels are within the competence of city and even district Party organisations. One recent estimate put the number of such elite posts, including those in the Soviet armed forces and those outside the *nomenklatura* proper who nonetheless enjoy similar privileges, at about 250,000.[32] These are men and women with an income of more than 450 roubles (£340) a month, and access to a wide range of restricted benefits and services – including the so-called 'Kremlin ration', under which they receive part of their salaries in foreign currency certificates; the use of special shops, special clinics and sanatoria, and restricted guesthouses and clubs; the right to good housing, and to educate their children in the best schools.

The number of Chinese 'high cadres' with living standards comparable to the Soviet elite is probably fewer than 50,000, reflecting the fact that it is a much poorer country. But the privileged existence of the ruling stratum, the 'new class', as Milovan Djilas christened it, is maintained and protected in exactly the same way.

The stretch of the Moscow River that flows past Brezhnev's *dacha*, a lovely old mansion house with balustraded marble stairways running down to the water's edge, is off-limits even to Russians. So, to Chinese, is Jade Spring Mountain, in the western hills outside Peking, where Deng Xiaoping has a weekend home. The Soviet leaders have villas at Oreanda and Pitsunda on the Black Sea coast, and hunting lodges in the north; the Chinese have villas at Beidaihe and Qingdao, on the coast of the Yellow Sea, and country houses amid the exquisite scenery of mist-shrouded Lushan, and Huangshan, the Yellow Mountain. Chinese, like Soviet, cities have special accommodation for visiting leaders. When, in 1974, Mao spent several months in his home province of Hunan, he lived in a heavily guarded compound in the centre of the provincial capital, Changsha; a subsequent visitor, Princess Ashraf of Iran, was surprised to find that the large and well-appointed bathroom was decorated entirely in red, with handholds set into the red tiled walls for the aged Chairman to hang on to as he was taking his shower. Less exotic, but certainly more elegant, was a guesthouse complex in Canton where the late President Liu Shaoqi used to stay. It consisted of eleven green-roofed colonial-style villas, sumptuously furnished with antique furniture and paintings, set in gardens of bamboo, magnolia and ancient pines, with grass that was springy underfoot. When I went there with a foreign delegation in 1980, guards with fixed bayonets stood at the gates, but only one building was in use; being reserved for the elite, the villas stood empty most of the year.

Unlike the Soviet Union and Eastern Europe, China does not have special shops exclusively for high officials. Nonetheless a special supply system exists which is only marginally different, disguised within the Party apparatus like the so-called 'Welfare Department' of the Soviet Party Central Committee. One of its few visible outlets is a modern five-storey building near the Forbidden City, bearing a discreet sign, 'Peking City Food Depot', where ministers, Central Committee members and senior generals send their drivers to obtain choice meat, seafoods, and other foodstuffs not easily available on the open market. Certain officials have the right to use the 'Friendship Stores', which have been opened in the larger cities to serve foreign residents and tourists and carry a wider selection of goods than is found in ordinary shops. And those who travel abroad, as the *People's Daily* ruefully admitted, 'come back loaded down with quartz watches, television sets and washing machines'.[33] Although there are no special hospitals, high officials are allocated private wards, and are sometimes sent for special treatment abroad; Luo Ruiqing – the old general who wept in his wheelchair at Mao's funeral – died in Frankfurt, after an operation on his broken legs failed. At a less exalted level, Party mandarins in the provinces order hospital equipment and medical teams transferred to their own homes to treat themselves and their families.[34] The gradations of privilege persist even beyond the grave: some crematoria are restricted to officials of a certain rank; one in Shenyang will only cremate 'those whose monthly salaries exceed 147 yuan'.[35] In education, as in the Soviet Union, officials' children fill the best schools. Under Mao, when admission was by political criteria, the product of one favoured establishment boasted that ninety-seven per cent of his graduating class had gone on to university, compared with one per cent for the country as a whole. After Mao's death, when academic achievement once again mattered, officials' children accounted for two-thirds of all university entrants.

Privilege at this level extends beyond the high cadres to a much broader elite, which can be roughly defined as those who have regular access to *neibu* or 'internal' benefits.

The term *neibu* can cover anything which is not to be disclosed to outsiders. Central Committee documents, outlining new policies, which are read out at briefings to the Party's 38 million members, are *neibu* (a similar system existed in the Soviet Union under Khrushchev, but was stopped by the more secretive Brezhnev). The newspaper, *Cankao Xiaoxi* (*Reference News*), which publishes translations from the foreign press, is *neibu* – even though it is available down to the level of production brigade leaders, and its circulation of nine million is more than that of the *People's Daily*. The tighter the restrictions, the greater the benefits. An estimated quarter of a million officials and intellectuals have access to closed screenings of Western films, ranging from *Star Wars* and *South Pacific* to so-called 'negative teaching material' such as *Last Tango in Paris*. They may also see restricted performances of plays judged too controversial for the general public, and obtain books which are not generally available. Some receive *Reference Information*, a much fuller, ninety-six page version of *Reference News*; and a still more restricted version, *Reference Materials*, is issued twice daily to a few hundred top officials. The *People's Daily* and most provincial Party newspapers also have internal journals, circulated among the elite, dealing with popular grievances and other matters considered too sensitive for discussion in the open press. At the very highest level, there are secret bulletins of domestic political intelligence, such as *Qingkuang Huibian* (*Confidential Information*), produced by a special department of the *People's Daily*, sometimes several times a day, for Politburo members.[36]

The Soviet Union also has closed film shows and 'white Tass' and 'red Tass' news bulletins for senior officials. But they are more limited in scope, and there is no system of 'internal' newspapers. If the Soviet

Politburo wants political intelligence, it gets it not from a special reporting unit in *Pravda* but from the KGB.

In both the Soviet Union and China, the elite jealously guards its identity, and is intensely conscious of the eminence that sets it apart from the common herd. In the Soviet Union this was most pronounced in the years immediately after Stalin's death. 'The attitude of the bulk of the white-collar class to the manual labourers,' wrote Edward Crankshaw in 1959, 'is very like the attitude of the upper and middle classes in Victorian England to the rabble. To hear the way some charming young woman, daughter of an army general or a high official or a big industrialist speaks of the masses makes the blood run cold.'[37]

Two decades later, Soviet society has become less rigidly stratified, and the dominant social trend, as in post-Victorian Britain, is the strengthening of the middle class. In the 1980s middle-class Russians behave more and more like their counterparts elsewhere, buying life insurance policies, paying off the mortgages on their flats and saving up to buy their own cars. And it is to middle-class values that the majority of Russians aspire.

In China, the weight of the past is heavier and class polarisation sharper. The 'masses', like the Roman plebs, are an amorphous multitude, spoken of only in the plural; the 'cadres' are the patricians who rule them.

When Chairman Mao's widow, Jiang Qing, and the rest of her so-called 'Gang of Four' were put on trial at the end of 1980, they were accused of persecuting 'large numbers of cadres and people' – as though the two were quite distinct. When a Chinese official goes out among the masses, he speaks of 'making a trip to the lower levels'.[38] The barrier between one world and the other is symbolised by the black net curtains fitted to official cars to shield their occupants from common view. In the words of the newspaper *Guangming Ribao*,

> In feudal times, people could tell the rank of officials by the colour of their sedan chairs. Today, people tell the rank of officials by the kind of car they use. When an important leading cadre goes out, the number of bodyguards who accompany him, the extent to which he is separated from the people and the fear of the masses that is shown, surpass those for high officials in capitalist countries.[39]

'We must guard against degenerating into overlords, sitting on the backs of the people,' said the *People's Daily* in 1979. In Liaoning, in North-East China, a few months later, a case was reported of a factory Party secretary who had built an earthquake shelter outside his house in such a way that it blocked the doorway of his neighbour, a worker. For two years, the worker and his family had to enter and leave their dwelling by crawling through the window. Eventually higher authority intervened and the shelter was demolished – but the secretary was not punished for what he had done; losing the shelter was considered sufficient.[40]

The arrogance and contempt of even petty officials for the 'lower levels' – the lower orders, as the Victorians called them – shows most clearly in family relations. When a cadre's son or daughter wants to marry a worker or, still worse, a peasant, not only the family but often the local Party committee brings intense pressure to bear to make them break off the relationship, arguing that 'the official is made to lose face', and 'young people cannot marry when their social position is not equal'.[41]

The son of a Deputy Secretary of the Party Discipline Inspection Commission at Tangshan, the city razed by the 1976 earthquake, seduced a girl at the factory where he was working. Twice she became pregnant, but each time he persuaded her to have an abortion, telling her that unless she did so it would make it harder for them to marry. Afterwards he informed her that 'because his father was a high-ranking official, he could not marry the daughter of an ordinary person', and she should forget about him. When, in desperation, she took her story to the factory Party committee, his father mobilised powerful allies, including a deputy mayor, to have the affair hushed up.[42]

Another young man, Zhou Shaogong, the son of a leading city official in Wuhan, 'twice skipped work and enticed two girls to accompany him to Nanjing, Guangzhou and elsewhere for a so-called "travelling marriage"'. He also allegedly raped women. But when the police came to arrest him, his father warned them off, saying he had influential connections and they should not pursue the case. In the event his connections failed him; Zhou Shaogong was given three years in a labour camp, and his father was denounced in the press (though not otherwise punished) for trying to pervert the course of justice. At Changchun, in the north-east, the son of another city official and two other young men were executed in June 1980 for leading a group of youths who had raped and gang-raped ninety-two young women over the previous six years. As though by some unwritten *jus primae noctis* they had been permitted to continue their depredations because the police were afraid of their parents' high positions. The reaction had been, as the New China News Agency put it: 'Are you out of your mind to touch those influential people?'[43]

Commenting on the Changchun case, the *China Youth News* said:

There are people influenced by feudal ideas who think that because their fathers are ranking officials they can do whatever they like . . . There are leading cadres who do everything they can to let their relatives get away with crimes . . . They practice the old feudal custom of 'mandarins protecting each other'.[44]

Wen Hui Bao complained that

the feudal dross of the son sharing the glory of the father has become candied fruit in the minds of the people . . . Such things as the concept of rank and the 'special privilege' mentality have become ugly sores in our society.[45]

It was left to the intellectuals' newspaper, *Guangming Ribao*, to try to explain why these problems persisted:

Most of our officials come from peasant smallholder stock. In their minds there is still the idea of 'overthrowing the Emperor and ruling the country'. The corruption of power comes very easily to some people. It is nothing new in history for the leader of a peasant uprising to degenerate after he becomes Emperor.'[46]

Part II

Stalin and Mao

Report of the Special Case Group, October 25th:

'The liver cancer suffered by the subject of the case has worsened. According to the doctor's diagnosis, he might die at any time . . . We have agreed with the view of the investigation committee . . . that the subject be given improved treatment in the prison to prolong his life and, at the same time, be subjected to shock interrogation.'

Report of the Special Case Group, November 9th:

'On 26 October the subject's condition worsened drastically. On 28 October he was transferred to the military hospital. Thanks to the intensive care he received, he did not die until 1 November, thus giving us altogether an extra seven days for interrogation . . . In the 27 days between his arrest and his death we interrogated him 21 times, bringing increasing pressure on him, and finally forced him to confess . . .'

Those clinical police reports could come from the case file of a political prisoner under either Stalin or Mao. They actually describe the last days of an elderly Chinese professor in 1967.

Not even the investigators claimed he had done anything wrong. But twenty-five years earlier the wife of China's Head of State, Liu Shaoqi, had been one of his students, and he was asked to provide information for Mao to use against her as part of the campaign to have Liu expelled from the Party. The old 'granite-head', as the investigators called him, refused, and the confession eventually extracted was so incoherent as to be unusable.

The special case group reports were approved by the Minister of Public Security, Xie Fuzhi, and Mao's wife, Jiang Qing.

Thirteen years later, they were made public during Jiang Qing's trial. Peking Television broadcast a tape recording of part of the interrogation, in which the moans and shrieks of the dying man could be heard, punctuated by the shouts of his inquisitors.

For the last four days he was kept alive by an intravenous drip. The final session of questioning went on without a break for fifteen hours, ending at midnight on October 31st. He died two hours later.[1]

*

Stalin and Mao built their revolutions on the totalitarianism of Lenin, who was brutal and ruthless as well as wise and benevolent. Stalinism, in the view of Milovan Djilas, was

> Leninism applied and further developed (if that is the right word) under Russia's peculiar conditions. When Lenin died, communists had, broadly speaking, three roads to choose from: (*1*) Bukharin's programme for a more democratic and equitable communist society; (*2*) the internationalist Utopianism of Trotsky coupled with the prospect of a dictatorship even fiercer than Stalin's; and (*3*) the bureaucratic despotism of Stalin. Stalin's form of patrimonial tyranny was closest to Russian traditions and best attuned to the interests of the emerging new establishment.[2]

Maoism was Leninism applied and developed under Chinese conditions.

The similarities between the two systems reflect their common origin in what is, essentially, a Russian mutant of Marxism; concepts such as 'the dictatorship of the proletariat', which have underpinned both Soviet and Chinese rule, come not from the West European, Marx, but from Lenin, the Russian disciple who filtered his ideas through a prism of autarchy and revolution to create a specifically Russian political form.

The differences reflect the vastly different cultures in which each developed, Christian in Stalin's case, Confucian in Mao's. This is not to belittle the role of the leaders themselves. It was Mao's genius that he was able to use a doctrine as alien to Chinese thought as Leninism and transmute it into a source of moral authority which would sustain a revolution among a quarter of mankind. Stalin's achievement was to continue where Lenin left off, perfecting a system of personalised dictatorship which gave him power more nearly absolute than that of any other major ruler in modern times.

But revolutions are the saddest proof of the old saw, the more things change, the more they are the same. Mao and Stalin built their new order in the image of the old.

It was when Stalinism was at its most extreme, in the 1930s, that it most resembled the rule of Ivan the Terrible – with one difference: at the height of Ivan's terror, in the sixteenth century, ten to twenty people were killed daily; in 1937–38, there were days when a thousand men and women were shot in Moscow alone. Stalin himself was aware of the parallel. He spoke of 'the progressive role played by the *Oprichnina*' (Ivan's secret police), and blamed Ivan only for not being decisive enough in liquidating his enemies and spending too much time praying for forgiveness. In Stalin's later years, no criticism of the tsar was tolerated. Writers such as Kostylev and Yazvitsky glorified Ivan's bloodstained rule, portraying him as a just and affectionate man, and praising his chief executioner, the infamous Malyuta Skuratov, as 'a model of love for the homeland' with a humane, Russian heart.

Stalin's terror had one aim: to remove all who might challenge his power. The Cultural Revolution was more complex. Mao wanted to destroy not only his political opponents, but the ideas they stood for. Like Qin Shi Huang, who, 2,000 years earlier, burnt the Confucian classics and buried the scholars alive, Mao sought to obliterate the former orthodoxy through campaigns against the 'Four Olds' ('old thinking, culture, customs and ways of life') and, later, the movement to 'criticise Lin Biao and Confucius'. During Mao's last years, criticism of Qin Shi Huang was regarded as criticism of Mao himself. Yet it was precisely during the Cultural Revolution that Mao's rule most resembled that of a feudal emperor, at the apex of the Confucian system, surrounded by all the panoply of cult worship and adulation.

Mao's communism was Confucian in the same way as Western atheism is founded on Christianity. In Mao's view, society should be regulated not by laws and institutions but by a collective moral order, spreading down from the ruler (the Party) to the humblest of his subjects; political change must be engineered by social mass movements. In Stalin's view, change should be ordained by the word of the *Vozhd*, the Leader, and society should be regulated by the discipline of fear. Stalin launched the blood purges of the 1930s by engineering the assassination of Kirov and using it as a pretext to uncover layer upon layer of spurious conspiracies, in which not only his potential enemies but also his loyal followers were struck down – until the entire country was in thrall to his despotism, and none had the will to resist.

'O great Stalin; O leader of the people, you who created man, you who populated the earth, you who made the centuries young, you who made the springtime flower' – rhapsodised *Pravda* in 1936, a year in which at least 100,000 people were shot as the purges were getting under way. A decade later, a Soviet writer described how, visiting the Kremlin, 'we walk on stones which he may have trod only quite recently. Let us fall on our knees and kiss those holy footprints!'[3] The only change, as the years passed and the cult became an institution, was that the tone of veneration grew more reflective. On Stalin's seventieth birthday, in 1950, *Pravda* wrote:

If you meet with difficulties in your work or suddenly doubt your abilities, think of him, of Stalin, and you will find the confidence you need. If you feel tired in an hour when you should not, think of him, of Stalin, and your work will go well. If you are seeking a correct decision, think of him, of Stalin, and you will find that decision . . . 'Stalin said' – that means the people think so. 'The people said' – that means Stalin thought so.[4]

Stalin's very name became a talisman, shouted out by soldiers going into battle, and officials being taken to be shot. In this, too, he resembled Ivan the Terrible. A nineteenth-century historian has described how 'Prince Repnin, impaled on a stake and dying slowly . . . praised the Tsar, his lord and executioner.'

In China, the veteran communist Ma Mingfang, dying in a prison hospital after being tortured so badly he could not walk, remained 'unshaken . . . in his confidence that Chairman Mao would eventually come to his help', and told his wife and children: 'If I should die, you should try to pass the word to Chairman Mao that I, Ma Mingfang, am a good man.' In 1974 Marshal Peng Dehuai shouted, as he lay dying in detention, 'I have never opposed Chairman Mao.'[5]

If the Soviet Party under Stalin was, in Roy Medvedev's phrase, 'an ecclesiastical organisation, with a sharp distinction between ordinary people and the leader-priests, headed by their infallible pope', the Chinese Party at the height of Mao's power was a fully-fledged Church, with its own liturgy and rites.

Even before the Cultural Revolution, Maoism offered Chinese a much more complete system of personal philosophy for coming to terms with the world than Stalinism offered Russians. Its clergy (the Party cadres) preached that the path to heaven (communism) lay through right thinking, meritorious deeds and self-purification, achieved by the confession of sins (criticism and self-criticism).

In the late 1960s, these tendencies were developed to an extreme. The Chinese people began each day with a 'loyalty dance': 'You put your hand to your head and then to your heart, and you danced a jig – to show that your heart and mind were filled with boundless love for Chairman Mao,' one Party member recalled. Then came 'Asking for instructions in the morning, and making a report in the evening':[6] before starting work, factory workers and commune peasants gathered in front of a portrait of Mao to read quotations from the 'Little Red Book'; at the end of the day they returned to 'report' to the portrait what they had done, and to 'confess' impure, unproletarian thoughts – like Christians before taking the Sacrament.

'The faithful prayed before living idols,' the Shanghai newspaper, *Wen Hui Bao*, wrote ten years later. 'Crowds of people who had suffered persecution would bow deeply to the Leader's portrait, "admit errors and ask for punishment".'[7]

It became impossible to make a telephone call or a purchase in a shop without first reciting a Maoist catechism. A notice in a photographer's window in Canton declared: 'Revolutionary masses who enter our revolutionary photography studio for revolutionary photographs to be taken must, upon entering, first shout a revolutionary slogan.' At meetings, the 'Little Red Book' had to be 'held over the heart and raised high, especially on the "left" side'. There was a 'movement to chant Chairman Mao's quotations set to music'. All official correspondence had to begin with one of his quotations, and in the newspapers his words were printed in bold type – just as, in imperial China, a statement by the emperor had to be placed at the top of the page.[8]

'Mao Zedong Thought is everlasting, universal truth,' wrote the then Defence Minister and heir apparent, Lin Biao. 'One single sentence of his surpasses 10,000 of ours.' To maintain this pretence, it was later admitted, Mao's writings were repeatedly revised to make them conform to each new twist of the political line, and a secret directive was issued, making it a criminal offence to trace them back to their original versions. All publications containing original texts of Mao's works were designated state secrets and confiscated.[9]

Another directive laid down that the characters forming Mao Zedong's name should never be divided and printed on separate lines 'because separating a name by printing it on two lines was regarded as an evil omen'.[10]

If an editor, while correcting an article, crossed out Mao's name or one of his quotations, 'it would be treated as a major case of disrespect', wrote the *People's Daily*. 'Whoever damaged a badge bearing the great man's portrait . . . was punished on charges of counter-revolutionary vicious attacks.'[11] Nor was it only Mao whose name was invulnerable. In Nanjing a railway worker was sentenced to five years' imprisonment for saying, 'Chairman Mao is glowing with health, but Lin Biao is as thin as sticks of kindling.' Another worker received a seven-year term for stumbling over a phrase when reading aloud a big-character poster.[12]

The writer, Bai Hua, reflecting on those years, drew a parallel with the time before the 1911 revolution, 'when anyone who smashed an idol was surrounded and beaten to death'.[13] *Guangming Ribao* looked back still further:

The 'god-building' movement . . . brought a return to the barbarism, darkness and terror of medieval times . . . In the Middle Ages, the words of the Bible had the authority of law . . . [In the Cultural Revolution] the Quotations [of Chairman Mao] had the authority of law. The Quotation tribunal became a latter-day Inquisition.[14]

149

When Brecht's play, *Galileo*, was performed in Peking in 1978, the scenes of the Inquisition were taken by Chinese audiences as a parable on their own experiences.

The contradiction between revolutionary intentions and reactionary, feudal means is fundamental to any understanding of the Cultural Revolution and the Stalinist terror, and indeed of all totalitarian communist regimes. Pol Pot in Kampuchea resurrected the slave system of Angkor in the name of an egalitarian Utopia. Mao's supporters, as his successors have acknowledged, 'shouted "Down with the Four Olds!" while setting society back to a state of ignorance even more "Four Old-ish" than the "Four Olds"'.[15]

Stalin and Mao built their cults in the tradition of the feudal autocracy which the revolution had replaced. Both were corrupted by the power they wielded and the adulation they received: in Stalin's case, it fuelled his megalomania; in Mao's it cut him off from reality.

Old film clips show him standing on Tian An Men, a brutal hulk of a man, shattered and scarred by decades of ruthless political warfare, reviewing the great parades, which took place in the early days of the Cultural Revolution, of a million Red Guards, chanting and screaming like Western teenagers at a rock concert, with an orgiastic light of frenzied ecstasy shining from their faces – and on Mao's ravaged, exultant face, lapping up the worship, a cynical smile of triumph.

'All this marching up and down and cheering and waving flags,' one of Orwell's characters says in *1984*, 'is simply sex gone sour. If you're happy inside yourself, why should you get excited about Big Brother and Three Year Plans?'

Orwell had Stalinism in mind when he wrote of the link between 'sexual privation . . . and warfever and leader worship, [and] . . . chastity and political orthodoxy'. In Russia in the 1930s a woman who wore make-up and tried to dress attractively was not only liable to be hauled before local officials for showing bourgeois tendencies, but would be loudly condemned by passers-by on the streets. Femininity was suppressed so harshly that sexual frigidity became a national blight, affecting, in the estimate of Dr Mikhail Shtern, sixty to eighty per cent of Soviet women. In China repressed sexual drive was used even more blatantly to propel the Cultural Revolution. Any form of individualism in clothes or appearance was denounced. Make-up was banned. The young were urged to wear identical blue or olive-green work-clothes to show their proletarian spirit.[16] Xenophobia – which in the Soviet Union manifested itself in a crawling fear of spies and enemy agents – was whipped up in China to insane heights. 'Ferocity,' Orwell wrote in *1984*, 'was directed outwards, at . . . foreigners, traitors and saboteurs.'

Where Orwell described the imaginary 'Two Minutes' Hate' as a fictionalised expression of Stalinist thought control, China perfected the reality of the struggle meeting:

> The struggle . . . is a peculiarly Chinese invention, combining intimidation, humiliation and sheer exhaustion. Briefly described, it is an intellectual gang-beating of one man by many, sometimes even thousands, in which the victim has no defence, even the truth . . .
> The struggle was born in the Thirties, when the communists first began making headway in the great rural stretches of China. Developed over the years by trial and error, it became the standard technique for interrogating the landlords and other enemies who fell into the hands of the rebellious peasants, [before whom they were] . . . forced to kneel and bow [their heads] . . .
> A struggle is rarely resolved quickly; that would be too easy. At the beginning, even if the victim tells the truth or grovellingly admits to any accusation hurled at him, his every word will be greeted with insults and shrieks of contradiction. He is ringed by jeering, hating faces, screaming in his ear, spitting; fists swipe menacingly close to him and everything he says is branded a lie. At the end of the day he is led to a room, locked up, given some food and left with the promise that the next day will be even worse. . . .
> In China, the thought counts as much as the deed, and the struggle is one of the most effective weapons for weaseling into a man's mind to control his thoughts.[17]

In Mao's China, as in Stalin's Russia, culture was stifled by revolutionary mawkishness. Readers of the Soviet novel, declared the critic Pomerantsev shortly after Stalin's death, had been 'deafened by the triumphant roar of tractors'. In Soviet plays, lamented Konstanin Simonov – in terms identical to those used in China after Mao's death – 'the better competes with the good, and the perfect with the best'. Shostakovich and Prokofiev were hounded to write songs that the moronic blonds of the new order could sing as they worked in the fields.[18] In *1984*, songs are composed, and novels and plays written, by machine. In China, in the Cultural Revolution, they were written by committee.

For both Mao and Stalin, the cult of the leader was an essential political instrument, consciously created and deliberately used. 'By [1966],' Mao told Edgar Snow, 'I thought . . . we needed some personal worship.'[19]

In each country, however, its purpose was slightly different. For Stalin, the cult provided a counterpoint to the terror. The Russian writer, Pismenny, has argued that an honourable person living in the Soviet Union in the 1930s had little choice but to believe in Stalin; the alternative, 'that all social actions could be prompted by the criminal designs of a single man who had appropriated the full plenitude of power, and that this man was Stalin', was so monstrous as to be beyond rational belief. So the Soviet people did believe in Stalin; they believed that Zinoviev, Kamenev, Rykov, Bukharin, Krestinsky, and the others *were* 'enemies of the people'. The cult fed on this belief, and as it grew, it shielded Stalin from any personal imputation of blame. The excesses which people could not justify to themselves were attributed to the NKVD. To have blamed Stalin himself would have been akin to blasphemy. Conversely, to have recognised the purges for what they were would have brought a moral imperative to take a stand against them. Russians wanted to believe, because it salved their consciences. Until the end of the Second World War, and, for many, even up to his death, Stalin remained a popular ruler who was genuinely loved.

In China, there was never any question of Mao distancing himself from the Cultural Revolution. It was Mao's creation, which 'he personally launched and led', as the propaganda endlessly repeated. Without his immense personal prestige it could not have been started, and without his cult it could not have been sustained.

Where the Stalinist terror was executed by a professional elite – the secret police, elements of the judiciary and the Party *apparat* – Mao's terror was the product of a mass movement. Russians now in their sixties and seventies may, as young men and women, have informed on each other and betrayed their friends. They may have sanctioned the arrest of their subordinates, and voted for their expulsion at Party meetings. Many did all these things. But the torture and killing were carried out by a small group, probably comprising fewer than 100,000 men, within the NKVD. In China, tens of millions took part in the struggle meetings and street battles. The tour guide who meets you at the airport, or the engaging young official from the foreign trade corporation with whom you are negotiating, may as students have beaten their professor to death with their bare hands. Many did.

The number of Stalin's victims was so huge as to be almost beyond comprehension. In the years 1936–38, one million Soviet citizens were executed and eight million imprisoned. From 1936 to 1950, it is estimated, 12 million prisoners died in the camps from maltreatment and exhaustion, and at least seven million deaths occurred before 1936 in the collectivisation famine and associated deportations. During his two decades in power, Stalin killed ten per cent of the Soviet population, and a further ten per cent died in the war: in other words, one Soviet citizen in five died violently.

Stalin's use of terror was nonetheless controlled and highly central ised. In 1937–38 alone, he and Molotov signed some 400 execution lists drawn up by the NKVD, each containing the names of several hundred senior officials. But at least there were lists: the scale of the purge was precisely defined.

In the Cultural Revolution, that was not so. The terror that Mao unleashed was general and uncontrolled. More important than merely destroying his enemies, it was an apocalyptic revolution, a last doomed attempt to re-make men's minds and re-fashion social behaviour in accordance with an idealistic revolutionary vision. 'The Chinese people are poor and blank,' Mao once said. 'On a blank sheet of paper, you can write the most beautiful poem.' In the 1950s, he told Nehru that a nuclear war would not be a bad thing, because even if it destroyed half of

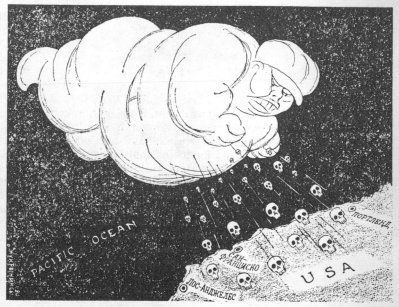

Pravda, 1980

mankind the other half would survive, and imperialism would vanish. The Cultural Revolution involved applying that principle within China – with the same total ruthlessness and imperious disregard of human suffering.

153

The Abuse of Terror

Most of what we now know about the Stalinist purges was disclosed after the dictator's death. That has also been the case with the Cultural Revolution.

In 1980, Hu Yaobang, then the Party's General Secretary, said that in the decade of political upheaval from 1966 to 1976, one million Chinese had died, 30 million had been persecuted and 100 million had been 'affected', meaning that they had been discriminated against because of their class status or occupation, or because they had relatives in political trouble.

Other figures are generally consistent with a death toll of this order. In Guangdong, according to the provincial governor, 40,000 died out of a population of 50 million; in Longyan prefecture of Fujian, 1,700 out of two million; at the Hongqiao Commune near Shanghai, a showplace visited by foreign dignitaries including the Duke of Kent, 'more than 20' out of 30,000.

In the Guangxi autonomous region, bordering Vietnam, where the violence was particularly fierce – in street battles in the regional capital, Nanning, machine-guns and bazookas were used, according to one participant – 67,400 people reportedly died, out of a population of 34 million. That figure comes not from an official source but from a wallposter, put up in Peking in August 1979. It named a thousand of the victims, on fifty cyclostyled sheets, together with details of how they died and the names of those who killed them, where known. Most had been beaten to death, but one group of forty-eight young women had been subjected to a mass rape.

'They were then tied up and their nipples cut off,' the poster said, 'and after they died their bodies were mutilated.'

Such atrocities were common in those years. The pianist, Fou Tsong, whose parents committed suicide in Shanghai after being forced by Red Guards to kneel for three days in the street outside their home, said it was as though all the ingenuity and creativeness of the Chinese character had been turned inwards, to take a fiendish delight in viciousness, cruelty and torture. In Peking, the Director of the PLA General Logistics Department, Qiu Huizuo, ran seven private prisons, guarded by his own troops, in which, according to evidence given at his trial, 'several dozen methods of torture were employed'.[1] In Inner Mongolia, the Red Guards' repertoire ran to seventy-five different tortures, each with its own special name. In Fujian, a former Red Guard described how his favourite teacher at Middle School No 8 in Amoy was beaten to death with broomsticks:[2]

> He passed out several times but was brought back to consciousness each time with cold water splashed on to his face. He could hardly move his body. His feet were cut with glass and thorns. He shouted, 'Why don't you kill me? Kill me!' This lasted for six hours. They tried to force a stick into his rectum. He collapsed for the last time.

The brutishness of the Cultural Revolution – and Mao's responsibility for it – cannot be overstated.

Unlike Stalin, Mao signed no death warrants; unlike Stalin, he did not kill those of his close colleagues he purged – with some exceptions, they survived. But by calling for total revolution, and demanding that each individual struggle against those around him to defend the 'revolutionary line', Mao legitimised violence and deliberately encouraged its use. To him, in the final analysis, violence was the *sine qua non* of revolutionary transformation. It was through the violence of war that the early members of the Communist Party has forged their commitment to revolution. It was through the violence of the land reform that the peasantry was committed to the revolution: by killing their landlords, they became bound to the communist cause. In the late 1940s and early 50s, with the Party's encouragement, some 800,000 landlords and other 'counter-revolutionaries' were executed in this way.

From 1966 to 1968, Mao tried to apply that experience to revolutionising the whole of Chinese society. Then, when the political struggle had degenerated into aimless factional warfare, and he realised that he had failed, he called a halt, and sent in the army to restore order.

In this scheme of things, the deaths of one million people were simply part of the revolutionary process, to be shrugged off as insouciantly as the 'excesses' of earlier political movements.

The great majority of those who died fell victim to generalised, grass-roots violence, generated in response to Mao's line but not directed by him. Anyone who had been identified with the pre-Cultural Revolution establishment, whether as an official, a teacher, a doctor or a scientist, became a potential target. The struggle against such people was not simply imposed from above. Xu Wenli, former editor of the unofficial Peking magazine, *Siwu Luntan* (*April 5th Tribune*), has argued that it was often widely supported by a populace bitterly resentful of the arrogance and privileged lifestyle of the Party bureaucrats who had become the new ruling caste. As the disorder grew and factional violence proliferated, that support faded away. But by then, all high-level resistance to Mao had been smashed; he was being worshipped as the Son of Heaven – the Great Helmsman, the Reddest, Red Sun in Our Hearts – and the Cultural Revolution had become unstoppable.

Many died in feuds between rival factions, each of which claimed to be more Maoist than the next; many died in the settling of old scores under cover of political struggle. The new leaders who emerged from the carnage and chaos were those who were able to ride out and manipulate the factional rivalries: Hua Guofeng in Hunan; Ji Dengkui in Henan; Chen Yonggui in Shanxi; and certain military figures, such as Chen Xilian in the north-east.

In some cases widespread violence followed provincial purges ordered directly by the central leadership. Mao had set up a Cultural Revolution Group to serve as a loyal instrument, bypassing the Politburo, to carry out the Cultural Revolution. Its prime movers were his former secretary, Chen Boda; his wife, Jiang Qing; and the secret police chief, Kang Sheng. In 1968 Kang concocted a case against the Inner Mongolian leader, Ulanfu, whom he alleged had established a so-called New People's Revolutionary Party. In the ensuing purge, 16,222 people died and 346,000 were persecuted, out of a population of eight million.[3] Not even the smallest hamlets were spared: among the 130 inhabitants of Xiaoyingzi production brigade, seven died, and seventeen were beaten so badly they were permanently disabled.[4] Another huge regional purge, ordered by Kang Sheng in Yunnan, caused the deaths of 14,000 people, out of a population of 30 million. In the same province a PLA regiment was 'suppressed by armed force' and four other big purges were carried out to smash spurious 'counter-revolutionary cliques' which existed only in the imaginations of those charged with their liquidation.[5] Yunnan and neighbouring Sichuan were both officially described as being in a state of civil war in 1967–68.[6]

A further regional purge deliberately triggered by a central leader occurred in Eastern Hebei, where, in December 1967, Chen Boda accused the local Party organisation of being infiltrated by renegades, and named the First Secretary, Yang Yuan, and the Mayor of the city of Tangshan, Bai Yun, as 'Guomindang elements' and 'big Manorial lords'. A 280-member special-case group was set up to 'trace the roots of the "Yang-Bai Group" and ferret out its social foundation'. In the next two years, 84,000 people were persecuted, of whom 2,995 died and 763 were maimed. Yang and Bai themselves were sent to labour camps. By the time the investigation ended, in 1969, a further 1,604 officials scattered over twenty-four provinces had been implicated with them.[7]

Large-scale violence in the provinces, however, was more commonly initiated by local leaders as part of their struggle for power. In one such period of 'white terror', in Caozhuang in Shandong province in July 1967, 10,659 people were beaten, 692 were permanently disabled and ninety-four died.[8] Even in rural counties on the outskirts of Peking that year, according to *Beijing Ribao*:

Large-scale struggles by force . . . lasted a full month [in July and again in December] . . . More than 1,190 leading cadres in Fangshan county were struggled against, resulting in many astounding cases of persecution . . . Xu Qingwen, Secretary of the Nanhanji production brigade . . . was beaten until he lost consciousness and finally had to leave his native village. Even Xu's family was not spared. His old mother suffered a broken rib and his wife became a cripple as a result of beatings; his father and small daughter died of starvation. Wu Chunshan, another brigade Party Secretary . . . was branded a 'second landlord' and forced to kneel on the snowy ground in a severe winter. Then he was forced to crawl along the street with a stone on his body weighing more than 50 kgs until he nearly died of exhaustion . . .

[In Songzhuang village in Tong county] many people were hung up to be beaten, and more than 10 were severely injured . . . They also held kangaroo courts, set up private prisons and tortured their victims during illegal interrogations . . . More than 90 people in the village were severely beaten – of whom two died, five committed suicide and 10 were crippled.[9]

In Xiao county in Anhui, leftist leaders

built prisons and erected torture chambers . . . A woman Party member who had written a big-character poster against them was actually hung from the beams of the county court building and beaten almost to death. At one private prison they built, 900 people were illegally locked up . . . and subjected to all kinds of tortures . . . Some were beaten unconscious many times.[10]

In Jinjiang prefecture, in Fujian, a so-called 'Children's Corps', formed by young Red Guards, operated 'an underground jail with several dozen kinds of torture devices'.[11]

Guns and bombs were looted from armouries, and in the southern provinces from trains taking military supplies to Vietnam.[12] Some provincial leaders set up 'hit squads' and special intelligence groups.

157

Chen Ada, one of the Red Guards' 'five tiger generals' in Shanghai, organised a so-called 'reform section'. According to Radio Shanghai, young women detained by the section were stripped naked and beaten. In one case the screams of a man being clubbed were tape recorded and played to his family until he was persuaded to 'confess'.[13] Another Shanghai group, the '244 Group', was formed by a journalist named You Xuetao to serve the city's Mayor, Zhang Chunqiao, one of the quartet of leftist leaders later known as the 'Gang of Four'. According to evidence produced at his trial,

> Zhang Chunqiao used the group to make house searches, tail and kidnap innocent people, extract confessions by torture and collect information . . . A Shanghai actress, Zhuang Ruiyun, who had been a member of the . . . group, [testified that] . . . the methods they used included 'sex traps' . . . The group had its own headquarters, its own special funds as well as cars, motorcycles, guns, hand-grenades, cameras and miniature tape recorders.[14]

From 1967 to 1970, the '244 Group' detained and tortured 183 people, of whom five died. Several cases were described in detail in court:

> One of the victims was the head of the former Shanghai Xiqu [Opera] School's organisation section . . . He was forced into a car in the middle of the night, blindfolded, dragged to a dark basement, and subjected to continuous interrogation for four days and nights without food or sleep. When he could stand it no longer and fainted and fell down, he was kicked until he opened his eyes again, and then subjected to further interrogation.
>
> Another victim was a script writer . . . Because he had opposed Zhang Chunqiao, he was illegally detained . . . They forced two-inch steel needles into his fingers and toes.
>
> Yet another victim was a woman teacher . . . She was also detained because of her opposition to Zhang Chunqiao. She was whipped with a sprung leather whip. She was also forced to kneel down on a bench with her hands stretched out in the air and her neck in a ring of wire from which six bricks hung. She was sometimes tied to a bench with bricks underneath her thighs for the torture known as the 'tiger's bench'. While she was being clubbed, she was forbidden to utter a sound until 50 strokes had been administered, otherwise the clubbing would start again from the beginning.[15]

In the hysterical atmosphere of that time, horror became commonplace. In the villages, there was looting and rape. In the towns, in 1969, intellectuals were rounded up and sent with their families to do manual labour. In Liaoning province alone, more than a hundred thousand families were rusticated. 'The old, the weak, the sick and disabled were not spared,' the *People's Daily* wrote later. 'Some were even carried from their hospital beds and sent to the countryside with oxygen bags, with the result that they died on the way.[16] Elsewhere the authorities behaved less harshly, but altogether several million families were involved.

Intellectuals were especially vulnerable. China's leading economist, Sun Yefang, was kept for seven years in solitary confinement in a prison cell. He was never told why he was arrested, or why he was released. Jian Bozan, a seventy-one-year-old historian with an international reputation, was made to lie full-length on the ground at struggle meetings, under a pile of lavatory paper covered with excrement, while Red Guards beat the soles of his feet. He eventually committed suicide. In Shanghai, several hundred scientists were arrested as 'secret agents'. Some, including the laser expert, Huang Wuhan, who was accused of being a British spy, died in prison.[17]

Similar repression took place all over China. Incomplete figures made public in 1980, drawn from about half China's provinces, showed that the number of scientists persecuted exceeded 53,000; the number of teachers, 142,000; and, in the medical field, 500 out of 674 professors in the country's leading health colleges.[18]

Writers and artists were prime targets because it was a *Cultural* Revolution, concerned as much with ideology as with political power, and Mao's wife, Jiang Qing, regarded culture as her special preserve. The *People's Daily* recounted:

> As to those . . . who refused to dance to their tune, and to those influential literary and art workers, they [Jiang Qing's supporters] tried to kill them in order to vent their feelings. If their target was a singer, they tried to break his nose. If their target was a dancer, they tried to break his legs. If their target was a musician, they tried to break his hands.[19]

In Peking, where the level of violence was average – according to official figures, 10,289 people died out of a population of eight million – the Red Guards ransacked 33,695 homes between mid-August and the end of September 1966; in those six weeks, 85,000 people were driven out of the city, and 1,772 died.[20] One of them was China's foremost novelist, Lao She. Years later his widow described how

> that summer the weather was unbearable, stifling! The atmosphere, both climatic and political, was so bad that people could hardly breathe. Fascist atrocities like a plague descended on us, with people fighting, houses being searched, people being paraded through the streets, people being beaten to death. Everyone felt in danger; each family became tense.

On the afternoon of August 23rd, Red Guards burst into the Peking Federation of Literary and Art Circles building and herded Lao She and some twenty other well-known writers into a lorry. They were taken to a struggle meeting, where they were severely beaten. Lao She returned home at two am, 'his head injured and his face covered in blood'. The following morning he left the house. Two days later his body was found, drowned in a lake in the west of the city.[21]

In one of the countless acts of petty cruelty which typified so much Chinese behaviour in those years, the bereaved woman was not allowed a last look at her husband's body, nor was she permitted to have his ashes.

Another ransacked house belonged to the family of China's most famous opera singer, Mei Lanfang, whose legendary status was comparable to that of Caruso or Patti in the West. Since his death in 1961, the house had been turned into a museum. In 1966, his family were driven out. His widow was accused of indulging in bourgeois pastimes because she kept nine white, long-haired cats; her head was shaved and her back broken. Mei's son, who had followed him on to the stage, was sent to do forced labour.[22]

During the Cultural Revolution, nearly one-third of the 224 National Committee members of the Federation of Literary and Art Circles were persecuted to death. The scriptwriter, Zhang Haimo, was beaten to death on a brightly-lit film set.[23] Ba Jin – who, with Lu Xun, Lao She and Mao Dun, is one of the four leading twentieth-century Chinese writers – spent three years cleaning the drains at the Shanghai Writers' Association building. 'At least,' he told me wryly, 'when the sink in my flat gets blocked up, I don't need to call a plumber.' Another old writer, Shen Congwen, was sent to a May 7th school, a work-study farm where officials 're-moulded themselves' through manual labour. 'Cows are relatively decent,' he reported to his family, after being put in charge of the vegetable plot, 'they'll let you drive them away. Pigs are no good. They look stupid but they're very crafty. When you're driving them along, all of a sudden they give you the slip and race back . . .'[24]

The singer, Xin Fengxia, was made to work digging air-raid shelters – which ruined her health and left her a cripple: like the Moscow underground, built as a showpiece by Kaganovich and Khrushchev, using camp labour in the 1930s, the tunnel systems beneath China's big cities were constructed partly with forced labour.

Even the 'organs of dictatorship' – the police, the procuratorate and the courts – were not exempt. After the autumn of 1967, six of the seven vice-ministers of Public Security were arrested; 34,400 policemen and prison officers were persecuted, of whom 3,600 were disabled by beatings and 1,200 died.[25] In Gansu province, in North-West China, only fifteen per cent of the provincial police force remained at their posts.[26] In Heilongjiang, 30,000 grass-roots public security committees – set up in every neighbourhood and village – were disbanded, and several dozen labour reform farms and factories were closed and the prisoners freed.[27] In Guiyang, in the south-west, according to the provincial radio station,

> Monsters and freaks of all descriptions turned out and evil spirits of all kinds danced in a riotous revelry and frantically attacked the dictatorship of the proletariat. They . . . stormed prisons, looted confidential files and guns and swept public security cadres and policemen out like rubbish . . .
>
> The roofs of the communications centre and the message centre of the municipal Public Security Bureau were destroyed, and the bureau's garage and office were completely smashed.[28]

In Anhui, policemen were beaten up: 'Some died, and some went insane.'[29]

Some of those purged ended up in the very camps which previously they had administered. But most of the Cultural Revolution's victims, whether in the police force or elsewhere, were exiled to remote rural areas to do manual labour under surveillance, or held in private prisons known as *niulan*, 'cowsheds', a term which could cover anything from a real cowshed to house arrest.

In the whole decade, 1966–76, only 270,000 political cases were handled through the courts, and of those nearly two-thirds were later admitted to have been trumped up.[30]

The public security apparatus played a minor role in the Cultural Revolution – insignificant compared to that of the NKVD in Stalin's purges – partly because it belonged to the old order which Mao was trying to smash, and partly because Mao was committed to wholesale revolution, engineered by mass political campaigns, while Stalin's aim was more limited and precise. If those repressed in China by extra-judicial means are taken into account, the number of victims increases a hundred-fold. An investigation after Mao's death showed that in Shanghai alone, 150,000 people had been unjustly detained or purged, equivalent to 15 million nationally. In a rural county in Jiangxi, in South-East China, 10,000 people, one in twenty of the local population, were 'erroneously ferreted out', which would correspond to 40 million victims.[31] The truth must lie somewhere between.

Neither the Stalinist terror nor the Cultural Revolution descended out of the blue. Each was the culmination of a process long in development.

From 1928 to 1933, Stalin fashioned the OGPU – the predecessor of the NKVD – into an instrument of personal power, and mastered the technique of the show trial, soon to become his preferred political device. At the same time he picked off, one by one, his Politburo opponents: Zinoviev in July 1926; Trotsky and Kamenev in October; Bukharin, the ablest of the younger men, whom Lenin had thought of as a successor if Trotsky were killed, in 1929.

Three decades later, beginning in 1954, Mao developed the political movement – the *cheng feng*, or 'rectification of [unorthodox] tendencies' campaign, used at Yenan in the early 1940s as a means of thought reform and ideological control within the Party – into an instrument for manipulating state policy. That year saw the first top-level purge since he had assumed the Party leadership, twenty years before: the Manchurian leader, Gao Gang, and eight other high Party officials were overthrown. A few months afterwards Mao launched an assault on the intellectuals. Campaigns against the literary critic, Feng Xuefeng, and the poet and essayist, Hu Feng, stamped out heterodoxy and laid the basis for the cultural sterility of the 1960s and 70s.

Mao decreed at Yenan that art must serve the workers, peasants and soldiers, by which he meant in fact that art must serve the Party. Hu Feng demanded that writers have the freedom to write as they wished. When the campaign reached its climax, in the summer of 1955, he was declared to be the leader of a counter-revolutionary clique and arrested with ninety-two of his supporters.[32] Mao personally wrote in the *People's Daily*:

> Hu Feng's elements who have appeared in disguise are counter-revolutionaries . . . They were regarded just as cultural figures in the past, but this is . . . wrong. Their members sneaked into various departments, such as the political, military, economic, cultural and education departments . . . Their basic ranks include special agents of imperialism and the Guomindang, Trotskyites, reactionary military officers or traitors to the Communist Party. A counter-revolutionary faction and an underground independent kingdom have been set up in the revolutionary ranks with these people as the backbone elements. The task of this counter-revolutionary faction and underground kingdom is to overthrow the People's Republic of China and restore the rule of imperialism and the Guomindang.[33]

Not one word of this was true. Hu Feng and his friends were poets, with purely literary concerns. But it served Mao's purposes to paint them as black as he could, in a technique derived from Lenin and Stalin at which he became supremely skilled.

What should have been an academic debate was made the pretext for a reign of terror, in which 2,100 people were implicated, and many committed suicide.[34] Yet it did not completely destroy creative independence, and Mao's objective of subordinating art to politics was still not entirely achieved. That came two years later, when, in the wake of the '100 Flowers', the short-lived period of liberalism and tolerance which followed de-Stalinisation in 1956, Mao reasserted the primacy of the Party through the anti-rightist campaign.

From June 1957 to March 1958, 400,000 intellectuals were labelled as 'rightists' and sent to the countryside to re-mould themselves through manual labour. Most remained there three years, but their labels were never removed, and when the Cultural Revolution began in 1966 they were sent back to the countryside under much harsher conditions. The writer Xiao Chen, educated at King's College, Cambridge, was sent with his wife and children to a remote part of Hubei province. There they were given bricks and wood and told to build themselves a house and live on what they could grow. Their daughter, aged fourteen, could not endure the back-breaking labour and became mentally ill. Years later it was officially admitted that more than ninety-five per cent of those accused of being rightists for allegedly opposing the Party had been wrongly condemned.[35] But in the meantime the resistance of the intellectuals had been smashed.

To Bai Hua, then one of the youngest victims of the anti-rightist campaign, it was 'the watershed – the harbinger of the Cultural Revolution', a foretaste of the ferocity to come. Xiao Chen compared the two by quoting a cruelly barbed proverb: 'The man who has no shoes complains until he meets the man who has no feet.'

Both Stalin and Mao at this point in their respective careers – 1929 for Stalin, 1958 for Mao – launched dramatic programmes for the transformation of their countries' economies.

The Soviet Union underwent collectivisation, and 'crash industrialisation'. The Five Year Plan was to be completed in four years – even, at one stage, in three; coal production was to triple, oil production to increase four times, iron ore mining, five. 'We are fifty to a hundred years behind the advanced countries,' Stalin said. 'We must make good this distance in ten years.' In the countryside, fifty per cent of the peasantry were collectivised in seven weeks in the spring of 1930.

The Chinese equivalent was the Great Leap Forward. In fifteen years – later in four years – China was to overtake Britain; in one year, grain and steel production were to double. In six weeks virtually the entire agricultural population, 122 million peasant families, was brought into the communes.

In both countries these *Sturm und Drang* tactics were preceded by assurances, made under conservative pressure, that cautious and gradualist policies would be followed. In both countries, the results proved catastrophic, and within months Stalin and Mao were blaming low-level officials for 'excesses'. The situation was worst in the Soviet Union, where the peasants killed their livestock and refused to carry out the spring sowing. By June 1930, Stalin's policy lay in ruins, and most of the peasants had been permitted to leave the collectives and farm on their own again. In China, in December 1958, the Central Committee likewise sounded the retreat, and it was announced that the following year Mao would step down as Head of State in favour of Liu Shaoqi.

But while both Stalin and Mao were much weakened politically, in neither case did their opponents seize the initiative and move on to the attack: instead, in this time of crisis, the Party closed ranks behind them. In July 1930, Tomsky, the trade union leader, and in December, Rykov, who had succeeded Lenin as Premier, were expelled from the Politburo, which became henceforward a purely Stalinist body. In August 1959, the Chinese Defence Minister, Marshal Peng Dehuai, was dismissed for having criticised the Great Leap and replaced by the colourless Maoist, Lin Biao.

In the Soviet Union, Stalin's reaction to his initial failure was to return to the task with even greater ruthlessness. By the end of 1932, collectivisation was three-quarters completed – at staggering cost. Lev Kopelev was one of the young idealists who enforced the Party's will:

With the rest of my generation, I firmly believed that the end justified the means. Our great goal was the universal triumph of communism, and for the sake of that goal everything was permissible – to lie, to steal, to destroy hundreds of thousands and even millions of people, all those who were hindering our work or could hinder it, everyone who stood in the way . . .

That was how I had reasoned, and everyone like me, when . . . I saw what 'total collectivisation' meant – how they 'kulakised' and 'de-kulakised', how mercilessly they stripped the peasants in the winter of 1932–3. I took part in this myself, scouring the countryside, searching for hidden grain, testing the earth with an iron rod for loose spots that might lead to buried grain. With the others, I emptied out the old folks' storage chests, stopping my ears to the children's crying and the women's wails. For I was convinced that I was accomplishing the great and necessary transformation of the countryside . . .

In the terrible spring of 1933 I saw people dying from hunger. I saw women and children with distended bellies, turning blue, still breathing but with vacant lifeless eyes. And corpses – corpses in ragged sheepskin coats and cheap felt boots; corpses in peasant huts, in the melting snow of old Vologda, under the bridges of Kharkov . . . I saw all this and did not . . . curse those who had sent me to take away the peasants' grain in the winter, and in the spring to persuade the barely walking, skeleton-thin or sickly-swollen people to go into the fields in order to 'fulfil the Bolshevik sowing plan in shock-worker style'.[36]

Collectivisation brutalised the Soviet Party, preparing the way for the terror three years later. Stalin told Churchill at the end of the Second World War that 10 million kulaks had been dealt with, of whom the great majority had been 'wiped out'. In the post-collectivisation famine, three million died in the Ukraine alone – not because the harvest was bad, but because state procurements of grain were increased by forty-four per cent; while the people starved, nearly two million tons of grain annually were exported to finance the crash industrialisation pro-gramme.

Pol Pot, in Kampuchea, exported rice in 1977 and 1978 while the Khmer nation gnawed roots and grasses; in the three-and-a-half years of his rule, one million people – one in seven of the population – died. In Soviet Kazakhstan, during Stalin's collectivisation drive, one person in five died.

But it was in China that the most devastating famine of all occurred. As Mao and the other leaders whipped up a 'wind of communism', local officials demanded that the peasants achieve impossible yields. In some areas rice was planted so close together that it would support the weight of a child. In the expectation of a miraculous harvest, the country was urged to eat its fill; people discussed what they would do with all the surplus grain. But the rice died; the granaries stood empty; and then came a calamitous drought. Proportionate to China's population, the death toll was lower than in the Soviet Union or Kampuchea. In absolute terms it has been exceeded only once this century, by all the dead of every country involved in the Second World War. From 1959 to 1962, 20 million Chinese died of starvation or related diseases, 10 million of them in 1960 alone, despite a draconian rationing system under which most people were permitted a maximum of 125 grams of grain a day.[37] The disaster, said Liu Shaoqi, in a speech castigating Mao in 1962, was 'seventy per cent man-made, and thirty per cent due to natural causes'.

No Chinese Kopelev has chronicled the agony of the peasantry in those years. A wallposter at the time described how 'the people, their faces and legs swollen with hunger, are eating wild plants and leaves'. In some villages cases of cannibalism were reported. In the labour camps, men ate worms and undigested grains of wheat they found in horse manure.[38]

In name the commune system was kept intact, but in reality it was greatly modified and in the poorest areas, at Liu Shaoqi's urging, individual families were for a time allowed to farm on their own.

The effects of the Great Leap on industry were equally disastrous. Unlike Stalin's crash industrialisation drive, which, costly and wasteful though it was, did in the main succeed, China's backyard furnaces did not. The iron they produced was unusable, and they consumed so much of the country's coal supply that railway engines had to run on wood shavings. When supplies of iron ore ran out, recalled Albert Belhomme, an American working in a factory in Jinan:

> Members of the street committees went from house to house confiscating pots and pans, ripping up iron fences, and even tearing locks off doors. When people complained, they were told that their utensils were unnecessary, since they would soon be eating in communal mess halls . . . They tore the radiators out of our shop at the paper mill and melted them down.[39]

The belief that the human will could triumph over material and natural laws was raised to the heights of lunacy. All over China, machines were ruined by being run at twice and three times their maximum permitted speed. Whole factories came to a standstill. And the chaos was compounded by the Soviet Union's decision to repatriate thousands of technicians and stop work on 160 aid projects at the start of the Sino-Soviet split.

By the time the madness passed, Chinese industry was so laid waste that not until 1963 did production regain the level of 1957.

Twenty million workers – nearly half the industrial workforce – were laid off and resettled in the countryside, because the towns could supply neither food nor work.[40] They were promised that when the economic situation improved they would be allowed to return – but the promise was never kept. And even in these conditions, the political movements did not end.

In 1959, after the disgrace of Peng Dehuai, there was a campaign against right-opportunism; in 1963, a so-called Socialist Education Movement in the countryside; and in 1964, the 'Four Clean-ups' campaign, to restore ideological discipline after the famine. In one province, Gansu, more than 80,000 people were purged in these movements, suggesting a national total of four million victims.[41]

The Great Purge and the Cultural Revolution

By 1934, Stalin in the Soviet Union, and by 1954, Mao in China, both found themselves blocked by their Politburo colleagues.

That February Stalin presided over the Seventeenth Party Congress, called the 'Congress of Victors'. Collectivisation had been accomplished; the crash industrialisation drive had been scaled down and was succeeding. Stalin's slogan was, 'Life has become better, comrades, life has become more joyous.' Now that the worst seemed over, his fellow leaders hoped to revert to more normal methods of rule. Already in 1932 and 1933, Stalin's efforts to arrest and execute political opponents had been blocked by more moderate elements, including the Georgian, Ordzhonikidze, the Leningrad leader, Kirov, and the Soviet President, Mikhail Kalinin. At the Seventeenth Congress, in 1934, there was talk of Kirov coming to Moscow and of Stalin delegating some of his power.

Nine months later Stalin contrived Kirov's murder, providing himself with the pretext he needed to set in motion the machinery of the purge trials. Kamenev and Zinoviev were shot in 1936. Tomsky and, later, Ordzhonnikidze, committed suicide. Bukharin, Rykov and four more Politburo members were shot in 1938 – and with them more than a million less exalted citizens. By 1939, the year of the Eighteenth Party Congress, Stalin had achieved his objective: his power had been made absolute and the Party had been enslaved. The terrible amalgam of cult-worship and police terror by which he would rule Russia until his death was firmly in place.

Mao suffered a far graver reverse as a result of the Great Leap Forward. He lost much of his power, and in the early 1960s was little more than a figurehead. For the sake of unity, the Party had rallied to him against the challenge made by Peng Dehuai. But Mao had not had enough support to purge Peng completely, as he had Gao Gang, four years earlier; although disgraced, Peng remained a member of the Politburo, and as the full effects of the famine and the industrial disruption became clear, Mao's colleagues openly acknowledged that the old Marshal had been right.

In April 1959, Liu Shaoqi took over as head of state, and thereafter he also oversaw the work of the Central Committee; Deng Xiaoping, as General Secretary, ran the Party secretariat; Zhou Enlai was in charge of the government. Apart from the Party's Military Commission, headed by Mao's ally, Lin Biao, all the levers of power had been taken out of his hands.

Had Mao's colleagues used their power to follow policies of which he approved, all might have been well. But they did not. Instead, they reverted to the cautious, pragmatic programmes of the mid-1950s, which Mao later characterised as 'taking the capitalist road'. All his attempts to put China on a more radical, revolutionary course were ignored or turned aside. 'They treated me with the respect they would have shown their dead father at his own funeral,' he said afterwards – and by January 1965, he decided they would have to go. The method he used was, as always, the political movement; his weapons were those Stalin had chosen, three decades before: cult-worship and mass terror.

If I have dwelt on the similarities between Stalin's progress from the 1920s to the Great Terror, and Mao's from the 1950s to the Cultural Revolution, rather than the differences – Stalin and Mao were, after all, very different personalities, and China and the Soviet Union are very different countries – it is not to imply that the one was simply a mechanistic repetition of the other. Mao would have launched the Great Leap Forward and the Cultural Revolution, or something very like them, regardless of Stalin's experience. In a sense he did so, by refusing to heed the warning of Khrushchev's Secret Speech, which, a full decade before the Cultural Revolution, had exposed the consequences of such policies for all who had eyes to see.

Mao's view of de-Stalinisation was dominated from the start by his perception of the parallel between Stalin's position and his own. The Sino-Soviet split had many causes, chief among them the nationalisms of China and Russia. But there was a sort of symmetry in its beginnings: when Khrushchev rejected Stalin, Mao – Stalin's Chinese counterpart – rejected Khrushchev. As the years passed, Mao's assessment of 'revisionism' at home (Liu Shaoqi's departures from his own policies), which led to the Cultural Revolution, and his assessment of 'revisionism' in Moscow (Khrushchev's departures from Stalin's policies), which led to the Sino-Soviet split, became inextricably linked. Much of the theoretical basis for the Cultural Revolution was first elaborated in polemics with Moscow, and when the revolution finally began, Liu Shaoqi was labelled 'China's Khrushchev', to imply that he had tried to do to Mao what Khrushchev had done to Stalin.

The constant agonising over the Stalin question was reflected in

Chinese pronouncements throughout that decade. The first author-itative commentary on the Secret Speech, in the *People's Daily* on April 5th, 1956, was at pains to defend Mao from any imputation of Stalin's errors. 'Stalin made the mistake of exaggerating his own role to an inappropriate proportion,' it said, but it would be 'utterly wrong to deny the role of the individual, the role of forerunners and leaders'.

In August 1956 Mao warned against uncritically copying de-Stalinisation. But other Chinese leaders, notably Liu, Peng Dehuai and the Mayor of Peking, Peng Zhen, insisted that a lesson must be drawn. In September, the new Party constitution dropped references to Mao Zedong Thought, which had been inserted in 1945, and included a statement that 'no political party or person can be free from short-comings and mistakes'. Presenting the new constitution at the Eighth Party Congress, Deng Xiaoping reported:

> It is obvious that it is against the principle of the establishment of a communist party to have important issues decided by one person. It will certainly lead to mistakes . . . In essence, our affection for the leader should be expressed through our concern for the interests of the Party, the class and the people, and not the deification of the individual . . . The Party Central Committee has always opposed the . . . exaggeration of the role of leaders in literary and artistic works. Of course the personality cult is a social phe-nomenon of long historical standing and we just cannot help having certain manifestations of it in our Party and social life. Our task is to persist in the Party Centre's opposition to giving prominence to and eulogising the individual.

Mao's sensitivity to these moves was shown during the Cultural Rev-olution, when Liu and Deng were fiercely criticised for having tried to downgrade him at the Eighth Congress. But while Mao tried to defend Stalin (and hence, indirectly, himself), he did not deny that the Soviet leader had faults: 'Seventy per cent good, thirty per cent bad', in his judgment. He went on to ask which were the weak links in the system which had allowed those faults to develop and how they could be reformed.

His conclusions were set out in a major speech, 'On the Correct Handling of Contradictions among the People', in February 1957, which explored the question of how to manage the conflict between rulers and ruled under a communist system. To the American academic, Benjamin Schwartz, it was 'a vision of totalitarianism by consent'. Isaac Deutscher called it 'by far the most radical repudiation of Stalinism' produced by any communist country. Yet it remained a vision. When Mao tried to put it into practice later that year under the slogan, 'Let a hundred flowers bloom, let a hundred schools of thought contend!', it produced such an outpouring of pent-up frustration from China's intellectuals that within weeks he reversed course and launched the anti-rightist campaign. To preserve his aura of infallibility, he claimed that it had been from the start a trap, an 'open plot' to lure 'the demons and hobgoblins out of their lairs . . . [in order] to wipe them out better'. But Mao's colleagues, and the Party, knew better.

Efforts to strengthen the rule of law and to democratise the leadership system were also made at this time in response to de-Stalinisation (and, twenty years later, would be replicated by Mao's successors as they grappled with de-Maoisation). When, in December 1958, Mao announced that he would step down as head of state, it was not simply a response to the failings of the Great Leap. His decision had been disclosed within the Party ten months before, and had originated in 1956, when he had decided gradually to withdraw from active leadership to let Liu, Deng and other younger leaders acquire experience, so that they would not act after his death as Stalin's successors had done. As he explained later,

> For the sake of state security and in view of the lessons in connection with Stalin of the Soviet Union, we created the first front and the second front. I was with the second front, while other comrades were with the first front.
> I wanted to have their prestige established before I died, but I had not expected that things would turn out the other way.[1]

In the event, none of Mao's efforts to draw positive lessons from de-Stalinisation turned out as he had hoped, and one by one they were abandoned as he reverted to what was, in effect, a neo-Stalinist course.

In 1937, as a means of justifying the blood purges, Stalin propounded the theory that class struggle becomes ever sharper. 'The greater our progress,' he said, 'the fiercer the remnants of the defeated exploited classes become . . . and the more desperate their methods of struggle.' In 1956, Mao repudiated this doctrine. Class struggle was 'basically over', he said. 'We should not follow Stalin's example in continuing to stress the intensification of class struggle after the elimination of classes.' But by 1962, Mao was urging the Party to 'emphasise class struggle every day, every month and every year'. By 1966 the wheel had gone full circle. Mao said, paraphrasing Stalin: 'The deeper the socialist revolution, the greater [the] resistance, and the more . . . anti-Party and anti-socialist inclinations are exposed.' Where in 1956 Mao had acknowledged that 'Stalin indulged more and more in the personality cult and violated the democratic centralism of the Party', ten years later he argued, ostensibly apropos of Stalin, but also of himself: 'The so-called "opposition to the personality cult" is against Lenin's complete teaching concerning the relationship among the leader, the political party, the class and the masses. It is sabotaging the Party's principle of democratic centralism.'

In 1934, during the build-up to Stalin's terror, decrees were passed setting up the NKVD Special Board, which, without reference to the courts, could impose a term of imprisonment nominally limited to five years, but often in practice longer. In 1957, during the anti-rightist campaign, China enacted legislation authorising the police to send people to re-education camps for an indefinite term by administrative decision.

After Kirov's murder, in December 1934, normal legal procedures were suspended. The so-called 'Terror Decree', drafted by Stalin, directed the NKVD to speed up the investigation of cases involving terrorist activity, and authorised the immediate execution, without possibility of pardon, of all those convicted. After 1937, the courts were frequently replaced by 'Troikas', consisting of the local Party first secretary, an NKVD official and a prosecutor, which sentenced hundreds of thousands to death without reference to any written law. In China, during the Cultural Revolution, legal safeguards were also suspended. A 'Six-Point Regulation on Public Security Work' was drawn up, under which anyone who maligned Chairman Mao or Lin Biao, who uttered a 'reactionary slogan' or wrote a 'counter-revolutionary letter or poster', was to be treated as an 'active counter-revolutionary' and imprisoned or shot.[2]

During the Great Terror of 1937–38, the NKVD operated on a quota system. A telegram from the NKVD chief, Yezhov, the 'bloodthirsty dwarf', to the regional NKVD office in Frunze, Soviet Kirghizia, stated: 'You are charged with the task of exterminating 10,000 enemies of the people. Report results by signal.' The reply was a numbered list of those who had been shot. One small town in Siberia, ordered to liquidate 500 'enemies', could not find enough, and NKVD officers had to shoot priests and their relatives to make up the number.[3]

During the Cultural Revolution – and other political movements – the *People's Daily* later admitted, 'we often arbitrarily fixed a certain ratio for allocating punishments. To "make up the number", some people were wrongly punished.'[4]

The terms 'enemy of the people' and 'active counter-revolutionary' were coined for the same purpose: they placed those to whom they were applied outside the law and the normal protection of society.

Yet most of Stalin's 'enemies' were shot, whereas most of Mao's 'counter-revolutionaries' survived. Relative to population, twenty times more Russians died from political violence when Stalin was in power than Chinese under Mao. From 1934 to 1939, more than seventy per cent of the Soviet Central Committee were shot, many after terrible tortures. In China, in the 1960s, a similar proportion of Central Committee members were denounced as 'enemy agents', 'renegades', 'elements having illicit relations with foreign countries' or 'anti-Party elements', but fewer than five per cent perished.[5]

These are substantial differences and they should not be underrated. If Chinese were as severely traumatised by the Cultural Revolution as Russians were by the Terror, it was not because of a comparable death toll. It was because, in China, an entire nation was made the instrument of its own terror: no one was immune. Yet the parallels with the Stalinist police state are compelling, as the Chinese themselves have acknowledged since Mao's death. 'History is a mirror,' wrote *Guangming Ribao*. 'We made similar mistakes to those made by Comrade Stalin. We even reached the limit in making this kind of mistake.'[6]

From September 1963 to July 1964, China published a series of open letters to the Soviet Party, known as the 'Nine Comments'. They are the most comprehensive indictment of revisionism that Mao ever put forward, and are written from an uncompromisingly radical, leftist stand. As the 'Comments' were presented as a denunciation of Soviet and Yugoslav heresies, they seemed to have little connection with China's own internal policies, and gradually the leftist political programme they outlined, still masked by its foreign-policy wrapping, won widespread acceptance.

Mao first attempted to apply these ideas within China in January 1965, by turning the 'Four Clean-ups' movement into a full-blown campaign against 'capitalist-roaders'. This move, like Mao's earlier efforts to radicalise Party policy, was quickly headed off by Liu Shaoqi and the Party *apparat*, so convincing him, he later told Edgar Snow, that Liu would have to be overthrown.

Mao's next try was more successful. At a Politburo standing committee meeting the following September, he renewed his oft-repeated claim that Chinese writers and artists were showing revisionist tendencies, and called for a 'Cultural Revolution' to correct them. At first it seemed that, like so many of Mao's schemes, it would be blunted by the Party and harmlessly fizzle out. But in November, the Shanghai newspaper, *Wen Hui Bao*, published an article entitled, 'A Criticism of the New Historical Play, *Hai Rui Dismissed from Office*', by an obscure journalist named Yao Wenyuan, later a Politburo member and one of the so-called 'Gang of Four'. Mao regarded *Hai Rui*, which described the wrongful dismissal of an upright official in the Ming dynasty, as a veiled attack on his own dismissal of Peng Dehuai, and the article, which he personally revised, denounced the work as a 'poisonous weed'. The content, however, was less important than the target. The play had been written by Wu Han, a Vice-Mayor of Peking, and had been published with the blessing of Peng Zhen. It was on Peng Zhen that Mao had set his sights.

'A Criticism of *Hai Rui*' proved to be the opening salvo of the Cultural Revolution. It was supported by the *Liberation Army Daily*, under the control of Mao's ally, Lin Biao, and eventually reprinted by the *People's Daily* and most other newspapers. Wu Han made a self-criticism at the end of December, but it was not enough, and by February 1966 Peng Zhen was prepared to sacrifice him. That was not enough either: a month later Peng Zhen himself appeared in public for the last time.

Mao was able to parlay a charge as flimsy as permitting the publication of a doubtful play into the purge of one of the most powerful men in the Politburo for essentially two reasons. One was the failure of Peng's colleagues to defend him. The other was the support he had from the armed forces under Lin Biao, whose last serious opponent in the high command, the Chief of the General Staff, Luo Ruiqing, had just been removed.

Luo's overthrow was brought about in typical Maoist fashion. Relying on factional loyalty, Lin persuaded the airforce commander, Wu Faxian, and the navy commissar, Li Zuopeng, to fabricate evidence that Luo had tried to usurp the army command. This was then presented to the Politburo and the Military Commission, where 'Comrades [Liu] Shaoqi, [Zhou] Enlai and [Deng] Xiaoping did not take a stand on Wu Faxian's claims'.[7]

This was to be the standard pattern for the years that followed: Mao and his supporters would trump up charges – 'Chairman Mao's tricks', as Deng Xiaoping later called them; those who disagreed would signify their dissent by keeping silent. Whether on policy or personality issues, they would never stand up and confront Mao directly. Had they done so over Luo Ruiqing, or even over Peng Zhen, the Cultural Revolution might have been averted, and Mao forced into embittered retirement. But at each new test they tried to save, and, in some cases, advance their own positions by sacrificing others, until eventually they were sacrificed themselves. Stalin's victims, in the years leading up to the Great Terror, had done exactly the same.

Luo was also accused of participating, with some of Peng Zhen's supporters, in a spurious plot to surround Peking with troops in preparation for a military coup, the so-called 'February Mutiny'. On March 18th, he tried to commit suicide. Ten days later Mao for the first time denounced Peng Zhen by name. On April 3rd Luo was dismissed, and three weeks afterwards formal criticism of Peng began within the Party.

With the ideological rectification campaign growing shriller and more heated, Liu and his conservative supporters were now placed on the defensive. To raise the temperature still further, Mao's cult was vigorously promoted. At an enlarged Politburo meeting on May 18th, Lin Biao warned:

> Mao Zedong is our Party's greatest leader, and his every word sets a standard for our movement. The whole Party will settle scores with those who oppose him, the whole Party will criticise them. Mao Zedong has done a great deal more than Marx, Lenin or Engels . . . Mao Zedong is the greatest man in our country and in the whole world.

The same meeting approved the so-called 'May 16 Circular', drafted by Mao, which called for criticism of all the 'representatives of the bourgeoisie who have infiltrated into the Party, the government, the army and cultural circles'. It added, threateningly:

> Some of them we have already seen through. Others we have not. Some are still trusted by us and are being trained as our successors – persons like Khrushchev, for example, who are still nestling beside us.[8]

The circular was of crucial importance because it broadened the scope of the movement from culture alone to the whole range of Party and state activity. With hindsight, it is hard to understand how Liu Shaoqi and the others could have endorsed a directive so laden with menace for their own positions. But at the time it may have seemed no more than a logical response to the purging of Luo Ruiqing and Peng Zhen. For no one then realised how far Mao was prepared to go in destroying the Party and his own closest colleagues in order to put China back on what he regarded as an ideologically correct path. It was not until six weeks later that Liu told his family he believed Mao was fomenting a 'big split' in the country.[9] By then it was too late. Mao's trap was already sprung.

Even before the May 18th meeting, on Mao's instructions, the secret police chief Kang Sheng, sent a 'Central theoretical investigation group' to Peking University, with orders to 'kindle the flames'.[10] On May 25th, at the urging of this group, a woman lecturer named Nie Yuanzi put up a wallposter attacking 'bourgeois representatives' on the university Party committee. A week later, Mao praised it as 'China's first Marxist-Leninist big-character poster', and ordered it broadcast by Radio Peking to spread the gospel of radical insurrection to universities throughout the country. Liu repeatedly asked Mao for instructions; but the Chairman, ensconced in his retreat in Hangzhou, 'refused to give clear answers'. When, in June, Liu and Deng Xiaoping flew down to invite him to take personal charge of the movement, he again refused and told Liu to deal with it 'as he saw fit'.

The situation was now rapidly deteriorating. In one incident, at Peking University,

> Over 60 cadres were crowned with tall paper hats, their faces smeared with ink and big-character posters attached to them. They were forced to kneel and their hair and clothes were torn to pieces. They were beaten up, paraded through the university and struggled against. What was more disgusting was that hooliganism occurred in which women comrades were insulted.
>
> [Elsewhere] more and more people became the target of struggle, and the means of struggle became worse. In some schools, people were beaten to death. Some committed suicide because they did not understand what was happening.[11]

The choices before Liu Shaoqi were either to go along with this radical upsurge, as Zhou Enlai was to do, leaving himself defenceless against the radicals' attacks; or to send in Party work teams to control the movement, which would render him liable to accusations of ordering its suppression.

In the end, he sent in work teams. Mao waited a month for sufficient evidence to accumulate that Liu had mismanaged the movement, and then plunged back into the political fray, signalling his return by swimming the Yangtse. Back in Peking for the first time in four months, he accused Liu and Deng of suppressing the student masses.

'Some people,' Mao said ominously, 'talk about the mass line, talk about serving the people every day, but they actually follow a capitalist line and serve the bourgeoisie.'[12]

Shortly after this the work teams were abolished and the Red Guards brought into being, created by the same technique as Nie Yuanzi's poster. A letter from a group formed 'spontaneously' at Qinghua University was endorsed by Mao and given nationwide publicity to serve as a model for youths all over China.

On August 1st, the Central Committee met in plenary session. Against a background of huge rallies and inflammatory editorials in the

People's Daily, now controlled by Chen Boda, Mao denounced his opponents:

> Some leading comrades from the central down to the local levels . . . have enforced bourgeois dictatorship and struck down the surging movement of the Great Cultural Revolution of the proletariat. They have stood facts on their heads and juggled black and white, encircled and suppressed revolutionaries, stifled opinions differing from their own, imposed a white terror and felt very pleased with themselves. They have puffed up the arrogance of the bourgeoisie and deflated the morale of the proletariat. How poisonous they are![13]

By a narrow majority, the Committee approved the nomination of Lin Biao as Mao's sole deputy, and downgraded Liu Shaoqi, Zhou Enlai, Zhu De and Chen Yun from vice-chairmen to ordinary Politburo members. Liu was further demoted from second to eighth place in the ranking order. A 'Decision on the Great Proletarian Cultural Revolution', passed on August 8th, set out the methods of struggle to be used and identified their main target: 'Those persons in authority taking the capitalist road.'

Over the next two years, China was torn apart as Mao pursued his twin objectives of recapturing nationwide power and 'large-scale struggle to transform men'. The radical political programme which he had embedded in the 'Nine Comments' against Moscow in 1963–64 was unveiled as a charter for China itself. All those who had previously opposed him were criticised, struggled against, disgraced or driven to death.

The treatment of Liu Shaoqi set the pattern for many others. At first he was allowed to remain with his family at his official residence in Zhongnanhai. Although stripped of influence, he was still head of state and a member of the Politburo. At the end of November, wallposters began attacking Liu by name. At midnight on January 13th, Mao summoned him to a meeting in the Great Hall of the People, at which Liu made a last attempt to retrieve the situation by offering to resign 'in order to end the Cultural Revolution quickly'. 'Chairman Mao muttered to himself, smoking furiously, and said nothing.'[14]

Two days later, their home was surrounded by 'revolutionary rebels'. The head of state and his wife, Wang Guangmei, were made to stand on a table, where they were harangued by Red Guards. Shortly afterwards, their telephone was cut off and all contact with other leaders severed. In July 1967, while they were being paraded before another Red Guard rally, Liu's residence was ransacked and searched for evidence against him, and he was separated from his family for the last time.

This marked the beginning of a year-long investigation to fabricate a case against Liu which would justify his expulsion from the Party. The method used was Stalinist: the application of torture to extract false testimony. At least four people died under interrogation in 1967 and early 1968 as the Special Case Group tried to prove that Liu had betrayed the Party during strikes in 1927 and 1929, and that Wang Guangmei, and hence Liu himself, had links with the US Strategic Intelligence Service. 'We must interrogate,' Jiang Qing was quoted as saying. 'If someone dies, let him die . . . They themselves want to die. The King of Hell has invited them to drink white spirit.'[15]

Three hundred Red Guards were sent to Manchuria to sift through 2,450,000 documents in the hope of uncovering evidence of Liu's supposed treachery when he served as secretary of the provincial Party committee there. Two veteran communists who worked with him in the 1920s, Meng Yongqian and Ding Juequn, were coerced into incriminating him, and when they tried to retract their 'confessions' were threatened with charges of counter-revolution. Another man, an illiterate policeman, was made to fingerprint a confession he had never seen.[16]

On October 13th, 1968, an enlarged plenum of the Central Committee, packed with Mao's supporters, met to consider Liu's crimes. The indictment, which labelled him a 'renegade, traitor and scab', was read out by Zhou Enlai. It was duly ratified, and Liu was expelled from the Party 'for ever'.

Within the leadership, only the ageing Zhu De and a veteran woman labour organiser named Chen Shaomin raised dissenting voices.[17] But in the country as a whole, more than 22,000 people were arrested as Liu's sympathisers. His cook, Hao Miao, was jailed for six years. A nightsoil collector, with whom Liu had been photographed shaking hands at a model workers' conference in 1959, was paraded through the streets with a placard round his neck and maltreated until he became deranged.[18]

Liu himself became seriously ill with pneumonia and diabetes. Orders were reportedly given that he be kept alive 'to serve as a living target for the Party's Ninth Congress', held the following April.[19] Once the Congress was over, however, Lin Biao issued instructions that all top-level political prisoners should be moved from Peking. Kept alive by a drip-feed, Liu was taken on a stretcher and flown secretly to Kaifeng, in Henan province, where he was held under heavy guard at an improvised prison in a former bank. Denied proper medical treatment, he died four weeks later, on November 12th, 1969, a few days short of his seventy-first birthday. His guards were kept in ignorance of his identity, and his cremation was carried out under a false name.[20] Such was the atmosphere of conspiracy that even his family was not told of his death until three years later.

At about this time, Lin Biao ordered the execution of Wang Guangmei, who had been detained at Qincheng Prison near Peking. But Mao countermanded it and she was spared.[21] Three of Liu's older children were also in prison or under house arrest, and one, a son by a previous marriage, had been killed by lying – or being tied – across a railway track. Of the younger children Yuanyuan, seventeen, was living rough in the countryside, supporting himself by selling his blood, while Tingting, fourteen, and Xiaoxiao, six, were apparently confided to the care of the local authorities.[22]

Other children of purged leaders spent five years in a residential 'study class' run by the Peking Public Security Bureau. According to an official account, they were made to haul carts weighing 1,000 kilos, kept constantly hungry, denied medical care, and 'forced to curse their own parents by name'.[23]

By 1972, these child prisoners were beginning to be freed, and late that year Liu's children were allowed for the first time to see their mother. A woman of unusual beauty, whose charm and sophistication had captivated such worldly men as President Sukarno of Indonesia, she was now 'unable to stand, her hair falling out and coughing up blood'. They broke the news to her, conveyed to them in a message from Mao a few days before, that her husband was dead.[24]

The fate of Tao Zhu, Party chief in Southern China who was appointed head of the Propaganda Department and promoted to fourth position in the leadership at the start of the Cultural Revolution, showed the same gratuitous cruelty.

With Peng Zhen, Liu and Deng Xiaoping, Tao was one of the four principal victims of the Cultural Revolution, and a chief target of Red Guard rallies and wallposters throughout the first half of 1967. He was arrested a few days after Liu and, like him, remained under guard at his home in Zhongnanhai for the next two years. In 1969, at the age of sixty-three, he was dying of cancer. When the order came for him to leave Peking, his wife was ordered to choose between accompanying him and cutting all ties with their daughter, or staying with the child and leaving him to die alone – on the grounds that no one could be permitted to know where he was being held.

Six weeks after they parted, Tao died in prison in Hefei. His body was cremated as a nameless corpse and his family refused permission to have his ashes.[25]

Deng Xiaoping, Party General Secretary and 'the No. 2 person in authority taking the capitalist road', was treated less harshly, apparently on Mao's personal instructions. Arrested at the same time as Tao Zhu, he was sent to a May 7 school in Jiangxi to do manual labour. But he, too, had his share of tragedy. His eldest son, Deng Pufang, a physics student, was thrown from a second-floor window at Peking University. As he was Deng's son, the other students were too frightened to come to his aid, so he lay there all day until a janitor moved him. Then no doctor was willing to operate. He survived, but was paralysed from the waist down.

Others fared worse. The Minister of the Coal Industry, Zhang Linzhi, a man of nearly sixty, was interrogated fifty-two times in thirty-three days. He was severely beaten and forced to wear a cast-iron hat weighing thirty kilograms at struggle meetings:

On January 21st, 1967, Zhang Linzhi was paraded at the Mining Institute campus and tortured until that night, when he died . . . The post mortem showed that he had a fractured skull, and 30 wounds on his body.

It was said later that he had been whipped to death.[26]

Marshal He Long, who as a boy of seventeen had commanded an army of several thousand peasants while Mao was still a library assistant, was arrested as a 'three-anti element – anti-Mao, anti-Party, anti-Mao Zedong Thought'. Instantly recognisable by his huge handlebar moustache, he was one of the most colourful of the early communist military leaders, bringing to the Party the flamboyance and panache of the outlaws and secret societies. In prison in Peking in 1969, his rations were reduced until he gnawed the cotton of his mattress in his hunger and caught rainwater to drink. He died that June.[27]

Marshal Peng Dehuai was placed under house arrest in Western Peking and confined to a darkened room whose one window had been pasted over with newspaper to prevent him seeing out.[28] He died in November 1974.

Liu Ren, Vice-Mayor of Peking and Political Commissar of the city garrison, was kept in handcuffs for five years. When his wife was permitted to visit him, 'she found all his clothing stained with blood, urine and excrement' from the tortures inflicted on him. He died in detention in 1973.[29] Tang Ping, a senior general attached to the Party's Military Commission, was tortured until he was unable to walk: at the time of his death, he weighed thirty kilograms – about the same as a Nazi concentration-camp victim.[30] Liao Mosha, an official of the Peking Party Committee, was jailed as a spy, and had all his teeth knocked out by prison guards.[31] Wang Kunlun, a leader of one of the small democratic parties, received similar treatment:

I was tied down and hit and kicked to the extent that my teeth were broken, my head swelled up and I could not walk. At the same time, all my family were persecuted. They not only considered my wife to be a 'spy', but also wanted falsely to accuse all my brothers and sisters and my daughter, Jinling, as 'spies' or suspected 'spies'. Even the third generation, my granddaughter, who was only 14 or 15 at that time, was not spared.[32]

In the 1930s, Stalin systematically liquidated Old Bolsheviks, particularly from his native Georgia, who knew too much about his past, or whose contributions had at one time exceeded his own. His purpose was to protect the myth of his unique wisdom, whose glorification formed the core of his personality cult.

For similar reasons, Mao's victims in the Cultural Revolution included many of his mentors and colleagues from the period before he became Party leader in 1935. Li Da, seventy-six, one of the twelve founder-members of the Party, died in Wuhan after being assaulted by Red Guards and denied hospital treatment. Li Lisan, sixty-eight, a fellow Hunanese whose policies dominated the Party from 1928–30, was arrested in June 1967 and died in detention six days later. His Russian-born wife spent the next eight years in prison. The underground Party organisations which had operated in the major cities, independent of Mao, in the 1930s and 1940s, were also attacked. In Canton 7,100 former members were accused of being 'renegades and spies', and eighty-five were killed.[33] In Shanghai, 3,600 were persecuted and four died. Nothing was to detract from Mao's aura as the sole architect of the Chinese revolution.

Even early communist martyrs were not spared. The first Party leader to organise the peasantry was not Mao but Peng Pai, in Guangdong province in 1924. Three years later Peng founded the first Chinese Soviet government, before being captured and executed by the Nationalists in 1929. In 1967, it was claimed that commemorating Peng's government was 'boycotting Mao Zedong Thought'. Books about Peng were confiscated, relics of his life destroyed, placenames changed, and his family subjected to what the *People's Daily* afterwards called, without hyperbole, 'truly shocking persecution':

Peng Hong, Comrade Peng Pai's son, died of persecution . . . The whereabouts of his body are not known even today. Peng Ke, Comrade Peng Pai's nephew, was beaten to death. His head was cut off with a knife and put on public show in the town centre for three days as a warning. Comrade Peng Pai's cousin was cruelly shot to death. His 95-year-old mother was secretly imprisoned and tormented to death. The rest of his relatives were all subjected to struggle or put in prison.[34]

Another veteran, the brilliant young guerrilla commander, Liu Zhidan, who secured the Shaanxi base area while Mao was on the Long March and was later killed at the age of thirty-four, became a non-person. His brother was imprisoned, and a woman who wrote a novel about his life was labelled an anti-Party element. One of the charges against her was that she had 'belittled and negated Chairman Mao' by writing that Liu had used the phrase, 'a single spark can start a prairie fire', two years before Mao first used it. In the ensuing campaign, several thousand people were criticised for alleged links with the book.[35]

This relentless thoroughness was common to Stalin and Mao. When Wu Han, who wrote the play which Mao used as a pretext to launch the Cultural Revolution, was imprisoned, not only did his family suffer – his wife died after being kept in a latrine without food, and their daughter committed suicide – but even the actors who performed the play were persecuted to death.[36]

The writer, Ding Ling, who herself spent five years of the Cultural Revolution in a 'cowshed' in solitary confinement, said later: 'Under the emperors, when a man was banished, all his relatives were banished with him up to the ninth degree. We communists have done better. It's not just your relatives – even your readers are punished if your books are found in their homes. Under the emperors, repression was limited to one area. If you could flee you would be safe. Under us there is no escape. Repression covers the whole country.'

Most of those Mao purged were imprisoned or killed for political reasons. But his wife, Jiang Qing, who found herself, for the first time, able to exercise almost unlimited power, often acted for purely personal ends.

Throughout the Cultural Revolution, she had a nagging fear that her enemies might uncover details of her Bohemian private life as a young actress in Shanghai in the 1930s. In October 1966, she ordered a secret search of the homes of a number of writers and actors she had known there, in case they had kept her letters and photographs. The operation was entrusted to an airforce unit and carried out with military precision in the early hours of the morning by a group of young men, travelling in unmarked lorries, disguised as Red Guards. The local authorities were kept in ignorance of the operation and promptly launched an investigation to try to discover the identity of the raiders. An internal Party report noted:

The special point of these people in ransacking these homes was that they only ransacked documents and cultural relics and nothing else. Their actions were secret . . . At a little past 0100 on 9 October, about 10 people, ranging from 25 to 30 years old, wearing 'Red Guard' armbands, entered the Wukang [apartment] building, locked the gate, placed the lift operator under their command and commandeered the telephone. Some went upstairs and entered the home of [the writer] Zheng Junli. These people moved and spoke softly . . . They made a very careful search, covering not only every corner but also the clothes and shoes Zheng was wearing. Their movements were very skilful. When they left they told Zheng not to tell anyone about the search or they would blow his head off . . .[37]

The proceeds of the searches were flown to Peking and a sackful of material, which Jiang Qing judged to be sensitive, was burnt in her presence by the Minister of Public Security, Xie Fuzhi, in a kitchen stove at Lin Biao's home. A year later, several of those searched were arrested. Two died in prison and a third, the film actor Zhao Dan, was held for five years as an 'enemy agent'.

In 1968, five students from the Peking Cinema Institute, who had gone to Shanghai to do research work on the art of the 1930s, were arrested on charges of 'collecting slanderous material on Jiang Qing'. They were imprisoned for five years. Sixty-two library workers who had helped them were also implicated. A former maid-servant, Qin Guizhen, who had befriended Jiang Qing in the 1930s, was jailed for seven years as a 'counter-revolutionary and anti-Party element' because she 'knew too much about her'. Another Shanghai acquaintance, a veteran Party official named Wang Shiying, was persecuted to death. According to *Da Gong Bao*, 'his family members were also persecuted and suffered grievously. Some lost their sanity while others died unjust deaths.' Even those who helped her cover up her past were imprisoned, to silence them.[38]

The combination of political campaign and personal vendetta, violently pursued at every level of the system, resulted in a purge of staggering dimensions. In Inner Mongolia, ninety per cent of senior officials in the Party, the government and the army were overthrown. The same proportion was purged among senior officials in Peking, and at all levels in the capital, one official in five was hauled out for investigation.[39]

Most of these men and women were sent to 're-mould themselves through labour' on farms in the countryside, under the surveillance of local officials. The top leaders, however, were, with few exceptions, detained in special prisons. Chief among these was Qincheng, a few miles north of the county town of Zhangping between Peking and the Great Wall, which held not only Wang Guangmei, but Peng Zhen, Vice-Premier Bo Yibo, the former head of the Propaganda Department

Lu Dingyi, and Li Lisan's wife, among others. An account of life there, compiled from interviews with prisoners' relatives, was published in 1979 by the unofficial magazine, *Tansuo (Exploration)*:

A covered walk-way leads [from the entrance] to the central section of the prison, [where] . . . there is an iron gate with two sentry boxes. Beyond, there is a broad, paved strip, with courtyards leading off on either side. On the east side, many new buildings were put up to cope with the increase in the number of prisoners during the Cultural Revolution. But on the west side, there are fruit trees growing . . . The architecture is pleasant, and with greenery all round it is a rather beautiful place . . .

The prison is directly under the jurisdiction of the Public Security Ministry, and even its existence is secret . . . The food allowance for prisoners is divided into four grades, costing from 40 to 8 yuan [£12 to £2.50] a month [and each prisoner receives a cash allowance of between 200 and 60 yuan (£60 and £18) a month] . . .

Each prisoner is kept in a separate narrow cell with a wooden bed, thin quilt, nightsoil pot and water-tap. One suit of prison uniform is provided in winter and another in summer . . . Favoured prisoners are allowed to borrow works by Marx, Engels, Lenin and Stalin, and to read the *People's Daily* . . . Each prisoner has an individual exercise-yard, partitioned off from the others. There are many irrational regulations. For instance, they must sleep facing the door . . . If a man turns over while asleep, the guard will wake him and make him turn back . . .

Prisoners are not allowed to speak to each other . . . Their only chance to talk is when they are being interrogated.[40]

According to *Tansuo*, prisoners were frequently beaten, and some subjected to electric shock treatment and sedation, though this is not confirmed by other sources. All accounts agree, however, that the most debilitating aspect of the special prisons was the total absence of physical activity. 'Physical labour would have been a luxury,' wrote a former guard at a special prison in Guangdong, 'but some did not even have the right to go out into the fresh air.'

The prison where he served, known as 'Office No. 31', was in a bare, mountainous region, 140 miles north of Canton. Those held there included several provincial Party secretaries.

It consisted of two ordinary-looking one-storey houses about 20 feet apart, one containing cells and the other the interrogators' living quarters built on a hillside. It was surrounded by a 10-foot high wall . . . topped by thick black wires. Outside was a rolling tea plantation, and beyond that, barren emptiness . . . The atmosphere was more severe than ordinary prisons. There were armed guards outside and, inside, a roving sentry . . . Everyone was kept in solitary confinement, and the lights in the cells were kept on all night.[41]

In 1975, when for a brief period the political climate eased, many of the provincial special prisons were closed and some of the prisoners at Qincheng, including Peng Zhen, were exiled to remote villages.

Even after their arrests, few, if any, of the senior Party leaders voiced open opposition to Mao. Like Stalin's victims, they played along by the rules. But lower down in the Party and outside it, a few Chinese did find the courage, or recklessness, to speak out.

A worker in Guizhou named Wu Zhenmou wrote to Jiang Qing: 'You put on a red cloak but commit murder. It seems you will not be happy until you have tortured all the Chinese people to death . . . You are all like wild beasts that have gone mad.' Wu was lucky: he was let off with fifteen years' imprisonment; the usual penalty was to be shot. Executions for such offences continued at least until December 1976, three months after Mao had died and Hua Guofeng succeeded him.[42]

The most notorious case was that of a forty-five-year-old woman official of the Liaoning Party Propaganda Department named Zhang Zhixin. Arrested as an 'active counter-revolutionary' in 1969 for criticising Mao's 'left-deviationist errors', she was sentenced to life imprisonment. Because she refused to recant, she was held in handcuffs and leg-irons weighing four and a half kilograms each, and confined for one year, six months and twenty-six days in a 'small cell', a cell so constructed that a prisoner could neither lie down in it nor stand upright, normally used for convicts awaiting execution and then for a maximum of ten days.

To 'deflate her arrogance' she was repeatedly taken to witness public executions. But she 'obstinately clung to her reactionary stand', and in 1975 the provincial Party leadership, which included Mao's nephew, Mao Yuanxin, resolved that she should be sentenced to death. On April 3rd, on the orders of the provincial first secretary, Chen Xilian, she was taken to the office of the prison discipline section. 'In the room were ten people, three of whom were dressed in the white robes of medical orderlies. On a desk was placed a medicine chest, with surgical knives, scissors and clamps arranged alongside. On the floor was a bucket of water, and in the centre of the room was a brick.' She was pinned to the ground, her head resting on the brick, and her windpipe cut to prevent her shouting revolutionary slogans at the execution ground. A stainless steel tube was inserted through the open wound in her throat so that she could breathe.[43]

Next morning she was made to watch two other prisoners being shot, and was then executed herself.

Such refinement of cruelty was not exceptional, even as late as 1975. The man who cut Zhang Zhixin's windpipe did the same to forty-eight other prisoners.[44] According to General Ren Zhongyi, the practice went back to the early years of the Party, when 'once a person was believed to be a class enemy, he lost any protection under the law and no act against him was regarded as excessive'.[45]

In Shanghai, in 1968, a young woman named Lin Zhao was shot for criticising Mao's cult. Afterwards, the police demanded that her aged mother pay them five fen (about a penny) to cover the cost of the bullet which had been 'wasted on a counter-revolutionary'. Others, placed under house arrest, were made to pay a 'dictatorship fee' to cover the wages of their guards.[46]

'In some socialist countries,' commented the Spanish Communist Party leader, Santiago Carillo, to an audience of Chinese officials in Canton a decade later, 'the political sectors of the superstructure remind people of fascism. Their manifestations are almost the same as fascism.'[47]

Stalin, in the 1930s, used to urge the Soviet people to 'scold' their leaders and criticise their mistakes. 'We must ensure,' he said, 'that leaders will not become conceited and self-important, and that they will never become isolated from the masses.' Mao's lip-service to the 'mass line' was equally hypocritical. The intrigues and ruthlessness of the Cultural Revolution were paralleled by policies which negated all the individuality of the Chinese people.

In the communes, the peasants' private plots were taken away, and they were limited to a maximum of one private fruit tree outside their houses, one private pig and four chickens. Following the lead of the Dazhai production brigade, headed by Chen Yonggui, the distribution of grain and workpoints was progressively equalised, so that a man earned the same whether he worked or not. In industry bonuses and overtime were banned. Private commerce was prohibited in the name of 'cutting off the tails of capitalism'. All over China tens of thousands of small family-run shops and restaurants closed.

Politics was held to be the key to everything. If a field of cotton withered and died, it was treated from a 'class viewpoint'. The correct response was not to buy pesticide, but to 'ferret out and struggle against a former landlord'.[48]

185

The slogans of the day urged, 'Better a socialist train that's late than a capitalist train that's on time'; 'We would rather have socialist weeds than capitalist seedlings'; and, to discourage private ownership of livestock, 'Don't let capitalist sheep eat the socialist grass!'

'Even the planets weren't allowed to overstep the class orbit,' *Guangming Ribao* wrote later. 'Otherwise, why should the nine planets revolve around the red sun?'[49]

For four years, all universities and secondary schools were closed. When they reopened, university entrance depended on political, not academic, criteria. Examinations were abolished, courses were shortened, and students spent up to three months a year on *kai men ban xue*, 'open door schooling', in which study was combined with manual labour in communes and factories, to ensure that they did not become divorced from 'the masses'. As a result, standards fell so precipitously that by the late 1970s they were on average four years below pre-Cultural Revolution levels: a sixteen-year-old had the knowledge of a twelve-year-old. It was hoped to catch up again by 1983.[50]

In Inner Mongolia, Tibet and Xinjiang, the use of minority languages was discouraged, local cultural troupes disbanded and customs suppressed. Tibet, in the 1950s, supported 2,000 Lamaist monasteries. By 1971, there were fewer than ten, and even they were closed to the public. Many, like the Gadan, the oldest of the three great monasteries of Lhasa, had been razed to the ground. In Kashgar, a devoutly Moslem city in the far west of Xinjiang, the number of mosques fell from 500 to four. The deputy director of the city's religious affairs bureau, Abdel Lahai, told me:

> During the Cultural Revolution, I saw with my own eyes, before the Great Mosque in Kashgar, piles of Korans and other books being burnt. Some people ordered the Moslems to burn these copies themselves. Some refused, and people rushed into their homes and took out the copies. I also saw people trying to pull down the minarets beside the Great Mosque. The masses were very indignant, but they could do nothing.

Other religions suffered even more. From 1966 to 1974, for a quarter of the world's population not one place of Buddhist or Christian worship remained open. At the holy mountains, Wutaishan and Emeishan, and in Peking, Shanghai, Xian, Kunming and other large cities, the temples were sacked and the sacred groves around them cut down and burnt. In many areas the destruction was systematic: in the name of destroying the 'Four Olds', Red Guards divided into groups, each assigned a particular task. Steles and statues were smashed with sledgehammers, sutras and Bibles burnt and frescos scrawled across with Maoist slogans. Today, most Chinese pagodas have their statuary broken off up to a height of eight feet, as far as a hand holding a hammer can reach.

In the iconoclasm that swept seventeenth-century Britain, Cromwell's troops used the churches as stables. In China, buildings of all religions were taken over as factories, warehouses or army stores.

Other monuments to the beauty and greatness of China's civilisation were also despoiled. Four of the eleven world-famous classical gardens at Suzhou were wholly or partly taken over by industrial plants. Large sections of the Great Wall – amounting to thirty miles in length near Peking alone – were pulled down by peasants and soldiers seeking building materials for housing and barracks.

The tombs of Confucius (symbol of traditionalism and feudal ideas) and of Genghis Khan (symbol of minority nationalism) were damaged, as were those of early communist leaders such as Wang Refei, whose ideas were no longer in tune with the new Maoist line. The same treatment was meted out to modern 'scholar-tyrants'. As a warning to others, the urn containing the ashes of a well-known zoologist, who died just before the Cultural Revolution, was 'removed from Babaoshan cemetery and smashed with a hammer. Petrol was poured over it and it was set on fire in front of a large gathering of scientists.'[51]

A few institutes engaged on military nuclear programmes were given special protection, but most intellectuals were made to spend several days a week on political study. Afterwards, for relaxation, there was only more politics.

Cultural life was totally devastated. All traditional stage performances were banned, and replaced by eight 'model revolutionary works' sponsored by Jiang Qing. All creative writing of any merit ceased, to give way to sterile political homilies. Pre-Cultural-Revolution novels and translations of foreign works were no longer sold. No new films at all were produced for six years, and when the studios did start working again, the ideological limits were so narrow that a film called *Pioneers*, on the theme, 'Thinking of Chairman Mao, the harder we work and the happier we feel', was banned for not giving politics sufficient prominence.[52]

Chess was denounced as 'a bourgeois pastime'. Stamp-collecting was counter-revolutionary. Keeping pets was bourgeois. Goldfish survived in China only because the children hid them under their beds, where they became so used to the dark that they would swim blindly into the walls of their jamjars if brought out into the light. The villages were plagued by rats, because all the cats and dogs had been killed. Even flower shops were closed for 'peddling revisionism' and, in public places, flowerbeds were pulled up and ornamental fruit trees cut down as 'bourgeois tails'.[53] In short, everything which gave colour, variety and amusement to life was summarily forbidden so that the Chinese people should have no distraction from 'making revolution'.

All over the country, groups of Red Guards went from house to house, searching the homes of 'doubtful elements'. Old books were seized and burnt, or, later, sent to be pulped at paper mills. One mill in a suburban county of Peking disposed of 2,000 tons of books. The total quantity destroyed in this way is not known, but the number recovered after the frenzy had subsided – representing only a small fraction of what had already been pulped – included two million rare and ancient volumes, some of which dated back to the Song dynasty.[54]

Intellectuals smashed their collections of antique porcelain in the knowledge that it would be smashed by the Red Guards anyway, and at least, by destroying it themselves, they would avoid the political stigma attached to its possession.

A few were more courageous, and caches of old books were later uncovered in the walls of houses demolished by the Tangshan earthquake. In the same way, 2,000 years earlier, Chinese intellectuals had hidden the Confucian classics to save them from the destruction decreed by Qin Shi Huang. By 1980, porcelain which had been buried at the start of the Cultural Revolution was being dug up again, and muddy pots and vases began to appear in commission shops.

The campaign against the 'Four Olds' showed another side of the leadership's hypocrisy. Mao buried himself in books of ancient Chinese history and philosophy. Kang Sheng amassed a collection of more than 40,000 works of art, seized by the secret police from shuttered-up museums and the homes of imprisoned intellectuals.[55] But for an ordinary person to possess an old book or an antique was a political crime.

The possession of a foreign book, or any 'foreign thing' was even more serious. If the Red Guards found it, the owner would be forced to crawl on his knees and be struggled against. Listening to a foreign radio station was punishable by imprisonment. 'The ability to speak a foreign language or a past visit to a foreign country became "evidence" of being a "secret agent" for that country,' a Chinese report said later. 'Filling in a registration form for foreign language translators was regarded as participation in a "secret agent organisation".'[56]

This obsessive fear of contact with the outside world not only had parallels with the hysterical anti-foreignism of the Soviet Union in the 1930s and late 40s, it was also consciously rooted in China's own history, as some of Mao's most extreme supporters acknowledged. In March

1967, the ultra-leftist Qi Benyu published an article entitled, 'Patriotism or National Betrayal?', attacking Liu Shaoqi, which implicitly compared the Red Guards with the Boxer rebels of 1905 and endorsed their xenophobia:

> Wearing red kerchieves, red belts and shoes trimmed with red lace, and holding big swords and spears, [the Boxers] had an awe-inspiring look . . . They changed the names of Dong Jiao Min Xiang Street to Slicing Foreigners Street, and the Imperial Moat Bridge to Stopping Foreigners Bridge. With the masses looking on during parades, the Boxers would often shout in unison, 'Kill the foreigners!' This sent cold shivers down the foreigners' spines . . . Among the Boxers, young people formed a most active and enthusiastic force and performed immortal feats in this great revolutionary movement.[57]

During the Boxer rebellion, the changing of street names reflected the Confucian doctrine that if a thing is named correctly, people will act accordingly. In 1967, in unconscious obedience to this tradition, Nandi Lu in the former Legation Quarter was renamed Anti-imperialist Street, and the road leading to the Soviet embassy became Anti-revisionist Lane.

That summer foreigners were subjected to constant petty harassment. Even long-time foreign sympathisers living in China were arrested as spies, and several diplomats were physically attacked. The climax came with the burning down of the British legation in August. After that the tide of hatred began to recede, but acquaintance with a foreigner was still enough for a Chinese to be arrested as a 'suspected enemy agent', and in 1970 a full-scale 'movement to criticise worshipping, admiring and relying on foreign things' was launched.[58] Two years later, a Chinese woman was detained by plainclothesmen for waving at the procession of cars bringing President Nixon on his first visit to Peking. She was released only after being able to prove that she had been waving to her niece, an interpreter assigned to the Nixon press corps.

The anti-foreign campaign weighed most heavily on Chinese with relatives abroad. They were said to form a 'reactionary social base', and were listed with landlords, rich peasants, counter-revolutionaries, bad elements, rightists and enemy agents as one of the 'seven kinds of sinister people'. The two southern provinces of Guangdong and Fujian, where most of the population has overseas connections, were labelled 'a United Nations of enemy agents', and in Guangdong, a 'Six-point Regulation' was issued, under which officials were forced to sign pledges that they would break off all contacts with relatives overseas.

Sending letters abroad was qualified as 'maintaining illicit relations with foreign countries'. In some areas, Chinese with 'overseas connections' were excluded from the Party, the Communist Youth League and the army, and even refused employment or permission to marry. Their houses were confiscated and bank accounts frozen. In Fujian, eight were tortured to death and 300 imprisoned as American spies.[59]

Dying Years

The Soviet Eighteenth Party Congress, which marked the formal ending of the Great Terror, was held in March 1939, as the clouds of war gathered across Europe. The Chinese Ninth Congress, in April 1969, at which Mao summed up the initial results of the Cultural Revolution, took place a month after Soviet and Chinese troops clashed on the Ussuri River.

In each country these external pressures brought radical changes in policy towards the West. In 1941 the Soviet Union reluctantly joined the Western alliance in the war against Germany (in which the Chinese communists also fought on the allied side, against Japan). In 1971 China inaugurated ping-pong diplomacy with the United States.

The Soviet Politburo which emerged from the Eighteenth Congress included Molotov, Mikoyan, Kaganovich, and two new faces, Nikita Khrushchev and Andrei Zhdanov. Lavrentii Beria, who had taken over from Yezhov as secret police chief, came in as an alternate member.

So long as the Soviet Union was fighting for its life, Stalin left his new team alone. But as the memory of the war receded, the terror, which had never completely ended, returned. In 1948, Zhdanov, considered a possible successor to Stalin, was sent abruptly into retirement, apparently because Stalin was jealous of his popularity. Soon afterwards he died, officially of a heart attack, triggering the so-called Leningrad Affair, a purge which decimated the Party apparatus of that city and led, in 1950, to the planning chief, Voznesensky, and several other Central Committee members being shot.

Three years later, in January 1953, after Georgi Malenkov had become heir-apparent, it was announced that Zhdanov had been murdered by a group of Jewish doctors in the Kremlin Hospital. Harrison Salisbury was then the *New York Times* correspondent in Moscow:

> I will be frank and say that the hair rose on the back of my neck when I read this statement and the editorial which accompanied it in *Pravda* . . . It was quite apparent that Russia stood on the brink of a reign of terror beside which that of the 30s would seem trivial . . .
>
> It took no analytic ability to see two obvious and immediate targets of this campaign. One was Beria, chief of the security services. The other was the

Jews . . . Each new batch of provincial newspapers that was brought into my office reported new scandals, new exposures, new arrests . . .

The target quickly broadened out. Khrushchev was involved, because his Party chiefs were being attacked . . . Mikoyan was involved deeper and deeper, because of the alleged scandals in the trade organisations. And Malenkov was dragged in, because in one city after another, his Party lieutenants were implicated.

But, most deeply and dangerously of all, was implicated that dry, pedantic little man who had survived so much before, Vyacheslav Molotov . . .

As February wore on, the terror deepened in Moscow. Every day the rumours circulated. There had been arrests in Tass, the news agency. The head of the agency, Palgunov, a man known for years to be very close to Molotov, had vanished . . . arrested. Madam Molotov (a Jewess) had disappeared . . . banished to Siberia . . . Arrests in Moscow University . . . Arrests in the Academy of Sciences . . . More Jews dismissed . . . Protectors of Jews arrested . . . Arrests in the Central Committee.

Who in the Politburo could feel safe by late February? No one, I thought. Not Molotov. Not Malenkov. Surely not Beria . . . There wasn't a safe name on the list.

And what of Stalin himself? In the pink of condition . . . Good health. Lively mind. That was the verdict of three foreigners who saw him in February . . .

Only Menon [the Indian ambassador] had one strange thing to report . . . Throughout the interview, the old man kept doodling wolves . . . And presently Stalin began to talk, too, about wolves. Russian peasants, he said, knew how to deal with wolves. They exterminated them.[1]

On March 5th, Stalin died in his bed after suffering a stroke, and the terror passed, like an evil dream.

The China which emerged from the travails of the 1960s was also a joyless, frightened country, clothed in shabbiness and political hypocrisy. 'It was almost normal,' Orwell had written in *1984*, 'for people over thirty to be frightened of their own children.' That was to be true until well after Mao's death.

Yet the limitless capacity of the Chinese to dissemble and deceive, to present only those fragments of China's truth that serve their interests, continued to work its spell on the small groups of privileged Westerners who were allowed to come and exclaim over Mao's new society. In 1960, when the Chinese population fell by 11 million due to famine deaths, Western students living in China had been prevented from seeing even one case of serious malnutrition. In August 1971, as experienced an observer as Robert Guillain told readers of *Le Monde* after an extensive tour of the country: 'No longer are there any traces today of the storms of yesterday. With that amazing gift of knowing how to heal and restore herself very rapidly, People's China of 1971 gives an impression of ease, order and peace.'[2]

Exactly one month later, Lin Biao was killed in a plane crash while fleeing to the Soviet Union, and Chinese officials began leaking stories of a sensational plot to assassinate Mao.

Lin had been confirmed by the Ninth Congress as Mao's deputy and successor, sharing membership of the Politburo Standing Committee with Zhou Enlai, Kang Sheng and Chen Boda. But, unlike the Soviet Union, where war enforced internal unity, the political intriguing in China did not stop. Within a year, Mao – like Stalin in 1948 – was worrying about his heir-apparent's power. When, in August 1970, Lin proposed at a Central Committee plenum in Lushan that the post of head of state be filled, phrasing the proposal in such a way as to make clear that he wanted it himself, Mao became convinced that his suspicions were justified: Lin was aiming to supplant him.

Mao was not necessarily correct in this. Lin might well have been prepared to remain head of state until Mao's death, without ever trying to seize supreme power. But having decided that he was a threat, Mao was not disposed to wait and find out. The proposal was rejected, and Mao began a long campaign to isolate Lin by picking off his supporters. The first to go was Chen Boda, 'placed under investigation' for ideological errors. Immediately afterwards, the personality cult, of which Lin and Chen had been the prime creators, was partially dismantled; Maoist slogans on public buildings were painted over, Mao badges no longer worn and the 'Little Red Book' less frequently cited. In April 1971, Lin's chief associates in the army, Huang Yongsheng, Qiu Huizuo, Wu Faxian and Li Zuopeng, known collectively as 'the four great God-protectors', were forced to make self-criticisms for having formed a faction at Lushan.[3]

By the autumn, Mao was closing in on Lin. In August he left Peking by special train on a journey through Central and Southern China to line up support from regional army commanders in preparation for a showdown.

Throughout this period it was not Lin Biao who was plotting against Mao, as official Chinese historiography has it, but Mao who was plotting to purge Lin. In April he had assured the generals, after their self-criticisms, that the Lushan affair was over. But four months later he told army commanders in Wuhan:[4]

There was a person who wanted hurriedly to be head of state and to usurp power . . . The thing which happened at Lushan is not finished yet. It remains to be settled. There is a person who is standing behind Chen Boda.

Up to this point, Lin, like Liu Shaoqi five years before, was still hoping to ride out the storm. There is little to suggest, and much to disaffirm, that he was behind the extraordinary and improbable plot later unveiled by the Chinese authorities as the 'Outline of Project 571'. Lin was one of the great strategists of modern Chinese history, a veteran of the Long March and of decades of civil war and ruthless political intrigue; that he should have authorised such an incompetent venture is hardly credible.

Project 571 did exist. But it was the work of Lin's twenty-seven-year-old son, Lin Liguo, and a group of young airforce cronies. At first the 'Outline' was merely a general statement of the need to overthrow Mao and seize power, couched in juvenile terms and full of schoolboyish code names: '571' was a homonym for the Chinese characters meaning 'armed rebellion'; Mao was called B-52, after the American bombers then pounding Vietnam. However as Mao drew the noose tighter, concrete methods of assassination were proposed. According to an official Chinese account:

> They plotted to attack Chairman Mao's train with flame-throwers and 40mm bazookas; dynamite the Shuofang railway bridge near Suzhou; bomb the train from the air; blow up the oil depot in Shanghai, near which the special train would pull up, and then assassinate the Chairman in the ensuing commotion; or let Wang Weiguo [a member of the group in Shanghai] murder Chairman Mao when being received by him.[5]

No attempt was made to carry out any of these schemes, and in 1980, when the four generals were put on trial, no shred of evidence was produced that they had even been aware of an assassination plot. They merely confessed that their actions had, in the Stalinist phrase, 'objectively assisted it'. Lin Biao must have known more, at least in the final days, but the only proof offered was that he was directly implicated was a fragment of paper on which he had written, 'I hope you will act according to the instructions transmitted by Comrade Lin Liguo . . .' Had any better evidence existed it would surely have been produced.

Mao returned to the capital on September 12th. Lin was then staying with his wife at Beidaihe, a resort on the Yellow Sea coast 100 miles north-east of Peking, under the discreet surveillance of the Central Guard Bureau.

At ten thirty pm Premier Zhou was called out of a meeting in the Great Hall of the People to be told that Lin was planning to fly to Canton early next morning. The official explanation is that the move was precipitated by the failure of the assassination plot, but it is equally likely that Lin had wanted to keep his options open as long as possible – either to flee northwards, or to retreat to the south and try to bargain things out. Whatever the reason, the delay proved fatal. Zhou gave orders that his plane be grounded.

Events now moved extremely fast. Lin learnt of Zhou's order within minutes. At eleven twenty-two pm his wife, Ye Qun, telephoned the premier to stall for time. By eleven forty, Lin and his entourage were racing at sixty mph along the narrow country roads to Shanhaiguan airport, where Lin's plane, a British-made Trident airliner, was waiting. On the way they overtook two lorries full of troops, sent by Zhou to prevent it taking off.

At twelve twenty-nine am the aircraft began taxi-ing across the apron. Its doors were still open and it was only half-refuelled. In the darkness one wing scraped a petrol lorry. A bodyguard, realising something was wrong, began to remonstrate with Lin; the man was shot dead. Three minutes later, without lights and in total blackness, the plane was airborne.

It flew first due west, across Inner Mongolia, before turning abruptly northwards, towards the Soviet Union. At one fifty am it crossed the border and disappeared from Chinese radar screens. For the next thirty-six hours, Mao and Zhou frantically prepared for every possible contingency from civil war to a Soviet invasion aimed at restoring Lin to power. Then, at two pm on September 14th, a mystified cable arrived from the Chinese embassy in Ulan Bator asking for instructions on how to deal with a Mongolian protest that a Chinese aircraft had violated Mongolian airspace and crashed near the settlement of Undur Khan, killing all nine people on board.[6]

Forty minutes after leaving China, the aircraft had run out of fuel and attempted an emergency landing in the desert. From the skid marks, it appeared that one wing had hit a sand dune, forcing the plane up into the air. It had crashed back and burst into flames.

For the next five years, until Mao's own death in 1976, all major political developments in China were centred on the urbane, statesman-like figure of Zhou Enlai, a man who seemed the antithesis of all that the Cultural Revolution had stood for.

Zhou's unqualified loyalty to Mao had enabled him to survive the assaults of the Red Guards and the sniping of radicals such as Jiang Qing and Kang Sheng, and to shield with his own prestige many lesser figures who would otherwise have been purged; at one stage, more than twenty ministers were living under his protection in Zhongnanhai.[7] In return for this influence, he followed unquestioningly each new shift in Mao's political line, never opposing him but quietly biding his time, waiting for the day when the tide would turn.

At the Lushan plenum, the tide did turn. In the campaign against Lin Biao, Zhou acted as Mao's right hand, and for nine months after Lin's death he was given complete control of both Party and government, which he used to try to return the country to a path of stability and economic development. However, by the late summer of 1972, Mao was beginning to worry that this was leading to the dilution of too many Cultural ·Revolution policies. A campaign against ultra-leftism was abruptly halted, and Zhou, like Liu Shaoqi and Lin Biao before him, began to learn the hazards of being Mao's number two. No longer was there a group of senior leaders on Zhou's right, whom he could criticise as Mao's opponents. The political spectrum had shifted. Zhou himself, vulnerable in his new eminence, was now the chief representative of the moderate, pragmatic element of the Party.

Against this background, Mao began once more considering the question of a successor. At the Tenth Party Congress, held in August 1973, thirty-eight-year-old Wang Hongwen, a protégé of Jiang Qing and the Shanghai leftists, who had enjoyed a meteoric rise through the Shanghai power structure, was appointed a Party vice-chairman ranking third in the Party hierarchy. A few months earlier a horse of a very different colour had reappeared. A short, stocky man, wearing a high-collared Chinese suit set off incongruously by white socks and black sandals, walked down the deep red carpet of the Great Hall of the People, accompanied by Mao's niece, Wang Hairong, to attend a banquet for the Cambodian leader, Prince Sihanouk: Deng Xiaoping had come back from the wilderness, the first major victim of the Cultural Revolution to be rehabilitated.

It was not Zhou Enlai but Mao who decided to bring Deng back, and the reasons were personal as well as political. Until the failure of the Great Leap Forward, Deng had for thirty years been one of Mao's most trusted followers.

He was born Kan Zigao, the second son of the second wife of a Hakka landlord near Chongqing, in Sichuan. In 1920, shortly before his sixteenth birthday, he sailed with a group of ninety-one other Sichuanese students to France, where he spent the next five years as a worker in a shoe factory. In 1924 he began helping to produce a cyclostyled fortnightly magazine, *Chiguang* (*Red Light*), put out by the infant Chinese Communist Party's French branch, headed by Zhou Enlai, which he did so efficiently that he was nicknamed 'Doctor of Mimeography'. A year later he became a Party member and took the name Deng Xiaoping.

After some months in Moscow, where he attended the Sun Yatsen University for Asian revolutionaries, Deng returned to China to become a full-time Party cadre. He was assigned first to Xian, to teach at a military academy run by the warlord Feng Yuxiang. Then, as a Red Army political commissar, he helped to found the You Jiang Soviet Government, based at Baise, near the border with Vietnam, before leading his troops to join up with Mao's forces in the main Soviet base area in Jiangxi in 1930. Three years later, Deng was temporarily disgraced, together with Mao's brother, Mao Zetan, when Mao's guerrilla warfare strategy came under criticism. He stuck with Mao through the Long March, supporting his successful bid for Party leadership at Zunyi, and after a year at Yenan became First Political Commissar under Liu Bocheng, 'the One-eyed Dragon', possibly the most able of all the Red Army field commanders. The Liu-Deng Army, as their forces were known, fought first the Japanese, and then in the final years of the civil war, a series of bloody battles against the nationalists in Central and South-Western China.

In 1945, Deng became one of the forty-four full members of the Central Committee. Evans Carlson, a US military observer who met him during the war, wrote that he was 'short, chunky and physically tough, and his mind was keen as mustard. One afternoon we went over the entire field of international politics, and I was astonished at the extent of his information.'[8] Even Chen Boda acknowledged sourly that he gave the impression of being a living encyclopedia. Articulate, decisive and of an impatience bordering on arrogance, Deng made enemies as well as admirers. But his prodigious organising abilities were disputed by none. After 1952 he was a member of virtually every important government committee, a vice-premier and Minister of Finance. Mao called him 'our little bit of gold', and elevated him to the Politburo and the general secretaryship of the Party, a post of such power and sensitivity that it could only have been entrusted to a man Mao regarded as completely loyal.

During the Cultural Revolution, Mao was to reproach him for betraying that trust. 'Deng Xiaoping is deaf,' he told a work conference in 1966. 'Whenever we are at a meeting together he sits far away from me. For six years, since 1959, he has not once made a general report of work to me.'[9] Yet still Mao continued to give him protection. And in 1973, when, at the age of eighty, Mao began to cast round for a younger man with the stature to inherit his mantle, Deng was all too obviously the only serious candidate. Zhang Chunqiao, the Mayor of Shanghai, was able and intelligent, but lacked national stature; moreover, he was not personally close to Mao. Wang Hongwen was a Cultural Revolution symbol. All the others were supporting figures.

Although Mao wanted Deng to succeed him, he also wanted Cultural

Revolution policies to be maintained. Until his death, these two aims were in permanent and irreconcilable conflict.

In January 1974, Deng's readmission to the Politburo was counter-balanced by a blistering attack on Zhou delivered by Mao himself. A certain person, Mao said, was 'colluding with foreigners and hoping to set himself up as an Emperor'. Shortly afterwards an interminable campaign was launched to 'criticise Lin Biao and Confucius', in which Zhou was obliquely accused of compromising with capitalism and revisionism. A year later Deng was appointed a Party vice-chairman, senior Vice-Premier and Chief of the General Staff, and took over from Wang Hongwen the day-to-day running of the Central Committee. That was offset by the appointment of Zhang Chunqiao as a member of the Politburo Standing Committee, second Vice-Premier and Director of the army's General Political Department.

Early in 1975, Mao's support for Zhou was so lukewarm – 'the Premier is still the Premier', he was quoted as saying – that it actually undermined Zhou's position further. When Zhou presented to the Chinese parliament, the National People's Congress, his programme for the 'four modernisations' (of agriculture, industry, science and defence), to make China a major world power by the end of the century, Mao pointedly stayed away and soon launched a movement to study 'proletarian dictatorship', to draw the country's attention away from the problems of development, back to the ideological concerns which he regarded as paramount. As a rallying point for China's 'moderates', Zhou was criticised even when he lay dying in hospital from cancer. The 'Water Margin' campaign, like the criticism of Confucius eighteen months earlier, was launched by Mao to accuse him of 'capitulationism'. In the final months of 1975, Mao met numerous foreign leaders, but he did not visit Zhou on his sickbed even once. And when Zhou died, on January 8th, 1976, Mao all but ignored it. He neither attended the funeral, nor issued any statement.

As a matter of practical politics, Mao knew that the leftists were not strong enough to carry the day. In a letter to Jiang Qing, in 1975, he wrote prophetically: 'Man's life is limited, but the revolution knows no bounds. In the struggle of the past 10 years, I tried to teach the Chinese people revolution, but I failed. If you try to reach the summit and also fail, you will fall into an abyss and be totally smashed.'[10] But as Mao's health declined and his isolation increased, his mind kept harping back to 'the struggle to transform men', and his old, unrealised Cultural Revolution goals.

Despite the attacks on Zhou, Deng retained Mao's confidence until the summer of 1975, when he began to implement the modernisation programme. Then Mao turned against him. 'He said he would "never reverse verdicts", but this cannot be trusted,' Mao commented later. Deng was criticised for approving draft plans, later dubbed the 'three big poisonous weeds', to promote economic development and restore discipline and professionalism in industry and science. By November, he was also under attack for reversing Cultural Revolution policies on education. A few weeks later Zhou's death removed his principal source of support and precipitated a decision on the choice of a new premier.

Deng appeared for the last time to read the eulogy at Zhou's funeral on January 15th. At the end of that month, after two weeks of bitter argument, the Politburo appointed a comparative unknown, Hua Guofeng, to be acting premier. On Mao's proposal, he was also to take charge of the day-to-day work of the Party Central Committee.

The leftists had been championing Zhang Chunqiao for the post, and in private their supporters spoke disgustedly of 'Mao's balancing act'.[11] It would have been truer to call it an admission of failure, of Mao's inability to choose between the left, whose policies he endorsed but which was too weak to govern, and the right, which could govern but not in the way he wanted.

In these circumstances the choice of Hua as a compromise was less surprising than first appeared. Born into a peasant family in Shanxi, he joined the Party during the war at the age of seventeen, working his way up to become a county Party secretary in Mao's home province of Hunan. There he wrote a series of articles on collectivisation. Three of these were singled out by Mao for praise, and included in a collection published in 1955 under the title, 'Socialist Upsurge in the Chinese Countryside'. Two years later he was promoted to the provincial Party apparatus for his activity in the anti-rightist campaign. In 1959, at the Lushan plenum, he provided Mao with materials showing the success of the Great Leap Forward, which Mao used to rebut the criticisms of Peng Dehuai. For this, he was appointed Vice-Governor of Hunan and a secretary of the provincial Party committee at the age of thirty-nine. According to Tan Zhenlin, from then on Hua was numbered among the up-and-coming local leaders whom Mao regarded as his personal followers.

Through the 1960s the connection was maintained. Hua oversaw the construction of a vast irrigation scheme in Mao's home district of Shaoshan. Emerging from the Cultural Revolution as Party leader of Hunan, he was appointed to the Central Committee in 1969, and two years later was brought to Peking as a Mao loyalist to take part in the investigation of the Lin Biao affair. Under the patronage of Kang

Sheng, he became Minister of Public Security, and at about the same time, in 1973, entered the Politburo.

None of this, however, meant much outside China, or even within the country outside the Party elite. An *apparatchik* who had spent his entire career within the bureaucracy, Hua was so lacking in charisma that even after he had been in power for a full year, the physical presence of his colleagues overshadowed him. Long-faced and jowly, he seemed undistinguished to the point of anonymity. His personality was subordinated to the role he played, and natural self-effacement combined with prudence kept his family life so completely in the background that, years later, few Chinese even knew the name of his wife.

However appearances were only part of the picture. Hua was one of those whose career had benefited from each new leftward spasm of Mao's progress, from the anti-rightist campaign to the Tenth Party Congress. But his long schooling in the rough and tumble of provincial politics had taught him the value of compromise and political bargaining. Unlike Jiang Qing and the Shanghai leaders, Hua was no doctrinaire leftist. His main Politburo allies were Wang Dongxing, Director of the Central Committee's General Office, a flabby figure with a bloated face and heavy-lidded eyes, who took over as secret police chief after the death of Kang Sheng in 1975; another security official, Ji Dengkui, whose career had paralleled his own in the neighbouring province of Henan; and the Chairman of the Peking Revolutionary Committee, the benign-looking, silver-haired Wu De. But he also cooperated with Zhou Enlai on plans to mechanise agriculture, and with Deng on the draft plan to revitalise science, shrewdly building bridges to other groups in the leadership, so that, if his influence and prestige were limited, he was at least acceptable to all.

Hua's appointment was made known within the Party on February 2nd and to the country as a whole five days later. At the same time, a full-scale campaign was launched to criticise 'unrepentant capitalist roaders' and 'beat back the right-deviationist wind of reversing correct verdicts'. Deng was named in leftist-inspired wallposters but not in the press, and as late as March, it seemed that Mao was reluctant to have him purged outright. But then occurred one of the most extraordinary events in the history of communist rule in China: the masses, the human clay that Mao had moulded and re-moulded through decades of ideological movements and campaigns, finally gave warning that their patience was running out.

Two thousand years earlier Mencius had written, 'When the ruler loses virtue, the people have the right to rebel.' In April 1976, the Chinese people did rebel.

The trouble started when the Shanghai newspaper, *Wen Hui Bao*, publicly attacked the memory of Zhou Enlai. In an article on March 25th, it charged: 'That capitalist-roader in the Party wanted to put back in power a capitalist-roader who had been toppled and is unrepentant to this day.' Thousands of letters and telegrams of protest poured in to the newspaper and to the Central Committee. Public discontent, which had already been aroused by earlier attempts to curtail mourning activities for Zhou, was inflamed by an internal directive, read out at workplaces, advising people not to attend ceremonies for the traditional Qing Ming, the Festival of Souls, the following week.

In Nanjing, student demonstrations broke out on March 29th. Starting that night, slogans were daubed on trains to Peking and other cities, warning: 'If anyone dares to oppose Premier Zhou, we will smash his donkey head!' and 'Be vigilant against the usurpation of state and Party power!'

In Peking, wreaths had appeared even earlier at the Martyrs' Monument in Tian An Men Square, and by Qing Ming itself, April 4th, they were piled up to a height of thirty feet, while the hedges around were white with slips of paper, each bearing a poem written in Zhou's memory. Some made oblique attacks on Jiang Qing and the leftists; some alluded to Mao by analogy with the Qin emperor. In the provinces people were blunter: 'Down with the big careerist and big conspirator Zhang Chunqiao!' one wallposter proclaimed.

Shortly after midnight on April 5th, Wang Hongwen arrived at the police station which then stood at the south-eastern corner of Tian An Men Square. Under his direction, every wreath was removed, thrown into lorries and taken to the Security Ministry nearby. Three lines of armed guards were posted round the monument with instructions to say it was 'closed for repairs'. At five am, Wang left.

That morning, the square filled with sullen, angry people. Foreigners who went there were told roughly to go away; it was an 'internal matter', for Chinese to settle themselves. A fight started when a plainclothesman was accused of slandering Premier Zhou. He broke away and ran up the steps into the Great Hall of the People, with several thousand furious citizens at his heels. They were stopped by PLA soldiers. Another man, suspected of calling Zhou a capitalist-roader, was beaten unconscious.

A police loudspeaker van arrived and began urging the crowd to disperse. It was surrounded and overturned. Then the crowd besieged the police station, demanding that their wreaths be given back. When there was no response, they set fire to a police car and two jeeps, parked nearby. Later a minibus, bringing food for the guard unit, was also burnt.

By mid-afternoon, a hard core of some 10,000 people remained. They sang the Internationale, and agreed to form a 'Peking People's Committee for mourning Premier Zhou'. Young men read out poems, written in their own blood, pledging their lives to defend Zhou's memory.

A few minutes after five pm, the police station was set on fire and gutted. The Mayor of Peking, Wu De, appealed for calm over the square's public address system, calling for vigilance against 'bad elements and counter-revolutionaries'. As dusk fell, amid further warnings that the square must be emptied, the crowds gradually left. At nine thirty pm, all the illuminations were suddenly turned on, and militiamen armed with wooden clubs drove out those who remained, making several hundred arrests. Peking lore has it that a number of the protesters were killed, but this has never been proved. However the suppression was certainly violent, and men and women were seen being dragged away, their faces covered in blood and their arms bound behind them with lengths of barbed wire.

In a dozen other cities, smaller-scale disturbances were similarly put down.

On April 7th, the Politburo confirmed Hua as Premier and appointed him First Vice-Chairman of the Party. The Tian An Men riots were labelled 'a counter-revolutionary incident', and Deng was stripped of all his posts. He was, however, permitted to retain his Party membership 'to see how he behaves'. In fact Deng had already been under house arrest since March, 'in utter isolation from the outside world', as a Chinese account afterwards put it.[12] For the remaining months of Mao's life, he became a cipher, existing solely as a target for leftist attacks.

Instability and unrest continued. At the end of April a bomb was thrown at the Soviet embassy. For the first time since 1949, bank robberies were reported. As the country lurched once more violently to the left, peasants abandoned their communes and divided up the land, taking advantage of the breakdown of discipline that leftist policies entrained. Workers stayed away from their jobs, and industry was crippled by politically motivated strikes. Fujian, Zhejiang and several other southern provinces were in a state of anarchy exceeded only in the Cultural Revolution, eight years earlier; Vice-Premier Li Xiannian was reduced to telling foreign leaders that they could not visit the famous resort of Hangzhou because the lake there was 'under repair'. Economic output in 1976 registered its sharpest decline since the Great Leap Forward.

Mao himself, hardly able to speak, gripped by the last stages of Parkinson's Disease, was turned into a venerated dummy, to be manipulated by the left in whatever way would advance their cause. Like Stalin, he became totally divorced from the people, ignorant of the conditions in which they lived and cut off from the reality of national feeling. Physical frailty, coupled with suffocating security precautions, left him as much a prey to the manoeuvring of those around him as the emperors in the Forbidden City, surrounded by eunuchs. When a foreign leader was taken to see him, he was made to promise not to say where the meeting took place for fear that the curtain of secrecy would be lifted. Even Jiang Qing, when she travelled, was assigned a personal guard unit of 300 men.

At the same time, constitutional safeguards for government and Party activity were totally disregarded. In Russia, after 1939, the supposedly quinquennial Party Congress was not held for thirteen years. In China in 1975, when parliament was to meet for the first time for eleven years, not even the deputies were told why they were being summoned to Peking; one man assumed he must have committed a political error and was about to be arrested.[13]

Life in China took on the same nightmarish quality as it had for Russians in Stalin's last years. The secret police had free rein. The regime preached puritanical dogmatism and xenophobia, and under a smokescreen of revolutionary jargon, reverted to the old Confucian principles that had sustained all earlier feudal rulers. In August 1976, the Chinese press related the story of a worker after the Tangshan earthquake, who was faced with a choice between rescuing his two young children or an old Party official, buried under rubble when a building collapsed. He saved the old official, and his children died. An almost identical story is told in a fourteenth-century neo-Confucian classic. Loyalty to the Party was the highest form of filial piety.

The earthquake, the most destructive in modern times, killed 250,000 people. In the villages of North China, it was taken as an omen of the end of the dynasty: rumours that the Mandate of Heaven was about to change became so widespread that the *People's Daily* was obliged to deny them. Then, six weeks later, Mao died.

In the Soviet Union, if contemporary accounts are to be believed, the struggle for power began even before Stalin's body was cold: Beria drove straight from the old despot's deathbed to the Lubyanka, to deploy NKVD troops around Moscow. Within twenty-four hours, the Politburo, which Stalin had enlarged in 1952 by the appointment of a number of younger men, including Brezhnev and Kosygin, in preparation for a purge of the old guard, was reduced to its former size and the new appointees were unceremoniously shoved aside. Malenkov became premier, and with Beria and Molotov formed the ruling triumvirate. *Pravda* began to build up the new leader's image by publishing a retouched photograph of Malenkov with Stalin, in which the other Politburo members had been crudely painted out. But Malenkov over-reached himself. Eight days later, he was forced to relinquish his concurrent post of senior Party Secretary to Khrushchev, then placed fourth in the Politburo ranking order.

For three months, the triumvirate coexisted uneasily at the head of a collective leadership. Then, after two days of riots in East Berlin in June, caused indirectly by the loosening of Stalinist controls in Eastern Europe, Beria was arrested, supposedly to forestall an NKVD coup. *Pravda* set out the case against him:

> Irrefutable facts prove that Beria lost the face of a communist and changed into a bourgeois renegade and became an agent of international imperialism. An adventurist and hireling of foreign imperialist forces, he hatched plans to grab the leadership of the Party and the country with the aim of . . . bringing about ultimately the restoration of capitalism.[14]

He was denounced as a 'bandit' and 'despicable traitor', and accused of trying to disrupt the Soviet Union's food supply and suppressing minority nationalities.

Twenty-three years later, when Jiang Qing and the other members of the 'Gang of Four', Zhang Chunqiao, Yao Wenyuan and Wang Hongwen, were arrested in Peking, the same hackneyed epithets were used against them. They, too, were 'renegades, imperialist agents and newborn bourgeois elements'; they, too, were accused of 'wanting to restore capitalism'. So much for the originality of communist phrasemakers.

As with Stalin, so with Mao; the rows began even before the funeral. Divisions over the key question of who should become Chairman were reflected in a failure to agree even on such practical points as whether or not Mao's body should be embalmed. With the leadership split and no compromise in sight, Hua and the Defence Minister, Ye Jianying, supported by the army command, decided to act. In justification they claimed afterwards that the 'Gang of Four' had been plotting an armed rebellion, but evidence at Jiang Qing's trial in 1980 made clear this was not so. The 'Gang of Four' had feared, correctly as events turned out, that Hua and the army might stage a coup against them, and had discussed what countermeasures they might take. But they made no preparations, and the only talk of insurrection was among their supporters *after* their arrests.

The four were detained in their homes at around two am on October 6th by troops of the Central Guard Bureau headed by Wang Dongxing. They were held first at the Peking Garrison Prison, under the control of the Military Region Commander, Chen Xilian, and then transferred to Qincheng. Jiang Qing was housed in a specially built padded cell, for fear she might try to kill herself.[15]

Some thirty others, including Mao's nephew Mao Yuanxin, were arrested the same night. The Commander of the Nanjing Military Region, Ding Sheng, was said to have resisted and was shot dead. Another leftist, the Culture Minister, Yu Huiyong, committed suicide in prison. Five more ministers, including Foreign Minister Qiao Guanhua, were detained subsequently. In 1981, one of these, the former Sports Minister, Chuang Zedong, was released and given a job as a table-tennis coach.

In the Soviet Union, Beria was shot in December 1953, together with the Minister of State Control, Merkulov, and four other high officials. The following year, the Minister of State Security, Abakumov, and the man Stalin had put in charge of the 'Doctors' Plot', Ryumin, were also executed. As the purge broadened, one-third of the members of the Central Committee were disgraced, roughly the same proportion as in China two decades later; of the 133 full members appointed at the next Soviet Party Congress in 1956, fifty-three were new. That year saw the last known Soviet political execution, of one of Beria's allies, the Azerbaijani leader, Mikhail Bagirov.

From then on, post-Stalin Russia, like post-Mao China, sought new methods of regulating its internal political struggles. Each country began a quest, which is not yet over, to come to terms with its past and with the titanic figure who had ruled it.

Part III

The Peking Spring

The creaky red and cream buses which ply back and forth, bursting at the seams with people, along Chang An Da Jie, the Avenue of Eternal Peace, retire each evening for what seems must be their final rest to a depot near the Xidan crossroads, a mile-and-a-half west of Tian An Men Square. At least, they used to; after 1980, they were gradually being replaced, as part of China's modernisation programme, by a smart new blue and white model. But the depot remained, as did the wall which separated it from the road. Seven feet high and a hundred yards long, made of grey brick, it looked on to a strip of bare, dusty earth, planted with a row of poplars and a few anaemic firs, set well back from the pavement. Beyond the bus depot, across a lane, the wall continued for another eighty yards towards the post office building, whose clocktower marked the hours by chiming the Maoist anthem, 'The East is Red'.

It was here, on Sunday, November 19th, 1978, that a poster appeared which changed the whole complexion of Chinese politics: for the first time, Mao was publicly criticised by name.

'Because in his old age, his thinking became metaphysical, and for other reasons,' it said, 'Chairman Mao supported the Gang of Four in raising their hands to strike down Deng Xiaoping.' The poster softened the blow slightly by treating it as a case of 'mistaken judgment'. But it was the first open breach of the fiction, which until then had been sedulously maintained, that Mao's policies were intrinsically correct but the 'Gang of Four' had distorted them.

By arguing that the disgraced leftists were able to act as they did because they had Mao's support, the poster implied that Mao himself should share the responsibility for their 'crimes'. It initiated a line of questioning which ultimately would ask – as Khrushchev asked about Stalin – whether Mao's leadership in the last twenty years of his life was a benefit to his country or a bane? Whether, since the mid-1950s, his achievements outweighed his failings?

Today, such ideas seem obvious, even banal. At the time they were absolutely electrifying. I know of no one, foreigner or Chinese, whose first reaction to that poster was not disbelief. Even two years after Mao's death, the notion of censuring him directly was close to blasphemy.

The fourteen sheets of closely written notepaper which carried these shattering implications were signed 'Worker No 0538, Motor Vehicle Repair Workshop, 57 Wang Fu Jing Street'. They had been pasted up during the morning by a thirty-five-year-old mechanic named Lu Pu, who then went home, told his wife to put a toothbrush and a change of underwear into a bag, and sat down to wait for the police. They came, a day later, but simply to tell him that they were aware of what he had done and there was no need for him to worry.

Throughout the afternoon, the poster was surrounded by a strangely quiet crowd of mainly young people. No attempt was made to take it down, and at 2 am next morning it still attracted the occasional late-night passer-by, who stopped to read it by the faint light of the streetlamps. Nearby a bored-looking soldier with fixed bayonet stood guard.

The Second Coming of Deng Xiaoping

It was not chance that the wallposter which launched the Peking Spring took Deng's disgrace as its theme. The triangular relationship between his fall, Hua's rise and the looming shadow of Mao behind them was the dominant political issue of the time, and had been throughout the previous two years.

The press campaign against Deng began to fade as soon as the 'Gang of Four' were arrested and by December had stopped altogether. Deng wrote to Hua, pledging his loyalty.[1] Most of those detained in the Tian An Men riots were quietly released, and sympathetic officials began telling foreign delegations that Deng's return to power was no longer impossible.

As the New Year, 1977, began, it looked as though Deng might be back in office within weeks. That impression was soon reinforced by wallposters and demonstrations in Tian An Men Square, marking the anniversary of Zhou Enlai's death. 'There's no need to keep 800 million people waiting,' one poster grumbled. 'We want Deng Xiaoping to be premier right away!' 'We hope the Central Committee will make arrangements quickly, so that all hearts under heaven may be at peace,' said another. Similar shows of impatience were reported from other cities. But then nothing happened. The posters were scraped off by municipal workmen. Deng remained a non-person, in political limbo.

The problem was that a majority of the Politburo opposed his reinstatement, or at least had strong reservations about it. Hua's allies, Wang Dongxing, Ji Dengkui and Wu De, saw it as a threat to their own positions. Wu De, in particular, was vulnerable. He had been the first Politburo member to attack Deng by name after the April 1976 riots, and on November 30th was the last to call for the anti-Deng campaign to continue. Both he and Chen Xilian, the Peking Military Region Commander, were strongly criticised in the wallposters in January for the part they had played in suppressing the riots. Chen Yonggui, who headed the leftist Dazhai agricultural brigade and had close links with both Jiang Qing and Hua, also opposed Deng, and said so in as many words at an agricultural conference in December. These five were all beneficiaries of the Cultural Revolution, and at the Politburo meeting the previous April, all had voted for Deng's dismissal.

Ranged against them were Marshal Liu Bocheng, Vice-Premier Li Xiannian, and the two southern military leaders, Xu Shiyou and Wei Guoqing. The other regional commander, Li Desheng in Manchuria, adopted a neutral position. None had been present at the April Politburo meeting.

Hua himself was in the invidious position of owing his rise to Deng's fall. Yet he seems to have realised very early on that Deng commanded enough support in the Party and the army to make his eventual reinstatement inevitable. Having accepted that, his strategy was aimed at ensuring that Deng's return took place in such a way as to do his own standing the least possible harm.

In this, Hua was supported by the octogenarian Defence Minister, Ye Jianying. In appearance, Ye resembled a doddery old professor, comfortable, well-rounded and completely bald, with an air of permanently shuffling about in carpet slippers. I once watched him being prepared for a public appearance. Two attendants straightened his jacket, buttoned his pockets and puffed him up like a cushion, before taking him by the arm and carefully propelling him towards his place. Yet it was this old man, whose career stretched back to the 1911 revolution which overthrew the last Qing emperor, who played the pivotal role in China in the year after Mao's death.

When it was a choice between Deng and the 'Gang of Four', Ye supported Deng, and showed it by refusing to attend the April 1976 Politburo meeting. But when the choice lay between Deng and Hua, Ye preferred Hua. As he explained later, in what sounded like a catalogue of the virtues Deng lacked, 'Chairman Hua is . . . prudent and steady, wise and resolute . . . He [is] worthy of being called Chairman Mao's good student and successor.'[2] An additional consideration was that Ye could influence Hua, whereas Deng, if he returned to power, would go his own way, and Ye had his suspicions about where that way would lead.

The old Defence Minister's commitment to Hua remained a constant factor in all the political manoeuvring that followed. In the first few months, whenever Hua appeared, Ye was at his shoulder, one step behind. His position was summed up in a poem, published by the *People's Daily* to mark his 80th birthday:

> There is a successor to the cause of the Long March!
> Old men enjoy writing verses in praise of dusk,
> I see the setting sun over the green mountain.[3]

On March 9th, 1977, the question of Deng's future was taken up in earnest at a secret two-week-long work conference of the Central Committee. Hua played off Deng's opponents and supporters in the Politburo against each other, while himself occupying the middle ground. These tactics were to become the hallmark of his style of rule, gaining him freedom of manoeuvre yet often enabling him to take the credit for whatever consensus was reached.

Against a background of inspired leaks that Deng would be back at work by April 7th, the anniversary of his fall, Hua told the Committee that although he had made serious errors, investigations had shown he was innocent of complicity in the Tian An Men riots.[4] However Wang Dongxing and others spoke against his reinstatement, quoting a phrase which had been inserted for the purpose in a *People's Daily* editorial a few weeks earlier: 'We resolutely defend whatever decisions Chairman Mao made, and we unswervingly follow whatever instructions Chairman Mao gave.'[5] How, then, he asked, could Deng be returned to power, when it had been publicly stated that he had been dismissed on Mao's proposal?

This was much more than just a matter of words. Hua's legitimacy as Party Chairman was based on Mao's approval. At a mass rally on October 24th, 1976, two weeks after he took power, it was announced that Mao had told him: 'With you in charge, I'm at ease.'[6] In November he started to build a tentative personality cult, using publicity material from his old power base in Hunan. He has 'remarkable quality, outstanding ability, revolutionary boldness and far-sighted vision', one article declared. 'His brilliant image is engraved on the minds of the masses.'[7] He even abandoned his crew-cut for a slicked-back hairstyle which heightened his physical resemblance to Mao. And articles, originated in Hunan, claimed quite fraudulently that he had enjoyed an especially close relationship with Premier Zhou.[8] On television and the stage, song and dance troupes presented sketches depicting Hua as the beacon of China's future. One I saw performed at an army camp the following summer had a final tableau of workers and peasants immersed in grief beneath black-bordered portraits of Mao, Zhou and Zhu De, projected on to a screen at the back of the stage. As they gradually faded, the music swelled, the screen turned a clear blue, the workers struck heroic, joyful poses, trumpets sounded and banners swirled, and in place of the sun there appeared, haloed in light, the face of Chairman Hua. If Mao was the demiurge who created the new order, Hua was to be the son of god. To the extent that the old godhead should be shown to be flawed, Hua's authority would also diminish.

The compromise which emerged from the March meeting (put forward by Hua himself)[9] was that Deng should be rehabilitated, but the

213

April 1976 Politburo resolution would be left untouched. It was agreed that more work was needed, inside and outside the Party, to prepare opinion for his reinstatement, and that a full-scale Central Committee plenum should be convened to make the announcement. Its timing was to be decided by the Politburo.

For Hua, this meant that the impact of Deng's return could be blunted by combining it with his own confirmation as Party Chairman and the expulsion of the 'Gang of Four' from Party membership. It also gave him longer to consolidate his position and to arrange for the rehabilitation to take place in the way most favourable to himself.

The *quid pro quo* was set out in a letter Deng wrote on April 10th, in which he acknowledged that he had made mistakes, and praised Hua as a leader who would be able to lead China to the end of the century and beyond. Together with his earlier pledge of loyalty to Hua, it was circulated within the Party as a Central Committee document on May 3rd.[10] Their message was that Hua's primacy would not be affected by Deng's return, and Deng himself, addressing the Central Committee just before his rehabilitation was announced, promised to spend his remaining years 'being a good assistant to Hua'.[11] Meanwhile, to prevent further displays of public support for Deng, all demonstrations during the anniversary of the Tian An Men riots were banned.

In mid-May the New China News Agency, Xinhua, issued a photograph of the Chinese leaders attending an industrial conference. In the middle stood a short stocky figure with the face of the Xinjiang leader, Saifudin. But at the time of the conference, Saifudin was visiting Yugoslavia. The small man with the borrowed face was unmistakably Deng Xiaoping. Two months later, after a flurry of preparatory articles in the press, a red wallposter sixty feet long went up outside the Ministry for Economic Relations with Foreign Countries, announcing in two-foot-high black characters that the Central Committee was in session and Deng had been restored to all his posts.

The official communiqué was broadcast at eight pm on July 22nd. The people of Peking had been told a few hours earlier at briefings at their places of work, and as soon as the broadcast ended the staccato clatter of firecrackers broke out from different parts of the city. Government buildings were illuminated with strings of lights. The air turned blue with the smoke of gunpowder, and big pink and black posters exhorting, 'Warmly welcome the decisions of the Third Plenum!' sprouted like an exotic fungus on the walls.

That night and for the next two days, Chinese in their millions poured on to the streets to march through Tian An Men Square, waving flags and beating gongs and drums. As always, the celebrations were carefully orchestrated, but for once they were marked by genuine jubilation. The masses who, fifteen months earlier, had reluctantly marched in enforced support of Deng's fall, now came out with a will to mark his return. A carnival atmosphere prevailed: children threw fireworks at each other, musicians perched on the backs of bicycle-carts, and elaborately decorated lorries moved in an endless procession along the broad thoroughfare of Chang An.

Next morning, at the newspaper display case outside the *People's Daily* office, people stood five deep to see the photograph of Deng next to Hua and Ye. At seventy-two, he looked older and more tired than at the time of his fall, but to those who cheered him, he represented an end to Maoist turbulence and the hope of a better life.

Although hardly what Hua would have wished, he made the best of it. Deng's rehabilitation, the newspapers explained, is 'yet another proof that . . . Chairman Hua is of one heart with the masses'.[12]

In the Soviet Union, new policies are introduced when a majority of the Politburo favours them. Rarely is it felt necessary to hedge them around with elaborate theoretical explanations. In China, Mao held that 'ideology decides everything': policy is implemented by people, but is determined by ideas. So when his successors wanted to change his policies, they had to provide a theoretical basis for doing so.

The first step was taken in May 1977, when the *People's Daily* published for the first time Mao's judgment, made a year previously, that the Cultural Revolution had been 'seventy per cent correct and thirty per cent mistaken'.[13] The 'mistakes' were ascribed to the 'Gang of Four', who were accused of 'having done things behind Chairman Mao's back which ran counter to his teachings'.[14] In theory it now became possible to reject Cultural Revolution policies as leftist distortions which Mao himself had repudiated. In practice, however, this required a suspension of disbelief – the ability, which Orwell described in *1984*, 'to tell deliberate lies while genuinely believing in them, to forget any fact that has become inconvenient . . . to deny the existence of objective reality and all the while to take account of the reality which one denies'. In the year after Mao's death, every Chinese official knew that the 'Gang of Four' had been Mao's closest followers; and every Chinese official without exception depicted them as Mao's most vicious enemies. To live in Peking at that time was to be the only person with a memory. Every official conversation began with the words, 'Because of the interference and sabotage of the Gang of Four . . .' – followed by a litany of the sins they were alleged to have committed.

The Chinese people were asked to believe that Mao had personally

215

initiated and led the struggle against the 'Gang of Four', but had been unable to complete it before his death. When Hua had had them arrested, he was 'carrying out Chairman Mao's behest'.[15]

Even for a nation inured to devious reasoning and a constantly shifting official line, this was too much to swallow. I remember one young man that summer, a China Travel Service guide, patiently explaining it all to a group of Hong Kong Chinese during a visit to the Imperial Summer Palace. As they moved off he added, to himself as much as anyone else, 'But what I don't understand is, if he was so great, why did he let all this happen?'

It was a question many Chinese were asking. But officially it was ignored. The autumn of 1977 marked the high point of Mao's posthumous cult. Millions of pounds were spent on a huge mausoleum in Tian An Men Square, resembling an imperial tomb, where his remains were enshrined in a crystal sarcophagus at the beginning of August. A few days later, at the opening of the Eleventh Party Congress, Hua pronounced a panegyric:

> Chairman Mao was the greatest Marxist of our time. His contributions . . . are immortal. We must hold high the great banner of Chairman Mao and resolutely defend it . . . We must cherish the great banner of Chairman Mao as our precious heritage and hand it on from generation to generation. Let the glory of the great banner of Chairman Mao illuminate the ages to come![16]

As the anniversary of Mao's death on September 9th approached, the press was flooded with commemorative articles. A film was made about the cottage where he had lived at Zhongnanhai, with books everywhere, even piled up on the bed, as it must have been during his life, and a patched dressing gown hanging nearby. Hundreds of wreaths of gaudily coloured paper lined the stone tribunes on either side of Tian An Men and engulfed the base of the Martyrs' Monument. Squads of Little Red Guards, ten or eleven years old, in uniform of white shirts and red neckerchiefs, drew up to pledge allegiance to Mao's policies and recite the Chinese schoolboys' catechism, 'March on to Communism'. Yet, unlike the anniversary of Zhou Enlai's death, few signs of real grief were evident. The wreaths came not from individuals, but from factories and Party organisations.

Speaking at the opening of the mausoleum, Hua said Mao should be credited with all the victories of the Chinese revolution. 'Like a great beacon,' he affirmed, 'Mao Zedong Thought has shone through the darkness . . . as it will do for ever.'[17]

In fact, Mao Zedong Thought was already beginning to change. In his letter to Hua on April 10th, Deng had proposed that a new approach be adopted to Mao's words. He explained to the Central Committee in July:[18]

> We must *comprehensively and correctly* implement Mao Zedong Thought. This is very important. Chairman Mao's thought is a great and unified entity. To implement it in every aspect, *we must absolutely not take one sentence in a distorted way and use it as a signboard*. Mao Zedong Thought must be taken as a whole and cannot be applied one-sidedly. (Emphasis added)

By August Hua had endorsed the 'comprehensive and correct' formulation, and the new line was set forth in a joint editorial, published on the anniversary of Mao's death, a month later:[19]

> We must not mechanically apply stray quotations from Chairman Mao's works in disregard of the concrete time, place and circumstances, but must have a true grasp of the essence of his works as a whole. Chairman Mao's statement on a particular question at a given time and in given circumstances is correct, as is his statement on the same question at another time and in other circumstances. But statements made on a particular question at different times and in different circumstances may sometimes differ in the degrees and points of emphasis and even in formulation. That is why when we deal with problems of a given aspect or in a given field, we must strive to understand correctly the entire body of Mao Zedong Thought.

As a Chinese commentator later admitted, this was 'pitting one set of quotations against another',[20] and it did nothing to answer the young tour guide's question – Why did Mao let it all happen? Yet it gave the leadership a theoretical weapon with which to beat the 'Gang of Four'; their policies, it could now be claimed, were based on individual quotations taken out of context. It preserved the myth of Mao's infallibility. And it disarmed potential critics of the retreat from Cultural Revolution policies. Who, if not the Politburo, was to say what constituted a 'correct understanding' of Mao Zedong Thought and what did not?

For the next eight months, until the early summer of 1978, this approach remained unchanged. 'Chairman Mao's banner is being held so high,' a British diplomat commented, 'no one can read what's written on it any more.'

The first, cautious steps away from leftist policies came as soon as the 'Gang of Four' fell. Hua reaffirmed the 'four modernisations', put forward by Zhou Enlai in 1975, and encouraged a revival of cultural life under the Maoist slogan, 'Let a hundred flowers bloom!' Volume 5 of

Mao's *Selected Works*, published in April 1977, expounded the moderate policies Mao had favoured in the early 1950s, and, shortly before Deng's reinstatement, his 'three big poisonous weeds' – the guidelines for development drafted on his orders two years earlier – were publicly exonerated.

By July 1977, the political clock had been put back two years, and the stage was set for an astonishing leap back into the past which in ten months would reverse almost all the new policies which Mao had introduced in the previous decade. With the ideological groundwork laid, one by one the 'new-born things' of the Cultural Revolution were pushed aside to make way for the policies they had earlier displaced. An entire period of China's development was turned on its head.

First to go were the 'model theatrical works' which had been the personal fief of Jiang Qing. Traditional Chinese opera reappeared in the provinces and, in January 1978, in Peking. Balladeers, reciting old stories to the rhythm of a wooden handbell, dragon dancers and child acrobats, balancing on monocycles on the rims of open umbrellas, turned out for holidays and street processions.

It was announced that of the thirty-six films under preparation in 1976, thirty-two were about 'capitalist roaders' and were being scrapped. Instead the cinemas and television showed films from the 1950s which Jiang Qing had banned, and an occasional foreign production, usually from Yugoslavia or Rumania. Chinese translations of Balzac, Dickens, Shakespeare and Tolstoy were reprinted in small editions, as were some Chinese classics. The first Western orchestras and musicians started coming to China, and concerts of Beethoven and Brahms, and of classical Chinese music, were occasionally broadcast on the radio. The slogan of the day was 'Let the old serve the new; let foreign things serve China!'

The political relaxation was reflected in the mood of the people. A particularly bold couple might hold hands in public. Young men let their hair grow longer and sported moustaches. Girls, and later older women, began affecting curls, and in a weighty decision in March 1978 a conference of Chinese hairdressers, rejecting what they called the 'theory of bourgeois hairstyles', resolved that in future they would wave and curl hair on demand. (Previously Chinese women had had to show a letter of authority from their units, explaining that they belonged to an amateur theatrical troupe or had another valid reason for wanting something more elaborate than a simple pudding-basin cut.) The leftists' view that the duller life was, the better communists people were, was 'a slander against socialism', the conference declared. That summer more young women took to skirts, instead of the ubiquitous baggy trousers. The first dresses, having reappeared in Canton under the influence of Overseas Chinese visiting from Macao and Hong Kong, made their way to Peking. And a few brave spirits experimented discreetly with make-up, and had their shapeless white blouses taken in to show a hint of a figure beneath.

Since the arts had been so completely under Jiang Qing's control, it was not hard to justify reversing her policies. Mao was quoted as saying her views were 'Shit! Wide of the mark', and that 'model operas alone are not enough . . . Others are not allowed to offer any opinion. That's no good.'[21] The leftists, it was claimed, had 'distorted the essence of [Mao's] directives while flaunting his banner'.[22] But why he had been unable to prevent this was still not explained. Other reversals of cultural policy strained credulity much more, particularly in the field of education, where all the key reforms were the work of Mao himself. University entrance exams were restored, and it was announced that as teaching standards improved in the secondary schools, students would be allowed to continue directly to higher education, instead of having to spend at least two years in between working in a factory or on a commune. 'Open door schooling', whereby part of the academic year was compulsorily devoted to manual labour, was phased out in the universities on the premise that it was being continued in secondary schools, and phased out in secondary schools on the premise that it was being continued in the universities. The authority of teachers was strengthened (in theory, students could now be expelled), and the work teams of 'workers, peasants and soldiers', sent in during the Cultural Revolution to ensure that academic work followed a proletarian line, were quietly withdrawn. New teaching materials and curricula were prepared. Even the pre-Cultural Revolution system of key schools and universities was revived, allowing the best teachers and resources to be concentrated in a few institutions to which only the brightest students were admitted.

The explanation eventually offered for this wholesale reversal of Maoist thinking was totally unconvincing. Mao himself, it was claimed, had acknowledged in 1971 that the old education policy had, after all, been 'on the whole correct'; however, the 'Gang of Four' had 'tightly suppressed' his statement and prevented it being acted upon.[23] In other words, people were asked to believe that for the last five years of his life, Mao had been powerless to have his instructions carried out.

Implausible though it was, the claim helped to legitimise the new policies, not just in education but in science and culture as well. In August 1977, Hua told the Party Congress that the number of intellectuals who 'take the stand of the proletariat are in a minority'. But by the

219

following March, Deng was able to assure a conference of scientists that the 'overwhelming majority' of them were 'part of the proletariat'.[24]

Research programmes got under way again. Disbanded institutes were reconstituted, and an ambitious eight-year development plan was drawn up to bring Chinese science to the world level of the mid-1970s by 1985. In other fields the first steps were taken to restore the legal system, contacts with (and investment by) Overseas Chinese were again encouraged, the gradual opening of China to foreign tourists was speeded up, foreign trade was developed – particularly imports of Western technology and exports of Chinese oil and minerals – even international sports exchanges increased; and all the blame was heaped on the 'Gang of Four' for 'sabotaging' Mao's policies.

For Chinese workers, the most dramatic development was the announcement at the end of 1977 of a ten per cent wage rise for the lower paid, the first for six years, followed by a vigorous press campaign to promote the use of piecework rates, bonus schemes and other forms of material incentives. This was a change so inconceivable that at first Chinese translators refused to use the word 'incentives', maintaining that what was being talked about was material 'encouragement', supposedly quite a different proposition. Nevertheless, incentives they were, the same for which Liu Shaoqi had been denounced and which had been damned throughout the Cultural Revolution as out-and-out revisionism. '"From each according to his ability, to each according to his work" is a socialist principle clearly affirmed by Marx, Engels, Lenin, Stalin and Chairman Mao. It is also common sense,'[25] the *People's Daily* said primly.

In April 1978, in another reversion to pre-Cultural Revolution practice, it was announced that factory managers would be appointed to replace factory revolutionary committees. The need for industrial discipline and for a system of personal job responsibility was affirmed. Even the much-abused profit motive was rehabilitated. 'It's glorious to make profits for the state and shameful to make losses' became the new slogan.[26]

In the countryside, peasants were again permitted to have private plots. All over China, from the spring of 1978, village trade fairs resumed after a break of twelve years; not only foodstuffs could be bought and sold, but also basketware and rush mats, and soon winesellers, cobblers and watch-repairers added their wares. In the fields, as in the factories, the fruits of collective labour, instead of being shared out equally among the workforce, were to be distributed on the basis of 'more pay for more work, less pay for less work, and no pay for no work', and the old Leninist slogan, 'He who does not work, neither shall he eat', was revived. The *People's Daily* set the target of raising the income of ninety per cent of commune members each year.[27]

The last of the 'four modernisations' was defence. Mao's doctrine of 'people's war' held that poorly armed troops could defeat a well-equipped enemy by concentrating their forces to achieve numerical superiority and relying on men rather than weapons. His successors recognised that modern warfare required both a highly trained professional army and the weaponry with which to fight. The purpose of the modernisation programme, according to Hua, was 'to strengthen ourselves economically and heighten our defence capabilities at top speed'.[28] But which was to come first – and should the stress be put on conventional or nuclear weapons?

The conclusion eventually reached was that the economy must come first, 'so as to lay a reliable material foundation for defence construction', and that conventional weaponry should be selectively upgraded. Chinese leaders expressed interest in the Harrier jet fighter from Britain and anti-tank missiles from France.[29] The Science and Technology Commission for National Defence said it was 'foolish and even criminal' to think China could 'use broadswords against guided missiles', and urged that weapons development begin now: 'It is not a good idea to wait until one is thirsty to start digging a well.' The army newspaper, the *Liberation Army Daily*, put it even more bluntly: 'Material strength can only be destroyed by material strength . . . A "red heart" cannot smash the enemy's iron tank.' It added, in the weary tones of a schoolmaster explaining to a particularly dim child, 'Just as workers should work and peasants should farm, the job of an army is to fight . . . If the army cannot fight, what is the use of having it?'[30] The length of service for army conscripts was increased from two years to three, discipline was strengthened, and a 'mass military training movement' was launched. A company in Hebei declared it was ready for 'the breaking out of war tomorrow morning'.[31]

The modernisation programme was also intended to meet other needs. Deng Xiaoping spoke of raising living standards, and consolidating China's socialist political system. The *People's Daily* touched on an even more fundamental issue, that of national pride:

In the present-day world, to be backward economically and in technology means to be beaten. For a whole century following the Opium War, China was beaten . . . Why was our country subject to such humiliation? Why was she trampled on so? The corrupt social system was one factor, and economic and technological backwardness was another.[32]

Mao said in the 1950s that China would 'cut a sorry figure' if, with its territory, resources and population, and the benefits of the socialist system 'which is supposed to be superior', it could not overtake the United States by the beginning of the next century.[33] As an initial step in that direction, Hua told the National People's Congress in February 1978 that by 1985 steel production would nearly triple to 60 million tons a year, agriculture would be eighty-five per cent mechanised, and grain production would increase by forty per cent to 400 million tons a year. 'The tasks are gigantic,' he said, 'but the job can be done . . . We are sure this splendid plan of ours can be fulfilled.'[34]

It was all stirring stuff, and all too reminiscent of the grandiose but impossible plans of two decades before, which crashed when the Great Leap Forward failed. Whatever its inadequacies, however, it served to fire the enthusiasm of a nation which desperately wanted to believe.

With the return of pre-Cultural Revolution policies came the return of those who had flourished under them. Huang Kecheng, PLA Chief of Staff under Peng Dehuai in the 1950s, was brought back from twenty years in the wilderness to act as an adviser to the Party's Military Commission. China's foremost novelist, Ba Jin, and the playwrights Cao Yu and Xia Yan reappeared, along with Zhou Yang, Mao's cultural commissar until 1966. The Panchen Lama re-emerged, as did the Xinjiang Islamic leader, Burhan Shahidi, and the Roman Catholic Archbishop of Shenyang, Mgr. Ignatius Pi Shushi, in the first signs of renewed religious tolerance. In February 1978, the Chinese People's Political Consultative Conference (CPPCC), a long dormant united front organisation, was revived, with Deng Xiaoping as its new chairman, to serve as a back door through which once-purged veterans could be discreetly re-inserted into political life. In April, in its first effort at a general rehabilitation, the Party Central Committee ordered a case-by-case review of all those purged in the 1957 anti-rightist campaign. Those found to have been wrongly convicted should be compensated, the document said, and where age and health permitted, given new work assignments by the State Planning Commission; where the original verdicts were upheld, the victims' 'bourgeois rightist' labels were simply to be removed and their political rights restored.

Many of those brought back, former governors, vice-governors, commanders of military regions and districts, as well as lower officials, were unknown outside China. Yet they had once administered provinces as populous as France or Britain, and could do so again. What rehabilitation meant to them was described in a bitter-sweet short story, published by *Peking Spring*:[35]

I have only been in this organ for two weeks, but everyone knows I am the Commanding Officer's son-in-law.

I notice that people's expressions have become friendly, those who ignored me before now greet me, and even some upper-level directors also wish me good-day.

Three years ago, I joined a production brigade in X X County. The name of the village was Taoyuan. It had only two bare hills, very little water and one road leading to the provincial capital.

There was a PLA post at the side of the village. Even now I don't know what it did. Inside the post were several rows of two-storey buildings. The unit was of about battalion strength, and there were cadres, soldiers and some people who wore glasses whose job I couldn't figure out.

The unit reclaimed several hundred mou *of river flood land and its members took turns to labour. They also performed weekly labour in aid of the villagers, and their relationship with the production brigade was cordial.*

I was then in charge of the water in the brigade's paddyfield and often had dealings with the soldiers. As time went by, I got to know them well. Several of them often came to visit the compound where we youths who'd been sent down to the countryside were living.

One day I noticed an old man working with the soldiers. His hair was grey, and he looked about sixty years of age. He wore an old army uniform without collar or insignia.

The old man never said a word while he worked. He often stopped to take a breather. Apparently he was not a manual labourer. His hands looked white and soft. The skin of his face, once well cared for, had been roughened by the wind and hung loosely on his cheeks.

He was doubtless a 'target of investigation', what people call a 'monster and demon', a 'capitalist-roader'.

The soldiers addressed him as 'Old man' or 'Fatty', never by name.

When the soldiers rested, he was told to rest. But he always sat by himself away from the others.

Once I asked a soldier who he was.

'Don't know. Seems he was a high official.'

'I hear he's a commander,' interrupted another.

'What mistake did he make?' I asked.

'Who knows? Probably followed the wrong line.'

I looked at the figure of the old man, the wind fluffing his grey hair, his weak chest rising and falling, panting, screwing up his eyes, gazing at the distance, his thoughts unknown.

Later, finding an opportunity to approach him, I said in a low voice: 'Anything you want me to do, I'll do it for you.'

223

He stared at me suspiciously and shook his head covered with grey hair:
'*Thank you. Nothing.*'

I could imagine how he was treated. One day, I wrapped a piece of cooked pork with paper and stuffed it into his pocket when no one was looking. He turned, felt it, and without a word averted his head and pretended to rub some sand from his eyes. He wept.

One afternoon after work, I was near where the soldiers were working, and the old man, picking up his jacket, pointed to a stone on the ground, looked at me and walked away.

After they had gone far enough I lifted the stone and next to a nest of busy black ants I found a neatly folded letter.

When I opened it, a slip of paper fell out: 'Xiao Jiang, help me send this letter.' It was addressed to his wife and there was another to his daughter, Yanyan.

Some days later, when I had finished work and was returning to the village, a child came to tell me: 'Your aunt on your mother's side has come.'

An aunt? I had no aunt on mother's side. Then I understood. It was they who had come. I hastened home and on opening the door saw a stout woman of about fifty and also a girl of about twenty with small pigtails who was looking curiously at our messy room.

I opened my mouth but stopped myself. There were two other students in the room. Then I called out to her: 'Auntie!' She smiled and pressed my hand, and began to cry. The girl also cried and, I don't know why, I began to cry too.

The two students looked at us mystified and left the room.

The next day I led them to the place where the old man was working, having admonished them to be very careful not to give themselves away. As we approached the small group we saw already from afar the old man's white head.

The 'aunt' went forward with an unsteady gait, faster and faster, with the 'niece' finally almost running. I went in front, reminding them in a low voice: 'Slow down, people will notice you.'

About a hundred metres away I stopped them. 'Sit here, don't cross over there.'

Aunt's face was bathed in tears. She plumped herself down on the ground, pulled out her handkerchief and vigorously rubbed her face, almost ready to cry again.

Yanyan stared blankly, without emotion, gazing at her father's figure. He also had seen them. He waved his shovel. He should have looked this way but I don't know for what reason, his head was drooping lower and lower. They sat there like this as though separated by a mountain torrent, yet actually there was nothing between them but a field which would have taken only half a minute to cross. 'Aunt' had stopped crying and was also staring with a blank expression. The wind had dried her tears.

The following day the letter I pulled out from under the stone told them to return home immediately. Attached was a sheet of material written closely in very small writing, which he asked them to send to the premier. I asked for leave and escorted them back to town.

One month passed.

One day I went as usual to see the old man on the side of the ricefield, but he was not there. I pulled a long face and asked the soldiers: 'Where's the old man?'

'He was taken away yesterday. One of those big Hongqi limousines came for him!'

Two days later another Hongqi limousine came. This time it was for me. Yanyan was sitting inside.

'Father has been released!' Those were her first words. Her smile indicated that her family tragedy was over. For her it was the transition from one era to another. We went back to her house and when we stepped out of the car, her parents came out to welcome us. It was no longer the one simple, primitive room, but a small Western-style villa. The whole day the entire family was around me all the time.

I had from beginning to end only one thought, namely to get home as quickly as possible. But they sent Xiao Zhang to fetch my parents. Xiao Zhang was the driver of the Hongqi limousine. So I had no choice but to stay.

That evening, when we reached home, father began to tell me something. 'Commander Yu,' he said . . .

I was startled. 'What Commander Yu?'

This amazed father. 'Don't you know that he is Commander of our Military Region?'

In this way I came to know that he was such a high official – not the 'run-of-the-mill high official' I first thought.

What followed is known to all. I joined the PLA, was promoted to become a cadre, and married my 'cousin' Yanyan.

A long section of Hua's political report at the Eleventh Party Congress was devoted to explaining why such men should be brought back. 'The Gang of Four,' he said, 'perverted Chairman Mao's teaching on the question of capitalist roaders within the Party, thus creating much confusion . . . They equated veteran cadres with democrats, and democrats with capitalist roaders.' Using this device, Hua added, they had tried to overthrow veteran officials who refused to follow them, even though the 'overwhelming majority' of these men were loyal to Mao and had become the mainstay of the country's administration.[36]

Rehabilitated veterans accounted for half the ninety-one new Central Committee members the Congress appointed. Their return to power was portrayed as part of a much broader united front policy, whose aim was to mobilise all sections of Chinese society, communist and non-communist, behind the new regime. But the veterans had special importance because they were the only experienced administrators the leadership could rely on to restore discipline and promote its policies. Younger officials, in their thirties and forties, even if they had no direct connection with the leftists, had risen to power and had formed their political outlook during the Cultural Revolution and the Great Leap Forward. The veterans had been struck down because they believed in the pre-Cultural Revolution policies which Deng Xiaoping was now bringing back. They still believed in those policies. This was their second and last chance to make them work.

Politburo Intrigues: The Wind Faction, the Slippery Faction, the Earthquake Faction and the Cover-up Faction

The manoeuvring for power which delayed and complicated Deng Xiaoping's rehabilitation grew sharper after his return. In July 1977, he had told the Central Committee: 'We must tell the whole truth, the honest truth. Of the comrades here, some old scoundrels were affected by bad habits and do not speak the truth. This cannot be forgiven.'[1] He made the same point, more discreetly, at the Eleventh Party Congress, and his ally, the veteran PLA Marshal Nie Rongzhen, newly restored to the Politburo, warned that anyone who 'covers up mistakes in order to gain honour and keep his position at the expense of the Party's cause . . . will in the end have his falsehoods exposed'.[2]

These attacks were directed at Wu De and Chen Xilian, still the objects of widespread public anger because of their role in suppressing the Tian An Men riots, and at Wang Dongxing, now elevated to the post of Party Vice-Chairman ranking fifth in the hierarchy after Hua, Ye, Deng and Li Xiannian. Wang's promotion, nominally in recognition of his role in the arrests of the 'Gang of Four', was the most important of three Hua obtained at the Eleventh Congress, for as head of intra-Party security he wielded great power. The others were Ni Zhifu – a model worker who had once invented a special drill-bit, and was now, at forty-four, the youngest member of the Politburo – promoted from alternate to full membership; and Chen Muhua, Minister for Foreign Economic Relations, brought in as an alternate member to be the Politburo's token woman. Deng, on his side, was partly responsible for the strong military bias of the new body, ten of whose twenty-three members were PLA men, and for the entry of the Sichuan leader, Zhao Ziyang, as an alternate member.

Hua supported Wang and the other leftist Politburo members, and their counterparts at lower levels of the system, partly for tactical reasons. At the highest level of leadership, the power of the Party Chairman came from balancing one faction against another. If the leftists were removed, that power would be lost. Moreover, Hua needed them as protection for his own left flank; without them, he risked finding himself dangerously exposed at the leftist end of the Politburo spectrum. Within the country as a whole, Hua hoped to build a constituency among the huge, silent majority of Party bureaucrats who had gone along with the 'Gang of Four', and were anxious that it should not be held against them.

Deng's campaign against the leftists, both in the Politburo and the Party at large, was the first major issue on which he and his supporters, on one side, and Hua and Ye, on the other, publicly disagreed. Deng wanted the leftists out in order to move his own men into the key positions, and all through the autumn his aides wrote articles in the Party press, calling for a 'merciless purge' of the 'Gang of Four's' followers, and warning that if the campaign against them were not carried through to the end, 'earthquakes may occur again'.[3] But Hua, in his speech to the Eleventh Congress, called for moderation, arguing that 'only a handful' of people had been deeply involved, and that the campaign should be wound up by early 1978.[4]

Hua's leftist allies also hit back directly. In September, a directive was issued from the Central Committee's General Office, controlled by Wang Dongxing, calling for 'blows to be struck against reactionary speeches which harm and discredit Chairman Mao's great banner and attack and split the Party Central Committee headed by Chairman Hua'. This was answered a month later by Luo Ruiqing, the former PLA Chief of Staff whose legs had been broken in the Cultural Revolution. 'When dealing with careerists who try to usurp power,' he wrote in the *People's Daily*, 'if we compromise with them, yield to them and appease them, they will haunt us like ghosts and eventually bring disaster.' Another *People's Daily* article on October 14th warned: 'Those who have erroneous "leftist" ideas are often inclined organisationally to sectarianism . . . Numerous facts show that such a danger really exists.'[5]

By the end of that month, Deng's offensive was beginning to bring results. Hua conceded that 'some members of revolutionary committees have committed grave errors . . . but have refused to repent', and said that 'smash and grabbers' promoted during the Cultural Revolution should be resolutely excluded. Commenting on his statement, the *People's Daily* said it meant that in future, 'leading bodies which enjoy public confidence' should be appointed at all levels.[6]

Wei Guoqing, First Political Commissar of the Canton Military Region, became Director of the PLA General Political Department, a post which had remained unfilled since the arrest of Zhang Chunqiao the previous year. Wu De and Chen Xilian made token self-criticisms, acknowledging that they had made mistakes in 1976. In November, Hua succeeded in placing one of his old Hunan associates, Zhang Pinghua, in the post of Director of the Central Committee Propaganda Department. But the following month his move was countered when the office building of the Organisation Department, which controls Party appointments, was plastered with wallposters naming as its new director one of Deng's closest allies, Hu Yaobang.

Hu's promotion was the most important achievement of Deng's first months in power. Though none could have foreseen it at the time, three years later he would replace Hua as Party Chairman.

A tiny, crew-cut man, less than five feet tall, with expressive, lively features, he is one of the very few top Chinese officials of genuine poor peasant origin. At the age of fourteen, Hu ran away from home in his village in Hunan to become a child soldier, one of the so-called 'Little Red Devils' in the Red Army base area at Jinggangshan. Five years later, in 1934, he took part in the Long March, which only three soldiers in ten survived.

Hu first met Deng in 1941, when he served under him in the General Political Department of the 18th Army Corps in the barren Taihang Mountains, in Central China. For most of the next four decades, their careers ran in parallel, linked by personal friendship, common political ideas and a shared passion for bridge. When Deng fell at the start of the Cultural Revolution, Hu fell with him and spent two years living in a stable. When Deng was rehabilitated, Hu also returned, and helped to draft the 'three big poisonous weeds' in 1975. The following year, when Deng fell for the second time, Hu again disappeared.

But for all his closeness to Deng, Hu is no placeman. A powerful personality in his own right, he has great clarity of mind and as keen a sense as Deng himself of where China should be going – a vision which does not always coincide with that of his mentor.

The general purge of leftists which began at the end of 1977 lasted a year. The cast of characters was straight out of Peking opera, a Chinese variant of an old Stalinist technique, whereby such extravagant labels were pinned on opponents that any possibility of a reasoned defence was lost. In Henan province, the 'black ace generals and black claws of the Gang of Four' were said to have established a factional network of 'beaters, smashers and looters, corrupt elements, speculators, so-called old cadres who sold themselves and monsters and freaks'. In Hubei a 'female black ace general, a faithful running dog of the Gang of Four' was aided by a 'dog's head army officer and ferocious hired ruffians'. In Jiangxi, the 'little overseer and the filial scion of the landlord class' were said to have 'ganged up with renegades and alien class elements to hatch plots, shoot arrows in the dark and create splits'. In Liaoning 'the despotic ruler of the south and the local tyrant' were ferreted out. In Guangdong the purge exposed 'a ringleader who held black meetings, fanned up evil winds and fires, fabricated black materials, laid black charges and bombarded and attacked to seize power amid confusion . . . and held a black, mid-autumn dinner gathering'. In Shandong there were 'black melons of a poisonous kind, and jackals of the same lair'; in Xinjiang, a 'fox's tail'. All over China, 'struggle and criticism rallies' were held to denounce backstage directors, sinister henchmen, cats-paws, mad dogs, confidants and cohorts, factional chieftains and 'accomplices with bristles covering their bodies'.

At a typical rally, 'the army men and people roar, and all their hatred erupts like a volcano'.[7] Shenyang Radio in November 1977 described one session in the city's gymnasium at which, 'amidst the explosive shouting of slogans, an arch-culprit of beating, smashing and looting and active counter-revolutionary, Li Peiyuan, who had committed bloody crimes, was brought in . . . With a host of startling facts, comrades of Liming Machine Works of Shenyang municipality exposed . . . [his] fascist atrocities.'[8] Li and his associates were apparently imprisoned. Others were less fortunate. In Anyang, an industrial city in Henan province, that autumn, the former chairman of the county revolutionary committee, his deputy and ten other men, were taken from the Municipal People's Court after their trial, put on the backs of lorries, and driven slowly along the main street. Placards hung round their necks identifying them as counter-revolutionaries, and a loud-speaker van drove in front, recounting their crimes as 'unrepentant followers of the Gang of Four [who had] struggled by force . . . [and] carried out armed attacks'. The lorries were followed by brightly coloured floats, depicting the downfall of the disgraced leftists. Tumblers and child-acrobats performed, and some of the police sucked ice lollipops. Then the twelve were shot.[9]

Among those worst hit by the purge were former Red Guard leaders and 'rebels' who had been shock-promoted to local Party committees. This was true even of those who had been removed from power before the 'Gang of Four' fell. In Sichuan, a middle-aged couple, Liu Jieting and Zhang Xiting, had become vice-chairmen of the provincial revolutionary committee in the 1960s by manipulating competing Red Guard factions. In late 1977 and early 1978, they were taken from one part of the province to another and paraded before struggle rallies fifty-three times in six months; altogether, 13 million people screamed and spat at them.[10] Yet they had been dismissed from all their posts as early as 1971.

This was the revenge of the newly rehabilitated veterans who had themselves been tormented when Liu and Zhang were in power. As the campaign progressed, such cases became widespread, and articles appeared in the press urging the veterans not to bear grudges, but instead to blame Lin Biao and the 'Gang of Four' for what had happened to them.

No official figure has been given for the number struck down, but it was certainly far smaller than the number rehabilitated, which eventually reached three million. At the highest level in the provinces, the weeding out of leftists was comparatively thorough. By February 1978, seventy per cent of the chairmen and vice-chairmen of provincial revolutionary committees in power when Hua took over had been removed and not identified as reappearing elsewhere. But this pattern was not repeated lower down the scale. At a scientific institute in Changchun, where leftist influence had been particularly strong and 'almost all the responsible members . . . had been replaced', 166 scientists and officials were rehabilitated. Yet only one man was purged, five others suspended from Party membership, and 'a few' demoted.

This reflected both resistance from below – there was constant grumbling in the press that individual local leaders were 'clamping down the lid' – and restraint from above. The desire to avoid excessive upheavals was widespread, and led one provincial newspaper to conclude: 'We should punish some of those who have aroused the people's indignation, but not all of them. That is because, if we punish all of them in accordance with the law and general rules, there will be too many people involved.'[11] Three factories I visited in Harbin and Shanghai in the winter of 1977 admitted to an average of nine 'troublemakers' among 10,000 workers, equivalent to 85,000 in industry as a whole. Others denied having had any leftists at all.

In the armed forces the purge was almost totally blocked. In February the *Liberation Army Daily* warned that 'very serious evil will ensue if the army cadres are not purified', and called for blows to be struck against 'those who everybody knows have committed serious mistakes and have behaved very badly'.[12] Nevertheless, apart from a few senior commanders who had become deeply enmeshed in leftist politics, the army looked after its own: officers dropped from sight, seemingly purged, but in fact were moved sideways, out of the limelight, to reappear in new positions several months or a year later.

My own estimate is that, by the end of 1978, the purge had caught up some hundreds of thousands of people; the evidence is too fragmentary to try to be more precise.

After the Eleventh Congress, Deng's prestige steadily grew. Within weeks, demands inside the Party for him to take over the premiership reached a point where the Central Committee felt obliged to call on Party members to 'spontaneously uphold, ardently propagate and resolutely defend Chairman Hua's leadership position', and Deng himself moved to lower the temperature by telling a visiting Japanese delegation that he did not want the job. His words, as quoted by the Japanese, were reported by Western news agencies, and then made known within China through the *Reference News*, *Cankao Xiaoxi*. Nevertheless in January 1978, when he visited Burma and Nepal, he was treated as a head of government, and during a stopover in Chengdu, in his native Sichuan, the crowds which gathered to see him were so dense that his motorcade could not pass.

That month, the press for the first time began timidly to grasp the nettle of the Tian An Men riots, which remained a point of extreme sensitivity for the whole of the left. The Party journal, *Red Flag*, said the 'Gang of Four' had 'distorted the nature of the masses' activities commemorating Premier Zhou', and Hua accused them of 'trumping up charges' against Deng. But it was still maintained that 'counter-revolutionary elements' had played a part.[13]

This was a typical Hua compromise, which exonerated Deng; half-satisfied public pressure for the exculpation of the rioters, but without in any way endorsing their actions; and attempted to protect Politburo members such as Wu De, Chen Xilian and Ni Zhifu (Commander of the Peking Militia at the time of the riots), who were directly or potentially implicated in their suppression, by affirming that counter-revolutionaries had been involved. But the problem was not about to go away so easily; stop-gap measures might delay the reckoning, but eventually a settlement would still have to be made.

Hua and his supporters had other problems that spring. On January 4th, the *Liberation Army Daily* published an article entitled, 'A Portrait of the Wind Faction'. It took its title from Luo Ruiqing's article, three months earlier, which had attacked careerists who 'trimmed their sails according to the wind', and it was aimed at 'certain comrades' who, as the *People's Daily* put it, 'have no direct connection with the Gang of Four organisationally, but . . . reek with the Gang's stench'.[14] Brilliantly written, it set the tone for a sustained campaign against opportunism at the highest level.

'The followers of the Wind Faction,' the *Liberation Army Daily* said, 'have necks on ball-bearings, and wear anemometers on their heads . . . They change colour as they scent what the wind brings them. Having a weakness for speculation, they sell their souls at auction, and call "mother" anyone who gives them suck.' During the Five Dynasties period, in the tenth century, it continued, the mandarin Feng Dao served as chief minister for fifty-four years under five successive emperors. 'Can we not see in today's "followers of the wind" the shade of this old opportunist of classical times?' it asked. 'They are thick-skinned and ambitious, and their bones are soft and flexible . . . They are shameless, and with their honeyed phrases, they can pass off the dead as living, black as red, turn a bandit into a wise man and a wolf into a sheep.'

In an allusion to Deng's statement to the Central Committee plenum the previous July, it said leaders must be 'honest men who speak honest words and do honest deeds', and warned that those of the Wind Faction would not be able to 'switch winds for ever'.[15] A second article, some days later, levelled a similar barrage against what was termed the 'Slippery Faction', which was accused of trying to hide its errors and 'slip away'. Some people in this faction, the article declared, are 'not only like balancing dolls, which can never fall over, but they have risen to high posts'.[16] On January 15th it was the turn of the 'Earthquake Faction' – 'strange animals with horns that were not oxen, for they had bristles which the ox does not have, and were not porcupines, for the porcupine has no horns'. These people 'made trouble all day long', creating earthquakes as a means of advancing their own positions.

The attack was so broad that no leader who had survived the Cultural Revolution unscathed could feel safe – Hua and Ye, as much as lesser figures such as Wu De and Chen Xilian. In December, after a tense debate, held as usual in secret, the Peking People's Congress had re-elected Wu Chairman of the Municipal Revolutionary Committee. But the following month, on the second anniversary of Zhou Enlai's death, he came under renewed attack in wallposters for preventing publication of an unofficial anthology of commemorative poems written at the time of the Tian An Men riots. Several hundred crudely-printed sheets were pasted up in front of the bus depot at Xidan. It was the first time posters had appeared on what would later become known as the 'Democracy Wall'. More attacks on Wu followed during the anniversary of the riots in April, including a cartoon depicting him as the 'balancing doll' the *Liberation Army Daily* had described. The caption read: 'Swing to the Left + Swing to the Right = Will he fall?'

Chen Xilian also came under attack in January as 'an agent of Lin Biao and the Gang of Four' in posters put up by railway workers in Shenyang, where he had been Military Region Commander until 1975. But the more important targets were Ye and Wang Dongxing. By the end of 1977, Ye had become the major obstacle to Deng's plans: not only was his personal commitment to Hua undiminished, but his ceaseless glorification of Mao and of the Cultural Revolution was increasingly out of tune with the new political line. In the autumn he had proposed that stress be placed on promoting 'outstanding people who have come to the fore in the Cultural Revolution'.[17] In December he was instrumental in promulgating a 'Central Regulation' that the campaign against the 'Gang of Four', which Deng had been trying to broaden to include followers of Lin Biao, be limited to the period after the Tenth Party Congress in 1973.[18] The broadsides a few days later against the Wind Faction and the Slippery Faction denounced those who had embarked 'both on the pirate ship of Lin Biao and the factional wagon of the Gang of Four'. Another article accused them of 'creating taboos . . . to cover up for themselves'.[19] Ye, Wang and Hua were all open to that charge.

Before the campaign was over Hua himself was attacked in a poster in April about the Tian An Men riots. 'Who was in charge of Central work at that time?' it asked. 'Who was holding the instruments of dictatorship?' This poster, however, unlike those attacking lesser figures, was quickly removed by the police.

Hua had been obliquely criticised even earlier, in an abstruse historical allegory in the intellectuals' paper, *Guangming Ribao*, entitled: 'In studying calligraphy learn from Yen.' Hua's handwriting was in the calligraphy style of the classical writer, Yen Chenching, and the article was ostensibly devoted to praising the school which Yen had founded, comparing him, for that purpose, with another ancient hero named Zhou Bo. Both Yen and Zhou successfully subdued rebellions, in Zhou's case that of the Empress Lu. This showed, *Guangming Ribao* said, that 'Yen was as dignified as Zhou Bo, as simple and pure, as staunch and unyielding.'

At first sight, this might be taken as discreet flattery of Hua. For although the article did not name him, he, like Zhou Bo, had subdued a rebellion, and Jiang Qing had sometimes compared herself to the Empress Lu. The sting lay in what *Guangming Ribao* did not say, but every educated Chinese reader would have known: as a reward for his services in overthrowing the Empress Lu, Zhou was made Prime Minister, passing over the elder statesman who would normally have taken that post, Chen Ping. But as time went on it emerged that Zhou had little knowledge of statecraft, and the Emperor grew dissatisfied, eventually removing him and installing Chen Ping in his place. If Zhou is Hua, Chen is Deng Xiaoping: the moral of the tale was that Deng would eventually supplant Hua as China's leader.

Even Mao, except at the height of his power, had been unable to confront head-on this kind of innuendo. At one level the *Guangming Ribao* article was about calligraphy. At the next it was in praise of Hua.

Only at a still deeper level was its true meaning apparent as an attack on the very person it seemed to praise. The writer of such an article could be killed, as Stalin would have done, and as Mao did in the Cultural Revolution, but there was no rational way he could be pinned down and censured. The same was true of the attacks on the Wind Faction: who could reasonably complain about attacks on opportunists without inviting the counter-charge, 'If the cap fits . . .'? For this reason control of the press remained as important under Hua and Deng as it had been under Mao. The charges were too vague to be rebutted, but clear enough to chip away at a man's prestige and position unless convincingly answered. And they could only be answered in kind.

The contest that unfolded in the spring of 1978 was a game of power played by master tacticians: Deng, the seasoned, charismatic veteran, with fifty years of political intrigues behind him; Hua, the self-effacing political manipulator – each seeking with total ruthlessness to circumscribe the power of the other. Their political styles and aims were as different as their characters and personal histories. Hua, with Ye's support, saw himself as Mao's heir. He took the view that, where possible, Maoist orthodoxy should be preserved, and his speeches, always cautious and compromising, rarely original, were full of the Maoist sayings and jargon on which he had cut his political teeth, twenty years before. Deng, who had grown up before the Chinese Communist Party was formed, and had climbed to power alongside Mao – and sometimes in opposition to him – was altogether blunter: when he could, he spoke his mind; when he could not, he remained silent.

Their contrasting approaches showed up particularly sharply at a national conference on science, held in March. The opening address was given by Deng, who spoke almost entirely about the position of intellectuals:

We must see with a clear head that there is still a very big gap between our science and technology and advanced world levels . . . Will factually pointing out this backwardness make people lose heart? There may be such people. They do not have half a whiff of Marxism about them. Backwardness must be perceived before it can be changed. A person must learn from the advanced before he can catch up and surpass them . . .

We cannot demand that scientists and technicians, or at any rate, the overwhelming majority of them, study a lot of political and theoretical books, participate in social activities and attend lots of meetings unrelated to their work . . . The basic task of scientific research institutes is to produce scientific results . . . The main criterion for judging the work of the Party Committee of a scientific research institute should be the successful fulfilment of this basic task. Otherwise putting politics in command will remain mere empty talk.[20]

Hua, speaking six days later, took a very different line:

The modernisation of science and technology should not be regarded as a matter only for scientific and technological organisations, nor should it be left to a few people in research institutes or universities. The most powerful base and inexhaustible source of strength for the modernisation of science and technology in our country is the masses of the people in their hundreds of millions . . .

Far from being weakened, political and ideological work should be strengthened in the new period of development in our socialist revolution and construction . . . Politics is the commander, the soul in everything, and it won't do not to grasp political and ideological work . . .[21]

Here it was not just vocabulary and style which differed; a clear divergence over policy was also evident. Each man was addressing his own constituency – Deng, the intellectuals and the technocrats; Hua, the masses of the Party faithful. While avoiding confrontation, each was looking for leverage against the other.

Hua could do little to stop the attacks on the Wind Faction at source, because the *Liberation Army Daily* was controlled by Wei Guoqing, at that time one of Deng's allies. But through Zhang Pinghua, in the Propaganda Department, he succeeded in discouraging other newspapers from following suit. This was of crucial importance as the campaign had been intended to put pressure on him during the bargaining for state and government appointments which preceded the National People's Congress in February. In the end the only top-level victim was the Xinjiang leader, Saifudin, who was accused of 'following the wind' and removed from all his provincial posts. Yet even he was allowed to continue as an alternate Politburo member.

Hua's success in countering Deng's offensive was shown by the list of appointments the NPC announced. The veteran Marshal Xu Xiangqian became Defence Minister in place of Ye, who thereby surrendered part of his power and took over the honorific post of Chairman of the NPC Standing Committee, equivalent to head of state. Deng himself was named first among the vice-premiers, and a long-standing ally, Hu Qiaomu, who had worked with Hu Yaobang on the 'three big poisonous weeds' in 1975, was appointed president of the newly-formed Academy of Social Sciences. People dubbed these last two Deng's *erhu*, in wry recognition of their dominance within his inner circle; the term means literally 'two Hus', but is also the name of the Chinese two-stringed fiddle which drowns all the other instruments in the orchestra. At this time, too, Deng became Chairman of the CPPCC. Hua, on his side, was confirmed as premier as well as Party Chairman, so in theory holding more of the levers of power than even Mao had done. Chen Xilian remained a vice-premier, and an unhappy-looking Wu De and Saifudin hung on as NPC vice-chairmen. Closing the session, Deng called it 'a meeting of unity, a meeting of victory'. For Hua that was certainly true. He had ridden out the turbulence created by Deng's return, and by diluting the attacks on the leftists he had maintained the balance in the Politburo and held off a challenge to his power.

The appointments were made public with much fanfare on March 5th. Street demonstrations were organised, and Chang An Da Jie, the Avenue of Eternal Peace, was blocked by hundreds of thousands of people marching in procession: workers with red silk flags; dancers in the costumes of China's minorities; students holding up portraits of Hua and Mao; and columns of tiny children, chanting praise to the leaders. First-aid posts were set up along the route to treat firecracker accidents, and loudspeakers blared out patriotic songs.

The decisions had in fact been taken some days before the NPC meeting began, at a Central Committee plenum which opened on February 18th. Once that was accomplished, the campaign against the Wind Faction could do no real damage, and Hua was able to relax his grip on the press. On February 22nd, as the plenum was ending, the *People's Daily* broke its silence with a vituperative article which was, in fact, an admission of the campaign's defeat. It was entitled, appropriately, 'The Cover-up Faction', and said:

> Those people who have the character of the Wind, the Slippery and Earthquake factions still have power in their hands, and are covering up the lid in order to defend themselves . . . They are like the man in the legend who put up a sign saying, 'There is no silver buried here', over the place where he had hidden 300 ounces of stolen silver . . . They parade themselves as persons who are really holding high [Chairman Mao's] banner, but the one thing they do not want to do is expose and criticise the Gang of Four . . . Why can they still cover up? Because they hold power, and still have a 'gang' under them. With power in the hands of such people, are the masses satisfied?[22]

Another article, in March, attacked 'hyena-like people' who neither opposed 'killing' – meaning the attempt to overthrow Deng in April 1976 – nor were sufficiently ferocious to take a direct part in it, but prowled nearby hoping to benefit when it was completed.[23] References to the Wind Faction continued to appear intermittently for a few months more, but they now had little significance, and before long were being countered by renewed calls for moderation.

By the early summer of 1978, China had become a more unequal, more vital country than it had been possible to imagine while Mao was still alive. The uneasy legacy of anarchism and conformity, bequeathed by the Cultural Revolution, was being replaced by order, and a restored sense of the individual. On paper, at least, politics were giving way to professionalism, laxness and irresponsibility to discipline and hard work.

The army was instructed to spend two-thirds of its time on military training, and only one-third on political work – not the other way round as in the past. Scientists were to spend at least five days a week on research, and not more than one day on political study. Academic and professional titles were restored. In awarding university places to students and bonuses to factory workers, the emphasis was to be on results, with political attitude a secondary criterion. Egalitarianism was openly denounced as a petty-bourgeois concept with 'nothing in common with Marxist socialism'. Even if all wages were made equal, the *People's Daily* argued, workers with small families would be better off than workers with large ones; likewise it was an 'objective fact' that some students were brighter than others. These problems would remain until full communism was achieved, and that could only be brought closer by a sustained increase in production, or, as Deng Xiaoping put it at the Eleventh Congress, 'more hard work, and less empty talk'.

These common-sense, pragmatic policies sat less and less easily, however, with the continuing cult of Mao. The abandonment of his ideas and the rehabilitation of his former opponents eroded his image even as his name was being praised. In some provinces, almost every surviving official who had held a leading post before the Cultural Revolution was now back at work, and newspapers were for the first time admitting that innocent people had been beaten to death.

Yet the official view remained, in Hua's words:

Beyond any doubt, the Great Proletarian Cultural Revolution will go down in the history of the dictatorship of the proletariat as a momentous innovation which will shine with increasing splendour with the passage of time.[24]

Both he and Ye, moreover, warned that 'political revolutions in the nature of the Cultural Revolution will take place many times in the future.'

This did not stop small presentational changes – Mao's sayings

ao and Stalin with Bulganin (centre)
Moscow in 1950.

Deng Xiaoping,
visiting America in 1979.

Nikita Khrushchev

The arrest of Ren Wanding (wearing glasses) at Democracy Wall in April 1979. The plain-clothes policeman (right) is trying to put his hand in front of the camera

Chairman Hu, aged sixty-five when his appointment was announced in June 1981

Brezhnev's choice as successor,
seventy-year old Konstantin Chernenko

ceased to be featured on the masthead of the *People's Daily*, and when cited in articles they were no longer printed in bold type. But that hardly diminished the blatant contradiction between Maoist form and non-Maoist substance. The result was growing resistance to, and distrust of, the new political line.

Officials obstructed or delayed rehabilitations; deferred investigations of leftists; procrastinated and evaded implementing new policies; and when forced to act, 'erred to the "Left" rather than the Right' – for fear that they would be accused of 'denying the Great Cultural Revolution', and that 'the verdicts on a movement of one year may be reversed three years later'.[25] Among intellectuals this problem of 'unforgotten trepidation', as it came to be called, was especially marked, and not without reason: they had been the prime targets of almost all Mao's campaigns, and that spring renewed grumbling was heard in the Party that 'intellectuals are getting cocky again'.[26] In Shanghai and Peking, I talked to teachers, writers, musicians, opera singers – all wanted Deng to succeed, yet all feared that as had happened so many times in the past the left would stage a come-back, and he would fail. Their fears were made more acute by the visible differences within the leadership, and Hua's tendency to lean to the left for his own tactical, political needs. So they played safe, and did not stick their necks out.

It was a time when, on the surface, immense changes had taken place, but much of the bedrock below remained unaltered; when policy had been reformed, but practice had not. Cultural life was in theory now unfettered, but there were days when in Peking, the capital city of a quarter of the world's people, there was not a single stage performance of any kind, and only half-a-dozen old films. Western classical music was back in favour, but apart from a few token performances for visiting dignitaries, it was never played. The new education policies were criticised as elitist. Not only in the spring but all through that summer, not one factory I visited had introduced a bonus scheme or replaced its revolutionary committee; the reason was always that they were 'waiting for instructions from above', instructions which never came because nothing Mao had ever said could be found to justify them. No matter how much the press inveighed against the passivity of leading bodies, the bureaucracy was not sticking its neck out either.

Even the purge progressed more slowly than intended. In May 1978, two months after it was said to be 'in the main completed', the *People's Daily* indicated that in a quarter of all Chinese units, leftists were still in power, and that in many others the campaign against them had been half-hearted.[27]

The problem was that Deng and the reformers who supported him were blocked on all fronts – organisational, political and ideological. The barrier was the colossal figure of Mao. Organisationally, the campaign against the Wind Faction had failed, and the left-leaning members of the Politburo had held on to their power, because, as the *People's Daily* commented, 'they use [Chairman Mao's] great banner as a tiger-skin to cover themselves and intimidate others'.[28] Politically, the need to justify everything in Maoist terms meant what could not be done in his name could not be done; and what could not be done in his name convincingly might be announced, but would not be carried out. To break out of this straitjacket a wholly new approach was needed.

Mao Dethroned: Seeking Truth from Facts

In July 1937, Mao coined the formula, 'practice is the criterion of truth'. Like the concept, 'one divides into two', meaning that nothing is either completely bad or completely good, it was designed to combat leftist dogmatism in the Party.

In similar circumstances, after the fall of the 'Gang of Four', forty years later, Marshal Nie Rongzhen declared that these principles were the philosophical foundation of Mao Zedong Thought.[1] Deng Xiaoping spoke of them at the Central Committee meeting which approved his rehabilitation, urging the Party to 'seek truth from facts', and in the summer of 1978 he turned that slogan into his personal banner. It did not happen all at once: all through the spring, stirrings of independent theoretical discussion were beginning to be heard. But in April, after the campaign against the Wind Faction had clearly failed, Deng and Hu Yaobang took a conscious decision to use against Mao the weapons he himself had used against his leftist enemies in the 1930s.

The debate that followed profoundly altered political attitudes in China. It was launched by an article in *Guangming Ribao* on May 11th:

Revolutionary teachers . . . did not think that their theories were the 'peak', or absolute truth, or that they were free of the need to be tested by practice; nor did they think that their . . . conclusions were unchangeable . . . They never allowed others to worship their words as a 'Bible'. There is no doubt that the fundamental principles of Marxism, and the basic Marxist stand, viewpoint and method must be firmly upheld. But the treasury of Marxism is not a pile of petrifying dogma. In the course of practice, new viewpoints and conclusions will be added to it, and old ones which no longer meet the needs of new circumstances will be discarded . . . All ideas and theories without exception must always be tested by practice. Any idea or theory even if it has been proved to be true at a given stage of practice, must be further verified by new practice, so that it may be complemented, enriched or corrected.

What this meant was that any policy, whether it had been formulated by Mao, by Lenin, or by Karl Marx himself, could be scrapped if it was found not to work.

Such a radical, not to say revolutionary proposition could not fail to produce a furore. It was rather as though *The Times* had published a long, insulting article about the Queen. For several days *Guangming Ribao* was inundated with telephone calls, telegrams and letters. While the leftists denounced it as 'theoretically specious, ideologically reactionary and politically against Mao', others, including Li Desheng, the powerful Commander of the Shenyang Military Region, voiced support.[2] Deng himself endorsed the new formulation on June 2nd, in a speech to an all-army political conference.[3]

Hua remained neutral, declaring that the 'system' of Mao Zedong Thought was 'incontrovertible truth', but declining to be drawn on the practice criterion itself.[4] Since his success at the NPC he had grown visibly more self-assured. In May he had made his first visit abroad, to North Korea, and later that summer travelled to Rumania, Yugoslavia and Iran, where daily satellite coverage on Chinese television showed him taking part in a folk-dance with President Ceausescu in Bucharest, and relaxing with President Tito on an Adriatic cruise. No Chinese leader before had been presented to the people in this way: Mao had looked down from an Olympian height; Zhou had always been in Mao's shadow. Hua still found it painfully difficult to project a sense of presence, but he was no longer the hole in the crowd he had been two years earlier. He plainly felt his best course was to cultivate an image of statesmanship, which would provide a rallying point for all who wanted to prevent Deng rocking the boat. His slogan was 'stability and unity', and every speech he made was larded with it. In this new role, Hua tried to stay above the 'practice' debate.

The army conference saw the collapse of Ye Jianying's attempt to prevent the criticism of Lin Biao. The 'Gang of Four', Deng said, had been Lin's partners, and had stopped his crimes being properly exposed. Now it was 'imperative' to repair this omission. Disingenuously, he argued that far from negating the Cultural Revolution, criticising Lin Biao was 'precisely . . . to protect the great gains of the Cultural Revolution, which Chairman Mao personally initiated and led'. It was wrong, he told Hua, to argue that this was detrimental to unity, because there could be 'no basis for unity' unless followers of Lin Biao and the 'Gang of Four' who 'refused to correct their errors' were purged.

The 'practice' campaign, Deng told the conference, was directed against

> those comrades who talk about Mao Zedong Thought every day but maintain that whoever persists in seeking truth from facts, proceeding from reality and integrating theory with practice is guilty of a heinous crime. In essence their view is that one may only copy direct from Marx, Engels,

Lenin, Stalin and Chairman Mao . . . and to do otherwise is to go against Marxism-Leninism-Mao Zedong Thought.[5]

The leader of this group was Wang Dongxing. Its members included Wu De, Chen Xilian and Ji Dengkui. Collectively they became known as the 'Whateverists', because of their insistence on defending 'whatever decisions Chairman Mao made and whatever instructions Chairman Mao gave', the formula coined in the spring of 1977 to delay Deng's return to power.

Hua's decision to detach himself from the political fray meant the Whateverists could do little to obstruct Deng's offensive, particularly since all his arguments were carefully buttressed by quotations from Mao's works. The *Liberation Army Daily* cited Mao to show that 'Mao Zedong Thought itself also needs to be tested through practice'.[6] And Deng himself, in his speech to the PLA, quoted him no less than nineteen times.

The campaign reached its climax on July 1st, when, to mark the Party's fifty-seventh anniversary, every newspaper in the country printed a previously unpublished speech Mao had made in 1962, dealing with errors during the Great Leap Forward. To a Western reader, conditioned by pre-digested news flashes and banner headlines, a few sentences lost in the middle of a sixteen-year-old document, 25,000 words in length, may sound less than sensational. But to Chinese, they were electrifying. For the first time, the Party was acknowledging to the people that Mao was fallible: he had made mistakes.

'In socialist construction,' Mao had said, 'we are still acting blindly to a very large extent. Take me, for example . . . When it comes to productive forces I still know very little . . . Haven't we done many foolish things during the last few years? For shortcomings and mistakes in our work during the last few years, the responsibility rests first with the Central Committee, and in the Central Committee, primarily with me.'[7]

Much of the speech was devoted to the need for collective leadership and democracy, and it opened the way for an initial attempt to come to terms with the question – why, if Mao was so great, did Lin Biao and the Gang of Four come to power? 'The emergence of such anti-Party cliques,' answered the *People's Daily*, 'has something to do with imperfections in the implementation of democratic centralism.'[8] In other words, it was because democracy had been suppressed, the implication being by Mao. The speech also provided the first public admission since before the Cultural Revolution that the Great Leap Forward had been less than a complete success. And it hinted at a reassessment of Liu

Shaoqi, for it was Liu and Deng who had forced Mao to make his self-criticism. Liu was still being criticised publicly by Hua and Ye, but Deng never mentioned his name.

Mao's confession of error served to dramatise Deng's contention that nothing would be exempt from the practice criterion. Wang Dongxing and his allies, with support from conservative elements in the bureaucracy, continued to hold that Mao's teachings were themselves a criterion of truth, but this was not an argument that could easily be sustained.

Two years after Mao's death, China was at last beginning to move out from under his shadow. Slowly but surely, his role was being whittled down from that of a demiurge whose words were Holy Writ, to be interpreted and manipulated as scripture by his successors, to the more modest status of a great man with human limitations. Inch by inch, he was moved away from the centre of the political stage. The historians had a field day with allegories about the faults of Qin Shi Huang. On September 9th, the anniversary of Mao's death, no official ceremony was held, and only five small wreaths were laid at the monument in Tian An Men Square. A provincial leader wrote: 'We are convinced that if Chairman Mao were alive today, he would not repeat what he had said before, but would give new instructions in the light of the new situation, or make alterations or additions.'[9]

This slow ritual of attrition was accompanied by increasingly frontal attacks against the Whateverists and their supporters in the provinces. In June, as the campaign was starting, the leftist leader in Tianjin, Xie Xuegong, was removed – the first province head to fall since Saifudin in January. A month later, the *People's Daily* criticised 'forces that go against the tide and block the surging historical current', and warned that 'the day will come when they will be bidding their ladies farewell' – one of the communist world's more elegant euphemisms for being purged.[10] *Red Flag* published an article by one of Deng's supporters grumbling that 'some people are like tigers whose arses no one dares touch . . . They won't let the masses speak out honestly and according to facts.'[11]

More provincial Party chiefs were replaced in the autumn. In Peking, at a meeting held to rehabilitate those who had been wrongly arrested after the Tian An Men riots, a young worker named Han Zhixiong caused a sensation by accusing the city's Youth League Committee, and by implication the authorities under Wu De, of 'holding down the lid'. This was followed by articles in the *Peking Daily*, criticising Wu's administration.[12]

Matters now came abruptly to a head. Early in September, Wang

Dongxing ordered the suppression of the first issue of the newly-revived magazine, *China Youth*. One article in it, written under the aegis of Hu Yaobang, criticised the cult of Mao as a religion; another described the Tian An Men riots as 'a demonstration of real and full socialist democracy on the part of the people'. The ban was accompanied by an article in *Guangming Ribao*, signed by Fu Zuo, a homonym for 'Assist-the-Left', calling for a halt to the erosion of Mao's ideas.[13] Wang's action was implicitly supported by *Red Flag*, and by Ye Jianying, who told the NPC Standing Committee on September 13th: 'Sayings which are not beneficial to unity should not be said, and deeds which are not beneficial to unity should not be done.'

Six days later, all the main newspapers published a commentary implicitly comparing Wang with Zinoviev, whom Stalin had attacked for dogmatism in 1926.[14]

Rumours of a split in the Central Committee were now openly bruited about in wallposters. Hua had been sniped at for his insistence on the primacy of politics – 'Is politics still the commander,' asked the *People's Daily*, 'if there is nothing for it to command?'[15] – but otherwise, in his new aloof role, steered clear of criticism. However he did so at the cost of losing part of his freedom of manoeuvre. In the last week of September, the Politburo met in enlarged session, and the two sides set out their respective positions. Representing Deng's viewpoint, a *People's Daily* commentary declared:

In verifying who is truly holding something high and who is doing so falsely . . . we have never depended on statements or declarations, but on practice. A single concrete step is more important than a dozen self-criticisms. We do not trust promises easily. We do trust practice.[16]

The following day, *Guangming Ribao*, for the leftists, replied:

If today there are people who have made mistakes in line . . . we should wait and see . . . We should be prudent in reaching organisational conclusions on those who have made mistakes . . . People should not act with undue haste.[17]

Such pleas notwithstanding, the meeting decided to remove Wu De as Party leader in Peking. His replacement, Lin Hujia, a hatchet-faced, balding official, who had spent the previous two years running the anti-leftist purge in Shanghai and Tianjin, made his first official appearance accompanying Deng on an inspection tour in the city three weeks later. The change was greeted by the populace with undisguised jubilation – not just because Wu had been hated politically, but also because he had been a poor administrator: during his tenure of office, living conditions, hard anyway, had grown still worse, and crime was rising. One of Lin's first actions was to order a police dragnet, in which some 3,000 petty criminals were picked up and deported to the countryside. A wallposter, put up by workers at a television factory, summed up the general mood. 'With pleasure we send off Wu De,' it said, and quoted a couplet from one of Mao's poems:

> We ask the God of Plague, 'Where are you bound?'
> Paper barges aflame and candlelight illumine the sky!

The meeting also reversed the ban on *China Youth*, with the face-saving formula that an extra full-page photograph of Mao should be inserted. And it decided to re-examine the historical role of Liu Shaoqi, to see whether his case should be re-opened. *Guangming Ribao*, a week earlier, had drawn attention to the leftist practice of holding that 'the good is absolutely good, perfect, and to be lauded to the skies; the bad is absolutely bad, to be charged with fabricated crimes and driven into hell'. This meant, it noted, that if a person committed an error, all his past good points were rejected.[18] The unstated question was: 'If Mao is no longer absolutely good, are his enemies still absolutely bad?' It was still too early for an answer, but soon after this all criticism of Liu Shaoqi ceased.

The new situation was reflected in a speech Hua made at a state reception in the Great Hall of the People on October 1st, National Day. On the one hand he affirmed the achievements of the 'first' Cultural Revolution. On the other he urged the nation to 'emancipate the mind a little more' – a 'little', however, not a lot: Deng, four months earlier, had demanded 'a great emancipation'. He ended with an appeal: 'The stronger our unity, the greater will be our strength and the better we shall be able to manage our affairs.' It was an unusual note to strike on such a formal occasion, and betrayed a deep unease about the direction events were taking.

By now Deng had built up a momentum that was unstoppable. In each province and military region, Party committees were holding study meetings on the practice criterion, at which their leaders were having to stand up and be counted: for Deng or against him.

As the leftists were weeded out, the degradation of Mao's status accelerated. The press, which had always called him 'Our Great Leader and Teacher, Chairman Mao', started writing of him simply as 'Comrade Mao Zedong'. Zhou Enlai was quoted as having said, 'Mao Zedong is a great man born in the land of China, but . . . we must not view him as a god.'[19] The leftist thesis that Mao was an innate genius was rejected. 'The principle of "one divides into two" applies to every political party and every person,' wrote the *People's Daily*. Another article implied that the letter of what Mao wrote could now be ignored: instead, one should grasp the 'spiritual essence' of his writings, and use their 'stand, viewpoint and method . . . to solve practical problems'. Others said Mao Zedong Thought was 'not the ultimate truth', and that 'even the basic principles will be replenished, enriched and developed in the course of practice'.[20] The paraphernalia of the Cultural Revolution were reassessed. The Little Red Guards were renamed the Young Pioneers. The Red Guards themselves were described as naive youths who 'more often than not were misled into picking the wrong target to rebel against'. Their five former leaders, including Nie Yuanzi, the woman whose wallposter ignited the Cultural Revolution, were quietly arrested. And the 'Little Red Book' was accused of 'dismembering Mao Zedong Thought'.[21]

At the end of October, Deng left for a week's visit to Japan. He was the first top Chinese leader to go there since the Second World War, and his journey symbolised the two countries' reconciliation after the brutality of the Japanese occupation. It turned out to be a phenomenal success. The Japanese press talked of 'Deng Xiaoping fever', and he delighted his hosts by telling them, 'There is no use in an ugly person pretending she is beautiful . . . To have a poor friend like China must be troublesome, but please help us.' At home his travels were publicised on television and in the newspapers on a scale previously reserved for Hua alone.

Meanwhile the fall of Wu De had opened the floodgates for a wholesale reappraisal of the Tian An Men riots. The *People's Daily* carried accounts of how young people had gone to the square to support Deng against the leftists, and had refused to recant under arrest. A play, *Where the Silence is*, depicted the witch-hunt which followed the riots, and in the process gave a harrowing glimpse of the reality of the Cultural Revolution. The Tian An Men poems were exalted as the 'literature of rage'. The *China Youth News* compared the events of April 5th, 1976 with the student demonstrations which gave birth to the 'May the Fourth movement', the great revolutionary ferment in 1919 which shook China out of its feudal lethargy and changed the course of history.

The problem for Deng was how to translate this pressure into an irreversible political gain. Within the Politburo, relations had become so poisonous that Nie Rongzhen and Wang Dongxing were no longer speaking to each other. The historian, Li Shu, complained that some 'gentlemen whose heads must have been made of granite, so that they did not know that the era of Lin Biao and the Gang of Four was ended', were continuing to use 'stern language' to oppose the exoneration of the Tian An Men incident 'as though there were still something in their hands that could be used to suppress the revolutionary masses'.[22] Wu De and Chen Xilian were not named, but it was to them that he was referring.

In the end, Deng resorted to a ruse to force a conclusion. At his instigation, on November 2nd, Lin Hujia told an enlarged meeting of the Peking Party Standing Committee that the Tian An Men incident had been 'completely revolutionary' and that all who had been persecuted for their part in it should be rehabilitated. Lin's statement could not be made public, however, because the original verdict that the riots were counter-revolutionary had been passed by the Politburo, and only the Politburo or the Central Committee could change it. The effect of the move, therefore, was that the leadership now had no choice but to confront the issue and make clear its stand.

Eight days later, on November 10th, 1978, the Central Committee began one of the most important meetings since the communists had come to power. It was no longer quite the same body as had been elected at the Eleventh Party Congress when Hua's line dominated: at least twenty of the 201 full members had been purged as leftists. Deng was again away, this time in South-East Asia, when the work conference opened, but flew back on November 14th. The following day the Peking Party Committee promulgated the decision to reverse the verdict on the riots, and announced city-wide struggle rallies to criticise Nie Yuanzi and other arrested Red Guard leaders.

The shock waves these measures set off reverberated throughout the country, triggering an orgy of glorification of the riots and all who took part in them. In a dozen provincial cities, victims of similar incidents were publicly exonerated. The Peking Public Security Bureau announced that contrary to all previous official claims, not *one* of those arrested at Tian An Men Square had been a counter-revolutionary. The newspapers all carried pages of photographs taken in 1976 showing demonstrators declaiming poems to the crowd, and children tying white paper flowers to the hedge around the Martyrs' Monument, half-buried under an avalanche of wreaths. 'A brilliant page in China's revolutionary history,' one editorial called it. 'A real, spontaneous democratic revolution!'[23]

The timebomb Hua had been living with for the previous two years spewed out political shrapnel. Why, if ordinary people had stood up for Deng against the 'Gang of Four', had their leaders not done so? Why, if ordinary people had been right to demonstrate, had Hua and the others not resisted the leftists' demand to brand them as counter-revolutionaries? And, more ominously, if the Politburo resolution, approved by Mao, condemning the riots and stripping Deng of his powers, was now shown to have been wholly wrong, what was the status of the other Politburo resolution, also approved by Mao, which had been passed at the same time, appointing Hua premier and First Vice-Chairman?

Hua's reaction, as at the time of Deng's rehabilitation, sixteen months earlier, was to try to brush such considerations aside by appropriating the credit for what had happened. The reversal of the verdict on the riots, the press declared, had been achieved 'under the leadership of the Central Committee headed by Chairman Hua Guofeng'. On November 18th, Hua wrote a title inscription for a volume of Tian An Men poems, which was printed prominently in the newspapers and welcomed at the printing press with red banners and cheering crowds. This, said the *People's Daily*, using almost the same words as in July 1977, showed that 'Chairman Hua is indeed at one with the people'.[24]

But what had been convincing in 1977 looked rather threadbare a year later. This time the contradiction was drawn more sharply, and on a much broader canvas. The damaging, unstated questions did not go away. On Monday, November 20th, the *Liberation Army Daily* said the fall of the 'Gang of Four', which had previously always been ascribed to Hua's 'wise and courageous leadership', was 'an inevitable result' of the Tian An Men incident. During the weekend, posters went up calling for a special commission to investigate the suppression of the riots and identify those responsible. Two days later a writer who signed himself *Wu Wen*, meaning 'Without [the] Cultural [Revolution]', hinted that Hua was to blame for the delay in rehabilitating the rioters: there had been too much of 'the "wise" decision kind of empty talk', he declared. Another *Wu Wen* poster went further. The two Politburo resolutions of April 7th, 1976, it said, 'are not Marxist, but a product of dictatorship. They have violated democracy and the will of the people . . . They are a product of the criticism of [Deng Xiaoping's] supposed "right-deviationist wind".' The resolutions, it added, were also inadmissible because in a 'people's republic' officials should be appointed and removed by the people, not by 'the will of a few chiefs' as in feudal times. Not only Deng's dismissal but also Hua's appointment had been engineered by the 'Gang of Four' and were fundamentally undemocratic.

Deng was asked about the resolutions at a meeting with a Japanese delegation the following weekend. His reply was double-edged. Hua, he said, bore no responsibility for them because he had not had access to Mao; moreover, by April 1976 Mao was already too ill to make correct decisions. This was a perfectly adequate explanation of the reversal of the verdict on the riots and of Deng's own rehabilitation. But it carried the clear implication that Mao was also too ill to make a correct decision when he proposed Hua's appointment.

Nonetheless, popular feeling was not against Hua. I asked a crowd of a couple of hundred young Chinese, at the Xidan wall when the *Wu Wen* posters appeared, whether they wanted Deng to become premier. The answer was a roar of agreement. When I asked whether they also supported Hua, the response was another roar, as enthusiastic as the first. An older man in padded blue workclothes explained why: 'Chairman Hua smashed the Gang of Four. That was a major achievement. And he rose through the ranks, not like they did.' The intellectuals might prefer Deng, but ordinary people approved of both men.

Yet Hua had not been wrong to be wary of reversing the verdict on the Tian An Men incident, for it marked the moment of his eclipse. The initiative slipped from him, and passed to Deng. That month it was not he but his senior vice-premier who made the important statements. It was Deng who intervened when the wallposter movement got out of hand. And it was Deng whom the newspapers praised (until he ordered them to stop) for his 'radiant and piercing eyes, and his disarming smile . . . and his look of striking vigour'.[25]

The same day that the decision on the Tian An Men incident was made public, *Guangming Ribao* carried a long article which for the first time depicted the Cultural Revolution, not as a revolutionary movement which had been subverted by Lin Biao and the 'Gang of Four', but as fatally flawed from the very start. It denounced Yao Wenyuan's commentary on the play, *Hai Rui Dismissed from Office*, which he had written on Mao's instructions to launch the Cultural Revolution, as 'a counter-revolutionary signal for practising fascist ideological dictatorship', and described what followed in these terms:

Dark clouds spread over China . . . Our ancient culture was cancelled; people's thinking was put in a straitjacket; and public opinion was controlled. In such a big country as China, there was only the dictatorship of the Gang of Four. There was no freedom of the people . . .

The article ended with a warning: 'If injustices are not corrected, the people will not be happy. If the victims of unjust cases are not exonerated, the people will not be pleased.'[26]

The *People's Daily* echoed this demand for redress and called for special efforts to tackle 'prickly and complicated cases', no matter who had taken the original decisions. However it took a very different line on the question of the Cultural Revolution itself. 'Correcting mistakes in the Cultural Revolution' did not mean 'denying its fruitful results', it said. 'The mainstream of each of the political movements led by Chairman Mao was correct.'[27]

This reflected Hua's position, which once again was a compromise: rehabilitation work should be done well; Mao and the Cultural Revolution should be spared. But the tide of events was now against Hua. The first open criticism of Mao appeared at Xidan four days later.

The Democracy Wall

If the wallposter campaign which developed in November 1978 had been concerned merely with abstract political theorising and the in-fighting among China's leaders, it would have remained just an adjunct to the manoeuvring at the top, one factor among many in China's efforts to claw its way forward out of the Maoist past. That it turned into a movement which would shake the very fabric of the Maoist system was due to another, more potent force at work. Not for nothing was the wall at Xidan renamed at this point *Minzhu Qiang*, the 'Democracy Wall'. The new element was pressure from the people for more say in running their own affairs, and the realisation by Deng and other leaders that without more democracy, China could not progress.

Mao's successors did not start out with that view. Hua's style was of schoolmasterish authoritarianism, and the first year of his leadership was marked by a wave of executions. Court proclamations which came to the notice of foreigners included more than a hundred death sentences, and the figure for the whole country may well have been in the thousands.

Most of those shot were common criminals, but some were political offenders convicted of crimes such as 'uttering counter-revolutionary slogans', keeping a 'revisionist diary', and trying to form a political party. One man was even condemned to death for defacing a wallposter announcing Hua's appointment as Party Chairman in October 1976. The slogan of the time was, 'Grasp the key link of class struggle and bring great order across the land', and new Party and state constitutions were passed which brought a return towards the Marxist-Leninist orthodoxy of the 1950s.

Correspondence columns for airing grievances reappeared in the newspapers, and Party organisations were urged to be more responsive to the masses' complaints. These freedoms had to be realised through official channels, however. The purpose of more democracy, Ye Jianying explained, was to strengthen that 'iron discipline' without which the revolution could not succeed: democracy must have central-ised guidance, otherwise it would go astray.[1] Despite a marked liber-alisation of cultural policy and freer academic debate, this hard-line stance did not change until the start of the 'practice' campaign and the publication of Mao's 1962 speech on collective leadership.

Pragmatism connotes pluralism. In Deng's phrase (formally rehabilitated a few months later), 'It doesn't matter if the cat is black or white so long as it catches the mouse.' To accept this means to accept an element of political choice: there is no longer a unique correct path; any path which practice proves effective is correct. But if policy is to be determined by practice, there has to be debate; people must be allowed to state different views. *Red Flag* commented in July 1978, in an editorial on Mao's 1962 speech:

> By democracy we mean letting people speak out . . . If speaking out is not permitted within our Party and among the people, what democracy is there? Our comrades must draw a clear line of demarcation between us and the Gang of Four, who constantly labelled others as 'counter-revolutionaries'. Problems should be brought out into the open, both inside and outside the Party, and the masses should be allowed to speak out even if they abuse us.[2]

Four months later, this was to provide the authority on which the democracy movement would be based.

Meanwhile the authorities took a number of steps which encouraged the young in particular to be more adventurous. It was announced that several thousand Chinese students would be sent to study abroad, awakening in millions of young minds the previously undreamed-of hope of foreign travel – provided they could learn a foreign language. Television courses started in English, French and Japanese, and after a Central Committee member had publicly pointed out the absurdity of encouraging Chinese to learn languages but preventing them from practising their skill, word went out to the police not to intervene if they saw young people striking up conversations with foreign tourists. In four months, in Peking alone, more than a million English course books were sold; and unlike the last big foreign-language campaign, to study Albanian just before the Cultural Revolution, this time people really wanted to learn. After twenty years in which foreigners found it all but impossible to have any casual contact with Chinese, it became difficult to spend five minutes in a park without an eager youth descending on you wanting to try out his verbs. The prospect of an end to China's modern isolation fired the imagination of people of all sorts. One old lady grumbled to my wife about her eight-year-old grandson, who always got poor marks at school. 'I tell him,' she said, 'if he'll work, one day he can go overseas.'

All the elements from which the ferment of the coming weeks would grow were now present: explicit, official recognition that people should have the right to speak their minds; a more liberal cultural climate and easier acquaintance with foreigners and foreign ideas – even the ban on listening to foreign radio stations was lifted; the acknowledgement of Mao's fallibility and reversal of most of his policies; and the obvious disarray at the highest levels of the leadership over how to assess the Cultural Revolution.

Together these created that mood of doubt and questioning which must accompany any attempt to emerge from credulous feudal certitude into the real world. But like a damp sheet of paper which smoulders and will not burn, it needed the spark from the exoneration of the Tian An Men incident to make it catch. By declaring the riots to have been revolutionary, the leadership, in spite of itself, endorsed the right of the people to take spontaneous political action against men and policies they disliked. As the *People's Daily* wrote: 'Nobody gave the call. Nobody mobilised and organised. Nobody fixed in advance the target of the struggle or the banner. The masses of the people themselves were the fighters, the organisers and the commanders of the movement.' To argue that the people should have waited for the Party to lead them, it declared, was tantamount to saying that 'the people should always be a passive force in history to be butchered by anyone'.[3]

Lu Pu's first poster criticising Mao and the *Wu Wen* attacks on Hua were followed on Tuesday, November 21st, by an anonymous broadside against all the Politburo leftists.

> There is a small group of highly-placed feudal, fascist despots who are still holding leadership power . . . We tell this small group that the people have seen this very clearly. We are going to bring you down. You have not many days to go.

It hinted at Wang Dongxing, Chen Xilian and Ni Zhifu, but mentioned by name only Wu De – who was also the butt of numerous other posters. One, which caused endless merriment among the crowds, was a word-play on two homonymous characters meaning 'without virtue'. 'Old Wu, Old Wu,' it said, 'you really are the same as your name. You really are "without virtue".'

Pictures of 'militia heroes' who had helped to suppress the Tian An Men riots were pasted up, with crosses scrawled across their faces and a caption declaring them to be 'running dogs under Wu De's hand'. A poster, signed 'the Xidan-Hyde Park observer', proposed that 'criminals who have sneaked into senior Party positions' be punished according to law. Speakers' Corner at Hyde Park, it turned out, was known to most educated Chinese because it is mentioned in the writings of Karl Marx.

The attacks did not stop with the living. Wu De's predecessor as Party boss of Peking, Xie Fuzhi, who had died in 1972, was accused of persecuting veteran officials during the Cultural Revolution when he was Public Security Minister under Kang Sheng. The 'venerable Mr Kang' himself, who as late as August 1977 was still being fulsomely praised by Hua and Ye for his 'outstanding services to the revolutionary cause', was likewise denounced and appeals were made for the rehabilitation of his victims. One poem summed up the feelings of many:

> Tao Zhu was blameless,
> And the merits of Peng Dehuai
> Greatly outweighed his mistakes.
> Kang Sheng will stink for ever,
> And the body of Xie Fuzhi
> Should be whipped 300 times!

Calls were also made for the return of Peng Zhen, the only living member of the pre-Cultural Revolution Politburo still in disgrace. Without naming him, the Peking Party Standing Committee praised the way the city was run in the early 1960s when he was Mayor, and *Gongren Ribao* reported that a slogan was circulating which ostensibly meant, 'we want truth', but by a play on the Chinese character for truth, *zhen*, actually conveyed the meaning, 'we want Peng Zhen'.[4]

These issues of personality temporarily overshadowed, but did not displace altogether, the deeper import of the wallposter campaign, which had to do with democracy. The same Tuesday, November 21st, which saw the first attack on the Politburo leftists, a poster went up, signed by a worker in a radio factory, warning: 'To make people think that democracy and human rights are only slogans of the Western bourgeoisie, and that the Eastern proletariat needs only dictatorship – especially all-round dictatorship in all spheres of the superstructure – cannot be tolerated any more.' A day later a railwayman wrote:

> Our country is now entering a new historical period. The Chinese people are thinking where China will go. Without a tremendous spiritual revolution in China's ideas, the revolution cannot continue. A great spiritual revolution leads to a great social revolution, which leads to great economic reforms.

The poster went on to affirm that Mao had been a great leader, whose historical contributions were indelible. 'But,' it said, 'this does not mean he did not make mistakes.'

Try to ask yourself, without Chairman Mao's support how could Lin Biao have come to power? How could the Gang of Four have stirred up the anti-right deviationist wind, aimed at overthrowing Comrade Deng Xiaoping? How could the Tian An Men incident have been called counterrevolutionary? . . . Only by pointing out on what questions Chairman Mao made mistakes . . . can political swindlers like Lin Biao and the Gang of Four be prevented from usurping power, and can the historic tragedy be prevented from occurring again. If, on the contrary, people are not allowed to speak their minds about Chairman Mao, freedom of speech and democracy will be empty words.

The graffiti the poster attracted was revealing. 'The people should dare to criticise the emperor!' one person wrote. 'Very good that he raised his opinion! Resolutely support him!' scrawled another. A third wrote simply, 'This man has got courage.' Only one comment was hostile. 'I want to criticise the reactionary viewpoint of this poster,' it said. 'Workers, peasants, soldiers, cadres and intellectuals will not allow Chairman Mao's great banner to be slandered!' This had been crossed out, and someone had written in a different hand: 'Don't start by putting hats on people. You should give your reasons. Chairman Hua and Vice-Chairmen Ye and Deng are listening to the voice of the people, and they are wiser than you!'

Other posters on Thursday and Friday accused Mao of becoming muddled in his old age, and losing touch with the people. 'Why did the people not love you as they loved Premier Zhou Enlai?' one asked pointedly. 'How we wish Chairman Mao could listen modestly to what is being said about him now!'

The most important poster of the week went up on Friday afternoon, not at the Democracy Wall but on a wooden fence along one side of Tian An Men Square, directly opposite Mao's mausoleum and only a stone's throw from the Public Security Ministry. It was nearly 20,000 words long and stretched for fifty yards, on sixty-six beautifully calligraphed sheets, the first of which showed a flaming torch. The work of eight rather nervous young men from the remote south-western province of Guizhou who called themselves 'The Enlightenment Society', it was an impassioned, sometimes inflammatory attack on feudalism and idolatry. 'Down with modern superstition!' it said. 'And down with the modern deification of the imperial power of today! The day when deification disappears from the life of mankind will be the day of mankind's awakening.' The feudal state of Qin Shi Huang had gone and would not return, it declared. 'The spiritual Great Wall of thousands of years of dictatorship has been smashed, and the people must march through onto the path of democratic freedom.' It concluded, in huge characters:

THE CULTURAL REVOLUTION MUST BE REASSESSED. MAO ZEDONG WAS 70 PER CENT GOOD, AND 30 PER CENT BAD.
Chinese, Arise! The moment has come to launch an attack against dictators of all kinds, and to settle accounts with them once and for all. Judge them, and prepare for the final struggle against them!

By this time many foreign embassies in Peking, including those of Britain and the United States, were reporting back to their governments that the wallposter campaign was being orchestrated by Deng to exert pressure on the Central Committee work conference.

This was a perfectly reasonable assumption. The first big poster campaign after the communist victory, against the rightists in 1957, was launched on Mao's instructions and popularised by Party committees. In the Cultural Revolution, Nie Yuanzi's first poster was inspired by Kang Sheng. And in 1976, the campaign against Deng and the 'right-deviationist wind to reverse correct verdicts' was whipped up by the 'Gang of Four'. But this time the assumption was wrong. Deng welcomed the campaign, and tried to guide it into directions useful to himself, but he did not initiate it, nor was it ever really under his control.

One reason for this was given by Ren Wanding, a former Red Guard who emerged as one of the democracy movement's leaders. Disillusioned, like millions of other young people whom Mao had discarded at the end of the Cultural Revolution, when they had served their political purpose, Ren had fallen foul of local officials and had been designated a 'bad element', a label not removed until 1978. Now aged thirty-four, married with a small daughter, he worked as an electrician; a stocky man, always clad in quilted blue workman's clothes, he soon became a familiar figure at the Democracy Wall, peering myopically through a pair of spectacles, one lens of which had been shattered by, of all things, a ping-pong ball.

Ren argued that any leader who tried to meddle in the campaign ran too great a risk of being charged with factionalism if found out. And certainly Deng's allies were careful to do nothing which might lay them open to such charges. When Xia Xunjian, who started an unofficial magazine called *Reference News for the Masses*, approached Hu Yaobang for support, Hu's secretary showed him the door and told him not to come back. Even those who did have high-level connections were not involved in the democracy movement at the start. Zhou Weimin, a Communist Youth League Central Committee member, together with

Han Zhixiong, the young man who had spoken out against the Peking Youth League Committee in August, and a third CYL Committee member, Wang Juntao, founded the magazine *Peking Spring*, but not until some weeks after the movement had started. Initially Zhou opposed the Democracy Wall, arguing that there was no need for it. As for Lu Pu, whose poster criticising Mao began it all, he and his friends had no back-stage support. 'If we had,' one of them told me a year later, when the wheel had turned full circle and the democracy movement was being suppressed, 'would we be in the position we're in now?'

Like the Tian An Men riots, from which it drew its inspiration, the democracy movement arose spontaneously. Yet it was not without antecedents. In November 1974, three young men in Canton, with support from an official at the provincial radio station, wrote a long wallposter under the pen-name Li Yizhe, entitled 'On the Democracy and Legal System of Socialism'. It attacked feudalism and 'modern superstition' and propounded a down-to-earth, moderate political programme which in those days of leftist dominance was viewed as the blackest heresy.

'What makes us marvel,' wrote *Peking Spring*, four years later, 'is that under the peculiar conditions of that time young people could correctly reveal the essence of so many important political problems.' Those words were also applicable to *Peking Spring* itself, and to the unofficial democracy movement to which it gave its name. Despite twenty years of relentless leftist propaganda and total isolation from alternative ideas, there was no lack of young Chinese who were able and had the courage to think for themselves, often with startling clarity.

The most astounding of all the revelations from the Democracy Wall was the extent to which independent thought had been kept alive even through the worst periods of ideological repression. Malraux's cruel dehumanising image of 'a nation of blue ants' was not only not true now, it had *never* been true. Until 1978, foreign writers and journalists, even foreign governments, by and large accepted the official picture of China as a new, revolutionary land, whose people were somehow above the normal rules of human behaviour and to whom the criteria of happiness or misery that they would use in their own countries were not to be applied. The Chinese themselves, not being endowed with such credulity, held on silently to the old values, waiting for the day when the storm would subside.

Li Yizhe's poster in 1974 had a predictably hostile reception. The three young writers were taken to criticism meetings and eventually imprisoned. But four years later, the political climate had become very different. Xu Wenli, who helped to found, with Lu Pu, the first of the

Peking unofficial magazines, the *April 5th Tribune*, explained the wallposter movement as 'something we felt we now had a right to do'. This time the leadership concurred, at least to the extent of instructing the police to let it run its course.

So began one of the most extraordinary weeks in China's recent history. In the early hours of Saturday morning, November 25th, a carload of police arrived to photograph the Enlightenment Society's poster. Crowds began gathering soon after dawn, and throughout the weekend there were rarely fewer than five or six hundred people standing in front of it, animatedly discussing its contents.

At the Democracy Wall, foreign diplomats and journalists were mobbed by eager youths, asking about life in the West and about what the West thought of China. Did France have food rationing? Could Americans really dismiss their leaders? Could people abroad travel freely and choose their own jobs? Could they live where they wanted to? Did foreigners think China would also one day have these freedoms?

I asked one such group what *they* were seeking:

Human rights should be protected. The democracy of every person should be protected. Now there is no such protection. We want the freedom of going to other provinces, the freedom of ideas, of speech . . .

But now at least you have some freedom of speech. A month ago you couldn't have talked to me like this.

(Laughter, shouts of 'No, we couldn't'.) I don't think democracy is yet fully developed. In my understanding, we now have to develop it. There seems to be freedom. You can put up wallposters in Tian An Men Square and here at the Democracy Wall, and the officials won't arrest you. But when you get back to your factory your comrades there will discriminate against you, and you'll have trouble. If you are very cautious, you may not be discriminated against, but if you want to speak more, disaster will come.

What sort of disaster?

It's very difficult to say. Perhaps you will meet some huge disasters. (Gesturing at others in the group.) They don't like to say.

You mean, you might be arrested?

(After heated discussion.) They say they want to get rid of the secret police. They say the secret police are everywhere, whether at the Democracy Wall or in Tian An Men Square or other places. They want to get rid of them. This is one of the things they want. (Another speaker.) We also want freedom of speech, but not for its own sake. We want to use it to

contribute to China's modernisation. At the moment freedom of speech does not actually exist.

What other freedoms do you want?

Many! Freedom of forming societies and associations, freedom to strike. People should get whatever rights they are supposed to enjoy. It's written in the constitution that workers can go on strike, but it's only written on paper. It's nothing! It's nil! And the people still have no freedom of going from province to province and no freedom of occupation.

How will you try to bring about change?

We must rely on the people to bring change. What we can do now is to import the ideas of foreign countries. We want to use human rights to educate the people. Many people now are beginning to understand human rights, and we want to do some sort of education work. The human rights problem is getting sharper and sharper. The question is rising – sharply!

The fear of police informers was widespread. I listened to a tall, gangly youth denouncing Wang Dongxing. 'He is an animal, a bandit,' he said of China's fifth-ranking leader, who also happened to be the country's security chief. As he spoke he drew meaningful looks from an older man nearby, who eventually could bear it no longer, and burst out, in fractured English, 'I afraid. There too many policemans here.'

Plainclothesmen in most countries have their particular characteristics. In the Soviet Union they are called *shlyapki* – 'hats' – on account of their distinctive headgear, a kind of Russified trilby. In China they are large, clean-cut young men, usually in their thirties, slightly better turned out than the average and wearing leather, not cloth, shoes. Ordinary people loathe them. When a student was detained at the Democracy Wall during an argument with two of these *Gonganju* agents whom he had caught noting down bicycle numbers, a poster went up giving an eye-witness account of his arrest, accompanied by a slogan in foot-high characters, declaring: 'We want socialist democracy, we don't want the KGB! We want stability and unity, we don't want blue terror!'

Saturday, November 25th, also saw the founding of the *April 5th Tribune*. 'We thought that wallposters were not enough,' Xu Wenli explained. 'They didn't reach enough people. Nothing had been published by the people themselves since 1949, and we felt that now we could do it.' By the end of December more than a dozen other unofficial magazines followed, and in the succeeding months, altogether about eighty appeared.

That evening a crowd of several hundred people marched from the Wall to Tian An Men Square, for a rally at the Martyr's Monument. They chanted, 'Long Live Democracy!' and 'Long Live the People!' and sang the Internationale. Earnest young men stood up to denounce 'feudal socialism' and the 'Gang of Four and their present-day followers'. A soldier, in olive-green PLA uniform, pointed to the Great Hall of the People, where the Central Committee was in session, and told the crowd: 'The people sitting in there should represent us.' An older woman complained that people had been afraid to speak their minds not just since the Cultural Revolution, but since the anti-rightist campaign in 1957. The sentiments were startlingly direct, but the atmosphere remained calm, and soon after nine pm the participants dispersed after agreeing to meet again.

At this point Deng made his first public appearance for two weeks, at a meeting on Sunday morning with the Chairman of Japan's Democratic Socialist Party, Ryosaku Sasaki. The initial bland communiqué merely quoted him as saying that China was concentrating its energies on its modernisation programme, and that stability and unity prevailed. But through unofficial channels – 'xiao dao xiao xi' or 'small path news', as the Chinese call it – word spread quickly that he had in fact endorsed the wallposter movement, and had said the authorities would not suppress it. This was confirmed on Monday at the third of the rallies now being held nightly at the Wall and at Tian An Men Square. By then Deng had had a further meeting, with the American columnist Robert Novak, and a summary of what he said was relayed by a fellow journalist to the 3,000-strong crowd. The wallposter movement was 'a good thing', he told Novak, even though some individual posters were not correct. In particular, Mao was better than seventy per cent good, thirty per cent bad, as the Enlightenment Society had judged him. 'Chairman Mao's contributions in Chinese history are beyond words,' Deng said. 'Every Chinese knows that without Chairman Mao there would have been no new China.'[5]

Asked about the premiership, he said it was not a job he wanted, both because of his age – at seventy-four he was too old – and because he wished to keep his hands free to look after China's modernisation. As for his relations with Hua, 'Well,' he said, 'didn't Marx have Engels?' Whom he was comparing with Marx, and whom with his amanuensis, was left delicately unsaid.

The effect of Deng's qualified approval was to lend added momentum to a movement which was already growing extremely fast. Local 'democracy walls' had started in Canton and Hangzhou, and that weekend several thousand young people gathered in the People's Square in Shanghai for discussions similar to those in Peking. Before long, every provincial capital had its wall, even Lhasa in distant Tibet.

As the leadership began to grasp the potential scope of the forces that had been unleashed, and with the lesson of the Cultural Revolution still fresh in their minds, it was decided that Deng's statement must be complemented by measures to damp things down. On Monday afternoon, a suspiciously official-looking poster, ostensibly written by a group of Qinghua University students, condemned what it termed 'the Hyde Park kind of democracy', and urged people 'firmly to rally round the Central Committee headed by Chairman Hua'. The *Reference News* carried an account of Deng's talk with Sasaki, in which he said it was wrong for posters to criticise Mao by name. The following morning parts of his remarks were published on the front pages of all the main newspapers:

> To write big-character posters is allowed by our country's constitution. We have no right to deny this or to criticise the masses for making use of democracy and putting up big-character posters. If the masses feel some anger, we must let them express it. Not all the opinions of the masses are carefully thought out, nor can we demand that they all be entirely correct. That is nothing terrible. It is wonderful to see the ability to distinguish right from wrong and the conscientious care for the destiny of the country shown by the overwhelming majority of the masses . . . They demand stability and unity and consider the overall picture. The masses have their doubts on some questions; some utterances are not in the interest of stability and unity and the four modernisations. We have to explain matters clearly to the masses and know how to lead.[6]

The repetition of the phrase, 'stability and unity', and the *People's Daily*'s reassuring headline, 'The Party Central Committee led by Chairman Hua is united and full of confidence', were clear calls for restraint. But in trying to control the movement, Deng had given it legitimacy. The crowds going each evening to Tian An Men Square diminished, but the feeling of euphoria did not. Every politically minded Chinese was aware that the system was being shaken, and no one could say where it would end. To some, anything seemed possible. When I asked a normally staid Chinese official whether he thought the country would still be Marxist in fifty years' time, the reply was: 'Who knows?'

For the next few days, posters continued to go up attacking Wang Dongxing for his opposition to 'Prince Deng'. 'He is an opportunist, hungry for power,' one declared. 'Blast him out, this insect! The Politburo cannot keep him.' Abuse was also piled on the heads of Wu De and Ni Zhifu, notably in a poster which made a homonymous play on the characters *wu ni* meaning 'sewage'. Ni Zhifu, it said, was a 'criminal butcher' who had helped to direct the suppression of the Tian An Men riots: 'Bastards like Ni Zhifu can bugger off!' Deng himself, despite having told Novak he was against personal praise, was eulogised as 'the living Zhou Enlai', and there were renewed calls for the exoneration of Peng Dehuai and Liu Shaoqi. Deng had confirmed that Peng would shortly be rehabilitated, but when Novak had asked him about Liu, he remained silent. 'Did Liu Shaoqi really want to lead China into darkness?' one poster asked. 'Or did he just have a different opinion from Chairman Mao? Why must people always be overthrown if they have different opinions?' Another excoriated Mao for his support of the 'Gang of Four'. 'They acted under the leadership of Chairman Mao,' it said. 'Without his support, they would not have been able to achieve their aims . . . Without his prestige, they could not have stayed in the Politburo a single day.'

On Wednesday, November 29th, Deng met another Japanese delegation, to whom he hinted that the crucial decisions at the Central Committee work conference had now been taken. All political measures, he said, must be directed towards ensuring stability. Some leaders had made mistakes and were therefore being criticised for it, but the Party was taking a 'long view' of their cases.

It marked a turning point. The attacks on individual Politburo members gave way to speculation about possible promotions with a rapidity which provided impressive evidence of the accuracy of the information filtering out from the work conference through senior officials' children. Those being considered for Politburo posts were said to include the Anhui Party leader, Wan Li, who had fallen with Deng in 1976, Lin Hujia, Hu Yaobang, Vice-Premier Wang Zhen, Zhou Enlai's widow, Deng Yingchao, and Chen Yun, the veteran economist who drew up China's first Five Year Plan.

Posters went up complaining that the criticism of Mao had gone too far. Party youth leaguers took over the nightly rallies in Tian An Men Square, dinning out the official line, and on Friday they ended altogether. The same day Hua and other members of the Politburo Standing Committee, including Wang Dongxing, re-emerged in public, followed by the rest of the leadership at the weekend. The press, in chorus, called for stability, and the *China Youth News*, urging its readers to be patient, said it was impossible to solve major questions until the conditions were ripe, which required a process of preparation.[7]

But for all this display of unity, the reassertion of control was not entirely painless. 'You can silence the people,' one poster grumbled, 'but that won't solve anything.' Another took issue with Deng's remark about not criticising Mao by name. 'Whether a person is named or not doesn't alter the way people feel about him,' it said. 'Speeches can be banned, but ideas cannot.'

The Third Plenum and the Secret Speech

In February 1956, two years and eleven months after Stalin's death, Khrushchev's Secret Speech at the Twentieth Party Congress marked for the Soviet Union the divide between one era and the next. In China, two years and three months after Mao's death, that role was played by the Central Committee plenum, held from December 18th to 22nd, which ratified the work conference's decisions. Each country, in different ways, repudiated the legacy of its dead dictator. Each confirmed the dominance of the new leader who had emerged: Khrushchev in Moscow, Deng Xiaoping in Peking. Each moved decisively away from the known certainties of the past, into an unfamiliar present.

The Secret Speech was of the two the more momentous event, both because it came with so little warning and because of the political earthquakes it triggered, not only in Eastern Europe but throughout the world. The schism between the Soviet Union and China, the Cultural Revolution and the Prague Spring were all, in their different ways, as much a consequence of Khrushchev's words as the immediate repercussions in Hungary and Poland.

Even the wave of student unrest which overran the West in the 1960s and the emergence of terrorist groups such as the Weathermen, the Baader-Meinhof Gang and the Red Brigades, were not completely unrelated to Khrushchev's speech. Disillusionment with Soviet communism, born of his revelations, helped to lead a new generation of misguided idealists to look to more radical sources of inspiration instead of to Moscow, as their elders had done in the 1930s.

Internally, however, the Third Plenum may prove to have more far-reaching effects in changing China's system than the Secret Speech did in the Soviet Union.

After Beria's arrest in June 1953, pressure for reform came first from Soviet writers. The dramatist, Lavrenev, spoke out against plays in which 'the characters declaim excerpts from textbooks on the oil industry'. Ilya Ehrenburg, in October, asked literary bureaucrats to remember that 'statistics do not play the role in art that they play in industrial production'. Two months later the critic, Pomerantsev, appealed for sincerity in Soviet writing. And Alexander Tvardovsky, editor of the magazine *Novy Mir*, published a poem which began, sardonically:

> Here's your novel, all in order,
> Showing the new bricklaying method.
> The backward Assistant Director, the progressive Chairman,
> The old grandad, all marching towards communism!

With encouragement from Malenkov the controls were relaxed a little. Ehrenburg published a short novel, symbolically entitled *The Thaw*. Theatre audiences gave a rapturous reception to a play by Leonid Zorin, contrasting an idealistic old revolutionary with his privileged, bureaucrat son. The satirist Mikhail Zoshchenko, silenced in the Zhdanov purge, appeared in print again in the humorous magazine, *Krokodil*, for the first time since 1946.

The extravagant praise of Stalin, which had filled the newspapers in the years before his death, faded away. In its place collective leadership was urged, and there was a deliberate revival of Leninism. After the repudiation of the 'Doctors' Plot', anti-Semitic materials stopped appearing. Malenkov launched a campaign to raise living standards and make more consumer goods available, an area which Stalin, like Mao, had shamefully neglected. In August 1953 this was taken a step further when agricultural reforms were promulgated, including the virtual abolition of the tax in kind which Stalin had imposed on the produce of peasants' private plots. The Kremlin, which Stalin, in his morbid suspiciousness, had ordered closed on security grounds, was reopened to the public – as, twenty-five years later in Peking, were the parks north of the Forbidden City, which had been closed for the same reason in the last years of Mao's life. After the announcement that Beria had been shot, an investigative commission was set up to study the evidence of illegalities which had emerged at his secret trial.

As in Hua's first year in power in China, the changes came slowly. This was partly because Malenkov, though intelligent and able, was a colourless, uninspiring figure, in character not unlike Hua, and partly because, even more than in China, the Politburo was divided. Of its ten members, only the Stalinist old guard, Molotov and Kaganovich, and the 'liberals', Malenkov and Mikoyan, were consistent in the policies they supported. To the others, and above all to Khrushchev, policy choices were essentially instruments in the struggle for power. When the cultural relaxation Malenkov had favoured produced a flood of works showing the 'dark side' of Soviet reality, Khrushchev urged a clamp-down, which lasted through much of 1954. When Malenkov said another world war would mean 'the destruction of world civilisation', Khrushchev responded that it would 'end in the collapse of the world imperialist system'. When Malenkov, announcing his agricultural reforms, declared that 'the whole country is fully supplied with grain', Khrushchev said 'grain production does not cover all the needs of the national economy', and revealed that the Soviet Union had fewer cattle than in 1916. The fault, Khrushchev implied, lay in the Ministry of Agriculture – under Malenkov's control; the necessary corrective was a stronger role for the Party – under his control. In March 1954, he launched his so-called 'Virgin Lands' scheme, to open up for farming huge areas of marginal land in Kazakhstan and Southern Siberia.

By opportunism and shrewd alliances, Khrushchev chipped away at Malenkov's strength. From being merely senior Party secretary, he emerged at the September plenum in 1953 as 'first secretary', and soon afterwards 'First secretary', with the benefit of the capital letter. Then he set out to erode Malenkov's support in the provinces, cultivating his own followers in Kazakhstan, in the Ukraine and Leningrad – as Deng did in China in the second half of 1978. The instruments the two men used were different – more raw power in the Soviet Union, greater reliance on ideological levers in China – but the basic techniques for gaining control of the Party machine in Moscow in the 1950s and Peking in the 1970s were essentially the same. So were the outward signs of the struggle which appeared in the press. Where Hua was sniped at by innuendo, through abstruse historical analogies, Malenkov was taunted in the Aesopian language of Russian fable. 'A sparrow was appointed eagle,' one such parable began. 'Then the other birds wondered. "Is he really right for the job?"' [1]

Malenkov fell in February 1955 when Khrushchev finally succeeded in uniting a majority of the Politburo against him. His resistance had been sapped by murky hints the previous summer that he had helped Beria fabricate the so-called Leningrad Affair in 1948. However the issue which brought him down was his emphasis on consumer goods. This had encountered strong opposition from the military, the big industrial ministries and conservatives such as Molotov, all of whom wanted a return to the traditional Stalinist policy of absolute priority for heavy industry. Khrushchev could justify aligning himself with this group by arguing that Russia needed bread for the many before television sets for the few. Bread needed tractors and fertiliser, which in turn required steel and chemicals. Yet in fact Khrushchev was in agreement with Malenkov over the need for consumer goods, as he showed in later years when he adopted the same policy himself. His opposition was tactical.

In the last analysis, Malenkov fell because he was a weak leader, unable to steer a clear course through the conflicting demands set off by Stalin's death, and unable to carry the rest of the Politburo with him. That a man who had spent the last twenty years in Stalin's shadow, debilitated by constant fawning and fear, should prove an inadequate successor is hardly surprising. Less predictable was that someone of the pungency and flamboyance of Khrushchev would survive to become his rival.

The new premier was Marshal Nikolai Bulganin, fifty-nine, who represented the military in the Politburo and had been an ally of Khrushchev ever since they had worked together in the Moscow City apparatus in 1931. As the amiable, goateed straight man, he was a perfect foil for the rumbustious Khrushchev, and they quickly became known in the West as 'Mr B and Mr K'. Malenkov became Minister of the Electric Power Industry, but kept his Politburo membership. He was still a force to be reckoned with: in June, when Khrushchev's protégé, Shepilov, the new editor of *Pravda*, incautiously criticised Malenkov's ministry, he was forced to print a retraction the next day. But the witch-hunt for Malenkov's supporters in the provinces continued, and this he was unable to stop. A month later it was Molotov's turn. At a Central Committee plenum in July, he was out-voted, and strongly criticised by Khrushchev, for opposing a rapprochement with Yugoslavia.

Throughout that year, as Khrushchev was building up his power, he moved carefully. The grandiose attempts at innovation which marked his latter years would begin only after the Twentieth Congress. For the moment the priority of heavy industry was reasserted, though accompanied by more investment in agriculture, a drive to build new housing, higher minimum wages, better working conditions, and other consumer-orientated measures. The rift with Tito was patched over, Adenauer invited to Moscow and relations established with West Germany. And the policy, begun under Malenkov, of reining in the secret police and closing the labour camp complexes at Vorkuta and Kolyma was continued and expanded. In 1955 and 1956, perhaps five million prisoners were freed or had their sentences commuted to exile. Most of them, however, were amnestied without exoneration. By the time of the Secret Speech the number actually rehabilitated was only 7,679, compared with nearly three million in the same period after Mao's death.

Many of these measures implied de-Stalinisation, in that they constituted a determined move away from Stalin's methods and policies. The decision to remove Stalin's new appointees from the Politburo and to throw out the 'Doctors' Plot' and rehabilitate its victims, all within a month of his death, proclaimed more clearly than words that those methods were wrong. The mass arrests and purges ceased. Malenkov, despite his overthrow, was not executed or imprisoned, but remained a member of the leadership and in 1956 even visited Britain. Stalin's name was mentioned infrequently, and the anniversaries of his birth and death were marked half-heartedly or not at all. But apart from the emphasis on collective decision-making, and references to the 'cult of personality', which Marx, Lenin and Stalin were all said to have opposed, nothing was done directly to tarnish Stalin's image. Khrushchev in his memoirs, attempted to explain why:

> For three years we were unable to break with the past, unable to muster the courage and the determination to lift the curtain . . . [on] the arrests, the trials, the arbitrary rule, the executions, and everything else that had happened in Stalin's reign. It was as though *we were enchained by our own activities under Stalin's leadership*, and couldn't free ourselves from his control even after he was dead. Not until 1956 could we rid ourselves of the psychological after-effects of the hysteria which had gripped us during the hunt for enemies of the people . . . For a while we gave the Party and the people incorrect explanations about what happened; we blamed everything on Beria. He was a convenient figure. We did everything we could to shield Stalin . . . I repeat: not until 1956 did we set ourselves free from our subservience to Stalin. (Emphasis added.)[2]

Khrushchev was rationalising after the event. Inertia, opposition from Stalinist hardliners, and the sheer incalculability of the effects of knocking Stalin from his pedestal must also have played their part. For the Chinese, too, after Mao died, it was 'convenient' to blame the 'Gang of Four'.

The decision to start criticising Stalin openly, taken by the Soviet leadership in January 1956, was intended to free the repressed initiative of the workforce by loosening the stranglehold of the 'little Stalins' in the provinces, the hundreds of thousands of petty officials who kept rigidly to the old Stalinist ways. As *Pravda* explained, in terms which would be repeated word for word by the *People's Daily*, twenty years later:

> Some of these people act like political bosses who think they can make every decision themselves. They shout at people and take no one else's opinion into account . . . [They] feel they are incapable of making mistakes, and they regard every critical remark as being aimed at undermining them.

However no agreement was reached on how far or fast de-Stalinisation should go. When the Twentieth Party Congress opened on February

14th, the decision to make the Secret Speech had still not been taken, even though the materials for it – mainly the findings of the investigative commission – were all available. Instead, Khrushchev used his six-hour opening address, in the Kremlin's white and gold assembly hall, to present, as his own, refurbished versions of many of the policies which, a year earlier, he had been denouncing to bring down Malenkov. War, he said, was no longer inevitable, and communists could now win power by taking the parliamentary road (the two theses which later formed the basis for China's charges of revisionism). And while criticising those who 'tried to shift the emphasis from heavy industry to consumer goods', he agreed that light industry must develop quickly (and the growth rate envisaged by the new Five Year Plan was not much less than Malenkov had been calling for).

On Stalin, however, Khrushchev said merely that the Central Committee had 'vigorously condemned the cult of personality . . . and [the practice of] making a particular leader a hero and miracle-worker', adding: 'The currency of the cult of personality . . . at times resulted in serious drawbacks in our work.' The formulation was only a small advance on what had been said before, and attracted little notice.[3]

What then happened to make him deliver, eleven days later, an attack on Stalin so devastating that it rocked the communist world and brought Soviet-ruled Eastern Europe to the verge of disintegration? The crucial factor seems to have been the intervention of Mikoyan. On February 17th, as the Congress was torpidly winding its way through routine debate, the wily Armenian dropped a bombshell.

'For nearly twenty years,' he told the astonished delegates, 'we had in fact no collective leadership. The cult of personality flourished, a cult which had already been condemned by Marx and then by Lenin. This could not fail to exert an extremely negative influence on the internal situation of the Party and its activities.' He complained of 'self-glorification', and for the first time since Stalin's death attacked the old dictator by name, declaring that certain of his writings on economics 'hardly help us and seem not correct'. Stalin's *History of the Soviet Communist Party* (*Short Course*), which had a status analogous to that of Mao's 'Little Red Book', was 'unsatisfactory', Mikoyan said. And most dramatic of all, he charged that 'individual Party leaders' had been 'unjustly declared enemies of the people'.[4]

The British Kremlinologist, Edward Crankshaw, called it at the time 'the most sensational pronouncement made by a Soviet statesman for two decades'.[5] If today it seems rather tame it is because of all that has become known about Stalin since.

Was Mikoyan Khrushchev's stalking horse? Or did he deliberately set out to force Khrushchev's hand? It cannot have been by chance that the two examples he cited of Party leaders who had been unjustly cut down were men who had been purged by Khrushchev in the Ukraine in the late 1930s. Kaganovich, who spoke later, clearly opposed de-Stalinisation, while the others toed Khrushchev's line. Yet the picture was, as the *Economist* wrote that weekend, of 'Mr Mikoyan . . . leading, while Mr Khrushchev, the Party Secretary, follows behind'.[6]

In China Deng used de-Maoisation to remove ideological and political obstacles to the policies he wished to promote. But it was also a vital means to undermine Mao's successor, Hua, and Mao's followers, the Whateverists. In the Soviet Union, Khrushchev, too, wanted a more just and democratic society, and he knew it could only be brought about if the dead hand of Stalin were removed. Mikoyan's speech made him realise that unless he grasped the nettle of de-Stalinisation, he risked being overshadowed, and the Congress, 'the most important since Lenin's death', as Mikoyan had called it, would be a hollow triumph. By facing the challenge, he could present himself as the only man who dared to speak out, and win control of a powerful weapon with which to undermine his rivals. It was a make-or-break decision; having taken it, Khrushchev did not mince words:

Comrades! . . . Quite a lot has been said about the cult of the individual and about its harmful consequences . . . The cult of the person of Stalin . . . became at a certain specific stage the source of a whole series of exceedingly serious and grave perversions of Party principles, of Party democracy, of revolutionary legality . . .

Stalin . . . absolutely did not tolerate collegiality in leadership and in work and . . . practised brutal violence, not only toward everything which opposed him, but also toward that which seemed to his capricious and despotic character, contrary to his concepts . . .

Stalin abandoned the method of ideological struggle for that of administrative violence, mass repressions and terror . . . Arbitrary behaviour by one person encouraged and permitted arbitrariness in others. Mass arrests and deportations of many thousands of people, execution without trial and without normal investigation created conditions of insecurity, fear and even desperation . . .

Stalin showed in a whole series of cases his intolerance, his brutality, and his abuse of power . . . He often chose the path of repression and annihilation, not only against actual enemies, but also against individuals who had not committed any crimes against the Party and the Soviet government . . .

Many Party, Soviet and economic activists who were branded in 1937–38 as 'enemies' were actually never enemies, spies, wreckers and so on, but were always honest communists; they were only so stigmatised, and often, no longer able to bear barbaric tortures, they charged themselves (at the order of the investigative judges – falsifiers) with all kinds of grave and unlikely crimes. . . .

This was the result of the abuse of power by Stalin, who began to use mass terror against the Party cadres . . . Stalin put the Party and the NKVD up to the use of mass terror when the exploiting classes had been liquidated in our country and when there were no serious reasons for the use of extraordinary mass terror. The terror was directed . . . against the honest workers of the Party and the Soviet state . . .

It has been found that all the cases of so-called 'spies' and 'saboteurs' were fabricated. Confessions of guilt of many arrested and charged with enemy activity were gained with the help of cruel and inhuman tortures . . . Many thousands of honest and innocent communists have died as a result of this monstrous falsification of such 'cases', as a result of the fact that all kinds of slanderous 'confessions' were accepted, and as a result of the practice of forcing accusations against oneself and others . . .

It is clear that these matters were decided by Stalin . . . He was the chief prosecutor in these cases. Stalin not only agreed to, but on his own initiative issued, arrest orders . . .

Stalin was a very distrustful man, sickly suspicious . . . Everywhere and in everything he saw 'enemies', 'two-facers' and 'spies'. Possessing unlimited power, he indulged in great wilfulness and choked a person morally and physically. A situation was created where one could not express one's own will. When Stalin said that one or another would be arrested it was necessary to accept on faith that he was an 'enemy of the people' . . . What proofs were offered? The confession of the arrested . . . How is it possible that a person confesses to crimes that he has not committed? Only in one way – because of application of physical methods of pressuring him, tortures, bringing him to a state of unconsciousness, deprivation of his judgment, taking away of his human dignity . . .

Stalin sanctioned in the name of the Central Committee of the All-Union Communist Party [Bolsheviks] the most brutal violation of socialist legality, torture and oppression . . .

The power accumulated in the hands of one person, Stalin, led to serious consequences during the Great Patriotic War [the Second World War] . . . The necessary steps were not taken to prepare the country properly for defence and to prevent it from being caught unawares . . . Had this been done . . . our wartime losses would have been decidedly smaller . . . At the outbreak of the war we did not even have sufficient numbers of rifles to arm the mobilised manpower . . . Everything was ignored . . . Is this an example of the alertness of the Chief of the Party and of the state at this particularly significant historical moment? . . .

Very grievous consequences, especially in reference to the beginning of the war, followed Stalin's annihilation of many military commanders and political workers between 1937 and 1941 because of his suspiciousness and through slanderous accusations . . . During this time the cadre of leaders who had gained military experience in Spain and in the Far East was almost completely liquidated . . .

After the first severe disaster and defeats at the front, Stalin thought this was the end. In one of his speeches in those days he said: 'All that Lenin created we have lost for ever.' After this Stalin for a long time actually did not direct the military operations and ceased to do anything whatever . . . The threatening danger which hung over our Fatherland in the first period of the war was largely due to the faulty methods of directing the nation and the Party by Stalin himself . . . Even after the war began, the nervousness and hysteria which Stalin demonstrated, interfering with actual military operations, caused our army serious damage . . . [In the Kharkov operation alone] the Germans surrounded our army concentrations and consequently [as a result of Stalin's direct order] we lost hundreds of thousands of our soldiers. This is Stalin's military 'genius'; this is what it cost us! (*Movement in the hall.*)

Stalin considered that he never erred, that he was always right. He never acknowledged to anyone that he made any mistake large or small . . .

We must state that after the war the situation became even more complicated. Stalin became even more capricious, irritable and brutal; in particular his suspicion grew. His persecution mania reached unbelievable dimensions. Many workers were becoming enemies before his very eyes. After the war Stalin separated himself from the collective even more. Everything was decided by him alone without any consideration for anyone or anything . . . Stalin's mania for greatness led [him] . . . completely [to] lose consciousness of reality; he demonstrated his suspicion and haughtiness not only in relation to individuals in the USSR, but in relation to whole parties and nations . . .

Let us also recall the 'Affair of the Doctors' Plot' (*Animation in the hall.*) . . . Stalin personally issued advice on the conduct of the investigation and the method of interrogation of the arrested persons. He said that the academician Vinogradov should be put in chains, another one should be beaten . . . Stalin personally called the investigative judge, gave him instructions, advised him on which methods should be used; these methods were simple – beat, beat, and once again, beat . . . This ignominious case was set up by Stalin; he did not, however, have the time in which to bring it to an end (as he conceived that end), and for this reason the doctors are still alive . . .

Comrades! The cult of the individual acquired such monstrous size chiefly because Stalin himself, using all conceivable methods, supported the glorification of his own person . . . Stalin's *Short Biography* which he edited himself . . . is an expression of the most dissolute flattery, an example of making a man into a godhead, of transforming him into an infallible sage, 'the greatest leader', 'sublime strategist of all times and nations'. Finally no other words could be found with which to lift Stalin up to the heavens . . . Or let us take the matter of the Stalin prizes. (*Movement in the hall.*) Not even the tsars created prizes which they named after themselves . . . And was it without Stalin's knowledge that many of the largest enterprises and towns were named after him? Was it without his knowledge that Stalin monuments

273

were erected in the whole country – these 'memorials to the living'? . . .

Comrades: We must abolish the cult of the individual decisively, once and for all.

There was much more besides. It was Stalin, Khrushchev said, who had forced Ordzhonikidze to shoot himself. It was Stalin who had supervised the 'Leningrad Affair' after Zhdanov's death. It was Stalin's 'shameful role' which had caused the break with Yugoslavia. And it was Stalin, he hinted, who had had Kirov murdered.

One contemporary account said that thirty of the 1,600 delegates who heard the Secret Speech fainted or had seizures. The story is no doubt apocryphal, yet it conveys well enough the traumatic nature of the shock Khrushchev administered.

Devastating though it was, however, the Secret Speech was not a wholesale demolition of Stalin. His 'negative characteristics', Khrushchev said, became 'fully evident' only after the Seventeenth Congress; until then he had played a 'positive role'. And the speech included a remarkable passage which amounted to a partial exculpation:

Initially . . . Stalin was one of the strongest Marxists, and his logic, his strength and his will greatly influenced the cadres and Party work.

It is known that Stalin, after Lenin's death, especially during the first years, actively fought for Leninism against the enemies of Leninist theory and against those who deviated . . . At that time Stalin gained great popularity, sympathy and support . . . In the past Stalin undoubtedly performed great services to the Party, to the working class and to the international workers' movement.

This question is complicated by the fact that all that we have been discussing was done during Stalin's life under his leadership and with his concurrence; here Stalin was convinced that this was necessary for the defence of the interests of the working class against the plotting of enemies . . . We cannot say these were the deeds of a giddy despot. He considered that this should be done in the interests of the Party, of the working masses; in the name of the defence of the revolution's gains. In this lies the whole tragedy!

Not only did Stalin act from the highest motives, according to this argument, but the 'extreme methods' he used were not wrong in themselves. Lenin himself, Khrushchev noted, had 'when necessary, resorted ruthlessly to such methods'. Stalin's fault was that he used them excessively, and in cases when they were 'not necessary'; it was a question of degree.[7]

To Khrushchev, all the blame attached to the personality of one man – Stalin. He never asked, either in the Secret Speech, or later, in his memoirs, why the system was unable to prevent Stalin from behaving as he did. To him, the system was correct; the question of reform did not arise.

The Secret Speech has not, to this day, been published in the Soviet Union. It was delivered at a closed session, from which foreign delegates were excluded, on February 25th, the day before the Congress ended, and was then circulated within the Party together with Lenin's so-called testament, a letter written in 1922 questioning Stalin's suitability for leadership on the grounds of his 'excessive rudeness' and 'capricious temper'. Copies were sent to the Central Committees of foreign parties, and later a lengthy summary was read out at meetings of selected non-Party members in factories and institutes.

The first public sign that something extraordinary was afoot came from East Germany, where on March 4th *Neues Deutschland* published an article by the Party leader, Walter Ulbricht, saying that Stalin's works could no longer be considered as Marxist classics. *Pravda* and other Soviet journals began rehabilitating the reputations of old Bolsheviks whose names had not been heard for a generation, and by the middle of the month small groups of purged former leaders began emerging from the camps. History, one observer commented, was being 'unrewritten'.

In Moscow the Tretyakov Gallery abruptly withdrew from display all its portraits of Stalin. The marble busts of the dictator, which had occupied a place of honour in public buildings, were replaced by mirrors, aspidistras or whatever else came to hand. Where in China the 'Little Red Book' gradually faded from view, in the Soviet Union the *History of the Soviet Communist Party (Short Course)* and the *Short Biography* were removed from bookshops and kiosks overnight. Soviet historians began reassessing General Suvorov and Ivan the Terrible, whom Stalin had placed above criticism.

In Tbilisi riots broke out when the authorities failed to commemorate the anniversary of Stalin's death. Elsewhere, however, Khrushchev's injunction, at the end of the Secret Speech, against 'washing dirty linen in public', was generally heeded. Widespread private discussion of Stalin's merits and demerits took place, in the vegetable queues at the markets as well as among bureaucrats in their offices. But when, on March 17th, one day after the first accounts of the Secret Speech were published in the West, Ulbricht relayed its main themes at a public meeting in East Berlin, *Pravda* carefully deleted all references to Stalin from its report. When *Trybuna Ludu* in Poland was already calling Stalin a murderer and a despot, the Soviet press was still talking warily about 'disseminating the Marxist view of the part played by the individual in history, and the need to do away with the cult of personality'. Not until March 28th did *Pravda* criticise Stalin by name, and then in careful, measured terms scattered through an immensely long editorial.

This ferment stopped at the Chinese border. While politicians in most of Eastern Europe vied with each other to propagate Moscow's new line, China's leaders and newspapers remained completely silent. It was five weeks after Khrushchev had spoken before the *People's Daily* grudgingly reprinted *Pravda*'s editorial, and so informed the Chinese people that Stalin was no longer the 'everlasting sun'. At one level Khrushchev's handling of de-Stalinisation – in particular the lack of prior consultation – was the latest in a series of irritants to Sino-Soviet relations that had been accumulating through the 1950s. But Mao was more deeply disturbed by the substance of what he had said; as the Chinese later acknowledged, it marked the beginning of a parting of the ways.

Mao understood, as Khrushchev did not, the illogicality of damning Stalin while absolving the system. If the system was correct, in Mao's view, Stalin's rule was also mainly correct; if Stalin was mainly bad, it was because a bad system had let him be so. The latter possibility, that the Stalinist system was bad, and needed not piecemeal reform but thoroughgoing structural change – as Tito argued in November 1956, after the Hungarian revolt – Mao rejected all his life. In this, his first consideration was the parallel between Stalin's position and his own. His doubts on other questions, such as Khrushchev's theories on the avoidability of war, and on the possibility of a peaceful transition to socialism, did not become an issue until later on.

Accordingly China responded to the Secret Speech by affirming, in the *People's Daily* on April 5th, 1956, that Stalin's merits outweighed his faults. Although he had made serious mistakes – in enlarging the class struggle, in lack of vigilance on the eve of the Second World War, and towards Yugoslavia (and by inference also China) in the international communist movement – his achievements, the *People's Daily* said, entitled him to be regarded as an 'outstanding Marxist-Leninist fighter'. The following day Mao personally made this point to Mikoyan – who was then visiting Peking – urging the importance of making an 'all-round evaluation' of Stalin. The same themes were rehearsed in a follow-up article in December.

This remained China's view through the 1970s. By then, not only was all criticism of Stalin halted lest it reflect on Mao, but even Stalin's criticisms of Lenin were suppressed for the same reason.[8]

In these circumstances, Deng Xiaoping, in the winter of 1978, was extremely careful to avoid any suggestion that he was acting towards Mao as Khrushchev had acted towards Stalin. Nor was his caution unwarranted. Mao had used the Khrushchev label to pin down Liu Shaoqi; Hua now gave a veiled warning that he was prepared to use the same weapon against Deng. On November 20th, the day after Lu Pu put up the first wallposter criticising Mao, an editorial, reflecting Hua's views, appeared in the *People's Daily*. 'After Stalin's death,' it said, 'Khrushchev came out and made use of the people's dissatisfaction at the enlarging of the suppression of counter-revolutionaries . . . to stir up the fire and oppose Stalin.' In the days to come, it warned, 'anti-Party careerists' might also emerge in China to 'make use of the unfair cases during the Cultural Revolution to oppose Chairman Mao Zedong, Premier Zhou Enlai, Chairman Hua Guofeng and other leaders who practise Marxism'. Soon afterwards, a Central Committee document was issued which quoted Deng as saying 'the Chinese Communist Party and people will never behave like Khrushchev'. It was an assurance he was still repeating several years later.

The need to avoid accusations of 'Khrushchevism' was one factor inducing prudence. Another was the memory of the upheavals to which de-Stalinisation had led, which had caused Mao to be so contemptuous of Khrushchev's ineptitude. It was a memory made more actual by the continuing ferment all over China set off by the reversal of the verdict on the Tian An Men riots.

As a result the communiqué of the Third Plenum, made public on December 23rd, was not only far milder on Mao and the Cultural Revolution than the closed session Central Committee debate, but was also more circumspect than much of the comment which had been appearing in the press. Nonetheless, sandwiched between the eulogies of Mao as a 'great Marxist', it did make, at the most authoritative level of the Chinese Party, the two essential points: that Mao had made mistakes and the Cultural Revolution had had grave faults.

The great feats performed by Comrade Mao Zedong in protracted revolutionary struggle are indelible. Without his outstanding leadership and without Mao Zedong Thought, it is most likely that the Chinese revolution would not have been victorious up to the present . . . *Comrade Mao Zedong . . . always adopted a scientific attitude of dividing one into two towards everyone, including himself. It would not be Marxist to demand that a revolutionary leader be free of all shortcomings and errors.* It also would not conform to Comrade Mao Zedong's consistent evaluation of himself. The lofty task of the Party Central Committee . . . is to lead and educate the whole Party and . . . country to recognise Comrade Mao Zedong's great feats *in a historical and scientific perspective . . .*

The Great Cultural Revolution should also be viewed historically, scientifically and in a down-to-earth way . . . The shortcomings and mistakes in the actual course of the revolution . . . should be summed up at the appropriate time . . . However there would be no haste about this. Shelving this problem will not prevent us from solving all other problems left over from past history in a down-to-earth manner. (Emphasis added.)[9]

This was self-evidently a compromise, in which the decision to put off a definitive verdict on the Cultural Revolution was a concession to Hua and Ye. By the yardstick of the first comparable Soviet public statement, the *Pravda* editorial of March 28th, 1956, it was not very robust. But the woolly phrases were strengthened by the wave of rehabilitations which accompanied them. Memorial meetings were held for Tao Zhu and Peng Dehuai. During the Spring Festival, in January, Peng Zhen reappeared, having been flown back to Peking from his exile in Shaanxi five days after the plenum ended. With him were Wang Guangmei, Liu Shaoqi's widow, who had been released from Qincheng Prison barely a month before, and Lu Dingyi, who had been a vice-premier and head of the Party's Propaganda Department before the Cultural Revolution. Other former department heads and Central Committee secretaries followed, many of them among Deng's closest collaborators in the 1950s and early 1960s. By the middle of 1979, every important leader Mao had purged in the Cultural Revolution had been rehabilitated, except one – Liu Shaoqi himself – and in February the Central Committee had ordered a full-scale reinvestigation of his case.

By comparison Khrushchev, for all his strong words, did not clear the name of *one* of the major figures shot in the great show trials of the 1930s. Tens of thousands of lesser men were rehabilitated, and he implied in the Secret Speech that the liquidation of the 'Trotskyites, Bukharinites and Zinovievites' had not been justified. But, as he later acknowledged in his memoirs, the rehabilitation of Bukharin, Zinoviev, Rykov and the others was 'indefinitely postponed'. It was, he wrote, the 'one mistake' of the Twentieth Congress.

The mildness of the Chinese communiqué proved deceptive. Seven weeks later, in February 1979, it was followed by a Chinese 'Secret Speech' which caused almost as great a sensation, at a more restricted level, as did the original Secret Speech within the Soviet Party. The occasion was a Central Committee conference on theory, the speaker a deputy editor of the *People's Daily* named Wang Ruoshui:[10]

The Cultural Revolution should be correctly treated in accordance with what the . . . third plenum called, 'viewing it historically, scientifically and in a

278

down-to-earth way'. However, to regard what was obviously bad as good is not treating it correctly. It is also wrong to hold on to the personality cult. The Cultural Revolution was a great catastrophe for us and the whole people . . . It was an incorrect revolution, using the wrong method against the wrong targets . . .

Chairman Mao did not welcome criticism . . . He desired to find China's own road to the construction of socialism and even wanted to surpass Marx in his contribution to humanity. Therefore it is understandable that he was impatient and overstepped himself in certain things . . . However we cannot help saying that Chairman Mao became arrogant, impetuous and intolerant of criticism . . . Chairman Mao placed his personal prestige above the interests of the people. He could not tolerate the correction of his errors either before or after his death. In short, he could not tolerate anyone who infringed on his absolute authority . . .

During the Cultural Revolution, Chairman Mao's personality cult was further developed to its limit. This personality cult was personally encouraged by Chairman Mao.

The errors, however, did not begin with the Cultural Revolution, Wang Ruoshui said. There had been a whole series of leftist mistakes, starting from the anti-rightist campaign in 1957 – which had been 'taken too far' – and continuing through the Great Leap Forward and Mao's rejection of the criticisms of Peng Dehuai.

Wang's style was not Khrushchev's; it lacked his fire and bite. His criticisms of Mao were less forceful, and his approach less direct. Nonetheless the substance of what the two men said showed extraordinary similarities, even in matters of detail.

Khrushchev condemned Stalin for introducing a national anthem 'which contains not a word about the Communist Party, but contains the following unprecedented praise of himself':

> Stalin brought us up in loyalty to the people,
> He inspired us to great toil and acts.

Wang contrasted the Internationale, which contains the ringing declaration, 'There has never been a saviour, nor do we rely on spirits and kings!', with the Maoist anthem, The East is Red:

> The East is Red, the Sun rises,
> China has brought forth a Mao Zedong.
> He works for the people's happiness,
> He is the people's Great Saviour.

279

Where Khrushchev accused Stalin of adding self-adulatory passages to works which praised him insufficiently, Wang said that when Mao approved speeches and articles, he never objected to the adulation contained in them. Where Khrushchev recounted in numbing detail the fate of certain of Stalin's victims, such as Eikhe, who was shot in 1940, Wang asked why it was that 'during the long absence of He Long [who starved to death in prison in 1969] Chairman Mao never once asked where he was'. Khrushchev said that Stalin had fabricated the 'Doctors' Plot', and that Molotov and Mikoyan had been saved only by his death. Wang touched on a still more explosive subject, hinting that Mao, in his last years, had been trying to bring down Zhou Enlai, and that Zhou had been saved only by his own death.

Khrushchev asked whether Yezhov could have acted without Stalin's knowledge in creating the terror of 1937. He answered: 'No. It would be a display of naïveté to consider this the work of Yezhov alone. It is clear that these matters were decided by Stalin.'

Wang Ruoshui asked the question I had heard the tour guide ask nearly two years before, and millions of others had asked since: 'Why was it impossible for Chairman Mao to discover and frustrate the conspiracies of Lin Biao and the "Gang of Four" in time? Why did he allow them to commit so many crimes under his banner and with the aid of his prestige?' Because, he answered, 'there really were some "leftist" tendencies in Chairman Mao's thought' – in other words, because Mao supported them:

> Chairman Mao was dissatisfied with the 'Gang of Four'. This is the truth. But equally true is the fact that . . . all those who opposed the 'Gang of Four' met with an ignominious fate . . . It is true that the 'Gang of Four' deceived Chairman Mao and separated him from the masses. But Chairman Mao himself seemed to be quite at ease with such arrangements.

Where Khrushchev argued that Stalin's purges were redundant, because they occurred 'when the revolution was already victorious', Wang argued that the Cultural Revolution was unnecessary, because there were no economic, political or cultural grounds for it. The Third Plenum, he said, had been correct in stating that Mao had launched the Cultural Revolution to 'oppose and prevent revisionism', but 'Chairman Mao regarded all those who disagreed with his viewpoints as revisionists'. Stalin, by Khrushchev's account, regarded all those who disagreed with him as counter-revolutionaries.

All this would be striking enough if the comparison with Stalin were only implicit. But in key sections running through the speech, it was openly spelt out. Like Stalin, Wang Ruoshui said, Mao enlarged the class struggle to deal with his enemies – without heeding 'the lesson of Stalin's "leftist errors"':

> I think Chairman Mao did not fully learn the lesson of [what happened in] the Soviet Union. It is precisely because of this that he repeated Stalin's mistakes . . .
>
> Comrades, let us look at the two articles [on Stalin in the *People's Daily* in April and December 1956]. I think many of their opinions are still relevant today. The reasons for this is that these words were unheeded or simply forgotten for as long as 25 years . . .
>
> Chairman Mao discerned the seriousness of Khrushchev's anti-Stalinism, but failed to learn from the Stalin case. If Stalin had not made the mistake of his own personality cult and over-extended the movement to suppress counter-revolutionaries, it would have been impossible for Khrushchev to purge him. Likewise if Chairman Mao had not expressed the need to be worshipped but had persisted in the viewpoint held by the Party on the personality cult in 1956, it would have been impossible for Lin Biao and the 'Gang of Four' to . . . climb to the leading positions of the Party and state . . .
>
> One of the lessons we should learn is that we should never promote the personality cult nor give undue eulogies to any individual. The Soviet Union has had its lessons, and we have had ours. We should not commit such errors again.

There were two key differences between this and Khrushchev's Secret Speech. One was that Wang went on, as Khrushchev did not, to enquire into the causes of the cult:

> If we just blame the personality cult on the pride of one man or the conspiracy of a few persons, this cannot be regarded as an in-depth explanation. The personality cult has deep historical roots in our society. Our country has been primarily dominated by small producers . . . Patriarchal behaviour and the practice of 'what I say goes' is still a very serious problem among rural cadres . . . We lack a democratic tradition, while feudalistic monarchical thinking and autocratic rule have a long history in our country.

Wang acknowledged that no one in China could claim to be exempt from this failing. 'On reflection,' he said, 'did not we ourselves also cherish the personality cult of Chairman Mao?'

The other difference was that he and Khrushchev approached their subjects from opposite standpoints. Wang based himself on Deng's statement that 'without Chairman Mao there would have been no new China'. Although the charges he laid against Mao were similar to

Khrushchev's, the portrait of Mao which emerged was of a great leader flawed by great faults. Khrushchev's starting point was that Stalin did much evil. The portrait he drew was of a bad leader with redeeming features.

Nonetheless, in February 1979, Wang had gone much further than the Politburo was yet able to accept. Like Khrushchev, insisting that the Secret Speech 'must not get out of the Party', Deng personally gave instructions that the circulation of Wang's address be tightly restricted. Yet it proved to have an influence out of all proportion to the numbers of people who read it, or to its author's modest rank. Every important stage in China's treatment of Mao for the next two years can be traced back to his words.

For Hua, de-Maoisation had obvious implications in terms of personal power. Gone were the days when he could impress upon the National People's Congress, as he had done the previous February, that he had been appointed 'on the proposal of Chairman Mao'. Then his power had been at its height. Now it was slipping from him. At the Central Committee work conference in November he made a verbal self-criticism. The Third Plenum reaffirmed the principle of collective leadership, and the news media were instructed to give less publicity to individuals – after which he was no longer called 'the wise leader Chairman Hua', but simply 'Comrade Hua Guofeng'. Deng's increased stature, by contrast, was reflected in the plenum's praise: 'In 1975,' it said, 'when Comrade Deng Xiaoping . . . presided over the work of the Central Committee, there were great achievements in all fields of work.'

The extent of the shift in the power balance was shown by the fate of Hua's allies. Wang Dongxing, Chen Xilian, Wu De and Ji Dengkui all made formal self-criticisms. Wang lost his position as Director of the Central Committee's General Office, and Hua's old Hunan colleague, Zhang Pinghua, was removed from the Propaganda Department. Chen Xilian remained nominal Commander of the Peking Military Region, but without command responsibilities. Ji Dengkui was replaced as the region's First Political Commissar and lost his Central Committee responsibility for political and legal affairs. Chen Yonggui, the Politburo's token peasant, was severely criticised for exaggerating the achievements of his Dazhai production brigade, and lost his responsibility for agriculture.

Khrushchev's opponents suffered similar setbacks at the Soviet Party Congress in 1956. But the changes in the Chinese leadership went deeper than those Khrushchev managed to achieve. Molotov, Malenkov and the others still possessed considerable power, and a year later were to come within a hairsbreadth of bringing Khrushchev down. Wang Dongxing and his colleagues on the other hand had been reduced to mere shells, symbols around which the rest of the Politburo would manoeuvre in the struggle for power, but no longer able to influence the outcome of that struggle themselves. Khrushchev had been able to bring into the Politburo only one new full member – Mikhail Suslov, a conservative ideologue who was later to exert great influence as the *éminence grise* of the Brezhnev regime – and three new alternates: his protégé, Yekaterina Furtseva, who later became Minister of Culture; Marshal Zhukov, the hero of Stalingrad; and Leonid Brezhnev, whom he had recalled from the wilderness to take charge of the 'Virgin Lands' scheme. Brezhnev and Furtseva also became Central Committee secretaries.

Deng brought four new faces into the Politburo. Zhou Enlai's widow, Deng Yingchao, and Vice-Premier Wang Zhen became full members. The veteran economic specialist, Chen Yun, was made a Party Vice-Chairman and member of the Politburo Standing Committee, taking over from Wang Dongxing the fifth-ranking position in the leadership. And Hu Yaobang was appointed Party Secretary-General, the job which Deng himself had held from 1954 to 1956, when it was abolished to make way for the setting up of a full-scale secretariat. Yao Yilin, an economic administrator who had been purged in the Cultural Revolution and rehabilitated with Deng in 1973, became Director of the General Office and one of two deputy secretaries-general, the second being Hu Qiaomu, the other string in Deng's '*erhu*'. Another veteran, Song Renqiong, became Director of the Organisation Department, and Hu Yaobang concurrently took over the Propaganda Department.

The effect of these changes was not only to strengthen Deng's position in the Politburo, but to place the key levers of power in the Central Party apparatus firmly in his hands. Hua, the Party Chairman, no longer controlled a single Central Committee department. His ability to manoeuvre within the Party was eroded and circumscribed by Deng's appointees. It was the same technique which, twenty years earlier, Deng and Liu Shaoqi had used against Mao – to surround him with assistants who would gradually usurp his functions, leaving him with the shadow but not the substance of power. Mao had been able to turn the tables by launching the Cultural Revolution, but that was not a weapon Hua could use. Moreover he was now under pressure from another side: moves were under way to separate Party and government responsibilities in industry and in the provinces. If the same principle were applied to the central leadership, Hua would no longer be able to act as both premier and Chairman.

Neither Deng, at the start of 1979, nor Khrushchev in 1956 had achieved complete power. Each, in his different way, was still vulnerable; each was heir to a different political style, and each was operating under very different national conditions. The Russians could no more have endured the painfully slow dismantling that Mao's cult underwent than the Chinese could have tolerated the kind of shock Khrushchev administered. Khrushchev's epic pronouncements brought the appearance of deep change; Deng was more concerned with its substance.

The Twentieth Congress and the Third Plenum reflected differing emphases on personality and policy, outward form and inner reality, that create a constant contrast between the Soviet Union's efforts to come to terms with Stalin and China's with Mao. Khrushchev turned his back on Stalin, but said little about what should come after him. The Secret Speech was not intended to flatten a roadblock of Stalinist ideas barring the way ahead. Only a few sentences were devoted to the need to 'correct widespread erroneous views connected with the cult of the individual' in history, philosophy, economy, science and the arts, and 'to restore completely the Leninist principles of Soviet socialist democracy'. The Third Plenum said much less about Mao, but made a decisive break with his political ideas.

Ever since Mao assumed the leadership of the Chinese Party – indeed, ever since its foundation in 1921 – its *raison d'être* had been class struggle in one form or another (civil war, anti-Japanese war, land reform, anti-rightist campaign, Cultural Revolution). Even after Mao's death, the campaign against the 'Gang of Four' was carried out in the name of class struggle. Now, the Third Plenum declared, large-scale class struggle was over; the campaign against the 'Gang of Four' was to be stopped, and there should be no more mass political movements.

More than any other single factor, this marked the end of the Maoist system. Implicit in it was the view that man could not be transformed through revolution, as Mao had believed, but must work to transform his country through production, so that this economic transformation would bring about the transformation of man. China's priority, the plenum ruled, would from now on be its modernisation, and all methods of management and thinking which stood in the way of that goal must be resolutely changed.

To stimulate agricultural production, which was now for the first time admitted to be 'very weak', the rights of production teams were restored, which meant that, so long as state procurement quotas were met, each village could decide on its own what crops to plant and when, without having to follow arbitrary and often impractical directives from above. The procurement price for grain and other produce was raised, while the price of farm machinery was to be lowered, thus diminishing the so-called 'price scissors', the inequality in terms of trade which throughout the developing world depresses the countryside in relation to the towns. In agriculture, as other areas, inequalities were to be tolerated: 'In a country as vast as China,' one conference concluded, 'development can only be uneven.'[11] Peasants were encouraged to become rich, even if their neighbours remained poor. And the inheritance law was revived, so that wealth, once accumulated, could be passed on.

In industry the plenum proposed 'bold decentralisation'. Good workers and managers could be rewarded, and bad ones punished and demoted. Individual enterprises were to have greater decision-making powers, and administration was to be simplified.

Some of these ideas emerged from a debate on economic theory, led by Hu Qiaomu, which started in the early summer of 1978 and paralleled the political debate on the 'practice criterion'. Others were prefigured in Hua's speech to the NPC the previous February, but were not acted on at that time. Cumulatively, their effect was to undermine Hua's position further.

The plenum affirmed that henceforward, China would 'act firmly in line with economic law', in particular the law of value, which ran directly counter to Hua's 'Great Leap Forward' approach in formulating the Ten Year Plan. And it warned that 'we must not rush things, wasting manpower and material', the first public hint that the plan might be reconsidered. China's economy was to be run by more rational, practical methods, with the difference between hard work and laziness being recognised and rewarded.

The man chosen to preside over this new economic strategy was Vice-Chairman Chen Yun. A one-time typesetter from Shanghai, he had been a member of the Central Committee continuously since 1934. Already the Party's leading economist in the 1940s, he rose to become its fifth-ranking leader in 1956. But then he fell out with Mao over the 'Great Leap Forward', and for the next twenty years was stripped of power.

Despite poor health, Chen was known as a man of strong principle; with Hu Yaobang, he has been regarded as the most liberal of all the Chinese leaders. It was Chen Yun who led the campaign to have the labels removed from the 'bourgeois rightists'. In November 1978, it was Chen Yun who said: 'If Chairman Mao had died in 1956, he would have been remembered as the Chinese people's great leader. If he had died in 1966, he would still have been considered great. But he died in 1976, so what can we say?' And it was Chen Yun, the same month, who demanded an investigation into the evil done by Kang Sheng, who he said was 'not a man, but a devil'. The Third Plenum appointed him to head the newly-formed Discipline Inspection Commission, with Deng Yingchao and Hu Yaobang as his deputies, to investigate corruption and abuses of power and to ensure that the new political line was carried out, a task for which he was uniquely qualified, since for most of his career he had out-ranked every other living Chinese leader.

Many of the 'new' policies introduced at this time had first been tried in the 1950s. It was as though the Party were tacitly acknowledging that the twenty-year tangent, on which Mao had set off in 1957, had failed, and it was necessary to go back to the Eighth Party Congress in 1956, where Mao himself had declared that large-scale class struggle was over, and start again from the beginning.

But even if the leadership wanted to turn the clock back, some changes had occurred which could not be reversed. Whereas in 1956, China had fewer than 600 million people, in 1978 its population was nearing one billion. Under the altered conditions of two decades later, it was necessary to break completely new ground. The most dramatic move of this kind was the decision, announced in October, to accept foreign loans, which involved going against deeply-held fears of indebtedness stemming from China's humiliation at the hands of the imperialist powers a century before. A year earlier, even Deng had said such a step was unthinkable.

Efforts were also made to strengthen the united front. The Party Women's League, the Youth League and the Trades Union Federation all held congresses, and it was announced that the students' and youth federations would be revived. In January 1979, the Central Committee directed that all property seized from former capitalists during the Cultural Revolution should be returned, their previous salaries should be restored and neither they nor their children should be discriminated against. Former 'landlords, rich peasants, counter-revolutionaries and bad elements' except for 'the extremely few . . . who have not really yet re-moulded themselves' were also to be given back their political rights, and to prevent future discrimination, their children were to be reclassified as workers or peasants.[12]

This did much to end one of the blackest strains of persecution in the Chinese system. If your class origin or family background were 'wrong', then no matter how well you acted your life was blighted. Rong Guangxia, an educated youth in a commune in Zhejiang province, in South-Eastern China, sat the university entrance exam in 1977 for a place to read liberal arts. His marks ranked among the best in the province, but he was not selected. In 1979, he took the examination in science. Again his mark was over ninety per cent. Again he was not selected. The reason was that before 1949 Rong's father had worked as a clerk in an office of the Guomindang, the Chinese Nationalist Party. To the commune Party committee, which had to vouch for his political qualities before any university could admit him, that signified a reactionary background. As supporting evidence it was claimed that some years earlier Rong had put down insecticide which had killed his neighbour's ducks when they had come raiding his vegetable patch. Taken together, it was enough to wreck his career.

Because Rong's marks were exceptional, the provincial educational authorities made enquiries and overturned the Party committee's judgment. But how many thousands of others, whose marks were less outstanding but who also deserved university places, were similarly rejected, there is no way of knowing.

In China until 1978, if you had a landlord background, if one of your parents had fallen foul of the authorities politically, if you were the child of a capitalist, even, in certain cases, if you had relatives abroad, you were liable to be treated as a pariah, a member of a vast, unacknowledged, victimised minority, barred from joining the army, the Youth League, the Party, and from holding any official position. Even in the 1980s, the 'extremely few' landlords and rich peasants who have not had their rights restored are still ostracised, barred from production team meetings, given the nastiest jobs and paid least. But since the new directives, class hatred is no longer deliberately kept alive, and the problem has become less acute.

The decision to bring the businessmen and the former landlords and their families back into the mainstream of Chinese society formed part of a broader effort to rally the whole country behind the modernisation programme.

Within the next eighteen months, the new united front policy also saw the reopening of temples, mosques and churches, and the elaboration of a view of religion which effectively placed believers on the same footing as everyone else. '*They* believe in Buddhism or Christianity,' one young official commented, tongue-in-cheek, '*I* believe in Marxism-Leninism!' The old Maoist policy of assimilation towards minority nationalities was largely abandoned – most dramatically in Tibet, where the Dalai Lama was invited to return (but declined), and the restoration of 'full regional autonomy', defined as 'the right of Tibetans to decide things by themselves', was announced. Also a new flexibility, going far beyond the policies of the 1950s, was shown towards Taiwan. During the negotiations on normalising relations with the United States, in December 1978, Deng said Taiwan could retain its own armed forces, and its present social and economic systems, like Hong Kong or Macao, provided only that it accepted Peking's sovereignty, and the red flag with five yellow stars flew over Taibei. A month later he repeated this publicly before a group of American senators.

In short, pragmatism – meaning the use of the 'practice criterion' – as distinct from dogmatism, was elevated at the Third Plenum to become the Party's chief ideological guideline. Its application was not wholly consistent: Mao's links with the 'Gang of Four' were still camouflaged in evasions, and sacred cows such as the innate superiority of socialism remained inviolable. But in one way or another, it coloured every facet of policy. The *People's Daily* said the 'practice' debate was one of three great movements in China's modern history, the others being the May 4th movement in 1919 and the Yenan rectification campaign from which Maoism developed in the early 1940s.[13] No comparable claim was made after the Soviet Twentieth Party Congress. But Khrushchev did not create any comparable framework within which to carry out de-Stalinisation; he did not set out to reform the system, as the Third Plenum did.

It was to promote reform and the campaign to emancipate thinking, and to clear away the accumulated dross of leftist ideas, that the plenum called explicitly for more democracy:

> Bourgeois factionalism and anarchism must be firmly opposed. *But the correct concentration of ideas is possible only when there is full democracy.* Since for a period in the past democratic centralism was not carried out in the true sense . . . *and there being too little democracy, it is necessary to lay particular emphasis on democracy at present* . . . so as to make the mass line the foundation of the Party's centralised leadership. In ideological and political life among the ranks of the people, *only democracy is permissible and not suppression or persecution.* (Emphasis added.)

This was the charter on which the unofficial democracy movement based itself in the months that followed.

The Second '100 Flowers'

Khrushchev's debunking of Stalin at the Twentieth Party Congress led not only to a great upsurge, within the Soviet Union, of the political and cultural 'Thaw' which had been fitfully under way for the previous three years, but also, indirectly, in 1957, to the '100 Flowers' campaign in China. Both had much in common with the movement which accompanied the partial debunking of Mao in the winter of 1978.

The original '100 Flowers' began with what was known as the 'Unusual Spring'; its equivalent, two decades later, was called the 'Peking Spring'. Each was preceded by a period of political and cultural relaxation. Each had a 'Democracy Wall' – a name first given to the poster area opened during the '100 Flowers', on May 19th, 1957, at Peking University. René Goldman, who was then a student there, remembers 'a stormy outburst of long-suppressed feelings, demands, resentment and frustration. Hundreds of posters were stuck up every day expanding the targets of the movement and attacking the policy of the Party towards the intellectuals.'[1] Mass meetings were held, like those at Xidan and Tian An Men Square in November 1978, and within a week the unrest had spread to Tianjin, Nanjing, Wuhan and the north-west. In Peking, portions of Khrushchev's Secret Speech were posted up (and hastily removed by the University Party Committee). Students complained of excesses in the campaigns against counter-revolutionaries in the early 1950s, and called for the rehabilitation of Hu Feng, the writer Mao had purged in 1955. Posters condemned the arrogance of the Party, and asked why living standards had risen so slowly since the communists had come to power. All these issues were also raised in the second '100 Flowers' in late 1978 and early 1979. And very similar questions were being asked in 1956 and 1957 by students in the Soviet Union.

Contemplating the conservative monolith that the Soviet Union has reverted to under Brezhnev, with its apolitical youth and ideological dearth, it requires no small effort of imagination to recall the intellectual ferment when the Khrushchev 'Thaw' was at its height. In the late summer of 1956, Pasternak had just finished writing *Dr Zhivago*, and *Novy Mir* was about to publish Dudintsev's novel, *Not by Bread Alone* – a devastating indictment of the new Soviet bourgeoisie, which exposed the graft, the careerism and unscrupulousness of a corrupt, privileged class. The name of Dudintsev's villain, the factory manager, Drozdov, has passed into the language, and the book itself became the centre of an intellectual revolt, which, like the '100 Flowers' and the 'Peking Spring' in China, spread out from the capital to the provinces. 'Tell me your attitude to this book, and I will tell you what you are!' one Moscow student declaimed. 'Our literature has been the literature of a great lie,' said another. 'At last it is becoming the literature of great truths!'[2] All over the Soviet Union, at universities and technical colleges, students were launching magazines with names like *Heresy* and *Fresh Voice*, putting up wallposters (not, after all, unique to China) and issuing manifestos, denouncing the rottenness of Soviet society.

George Sherman, visiting Moscow in 1957, found Soviet students 'determined to find out about the outside world, to seize hold of the greater opportunity to hear different ideas'. They told him it was wrong for one group to hold a monopoly of power, and said they wanted regular changes of leadership with fewer and younger Party cadres.[3] In Peking, in January 1979, a young Chinese worker approached me for help in setting up an unofficial 'Chinese-American Friendship Society', because, as he explained, he and his friends 'didn't see why only the government should have the right to establish contact with foreign peoples'. Another young man wrote, in the Enlightenment Society's magazine, *Qimeng*: 'We want to go to the United States to look around as ordinary Chinese citizens . . . and see what kind of "monster" it really is (and not always have those government-designated officials acting on our behalf).'[4]

Chinese youth, like its Soviet counterpart, wanted a new way of choosing leaders. The magazine, *Jiedong* (*The Thaw*), suggested that they be elected by secret ballot, with a four-year term of office. 'Two terms of office are the maximum,' it added. 'We oppose any lifetime ruling position.'[5] *Peking Spring* went further and called for *all* cadres to be elected. 'The Soviet Union ruined its proletarian revolutionary cause,' it said, 'because it did not abolish in time the system of "appointing cadres and posting them according to grades" . . . China was to a large extent influenced by the Soviet Union, and traversed nearly the same course.' It, too, argued that fewer Party cadres were needed, and that 'the Party's leadership power . . . should gradually diminish, starting with units at the grassroots.'[6]

In the late 1950s, Russians openly derided their press. It was then that the joke was coined, '*V Izvestiakh nyet pravdi, i v Pravde nyet izvestii*' (In *Izvestia* [*The News*] there is no truth, and in *Pravda* [*The Truth*] there is no news'). Westerners visiting Moscow found themselves being asked: 'Is it also necessary to read between the lines in your newspapers to find out what has happened?'[7] In China, in October 1979, a West German correspondent went to meet a friend at Peking's new airport, which was supposed to have opened for traffic that day. Finding it deserted, he asked a policeman why it was not open when the *People's Daily* had said it would be. 'If our press says so,' came the reply, 'it's bound to be wrong.' *Reference News for the Masses* published an open letter on this subject, addressed to editors of the Party press. 'When goods are in short supply,' it said, 'you gentlemen conduct a "rhapsody on the flourishing market". When there is obviously a hard time, you force everyone to sing a "chorus of daily increasing prosperity". Unfortunately your spectacles are not coloured. They are made of wood. When you put them on you see nothing.'[8]

Both the 'Thaw' in the Soviet Union and the '100 Flowers' campaign in China ended in suppression, in the latter case, sweeping and brutal. From the first days of the Peking Spring, in November 1978, the possible parallels were disturbing. Older people saw this – and either watched warily from a distance, hoping that history would not repeat itself, or refused point-blank to have anything to do with the democracy movement. In January 1979, the *April 5th Tribune* reported a warning given by one such sceptic to a group of young people at Xidan:

Some cautious but well-intentioned person told everyone: 'The so-called freedom is limited to the Democracy Wall. Never use this freedom in your own unit or any other place where you are well-known. Remember the historical lesson of "luring the snake out of the hole" in 1957, and don't forget the label of "counter-revolutionary". Otherwise, what you say now is like money deposited in the bank. As soon as a movement comes, it will come back to you, capital and interest.'

Some nodded approvingly. Others remained silent. But some young people, like new-born calves that fear no tiger, indignantly retorted: 'What do we fear? The Constitution has given us freedom of speech, so we can talk anywhere without violating the law.'

The well-intentioned man replied slowly and calmly: 'Please don't forget there is another article in the Constitution, which comes before your freedom of speech. It reads, in part, "suppress all counter-revolutionary activities" . . . Young man, think of the past, and don't take the letter of the Constitution too seriously.'[9]

The *April 5th Tribune* concluded that the warning was apt, and then proceeded to ignore it. Other magazines and poster-writers rejected it outright. Those I asked simply insisted that a repetition of 1957 would not happen. China had learnt that lesson, they said. This time it would be different.

The activists linked the Peking Spring, not with the '100 Flowers' but with the May 4th movement (two decades earlier, their predecessors in the original '100 Flowers' had also made that connection). The call for 'democracy and science' had changed the face of China in the 1920s. The same slogan in different words – human rights and advanced technology – could do so again in the 1980s. So, at least, they believed, and it was in that expectation and hope that the Peking Spring went forward.

The posters and magazines addressed a bewildering variety of themes from feudalism to pollution and unemployment. In an overview they provided a window, which is available nowhere else and may not quickly be opened again, into the minds of politically aware, articulate young Chinese at the start of a crucial decade. It would be argued later, by Deng Xiaoping himself among others, that they were not representative of China's youth. Up to a point that is true, though not in the sense intended. For those who stuck out their necks and signed posters or launched magazines were not the timorous or the timeservers, but the most independent and strong-willed, the best and brightest of their generation.

Meng Ke, who launched the literary magazine, *Today*, was the son of a senior official in the State Planning Commission. Most activists were cadres' children, because, according to Meng, 'their educational level is higher'. But few actual students became involved, for fear of losing their university places. During the Cultural Revolution, Meng was sent down to the countryside, along with millions of others, and spent seven of his twenty-eight years there before being allowed back to the city. Then he was given a job as a factory messenger, which he quit in 1979 to devote himself full-time to writing. He was not concerned, he once told me, whether *Today* won official acceptance. 'All I want to do is to produce good poetry. If we are official and produce bad poetry, what use is that?' A strongly-built, elegant man, who in defiance of all Chinese mores lived with his girlfriend in two tiny rooms off a communal courtyard, he supported himself by selling his magazine and cyclostyled collections of his poems.

By comparison, Xu Wenli, of the *April 5th Tribune*, had a much more conventional lifestyle. A doctor's son, in his late thirties, married with an eight-year-old daughter, he worked as an electrician – 'nothing special, just the kind who fixes lights'. He and his family lived in two rooms of a communal flat, sharing the kitchen and bathroom with neighbours. Xu spent the Cultural Revolution in the army. He had the chance of going to university afterwards, but preferred to study on his own.

When the democracy movement was at its height, there were perhaps

300 committed activists like Meng and Xu in Peking, and a few thousand in the whole country. Many of the ideas they were struggling for were summarised in a '19-point Declaration', put up at the Democracy Wall on January 5th by Ren Wanding's Human Rights Alliance. It called for an independent judiciary, free elections, a genuine multi-party system, more openness in government, an end to the *neibu* system of restricted publications and films, and the freedom to travel abroad, subscribe to foreign magazines and visit foreign embassies.[10]

It concluded with an appeal for support from foreign governments and human rights organisations. To many older Chinese, this was not only politically dangerous, having overtones of treason, but also brought national loss of face. Two other posters put up in December, shortly before the normalisation of Sino-American relations, had also sought foreign help, and the reaction to them showed what a very raw nerve they touched. One, signed by a building worker, was addressed to President Carter's National Security Assistant, Zbigniew Brzezinski, and said that 'human rights in China are totally denied'. The other was to Mr Carter himself:

> In a country which regards Marxism as a new religion and which, in the name of the proletariat, uses oppressive methods, any citizen who expresses a different opinion is liable to be considered a counter-revolutionary and arrested, imprisoned, punished, exiled or even executed . . .
>
> We would like to ask you to pay attention to the state of human rights in China . . . China is a fourth of mankind. The Chinese people do not want to repeat the tragic life of the Soviet people in the Gulag Archipelago. This will be a real test of your promises of human rights, about which you . . . have said so much.

It was signed by the Human Rights Group, which turned out to be a forerunner of the Alliance, and within hours of being put up, on the evening of December 7th, was torn down – not, apparently, by the authorities, but by a reader who did not like what it said. Next morning it was violently attacked by an anonymous poster:

TO THE HUMAN RIGHTS GROUP

> When you were asking the 'democratic emperor', Jimmy Carter, for a little democracy and human rights, perhaps you did not know that at the same time 900 American Christians were committing suicide [at Jonestown, Guyana]. What a magnificent image of capitalist democracy and freedom! . . .
>
> The United States is the best place for dogs without masters. Please, gentlemen, go there soon! If that's where you want to be, GET OUT! . . .

Our country was once strong and prosperous. Yet you, you dogs of other nations, you beg from the imperialists and kneel before their feet. What a shame! . . . We are in China not Russia. If you want to play the part of Sakharov, please do! I hope you were paid a good price for your poster on the freedom wall.

The reactions this drew were mostly hostile. 'Read more Marxism-Leninism and make less scurrilous comments,' one person wrote. 'Abuse is a poor form of argument,' pencilled another. Two days later a second copy of the Human Rights Group's poster was put up, with a prefatory note saying that while some people might regard it as reactionary 'it is very important to let people express their views fully'. Tearing down wallposters was unconstitutional, it added, and those responsible should 'correct their unconstitutional behaviour'. A few hours later this copy, too, was torn down, by a middle-aged man who elbowed his way past the people reading it, shouting: 'This cannot have been written by a Chinese. It must be the work of a Soviet revisionist provocateur.' The self-appointed censor was quickly surrounded by several hundred angry people, who cursed him as a 'bad egg', and a 'little bastard', and demanded to know why he had destroyed the poster before others had had time to read it. No one spoke in his defence, and he was able to make his escape only after the police arrived to find out what the fuss was about.

These were the first posters to have been torn down since the Peking Spring had started, three weeks before. Their one distinguishing feature was that they called on a foreign leader to sit in judgment on China's affairs. But the thesis on which they rested was familiar from the May 4th movement, half a century earlier – the need to bring in foreign ideas as well as foreign machines, and to compare China, not merely with its own past, but with other countries' present. 'We must not only draw on Western science and technology,' said the Alliance's '19-point Declaration', 'we must also draw on Western traditions, democracy and culture.'

This led in several directions. Whereas, during the '100 Flowers', Chinese students asked why the country was developing so slowly, now the posters demanded: 'Why does our economy lag behind Taiwan, occupied by the Chiang Kai-shek clique?' Following Tito's visit to China and Hua's to Yugoslavia that summer, calls were made for 'Yugoslav-type socialism' and 'following the Yugoslav model'. The Human Rights Alliance went further. 'China and the Party have altered their understanding of Comrade Tito and his Yugoslav version of socialism,' it said. 'Major changes in our domestic and foreign policies in recent years . . .

have shown the bankruptcy of the notion of "revisionism". There is no objective basis for ideological differences and disputes between China and the Soviet Union. Citizens demand detente.'[11] *Exploration* (*Tansuo*) took up the same point: 'We do not want to see continuous bloodshed between the Chinese and Soviet people . . . Relaxing international tension is currently the main trend in the world.' This poster, too, was ripped down – an act which, *Exploration* said, 'manifested a guilty conscience. As people, do we not have the right to express our views on foreign affairs?'[12] It showed dramatically how far some young Chinese were prepared to go in questioning basic assumptions, not just of internal policy, where there was much unvoiced discontent, but of areas of foreign policy which were regarded as all but axiomatic both by China's leaders and by the vast majority of the people.

For most young Chinese, however, when they looked abroad, the country they looked to was the United States. It was a superpower and the richest country in the world – and the decision to exchange ambassadors and end nearly three decades of hostility, announced by Chairman Hua on December 16th, provided a fitting symbol of China's new, outward-looking policies, and the hopes they carried with them of a freer, more open society. To be an American in Peking that day was to

Rickshaw – Washington-style!   *Pravda* 1980

295

be mobbed. The *People's Daily* brought out a special issue, printed in red, which was pasted up next to the posters at the Democracy Wall. 'The Americans are rich,' one young man exulted. 'The Chinese people want to be rich too.'

This euphoria continued well into the spring. In January, several hundred million Chinese saw on television and in newsreels Deng Xiaoping being received by President Carter at the White House at the start of a visit as historic as that Khrushchev had made in 1959, which led to the end of the cold war and opened the way to detente. As though at the turn of a giant switch, the Chinese press, which a few months earlier had been depicting American life in terms of alcoholism and divorce, strikes and racial tension, printed stories about Disneyland, and photographs of Deng and his entourage disappearing under ten-gallon stetsons at a Texas rodeo. Through television, John Denver, Shirley Maclaine and the Harlem Globetrotters made their way into Chinese homes and community centres. A documentary on American life showed bronzed girls in skimpy bikinis romping on the beach, wall-to-wall traffic jams, San Francisco and the New England countryside, ultra-modern industrial assembly lines and a wedding party in a Chinese restaurant in New York, at which the young Chinese bride, looking shyly at her American husband, said she hoped relations between the two countries would prosper as her own new Chinese-American marriage. For a country where, a year earlier, Deng had had to intervene personally to authorise the first marriage between a foreigner and a Chinese for more than a decade, it would be hard to find a more emotion-charged symbolism for the new attitudes being created.

The wealth, the colour and variety, the sheer abundance of American life, stunned Chinese. Not only was it totally at variance with everything they had been told before about the decadence and misery of the capitalist world, but no attempt was made to provide balance by showing America's poor and dispossessed. Where Moscow television, assigned to show America to the Soviet people, would have chosen neutral pictures and filled its commentary with high rents, crime and inflation, Peking television offered the Chinese people a view which verged on the utopian. The climax came when a Chinese reporter visited what was described as the house of a typical American worker. He was actually a computer technician, earning 32,000 dollars a year – twice as much as a Chinese worker can hope to earn in his lifetime. The cameras spent ten minutes going from room to room, showing his children's electric train set, the deep-freeze and the dishwashing machine – all the paraphernalia which in the West are taken for granted as a part of everyday life, but are beyond the wildest imaginings of most Chinese.

To ordinary people in China, it came as a traumatic awakening to the reality of their country's backwardness, a shock so severe that in a matter of a week more seeds of real change were sown than in the whole of the previous three decades. To the democracy movement, which in mid-December had seemed to be flagging, the American connection brought a new lease of life.

'Why has the great banner of human rights been hoisted by a capitalist country like the United States, and not by us with an advanced social system?' asked *Qimeng*. Because, it answered,

> The United States is the world's most prosperous country today, and it is quite certain that its high social civilisation will harmonise with its high degree of democracy. Therefore, relatively speaking, it is the most democratic country in the world . . .
> Americans will not be charged with 'committing a crime' simply because they criticise their country's leader, and they will not be arrested or called 'counter-revolutionaries' or 'bad elements'. The supreme head of state also will not be excused from legal sanctions if he ever violates the criminal code. This is because, like any ordinary citizen, he is also subject to the limitations of the law, which commands an even higher authority than he does.

It quoted Montesquieu, Rousseau and John Strachey to argue that the United States represented 'the bright side of mankind', to be contrasted with the 'dark side . . . the undemocratic ways of the Soviet Union which cause people to suffer and bring only tragedy':

> Mankind has made new demands on democracy and human rights. The West is currently trying to satisfy these demands. The East is avoiding and suppressing them . . .
> Great Britain and Japan are monarchies . . . [but] these types of monarchy are in fact more democratic, more caring and respectful of people's rights than superficial republics . . . In today's world, the United States and Great Britain are two model nations that use the electoral system . . . In those countries the nation belongs to all citizens. The citizens change a government they dislike according to their will. It is considered natural and proper. This right is not interfered with or hindered by any means . . .
> Today we crave the freedom of speech of ancient Greece and the freedom of thought of the Warring States period in China, for we do not have as much freedom of speech and thought as people had then . . . Freedom does not mean unprincipled freedom. Exercise of the right of freedom is limited by non-interference in other people's freedom . . .
> In the West, publication is free. This situation, in which a hundred schools can contend through publication, is the basic reason underlying the Western

297

world's rapid development and high cultural achievements. In the East, publication is not free. This ideological and emotional singularity is the reason for our stagnation and lack of progress . . . This is the characteristic of a dictatorial society.[13]

Some writers proposed that China adopt an American style system of presidential elections. Others argued that more profound changes were needed. 'Look at the actual situation,' one poster said. 'Our elections are a mere formality. The undemocratic reality is given a cloak of democracy, and we, the people, are fooled.' Another, which appeared at the Democracy Wall in November, long before America became a general talking point, said:

> More than 2,000 years of feudal rule have left a legacy of blindness and superstition . . . Why can the people not raise their opinions about politics, economics, military and diplomatic affairs? In the United States there are opinion polls. Does anyone ask our opinion in China?
>
> I suggest we should create a 'people's opinion newspaper', where all the principal policy views, be they 'poisonous snakes' or 'beautiful women', 'fragrant flowers' or 'poisonous weeds', be published – and let the Chinese people judge!

Many of these proposals and arguments were unpalatable to China's leaders. Yet all through January and early February, Deng continued to affirm the essential correctness of the wallposter campaign. He told a delegation of American senators it could 'continue without restriction for generations'. The *People's Daily* said it was 'a good, not a bad thing', and derided 'comrades who became panic-stricken at the sight of the people showing their democratic spirit'.[14] In Canton the three young men who made up the Li Yizhe group, who could fairly claim to be the spiritual fathers of the Peking Spring, were released on instructions from the Central Committee, and publicly exonerated. The poster for which they had been condemned in 1974 contained 'many correct views', the provincial leadership announced.[15] Even the candid comparisons between China and the West (though not always the conclusions they led to) were officially encouraged, to overcome what the *People's Daily* called the 'smugness and stick-in-the-mudism' of Chinese workers and officials. 'While Westerners take the train,' it asked, 'should Chinese stick to the donkey?'[16]

This open support of the movement was strongly reinforced by other developments. The Cultural Revolution was denounced as a 'ten-year holocaust', and the press started to pick over its component parts, condemning developments which Mao had praised, and praising those which he had denounced.[17] Still more important, it was announced that the 'Gang of Four' would no longer be regarded as 'ultra-rightists' or even as 'sham left but real right', but as 'ultra-leftists'. This statement of the obvious was the result of fifteen months of tortuous ideological debate.* Under Mao it had been an article of faith that what was 'left' was good, and what was 'right' was bad, and on that basis officials preferred to 'err to the left rather than the right'. Now they were being told that leftist errors could be even more serious than rightist ones.

These moves were of vital importance in persuading local authorities to carry out the policies of the Third Plenum – policies which, for the last twenty years of Mao's life, had been continually denounced as rightist. They also opened the way for criticism of the anti-rightist campaign in 1957 when, it was now charged, 'honest comrades were persecuted' and 'the rights of Party members were not protected'; of the Great Leap Forward in 1958, when 'exaggerations and lies prevailed'; and of the campaign against Peng Dehuai in 1959, when 'right and wrong were confused'.[18] In short, Mao's policies for the last twenty years were acknowledged to have been a series of leftist errors, a point which Lu Dingyi, the former head of the Party's Propaganda Department, spelt out in an article in March:[19]

> Comrade Peng Dehuai's proposals at the Lushan meeting in 1959 were correct. It was not Comrade Peng Dehuai but the opposition to him that was wrong . . . It turned into a meeting to oppose the correct views of Peng Dehuai, and the tendency became increasingly 'left'. This erroneous 'left' tendency later developed into a line, and . . . lasted for 18 years, from 1958 to 1976. The damage it caused . . . continued, and to this day we have to go on recognising and overcoming it.

As every Chinese knew, the 'wrong opposition' was Mao.

Officials were urged to 'de-ossify their minds', and rid themselves of the feudal ideas which 'still penetrate many aspects of our life'. The Propaganda Department was told to be 'a liberal mother-in-law, not . . . a wicked one', and to let people speak out. Differences of political opinion within the Party and the country were legitimate, said the *People's Daily*, and must not be suppressed as counter-revolution.[20]

Nevertheless, the new surge of democracy, official and unofficial, only went so far. The *People's Daily* printed no articles proposing that the merits as well as the faults of Lin Biao and the 'Gang of Four' be

---

*To avoid unnecessary confusion. I have referred throughout to the 'Gang of Four' and their supporters as leftists. In China itself, however, this term came into use only after January 1979; until then, they were invariably described as 'rightists'.

recognised. Freedom of the press was displayed through articles sympathetic to the new line; it did not include the freedom to oppose it.

In Moscow, in 1957, a Soviet student told a Western visitor: 'You must not think we are basically against our system. After all, our fathers built it. What we want is change, to bring it back to the people in whose name it says and does so much.' In Peking, in 1979, Xu Wenli expressed the same thought: 'The majority of young people in China don't want a private redistribution of capital or the return of private ownership of land. But neither do they want a new bureaucratic class to rule over them.'

The Peking Spring, the Khrushchev 'Thaw' and the Prague Spring in Czechoslovakia in 1968, were all fundamentally different from present-day Soviet dissent. Their aim was to democratise communism – in Alexander Dubcek's phrase, to give it a human face – not to overthrow it. The actions of the authorities on the one hand, and the intellectuals and the people on the other, ran on parallel tracks, and were, in principle, mutually supportive. Soviet dissidents, with few exceptions, reject communism altogether, and their relations with the authorities polarise into confrontation.

The Peking Spring was played out in the streets and squares of China, more openly even than the 'Thaw' and the '100 Flowers' campaign, which took place mainly on university campuses and among intellectuals. In the Soviet Union today, the mere possession of *samizdat* material of any but the most innocuous kind is, technically, an offence. In China, and to a lesser extent in Moscow in 1956, unofficial magazines were printed on crude home-made presses, using waxed stencils cut on a typewriter, or, in some cases, by hand, which meant that hundreds or even thousands of copies could be made. The magazine *Peking Spring* was even able to persuade a commercial press to print one of its issues professionally. No unofficial printed journal has been seen in the Soviet Union since Khrushchev's death.

The literature of Soviet dissent, be it the humblest declaration, prepared by a dissident for his friends, or the most important *samizdat* journal, such as the *Chronicle of Current Events*, the literary magazine *Metropol*, or the independent Marxist review edited by Roy Medvedev, *Twentieth Century*, is typed in five or six carbon copies, the last one often scarcely legible, stapled together, and passed secretly from hand to hand. As with a chain letter, some of the recipients type new copies, and so the number grows. They are always given, never sold, along a network of contacts which exists solely on trust. Usually authors of *samizdat* sign their work, and it is that act of defiance, more than any other, which marks them out as dissidents. But in some cases, such as the *Chronicle of Current Events*, which the KGB tried for years to silence and eventually suppressed in 1977, the entire operation – the gathering of information, editing, production and distribution – was carried out in total clandestinity. Even the *Chronicle*, probably the best-known of all *samizdat* magazines, rarely achieved a circulation of more than about a hundred copies. Far more Soviet citizens than ever see a sheet of *samizdat* learn of the dissidents' views through the Russian services of the BBC, the Voice of America, Radio Liberty and Deutsche Welle, and the dissidents themselves are correspondingly anxious to ensure that their statements are broadcast. It is, in fact, the *only* way in which their voices can be widely heard.

Of all these radio stations only the BBC maintains a correspondent in Moscow, and I used to find that scarcely a week passed without a dissident reproaching me because the BBC had omitted to report some statement he had issued, vital to himself but of marginal interest to anyone else. In Peking that never happened. The stimulus of foreign reports about unofficial magazines and wallposters being broadcast back to China played virtually no part in the Peking Spring.

The officially supported main current was not quite the totality of the democracy movement, however. A side-current also existed, which had much in common with Soviet dissent. It rejected the Chinese system outright, and came to exert a disproportionate influence, both on the democracy movement itself and on the views of China's leaders. The Enlightenment Society, for all its ardent embrace of the American Dream, had stated its 'resolute support of the Chinese Communist Party and the socialist system'.[21] Even Ren Wanding of the Human Rights Alliance wrote from an avowedly Marxist perspective. But that could not be said of a poster which went up at the Democracy Wall on December 5th. It was called, 'Democracy, the Fifth Modernisation':

We have not heard so much about 'class struggle' on the radio and television and in newspapers and magazines recently. This is . . . because people are thoroughly sick of hearing about it, and are no longer deceived by it. But the old is replaced by the new, and heaven never disappoints the faithful. So now a new promise has been dreamt up, called the four modernisations . . . There are two old Chinese sayings, 'To draw a cake to satisfy one's hunger', and 'To look at plums to quench one's thirst'. Even in ancient times, people could satirise these fallacies . . . Yet for several decades the Chinese people, following their Great Helmsman, took the ideals of communism as a 'drawing of a cake' and the three Red Flags [the Great Leap Forward, the people's communes and the Party's general line] as 'the sight of plums', always tightening their belts and going forwards. Thirty years passed like a

301

day, and left us this lesson: the people have been like the monkey, fishing for the moon in a pond, and not realising there is nothing there . . .

Now some persons have pointed the way out. Go on, old yellow oxen, taking the four modernisations and 'unity and stability' as the key link, continue the revolution! You will reach your heaven in the end – communism and the four modernisations . . . I advise everyone not to believe political swindlers of this kind. We are no longer stupid.

The poster attacked Deng Xiaoping for having said, 'without Chairman Mao there would be no new China'. The truth was, it declared, that 'without *the people* there would be no new China' – and no 'Great Helmsman' or 'wise leader' either.

From this we can see that statements about the people being the masters of history are no more than empty talk. The people cannot control their own destiny, their merits are ascribed to another, and their rights are woven into his imperial crown. What sort of masters, then, are they? I say they are more like slaves.

Those who withheld democracy from the people, it continued, were 'shameless thieves, worse than the bloodsucking capitalists of old'. China was in the state it was because that 'bragging despot', Mao Zedong, had forced it down its present road:

It is said that this is the socialist road. Yet according to the founding fathers of Marxism, socialism means first and foremost that the people are the masters of the country. Ask yourselves, Chinese workers and peasants, apart from the little bit of salary you get each month to stop you from starving, what else are you masters of? . . . And what about every citizen having the right to be educated and to develop his abilities and so on? In our present society, we have none of these rights. All we have is the 'dictatorship of the proletariat', and a mutation of Russian-style despotism: Chinese-style socialist-despotism.

Is this the socialist road the people need? Does despotism produce happiness? Is this the socialist road envisioned by Marx? Of course not . . . It is a feudal socialism, a feudal monarchical system disguised in the cloak of socialism. Just because Russia has developed from social-feudalism to social-imperialism, does China have to follow suit?

While Chinese were begging in the streets, the poster said, 'political swindlers' like Mao gave away what the people had earned to 'bastards like themselves in Albania and Vietnam'. 'It is by no means certain,' it added, 'that the beggars would have agreed to rice being sent to somewhere called the Third World. But who would listen to their views?'

> The democracy enjoyed by the peoples of Europe and America is such that they could dismiss from office Nixon, de Gaulle and Tanaka, and, if they wished, could re-elect them to office later. No one can interfere with their democratic rights. But if the Chinese people so much as talked about that great man, Mao Zedong, what awaited them was the maw of prison and misfortune . . .
>
> Without [democracy,] the fifth modernisation, the other four modernisations are only a new lie. I call on the people to rally round the banner of democracy! Don't believe in the despots' 'stability and unity'. The slogans of fascism and totalitarianism can only bring us disaster. Democracy is our only hope.

The writer was a young man named Wei Jingsheng. His basic theme, that without democracy China could not modernise, was not in itself controversial. The *People's Daily* was saying as much. The difference lay in Wei's approach. If the views of Xu Wenli can be compared with those of a Soviet independent Marxist such as Medvedev, Wei Jingsheng is the Vladimir Bukovsky of the Chinese democracy movement. Although he committed blunders, his courage and fortitude have never been questioned. He alone dared to say out loud what many others merely thought, and he refused to be silenced.

When Wei wrote 'Democracy, the Fifth Modernisation', he was twenty-eight, a tall, slim figure who hovered around the Democracy Wall in nondescript grey workclothes and a brown corduroy cap. Like Meng Ke he is the son of a middle-ranking official, a deputy department director in the State Capital Construction Commission, who made him memorise communist texts from the age of twelve. Like many other activists, he is also a former Red Guard, radicalised and disillusioned by his experiences in the Cultural Revolution. Wei was sixteen when the Cultural Revolution was launched, and first joined one of the most extreme of the Red Guard factions. But he quickly found himself repelled by the totalitarian ultra-leftism of Jiang Qing, then, as ever, the extremists' mentor, and switched allegiance to a moderate group called 'Joint Action', made up mainly of the children of high officials, who blamed Jiang Qing for the attacks being made on their parents. In the turmoil of the 'January Storm' in 1967, when the leftist offensive was at its height, Wei was arrested, and though he was released three months later it completed his disenchantment with the ultra-leftist line. Jiang Qing, he decided, was using the Red Guards for her own personal ends. From there it was only a short step to conclude that Mao, as the prime mover of the Cultural Revolution, was doing the same, and that Marxism-Leninism itself was fundamentally undemocratic.

> It is not, as Lenin argued [Wei wrote], that democracy is an *inevitable* outcome of the productive forces and the relations of production reaching a certain stage of development. Rather, a democratic system is the precondition of all development . . . *The enemies of democracy always say that democracy will inevitably develop* . . . so there is no need to struggle for it. (Emphasis added.)

With other members of 'Joint Action', Wei spent the rest of 1967 travelling through China, 'making revolution' and trying to assemble a collection of 'black materials' on Jiang Qing's early life as a film actress in Shanghai. Their activities were discovered, and Wei fled to hide with relatives in Anhui. While he was there, and during the four subsequent years that he spent in the army, the last shreds of his belief in communism were destroyed by the sight of the wretchedness and misery of China's peasants. Not only was Maoism undemocratic, Wei decided, but it had brought no real benefit to China's people.

How many millions of others shared, in greater or lesser degree, Wei's disillusionment, is impossible to tell. In July 1979, Wang Xizhe, one of the members of the Li Yizhe group, published an article in the Canton unofficial magazine, the *People's Voice*, describing China as 'a capitalist country, without a bourgeoisie, governed by the dictatorship of the Party'. Yet Wang, for all the harshness of his criticism, retained a basic belief in Marxism. Wei was the voice of those who did not.

After the appearance of 'Democracy, the Fifth Modernisation', Wei and a small group of friends launched the magazine, *Tansuo* (*Exploration*), which quickly established itself as the most radical of China's unofficial journals. It was not without errors, of fact and interpretation, any more than were most of the others. Lenin did *not* say, as Wei quoted him as saying, that democracy was inevitable so there was no need to struggle for it, though most communist leaders since have acted as though he did. But that is hardly to be cavilled at. Wei's own knowledge of the finer points of Marxist theory was largely self-taught, in the years after he left the army, when he was employed as an electrician with the Peking parks department. His acquaintance with Western ideas stopped with a few old Russian novels, and articles on philosophy in a Chinese encyclopedia. What is remarkable is that on this slight basis he was able to think out for himself a critique of Marxism of great directness and force.

> The Marxist socialist experiment of using dictatorship to achieve the equal rights of man has been going on for decades. The facts have shown time and again that it simply won't work. A 'dictatorship of the majority' is only a utopian dream. A dictatorship is a dictatorship. A concentration of powers is bound to fall into the hands of the few.[22]

All dictatorial governments, Wei wrote, used some form of idealism to prop up their regimes; under the feudal dynasties it was religion, and under socialism, Marxism. All Marxist social systems, without exception, were undemocratic or anti-democratic autocracies.[23]

Exploration also carried reports on conditions in Chinese prisons, and, in its later issues, cases of police repression. These were subjects about which most unofficial journals had very little to say, in sharp contrast to Soviet *samizdat*, ninety per cent of which is concerned with police harassment, arrests, hunger-strikes, trials, and labour camp conditions. In part this reflects the underground nature of Soviet dissent, but it also has to do with the fragmentation of the Soviet movement into many different groups, most of which are primarily concerned with fighting for specific rights. The Jews and ethnic Germans want the right to emigrate; the Tartars want the right to return to the Crimea; the nationalists – Armenian, Georgian, Lithuanian, Moldavian, Russian and Ukrainian, among others – want greater autonomy, at least in culture and education; religious groups, such as Jehovah's Witnesses, Pentecostalists, and Russian Orthodox, Baptist and Buddhist dissenters, want the right to practise their faith and to proselytise; and artists and writers want the right to create. As a rule, it is only when these rights are denied, and those calling for them repressed, that *samizdat* material is produced; Jews who are allowed to emigrate do not write protests.

Only a very small number of Soviet dissidents, such as Sakharov and Andrei Amalrik, who wrote the book, *Will the Soviet Union survive until 1984?*, have tried to look at the broader issues of democracy with which the Chinese activists are concerned. Moreover, as Xu Wenli points out, many of this group are highly-placed intellectuals – scientists and university professors. That was also the case in China during the '100 Flowers', the May 4th movement and earlier reform movements in imperial times. But it was not so in the Peking Spring. Thanks to the anti-rightist campaign and the Cultural Revolution, most of its participants had no university education.

As a result, and taking into account the different conditions in China, the topics aired at the Democracy Wall were often more basic than those found in *samizdat*. Many of those who put up wallposters were less concerned with the right to emigrate than with calling for the abolition of the commune system, which 'makes a mockery of Marxism-Leninism, of Chinese history and of the destiny of the Chinese people'. Or grumbling about industrialisation: 'In Peking from morning till night, people are asphyxiated by a smoke-filled fog. The birds cannot stand it so they fly away. But people can't fly.' Or about the state monopoly: 'Even after boiling, tap water often tastes like sulphanila-mide. If the Peking waterworks were not the only concern, one would certainly change one's patronage.'

Rights which in the Soviet Union are generally taken for granted, in China still have to be fought for. They include the right to eat, and to share a home with one's family. A poster addressed to the 'Ladies and Gentlemen of the Peking Municipality' declared:

> Tens of thousands of people do not have enough to feed or properly nourish themselves. That is a fact, and we ask you, where has your communist humanitarianism gone? Go fuck yourselves with your socialism and communism in a society where people don't have enough to clothe and feed themselves decently.

Others demanded an end to the system whereby 'a citizen devotes his whole life to a unit . . . [with no] freedom of movement', and to the separation of husbands and wives forced to work in different parts of the country. 'We demand the right to live as human beings,' one poster said. Chinese should have 'three meals a day . . . [and] when it becomes time for marriage at 30, a small room with a bed', a reference to the shortage of urban housing.

Their content ranged from the profound to the pitiful, from the sensational to the merely silly. There were screeds of bad, adolescent poetry, and pages of mathematical formulae by a person who claimed to be a misunderstood genius. One man announced that he had written to Chairman Hua to suggest the abolition of the Communist Party, but had received no reply. Another charged that local officials were aiming death-rays at himself and his family.

By January 1979, wallposters were appearing not only at Xidan and in Tian An Men Square but all over Peking. Even the huge red billboards at street corners, carrying quotations from Chairman Mao, were plastered with them. Some were no more than a single scrap of paper, a few inches across; others were spread over a dozen or more sheets of plain or coloured paper, each several feet high. People would copy them down verbatim, to take back and discuss with their friends – no easy task when the winter temperature drops to −20°C and the wind howls down from Siberia, raising a choking dust which goes straight through the white gauze facemasks Peking people wear in an attempt to keep it out. By the time the blizzards had done their work, tearing the posters into shreds and exposing the peeling layers beneath, the city resembled the aftermath of a demented wedding, scattered with grubby, adhesive confetti.

The liberalisation of culture and society which the wallposters reflected was in most cases viewed from the narrow perspective of what was permitted and what was not. One diatribe tore into China's cultural commissars, 'at whose whim' it was decided which foreign films would be released and which foreign novels translated. Another declared that 'unless puritanism is eliminated, our literature and art cannot progress'.

> Certain people are afraid if we are permitted to see more foreign films we will also witness nude scenes. These scenes cannot harm us. They can only excite spectators, and will do nothing to damage their minds. [These people] . . . fear shots of naked bodies, women's breasts and the zeal of love. Why do they worry? They worry that married people will have abusive sexual relationships with others, and that unmarried young men will have sexual desires too early.

The Chinese people, no less than the authorities, the poster said, should take a more flexible view of sexual and romantic liaisons. Chinese should be free 'to have sexual relations when and with whom they like'. Someone had written across it that the author was 'an extremely bad poisonous snake'.

That poster appeared in response to the outcry over a Japanese film, *Sandakan No 8*, which had been screened in China in October. It was a curious choice, at a time when the only other non-communist foreign film that had been shown was Gregory Peck's *The Million Pound Note*, for it told the story of a Japanese prostitute in South-East Asia in the 1940s, and included scenes of love-making and violence which many Chinese found deeply shocking. People wrote in from all over the country to complain that it had 'had the effect of poisoning the minds of young people'. The *People's Daily* disagreed. It was not the appearance of the prostitutes' lives that was important, it said, but the conclusions audiences drew from it. 'In fact,' it added, 'most people leave the film with deep sympathy for the miserable life of the prostitute, and hatred for the dark and ruthless society in which she lived.' There was no need for China itself to make such films, it conceded, but it was 'not a serious attitude' simply to reject those made by others.[24]

Some additional cuts were made before *Sandakan* went on general release, but it remained highly controversial. Other films followed. The New Year holiday found every Chinese with access to a television set glued to Gina Lollobrigida, in a clinging, low-cut dress, dancing seductively in front of Anthony Quinn in *The Hunchback of Notre Dame*. Then came Charlie Chaplin's *Modern Times*, and Kris Kristofferson and Ali MacGraw in *Convoy*. One disgruntled Chinese parent told me he could no longer allow his children to watch television unless he or his wife were present, for fear of 'bedroom scenes'.

The new attitude which such films implied, that having a good time and enjoying oneself were not actually a bad thing (a proposition so irrelevant to Maoist propaganda that it had been simply passed over in silence), was looked at tongue-in-cheek in a poster which went up in December. The author wrote that he could not understand why, in such cold weather, people chose to spend their time getting tired and dusty at the Democracy Wall, putting up posters which made trouble, when they could be devoting their energy to making money. 'You should learn from me,' he wrote. 'Save up and buy a television set. Watch films like *Sandakan No 8*, listen to songs, and have a good meal and some tea!'

This vision of the good life was widely held. 'Facing us is a golden world filled with cars, television sets and refrigerators,' wrote a magazine called *Sihua Luntan* (*Four Modernisations Forum*). 'Let us greet it with both hands!'[25] The attitude was most evident in the two southern provinces of Guangdong and Fujian, due to the nearness of Hong Kong and the high proportion of families – forty per cent in Fujian – who have relatives or friends abroad. In the spring of 1979 people in Canton started erecting special TV aerials which enabled them to receive Hong Kong programmes. Canton television itself even relayed a Hong Kong beauty contest. The unofficial journal, *Qiushi Bao*, quoted a PLA officer, the secretary of his regiment's Party committee, as saying: 'This year I'm striving for a television set. Next year I'll try for a refrigerator and a washing machine.' What about ideological questions, he was asked, wasn't he still interested in them? 'Materialism has triumphed,' he replied. 'If I'm given the choice between a room with a TV set and a tape recorder, and a room with nothing in it, it's easy to tell where my preferences lie.'

On the whole, Deng Xiaoping encouraged such reasoning. If the country were to develop, people had to be aware of standards of living elsewhere. But it was not enough just to puncture their complacency. They also had to be shown that the dream held out to them was attainable. To this end, customs regulations were eased to allow Overseas Chinese to bring in one tape recorder or TV set as a gift for their relatives once a year. The result was a flood of consumer durables.

which rapidly expanded to include washing machines, air conditioners, deep freezes and almost anything else that was in demand, and finally assumed such daunting proportions that by the end of 1979, the authorities began to row back – not so much for ideological reasons, but because the flood had become a tidal wave. In 1979, 200,000 Overseas Chinese came home for the Spring Festival; a year later the figure reached 600,000. The crowds who struggled across the railway bridge which marks the Hong Kong border, with bundles of belongings hanging from one end of their bamboo carrying poles and boxes of electronic gadgetry from the other, were not, in most cases, wealthy. Many were ordinary workers and petty traders, often hard-pressed to make ends meet – but woe betide them if they did not satisfy their relatives' expectations. No longer was a colour television good enough; it also had to have remote control.

What had happened, although not expressed in these terms, was that Maoist egalitarianism had given place to 'keeping up with the Joneses'. Just as peasant production teams which happened to have fertile land were encouraged to become rich while their neighbours remained poor, so families who happened to have overseas relations were allowed to acquire the marks of affluence. Each was intended as a living proof, and therefore an encouragement to others, that prosperity could be achieved in China, so long as the prosperity of the whole was based on the prosperity of the individual, and not the other way round.

The stimulus provided by rich neighbours was backed up by advertising. First in the southern coastal provinces, then, in the summer of 1979, in Tianjin, Shanghai and Peking, billboards began to appear depicting not the workers, peasants and soldiers of Mao's day, but Sanyo and Hitachi televisions, Toshiba fridges, Japanese Dubakasi sunglasses, Philip Morris cigarettes and Hennessey Cognac. Advertisements were also accepted on the radio and in the press, including the *People's Daily*, franchised through an Overseas Chinese agent in Hong Kong. Even television got into the act, with a nightly advertising magazine programme. In the Soviet Union, the only commercial advertising of any kind, apart from a few token billboards for the benefit of foreign tourists near Moscow's international airport, is in a monthly consumer affairs magazine which covers only Soviet-produced goods and is determinedly informational in character. The idea of mounting window displays in department stores to show what, for example, an all-electric ultra-modern Japanese kitchen looks like, as China has been doing, is simply unthinkable. In Moscow, a Soviet citizen who takes too much interest in the display cases outside a foreign embassy is likely to find himself being questioned or moved on. Yet in Peking, Shanghai and other big Chinese cities, crowds were gathered permanently around shop windows full of Japanese digital watches and tape recorders.

Much of this was aimed at persuading people to ask their relations to bring them goods of a particular brand, a procedure made easier, early in 1980, by a decision to allow Overseas Chinese to remit the price of a television set or refrigerator of a designated model and make, to be collected by their relatives from stocks specially imported into China by the foreign manufacturer for that purpose.

Foreign consumer goods, particularly watches, radios and television sets, were also imported for direct sale to Chinese not blessed with relations abroad. In 1979 Seiko sold 60,000 watches in China; in 1980, the figure reached nearly half a million and the company opened its own showroom in Peking, the first foreign shop in the country since 1949. Its blue awning, fitments and gleaming interior were all imported from Tokyo, making it seem as though part of the Ginza had been transplanted and set down among the shabby local stores, unchanged since the 1940s, which occupy most of the city's shopping centre. The Chinese provide the salesgirls and take a hundred per cent mark-up on every watch sold; Seiko pays the rent and salaries, provides a Japanese technician to head the service department, and takes its normal profit on the basic selling price.

Along with foreign goods, more Chinese consumer goods were made available, and since the middle of 1979 they, and the lifestyle they represent, have also been advertised energetically. Maxam vanishing cream, Snow Lotus pullovers, Nie Er pianos and Chinese traditional medicaments guaranteed to restore 'vim and vigour' have all been featured on billboards and magazines, their attractions often enhanced by the presence of a beguiling Chinese lady. One of the best efforts depicted a renowned Tang dynasty beauty being offered a cup of wine. 'What did the Lady Yang drink?' it asked. 'Historically we don't know, it was so long ago. But today we can recommend SUNFLOWER BRAND CHINESE VODKA.'

The contrast between this unabashed promotion of affluence and the propaganda of the previous two decades, which demanded ideological rectitude and disregard of material comforts, was shattering. Outside war and revolution, few countries can have changed their value-systems so abruptly. Film stars and actresses who before had been kept as much as possible in anonymity, now looked out alluringly from the pages of calendars and youth magazines. In Shanghai, Peking and other big cities, wedding portraits in photographers' shop windows showed the bride in white, and the groom in a Western suit, with collar and tie, looking for all the world like a successful young man-about-town from Singapore or Hong Kong. It was pure show: the dress and the suit were hired, not for the wedding itself, but only for the photograph. In the same way, at an open-air photographer's stall near the Forbidden City, you could have your picture taken sitting at the wheel of a black 'Shanghai' sedan. It was not the reality but the image that was important. Once the image had been grasped, Deng believed, the reality would follow.

The whole strategy depended on Chinese workers and officials concluding that this 'golden world', being held out to them so tantalisingly, could be attained by hard work and only by hard work. Inevitably, there were many who tried to take short cuts.

Bribery and black-marketeering presented the biggest problems. Like other aspects of China's liberalisation, these were most in evidence in the south. From the spring of 1979, increasing economic interpenetration was permitted between Guangdong and Hong Kong and Macao, so as to encourage joint ventures using Hong Kong know-how and cheap Chinese labour. Hong Kong property companies were awarded contracts to rebuild part of Canton's city centre. Direct air, train and river-ferry services to the colony were opened. Even Canton taxis were run by a Hong Kong firm. The result was to provide local officials with almost limitless scope for crooked deals. Foreign businessmen found that a gift of a television set or a video-cassette machine not only improved their chances of winning a contract, but in some cases became a precondition to meaningful negotiation. Both legal and illegal emigration soared, as political controls were eased and corrupt police officers took bribes to approve far more than the normal quota of exit visas. In 1979 the population of Macao grew by twenty per cent, and at times more than a thousand illegal emigrants a day flooded into Hong Kong. Smuggling flourished as never before. In the small fishing port of Shanwei, in Guangdong, the fish catch plummeted in 1979 because, according to local officials, the fishermen were spending all their time smuggling illegal emigrants out to Hong Kong, and bringing back tape recorders and television sets. Most of the traffic was small-scale: contraband electronic goods in return for Chinese antiques, jade, musk, gold and silver coins. Black marketeers in the interior travelled to Canton or Fuzhou to obtain supplies. One racket, involving smuggled digital watches and Japanese silk scarves, had outlets in a dozen cities in Central and North-Western China. In some cases bulkier merchandise was involved. Chinese flat-bottoms, tied up in Hong Kong on some legitimate enterprise, could bring back almost anything, provided it could be unloaded at the other end. For communes along the coast and on the Huangpu River, that posed no problem; even bulldozers were smuggled in. One Hong Kong businessman hit on an ingenious solution to the question of how such imports were to be paid for by purchasers with no foreign currency. In return for six new fishing boats, a coastal production brigade delivered a third of its catch to Hong Kong, where the businessman had acquired part-ownership of a chain of fish restaurants to make use of it. His profits as a restaurateur repaid him handsomely for the outlay of his boatyard.

With native Cantonese wit, blood relationships across the border and the knowledge of how to wheel and deal in both the communist and capitalist worlds all playing their part, smuggling never stops entirely in Southern China, any more than does official corruption. In times of liberalisation they become blatant and widespread; in times of repression they go underground.

In the second half of 1978 and the spring of 1979, the whole country witnessed an upsurge of gambling and street crime. People grumbled that the clacking of Mahjong tiles kept them awake at night. Mustachioed young men, with sideboards and long, slicked-back hair, hawked home-printed copies of pornographic novels. Two soldiers wrote to the newspaper, *Gongren Ribao*, to complain that they had been offered 'filthy books and pictures' by railway attendants on the train to Inner Mongolia. 'They openly sold nude photos of beauties from Hong Kong, and songs like "When will you come again?", and "Friendship is stronger than wine"', they said. 'The department concerned should stop its people selling such decadent things.'[26] Similar cases of 'obscene cultural poison' being offered for sale were reported in many other parts of China.[27]

Groups of amateur players started giving uncensored performances of banned traditional operas with dubious plots. One, called *The 18 Strokes*, was widely staged during the Spring Festival in 1980. 'It is a story about a boy and two girls who have been sent to look after cattle,' reported a letter in *China Youth News*. 'This boy strokes one of the girls from her head to her feet and says some dirty words. Most of the people who saw it said that mean plays like this should not be put on.'[28] Even some professional troupes rejected the official bowdlerised versions of traditional operas, and went back to the old bawdy ones. And if they were still not sufficiently exciting, the *People's Daily* lamented, 'some opera groups unscrupulously changed the subject matter at random, and added obscene words and crude, insulting gestures to win cheap acclaim from the audience'.[29]

For hundreds of millions of Chinese, above all in the countryside, traditional operas are still, as they have been for centuries, the dominant cultural form. In Peking, starting from the Lantern Festival in 1979, peasants came in from the countryside to perform stilt-dances in the parks, weather-beaten old men, rouged and powdered, and wearing gaudy costumes, prancing and simpering at the audience as they played out well-loved scenes to the beat of gongs and drums. On holidays and feast-days, in small country towns, old-fashioned street processions resumed, and in Qinghai and Tibet, the New Year was greeted with butter sculptures. The ancient art of *Qigong* was revived. It means literally 'force-control', and an adept can snap a one-inch iron bar with his bare hands, or break a thick granite slab with his head.

One after another, the old ways, which were supposed to have been suppressed for ever in the Cultural Revolution, came out into the open again. Quacks and mountebanks promised miraculous cures. In small towns in the south street theatre reappeared, and gradually spread as far as Peking. Such shows were not for the squeamish. One group I came across, a grizzled middle-aged man and two youths, wore black trousers and red sashes, stripped to the waist, like the Boxers at the turn of the century. The performance began with each of the youths swallowing a fifteen-inch steel sword, until just the hilt protruded from his mouth. Then the older man swallowed a steel ball, more than an inch in diameter, and, after two or three minutes, during which saliva drooled continuously from his lips, brought it back up into his mouth – with a sufficient quantity of the noodles he had had for breakfast to prove that no trickery was involved. As the finale one of the younger men deliberately forced his arm out of joint and then snapped it back again, visibly enduring agonising pain. The 'show' lasted forty minutes, and after each 'act' the hat was passed round.

Witchcraft flourished. Ancestor worship was practised openly, along with geomancy and divination by drawing lots. Manuals of fortune-telling and palmistry, and almanacs which claimed to predict whether an unborn child would be a son or a daughter, also began to appear. Pedlars sold Taoist amulets and home-printed pictures of door gods. Old crafts revived. In the north-west, men carved apricot stones into tiny monkeys and boats, to sell for a penny each. In Fuzhou a street calligrapher wrote characters in multi-coloured ink-strokes, studded with ornamental dragons and inscribed with a couplet from a classical poem. People put paper-cuts in their windows and around the lintels of doors to mark weddings and holidays. Cage-birds and goldfish appeared again in the markets.

Some of these developments were officially encouraged; some were tolerated; some were disapproved of; and some were diametrically opposed to the new policies China's leaders were promoting. But all were part of the same pattern of re-establishing the historical and cultural links, broken by Cultural Revolution, between China's present and its past. The old was no longer contemptible. Articles appeared in the press praising antique collectors and connoisseurs for preserving China's heritage. Plans were announced to renovate temples and other historic sites which had been turned into factories or allowed to fall into ruin. The Great Wall was made the subject of preservation orders threatening imprisonment for anyone who damaged it, and one unfortunate army unit, which had totally destroyed a section nearly two miles long in order to build a barracks, was told it must pull the barracks down and put the whole lot back. An elderly intellectual even wondered aloud at a forum whether it had really been such a good idea to pull down the walls of Peking.

The re-emergence of Old China from beneath its revolutionary veneer was paralleled by the inflow of new cultural influences. Neither was brought about by a precise set of political instructions, any more than was the creation of the unofficial democracy movement. Rather, a gradual unwinding took place in the second half of 1978, as though the country were trying to find itself after realising it had lost its way. 'You don't know what a nightmare these last ten years have been,' a Foreign Ministry official told me. Returning to Peking that autumn after six weeks' absence, I found the change almost palpable. The Chinese genius for satire was back. One sketch by two popular comedians was built around a football match. One played the role of a radio commentator, but instead of describing the game he rhapsodised about the loving care and attention the Party lavished on sport, while the other, the listener at home, grew more and more infuriated as he waited, in vain, to learn the score.

Young couples promenaded hand-in-hand and arm-in-arm, untroubled by the shocked stares of their elders. In China's parks, in the evenings, and in the shadows where the streetlamps did not reach, romance was alive and well. The *China Youth News* warned its readers that 'kissing is dangerous for your health', and *Beijing Ribao* said young people must 'put love where it belongs' – after study, labour and the revolutionary cause.

High heels made their appearance – a modest one inch off the ground, and soon became so commonplace that peasant women complained there were no flat shoes to be found.[30] City girls started wearing brighter colours and more varied materials: silk scarves and imitation fur coats in winter; wide-brimmed silk hats in summer, with dresses and skirts which looked progressively less like gunny sacks and had a touch of 1940s glamour. In Shanghai and Canton the smart set sported tailored trouser-suits, or what the Chinese call 'thigh-huggers' with short velvet or brocade jackets. Handicraft shops began selling cheap jewellery, and some particularly daring young women appeared in *cheongsams*, the long dresses, slit to the thigh, which swept China in the 1920s. Waist-length plaits, the hallmark of Maoist pulchritude, went abruptly out of fashion, and vests were replaced by bras. In Peking, by the summer of 1980, girls clad in the shapeless uniform of Mao's day were the exception rather than the rule. Youths sported bellbottoms and leather jackets, Western suits with collars and ties, and started crazes of flower-pot hats, white plastic pith-helmets, and, for a few months in 1979, greased-back hair and a kiss-curl, like Bill Haley in the early days of rock'n'roll. A year later imported sunglasses became the rage, with the label still over one lens to prove that they really were imported; 'foreign cataracts', older Chinese called them. Beatle hair cuts were common, and a few young eccentrics, boys as well as girls, dyed their hair reddish-brown or blonde.

Conservatives of all ages found it shocking. 'I think a girl who wears make-up is rather queer,' an eighteen-year-old student at Amoy University told me. 'No one wants to marry someone who is rather queer.' In Peking, the younger, more go-ahead officials laugh at that kind of attitude, but in the provinces it is widely held. If, to a foreigner from Europe or the United States, Chinese dress in 1980 seemed still predominantly blue and grey, as it was in the 1950s, to Chinese eyes the changes were immense.

Two decades earlier, the period before the '100 Flowers' campaign saw a similar surge of tolerance. By the end of 1956, girls were wearing flowered blouses; the Women's League declared that beautiful clothes had nothing in common with bourgeois decadance; and Liu Shaoqi told broadcasting officials that their programmes should cover topics of popular concern such as fashion.[31] In the Soviet Union, Khrushchev's 'Thaw' ushered in drainpipe trousers, jeans, open sandals, winklepickers and flowered shirts. Today the flowered shirts and winklepickers have gone, but Western jeans are as much the hallmark of style for Soviet youth in the 1980s as they were in Khrushchev's day. In China, the stirrings of fashion in 1956 were crushed in the lurch to the left that followed, and then extinguished altogether in the Cultural Revolution. In the Soviet Union they continued regardless of the vagaries of the political line, whether under Khrushchev or Brezhnev, and that also promises to be the case in China in the 1980s.

In both countries the liberalisation of social behaviour was speeded up by the decision to permit large-scale foreign tourism. In 1959, 13,000 Americans visited Moscow, compared with a few hundred five years earlier. In mid-1978 the lobby of the Peking Hotel filled with blue-rinsed matrons, debating what dinner dress they should wear, and coaches marked 'Pan-Am tour group' could be seen on the road to the Great Wall. The bamboo curtain surrounding 'Red China' had been abruptly lifted: you could walk into a Hong Kong hotel, fill in a form for a weekend in Canton, and two days later your visa was ready. Soldiers guarding guesthouses for foreign tourists in the East China province of Shandong were told to beware of 'scenes of intimate relations between lovers' and 'maintain a healthy ideology', rather like a British unit being told to maintain a stiff upper lip.

China found it particularly difficult to adjust to Western permissiveness because the gap between the puritanism of the Cultural Revolution and the free-wheeling attitudes of Europe and America in the 1970s was far greater than that between post-war Moscow and the Europe of the 1950s. Neither the Chinese nor the Soviet leaders considered Western cultural and moral values desirable. In the Soviet Union their influx was a by-product of economic and foreign policy needs – the desire to earn tourist dollars, to import Western technology and to give some substance to detente. But in China such factors were compounded by the broader aim of opening to the West, to restore the country to its rightful place in the world, and to give its people a clearer notion of what that world was really like.

Until the middle of 1978, most Chinese were still ignorant of the fact that, ten years earlier, Americans had reached the moon. By the middle of 1979, the raising of the Stars and Stripes at the new embassy in Peking had been followed by Bob Hope (complete with bad jokes about Chinese laundries and chop suey) and a roadshow which included the black disco group, Peaches and Herb; Coca-Cola stalls at the Summer Palace (the Soviets, five years earlier, having opted for Pepsi); and frisbees, which soon constituted a serious traffic hazard. Muhammed Ali arrived, was photographed embracing Deng Xiaoping, and promised to return to train China's team for the 1984 Olympics; soon after this the ban on boxing, which had been in force since 1956, was quietly lifted, and a demonstration bout was held before an intrigued but sceptical crowd in one of the city's stadiums. Mikhail Baryshnikov danced the *pas de deux* from *Giselle* with a Chinese ballerina. That year the famous and the fashionable from all over the world made the pilgrimage to Peking: Yehudi Menuhin, Margot Fonteyn, Gunter Grass and the dress designer, Zandra Rhodes. It was the 'in' place to go, 'like Russia in the 1930s' one Western ambassador unkindly remarked.

One afternoon in March, Pierre Cardin gave a fashion show of *couture* clothes he had made up using Chinese fabrics, complete with electronic music and a shiny black-and-white catwalk flown in from Paris, on which three French models, bare-breasted beneath dresses of transparent silk, mesmerised an audience of Chinese textile workers. That evening the Boston Symphony Orchestra and the Peking Philharmonic, jointly conducted by Seiji Ozawa, played 'The Stars and Stripes Forever' before 15,000 people in a huge indoor stadium, while the American ambassador sat dabbing his eyes. A few months later it was the turn of Herbert von Karajan and the Berlin Philharmonic. The London Festival Ballet came, followed by Derek Jacobi in the Old Vic's production of *Hamlet*. The film, *Death on the Nile*, started a craze for the detective novels of Agatha Christie and Ellery Queen, and in 1980 some twenty of them were being translated into Chinese, to the disgust of certain intellectuals. 'Our publishers are so stupid,' one lady told me. 'All they want is to make money. Why can't they publish Iris Murdoch, instead of rubbish like this?' But even she agreed that Agatha Christie was more entertaining than the 'Little Red Book'.

By comparison the flow of Western culture into the Soviet Union during Khrushchev's liberalisation, when international contacts were still dominated by the cold war, was pitifully small. Yet even there, in 1956, *Kommunist* praised bourgeois writers for creating 'bright, typical characters' and accused Soviet authors of treating art as just another form of propaganda, producing works which 'gild reality, minimise our difficulties and do not show our shortcomings truthfully'.[32] In China, in the spring of 1979, a conference of film directors declared, 'People are sick and tired of the same old words and stories, which go on like a cracked record', and writers and artists were told 'not only to criticise capitalism, but also defects and wrongs in socialist society'.[33]

Taboos which had stood unchallenged since the mid-1960s suddenly collapsed. In November 1978, dances started, and in Peking, on New Year's Eve, several hundred young Chinese jived the night away to music from the film, *Saturday Night Fever*, and records of American rock groups. A year earlier Chinese staff at foreigners' parties signalled their disapproval by walking out as soon as dancing began, and many older people had reservations about its return. Dancing was all right, the *China Youth News* said, but rock'n'roll was going too far. Others were blunter. 'Now pop songs are heard in some places,' said the Shanghai paper, *Wen Hui Bao*. 'Some of them are rubbish from capitalist society, while others are lewd music and songs from the [city's] old dance halls.' Decadent music, it claimed, 'sapped the will of young people and ruined their minds', producing hooliganism. Besides, the newspaper added, 'if we lead befuddled lives and sing love songs all day long, how can we think of our country's development?'[34] In the Soviet

Union, in 1957, Shepilov, then editor of *Pravda* and a Central Committee secretary, denounced Western pop music as 'a chaos of meaningless sounds, wild shrieking, squeaking, sighing, wailing, roaring . . . the braying of asses, the amorous croaking of an enormous bullfrog . . . a wild cave-dwellers' orgy'.[35] And plenty of parents in the West would have been happy to agree with him. Yet in the subsequent two decades, the Soviet Union not only developed its own, somewhat anodyne, versions of Western pop groups, but since 1975 has allowed tours by singers such as Cliff Richard and Elton John, and the American disco group, Boney M. In music, as in dress, China seems destined to do the same.

Despite scare stories in the press of gang rapes, and complaints that private dance parties kept entire neighbourhoods awake, amateur bands were formed, reinforced by the electric guitars newly available in Chinese shops. On summer Sundays, in Peking, the sons and daughters of senior officials, including some Politburo members, would go in their fathers' cars to the Ming Tombs' reservoir, twenty miles north of the city, and dance in the open air to music from a portable cassette player. A whole underground network of contacts and connections developed, through which cassettes of the Taiwan singer, Teresa Teng, the Rolling Stones and pop stars from Hong Kong, were brought into China and dubbed on to blanks, which then changed hands among friends or through the young ticket touts who crowd the entrances of cinemas, until they could be found in any big city in the country.

By comparison with Gorky Street or Kalinin Prospect in Moscow, let alone a Western capital, the 'bright lights' of Peking (or Shanghai or Canton) are almost non-existent. Nonetheless, in 1979, the bigger cinemas and theatres sprouted neon signs, where three years earlier there had been only one in the whole country – on the Peking International Club; and in the staid cities of the north, a few restaurants, instead of closing at eight pm, stayed open an hour later. In Tianjin, an old German coffee house, Kiessling and Bader, a survival from the nineteenth-century concession, with monogrammed silver, art-deco chandeliers and a marble foyer, became a fashionable hang-out for the young. In Peking the Peace Café, a student drinking haunt of the early 1960s, reopened for the first time since the Cultural Revolution.

At such places, at dance halls and at the Democracy Wall, Chinese and Westerners could meet with a freedom unknown since the communists had come to power. For about eight weeks, early in 1979 when the Peking Spring was at its height, a Chinese youth or girl encountered casually on the street could walk back with you to your apartment or hotel, without hindrance from the PLA guards at the entrance, and without fear of subsequent arrest. The *apartheid* which separates Chinese from non-Chinese began to crumble. Intellectuals could come to see you without first seeking permission from their units, and you could visit them. There arose a sudden overwhelming curiosity about the outside world, after years when to show such an interest would have been politically dangerous. Chinese officials, even in quite senior positions, began asking foreigners how much they earned, just as Russians do. Radio Australia reported that its Chinese service, which received two letters a month from China at the beginning of 1978, received 20,000 a month a year later, and when, incautiously, it invited listeners to write in for a free calendar, that figure doubled overnight.

As happens in other countries, foreign men started going to dances to pick up local women (and sometimes the other way round). At the Peace Café, you could drink beer and Chinese champagne with the sons of well-placed cadres, students and workers, unemployed youths back illegally from the countryside, and pretty girls with lightly rouged cheeks and two buttons of their blouses undone, instead of the normal one.

Amateur prostitution, directed at foreigners, developed often not for money but, as in the Soviet Union, for a meal or a pair of nylons. Some young men pimped for their girlfriends, as though it were a novel way of offering international friendship. But mostly it was on a naïve, freelance basis, and there were old-fashioned difficulties about finding a place to go. Hooliganism became widespread. Students started cheating in exams (before there had been no exams to cheat in). Soccer vandalism started. And the nature of sport itself changed. After China's admission to the Olympic movement in November 1979, the old Maoist formula of 'friendship first, competition second' was quietly dropped. 'We must win glory for our country,' said the sports newspaper, *Tiyu Bao*. 'To win friendship we must first win gold medals.'[36]

In short, by the end of 1980, when Mao's successors had been in power for four years, young people in China were beginning to look and to behave much more like their contemporaries elsewhere. China had become a more normal country, with all the problems that normalcy brings. In the Soviet Union this social liberalisation has survived the zig-zags of Khrushchev, and the partial re-Stalinisation of Brezhnev. In China, too, it is continuing, despite twists and turns along the way.

The changes were most marked in the big cities, Peking, Shanghai and Canton, but were felt to some extent all over the country. Quanzhou, a town of 120,000 people on the East China coast, has hardly a single car and water is drawn from wells along the middle of the main street. Yet because it has close connections with Chinese communities

319

overseas, black-market Dunhill cigarettes and the latest albums by Teresa Teng, still in their original Taiwan wrappers, were sold openly at pavement kiosks, and on the wall of almost every other house hung a Hong Kong calendar with a picture of a pretty girl. Or take somewhere still more remote: Jiuquan, which is half as small again and lies 2,000 miles west of Peking on the edge of the Gobi desert, beneath snow-capped mountains at the northern end of the Tibetan plateau. Camel carts lurch through the streets, and in the middle of the ancient belltower, which stands at the centre of the town, the *yin-yang* sign and the eight trigrams – the magic symbols of old China – were repainted by the local authorities in 1979. Yet the commission store had a Japanese digital watch for sale, and smart young men in dark glasses and leather jackets picked their way past barefoot, ragged beggars, stretched out on the pavement asleep.

The contrast between the new images of urban affluence and the deep poverty of the countryside was shown most cruelly in Peking. In 1979, to mark the Spring Festival, China's leaders held a gala in the Great Hall of the People. Even by totalitarian standards, it is no ordinary building. A quarter of a mile long, with fourteen acres of floorspace, it takes up the whole of one side of Tian An Men Square, and is linked by underground tunnels to the leaders' offices in Zhongnanhai. Built in the monumental Soviet neo-classical style, with a flat golden-tiled roof to match the Forbidden City, its proportions make it look deceptively small, until the Lilliputian soldiers guarding the entrance force the eye to realise that it has been fooled: the granite pillars of the portico are a hundred feet high, and each window is as tall as a two-storey building.

On the evening of January 27th, this huge edifice was a blaze of lights. Outside, people were letting off firecrackers and rockets, and small boys, wrapped up like round balls against the bitter cold, carried traditional red paper lanterns on long poles. Inside, 30,000 people were enjoying themselves, milling around between the ballroom where an army band played waltzes and foxtrots, a variety show, comedians doing a cross-talk routine, halls of painting and calligraphy, games and sidestalls with all the fun of the fair. But opposite the entrance, some 200 ill-clad, wretched looking people, many with dirty, sickly children, stood holding banners written on sheets of old newspaper, and chanted: 'We want food! We want clothing! Down with oppression! Down with hunger!'

Hordes of poverty-stricken people, beggars and petitioners, had begun appearing in Peking and other big cities, for the first time since the 1960s, following the government's call for the correction of 'wrong and unfair cases' in the autumn of 1978. Most came to present grievances to the central or provincial authorities when local officials (often the very men who had condemned them) refused to change their original verdicts.

That winter, in Peking alone, they numbered at least 60,000. They spent their days weaving pieces of coloured plastic into mug-holders, toy animals and fish, to peddle to passers-by, or singing ballads at street corners, trying to earn enough to survive on coarse steamed buns and left-overs they could beg from restaurants. Often, in the evenings, at the smaller eating-houses, hungry ragged children waited outside the door, hoping someone would take pity on them. Once as a table was being vacated, I saw two grubby urchins dash in between the legs of the waiters, and carry off – with utter triumph written across their faces – a half-eaten fish, before it could be cleared away. At night, the lucky ones slept in the comparative warmth of the railway station, or in the Supreme Court building. Others, men, women and small children, curled up under rough shelters of straw matting on the pavements in the old legation quarter.

Many came to Peking only when they had reached the last stages of despair. Suicides were frequent, and on the coldest nights, when the temperature dropped to $-30°C$, some died of exposure.

The sheer number of petitioners testified to the magnitude of the problems Mao had left behind. A year earlier, the police would have arrested them all and shipped them back to the provinces from which they had come. Indeed, one man, from neighbouring Hebei, said he had been shipped back thirteen times since he started trying to get his case settled in 1976. But in the new and more open climate that emerged in the Peking Spring, much greater tolerance was shown. On January 8th, the anniversary of Zhou Enlai's death, when, as every year, tens of thousands of people gathered in spontaneous homage before the Martyr's Monument in Tian An Men Square, the petitioners staged a demonstration. It was followed, a week later, by a protest march along Chang An and a sit-in outside Zhongnanhai, to appeal to 'Deng the Incorruptible' to solve their grievances.

These were of every sort. Some wanted jobs, and food. Others, protection from corrupt local despots – just as, in times past, Chinese petitioned the throne to relieve them from oppression. One wizened old man, like a caricature of a small landlord of fifty years ago, said he was a 'historical counter-revolutionary', having served in the Guomindang army before 1949. He had been sent to the countryside in 1955, and ever since, he said, beginning to weep, he had been trying to rejoin his family in Peking. Zhao Haiyan, a young woman, twenty-five years old, carrying a bedroll on her back, had been dismissed from a machinery factory in 1976 for refusing to inform against her foreman during the campaign against Deng Xiaoping. She was seeking reinstatement.[37] Liu Zhitai, the former Party first secretary of Pi county in Sichuan, had been over-thrown as a 'capitalist roader' and expelled from the Party at the start of the Cultural Revolution in 1966. Now he was sleeping rough, keeping himself alive by selling plastic fish outside an underground station, while the Party's Organisation Department examined his case.[38]

The most explosive problem of all, however, was that of the 'educated youths', the millions of young people who had been sent to the country-side, particularly since the Cultural Revolution.

Together with the activists of the democracy movement, demanding intellectual rights, and the half-starved beggars and petitioners, de-manding the right to eat and to work, the educated youths formed the third strain of the ferment spreading across China that winter. Their grievances, and those of the petitioners, appeared in posters at the Xidan wall long before it became a vehicle for political debate.

By November 1978, the Party had admitted that the policy of re-settling young people in the countryside had not been a success, and should be modified and eventually phased out.[39] The decision was well-intentioned but for the 10 million young people who had been living unhappily on communes and state farms, in some cases since the late 1950s, it was a signal for revolt. For they were told, in effect, that whatever changes were brought in to benefit future school leavers, those already in the countryside would have to stick it out.

In Shanghai, crowds of youths up to 3,000-strong marched every day for a week to the municipal Party committee building early in Decem-ber, to demand the right to return to the city, or in the case of those who had already come back illegally, to have their status legalised and be given jobs. In Yunnan, in South-Western China, 50,000 educated youths went on strike and sent a deputation to Peking, where they staged a protest demonstration in Tian An Men Square on December 27th. A few days later they were received by Vice-Premier Wang Zhen, who, while telling them to 'be farsighted and consider the whole situation' and 'not to make trouble', also ordered measures to remedy their complaints about working conditions, most of which were found to be justified.[40] The troubles at Shanghai, however, were not so easily solved. Over the years, more than a million Shanghainese youths had been rusticated, and several hundred thousand of them returned to visit their families during the Spring Festival at the end of January. When the holiday ended, they refused to go back.

For several days, parts of the city centre were paralysed by vast crowds of demonstrators. On the afternoon of February 5th, militants seized the railway station, and held it until the early hours of the following morning. Sixty trains and 80,000 passengers were halted or diverted. Young men climbed on the tops of carriages and made inflammatory speeches. Rolling stock was damaged and running fights raged with the police. The railways put their losses at more than half a million pounds. For two more days, the centre of Shanghai remained immobilised, as youths disconnected the power lines to trolley buses and huge demonstrations surged up and down the waterfront. But then the repeated appeals for order being broadcast on radio and television and by loudspeaker vans, coupled with selective arrests of trouble-makers, began to have their effect. Smaller-scale disturbances, often involving the seizure of municipal offices and, in some cases, the roughing up of officials, were later reported from cities all over China.

The Shanghai incidents marked a watershed in the democracy movement. Previously China's leaders, at least in public statements, had given it their encouragement. Now they turned their attention to defining its limits. The press abruptly began taking a much more cautious line, and though articles encouraging democracy and the emancipation of people's thinking did not stop altogether, they became few and far between.

The new guidelines were set out by an unnamed Politburo member (probably Hua) sometime before February 7th, when they were announced at a meeting of the Shanghai Party Committee:

A leading comrade at the Central level has pointed out: firstly, democracy and freedom cannot be practised in violation of the fundamental principles of the Constitution. Secondly, the people's living standards cannot be improved without making efforts to develop production. Thirdly, individual interests cannot be placed above the national and collective interests. Fourthly, the universal Marxist principle is essential to any discussions about the emancipation of our minds.[41]

These themes were elaborated in an editorial in the *People's Daily* two days later:

In China today there are a hundred broken things to be mended and a hundred tasks to be accomplished . . . It is impossible to solve in a morning questions which have piled up over years. In many cases certain material conditions are needed to settle them, and it will take some time. China's economy at present is very backward. *For the time being it is unlikely that there will be big advances in living standards.*

We must tell people the truth about the situation and let them understand

323

that it is impossible to talk about raising living standards while departing from production . . .

Democracy and centralism are a unity of opposites. *We cannot over-emphasise one aspect to the neglect of the other.* Because there was too little democracy in the past, today *democracy* should be specially emphasised. But this *absolutely does not mean rejecting centralism. Democracy which is not under the leadership of centralism and democracy which is not controlled by discipline are not real democracy* of the people, but mere anarchism . . . We should try our best to guarantee the people's democratic rights, but we must also be good at guiding the people to use their democratic rights in a *correct way.* (Emphasis added.)[42]

This was aimed not only at educated youths, but also at the petitioners. Two weeks earlier Hua had spoken out publicly in their support, and provincial officials had been upbraided for not doing enough to help and 'jumping three feet in the air and feeling sick at heart' when the masses used harsh words to them.[43] Now the tone changed to condemnation of people's 'excessive and unreasonable demands'.[44]

'What kind of democracy is it,' asked the *China Youth News*, 'when people have the right to obstruct trains?' That was illegal even in capitalist countries. The *People's Daily* discussed the workings of the Riot Act in Britain, and demanded severe penalties for 'trouble-makers . . . who harbour ulterior motives'. And *Wen Hui Bao* wrote, 'By freedom we mean proletarian freedom, not bourgeois freedom, and still less that "freedom" which allows people to infringe on the freedom of others.' Freedom, it declared, was not an end in itself; its purpose was to mobilise enthusiasm for China's modernisation.[45]

These strictures had no immediate effect on the discussion of socialism and human rights taking place in the wallposters and unofficial magazines. But they prepared the way for the cold wind that followed.

Clampdown

The '100 Flowers' campaign lasted a bare five weeks, and when it ended Mao's prestige within the Party was in tatters. The Peking Spring endured longer, but followed a remarkably similar course.

When the '100 Flowers' began in 1957, 'anything seemed possible', according to Robert Loh, then a businessman in Peking – just as it seemed at the beginning of the Peking Spring, twenty years later. In 1957, Mao, too, derided Party officials who feared that 'the heavens will fall' if people spoke out. When it threatened to get out of hand, he warned that 'all words and actions that depart from socialism are completely mistaken' – just as his successors, after the Shanghai disturbances, reaffirmed the 'universal Marxist principle' as a guide to emancipating the mind.

Finally Mao sanctioned what were known as the 'six criteria', reasserting the primacy of the Party against its critics, and the *People's Daily* declared that 'while large-scale class struggle is over in our country, class struggle is not extinct, especially on the ideological front'.[1] A month later that was backed up by the statement that while exploiting classes had been eliminated in China, 'exploiting class remnants' might persist for a long time.[2] In 1979, to reassert the primacy of the Party, the Chinese leaders issued what were known as the 'four basic principles', and the *People's Daily* said that class struggle against counter-revolutionaries and criminals 'must not be relaxed'.[3] Two months later Hua told the NPC that while 'as classes, the landlords and rich peasants have ceased to exist . . . there will still be class enemies of all kinds in China for a long time to come'. The concept of 'class remnants' was invoked soon afterwards.[4]

In form, then, and in the processes through which it evolved, much of the Peking Spring was almost a carbon copy of the '100 Flowers'. Indeed, there were times in 1979 when it seemed the Chinese leaders were referring back to a twenty-year-old script in order to find out what to do next. But Deng Xiaoping's China was not Mao's. The Peking Spring may have begun when Mao's political credo, though tottering, was still intact – in November 1978 class struggle was still held to be the main contradiction in society – and it may have used Mao's method of 'blooming and contending', or, as it had been known since the Cultural Revolution, the 'Four Bigs' – 'big democracy, big blooming, big contending, big-character posters'. Nonetheless, by the time the 'four basic principles' were propounded, the Maoist era was passing. The Peking Spring not only saw a change of political line from Mao to Deng, analogous to the change from Stalin to Khrushchev, it also itself underwent a transition; after a Maoist beginning, it came to a Khrushchevian end.

In the Soviet Union, the clampdown which ended the 'Thaw' came in November 1956, provoked in part by the ferment within the country, then beginning to spread alarmingly from the university campuses to the population at large, but above all by the explosions in Eastern Europe, muted in Poland, but open and painful in Hungary. For Khrushchev, the weakening of Russia's hold on its East European empire was even more damaging than the outpouring of anti-Party sentiment that was Mao's reward for launching the '100 Flowers'. China, having no tributary states in its thrall, was spared that problem.

What occurred in Poland and Hungary, and, in a less dramatic form, in other Soviet satellites too, was the result of three separate Soviet policy initiatives, all of which bore Khrushchev's personal stamp. The reconciliation with Tito, to which Molotov had been so opposed, had shown that Moscow could be made to tolerate rebellion, and the consequent rehabilitation, in most cases posthumous, of satellite leaders purged as Titoists to appease Stalin, served to inflame anti-Soviet feeling. The Secret Speech undermined the vassal Stalins, Bierut in Poland and Rákosi in Hungary, even as it discredited the secret police on whom their rule depended. And Khrushchev's endorsement of the idea of 'different roads to socialism' allowed the East Europeans to hope for greater independence.

Until June 1956 Khrushchev was riding high. Kaganovich was moved to a more junior government post; Molotov was replaced as Foreign Minister by Khrushchev's protégé, Shepilov. Yet even before Molotov's replacement was announced, the first riots broke out at Poznan in Poland. Then came the publication in the West of a leaked version of the Secret Speech, causing the disillusionment of a large part of the rank and file of the world communist movement. From July, Khrushchev was on the defensive. Molotov and the Old Guard demanded and got a harder line towards Eastern Europe. But mere words were no longer enough. The Soviet position continued to crumble. By mid-November, Wladislaw Gomulka was heading a recalcitrant, tough-minded government in Warsaw, and Soviet tanks were in the streets of Budapest.

These events, particularly the intervention in Hungary – coupled with reports, filtering back from Soviet soldiers, that the resistance there came not from counter-revolutionaries but from ordinary workers – intensified the ferment within the Soviet Union itself. Students at Moscow University posted transcripts of BBC Russian Service news bulletins about the Hungarian revolt on notice boards, as a comment on the lying reports appearing in the Soviet press. Agit-prop lecturers were heckled at factory meetings, and wallposters were found in the naval academies at Kronstadt and Vladivostok. In the Baltic States, demonstrators called for the right of secession, and students boycotted Russian language lectures. If Khrushchev and his colleagues were united on the need to use force in Hungary, they did not agree on the responsibility for the debacle. Khrushchev blamed Stalin for creating a relationship with Eastern Europe held together by fear; Molotov and Kaganovich argued that de-Stalinisation had been too fast. Nor was there any consensus on how far to go in repressing dissent at home.

In late November, Khrushchev finally moved to bring the students to heel, and simultaneously the press reactivated a campaign, which had been sputtering fitfully since the summer, against 'rotten elements' and 'demagogues'. He acted partly because he really believed the students were going too far and must be stopped to prevent serious disorders, and partly to salvage his own prestige by showing the rest of the Politburo that he was able not only to initiate liberalisation, but also to control it.

In both aims Khrushchev was moderately successful. The expulsion of 200 students from Moscow University – including those who put up the reports about Hungary – coupled with a polite warning to the remainder that 'if you do not like our institutions, you can go out to work and others will come and study in your place' – had a salutary effect on restoring calm on the campuses.[5] And when the Central Committee met in December, he survived the criticisms of the Old Guard. Nonetheless, he lost a lot of ground. The leadership reverted to a collective. Molotov was put in charge of propaganda and ideological work. Khrushchev's economic plans were criticised, and Malenkov's supporter, Pervukhin, took over the State Economic Commission. Malenkov himself regained much of his former prominence, and de-Stalinisation was not only halted but reversed. 'We are all Stalinists,' Khrushchev declared at a Kremlin reception on New Year's Eve. Two weeks later, he called Stalin a 'model communist' in defending proletarian interests, and said Stalinism meant 'intransigence, refusal to compromise, and a fight to the end for the triumph of the working class'. For Khrushchev to say that, after all he had revealed in the Secret Speech, showed the extent of his retreat.

Yet even with Molotov in charge of propaganda and Khrushchev praising Stalin's ghost, the ferment did not end completely. The Party's writ was restored on the factory floor and in the lecture halls, but the questioning of the system continued, above all among the youth and the writers. Throughout the spring of 1957, there was an all-out campaign against Dudintsev's novel, *Not by Bread Alone*, and at the beginning of March Shepilov convened a meeting of the Moscow branch of the Writers' Union, so that Dudintsev could make a formal self-criticism and the assembly could publicly reaffirm the need for Party guidance. Yet in the event not only did Dudintsev refuse to recant, but many other writers supported him – and some of Moscow's most important literary figures refused to attend the meeting at all.

The writers had begun more cautiously than the students, but having committed themselves they were determined to make a stand. It took another two-and-a-half months before they knuckled under, and then it was only a partial capitulation.

The Chinese leadership was similarly divided in its attitudes to the Peking Spring, notwithstanding the support for it in the press and from Deng Xiaoping. On January 17th, after the big petitioners' march along Chang An, the Politburo met to discuss the situation. Hua reportedly described the leaders of the democracy movement as rightists. 'We do not want to take action against them,' he was quoted as saying, 'but it is no longer so simple, because others have entered the fray. We shall have to think again.'

Who the 'others' were became clear the following day, when police detained a young woman named Fu Yuehua who had been the chief organiser of the march, and an editorial in the *People's Daily* called for the first time for greater efforts to solve the petitioners' problems. Shortly afterwards, the Peking Party Committee issued a statement which was read out at closed meetings of Party members, complaining that the proliferation of wallposters was 'unsanitary' and suggesting that they be restricted:

Some bad elements . . . [and] enemies have smuggled themselves into the good forces. We must use the method of establishing who is our enemy and who is our friend in order to solve this problem. There are also some people who hate the Party and hate socialism, but who are not quite up to the level of being counter-revolutionaries. And there are some people who seem to feel that socialism isn't quite right. As regards this last group, we must try to stop them going further down the slippery slope. But as for the rogues and ruffians, we must detain those who should be detained and make them labour; and we should arrest and lock up those who should be arrested and locked up. For the rest we should strengthen education.

Where Mao had explained the anti-rightist campaign by saying that 'hobgoblins and demons' had been lured out by the '100 Flowers', and Khrushchev had accused 'rotten elements' and 'demagogues' of exploiting de-Stalinisation, so, in the Peking Spring, 'bad elements who hate socialism' were the pretext for a clampdown.

However, the Peking Committee's statement did not condemn the wallposters outright or call for the suppression of the movement altogether. Instead, like a *China Youth News* editorial on January 25th, which said people should not be 'frightened or anxious' if the young expressed wrong ideas, it merely hinted that wallposters might be better displayed within places of work.

But wallposters were not the Committee's only concern. The statement also betrayed profound unease about the growth of unofficial contacts between Chinese and foreigners. It charged that foreign embassies had 'stepped up their activities', and hinted at espionage by secret agents from Taiwan, as well as less dangerous but, to many older Chinese, no less shocking behaviour of another kind:

> Some Chinese have asked foreign embassies to provide them with duplicators, paper and printing materials . . . Some Chinese have been invited by foreigners to dinner. Such people are forgetting their national character, because not only do some of them go to the foreigners' residences to eat, they even ask for little gifts. This is a national disgrace. It impairs the dignity of the state.

In an article in *Exploration* on January 29th, Wei Jingsheng held the Peking Committee up to ridicule for these words.[6]

> What a solemn face has the dignity of our state! This face does not look like the face of the 1970s, but rather like the closed-door face of the Qing dynasty. We would like to ask this face a question. Can we describe Deng Xiaoping's dining with the Japanese emperor at the latter's invitation as a Chinese being invited by a foreigner to dinner? No doubt this also 'impaired the dignity of the state'. Is asking for printing materials from foreigners 'impairing the dignity of the state', and asking for hundreds of millions of yuan in loans and aid from foreigners not 'impairing the dignity of the state'? What kind of logic is this? . . .
>
> No one has entrusted you with the task of monopolising friendly relations, and no one has entrusted you with the task of ruling. You do not represent the people. Some bigwigs in the Peking Party Committee are afraid the people may enjoy real democracy. They are trying their very best to disrupt this present movement. The methods they have adopted are despicable.

Wei also rejected the attempt to control the wallposter movement: 'Are these the "limits" of democracy you have promised to give the people?

A thousand thanks for your kindness. These limits are not lower than the limits set when the "Gang of Four" ran wild.' And he derided the Committee for complaining about the petitioners' march:

> Since the constitution states that citizens enjoy the freedom of procession, why is it that some processions are described as bad? Probably because they were not organised by the government. If freedom must be organised by the government, is it then the government's freedom or the people's?

Next day seven of the main unofficial magazines in Peking, including *Exploration*, *Today*, *April 5th Tribune* and *Qimeng*, issued a melodramatic joint statement, declaring that if members of the democracy movement were 'persecuted to death' as a result of their activities, they would consider themselves 'duty-bound to publicise it . . . and to offer material support to their family members'. A rash of posters demanded the release of Fu Yuehua, including two huge yellow ones, each fifty feet long and in characters two feet high, on either side of Tian An Men. That weekend, 800 people attended a meeting at the Democracy Wall, the biggest of its kind since November, at which speakers pledged their readiness to spill their blood in the movement's defence.

But by then, unknown to them, the immediate threat had passed. The Politburo had ordered the Peking Committee's statement withdrawn.

For a Party directive to be countermanded ten days after being issued implies a situation of extraordinary fluidity. It was rumoured later that the Peking Party chief, Lin Hujia, had exceeded his brief, and certainly from this time on Lin's relations with Deng began to deteriorate. Unofficial accounts suggest that Deng did not attend the January 17th meeting, possibly because he was out of Peking preparing for his visit to the United States. Two or three days before his departure on January 28th, the Politburo met again, and decided, at Deng's insistence, that the restrictions on contacts with foreigners and on wallposters be deferred. Shortly afterwards, when the disturbances at Shanghai broke out, this decision was maintained. And even as late as mid-February, when the press, in chorus, was urging stability and unity in the wake of the Shanghai incidents, the *People's Daily* was still able to lash out at the foolishness of officials who wanted to call the police whenever a wallposter appeared.

Yet in March, when the democracy movement seemed at its least threatening, a clampdown *was* ordered, and in strikingly similar terms to those used by the Peking Committee two months before.

This second reversal of policy was due not to any single factor but to a constellation of causes, of which the most urgent was a swelling tide of discontent within the Party. From the provincial level right down to the grass roots, Party cadres were fed up with the disorders and difficulties the new policies were creating. They were harassed by petitioners and educated youths, and criticised in posters. Their authority was undermined by constant press accusations that they were blinkered and feudalistic. Many, having made their careers under Mao, were fearful of where de-Maoisation would lead; many regarded the Third Plenum as revisionist and a betrayal of Mao. Most were unsure how they would fare in the new, modernised China that lay ahead. The support Deng had among the people and in the central Party apparatus was much weaker in the layers between. Just as Mao himself, in the '100 Flowers', had become a focus for the disaffection of hard-pressed officials, so now Deng, as the architect of the Third Plenum, faced similar resentment. In the countryside, the decision to restore political rights to landlords and rich peasants encountered strong resistance. In the cities, objections were raised to restoring the wealth of former capitalists.[7] Leftists claimed that the plenum preached Khrushchev's doctrine of the 'dying out of class struggle', as indeed in a sense it did. 'Class struggle,' said the newspaper, *Wen Hui Bao*, 'can only develop in the general trend of gradual relaxation.' And traditionalists argued that by accepting foreign loans and entering into joint ventures with foreign companies, China was allowing its sovereignty to be diminished.[8]

The backlash of conservative thinking was reinforced by the genuine problems that political relaxation brought – recognised as such by Deng and other leaders no less than by the lower-level officials who had to deal with them. He, too, was concerned that the movement might suddenly rage out of hand. In 1957, during the '100 Flowers', Liu Shaoqi had warned, 'If we don't control things, in a jiffy millions of people will be on the move and then we won't be able to do anything – that wouldn't be to our advantage.' And Mao himself acknowledged to the former French premier, Edgar Faure, 'With a people like this it is necessary to observe certain limits.'[9] That was before the Cultural Revolution had shown the havoc a mass movement could wreak. In 1979, the lessons of the Cultural Revolution were never far from the leaders' minds. In January, Wang Zhen warned, 'We must never again allow a situation marked by anarchy and turmoil to emerge.' And the Shanghai Party leader, Peng Chong, also a Politburo member, compared the disruption of rail traffic there with an incident in November 1966 involving Red Guards led by Wang Hongwen. Was it exaggeration to draw such a parallel, asked *Jiefang Ribao*. 'It is not exaggeration at all; the line of demarcation is clear.'[10]

Increased crime, hooliganism and gambling, and the resurgence of old superstitions and customs, were accompanied by a sharp drop in the industrial growth rate – from twelve per cent in 1978 to six per cent in the first quarter of 1979. Peasants started dividing up communal fields and 'going it alone'. After being allowed to glimpse the wealth of the capitalist West, many young people concluded that 'capitalism is better than socialism'. And the hackles of Chinese of all persuasions were raised by a number of incidents involving foreigners.

At the Peking Language Institute, where foreign students learn Chinese before beginning university courses, girls from a nearby factory started turning up at weekend dances, offering sex for the modest sum of five yuan (about £1.50). There is a lingering suspicion that officials in the Peking Public Security Bureau, which violently opposed the new policies, deliberately allowed this to continue until it grew into a major scandal, in order to generate pressure for liberalisation to be curtailed. Then, in late February, just after the start of China's border war with Vietnam, a secret Defence Ministry document was leaked, giving casualty figures and a breakdown of the Chinese command. The information came into the hands of Wei Jingsheng, who passed it on to Western journalists.

If the war had been going well, this would have been bad enough. But the war was going badly. Chinese troops had not fought a large-scale engagement since the border conflict with India in 1962. There were problems of co-ordination – Chinese artillery units shelled their own infantry; logistical difficulties – tanks being unable to advance for lack of fuel; problems of communication, not only because of outdated equipment, but also because of the absence of ranks and uniforms, which made it impossible to identify officers; and problems of morale. It was not that China failed in its avowed task of 'punishing' Vietnam, for in the end its objectives were attained. Three Vietnamese provincial capitals were captured and razed to the ground, and every installation of economic value in the border areas was destroyed. But it took far longer than expected, and the human cost was high: at least 20,000 Chinese dead and wounded.

When it was all over, the ashes of those who had died were sent back to their families in red caskets – showing that they had been killed in action; or in white – meaning that they had been shot for cowardice.

February 1979 was a grim month for China. Apart from the problems of the war, the economic strategy which Hua had outlined with such fanfare a year earlier was found to be unworkable. On February 6th, the plan for nationwide agricultural mechanisation was dropped, and with it the Maoist policy of insisting that all areas be self-sufficient in grain. On February 22nd, US $2.7 billion in plant purchases from Japan were unilaterally suspended, as the Chinese leaders realised that they had committed themselves to far larger technology imports (US $23 billion in less than a year, according to Li Xiannian) than the country could possibly absorb. Two days later, it was announced that investment in heavy industry would be cut back, and the target of 60 million tons of steel a year was abandoned. Soon afterwards Chen Yun concluded that the imbalances in China's economy, first hinted at during the Third Plenum, were so severe that unless corrected they would make modernisation impossible. By April, the entire Ten Year Plan had been renounced.

This was a further blow to Hua, whose brainchild the plan was. The press inveighed against 'impetuosity and rashness' and setting steel targets which were 'arbitrary and irrespective of reality', and for the first time the parallel with the Great Leap Forward was drawn. Hua was also obliquely criticised for having called the 'Gang of Four' ultra-rightists, instead of ultra-leftists; for having helped Mao purge Peng Dehuai in 1959; and for doctoring Volume 5 of Mao's *Selected Works* to serve his own political line.[11]

Yet, perversely, the problems which came to a head in February – the economic setbacks and the war, which had no connection with the democracy movement, no less than the disturbances, the social problems and the leftist backlash, which did – proved in the end to be Hua's salvation.

In December and January, Deng had been riding high. The Third Plenum praised his 'remarkable successes'; his visit to America had been a triumph. But by the beginning of March, China was floundering. In every field – social, political and economic – there was a loss of purpose and direction. The old ideological props had been kicked away; the tidy Maoist vision of the world had given place to a much more complex reality. The leadership began to understand how incredibly difficult it was going to be to make its policies work. 'We were over-optimistic,' Hu Yaobang conceded later. The Sichuan leader, Zhao Ziyang, used the word 'imprudent'.

Against this sobering background the need for a general reassertion of discipline began to seem overwhelming. The pressure on Deng from the left and from the conservatives in the Politburo was reflected in an editorial in the *People's Daily* appealing to leading groups 'to seek common ground on major questions while reserving differences on minor ones'. It went on to deliver what amounted to an open rebuke to Deng for not mending his frayed relations with Hua, by citing the Peking opera, *The General and the Prime Minister are in Harmony*, which describes how a veteran general, during the Warring States period, is passed over for the post of prime minister in favour of a younger man. The general 'often intercepted the prime minister's carriage to make trouble and insult him'. But the prime minister 'exercised forbearance and restraint', and in the end the general 'awoke to his erring ways and apologised'. 'Is it conceivable,' asked the *People's Daily*, 'that we revolutionaries with a communist world outlook cannot do today what could be done by someone 2,000 years ago?'[12]

The sniping at Hua in the press ceased. He and Deng appeared in public together at a tree-planting ceremony. The Politburo directed provincial leaders to draw up regulations to restrict the democracy movement, and also, at their discretion, to deal with ancilliary sources of disorder: indiscriminate felling of trees and 'sinister theatrical groups' in Anhui; illegal sales of ration coupons in Shanghai; and even, in remote Qinghai, adjoining Tibet, 'unauthorised manure collecting'.[13]

On March 16th, the day Chinese forces completed their withdrawal from Vietnam, Deng addressed a meeting of 7,000 officials in the Great Hall of the People. He spoke about the war and the economic difficulties the country faced; but his main theme was the need for democracy to be controlled by a framework of laws. The policy of emancipating the mind was correct, he said, and must continue; the problems that had arisen were due to misunderstanding:

> When we say we must not follow Marxism-Leninism-Mao Zedong Thought dogmatically, they say it is no longer a guideline. When we expose the difficulties caused by Lin Biao and the 'Gang of Four' and by our own shortcomings and mistakes, they doubt the superiority of socialism. When we oppose feudal despotism . . . and advocate socialist democracy, they preach bourgeois democracy and advocate ultra-democracy. When we . . . correct wrong and unfair cases, they raise the question of 'defending human rights'. When we say we should learn from foreign science and technology, they think everything foreign is good and become intoxicated by the bourgeois way of life. When we say attention should be paid to the people's welfare, they demand that all problems be solved at once . . . This kind of behaviour has nothing to do with emancipating the mind, and is very harmful.[14]

The speech was defensive, but balanced. There was 'no need to make a fuss and bring unwarranted charges' if some people's views and actions were 'not completely correct'. But at the same time there was such a thing as the dictatorship of the proletariat. Fu Yuehua would be given a public trial. Chinese who consorted with foreigners to sell state secrets would be arrested. Anarchism would be resolutely opposed.

For the police and the provincial authorities this was music to the ears, and they needed no encouragement to act. Although the speech was not made public, word spread fast. The following evening I had dinner with two Chinese students, whom I used to meet most weekends, and found them depressed and nervous. A friend, whose father had attended the meeting, had warned them to have no further contact with foreigners because 'the axe is about to fall'. The next I heard was a telephone call six weeks later: they were all right, they said, but it was not safe for them to try to meet me again.

Others were not put off so easily. But when, that same week, officials ordered Chinese to leave a foreigners' dance and police began tailing foreigners who had meetings with Chinese, most non-official friendships lapsed.

The press lashed out in a xenophobic outburst which showed the intensity of the feelings that had been bottled up over the previous three months. The *Peking Daily* of Lin Hujia and the workers' newspaper, *Gongren Ribao*, controlled by Ni Zhifu, led the pack:

> How can foreigners offer China human rights and democracy? . . . Before liberation, the whip, the bayonet and the cannon of imperialism took no account of human rights and democracy. In parks one saw a notice at the gate, 'Chinese and Dogs Not Allowed' . . . The imperialists, when they ran their factories and companies, never treated Chinese workers like human beings. They used to say, 'You may not be able to buy a three-legged toad, but workers with two legs are easy to find.' The workers were fed like dogs and swine, and made to work like horses and cattle. They were always hungry, and often finished up being thrown into a communal ditch.[15]

Thus the *Peking Daily* on April 2nd. *Red Flag* took up the same theme. So did the *China Youth News*:

> Under the veil of the colourful history of capitalist civilisation is the bloodstained history of human rights violations. How can those millionaires fattened on workers' blood be fit to talk about human rights?[16]

Gongren Ribao charged that activists at the Democracy Wall were 'co-operating with foreign spy organisations to carry out disruptive activities'. But the prize for the most blatant, approved racism, went to an article in the *Peking Daily* on April 5th, written by a cook at the Peking Hotel, who said that having served foreigners for the last forty-three years, 'I really know what capitalist freedom and democracy are all about'. As though in proof, he told a long story about how a foreigner had once accused him of taking his wallet, only for it to be discovered that another foreigner had stolen it. The article went on:

A very few individuals want the 'democracy' and 'freedom' of the West, and put up wallposters all over the place . . . Some young people abandon themselves to the cult of decadent Western culture: the boys have long hair and wear bizarre clothes; the girls dress in questionable taste, and go to the big hotels to dance with foreigners and give themselves up to activities which are against the law, forfeiting not only their own dignity but also the dignity of China, which belongs to us all.

Thus spoke the voice of Chinese reaction. From mid-March until the end of April it was the dominant voice in China, and the views it expressed are still, today, the views of very many older Chinese. To them the young activists of the democracy movement, the girls who danced with foreigners, the petitioners who demonstrated outside government offices, the young prostitutes, hooligans, gamblers, confidence tricksters and violent criminals were all essentially the same. This was the view, too, of the police and of a broad sector of officialdom. As in the Soviet Union in 1957 – and as in the treatment of Soviet dissidents now – political, social and criminal problems were deliberately confounded so that each could be smeared by association with the other.

The Peking Revolutionary Committee declared:

Counter-revolutionaries hostile to the socialist system, criminals engaging in sabotage and followers of the 'Gang of Four' . . . with big- and small-character posters, speeches and private magazines, wilfully and viciously attack Party and state leaders and even openly call for the overthrow of the leadership of the Communist Party and the socialist system . . . Some people . . . storm government organisations, occupy offices, beat up and insult people, and obstruct normal work and social order. The masses are angered by such activities. They strongly demand that the problem be solved quickly . . .

Counter-revolutionaries, murderers, arsonists, rapists, embezzlers, swindlers, elements who engage in beating, smashing and looting, other elements who sabotage social order and criminals . . . will be resolutely punished according to law.[17]

Those who 'pervert social conventions' were lumped together with 'national scum who betray state secrets and damage the national interest'; those who 'act like riff-raff on the pretext of entertainment' with 'those who wave the signboard of democracy to gather crowds and make disturbances'; those who 'dance all night in the streets, affecting their work and study next day' (a complaint also voiced during the '100 Flowers') with 'pick-pockets and vagabonds sabotaging social order'.[18]

Even schoolchildren were not spared from the spate of all-embracing condemnations. Education authorities declared:

> Students must not get involved in fights, use vulgar language, smoke, drink, engage in billing and cooing, wear outlandish clothes, indulge in strange hairstyles or read pornography.[19]

To back up these restrictions, political study classes were assured that even though a few misguided young Chinese might 'blindly admire the capitalist lifestyle', young Americans were 'earnestly longing for socialist new China'. Workers in the United States, they were told, 'have very heavy burdens and are threatened by unemployment at all times'.[20]

This was part of an effort to tone down the glowing picture that had been painted of the West by focusing on what *Guangming Ribao* called the 'degeneration, crime and despair caused by the bourgeois way of life'. But because the gulf in living standards was so great, many of the facts cited tended to confirm, rather than discredit, the prevailing view of Western affluence. *Gongren Ribao* might report that 'Many American families are having less meat on the table. They are buying less clothes and keeping their cars longer. Because of high fuel costs, many families have turned off their heating and use blankets while watching television at night.'[21] But to most Chinese, with no television, no car, scarce meat and rationed clothes, that sounded like paradise. *Jiefang Ribao*'s indignation that some American states 'even go so far as to rule that workers who participate in the armed overthrow of the government are not entitled to unemployment benefit' hardly cut much ice in a country where unemployment payments do not exist.[22]

Unlike the Peking Committee's attempted clampdown in January, Deng's speech on March 16th did not give rise to any dramatic meetings of protest at the Democracy Wall. But as the press campaign gathered pace, a widespread feeling of betrayal developed. As usual it was most forcefully expressed by Wei Jingsheng, in a special issue of *Exploration* on March 25th:

> Is Deng Xiaoping worthy of the people's trust? . . . If he implements policies that benefit the people and if he leads them to peace and prosperity, we will trust him . . . Abolishing the people's right of expression under the pretext of social phenomena . . . is a habitual practice of all old and new dictatorial fascists . . . Deng Xiaoping has now found such a pretext . . .
> Do the people support Deng Xiaoping as a person? No, they do not! With the exception of his fight for the people's interests, he himself has nothing worthy of their support. He now wants to strip off his mask as the protector of democracy, and to suppress the democracy movement . . . He is following a dictatorial road after deceitfully winning the people's trust.[23]

Four days later, Wei was arrested and charged with counter-revolutionary activities. Chen Lu, of the Human Rights Alliance and another activist, Zhang Wenhe, were also detained. The same day, March 29th, police raided the office of the *April 5th Tribune*, and the Peking Revolutionary Committee approved a notice, along the lines recommended by the Politburo earlier in the month, restricting posters to a single site (the Democracy Wall) and requiring demonstrators to follow police orders when holding meetings and processions. That weekend, a battalion of cleaners went to work, scraping off accumulated layers of paper and glue from all the other poster walls that had sprung up around the city. Overnight Peking became a tidier and a duller place.

On April 4th, in a deliberate show of force, plainclothes police arrested Ren Wanding while he was putting up a poster at the Democracy Wall. But April 5th, the anniversary of the 1976 riots, passed without incident, and apart from *Exploration*, the *Human Rights Alliance* and the *April 5th Tribune*, which all protested at the repression, most activists decided to keep their heads down and write on non-controversial topics, arguing that this would at least keep the wall open. In the provinces even that was not possible. Some unofficial magazines survived, but wallposters were either banned outright, or, as in Hangzhou, restricted to a site so remote that in practice no one went there.

The Peking Revolutionary Committee's notice differed from those issued elsewhere by one additional clause:

> All slogans, posters, big- and small-character posters, books, journals, pictures, photographs and other representations which oppose *socialism, the dictatorship of the proletariat, the leadership of the Chinese Communist Party, and Marxism-Leninism-Mao Zedong Thought*, as well as the disclosure of state secrets and violations of the Constitution and the law are prohibited. (Emphasis added.)

The four phrases in italics, afterwards known as the 'four basic principles', were formally unveiled by Deng Xiaoping at a second closed meeting of senior officials on March 30th, marking the start of an intense propaganda campaign which lasted through much of the summer.[24] Like the 'six criteria', issued by Mao in similar circumstances in 1957, they could be used to forbid any criticism of the Chinese system and its leaders that the authorities disliked. Nor was the similarity in form and nomenclature unintentional. Five weeks earlier *Gongren Ribao* had published a signed article which declared, 'Should we not revise, enrich and develop the "six criteria" on the basis of actual conditions? I think we should.'[25]

On April 5th, the *People's Daily* demolished another of the foundations on which the democracy movement had been built – the right of the people to take spontaneous political action, as exemplified by the Tian An Men riots. The contrary proposition, that the struggle for democracy 'must and can only be under Party leadership', had never been completely abandoned. Now the contradiction was resolved by the Orwellian declaration that, in essence, the riots *had* been under Party leadership, and could not otherwise have had so great an effect.[26]

Yet all this was 'light rain and gentle breeze' compared with the thunderbolts unloosed at the 'rightists' in 1957. The Shanghai disturbances in February led eventually to three youths being sentenced to prison terms of between two and nine years. After similar student riots near Wuhan at the end of the '100 Flowers', Mao had the leaders shot. In the whole of China in 1979, perhaps two or three hundred people were detained in the clampdown on the democracy movement, and in most cases they were given short terms of re-education through labour. In 1957, 400,000 people were detained, most of them serving twenty-year terms.

If the 'blooming and contending' of the 'Second 100 Flowers' was halted much more gently than the first, Deng also got off more lightly than Mao had done twenty years before. But he did not escape attack altogether. Apart from the *People's Daily*'s suggestion that, like the veteran general in the Warring States, he should 'awake to his erring ways', he was obliquely criticised by the provincial authorities in Hua's stronghold of Hunan, for promoting 'individual affluence', and his ally, Hu Yaobang, as Director of the Propaganda Department, was sniped at in the *Peking Daily* for not giving sufficient emphasis to 'the black side of capitalist life'.[27] Months before, in December, voices had been raised in the Politburo – including Ye Jianying and Hua – warning that 'without the unified leadership of the Party deviations such as anarchism and ultra-democracy will come into being'.[28] Now they could tell Deng, 'we told you so', as Molotov and Kaganovich told Khrushchev after de-Stalinisation went sour. The *Peking Daily* came close to saying it publicly, by quoting members of the Peking Revolutionary Committee as commenting on the clampdown, 'This should have been done long ago!'[29] As everyone knew, it was Deng who had had it deferred.

In China, as in the Soviet Union, collective leadership was reasserted. Hua's role as Party Chairman was enhanced. The pressure on the Politburo leftists eased, and they began to appear in public again. The compromise, so laboriously worked out in December, whereby Mao's historical role was to be reaffirmed and questions such as how to assess the Cultural Revolution were to be set aside until a later date, was patched up, and the press once more wrote of the need to 'hold high Chairman Mao's banner'. Even his mausoleum reopened, after being closed 'for repairs' for four months.

In his speech on March 16th, Deng went as far in praising Mao as Khrushchev in praising Stalin in January 1957. If the reversal seemed less glaring, it was because Mao had throughout been less harshly attacked. But then, the clampdown as a whole was a huge reversal of all that Deng had stood for, and his failure was shown more graphically in his own words and those of his supporters than by anything his opponents said. Four weeks after the *People's Daily* had written, 'The method of suppressing criticism is a foolish one, used by those who lack confidence in the truth,'[30] and nine weeks after Deng himself had said that the wallposter movement could continue 'for generations', here it was, being suppressed.

Deng had no need to prove that he could be ruthless in dealing with dissent; his staff work for Mao in the anti-rightist campaign was sufficient testimonial to that. Also he was well aware of the damage that would result from an unconstrained crackdown on the right. But when he spoke on March 16th, he plainly underestimated the strength of feeling in the Party against the democracy movement. The torrent his words released swept away moderation, and left him for the next four weeks struggling to catch up – like Khrushchev weighing into the students at Moscow University, trying to regain the initiative. With tacit support from Hua and Ye, leftist and conservative officials at all levels of the Party tried to use the 'four principles' to negate the policies of the Third Plenum as 'un-Maoist'. For millions of cautious, hidebound functionaries, the 'principles' became a magic weapon to maintain the old Maoist ways, reject criticism and block change. This was not easy to counter, not merely because of the prevailing political mood, but because the 'principles' were Deng's own political creed as much as his opponents': he, too, believed that the Party was paramount and that dictatorship must be used against all who threatened its rule. Their differences were over how this should be done.

The outpouring of conservative, leftist bile in March and April was afterwards known as the 'Cold Wind in Spring',[31] and much of the summer was spent trying to undo its effects. All over China, the campaign to remove the labels from the landlords ground to a halt. Private plots were taken away, and private fruit trees cut down. 'Mopping-up squads' were formed, to 'mop up the peasants' small freedoms'. One such squad, in a wretchedly poor commune in Gansu, led by the local Party secretary in person, spent twenty days destroying vegetables and uprooting 10,000 saplings the villagers had planted around their houses. He explained afterwards that they had been 'implementing the four principles . . . and eradicating anarchist trends of thought'.[32]

By the autumn of 1979, the liberal new agricultural policies giving the peasants more say in the choice of crops and encouraging them to make more money, were being properly carried out in only ten per cent of China's communes. Elsewhere, commune and county leaders had either ignored or retracted them. The attitude of many local officials, and the broken hopes of the peasants, were summed up in a short story called *In Vino Veritas*, by a writer named Sun Yuchun. It recounts a conversation between Guo Shichang, an old commune secretary, and Erxi, a young production team leader who has put up posters suggesting a new crop plan:[33]

After the wine he had drunk, Guo's face had turned red and his forehead shone with perspiration. He paused for a while, and then pointed at the table. 'Take this table, for example,' he said. 'It was me who distributed it during the land reform, wasn't it? Now the Party tells us to be more democratic. You think I don't know what that means. But you've got some queer ideas. You think it means putting up wallposters against your leaders and kicking up a fuss! That's all wrong. You may have democracy, but I have centralism!' The more he spoke, the angrier he became, banging the table with his chopsticks . . . 'I'm warning you,' he said. 'A handful of troublemakers are using democracy to stir things up. Don't let yourself play into their hands. It will be too late to feel sorry if you do!'

Erxi was in a daze, as gradually he realised that the new rights for the peasants were nothing but an illusion. Frowning, he said nothing more . . . The secretary hiccuped again and scratched himself. In Vino Veritas, *as the saying goes. Guo struck the table and spoke his mind:*

'You think your little posters scared me? What crap! I don't give a damn about ten thousand posters, let alone your eight or ten! During the Cultural Revolution there were posters everywhere, but no one touched a hair of my head. You're too eager to get the right to decide. Too big for your boots! You demand this right and that right. That means seizing power from the working class . . . Give you an inch and you'll take a mile! Democracy? Shit! Yes, I mean it . . . Just you dare stick up another poster and sabotage the country's stability and unity. I'll have you arrested. Go ahead and try!'

Deng's response to the Secretary Guos of China – and those who offered them encouragement – was not long in coming. On April 5th, the Central Committee began a work conference, mainly to discuss the economy, but also to deal with ideological questions. On April 17th, the People's Daily, which alone among the press had continued to champion the need for democratisation, printed a commentary which went straight back to the days when the Peking Spring was at its height:

> Leading comrades usually do not object to hearing remarks which are pleasant to the ear or which they regard as correct. The problem is how to deal with remarks which they regard as wrong . . . If, when people speak out, they are attacked, punished, or retaliated against, who will dare to express his views? People will not dare to say things of which they are unsure. They may even avoid saying things which are obviously right . . . Thus opinions will be suppressed, and there . . . will be an oppressive situation in which ten thousand horses stand mute . . . This is not democracy at all . . . It is practically impossible to avoid saying wrong things. This world is complex, and . . . at times the unanimous view of the majority may not be entirely correct. On the contrary, the views of a few people or even an individual may be temporarily regarded by society as absurd and wrong, but may withstand the test of time . . . The propagation of Marxism underwent such a process.

It would be hard to make a more direct assault on the conservatives' position.

Hu Yaobang, Hu Qiaomu and the editor of the People's Daily, Hu Jiwei, were all accused at the work conference, as surrogates for Deng, of having 'gone too far' and 'mismanaged things after the Third Plenum'.[34] Wang Dongxing and the 'Whateverists', as surrogates for Hua, were attacked for 'placing the four basic principles in opposition to democracy and the emancipation of the mind . . . and to the discussion on the criterion of truth'. Deng, in his speech, said the 'four basic principles' were being opposed from two sides. From the right, they were under attack by 'a few anti-socialist elements' and young people who had confused ideas about socialism and capitalism. From the left, they were being opposed by 'comrades who try to reverse the wheel of history', who 'adopt a doubting attitude' and hold that the policies of the Third Plenum are 'rightist' and 'do not conform to Mao Zedong Thought'.[35]

By the time the work conference ended on April 29th this thesis of the 'two erroneous tendencies' had been formally approved. A week later, it was reluctantly endorsed by Hua. Speaking at a youth rally, he declared: 'If we deviate from the basic principles of Marxism-Leninism-Mao Zedong Thought, we shall lose our bearings and go astray. If we worship Marxism-Leninism-Mao Zedong Thought as unchangeable dogma, we shall also go astray.'[36] The rally was attended by virtually the entire leadership. But the façade of unity was hollow. The press, for the first time, began openly using the term, 'Whateverist', to describe the opposition from the left. Shortly afterwards the *People's Daily* said directly that it was the left rather than the right that constituted China's main problem.[37] And on May 11th all the leading papers published a devastating attack which not only revived the analogy between Wang Dongxing and Zinoviev, but also drew a parallel between Hua and Trotsky. It was one year to the day since Deng had launched the practice debate.

The new campaign developed with extraordinary speed, and was more open and uncompromising than anything that had gone before. The trouble was not that Deng's policies were too liberal, the *People's Daily* said, but rather that the minds of his critics were poisoned by ultra-leftist ideas. If young people doubted socialism, it was because the 'Gang of Four' had linked it with poverty; to doubt such 'sham socialism' was a good, not a bad, thing. It complained of a 'disease of left-sightedness', and said some officials were so deeply afflicted that they were 'quite beyond cure'. *Gongren Ribao* said there was 'a major problem of ideological ossification'; even the *Peking Daily* declared that the extent of China's advance depended on the extent to which the left was criticised.[38] During the summer, the discussion on the 'practice criterion' now described as 'the most fundamental principle of Marxism', was re-launched under the slogan of 'making up the missed lesson', as part of a 'great ideological line struggle' to rectify the Party.[39] The purpose, according to the *Liberation Army Daily*, was 'to make a clean break with those who adhere to the "two whatevers"' – in other words to isolate Wang Dongxing and the other Politburo leftists, and prepare the way for their eventual purge – and 'to eliminate the pernicious influence of the ultra-left line'. Of the two the second was by far the more difficult, and the newspaper itself acknowledged it would be 'an arduous, long-term task'.[40]

It was not simply a matter of opposition to the new policies. Even those who supported the reforms had 'lingering fears' or 'shared the same bed with different dreams'. Many worried that 'there might be another great reversal, and nobody knows when'; the old problem of 'unforgotten trepidation' was still there; and for all but a tiny handful of Chinese – unsurprisingly, after twenty years of indoctrination – it was still true that, as one newspaper put it, 'ultra-left theories hold their minds imperceptibly under a spell'.[41]

The problem was typified by a commune secretary in Liaoning, in North-East China, who solemnly went through all the documents that arrived on his desk, crossing out the words 'grow rich' and replacing them with 'increase income'.

Didn't he know [asked the *Liaoning Daily*] that it's the Central Committee's policy to allow peasants to grow rich? He did. Did he oppose the policy of allowing peasants to become rich? No. Then what on earth made him do such a thing? People say it was because the words, 'grow rich', sounded wrong to him.[42]

The obstacles really were that basic. 'Under the socialist system, to become rich is honourable,' pleaded a newspaper in Hainan. 'To become rich first is to be honourable first, and the richer a person is the more honourable he becomes.'[43] It was an uphill struggle.

The onslaught against the left was accompanied by a resurgence of the democracy movement. It began modestly: 'Like modernisation,' said the *People's Daily* at the beginning of May, 'democracy is a process to be realised step by step. However, we must keep to the path that leads forward.' But soon the editorials became more explicit. 'The Constitution guarantees freedom of speech,' said *Guangming Ribao*. 'If those who make criticisms are suppressed, imprisoned or even executed, what is the difference between that and slavery?' The *People's Daily* warned that a communist party which suppressed democracy would turn fascist, and pointed to the damage the anti-rightist campaign had done.[44] Others denounced the practice of 'grabbing people by their pigtails and fixing labels on them'. And throughout the summer and autumn a constant stream of articles asserted that the emancipation of the mind, far from being 'overdone', was only just beginning and would 'endlessly develop and be enriched'.[45]

But if, politically, the 'two' erroneous tendencies were in practice reduced to one – hardly anyone spoke about the problem of rightists any more – the democracy movement was now guided firmly on to a socialist path. The new, middle-of-the-road approach was set out by the Sichuan leader, Zhao Ziyang, who said in May that it was as wrong to think that democracy should have no limits and that the 'four principles' were being used to restrict it, as it was to think that democracy had gone too far and that they should be used to correct it.[46]

It was not bourgeois but socialist democracy that China was aiming for, its leaders declared; it was not a Western, capitalist modernisation programme that was being undertaken but a 'Chinese-style, socialist' one. The *People's Daily* said the 'four principles' were 'a precondition for the expansion of democracy'. The Heilongjiang leader, Yang Yichen, said 'support for socialism, not capitalism, is the political demarcation line for emancipating the mind'. The slogan, 'Only socialism can save China', was revived.[47]

That all this was wholly incompatible with Deng's insistence that practice was the sole criterion of truth – which meant that the validity of the socialist road, the Party's leadership and other 'basic principles' should themselves be tested by practice, and if found wanting, discarded – was evidently a contradiction with which the Chinese people would have to live. Beyond a certain point, neither Deng nor any other Chinese leader was going to try to be consistent; political survival instincts came first.

As 1979 wore on, the centrist approach was applied more and more widely – with all the contradictions it entailed. The *Peking Daily* was quietly rebuked for its anti-foreign outbursts – in a big nation like China, said the *People's Daily*, 'it's hardly surprising if half-a-dozen people lose their national self-respect; it's not worth making a fuss over'.[48] And the *Liberation Army Daily*, while calling for greater efforts 'to accept the good and reject the bad in Western life', declared that 'we cannot give up eating for fear of choking'. The good was said to include the 'activism' of Western society, and the bad, 'striptease and "praying to God"'.[49] *China Youth* deplored 'excessive faultfinding' with young people, and suggested that 'the length of a person's hair and the width of his trousers are not a reliable guide to the soundness of his ideology'. *Guangming Ribao* said the authorities should 'not be allowed to interfere' in such things.[50] Yet alongside these marks of tolerance, the Peking Public Security Bureau and, later, others elsewhere, promulgated regulations forbidding Chinese to have meals with foreigners in restaurants, visit them at their homes or give out their addresses, without specific authorisation from above.

Similar conflicts occurred on a more philosophical plane. In March and April, when the clampdown was in full swing, 'human rights' were decried as 'a bourgeois, not a proletarian slogan', 'a figleaf concealing the dictatorship of the bourgeoisie', which was advanced only by those who had 'not a jot of Marxism or patriotism in them'.[51] In June *Guangming Ribao* rejected these arguments as simplistic and unhelpful, declaring that the proletariat needed human rights no less than anyone else. But by October the paper had pulled back: while still insisting on the need to perfect the socialist system, it said the 'human rights' slogan should 'no longer be emphasised', because to do so would 'cause confused thinking'.[52]

Even painting was not exempt from the zig-zags of the middle course. In the autumn of 1979, a group of twenty-three young amateur artists, calling themselves the 'Star Society', staged an unofficial exhibition along the railings outside the Peking Art Gallery. The police, citing the municipal notice restricting posters to Democracy Wall, demanded that they take it down – and, when they refused, sent in plainclothes thugs to do it for them. But the gallery's staff then took the artist's part, and carried the paintings inside to prevent the police seizing them. Two months later, after high-level intervention, the exhibition was re-staged, with official backing, in a beautiful old summerhouse in one of the city's parks. It was a scene which by its very normalcy symbolised much of what was most positive in the changes of the previous two years: young couples, wrapped in scarves and heavy coats against the cold, snuggled up against each other on park benches, Strauss waltzes came over the loudspeakers and small children skated on the frozen lake. Yet to me there was a strong sense of *déjà vu*. Five years earlier, in the south-western district of Moscow, local Party officials had also sent thugs to smash up an open-air art exhibition. As is the Russians' wont, they were rather more thorough than the Chinese police; in full view of Western diplomats and their families, who had gone there for a Sunday outing, they used watertrucks with high-pressure hoses to demolish the exhibits, and burnt a number of paintings. Still not content, bulldozers were brought in to plough up the plot of wasteland where the exhibition had been held. An international outcry resulted, and some weeks later that exhibition, too, was re-staged, with official backing, in a park in the northern suburbs. Until 1979, when they were stopped, such unofficial art shows were the only form of cultural activity not directly under Party leadership which the Soviet authorities were willing to permit.

The controversy in Moscow was mainly over abstract paintings (which did not figure among the Chinese works) and the use of religious themes, the Orthodox Church being treated as a symbol of a non-communist political alternative. In Peking the politics was overt, and there were a number of wood carvings which could not have been shown in Moscow at all. The work of a thirty-year-old playwright named Wang Keping, they were fashioned from gnarled roots and branches and made use of the knots and peculiarities of the material to create repressive images of great power. One depicted a man's head in the shape of a fist with a single, lidless accusing eye, and someone's hand clamped across his mouth, silencing him in the moment of a scream. Another was a face, half filled by a great, round mouth, plugged by a wooden bung.

For most of the 33,000 people who saw the Peking exhibition, the biggest shock was not the politics but the nudes, which had been banned since the start of the Cultural Revolution. Artistically the less said about them the better. But the breakthrough they represented – if drawings of nymphs and an oil painting of a 1940s Hollywood-style sex goddess can properly be called a breakthrough – was followed at the end of the year by the publication of an art calendar, including reproductions of

Ingres's *Spring*, and Rubens's *The Rape of the Daughters of Leucippus*, and the unveiling of a large mural at the new Peking airport depicting the water-splashing festival of the Dai people in Yunnan.

Two nudes in the mural were 'washing away the poison spread by devils', explained the New China News Agency (Xinhua), adding that it was 'reminiscent of the style of Gauguin'. Whether or not Gauguin would have felt flattered by that comparison – the breasts of the nude bathers defied both gravity and the laws of anatomy – it marked a big advance on the workers, peasants and soldiers of Mao's day.

Traditionalists were outraged. 'They say it's bad enough having hooligans committing crimes,' *China Youth* reported, 'but now – naked paintings! What will it be next?' Yet, the journal commented, 'the genius of painters like Rubens and Ingres is known throughout the world. It is only in China that such works cause astonishment.' It was true, it added, that they might lead astray some young people whose minds had a tendency to wander – 'but we cannot ban the good and the beautiful in order to suppress the bad and decadent'. To back up its words, on the cover of its next issue it printed Delacroix's famous painting, *Liberty Leading the People*, which depicts the French Revolution as a bare-breasted woman striding militantly across the field of battle.

But conservatism in China dies hard. Protests continued, and the Dai people complained (or were persuaded to complain) that they should not be shown naked when Han Chinese were not. In April 1980 a curtain was put up, hiding the offending parts. For a few weeks, all across China, a tremor ran through the art world; models at life-drawing classes who had just screwed up the courage to pose without clothes, hastily put them back on again. Eventually a compromise was reached. Paintings of nudes would not be banned, but neither would they be encouraged; the mural would not be destroyed, but the curtain would remain in place.

Despite such equivocation, there were enough signs in the months immediately after the clampdown to convince the wallposter movement that it was safe to resume. In June 1979 the subject was debated at the NPC, and although demands were made for wallposters to be abolished – 'they waste a lot of ink and paper', one deputy observed – the majority agreed that they should continue. A few days later the *People's Daily*, in an extremely sympathetic commentary, said that when the mistakes of the young activists were being criticised, it was important not to negate the many 'valuable and correct ideas' they put forward.[53]

By late July, posters calling for the release of Fu Yuehua, Wei Jingsheng, Ren Wanding and Chen Lu began to appear – and the police, who were now being criticised for having in the past ignored legal procedures, left them in place. The following month, when America's Vice-President Walter Mondale visited Peking, several hundred young people gathered at the Democracy Wall to condemn the arrests and demand that public trials be held. Soon afterwards, a new issue of *Exploration* appeared, the first since March, edited by Wei's colleagues.

The petitioners, whom the police had shipped back to the provinces in April, streamed into the capital and staged almost daily demonstrations outside Zhongnanhai, sitting on the ground in neat rows, their bundles beside them, like big, sad children at a class in school. One man had tied a sign to his back: 'I am bursting with bitterness.' Some accused China's leaders of rehabilitating officials but doing nothing for ordinary people. 'We don't want to be refugees, we want to be citizens,' one poster delcared. Another, by a group of former workers asking permission to return to the city, was signed, 'The voice of the tramps, the voice of the jobless, the voice of the cheated'.

Many were simple peasants like Ruan Jun from Hunan. The official summary of his problem stated: 'He was smeared as a "new bourgeois element" for keeping a few private pigs. His house was confiscated, and the members of his family were forced to wander about destitute from place to place. Today his commune still refuses to consider his case.'[54] In September nearly a thousand people, including activists as well as petitioners, met in Tian An Men Square, to listen to speeches denouncing social inequality and injustice, and the privilege of senior cadres. Shortly afterwards the *People's Daily* lambasted local leaders who refused to deal with outstanding problems, and announced that a thousand officials were being sent to the provinces, backed by the full power of the Central Committee, to force them to take action. 'Most of the petitions are reasonable,' it said. Yet some local authorities behaved like feudal lords. It was 'completely wrong', it declared – in a clear reversal of the policy adopted in the clampdown – to 'look on the petitioners as "disturbances" and "nuisances" and apply a policy of arrest, intimidation and deception'.

Almost three years have elapsed since the downfall of the 'Gang of Four', yet the number of petitioners in Peking remains so enormous that it puts our work to shame . . . Some leading provincial officials, not to mention at prefectural, county and commune levels . . . have ignored wrongs and refused to redress them . . . They do not care about the serious plight of the people, and remain undisturbed even about life-and-death matters . . . This serious bureaucratic style of work is . . . a major factor in causing large numbers of people to present petitions.[55]

Not only petitioners were making protests. In October 1979 three thousand students and lecturers from the People's University marched through the centre of Peking, complaining that seventy per cent of their university buildings had been taken over by the Second Artillery, China's rocket forces, during the Cultural Revolution, and the soldiers refused to leave. They shouted slogans which had come down, unchanged, from the May 4th movement, sixty years earlier – 'We want science and democracy. We don't want warlords' – and carried a three-foot-high caricature depicting the unit's commander, Li Shuiqing, a member of the Central Committee, as a bloated general, smoking a fat cigar and sitting on a cushion marked, 'students' rights'. 'The people's army should serve the people,' it said. 'Down with army privilege!'

Poetry readings resumed in the parks. The artists staged a protest march. *Exploration* put up a wallposter criticising Hua for having said that when the 'Gang of Four' were tried, they would not be sentenced to death. Chinese began to speculate that Wei and the others would soon be released.

They could not have been more wrong. Days later, Wei Jingsheng was tried as a counter-revolutionary and sentenced to fifteen years in a prison camp. Exactly seven months after Deng first indicated that trials were being contemplated, the other shoe dropped.

In retrospect it is clear that the leadership never seriously wavered on the question of the trials, and that the related issue of much tighter restrictions on wallposters was also under discussion from the start. As early as April an article was written (but not published until nearly a year later)[56] arguing that the Cultural Revolution had shown wallposters to have fatal defects, and the time had come to ban them – or at least, if that were not possible, to make the writers sign their real names and to prosecute 'slanderers and rumour-mongers'. In June these suggestions were repeated, this time in public, during the NPC. And in September, Vice-Premier Wang Zhen told me, 'Some of them will go on trial and some will undergo re-education'.

Yet in the minds of many Chinese, such signals were outweighed by the liberal views being preached in the press. All through the autumn, the line taken in the newspapers was markedly more tolerant than the prevailing opinion in the Politburo. This discrepancy was not unusual in China; in the first half of the 1970s, the press was consistently to the left of the leadership. Now, as then, the cause was a lack of consensus. Old Maoists like Ye Jianying and the leftist members of the Politburo strongly opposed the democracy movement, but they did not want wallposters suppressed altogether, regarding them, correctly, as an integral part of the Maoist system, and one which the left might have

349

need of again. (Precisely the opposite consideration, the need to deny the left a possible weapon, was among Deng's reasons for wanting them stopped.) At the other extreme, Hu Yaobang and Chen Yun were also against wallposters being suppressed, but from totally different considerations. They had both opposed from the start the clampdown on the democracy movement, and even the arrest of Wei, for reasons Hu explained to NPC deputies in July:[57]

> Administrative orders cannot be issued in matters of this nature. I also advise you, comrades, not to grab people and struggle against them or lock them up. I am afraid that most people who raise this kind of question are not bothered about going to jail. Wei Jingsheng was arrested more than three months ago, but he has not yet written a self-criticism, and wants to go on hunger-strike in protest. You should not think that he is afraid of death. In fact he wants to die soon. When he dies he will become a martyr among the masses and in the eyes of the people. Martyrs are not necessarily buried at Babaoshan [the state cemetery in Peking]. There have been too many people of this kind in history.

In the same speech Hu acknowledged that other leaders disagreed with him, and that he had even been accused of 'engaging in so-called democratisation activities behind the back of the Central Committee'. 'But even though the majority oppose it,' he said, 'I still wish to reserve my viewpoint.' In the absence of any clear directive to the contrary, it was Hu's liberal views, as Director of the Propaganda Department, which coloured the content of the press.

Yet this still does not explain why the clampdown resumed in October, and in a much more determined fashion than its somewhat hysterical beginning in March. Wei's trial, when it came, was not merely the sentencing of one man, but the signal for a general offensive to strengthen Party control. At that time the democracy movement was not looking especially threatening. The students' outburst against the army must have worried the leadership, and certainly increased pressure for a clampdown from the military and from disciplinarians such as Peng Zhen. But the rusticated youths no longer posed a problem; the decision to send officials to the provinces to resolve the petitioners' cases had gone some way towards defusing that issue. The 'four basic principles' were generally being observed, and wallposters, in any case, were largely confined to Peking. As in March, the chief causes of the tightening up were to be found elsewhere.

The aimlessness and loss of direction which had contributed to the original decision to restrict the democracy movement had not only not gone away, it had developed into a general malaise, a 'lack of morale', as

350

Deng put it in an interview just after Wei's trial. To lifelong communists, with deeply ingrained totalitarian convictions, it was almost a reflex reaction to respond by reinforcing discipline. Moreover, Deng had come to realise during the summer that carrying out an ideological rectification campaign would not be enough to reform the Party bureaucracy; it had to be accompanied by a purge, to cut out the Maoist dead wood which could not or would not adapt. For this, too, discipline was needed. The wallposters which had been so helpful in November and December 1978, when Deng was battling with the leftists and promoting the idea of democracy as hard as he could, had outlived their usefulness. And whereas, in the spring, Deng's concern was to prevent the leftists using the clampdown to undermine his own position, in the autumn, when the left was in retreat, no such constraints applied.

The decision to move against the activists was almost certainly taken in September; the first hint of it came at the end of that month in a speech given by Ye Jianying, on behalf of the Central Committee, which for the first time in many weeks strongly re-emphasised the 'four basic principles'. This time, unlike in March, the clampdown was Deng's from the start. His was the iron hand which emerged from its velvet glove, and his the responsibility for what happened over the next three months.

Wei's trial, on October 16th, was timed by Deng to coincide with Hua's arrival in France at the start of a month-long tour of Western Europe, and proved so embarrassing to him that in Paris and London he withdrew from scheduled press conferences.

It was a show trial in the Stalinist tradition, staged *in camera* before a hand-picked audience, and filmed under television lights for senior officials to watch later. Wei's fiancée and friends were excluded – admission being only by special pass – and spent the day waiting outside the courthouse, a modern five-storey building completed only a few months before, watched over by plainclothes police. The only difference from the dissident trials I attended, or, rather, waited outside, in Moscow, was that the KGB were not there to photograph the crowd, China being more sparing of such technical resources.

As in Moscow, there was no pretence at legality. Wei appeared with his head shaven, the mark of a convicted criminal, and the official New China News Agency began describing him as a counter-revolutionary three hours before the verdict was announced. Tass once made the same mistake, in 1974, reporting the sentence on a Jewish activist before the judge announced it; in that case it was only a matter of minutes, and the error became known because it was the one dissident trial in the last twenty years to which a Western journalist was admitted. In both countries, in political cases, the verdict and, usually, the sentence, are

351

determined during the investigation; the trial itself gives a legal cloak to what the political authorities have already decided.

Wei was accused of 'providing others with state secrets' and 'counter-revolutionary agitation and propaganda' under Articles Six and Ten of the so-called 'Penal Code against Counter-revolutionaries', apparently a revised version, whose text has never been made public, of a law passed in 1951. The prosecution called two witnesses, Yang Guang and Liu Jingsheng, who had also been detained in the spring and had agreed to turn state's evidence in return for their freedom. Wei spoke in his own defence. The entire proceedings took less than five hours.

On the secrets charge, the indictment stated:

> The defendant Wei Jingsheng arranged secret meetings with *foreign agents* in Peking and supplied foreigners with important military intelligence . . . Our heroic border defence forces of the PLA engaged in bloody battles on the frontier. They suffered wounds and gave up their lives to punish the Vietnamese aggressors. Yet, at the height of this hand-to-hand fighting, the defendant Wei Jingsheng willingly became the running dog of Vietnam, being *a hidden enemy agent* and a traitor . . . Wei Jingsheng maintained *illicit relations with a foreign country* and betrayed his motherland. He is a scum of the nation and a criminal among the people. (Emphasis added.)

The whole basis for this statement, which virtually accused him of being a secret agent for Vietnam, was one meeting with a West European journalist, who was not even called to testify.

Under cross-examination, Wei acknowledged that it had been a mistake to pass on casualty figures and other details of the conflict, and said he had been worried at the time that 'it would harm me and bring me trouble'. But, he said, he had not regarded it as secret, nor did he think what he had done constituted a crime.

> The prosecutor says I committed treason in my conversations with British and French journalists. Does he mean that British and French journalists are enemies? When Hua Guofeng met with West European journalists, he called them 'friends' . . . When the Sino-Vietnamese war began, everyone was concerned about it, both inside and outside the country. In my conversations with foreign diplomats and journalists, it was impossible for the subject not to come up . . . Whether or not the information I mentioned was of a kind the government wanted released I had no way of knowing; as an ordinary person, my source was *xiao dao xiao xi* [small path news], not any government document . . .
> Of course, the prosecutor can say that, based on our country's customs, such things are considered secret. In the time of the 'Gang of Four', just about anything was secret, and speaking casually to a foreigner was treason-

able. Does the prosecutor wish to abide by the customs of the 'Gang of Four'? Or does he wish to abide by the law?

In any Western country, or even in the Soviet Union, where what is secret and what is not is defined in written laws, this reasoning would be specious. But in China, after the Cultural Revolution, when the Red Guards were encouraged to make public parts of secret documents incriminating Mao's enemies, all such distinctions were lost.

Wei's conviction was not in fact on the charge which was formally laid against him, of passing military secrets to others: had he passed them on to another Chinese, no case could have been brought against him, as was shown by the fact that no attempt was ever made to bring to court the persons who gave Wei the information, or to track down the person who would have been the chief culprit in Western law, the Defence Ministry official responsible for the leak. Wei's offence was rather that he breached the unwritten convention which in China divides the world into *nei* and *wai*, internal and external, Chinese and foreign, and only secondarily into friends and enemies. This was strikingly confirmed by the presiding judge, in cross-examination:

Judge: So at the time you said it, you knew, at the very least, that it could be harmful to you, and that it was against our country's custom. Yet you still said it. What was your motive? You should speak in the spirit of seeking truth from facts.

Wei: I felt that although, from the standpoint of our past custom I should not have said it, those customs were not correct . . . I could not see anything wrong in discussing it.

Judge: *Didn't you realise that you were talking to a foreigner?*

Wei: I knew it.

Judge: Well, given that *you knew you were talking to a foreigner*, didn't you take that into consideration?

Wei: I considered it.

Judge: *So you deliberately talked about it to a foreigner. That was the situation.* (Emphasis added.)

Had it been merely a question of sending Wei to prison, the secrets charge on its own would have sufficed; indeed, there would have been no real need to hold a trial at all. Like Ren Wanding and Chen Lu, he could have been shipped off under an administrative order to do re-education through labour, without the judiciary ever becoming involved. The purpose of bringing him to court was, as Deng freely acknowledged, 'to make an example of him'.[58] The trial was political theatre, a homily played out for the instruction of the Chinese people,[59] in which considerations of justice had no part whatsoever. Even the combination of charges was chosen to make the political points that Deng wanted put across. By smearing Wei as a traitor, Chinese were warned of the dangers of consorting with foreigners – as was underlined by the amount of time the judge spent questioning him about contacts with foreigners which bore no relation to the indictment. By trying him as a counter-revolutionary, they were warned of the dangers of criticising their system. As the indictment put it:

> The defendant Wei Jingsheng wrote many reactionary articles to carry out counter-revolutionary propaganda and agitation . . . and raised the so-called banner of freedom of speech, democracy and human rights to overthrow the dictatorship of the proletariat and the socialist system . . . The freedom of speech of the individual citizen must be based on the four basic principles . . . *The citizen has the freedom to support these principles, but not the freedom to oppose them* . . . *We should not only forbid such freedom, but should deal with it severely.* (Emphasis added.)

The 'four basic principles' appeared in no written law and had no legal force; the notice of the Peking Revolutionary Committee was simply a proclamation, which citizens were expected to obey. Yet, in Deng's China, as in Mao's, Chinese were now reminded, to express a contrary view was to risk imprisonment as a counter-revolutionary. Defiant to the end, Wei accused his accusers of themselves being counter-revolutionaries for going against the tide of democracy, and stood erect, showing no emotion, as the fifteen-year sentence was pronounced.

Next day, October 17th, it was the turn of Fu Yuehua. Like Wei she was charged on two counts, one criminal – she was said to have brought a false charge of rape against the secretary of her Party branch six years earlier; the other political – organising a demonstration in violation of public order. But this time the stage management broke down. A high official in the audience recognised one of the prosecution witnesses as a man he had had dealings with some years before, and stood up and denounced him as a 'hooligan'. Another spectator, a provincial judge, accused the trial judge of showing bias. Fu's statement in her own defence was so persuasive it was received with applause, even by an audience picked for political reliability. Finally, the hearing had to be halted altogether after she had described in intimate detail an abnormality on the Party secretary's body.

Amnesty International sent a telegram of protest. The State Department in Washington described Wei's sentence as 'surprising and disappointing'. Deng Xiaoping was unrepentant. Wei and Fu Yuehua, he

'Nuts Are for Cracking.'

said in an interview on October 18th, were 'shams and fakes'.[60] They were bad workers, and disrupted order in production and society. By punishing them China was not violating human rights, because 'if they were granted freedom, it would mean that the other 99.9 per cent of the people were deprived of freedom'.

The delay in Fu's trial proved in the end no help, nor could it have been, for as a political, not a legal, exercise, the verdict was predetermined. When the hearing resumed in December, the judge said Fu was 'morally degenerate' and plainly guilty of making a false charge;

however, for reasons he did not explain, that count of the indictment 'would not be pursued'. She was instead accused of theft, and although no evidence was offered, was sentenced to two years' imprisonment for this and for violating public order.

The trials were accompanied by a barrage of criticism and warning editorials in the press. The tone was set by the *People's Daily* the morning after Wei's conviction:

> For a period of time there were some people who tried to defend counter-revolutionary criminals like Wei Jingsheng, even calling him 'a forerunner of human rights' and 'a fighter for democracy'. Some of these people were perhaps deceived, not understanding Wei's true character. But there were also a very few people who had the same aim as Wei, trying to use the same criminal means to subvert the proletarian dictatorship and the socialist system . . . *We advise these people, your calculations are wrong; you should give up your illusions.* (Emphasis added.)[61]

The *Peking Daily* warned 'all counter-revolutionaries' that 'no matter how "fashionable" your banner, no matter how cunning your ways, in the end you will not escape the net of the people's justice.' 'We must shout at such people,' added the *China Youth News*, 'if you do not change your minds, realise your errors and mend your ways, you will bring disgrace and ruin upon yourselves. Is not the lesson of Wei Jingsheng . . . worthy of attention?'[62]

The anti-foreign refrain was cranked up again, though less stridently than in the spring. There were calls for 'strengthening the dictatorship apparatus', that is to say, the police. At meetings in factories and offices Wei's imprisonment was praised as 'a good education for the people' which 'slaked their hatred'. Even *Guangming Ribao*, the intellectuals' paper, said 'no one is allowed to talk about any "emancipation of the mind" that runs counter to modernisation' or that violates the class interests of the proletariat.[63]

This time, however, unlike in March, the clampdown on 'the erroneous tendency from the right', as it was once again called, was balanced by a continuing campaign against the left, which remained the leadership's first priority. The objective, as Zhao Ziyang explained, in a speech at the end of October, was to restore discipline and the primacy of the Party without the zigzags that had occurred in the spring:

> To uphold the four basic principles correctly, it is necessary to . . . wage a struggle on two fronts . . . While the main effort is being made to eliminate the pernicious influence of the ultra-leftist line, we must at the same time

prevent the tendency of bourgeois liberalisation. We must not oppose wrong things by using wrong things . . .

The Party is the core force leading our cause . . . A socialist country cannot do without the Party's leadership, there can be no doubt about that . . . If nobody listens to the Party Committee, if nobody takes any action at the Party Committee's command, if quarrels and bickering become a daily routine and if everybody is in the way of someone else, nothing can be done at all . . .

Democracy . . . must serve the four modernisations. We will be putting the cart before the horse if we place democracy above the four modernisations. This will only create turmoil . . .

Our leading comrades must remain sober-minded, and analyse the ideological trends . . . calmly . . . We must not relax our efforts in drawing a clear-cut line against rightist practices . . . simply because we are mainly criticising the ultra-left. Nor should we hold back our criticism until this kind of erroneous trend has become very serious . . . We cannot afford to go back and forth again.[64]

This was an important speech, for it set out the views which a year later Zhao would bring to the premiership. It was also the first public attempt to define, in a reasoned and thoughtful manner, the new 'middle course' with which China would enter the 1980s.

But neither the harsh sentence on Wei nor the warnings in the press were enough to bring the democracy movement to heel. Unlike the clampdown in March, which aroused little resistance, the trials provoked loud protests. Within a day of Wei's conviction, a poster at the Democracy Wall accused the leadership of 'trampling on the Constitution and using it to serve themselves'. Another asked, 'If you put your thoughts into words, does that constitute a criminal action? If so, how does one know what words are not going to be regarded as criminal? Can it be that as well as criminal actions, there is also thought crime?' And on October 21st, the *April 5th Tribune*, in an act of open defiance, put up on the wall the first part of a complete transcript of Wei's trial, which had been smuggled out of the courtroom. An accompanying poster, headed, 'An Unfair Sentence', asked whether the authorities had been afraid to allow the public to attend. 'How,' it went on, 'could our courts, which we are told are a thousand times fairer than capitalist courts, refuse even to permit those who were concerned with the case to be present in the courtroom?' It supported Wei's argument that in passing on military information, he had committed 'a mistake, not a crime', and noted that he had not organised uprisings or incited violence, but had merely had 'mistaken thoughts'. The severity of his sentence, it said, was 'far in excess of what he deserved'. The same themes were aired at a meeting at the Wall on October 21st, at which one of Wei's supporters made a speech declaring, 'the fascism of the "Gang of Four" still exists', and then gave his name and address for the benefit of the plainclothes police in the crowd, 'so that if I am wanted, that's where I can be found'. Afterwards 200 people sang the Internationale.

The courage of the young activists who refused to be intimidated by Wei's imprisonment was not the only problem confronting the leadership. In many ways more disturbing, and certainly less expected, was the resistance of the intellectuals, above all the writers.

Just as in the Soviet Union, in the spring of 1957, when Khrushchev was cracking down at the end of the 'Thaw', many who had at first been wary of the easing of literary controls decided to make a stand – so, in China, in October 1979, the intellectuals who had played little part in the first months of the Peking Spring felt that the time had come when they, too, must try to hold their ground. A front-page article in *Guangming Ribao*, a week after the trials, began with a paraphrase of Wei's best-known statement, 'without political democratisation, the four modernisations cannot come true' – one of the views which Zhao Ziyang explicitly rejected – and went on to declare, 'we must conduct independent theoretical exploration', rendering that term by the characters, *tan suo*, the name of Wei's magazine. Another commentary in the same paper was headlined, 'Methods of dictatorship must not be used to solve problems of the mind':

> In the early days of the Chinese revolution there was only a small number of communists . . . They were liable to be put in jail or sent to the gallows . . . Yet they had truth on their side, and their cries . . . shook the land . . . Is it not strange that in the past we could refrain from using force to disseminate truth under the most adverse conditions, but now we have to use force to solve people's ideological problems . . . at a time when the proletariat has seized political power?[65]

To many intellectuals, this was the crux of the issue. It was not that they agreed with all of Wei's ideas. But having lived through Mao's broken promises, and having listened to the promises of his successors, they were depressed and embittered that, yet again, force – in the shape of a fifteen-year prison term – was being used to solve ideological problems. The Chinese leadership could, and did, trot out one hack jurist after another to insist that 'Wei Jingsheng did not only write articles, he also put them up on street walls' and 'this is a counter-revolutionary crime, quite different from just expressing extremist ideas';[66] identical arguments are regularly used by Soviet officials. To all but the simple-minded, their very dishonesty only made matters worse. The result was wariness and profound mistrust of the leadership's intentions. Zhao Ziyang was criticised almost openly in the *People's Daily* for his warning against bourgeois liberalisation. 'Some people have a prejudice,' it said. 'Whenever the word "liberty" is mentioned, they attack it and equate it with "bourgeois liberalisation". Why should liberty always be an attribute of the bourgeoisie?' The same article said unequivocally, 'We must not arrest people for making counter-revolutionary statements. Legal punishment is aimed at action, not thought.'[67] That the Party's own newspaper should print such direct criticism of Wei's trial showed the extent of the dissension.

But it was the writers, some of whom had only just emerged from twenty years in the wilderness, who made the strongest challenge. Until the summer of 1979, they had been even more timid than other intellectuals. Then the renewed drive against the left began to convince them that this time it was different, and there was a sudden outpouring of plays, poems and short stories, dealing with such previously taboo subjects as juvenile delinquency, corruption, and the arrogance and privilege of officials.

On October 30th Deng opened a Writers' and Artists' Congress, the first for nineteen years. He promised an end to outside interference in the arts, but urged his audience to oppose the 'two erroneous tendencies', and, in a caution echoed by all the cultural bureaucrats, reminded them that they must weigh seriously 'the social effect of their work'.[68] Among the speeches that followed was one by the poet, Bai Hua, who appealed for help and sympathy for the young writers whose works were appearing in unofficial literary magazines. At a time when unsanctioned writing of all kinds was under attack, it was a highly unusual note to strike, and Bai went on to praise the young writers' courage and independence of mind. But the main part of his speech was a devastating indictment of the system, which went far beyond anything ever published before.[69]

Should we cover up the social contradictions which no one can cover up? Should we eulogise the state of ignorance for which we have made a great national sacrifice? Should we keep silent before bureaucracy which has tied us hand and foot? Should we preserve the prestige of the one who practised 'the rule of the man alone' [Mao], the practice of which has nothing in common with the Communist Party? The people will not allow us to do so . . .

Many kind-hearted comrades and readers often wrote to me. They said: 'You are far from safe.' I am very grateful to them for their kindness. It was very sensible of them to think so . . . *Over the past years . . . a social mentality took shape: Hypocrites are safe and the honest are in danger.*

I often heard some comrades who had children saying with great anxiety: 'My son will surely be put in jail in the future because he does not know how to lie.' Other comrades said contentedly: 'My son has a promising future because he is now a young double-dealer' . . .

Since the Third Plenum . . . fewer and fewer people have been punished for their speeches. However this does not mean that the 'all clear' has sounded . . . *What sort of socialist country is it where communists do not dare speak the truth at Party conferences, fathers, sons, brothers, sisters and friends do not have heart-to-heart talks among themselves, writers do not dare take notes and citizens are afraid to keep diaries?* . . . It is not yet time to say that writers and artists are relatively safe. *Are there not people who write and speak about arresting some people and putting labels on them again?* . . .

I condemn the thieves and ringleaders in the literary arena. I condemn those who go slow. I condemn the rumour-mongers . . . We must pluck up our courage. Without courage we cannot make a breakthrough. Without a breakthrough there can be no literature. (Emphasis added.)

Not only did Bai Hua himself have the courage to say all this, but Hu Jiwei at the *People's Daily* had the courage to print it in full, the only speech so treated apart from the opening and closing addresses. No Soviet writer has ever gone so far and got his words into print. The closest to it was an essay by Ilya Ehrenburg, published at the end of the 'Thaw', attacking authoritarian government:

What counts is not the personality of the tyrant, but the essence of tyranny. A tyrant may be intelligent or stupid, good or evil – but whatever the case, he is both all-powerful and powerless. He is frightened of conspiracies, he is flattered; he is decieved. *The prisons fill; the cowardly hypocrites whisper*; and the silence becomes so complete that the heart almost stops beating . . .

Even if the king is a saint, his government destroys art – not because it bans the subject of a painting, but because it crushes the souls of artists . . . Even though the ministers be the most honourable men in the world, toadyism, flattery and obsequiousness will still grow and flourish . . .

The fault lies with the society which demands hypocrisy, punishes truth, and stifles large feelings in the name of a host of conventions. (Emphasis added.)

But where Bai Hua spoke directly about present-day Chinese society, Ehrenburg had to disguise his words as an essay on Stendhal, and they were printed, not in *Pravda*, but in a specialist magazine.

Bai Hua's question, 'What sort of socialist country is it where communists do not dare speak the truth?' could not be asked in Moscow, let alone reported.

Even before the Writers' Congress, there were signs of the clamp-down intensifying. Deng's objective had been from the start to restore discipline and the authority of the Party, and there is no reason to doubt that he was ready, from the start, to bring to bear whatever pressure was needed to achieve that purpose. The defiance of the young activists and the resistance of the intellectuals had to be put down. The immediate result was a decision to close the Democracy Wall, almost certainly taken at the beginning of November as part of a package of tough measures to deal with the democracy movement and a growing wave of youth crime. At the time of Wei's trial, Deng was already disenchanted with the Democracy Wall, telling visitors that 'it cannot represent the genuine feelings of our people'. And six weeks later he was saying that while some of those who put up posters had good intentions, 'we may have made a mistake in allowing it to last for so long'.[70]

The first public hint of any of this came in the *China Youth News* on November 3rd, which said opinions should be raised 'at meetings or through other normal channels' because problems could not be studied seriously through wallposters put up in the streets. 'Facts have shown', it added, that posters are 'apt to be used by those who have ulterior motives to create confusion in production, work and society at large'.

Within days, the pack was in full cry. This time it was *Jiefang Ribao* in Shanghai which led the way:

> Criminal cases in the city are constantly increasing . . . Counter-revolu-tionaries confuse and poison people's minds, stir up trouble, steal and gather information, try to make contact with enemy spy organs and to set up counter-revolutionary organisations. There are criminals who commit rob-bery, violence, rape and theft; there are hooligans who gather people for gang-fights, beat up teachers and shop assistants, insult women in the streets, and carry out wild activities . . . We should severely punish these persons without showing any mercy. We must arrest those who should be arrested, try those who should be tried; and kill those who should be killed. We cannot be soft-hearted.[71]

This was the same formula as had been used in the spring, but with the significant addition of 'killing those who should be killed'. In case any were in doubt that the authorities meant business, a public execution was shown on television – a young thug being shot in the back of the head by a policeman. Mass rallies were staged to sentence hooligans, and police were urged to use 'the iron fist of proletarian dictatorship'.[72]

The *Peking Daily* declared that Wei Jingsheng had 'tried to seize power from the proletariat with a murderous look on his face', and a group of army officers said he ought to have been executed. A smear campaign was launched, portraying him as a ne'er-do-well and a thief.[73] After Fu Yuehua was sentenced, the New China News Agency produced a report on her life of such foulness that the *People's Daily* refused point-blank to print it.[74] In China, as in the Soviet Union – witness the campaign against Pasternak in 1958 – to kick a person who is down is a basic law of politics. The one modern Chinese writer of genius, Lu Xun, called it 'beating the dog in the water', and the saying is still quoted in Peking as an admirable precept to follow.

The tone used towards the petitioners changed. Where in September the bureaucrats had been blamed for not solving their problems, now complainants were told, 'Don't make trouble even if your demands are justified . . . Troublemaking will only delay a solution.'[75] At the beginning of November, alleged 'troublemakers' and 'black sheep' were arrested in many cities and, by the middle of the month, the petitioners had all been shipped back to the provinces. A campaign was launched to improve army-civilian relations, in response to the accusation of warlordism. Zhao Ziyang's speech was widely quoted, and long editorials were published against anarchism, and 'remnants of Lin Biao and the "Gang of Four"' . . . stirring up an evil wind'. Although there was not enough democracy, provincial newspapers said, the need for discipline was 'more urgent'.[76]

The Regulations on Re-Education through Labour, introduced in August 1957 as an instrument for Mao and Liu Shaoqi to suppress the 'rightists' after the '100 Flowers', were re-promulgated and revised. The 1951 Regulations on State Secrets were republished, ending with the catch-all phrase, 'all state affairs which should be kept secret are secret'.[77]

But it was at the Democracy Wall itself that the final scenes were played out. On Sunday afternoon, November 11th, a bus-load of uniformed police arrived, arrested three young men who were selling mimeographed transcripts of Wei's trial, and manhandled them into a waiting jeep. The purpose was transparently to intimidate, for a poster with the same content nearby was not touched. A hostile crowd shouted abuse as they left. The following weekend the process was repeated. Most of those detained were released almost at once, but Liu Qing, a co-editor of the *April 5th Tribune*, was sent for re-education through labour. For what? For making public the record of what was officially termed a 'public trial'.

For the activists this was the most wretched time of all. Everyone could see the axe hanging, but no one knew when or on whom it would fall. The general gloom was reflected in a letter I received from a Chinese friend:

It is possible that very soon I shall be going to prison. This is the only freedom we have in this country. I don't have any regrets. Everything that I have done is what a morally upright person should do. The only crime that I have committed is that I have demanded to be able to live and to think like a human being on this piece of earth. But that is not possible. One day the Chinese people may remember us. Maybe they will forget us for ever. It hardly matters.

Soon after this he was branded a 'dangerous element' by the secret police, and other workers at his factory were forbidden to speak to him.

On November 21st, *Peking Spring*, defying a directive from the Youth League to discontinue publication, made a last appeal to the leadership to change its mind. Many people were watching to see what happened to the Democracy Wall, it said, because they knew that 'when the lips die, the teeth are cold'. Suppression might solve the problem in the short term, but what about the long-term effect?

A week later, amid a blare of publicity, the NPC Standing Committee formally requested the Peking Municipality to 'deal with the wall'.[78] The municipality, on its side, said the wall had 'only bad points and no good points' and 'influences the fighting will of the masses, causes traffic jams . . . and has become an important contact point where people with ulterior motives sell intelligence to foreigners'. The foreign connection was now strongly played up. NPC members claimed that 'foreigners have been putting their oar in', and called for severe punishment of those who 'collude with foreigners and ask them for money and political materials to carry out activities against the socialist system'. The same themes recurred in the orchestrated campaign of indignant letters to the press and meetings of condemnation which in China and the Soviet Union pass for expressions of public opinion. All across the country, a scare was whipped up against 'enemy agents and spies', and there were dark claims that 'international reactionaries' were supporting the democracy movement.[79] Yet in fact the foreign input had been negligible. Apart from a 100-yuan (£30) loan to *Exploration* from a Western journalist, the only significant help the movement had from foreigners was an Amnesty International report on political imprisonment in China, given to *Exploration* in confidence by a British diplomat, who was then horrified to discover it next morning pasted up at the Democracy Wall, and a copy of the Czechoslovak Charter 77 Manifesto, which I gave to the Human Rights Alliance. The charges of foreign interference were a tactic to convince sceptics that the clampdown was necessary, and to divert attention from the fact that the most important means of political expression available to Chinese was being rapidly whittled away.

For twenty years the wallposter had symbolised the differences between the Chinese and Soviet systems; with its impending demise, China moved a big step closer to the regime of Khrushchev and of Brezhnev.

The Democracy Wall closed at midnight on December 7th, by order of the Peking Revolutionary Committee. An hour later a watertruck arrived, accompanied by fifty municipal workers, men and women, clad in regulation blue overalls, armed with scrapers and old-fashioned twig brooms. It took them till four am to scrub it clean, watched by two soldiers, a policeman, myself and several other Western correspondents, and an occasional carter, driving a wagon full of farm produce through the deserted streets. In its place a substitute wall opened in a suburban park, and, as had been suggested in April, poster writers had to register their names and addresses and take 'legal and political responsibility' for their views; it became known as the 'bureaucracy wall', and was generally ignored.

The Peace Café was closed, and two young men who encouraged 'strangely and seductively dressed female hooligans to hang around with foreigners and to profit from this' were arrested.[80] In the provinces another campaign was launched against the now familiar amalgam of political and criminal offences – 'Even if their acts do not constitute crimes,' wrote a commentator in Tianjin, 'we must never allow them to do what they please.'[81] In one of the most shameful cases, in a small town in Henan, a young man named Gao Shuzhang was sentenced to eight years' imprisonment and five years' deprivation of political rights for having put up posters 'openly appealing for the counter-revolutionary Wei Jingsheng'.[82] In the same province another youth, Mu Changqing, who helped to edit an unofficial magazine, committed suicide by throwing himself under a train after being ordered to undergo re-education through labour. Other activists went on trial in Shanghai and Wuhan.

'If you close the people's mouths and let them say only nice things,' one of the last posters at the Democracy Wall had warned, 'it keeps the bile inside . . . Loyal words, though unpleasant, are good for you. Good medicine, though bitter, cures illness.'

But once again it was a writer who spoke out most sharply. A young poet, Ye Wenfu, whose career and safety were already under threat because of an exposé he had written about a corrupt general, published a poem in the *People's Daily*, evoking the image of Yuan Shikai, the nineteenth-century warlord who at first supported reform, and then, when he saw the strength of the conservatives, changed sides, and helped them suppress the reformers:[83]

> I cannot guarantee
> That there will not be shooting from behind.
> Yuan Shikai's spectre
> Will perhaps have an evil influence on some minds.
> I cannot guarantee
> That every battle will be won.
> There will be shameless betrayal by renegades,
> But our revolution will go on . . .

The latter-day Yuan Shikai, whom Ye was accusing of betraying the democracy movement, was Deng Xiaoping himself.

In the Soviet Union, too, in 1957, the boldest of the young writers was a poet, Yevgeni Yevtushenko. In April of that year, when the cultural commissars in Moscow were still trying unsuccessfully to bring the writers back into line, Yevtushenko was expelled from the Komsomol. His response was published in *Novy Mir*:[84]

> There is no virtue in the zealotry of suspicion,
> Blind judges do not serve the people.
> It is worse by far to mistake in haste
> A friend for an enemy than an enemy for a friend.

The challenge was taken up by Khrushchev himself. In May he invited the writers of Moscow to a garden party at his dacha, where he spoke about the Hungarian revolt and the 'Petöfi circle', the Budapest writers' club which had helped to foment it. Much suffering could have been averted, he said, if the Hungarian government had had the sense to shoot a few of them and nip the trouble in the bud. Were that ever to become necessary in the Soviet Union, he declared, 'my hand would not tremble'. One of the chief targets of this attack, the poetess, Margaret Aliger, fainted and had to be carried out. It was the first time since Stalin's death that Soviet writers had been forcibly reminded that the weapon of terror, which they had all thought buried and gone, was actually still there, available if needed. By the autumn, all but a handful had returned to the fold.

Four days after Ye Wenfu's poem was published, on January 16th, 1980, Deng delivered a major policy speech which included two explicit warnings. The first was to the intellectuals:[85]

We must . . . not be naïve about the general tendencies and true aims of the so-called 'democrats' and 'dissidents' . . . Party members and cadres, especially high-ranking cadres, must take a firm and clear-cut stand in this struggle . . . It is absolutely impermissible to publicise any freedom of speech, publication, assembly or form of association which involves counter-revolutionaries. It is absolutely impermissible for any person to contact these people behind the Party's back . . . We must tell Party members who support their activities that their standpoint is very erroneous and dangerous, and if they do not correct it immediately and completely they will be liable to Party disciplinary punishment . . . There must be no sign of wavering or hesitation.

Some people might say, 'Is this another retraction?' We have never 'relaxed' on this question . . . When have we ever said we would tolerate the activities of counter-revolutionaries? . . . Frankly, at the moment we should act strictly not leniently on these issues . . .

The second warning was to the writers. The anti-rightist campaign, of which they had been the principal victims, had not been wrong, Deng said. It had been necessary, at that time, to attack those who had 'opposed socialism'; the only error had been that the movement became inflated. This was a less brutal way of putting it than Khrushchev's threat of Stalinist terror, but its meaning was the same: repression had been correct in the past, and repression could be used again. The writers fell silent.

Officials sympathetic to Deng afterwards put it about that he had been forced to take this hard line as a result of pressure from the army and from conservative elements in the Party. Such pressure certainly existed; but it was only one factor among many. In Moscow, in 1958, the story was likewise put round that the persecution of Pasternak had taken place without Khrushchev's knowledge. That was not true either: each was simply an attempt to allay criticism.

In the same speech, exactly a year after he had said that the wallposter movement would continue 'for generations', Deng declared that the 'Four Bigs' had 'never played a positive role', and should be deleted from the Constitution. 'When the "Whateverists" were still strong,' the Canton magazine, the *People's Road*, commented bitterly, 'who was it who first made trouble for Wang Dongxing? Who first revealed problems about Wu De?' 'Once the bird has been caught,' said Xu Wenli of the *April 5th Tribune*, 'the bow and arrow are put aside.'

After January 1980, none of the unofficial magazines could be sold openly. A handful, including *Today* and the *People's Road*, managed to soldier on until the summer. But they were not permitted to register and acquire legal status, and when new regulations on publishing were promulgated in July, they too were forced to close. The NPC met in August, and wrote the 'Four Bigs' out of the Constitution. The era of the wallposter, and of Mao, was over, and with it the Peking Spring.

Part IV

Crisis of Faith

At the Dragon Pool Lake in South-Western Peking, one mid-winter afternoon, a schoolboy named Bao Wenli fell through the ice while skating. A crowd gathered on the bank, attracted by his cries. But no one went to his aid. For twenty minutes, they stood stolidly watching as his struggles grew weaker. When at last three men did crawl across the ice to rescue the half-dead child, several of the bystanders jeered: 'Go on, you heroes, win a medal!'

'From this incident,' said the *People's Daily* in January 1980, 'people may see to what extent our social morality has been sabotaged.'[1] The Confucian values which had underpinned Chinese society for two thousand years had been obliterated in the Cultural Revolution. The new Maoist ideals had been discredited, and the promise of the Peking Spring had been lost. For the intellectuals and the young, that did not leave much to believe in.

Chinese had been allowed to see the prosperity of other countries in order to demonstrate the benefits of modernisation, shake them out of their complacency and encourage them to work hard. But many had drawn a contrary conclusion: capitalism was a better system, and China was on the wrong road.

'Capitalism is decadent but not rotten; socialism is excellent but not superior,' went one popular saying in 1979. The press inveighed against 'a few people who are currently deluded by the temporary prosperity of capitalist countries and the temporary backwardness of China', but the delusion did not go away. In 1980, Deng Liqun, a deputy director of the Central Committee's General Office, complained that it was not only the young who had doubts about socialism, but 'even among ourselves, members of the Party, there are some comrades who fail to see the superiority of the socialist system'.[2] A year later, in the summer of 1981, one such Party member told me: 'Look what Japan has done – not even Japan, look at the countries of South-East Asia. They are not led by a communist party. And then look at what we've done. India is a poor country, I suppose. Yet it has forty university students for every 10,000 people. We have only 10.5. I am not hopeful for China. The leaders talk, but the officials don't care.'

The authorities' only answer to such arguments was the bald assertion, endlessly repeated, that socialism was best. 'The socialist system was not dreamt up by someone out of thin air,' said the *Peking Daily*. 'Socialism must inevitably replace capitalism. This is a scientific con-

369

clusion reached by Marx and Engels more than 100 years ago.' The *Liberation Army Daily* argued that the failings of China's system reflected the influence of capitalist and feudal ideas, and 'things invariably develop tortuously, not along a straight line'. However, it added hastily, 'our socialist society will certainly travel the shortest tortuous road in history.'[3]

In private, Deng Xiaoping was more forthright. At a closed meeting of senior Party officials, in January 1980, he said it was understandable if some people felt disappointed with socialism. The Party 'must work patiently and confidently to effect a gradual change in their mental attitude':

> We lack experience, but now perhaps we can explore a relatively good road . . . We must and can produce much in the future to prove that the socialist system is superior to the capitalist system. This should be expressed in many aspects, but first in the speed and efficiency of economic development. *Without that, all our bragging will be in vain.* (Emphasis added.)[4]

The common point of all these declarations was that for the time being people must have faith: work hard now, and things will get better later. But in China, in 1980, after the twists and turns of the previous thirty years, faith was a commodity in very short supply.

An opinion poll, published in the *People's Daily* in February 1981, showed that, in a sample of 1,000 young people, one in three was sceptical about the advantages of socialism and one in two doubted whether China's modernisation programme would succeed.[5] Among students, the proportion was still higher. A poll carried out at Fudan University in Shanghai in September 1980 found that only ten per cent of those questioned were confident that China could be modernised. Thirty-seven per cent said they now had more doubts about communism than before, and only 1.6 per cent cited 'communist ideals' as their basic motivation for study; most said they were studying because there was a career at the end of it.

These figures are all the more telling when it is remembered that sixty-five per cent of China's population is under the age of thirty. But as the 1980s began, it was not only the young who lacked confidence. The Shanghai newspaper, *Jiefang Ribao*, explained:

> It seems that now there is a general mood prevailing, that when several persons gather together . . . some comrades are always full of grievances: the economic problem, the youth employment problem, the problem of leading cadres' privileges, and so on – the discussion never ends, and the

more they talk the angrier they get. At last they heave a sigh of despair: 'Alas, China's affairs are not going well!'

China's affairs are indeed not going well . . . The problems . . . have piled up . . . But the key is not how many problems we have but the people's mental state when dealing with them.[6]

Even at the very highest level uncertainty was voiced. I know of two instances in 1980 of Chinese living abroad being advised by friends in Peking, in one case by a Politburo member, in the other by a member of the Central Committee, not to come back and settle in China yet but to 'wait and see how the situation develops'.

If China's leaders were so wary, others could hardly be blamed for their lack of confidence. Scientists, educators, writers and musicians scrambled frantically for visas to go on study courses abroad lest the policy change and foreign travel again became impossible. And sure enough, by May 1980, the brain drain had reached such proportions that senior academics were barred from leaving the country except under government-sponsored exchange schemes.

Lower down the scale, there was a chronic shortage of history teachers: it was too 'political' and therefore dangerous a subject, so no one wanted to teach it. Similar problems applied to all the arts and social sciences. A friend of mine, a Chinese doctor, had a fourteen-year-old son who, unusually for a boy of that age, had a real gift for classical poetry. He was a born scholar, and wanted to specialise in literature at university. But his father insisted that the boy study science, even though he had little aptitude for it. 'If you're a natural scientist, you're safe,' he explained. 'If you're a social scientist, you have to take a political position in your work, and you may be struck down.' He and his wife agonised over it, he said, but much as they wanted to encourage their son's talent, they had to think of his future.

'If a man has been bitten by a snake,' a Chinese saying goes, 'he will be frightened of a coil of rope.' In a Fudan University opinion poll in 1979, ninety per cent of those questioned said a return to ultra-leftism was still possible. Many older Chinese thought the same.

The term, 'crisis of faith', first appeared in the press at the end of that year, but its roots went back much further, to the disillusionment that set in during the early 1970s after the fruitless turmoil of the Cultural Revolution and the purge of Lin Biao. A similar malaise gripped the Soviet Union in Stalin's last years. Russian soldiers came back from the war bringing tales of how much better life was in Germany and the other countries they had marched through, and with booty to prove it: dresses such as their wives had never seen before, nightgowns and silk underwear.[7] After all they had endured, Russians began to hope that they, too, might share in these good things. But Stalin had other ideas. To rebuild the war-shattered economy, even greater sacrifices were demanded of them; in the Ukraine, hundreds of thousands of people starved to death in 1948–49. The desirability of foreign ways was lambasted through the anti-cosmopolitanism campaign. The cold war began, and the terror resumed.

The deaths of Stalin and Mao, and the political relaxation that followed, heightened the mood of uncertainty and made it more vocal. Three years later, gradually in China, abruptly in Russia, each of the former demigods was dethroned – to be followed in each country within months by a bewildering partial retraction.

'Something approaching a crisis of conscience appears to exist among many Soviet young people,' wrote Harry Schwartz in the *New York Times* in September 1956. 'They were raised to believe that Stalin was all-good and all-wise; the recent revelations ·about him have caused many to develop doubts not only about Stalin but about his successors as well.' The East German leader, Walter Ulbricht, said honest answers must be given to awkward questions 'to restore the faith of the young'. Edward Crankshaw wrote of 'the failure of the Party propagandists to inspire large numbers of the younger generation with any belief in anything at all'. Two decades later, in China, the workers' newspaper, *Gongren Ribao*, also wrote of those who 'don't seem able to believe in anything at all', when describing the nihilism of young Chinese.[8]

The parallel was explicitly recognised in a commentary in *Wen Hui Bao* in January 1980:

> In 1957, after Stalin's personal superstition was demolished, a 'crisis of confidence' appeared. . . . Now that we have broken down the modern superstition [of the Mao cult] which ran amok in China for some time, the same situation has emerged again. From this people may see that these phenomena follow a law: after the collapse of a myth . . . those well-meaning people who were taken in by it, particularly the young, feel disappointed, depressed and uncertain . . .

To overcome such a crisis, the newspaper said, democratic methods and painstaking ideological work were required. 'In no way can we rely on dictatorship,' it warned; using Mao Zedong Thought as a club to be held over people's heads would only make matters worse.[9]

With certain glaring exceptions such as the trial of Wei Jingsheng and the Pasternak affair – rather more numerous in China than in Russia –

this approach was adopted by both Deng and Khrushchev. At a modern art exhibition in Moscow in 1962, Khrushchev bawled out Ernst Neizvestny, saying his paintings looked like the daubings of a donkey's tail. But Neizvestny was not arrested. Dissident trials in the Soviet Union became a regular feature only in 1965, the year after Khrushchev fell.

In China, too, writers were no longer purged if the Party found their works unacceptable. In 1980, when three play-scripts were banned for painting too black a picture of Chinese officialdom, Zhou Yang said writers must be persuaded to revise works which 'exaggerate the difficulties and spread pessimistic or hopeless views'. However it was accepted that they should have the right to defend their works in the face of criticism, and to reserve their position if no agreement was reached. A year later this was tested to the limit when a political storm blew up over a film called *Bitter Love*, written by Bai Hua. Although Bai was severely attacked, he was allowed to go on writing and the principle was upheld.

Not purging the Neizvestnys and Bai Huas of Soviet and Chinese culture was one way of building up confidence, albeit a negative one. To take positive measures to restore belief in the merits of the system was altogether more difficult. Nonetheless, each government tried.

In the Soviet Union in 1958, the Komsomol launched a campaign against the view that 'rudeness is revolutionary', and Soviet schools were directed to give lessons in morality and good manners. In China, in 1979, the *People's Daily* called for the creation of 'a strong public opinion that barbarous behaviour is shameful and civilisation is glorious'. Rudeness was so much the norm that one foreigner, a German lady, mistakenly concluded that Chinese equated courtesy with standoffishness and that to make friends it was necessary to be rude too. Two years later Chinese schools also introduced courses in civility, 'to revive traditional moral standards, debased in the Cultural Revolution'. Newspapers carried articles teaching people to say 'please' and 'thank you', words that had almost passed out of the language, having been regarded as expressions of bourgeois hypocrisy.[10]

As in the Soviet Union in 1956, there was a conscious effort to restore family life. 'The balance of dependencies between the generations has always been one of the stabilising factors in Chinese society,' one official said. 'After the Cultural Revolution, we feel it's time to get in touch with our traditions again.'[11] That point was underscored by a series of widely publicised cases of elderly people being driven to suicide through maltreatment by their relatives – a problem common to many countries, but particularly shocking as a sign of the social fabric breaking down among a nation whose Confucian traditions had for thousands of years emphasised filial piety and the veneration of the old.[12] One such case was described in the *People's Daily* in June 1980:

> The old man was named Cui Xinan, and he was 80 years old. His wife was aged 76. They had five sons and two daughters, plus grandchildren and great-grandchildren – 24 people in all . . . After liberation they worked hard and lived frugally, so that when each of their five sons got married, they could build him a house of his own . . . Last year, the family's annual income was more than 100 yuan [£30] per head. But no one would support the old people . . .
>
> During the Spring Festival in 1977 and 1978, the couple spent their holidays begging in the streets. Since the beginning of 1979 they could no longer cook for themselves, so they took their meals at their sons' houses in turn. But they never had enough to eat. In winter they had only a worn-out quilt to sleep on, and their cotton clothes were in rags . . .
>
> On March 24th, 1980, they asked one of their daughters-in-law to give them some soup, and she shouted abuse at them. The old couple could not tolerate their ill-treatment. They cried together for a long time, and at last they hanged themselves.[13]

When the case went to court, two of the sons were jailed for five and seven years. The provincial Party Committee said the lack of respect of the young for their elders had become 'a social problem of concern to everyone', and a year later national contests were organised to find the family that best showed 'the tradition of harmonious family relations, reverence for the aged and care for the young'.[14]

In Peking a campaign was launched to stop spitting, which, it was said, 'harms the prestige of the state and is out of harmony with the political status of the capital'.[15] Efforts were made to promote a sense of civic pride. Gardens were laid out along the main streets, where before there had been bare, grey earth. Shop fronts were re-painted in the traditional red, green and brown, and ancient carved wooden shop signs, plastered over in the 1960s in the interests of uniformity, were exposed to view again. 'We must let young people understand what is beautiful and what is ugly,' said Ren Zhongyi in Canton. 'Spitting everywhere, throwing litter around and paying no attention to social morality are by no means trivial acts.'[16]

In 1981, all these elements were brought together in a movement called the 'Four Beauties and Five Stresses' – beautification of the mind, language, behaviour and the environment; and stress on decorum, courtesy, cleanliness, discipline and morality.

But as Khrushchev learnt in the 1950s, once faith has been lost, no amount of exhortation will bring it back. The 'Four Beauties' had some effect in making China a pleasanter place in which to live, but as an attempt to generate revolutionary enthusiasm they were a complete flop. So were the various campaigns, which started in mid-1979, to learn from Lei Feng, a model soldier who died young and was canonised by Mao for use as a propaganda hero in 1963. Lei was portrayed in exhibitions all over China as a paragon of selflessness, who spent his life doing good deeds and writing them down in his diary. 'These exhibitions,' noted the Belgian sinologue, Simon Leys, 'contained remarkable photographic documents, such as "Lei Feng helping an old woman to cross the street", "Lei Feng secretly doing his comrades' washing", "Lei Feng giving his lunch to a comrade who forgot his lunchbox", and so forth. Only cynical and impious spirits will wonder at the providential presence of a photographer during so many private incidents in the life of that humble soldier.'[17]

The myth of Lei Feng was dusted off and refurbished whenever the Party wanted to stress self-sacrifice and idealism: first in the early 1960s, after the fiasco of the Great Leap Forward; then during the Cultural Revolution; and finally after the Peking Spring.

But to young Chinese in the 1980s, cynical and self-centred, bored by communist politics, interested only in bettering their own lives, Lei Feng with his avowed ambition to be a 'rustproof screw' in the communist machine was about as relevant as he would be to young people in Britain. *Red Flag* frankly acknowledged:

Some say that 'the Lei Feng spirit is outdated' . . . Some say that Lei Feng is like a block of wood, and what he did could be done by a robot. These disparaging remarks mean that Lei Feng was a simpleton who had no character, did not think independently, could be cut into any shape like a block of wood, and operated like a robot according to instructions . . .[18]

This was 'a very shallow and frivolous view', the journal complained. Nonetheless, it was the view of the majority.

When some naïve young person did take the campaign seriously, he was laughed at, as was shown by a pathetic letter published in the *China Youth News*:

Not long after I joined the army, a movement to learn from Lei Feng was launched in my unit. I took an active part in it and tried to be outstanding . . .

Very soon, on holidays and days off, I was always the one who was 'recommended' to stand on guard duty, and do the tiring and dirty jobs. Almost every day I found my basin full of dirty socks, clothes and shoes, which people put there for me to wash and clean for them . . . They told me: 'Just you keep up the good work. When the time comes, we'll all elect you as our "activist in learning from Lei Feng".' At first these lofty words excited me, but . . . facing up to the truth I felt ashamed and did not know whether to laugh or cry . . . I said to myself: 'Is this what Lei Feng did when he was alive?'[19]

The cynicism became so pervasive that nothing was immune from it. At a divorce hearing in Peking in 1980, a middle-aged woman complained that her husband beat her. 'How can this happen under socialism?' she asked bitterly. Guffaws from the public benches. In Shanghai, a year later, during a play about China's war with Vietnam, the hero picked up a grenade and pledged his willingness to die for the people: hoots and jeers from the audience, hats thrown into the air, and mocking shouts of 'Charge! charge!'[20]

Propaganda had been so abused over the years that people had become impervious to it. Ideological claptrap got short shrift: at best, indifference, at worst, open contempt. The leadership knew this, but seemed to have nothing better to offer. *Guangming Ribao* acknowledged wearily in 1981: 'The fostering of people of a new type, worthy of the socialist era, may take a long time, but we must persist.'[21]

Thought Crime and Reform

Stalin ruled the Soviet Union by the secret police. Mao, in China, used mass political movements to destroy his enemies. The Secret Speech, in 1956, and the Third Plenum, in 1978, repudiated those methods. Deng and Khrushchev set out to liberate the initiative of their peoples and build modern, dynamic societies.

In each case, within months, these ambitions were redefined in a more restrictive sense – by the promulgation of the 'four basic principles' in China in March 1979, and by the crushing of the Hungarian revolt and partial re-Stalinisation in the Soviet Union at the end of 1956. Initiative, it was made clear, would be encouraged only within the limits of the system, and the leadership would decide where those limits fell.

The question then was how to carry out reforms so as to allow people more initiative, but at the same time ensure that they used it as the leadership would wish. For it was on reform, and on raising living standards – Goulash Communism, as Khrushchev's detractors called it – far more than on ideological pleading, that Mao's and Stalin's successors were relying to overcome the crisis of faith and restore confidence in their rule. Either people had to be made to feel they had a real say in running the country, which meant more democracy; or they had to be bought off with higher wages and more consumer goods.

The first step, in both countries, was to instal rule by law, as a means of social and political control, in the place of rule by class struggle, in the form of terror and mass movements. It was not put that way. In Moscow, the new emphasis on 'socialist legality' was hailed as 'guaranteeing democratic norms'. In Peking the Third Plenum spoke of 'systematising democracy and writing it into law'; without a 'sound legal system', explained the *People's Daily*, 'it is hardly possible to realise a sound socialist democracy'. But the function of law is to punish as well as to protect, and China's Chief Justice, Jiang Hua, made clear that the restoration of the legal system had been seen from the start in those terms:[1]

> [It is] a weapon with which to protect the socialist system . . . to *suppress* all forms of treason and counter-revolutionary activity, to *punish* all traitors

and counter-revolutionaries . . . and to *compel* the class enemies to behave themselves . . . *We must also use this weapon to protect* the people's personal freedoms, democratic rights and rightful economic interests. (Emphasis added.)

In the Soviet Union in the 1950s, Stalin's 'Terror Decree' was repealed, along with other laws which had prescribed imprisonment or exile for the families of persons who fled abroad, for workers who left their jobs and peasants who gleaned wheat from collective fields. The NKVD Special Board, which had sentenced most of the political offenders during the Great Terror, was abolished; so, at the Third Plenum, were the Special Investigation Groups, set up by Kang Sheng to handle major political cases in the Cultural Revolution. The theory of Stalin's Prosecutor-General, Vyshinsky, that the accused's confession should be the main element of the prosecution case, which had fostered the widespread use of torture, was denounced, and to prevent fresh abuses a law was passed laying down that no one could be convicted on the basis of a confession alone. An identical provision, for identical reasons, was included in China's new penal code which came into force in 1980.

For the Chinese leaders, such changes were more momentous than they were for Khrushchev. A confession extorted by whatever means had been essential to Chinese notions of justice for 2,000 years; without it, a judge could not pass sentence. In practice that is often still the case in nationalist-ruled Taiwan, where coercion is regularly used to extract an admission of guilt before a person is brought to trial.

In the Soviet Union, restoring 'socialist legality' was a matter of reining in the secret police, scaling down the labour-camp system and repealing the most iniquitous of Stalin's repressive laws. In China, there was no legal system to restore. From the time of Qin Shi Huang, law codes had prescribed punishment – but how the verdict was arrived at was left to the individual magistrate in his *yamen*. After 1949, not even a law code existed, and attempts to draw one up foundered in the Cultural Revolution. So the entire system had to be redeveloped from scratch.

Trial by jury was reinstated. Except in cases involving state secrets, sexual offences and crimes by juveniles (the same restrictions as exist in the Soviet Union), hearings were to be announced in advance and open to the public. Defence lawyers were allowed to practise again. Legal aid offices reopened and the Ministry of Justice resumed work, having been closed in 1959 after the anti-rightist campaign. A criminal procedure law was enacted, providing for the first time some protection for the rights of the accused, and in 1981 a civil code was under discussion, promoting the notion, quite alien to the traditional Chinese concept of justice, that the law could serve as a reliable and impartial arbiter of civil disputes as well as a punisher of crime.

Much of the new legislation was deliberately modelled on Soviet laws. This was particularly evident over the status of the judiciary, and in the treatment of political offenders.

Counter-revolutionary offences, as defined in the Stalinist penal code, were those

> designed to overthrow, undermine or weaken the authority of the . . . workers' and peasants' government of the USSR . . . or to undermine or weaken . . . the basic economic, political and national achievements of the proletarian revolution.[2]

Under the Chinese penal code, they are offences

> for the purpose of overthrowing the political power of the dictatorship of the proletariat and the socialist system and jeopardising the People's Republic of China.[3]

All countries have 'political' laws, prohibiting sedition and armed insurrection. But, as Wei Jingsheng's trial showed, 'jeopardising the People's Republic', like Stalin's formula, 'weakening . . . the achievements of the revolution', could be applied to any form of opposition the Party wished to suppress. Under Khrushchev the term, 'counter-revolutionary', was replaced by 'anti-Soviet'. But that apart, the parallel continues, as was underlined a few days after Wei's trial when the KGB launched an investigation into a samizdat magazine which, ironically, bore the same name, *Poiski* (*Exploration*), as Wei's magazine, *Tansuo*. Its editors, Valery Abramkin and Yuri Grimm, were later imprisoned for 'disseminating slanderous inventions injurious to Soviet society and the state order'.

Both the Chinese and Soviet governments insist that none of their citizens is punished for his views, only for concrete acts. Yet quite what constitutes an 'act' has been the subject of much debate. In 1979, after the rehabilitation of Zhang Zhixin – the woman who had been executed after having her vocal cords cut for making counter-revolutionary statements – the *Peking Daily* declared:

> Thinking and acting are different. To consider a problem and express and maintain an opinion are the basic rights of a citizen as guaranteed by the constitution. To exercise these rights has nothing to do with committing a crime. Without words . . . there is no way to express thought. . . . Speech cannot be made a basis for carrying out legal punishments. It is provided in

the constitution that a citizen has freedom of speech. . . . If expressing differing opinions or raising criticisms or suggestions to the leaders is considered criminal behaviour . . . the provisions of the constitution are worthless wastepaper.[4]

Those arguments could have been taken verbatim from a poster on the Democracy Wall. Others were equally liberal. A vice-minister of Public Security said, 'We are firmly against resolving . . . the problem of dissidence by judicial or administrative means', and the *People's Daily* called on the law to 'differentiate between political offenders and criminals'.[5]

But in October, when Wei was put on trial, all that was swept aside. A high court judge declared that the touchstone for distinguishing counter-revolutionaries was 'whether they uphold or undermine the four basic principles'. By 1981, the *Peking Daily* had eaten its words:

Some people are of the opinion that . . . the uttering of counter-revolutionary speech is a problem of an ideological nature, and the law sets out to punish conduct not thought . . . This viewpoint is . . . a deliberate misinterpretation of socialist freedom of speech . . . Speech and thought are not the same thing . . . Speech enters the realm of reality . . . What is being punished here is not thought *per se*, but counter-revolutionary conduct . . . Counter-revolutionary speech is a defined legal concept.[6]

China had reached the same view of how the law should treat political dissent as had been arrived at in the Soviet Union, with much less heartsearching, under Khrushchev and Brezhnev.

China also adopted the other key feature of the Soviet legal system – the subordination of the judiciary to Party control. Shanghai Radio candidly acknowledged: 'Neither independent trial by the people's courts nor independent prosecution by the people's procuratorates is independent of the Party's leadership.' 'Law has to serve politics,' explained Vice-President Zhang Youyu of the Academy of Social Sciences.[7]

In theory this meant that local Party committees should 'guide, supervise and support' the operation of the courts but should not interfere in individual cases. In practice the scope for abuses and conflicts of interest was limitless. Peng Zhen told Party officials in September 1979:

When the courts act correctly, they must be supported [by Party Committees]. When they commit errors, they must be criticised and corrected, and when it is necessary, some of their responsibilities must be taken away from them.[8]

Who decided whether the courts were correct? Of course, the Party committee. The result was described by *Guangming Ribao* a year later:

> Sometimes a judge or a chief prosecutor is dismissed at the whim of the Party First Secretary . . . For example . . . there was a rape case in a city . . . The intermediate court sentenced the accused to a long term of imprisonment. On appeal, the high court reduced the sentence to three years' imprisonment. But the First Secretary of the city Party committee instructed the court to set the accused free, and change the verdict to 'not guilty' . . . [When the court refused,] he freed the criminal himself, and asked the court: 'Why did you not carry out the instruction of the city Party committee? Why instead did you seek instructions from the high court?' [After a second incident of this kind] . . . he dismissed the court president and his deputy and personally appointed new ones . . .
>
> The other side of the problem is that some judicial personnel are afraid of making mistakes and themselves refer cases to the Party committee for examination.[9]

By 1981, the leadership had begun to understand that the role of Party committees would have to be reduced and the courts allowed to get on with the job themselves.[10] But most cases were still decided before they ever came to court, and attempts to end this way of doing things were strongly resisted. The *Peking Daily* complained:

> It is useless to organise a public trial when the Party committee has already ruled on the guilt or innocence of the accused and on the nature of the sentence . . . [Yet] some comrades, particularly some leading comrades, cannot understand why the prior endorsement of verdicts by Party committees must be abolished.[11]

Another problem was that the machinery for dispensing justice operated on two levels: the courts, which dealt with offences among the people; and the Party's Discipline Inspection Commissions, which dealt with offences by Party members. As in the Soviet Union, a Party member cannot be arrested without the approval of his Party committee, and except in the most flagrant cases this is usually withheld. 'Very often,' said the Shanghai newspaper, *Jiefang Ribao*, 'Party discipline is substituted for state law.' It cited cases of Party officials being given a 'disciplinary demerit' for criminal offences ordinarily punishable by imprisonment, and of Party discipline, rather than the law, being used to deal with cases of embezzlement and forgery.

All this occurs in the Soviet Union as well as China: it has as much to do with their shared history of feudal autocracy as with the communist present. *Jiefang Ribao* explained:

> Once people become leading cadres, especially . . . in higher positions, they seem to be beyond the law . . . The worst thing that can happen to them is to be dismissed from office and cease to be an official. Is this not the same as 'punishing officials by taking away their titles' in feudal society?[12]

In China, however, the problems are more intractable because the tradition of an impartial legal system is absent. In Confucius's view, the purpose of the law was to 'uphold the rites', that is, to support the government, and this remains the view of China's leaders today.

In June 1980, Deng Xiaoping told a group of American journalists that the 'Gang of Four' were guilty of 'towering crimes', but 'since we now advocate socialist legality, the whole thing must be done by rule of law':[13] superficially a different method, but no less certainty about the result.

When the concept of legality is so weak at the highest level, it is hardly surprising if it is lacking lower down. Central and local authorities alike rule by edict, as they have done for centuries, promulgating regulations as and when the situation demands with no thought of seeking legislative sanction.

In civil cases, court judgments are regularly ignored. 'People say: "After all, it's not a criminal matter. If we take no action you can do nothing against us"', reported the *People's Daily*. 'Certain production brigades, communes and basic level organisations have even publicly torn up court documents and accused the people's court of . . . "taking a [politically] doubtful stand".'[14]

Nor is the judiciary itself always clear how the law should be applied. Confessions are no longer mandatory, but the old Maoist doctrine of 'leniency for those who confess, severity for those who resist' lives on. At the trial of the 'Gang of Four' in December 1980, when the former Chief of Staff, Huang Yongsheng, denied knowledge of a plot to kill Mao, the prosecution demanded that his punishment be increased because he refused to admit his guilt. Such logic discriminates against the innocent and undermines the right of defence and appeal. Indeed, attempts to establish the principle of the presumption of innocence have been firmly rejected (unlike in the Soviet Union, where it was restored in the 1950s); instead there is a tacit assumption that all persons brought to court are guilty. The role of the defence lawyer is limited to pleading mitigation, and if a defendant is reckless enough to appeal, the higher court usually orders a re-trial at which the sentence is likely to be increased. In the first half of 1980, less than three per cent of Chinese defendants were acquitted.[15] Moreover the safeguard of having hearings 'in public' is in practice nullified by limiting admission to the courtroom:

the purpose of an 'open trial' in China is not to show that justice is being done, but to serve as a lesson to the populace.

In the summer of 1979, the government launched a year-long campaign to explain the mechanics of the legal system. A conference of high court judges urged:

> Illegal practices that insult human dignity and violate personal rights, such as having the accused go from place to place to be criticised and struggled against, parading the accused through the streets to expose him before the public, having the accused go the rounds to be sentenced and so forth, must all be abolished.[16]

The Chief Justice, Jiang Hua, demanded that courts stop imposing sentences according to the offender's family background. Another supreme court judge warned that legal sanctions must 'absolutely not be extended' to an accused person's 'family, relations, friends and other innocent people'.[17]

But it was an uphill task, as was shown dramatically by efforts to end police torture. Article 136 of the new penal code stated that it was 'strictly forbidden to extort a confession by torture', on pain of imprisonment for up to three years. Peng Zhen told the NPC in June 1979 that this provision was 'absolutely necessary' because of what had happened in the Cultural Revolution.[18] A description of police interrogation techniques was published by the unofficial magazine, *Peking Spring*, in a grisly account of the maltreatment of a young worker named Yue Cunshou, after the Tian An Men riots in 1976:

> Six policemen surrounded him in a semicircle and started to belabour him with their boots, kicking his thighs, his belly and chest, and then hitting him with their fists. Someone pulled his hair and hit his head against the wall. The six men stopped when they got tired, and handcuffed Yue's wrists to the leg of a table . . .
>
> Blood was still flowing freely as Yue stared vacantly ahead. He saw the door of another room open. A small fellow of about 17 or 18 was standing in a corner . . . He was clad only in a vest and pants. A policeman walked up to him with a wooden plank in his hands . . . He swung the plank and hit him . . . on and on . . . The boy fell to the ground and remained motionless.
>
> The policeman . . . told Yue: 'You saw that. Now you had better think things over carefully. . . . The iron fist of the proletariat will beat you to a pulp' . . .
>
> Yue looked and saw a thick wooden plank from which four shining nails protruded . . . Several policemen held him down. The wooden plank went up, and one, two, three, four times the nails drove deep into Yue's flesh, drawing springs of fresh blood. With a loud shriek of pain, he became unconscious.[19]

In July 1979, a police conference declared that the use of torture was a 'chronic and stubborn disease' and a resolute struggle must be waged against it. Yet the press continued to report cases of policemen being arrested for beating suspects to death.[20] In Lanzhou in 1980, a young man named Li went to the railway station to see off his mother and got into an argument with a ticket collector. The *People's Daily* described what followed:

> Policeman Liu Changsheng, who was on duty at the ticket office, intervened, and without letting Li explain, dragged him by force to the railway police office. When he resisted . . . Liu beat him with his fists. After entering the room he wanted to sit down. Liu forbade him to do so, and when he persisted beat and kicked him unconscious . . . At about midnight, he was sent to an army hospital. The examination showed he was dead. The autopsy found that both his testicles were broken and blood had been extravasated. There was a three-inch-long wound on his forehead.[21]

Shortly after this incident it was disclosed that police in neighbouring India had been blinding suspected criminals by piercing their eyes with bicycle spokes and pouring in acid. India, through British rule, had been exposed for more than a century to Western ideas of legality. Yet after the blindings in Bihar, all but two of the police involved were reinstated and huge demonstrations were staged in their favour by Indians who insisted that what they had done was a legitimate way to keep down crime.

If that can happen in 'Westernised' India, how much harder is it to bring about change in China, which has no comparable experience of foreign legal concepts and where torture was officially sanctioned until a few decades ago?

The legal system with which China enters the 1980s is a far cry from the 'rule of law' demanded by the wallposters in the Peking Spring as a guarantee of democratic rights. It is highly politicised, non-independent and, to all intents and purposes, run as an adjunct to, if not a component of, the Party machine. Moreover it can be bypassed altogether: under administrative detention regulations, the police are empowered to send a person to do forced labour, to confiscate his goods or to sentence him to up to four years in a re-education camp (compared with a maximum fifteen-day prison term under the equivalent Soviet law) – all without reference to any court. The regulations are used for petty criminals and 'troublemakers' and those who commit 'minor counter-revolutionary or anti-socialist reactionary offences and whose criminal responsibilities have not been investigated and affixed' – in other words, political offenders whom the authorities do not wish to bring to trial.[22]

It is a measure of how much ground the Chinese legal system has to make up that in criminal, though not political, cases, a Russian has a better chance of justice from a Soviet judge than any Chinese can hope for in China. Yet just as the Soviet legal system under Khrushchev and Brezhnev was a huge advance on the personal despotism of Stalin, so the Chinese legal system today is a big step forward from the anti-legalism of Mao.

The forms of the rule of law have been established, if not yet their substance. Even Wei Jingsheng's trial showed that much: a legal process of sorts was observed, Wei was allowed to speak in his own defence, and on conviction a determinate sentence was publicly announced – which will probably be adhered to. (Fu Yuehua was freed at the due time, when she completed her sentence in May 1981.) In Mao's lifetime none of that would have been possible.

The establishment of a legal system was one of many proposals which were first aired unofficially during the Peking Spring, and later put into effect as part of the government's reform programme.

The Human Rights Alliance said in its 'Nineteen-point Declaration': 'Every Chinese citizen has the right to demand that the state make public the national budget, financial statement and figure for gross national product.' Five months later, in June 1979, the NPC, for the first time since the 1950s, did publish those figures and a wealth of other data besides. 'We cannot expect people to trust us,' a senior official told me, 'unless we are prepared to trust them.' Calls in wallposters for changes in the election system to allow a choice of candidates were reflected in a new electoral law, adopted in July 1979, providing for multi-candidate elections. And demands for a proper system of retirement for officials, including Central Committee members, were incorporated into a draft Party constitution, due to be presented at the Twelfth Party Congress in 1982.

This did not necessarily mean that the leadership took over proposals originated at the Democracy Wall; rather the unofficial debate during the Peking Spring paralleled and interacted with discussions under way within the Party. But there was a correlation between the two, which had not been the case at all in the Soviet Union in 1956.

There, in the ferment touched off by Khrushchev's Secret Speech, calls were also made for multi-candidate elections and even for a multi-party system.[23] All were immediately and unequivocally rejected. 'The Soviet system,' *Pravda* declared, was 'genuinely popular, lasting, unshakeable . . . and an example to others.' And it added, with more truth than it may have intended: 'Despite all the evils caused by the Stalin cult, it did not and could not change the nature of the Soviet socialist order.'[24] The leadership also rejected proposals for a revival of inner-Party democracy, such as had existed under Lenin in the first years after the revolution. Guarantees to 'exclude the possibility of any dissenting activity within the Party's ranks' remained necessary, the Twenty-Second Party Congress was told in 1961.

Two decades later, Soviet broadcasts were still blithely assuring their listeners that single-candidate elections offered plenty of choice, only it was exercised 'at the stage of nomination', rather than during the voting.[25]

Khrushchev curbed the secret police, freed the writers and artists by alternating liberalisation and pressure to conform, loosened the restrictions on the press and permitted, within definite limits, more freedom of debate and discussion than the Soviet Union had known since the 1920s. But neither he nor Brezhnev made any attempt to democratise the system by altering its basic structure.

In China, Deng Xiaoping took a very different view. Speaking at a Politburo meeting in August 1980, he argued that it was Mao's failure in the 1950s to 'solve the problem of the system' after Khrushchev had exposed the defects of Stalinism that had permitted the Cultural Revolution to break out ten years later. This was 'an extremely profound lesson', he said:[26]

> The question of system is of a fundamental, all-round, stable and long-term nature . . . Unless we resolutely reform the present defects in the system, certain serious problems that appeared in the past may recur in the future. Only if we carry out planned, measured, resolute and thoroughgoing reforms of these defects will the people trust our leadership, the Party and socialism.

Deng's objective was to strengthen the Party's rule by improving it. 'If we fail to put the socialist system on a sound basis today,' he told his colleagues, 'people will say: "Why is the socialist system incapable of solving problems that the capitalist system has already solved?"'

After 1979, the need for political reform was reinforced by the abandonment of the Maoist approach to mass participation in politics symbolised by the wallposter. As Xu Wenli, of the *April 5th Tribune*, argued: 'If you're going to stop posters, you have to come up with something better in their place.'

The first step, taken that year, was the decision to permit multi-candidate elections to People's Congresses (local parliaments) up to county level. Previously, direct elections had been held only at the lowest level, the commune, and then with only a single candidate, so that voting was a pure formality. In July 1979, Hu Yaobang told provincial officials:

> In many places [our elections] were . . . without any democracy to speak of . . . Lists of candidates were perfunctorily read out at meetings and even the most elementary election methods were avoided. All that was needed was approving applause and the thing was done . . . This not only violated the will of the masses . . . it was not at all prudent. It was the patriarchal system of 'what father says goes', and the people were treated like fools. Far from being representative, the deputies elected in this way were liable to arouse the masses' resentment . . . They were horse's-arse deputies, not people's deputies, and they got where they were by patting the leaders on the arse.[27]

Under the new system, anyone could stand for election to a commune or county congress, provided their nomination was supported by at least four voters, by the Communist Party, one of the small democratic parties or a mass organisation. If the number of candidates was too large, a preliminary election would be held, or the list would be reduced through 'democratic consultation' by a Party-controlled electoral committee, to not more than twice the number of seats to be filled.

In a typical election, in the East City district of Peking in November 1979, 7,866 candidates were nominated for 350 seats. Of these, the electoral committee approved 592, including 396 Party members. In the voting, 218 of the Party members and 130 non-communists were elected deputies; in two seats no candidate secured a majority in the first round and a second poll was held.

The chief limitation of this system lay in the method of drawing up the final list of candidates, which often enabled the local Party committee to block those it regarded as unsuitable. In theory, voters could write in the names of additional candidates on the ballot paper, but in practice it was virtually impossible for anyone not on the official list to obtain a majority. Moreover, the powers of deputies, even when elected, were not great. They supervised some of the work of local government, and elected local office-holders and, indirectly, the members of higher congresses, including the NPC, also with a choice of candidates. But on all major issues, the final say lay with the Party.

Nonetheless, for the first time since the communists had come to power, Chinese were allowed some measure of choice over who should represent them; that this was a real gain was shown backhandedly in 1980, when cases started coming to light of Party committees trying to annul elections in which their preferred candidates had been defeated.

Even though they lacked power, the new congresses provided a forum for airing grievances, and the authorities encouraged them, together with letters to the newspapers, as a safety valve for public opinion.[28]

This applied at the national as well as the local level. After 1980, the press carried daily parliamentary reports during each annual two-week session of the NPC, quoting deputies' criticisms not only of the implementation of government policy, but in many cases of the policy itself. Again there were limits: no one criticised Deng Xiaoping or attacked the basis of the communist system. Even if anyone had done so the criticism would have gone unreported, for apart from the formal plenary sessions, the NPC conducted its business *in camera*, and the press published only what the Party wanted to appear.

Yet the scale of grumbling, from attacks on ministers for inefficiency and waste to accusations against China's trading partners – 'China does not ask for war reparations from Japan, yet Japan . . . is cheating the Chinese people' – and demands for legislation to protect the right to strike, showed dramatically the extent to which the leadership was willing to countenance conflicting views, so long as they were expressed within the system, not outside it.[29] This message was reinforced in September 1980, when for the first time NPC deputies voted against government legislation. The numbers involved were derisory: on a citizenship bill, three-and-a-half thousand voted for and one against; on a marriage law, four abstained. But the principle was established that deputies could oppose the government without suffering retaliation.

Absorbing even these limited changes was a slow process. It took two years, until the end of 1981, for county-level elections to be completed, and only then could preparations begin for indirect elections to the provincial congresses and the NPC. In the meantime, there was considerable pressure for more far-reaching reforms.

From the start there had been calls for provincial and national elections also to be carried out by direct vote, and the decision to limit this method to county level and below had been portrayed as a transitional measure. The *People's Daily* said China needed to develop 'certain specific forms of bourgeois democracy', and went on, echoing Wei Jingsheng:

In some countries where the system of parliamentary democracy is relatively sound, the bourgeoisie are capable of controlling their officials. Even presidents and prime ministers can be toppled through democratic and legal procedures if they act against the will of the bourgeoisie. Yet in our country Lin Biao and the Gang of Four committed heinous crimes but the people could do nothing . . . From the above comparison, we can see how important a sound democratic structure is.[30]

Others were more cautious. Zhao Ziyang warned against 'mechanically copying the capitalist democratic system of the West', and Hu Yaobang said whatever system China evolved would have to preserve Party leadership.[31]

But both endorsed the need for further reform, and at the NPC meeting in September 1980 there was much discussion of how to give the People's Congresses real power over the work of government which was nominally under their jurisdiction. Xiong Fu, the editor of *Red Flag*, said NPC motions should have the force of law. 'The NPC Standing Committee,' he added, 'should supervise the State Council and the departments under it. Those [ministers] who are not qualified for their jobs should be impeached, and some of them should be dismissed.' Others proposed the setting up of parliamentary committees to deal with economic, defence and foreign policy, and a permanent commission on budgetary appropriations, which would examine all major government projects before funds were approved. 'An individual minister or vice-premier cannot decide such matters,' one deputy argued. 'If there is no report to the NPC and a handful of people still have the final say, what is the use of having an NPC?'[32]

Underlying all these ideas was the principle of the separation of Party and state. First discussed at the Third Plenum in December 1978, it had become by 1980 one of the main planks of the reform programme. But how it should be put into practice, while preserving the Party's absolute primacy, was altogether another matter, since by definition the NPC – the supreme organ of the state – could only exercise power to the extent that the Party was prepared to cede it. At the end of 1981, the situation was still, in the blunt words of one deputy, that 'the only power of the Congress is to approve the Party's decisions, and the only power of the government is to carry them out'.[33]

Unless this changed, *Guangming Ribao* warned, the NPC would remain 'a political ornament and a rubber stamp':

If the NPC and the People's Congresses in the localities cannot play the role of . . . organs of power, then the statement, 'All power in the People's Republic of China belongs to the people', solemnly declared in the constitution, will be empty words.[34]

At the NPC session in September 1980, these questions were turned over to a constitutional review commission, charged with drawing up a new state constitution incorporating elements of the experience of capitalist as well as other communist countries.

Parallel to the reform of the state system, measures were taken to reform the Party. Starting in 1979, a choice of candidates was allowed in elections to district and county Party committees. Later the principle was extended to the election of delegates to the Twelfth Party Congress. And in March 1980 the Central Committee promulgated a set of 'Guiding Principles' for every Party member to follow, which was intended to restore the discipline and idealism that had been lost in the Cultural Revolution, yet to preserve the right of dissent.

But neither the 'Guiding Principles' nor the plan to revise the state constitution confronted the key obstacle to reform, the archaic cadre system under which senior officials held their posts for life and there was no mechanism for demoting or dismissing them, no matter how incompetent they proved.

This problem was already under discussion in 1978, but it was not until more than a year later that Deng for the first time called for a systematic effort to promote men in their forties and fifties, particularly technocrats, and to persuade veteran officials who can 'no longer work eight hours a day' to relinquish their posts and become advisers.[35] In January 1980, in a review of the main tasks for the coming decade, he spoke at length about the importance of these measures:

> We must have a body of cadres which consistently follows the socialist road and has specialised knowledge and ability . . . No matter what your trade, if you are not expert . . . you cannot possibly claim to be Red. *We cannot accomplish the four modernisations unless we solve this problem*. Both internationally and internally there is a widespread feeling that we are overstaffed and bureaucratic . . . Many problems which could have been solved by one telephone call cannot be solved in six months. How can we carry out the four modernisations like this! Many foreigners say that *China has no hope of accomplishing the four modernisations in this way. People at home say so too. And it is indeed true, not false*. (Emphasis added.)[36]

The crux of the problem was the irrationality of the cadre structure: it contained too few professionals, and too many who were 'content with being laymen and indulging in political claptrap'.[37] For such men Deng had an unequivocal warning: 'If you cannot or will not learn a profession, you will just have to go. There is no other way, because you are holding things up.'

At the Fifth Plenum, the following month, it was agreed that the system of lifetime tenure should be abolished. But agreement was one thing – getting it carried out was another. By August 1980, Deng had realised that if the reform was to have any effect it would have to be more thoroughgoing. As he told the Politburo:

> Further amendments and supplements are needed. The key lies in putting on a sound basis the systems of cadre election, examination, appointment and dismissal, maintenance of standards through examinations, impeachment and rotation. We should make appropriate and clear-cut regulations in light of the circumstances regarding the tenure of all categories of leading cadres . . . and for their retirement and resignation. *No leadership post should be held indefinitely.* (Emphasis added.)[38]

Some of these ideas were incorporated into a draft of the new Party constitution which was being circulated at the end of 1980.

Its most striking proposal was that Central Committee members 'shall not be re-elected for more than three consecutive terms'. If approved, this would make it virtually impossible for a Chinese chairman or premier to hold office for more than ten years, and a single five-year term would be the norm – restrictions similar to those on the American presidency, which had been widely advertised as a model by the unofficial democracy activists during the Peking Spring, two years earlier. The draft also suggested that the average age of the Central Committee should be limited to sixty-five, and that lower age-limits should apply to local committees, down to forty-five at county level – though how they would be enforced in practice was not explained. The ban on holding office for more than three terms was also to apply at the local level, and advisory committees were to be set up to absorb veteran officials displaced by the restrictions, guaranteeing them their privileges and influence but without formal executive power.[39]

Discussion of these proposals continued in 1981. *Guangming Ribao* called for similar regulations to be drawn up governing the tenure of state officials, and Deng Xiaoping suggested that a system of state advisory committees be established.[40] In March that year the first concrete step was taken in this direction, when four elderly ministers were appointed advisers to the state council.

Exploring the Capitalist Road

In both China and the Soviet Union, the fate of political reform has been inseparable from the reform of the economic system. Deng wanted more political democracy because without it economic modernisation could not succeed. Khrushchev and Brezhnev refused to liberalise the Soviet economy because they feared the political consequences it would entail.

The blueprint for economic reform in China was drawn up by Hu Qiaomu, the President of the Academy of Social Sciences, in the early summer of 1978.

Hu called, firstly, for changes in the overall economic structure. Imbalances, principally shortages of power and raw materials, which kept factories idle, must be corrected, and proportionate development of the different economic sectors restored. The principle of self-sufficiency, which led every tin-pot enterprise to insist on producing everything it needed itself rather than rely on others, causing endless waste and duplication, was to be scrapped in favour of specialisation. And a thorough reform of the price structure should be undertaken, to end the glut of high-priced goods, which were profitable to manufacture, and the corresponding shortage of everyday items which no factory wanted to make because their prices were set too low to give an adequate return.

Secondly, Hu Qiaomu urged that enterprises should be made responsible for their economic results. Their relations with each other, and with state buying and marketing agencies, should be governed not by administrative links, like those between government departments, but by legally binding contracts, and economic courts should be set up to enforce them. If an enterprise failed to meet its obligations under a contract, it would be punished by being made to pay compensation. Managers should be made personally responsible for the losses of their units – Hu Qiaomu quoted Lenin as saying that managers of loss-making enterprises 'should stand trial . . . and be punished by having all their property confiscated and their freedom taken away for a long time'. Enterprises which did well would be given a bigger say in the use of their profits. Factories must meet labour productivity norms, and achieve an adequate return on their fixed assets. To encourage the efficient use of capital, bank loans were to replace subventions from the state.

These proposals were approved by the Politburo in September 1978. But before they could be tried out on any scale, the new leadership, dominated by Deng, formed at the Third Plenum three months later, became convinced that the disproportions in the economy were so severe that China was on the brink of a crisis – a conclusion which led to the panic suspension of plant imports from Japan, and indirectly helped to precipitate the suppression of the unofficial democracy movement. Consequently, when the Central Committee held a work conference on economic policy in April 1979, it decided that a much more sweeping readjustment of economic priorities was needed.

The root of the problem was that China was ploughing back into industrial and agricultural expansion schemes a greater proportion of the national income than the economy could stand. In the early 1950s, seventy-six per cent of the national income was consumed, and only twenty-four per cent re-invested. But during the Great Leap Forward, the proportion re-invested or 'accumulated' shot up to forty per cent. In 1978 it was still 36.6 per cent, a figure which the *People's Daily* said was 'obviously too high'.[1]

Because consumption was kept artificially low, the work conference was told, living standards stagnated; and because accumulation was excessive, far more projects were started than there were materials to complete or to operate.

In 1978, 100,000 projects were under construction in China, of which 1,700 required multi-million pound investments. But only enough cement was available for half of them. Timber was in even shorter supply. As a result, a large project took on average eleven and a half years to complete, twice as long as in the early 1950s.[2] Tens of billions of pounds were tied up in half-built schemes producing nothing. And because more projects were started than the country could handle, the *People's Daily* reported,

> Many items are postponed time and again. Some are discontinued at the half-way stage; because of poor organisation, design and construction, workers remain in enforced idleness, but their salaries have to be paid, equipment has to be maintained and the costs keep mounting. In the end, the waste is astounding.[3]

Of the 600 billion yuan (£180 billion) invested since 1949, it was estimated that 200 billion had been wasted.[4] Even of the rest, not all was productive:

Very often, the design of a project begins before any geological prospecting is carried out . . . Some collieries are built, only to find there is no coal underground. Some iron mines are constructed, only to find there is no iron there. This kind of fruitless investment has . . . reached astonishing proportions.[5]

In Shanghai in 1979, sixty factories making steel windowframes were operating at two-thirds of their capacity because there was no market for their products. Yet the planning authorities approved the construction of eleven more factories making steel windowframes. In Lanzhou, in 1978, twenty-four research institutes owned computers. Their utilisation rate was less than thirty per cent, yet nine more computers were approved. Over a three-year period, a government ministry in Peking imported seven sets of high-pressure modelling machines, and then discovered that it had no use for them.

Even if these new plants and equipment had been needed, many would have been unable to operate. In 1978, twenty to thirty per cent of existing industrial capacity, let alone what was being built, lay idle for lack of electric power; in some provinces the figure was as high as fifty per cent.[6] Transport was equally inadequate: some of the main trunk rail lines could carry only half the required volume of freight. And shortages of oil and coal were beginning, partly because China was so profligate in its use of energy (twice as inefficient as most Western countries) and partly because the development of new coalmines and oilfields and the expansion of existing ones had failed to keep pace with requirements.

An additional cause for concern was that the sheer size of the capital investment planned – Hua announced in 1978 that in the next eight years it would exceed the entire investment of the previous twenty-eight years – coupled with higher prices paid to peasants for their crops, higher wages and bonuses in industry, the cost of the border war with Vietnam and the payment of well over one billion yuan (£300 million) in back wages and compensation to rehabilitated purge victims, portended a large budget deficit and significant inflation.

A permanent solution to these problems, the Central Committee decided, required a fundamental shift towards the creation of a consumer society – the Chinese equivalent of the Goulash Communism for which Mao had so scathingly derided Khrushchev.

In practice this meant that the rate of accumulation was to drop (it came down to thirty-three per cent in 1980, and a little over thirty per cent the following year). Thousands of factories under construction were to be suspended, and new ones in the planning stage either cancelled or postponed. 'We must . . . resolutely cut out projects which are unrealistic in terms of construction possibilities or which are not badly needed,' said the Finance Minister, Wang Bingqian, in 1980. 'We must use our limited financial and material resources for those projects which will yield the best economic results.'[7] Economists such as Xue Muqiao urged that more money should be made available for depreciation funds, to end the anomalous situation in which it was easier for a factory to get money to buy new machinery than to maintain the machinery it already had. It was decreed that the main emphasis in industrial development should shift from expansion to upgrading. Construction crews taken off suspended projects were set to work on housing and urban improvement schemes.

The long-range target was to reduce the accumulation rate to twenty-five per cent, or even lower, and to ensure that around half the funds set aside for accumulation were used to improve social facilities rather than to expand economic production: in other words, the proportion of the national income ploughed back into industry and agriculture was to be cut to little more than a third of the 1978 level.[8]

The traditional Maoist and Stalinist order of priority – heavy industry, agriculture, light industry – was abandoned. An investment in light industry, it was argued, created jobs for three times more people and produced seventeen times more profit than the same investment in heavy inudstry.[9] Light industry had greater export potential, and required less raw material and only a quarter as much electricity. But, having been starved of funds, it had become 'like a locomotive entering a station, it makes a lot of noise and moves very slowly'. Light industry must therefore be encouraged to grow faster than heavy industry, whose growth rate would be reduced.[10]

By July 1979, this policy was beginning to show results. For the year as a whole, the light industrial growth rate was 9.6 per cent, as against 7.7 per cent for heavy industry. In 1980, light industry was given absolute priority over heavy industry for raw materials, fuel, power, transport and foreign exchange allocations; heavy industry was encouraged to turn surplus capacity over to making consumer goods; and the defence industry, which already in 1979 was devoting eleven per cent of its output to civilian production, was urged to make further efforts to beat swords into ploughshares. Munitions factories in Jiangsu began making motorcycles; the aircraft industry produced washing machines. In 1980, civilian goods accounted for twenty-two per cent of war industry production, and the following year the figure reached forty-three per cent.[11]

In 1980, light industry as a whole grew 18.4 per cent, compared with 1.4 per cent for heavy industry. The share of light industrial products in the total output of industry rose from forty-three per cent in 1979 to 46.9 per cent in 1980, and in January 1981, for the first time since 1965, accounted for more than half of all industrial production.

Within the slimmed-down heavy industrial sector, priority was given to expanding energy production, upgrading transport links and alleviating the shortage of building materials. An energy conservation campaign was launched in 1980, and petrol and oil supplies to most units cut by ten per cent. In 1981, each province was encouraged to impound and store non-essential motor vehicles, and it was announced that production of the hand-built Hongqi limousine, the ultimate status symbol for senior officials, was being discontinued because it was a gas-guzzler.

Meanwhile, steps were taken to reduce the number of enterprises running at a loss, which in 1979 accounted for twenty-four per cent of all state-owned industry. By the end of that year, 3,000 factories which produced low-quality or unsaleable goods, or consumed excessive amounts of energy, were shifted to other lines of production, merged or closed down. Workers made redundant were guaranteed their basic wage and given technical training until they could be found other work.

These measures, approved by the Central Committee at its April work conference, were unveiled gradually in the spring and summer of 1979 under the rubric, 'readjustment, reform, rectification and improvement'. At first it was hoped they would be completed in two years, but the time-limit was soon extended.

The readjustment policy was not only an economic imperative, it was also politically expedient. 'It is impossible for a government to survive,' said Vice-Premier Li Xiannian, 'if after it comes to power it does nothing to improve the economy and meet the needs of the people.' The *People's Daily* acknowledged: 'We used what was needed for consumption by the people to undertake construction. We must discontinue this practice.'[12]

But so dramatic a departure from the Stalinist model which China had followed for three decades was not easily accepted, and the press ran a long campaign to convince the faint-hearted that it was correct. Stalin's dictum that industrialisation should start with heavy industry was 'not a universal economic law', said the *People's Daily*. 'Our country has its own concrete conditions.' Others noted that Britain's industrial revolution began with the manufacture of textiles. Stalin himself was quoted as saying that 'men produce not for production's sake but to satisfy their needs', and Mao that agriculture and light industry should have priority over heavy industry.[13]

Correcting imbalances in the structure of the economy – between accumulation and consumption, heavy and light industry, energy production and demand – was one part of the new policy. The other was reform.

From 1979 onwards, the use of contracts became increasingly widespread, and more than a thousand courts set up economic divisions to enforce them. The Maoist doctrine of individual self-sufficiency was repudiated as a holdover from 'the small-producer mentality of a peasant economy', and efforts were made to break down administrative barriers preventing economic link-ups between different trades, ownership systems and regions, military and civilian projects and industry and agriculture.

By early 1981, 19,336 factories had merged to form 1,983 specialised corporations making products ranging from sewing machines to metal furniture and electric light bulbs. A typical merger in Chongqing brought together one large watch-making company and fourteen smaller ones, previously under the separate authorities of the province, the city, three counties, three communes, two neighbourhood committees and one army unit, and reorganised them as two large watch-making factories, one clock-making factory, a tool-making shop and a repair works. By eliminating duplication and making use of idle capacity, the production of watches increased by sixty-seven per cent, and of clocks by forty-three per cent. A more exotic scheme in the same city joined up factories which made hairdressing equipment, aluminium implements and machine tools, to form an enterprise turning out electric fans. Joint ventures between enterprises in different provinces, and integrated agro-industrial undertakings linking city factories and suburban communes were also encouraged.

The principle of specialisation was applied geographically, too. Where before each province had been expected to be self-sufficient in grain – a policy which so damaged the ecology of areas such as Gansu and Inner Mongolia that it will take generations to repair – now each province was told to concentrate on what it could do best: animal husbandry in the pastoral north-west, sugar cane and other industrial crops in Guangdong. Liaoning was to specialise in heavy industry, Shanghai in high technology ventures. Scenic cities such as Hangzhou and Guilin, fast being ruined by industrialisation, were to concentrate on tourism.

Restrictions on inter-provincial trade were lifted, and individual provinces and enterprises given greater financial autonomy. This was pioneered by Zhao Ziyang in Sichuan. Instead of handing over all their profits to the state and receiving back a fixed sum to cover bonuses and welfare, 100 selected enterprises were allowed to retain five per cent of their profits, provided they fulfilled the state plan, and twenty per cent of profits on production in excess of the plan. If any of the eight economic indicators covering such factors as quality and fuel consumption were below the norm, the retained profits were reduced by a tenth for each target missed. The enterprises taking part in the experiment were also given more scope to renovate and improve their equipment, to organise their own production and sell above-quota output directly to other enterprises, and to negotiate contracts with foreign companies, instead of having to go through the foreign trade corporations in Peking.

Since increased profits now meant increased bonuses, the Sichuan enterprises registered a growth rate in the first six months half as high again as the rest of the province, and by the end of 1980 the scheme had been extended, with some modifications, to 6,600 factories throughout China, accounting between them for sixty per cent of the output of all state-owned industry.

The next refinement, which in 1980 was being tried out in 191 factories, was to switch from profit retention to a Western capitalist-style system of corporate taxation, under which an enterprise functioned as an independent accounting unit, responsible for its own profits and losses. Charges were levied on fixed assets and working capital, which were treated as loans from the state on which interest had to be paid.

In other reforms, bank loans with punitive interest rates for late repayment replaced subventions from the state as the main means of financing capital construction projects. The aim was to cut down waste by making unnecessary or delayed construction prohibitively expensive to the now profit-conscious enterprise which commissioned it. A still more dramatic departure was the decision to permit certain enterprises to raise capital by selling shares to their workers. *Gongren Ribao* condemned the practice as a harmful retrogression towards private ownership, but the chief accountant of a Shanghai textile mill that was using the method, Ke Jianying, said it was beneficial because it lessened the burden of the state and gave workers a direct interest in their enterprise's economic performance.

'In the Soviet Union, Lenin advocated using capitalist management methods in socialist society,' he said, 'so even though shares are a capitalist phenomenon, we felt we could make use of them so long as there is no exploitation.'

At the Shanghai mill, shares could be sold only to the mill's own workforce and to a maximum value of 250 yuan (£75) per worker; they were non-transferable and had to be redeemed when the holder retired.[14] The *People's Daily* published a more radical proposal, whereby enterprises with surplus capital would be allowed to invest in those which were capital-deficient. It conceded that 'many problems would be encountered in issuing stocks for sale in a socialist country', but argued that these could be overcome and the method would help to 'pool scattered capital for use where it is needed most'.[15]

In all this, the underlying principle was to give greater play to market forces. Again it was Zhao Ziyang in Sichuan who first explicitly called for 'elements of a market economy within the planned economy', and the *People's Daily* later spelled out what this meant:[16]

> The needs of society are complicated and varied, and market conditions change with every passing day. How can the state plan be all-embracing?
> We must therefore give enterprises the flexibility to gear production to market needs. We must encourage those enterprises not fully occupied to seek production orders on their own after fulfilling their quotas – orders for various kinds of products which are needed.

The number of products in which the state held a trading monopoly was reduced, and it was proposed that eventually the monopoly should be abolished altogether. For non-restricted products, enterprises were encouraged to carry out market surveys, to advertise and compete for custom – whether they were selling heavy machinery or consumer goods. Factories were permitted to have direct links with retail stores, cutting out the state as middleman, and state wholesaling agencies were told to refuse to buy goods which were of poor quality or out of line with market needs.

For 300,000 small factories spread across China, it required a painful adjustment. In 1979, the Peking Electric Motor Factory made a profit by selling all its motors to the state, which distributed them according to a fixed plan and ignored the recipients' complaints. In 1980 the state announced that it would buy only half that year's production, and none at all in 1981: the factory would have to find customers itself. The trouble was that the Peking motors had plastic cooling fans, which were less efficient than the aluminium fans used by a rival factory in Dalian. 'What do we do?', asked the manager, Li Guisheng. 'Last year our clients had no choice, but this year they say they will buy elsewhere.'

The government was unrepentant. 'In the process of competition, a very small number of enterprises will be eliminated because their products are poor in quality,' said the *People's Daily*. 'What's wrong with that? It will encourage the advanced and retard the backward.'[17]

In Peking, Manager Li began negotiating to buy aluminium fans from an outside supplier. Salesmen were sent out to canvass business. A new slogan was pasted up in the workshops: 'We live or die by quality'.[18]

Nonetheless, getting across the notion of a mixed economy was not easy. The Gansu provincial Party committee discovered that although two million pairs of rubber-soled shoes were piled up in provincial warehouses, local factories continued making them in large quantities:

> The provincial leading comrades asked: 'Why is there such a huge supply of rubber-soled shoes?' The answer was that the shoes had not sold because the style was out of date. 'If the product is not selling, why is it still being produced?' The answer was that the factories still kept producing them because they had to fulfil production plans.[19]

The same was true of most branches of Chinese industry. At the end of 1979, the country had stockpiled nineteen million tons of steel and sixty billion yuan (£18 billion) worth of machinery. After a year-long campaign to reduce inventories, the steel stockpile rose to twenty million tons. In part this was due to hoarding, caused by the fear of irregular supplies: a steel mill stocks enough rollers to last it twenty-eight years; a knitwear factory imports thirty years' supply of knitting needles.[20] But the main cause was production unrelated to market needs.

To solve these problems, China looked to the experience of the West and of socialist states such as Yugoslavia and Hungary which had successfully moved away from the Soviet model.

'Capitalist management systems are . . . "cats which can catch mice"', not "tigers which eat people"', said *Gongren Ribao* in an allusion to Deng Xiaoping's dictum that 'it doesn't matter whether the cat is black or white so long as it catches the mouse'.[21] In 1980, eight Americans were hired with the help of the US Commerce Department to set up a management institute in Manchuria, headed by William Dill, dean of the New York University business school. After a four-and-a-half-month course, attended by 120 senior Chinese managers and officials, who grappled with such unfamiliar notions as price cuts to sell off slow-moving lines, production flow control and the application of behavioural science to enterprise management, all of which, as Mr Dill noted, 'would have been blasphemous only a few years ago', the government asked the Americans to extend the programme for another four years.

Even Taiwan was taken as a model from which to learn. In November 1980, a book was published in Peking, written by Taiwan entrepreneurs, whose purpose was said to be to 'acquaint readers on the mainland with modern enterprise management ideas'.[22]

The difficulty, as Zhao Ziyang frankly acknowledged, was 'how to combine this advanced foreign management experience with China's socialist system' – in other words, how the mixture should be weighted.[23] 'We do not advocate the restoration of capitalism,' said Xue Muqiao, 'yet we should not be overly afraid of it. It is all right to have a bit of capitalism since it is not time to exterminate capitalism yet.' Mao was quoted as having said in 1945 that feudalism, not capitalism, was China's main problem; 'indeed, we have too little capitalism'.[24] In Shanghai, *Jiefang Ribao* complained that too many people had 'capitalism-phobia'. In Chongqing, a watch factory manager said he saw little difference between the new system of independent accounting and tax payments to the state and the system in effect before the communist takeover in 1949.

In fact, not quite so: in a key speech, late in 1979, Zhao Ziyang set out the two basic limits which China must not overstep:

> In my opinion, the major principles of socialism are, *first, public ownership of the means of production*, and *second, a system of 'to each according to his work'* . . . When we talk about the socialist system of public ownership, we mean [public ownership of] the principal part of the economy, *not the whole of it*; by . . . the principle of 'to each according to his work', we mean we must not exploit others or use capital to exploit them. *As long as we adhere to these two conditions, we should adopt any system, structure, policy and measure* that can promote the development of the productive forces . . . We must not bind ourselves like silkworms in cocoons. On this issue *we really have to emancipate our thinking vigorously*. (Emphasis added.)[25]

Another constraint on free enterprise was the state plan, which imposed quotas that had to be fulfilled before market forces could even begin to come into play. In 1979, thirty-five per cent of China's output of machinery was sold on the open market, but only two per cent of its output of raw steel; the rest fell under the plan and was allocated by the state.[26]

However the biggest obstacles to economic innovation were the price structure and the system of utilising labour.

In theory, fixing prices by political criteria, so that rents and basic necessities cost next to nothing while luxury goods are highly priced to soak up spending power, has much to commend it. In practice, as both the Chinese and the Soviet experience has shown, it leads to economic lunacy.

Consider, for example, what happened in Peking when the municipal government built a street of high-rise apartment blocks. The rents were set so low that they did not cover the cost of the electricity to run the lifts, let alone the maintenance costs of the buildings. Accordingly the lifts were switched on for only a few hours a day, and the buildings remained half empty: even in accommodation-starved China, few are willing to walk up nine or ten floors several times a day. All over the country, the lack of money for maintenance means that new buildings degenerate into slums in the space of a few years. And the low rents actually worsen the housing shortage: since apartment buildings are a financial burden for the organisations that own them, there is no incentive to build. Yet to raise rents is unacceptable politically, and to increase state subsidies is impossible without unacceptable cuts elsewhere.

There are other paradoxes. The price of black-and-white television sets made by a factory in Shanghai is fixed at 245 yuan (£73.50) when the components cost 257 yuan. The more sets it makes, the more money it loses. The same applies to frying pans in Wuhan: the result – plan or no plan, the newly profit-conscious factories stop making them, and shortages set in. Conversely, excessively high prices offered for peony root, a Chinese medicinal herb, have resulted in a glut of such dimensions that one province has enough in its warehouses to meet worldwide demand for forty years.

The worst irrationalities occur in the prices of primary materials. In Japan, a kilogram of grain buys two kilos of chemical fertiliser; in China, it buys only a seventh of that amount. A Japanese farmer can buy a tractor for five tons of grain; a Chinese tractor costs thirty-five tons. Most Chinese coal is sold for less than the cost of extracting it. Communes pay more for electricity to irrigate their land than they get back from selling the produce.

Arbitrary pricing also makes a nonsense of the bonus system. The government experimented in 1981 with levying a surtax on enterprises which, because of the price structure, made disproportionately large profits and consequently paid excessive bonuses to their workers. But that did nothing to help those whose bonuses were disproportionately small because the goods they made were underpriced.

The leadership accepted early on that all these anomalies could only be resolved permanently through a comprehensive price reform. Its first step, announced at the Third Plenum in December 1978, was to change the terms of trade between the city and the countryside. A year later, price controls were removed from about 10,000 handicrafts and simple consumer goods, representing twenty per cent of retail trade, and in 1980, as the market expanded, this rose in some provinces to between thirty and forty per cent. That October, however, Xue Muqiao made clear that more thoroughgoing changes would have to wait until the readjustment policy had been completed and the economy was stronger.[27] The aim then would be to eliminate or greatly reduce subsidies on rents and food and to bring other prices into line with the law of value, offsetting the resultant rise in the cost of living by a large nationwide wage increase – a complete reversal of Mao's policy, which held that the higher the ratio of collective welfare to personal consumption, the more advanced socialist society was. In the meantime, only limited adjustments would be made to prices which had little direct bearing on living costs.

Raising labour productivity and improving managerial efficiency was an equally intractable problem because of the Chinese 'iron rice-bowl' system. An iron rice-bowl cannot be broken; a Chinese worker cannot be fired.

The result, wrote Xue Muqiao in 1981, was that

> not only is it impossible to raise productivity, but even discipline can hardly be maintained . . . As soon as workers receive their 'iron rice-bowl', they can only gain entrance, promotion and reward, and cannot be sacked, downgraded or punished – and the main factor in wage rises and promotion is order of seniority, not work ability and labour contribution . . . How can the economic effect of labour be improved like this?[28]

One early and successful method of overcoming the 'iron rice-bowl' mentality was to cut by up to fifty per cent the wages of management and staff in inefficient enterprises until economic performance improved. But it proved so unpopular that it was quickly abandoned. In theory, enterprises practising profit retention were permitted to dismiss workers, but it rarely happened. Like the price structure, the 'iron rice-bowl' system was too intimately connected with the vital interests of the population at large for the government to be able easily to change it.

More progress was made in improving the system of management. Starting in 1979, workers were allowed to elect their own workshop heads, foremen and team leaders from a list of candidates of their own choosing, instead of having them appointed from above. In 1980, this was extended on a trial basis to the election of factory directors. Some units advertised managerial vacancies, instead of waiting for replacements to be assigned by the state. Others experimented with a system of half-yearly opinion polls, under which any manager receiving the support of less than thirty per cent of the workforce had to resign.[29]

Potentially more far-reaching were moves to change from the pre-Cultural Revolution system of factory directors working under the leadership of the factory Party committee, which had been revived in 1978, to a Yugoslav-style system of directors working under the leadership of the factory workers' congress. By mid-1981, workers' congresses had been established in forty per cent of state-owned enterprises at and above county level, and it was proposed that they should become organs of power with the right 'to discuss and decide major issues and to elect and remove the leading administrative personnel'.

But like the plan to reform the political system by giving power to the people's congresses – the local parliaments – this proposal required the Party to give up some of its own power. And when faced with taking a decision to that effect, in the end the Party balked. Regulations published in July 1981 laid down that workers' congresses would elect factory directors 'subject to approval and appointment by the proper higher authorities'.[30]

The 'iron rice-bowl', arbitrary price controls, state planning, public ownership and restrictions on the individual use of capital constitute a formidable barrier to the development of free enterprise. Nonetheless, within certain limits it has managed to thrive.

In the two years to the end of 1980, the number of individually owned shops, restaurants and hotels in China increased from 12,000 to 390,000, accounting for one per cent of the business done by state- and collectively-owned commercial undertakings, and the number of licensed artisans and individual labourers grew to well over a million.[31]

For the first time since the early 1960s, pedicabs reappeared on the streets of Peking. Bootblacks, newspaper sellers, knife-sharpeners, scribes – who for a fee would write letters for the illiterate – pen repairers, piano tuners, itinerant barbers and bicycle repairmen made a triumphant comeback. The ban was lifted on peasants coming into the cities to sell their vegetables and poultry, and whole streets were turned into pedestrian precincts, where stall-holders cried their wares, and hawkers and pedlars sold candied fruit on wooden skewers, home-made clay toys, tiny figures made of coloured dough and paper-cuts to brighten the windows of people's homes.

'Socialism should be lively, not cold and cheerless,' the *People's Daily* declared. As long as individual traders did not profiteer or exploit others, their role was beneficial. It helped to reduce urban unemployment – still estimated at around 10 million in 1981 – promoted efficiency by competing with state-owned enterprises, and 'made the people's lives richer and more colourful'.[32] But compared with the nine million private workers in Chinese cities in 1953, they were still far too few to satisfy the need for services.

To encourage the growth of private businesses, tax rates, which operated on a sliding scale from seven to seventy per cent, were lowered, and for the first time since 1956, banks were empowered to give individual businessmen loans. Usually limited to 1,000 yuan (£300), they could cover anything from the purchase of a sewing machine for a tailor's shop to a piano to enable a musician to give private lessons. Even the prohibition against hiring labour was eroded: from mid-1980, private traders and craftsmen were allowed to take on one or two apprentices, and a year·later the number was increased to five and up to two assistants, 'so that they can meet public demand and provide more jobs for young people awaiting employment'.

Collective businesses and shops, previously discriminated against as politically less advanced than state-owned enterprises, were also granted loans and more favourable tax treatment. They provided jobs without requiring state investment, and were responsible for their own profits and losses. The *People's Daily* suggested that state enterprises might do well to learn from the collectives, rather than the other way round, and in one experiment in Liaoning, a state-owned bath-house, which had run at a loss for years, was contracted out to its workforce to run on a collective basis and immediately started making a profit.[33] Such is the power of worker motivation.

Yet still limits remained. In 1980, a technician named Wang Shicai hired two rooms from a local plastics factory, borrowed some machinery, bought on credit nine tons of raw materials, and co-opted thirteen local peasants to turn out 100,000 plastic bags. Had the scheme succeeded, the profit in the first six weeks would have been 14,000 yuan (£4,300). But, instead, he was arrested, accused of speculation, and sent to prison for four years.[34]

One group of people, however, was permitted to use wholly capitalistic methods: foreign entrepreneurs who invested in joint ventures in China.

The launching of the readjustment policy in April 1979 brought the hopes of Western businessmen for an economic bonanza in China crashing down to eàrth. The Japanese contracts suspended in February were reluctantly reinstated, but no more deals for turn-key projects were signed. The decision to renovate existing plants, rather than build new ones, sharply reduced the scope for machinery imports, and the *People's Daily* said China should buy 'more hens and fewer eggs' – more technology and fewer sets of equipment. Later this principle was extended to imports of motor vehicles and electronic goods, and there were calls for more protectionist policies to promote import substitution. By 1980 the leadership was beginning to realise that the most advanced Western technology, complex, highly automated and extremely difficult to maintain, was not necessarily what China needed or could even digest.[35]

Meanwhile, the full extent of the waste in the first few years, when Chinese officials believed that any problem could be solved by throwing foreign money at it, became apparent. It was disclosed in 1980 that forty-five per cent of all equipment imports since 1972 had been unnecessarily duplicated, and many could have been made domestically in the first place. Pro-communist newspapers in Hong Kong wrote scathingly of the 'Westernisation leap forward', and within China the *People's Daily* drew a devastating parallel between the incompetence of the country's new communist ministers and that of their imperial predecessors during the 'Westernisation movement' at the end of the Qing dynasty, a hundred years earlier:

> When the mandarin, Zhang Zhidong, established the Hanyang steel plant, he sent a cable to . . . the Chinese envoys in England to place an order for machines and furnaces before the iron deposits which were to supply the plant had been explored. The manufacturers on Teesside replied: 'Before a steel plant is built, you must first send us samples of the ore, stone and coke for tests. From the qualities of the coal and iron, we shall know what kind of steel can be obtained and what sort of furnaces will be needed . . .' However Zhang Zhidong ignored this . . . [and] boasted: 'China is a vast country which has all kinds of resources. Why do we have to find the coal and iron ore before buying the furnaces?' So two Bessemer converters and one Martin furnace were purchased regardless . . .
>
> The phosphorus could not be completely removed from the iron ore so the steel cracked easily . . . The coal supply was also unsuitable. There was no alternative but to buy coke from Germany . . . at twenty ounces of silver a ton . . . Eventually a huge sum of money was spent, useless steel was produced, and new machines and furnaces had to be purchased.[36]

To a Chinese reader in 1980, that was the story, word for word, of how the Minister of Metallurgy, Tang Ke, bought the Baoshan steelworks from Japan.

After this, large-scale imports of Western equipment were limited to the priority fields of energy and transport, to meeting ad hoc needs for the modernisation of existing plants, and to expanding light industry, particularly projects which would rapidly generate foreign exchange. No dramatic increase in foreign trade was anticipated until the second half of the 1980s, and even then Chinese buyers were expected to be more cautious and discriminating than in the spending spree which followed Mao's death.

The one exception was the joint venture. By 1980, this was already taking a bewildering variety of forms: an Italian firm signed a contract to hire up to 400,000 Chinese labourers for public works projects in third countries; Western and Japanese companies searched for oil in the East China Sea under agreements by which they would share in any eventual production; and a Shanghai factory made wheel-doors for the main undercarriage of McDonnell Douglas DC–9 aeroplanes assembled in the United States. But the commonest arrangement was where a foreign firm provided raw material for processing and re-export, or machinery to be paid for by future production (so-called compensation deals), or where the two sides formed a joint stock company, with investment and profits shared either indefinitely or for a fixed number of years.

By June 1981, China had signed more than 7,000 export-processing and compensation deals, twenty-eight agreements for joint ventures with permanent foreign equity participation, and some 330 contractual joint ventures whose assets would eventually revert to the Chinese side. The vast majority were concentrated in five special economic zones in the southern provinces of Guangdong and Fujian, where they attracted investment from Hong Kong, Macao and South-East Asia.

The main problems were the glacial slowness and inefficiency of the Chinese bureaucracy, and the authorities' reluctance to let foreign employers pay their workers enough to make them work hard. At worst, this caused the kind of disaster that befell China's first joint venture, a compensation deal with a Hong Kong textile firm, Novel Enterprises Ltd. Under the agreement, the Chinese side was to pay for £200,000 worth of machinery, provided by the Hong Kong firm, by making yarn from wool it supplied. According to Novel's Chairman, Billy K. P. Chao, the first sign of trouble came when building materials for the factory had to be sent across the border from Macao, because it would have taken too long for China to procure them. Then, Mr Chao said, Hong Kong technicians, sent to train the new factory's workforce, found 'it was very, very difficult to do anything because the Chinese workers weren't so keen on working'. When the factory opened, it failed to make a single batch of yarn that was of the required quality, and cost Novel £170,000 in lost business in its first year of operation. Absenteeism was so serious that on some days half the workforce stayed away. Workers who had been described as high-school graduates turned out to be illiterate. Machinery was ruined through lack of maintenance, and Novel's demands that unfit workers be dismissed were ignored. In desperation, the firm cut off wool supplies and complained to the State Council in Peking.[37] The case was taken up by the *People's Daily* as a warning to Chinese officials 'under no circumstances to allow this kind of problem to recur'. After a fifth of the workforce had been fired, production resumed, though still with a number of basic problems unresolved.[38]

In 1980, thirty of the 600 or so foreign firms engaged in joint ventures in the Shenzhen economic zone, adjoining Hong Kong, pulled out, some for similar reasons. But at best, the schemes could be immensely successful. A joint stock company, set up by the Swiss firm, Schindler, and a Hong Kong trading house to make lifts for the Chinese and foreign markets, earned US $4 million in profits in its first year of operation, giving the foreign partners a return on investment of twenty-three per cent. The terms of the agreement gave them a virtual veto on all major decisions, and the workforce of 2,000 received an average wage of 170 yuan (£51) a month, three times the norm for state-owned industry, with the prospect of a sixty per cent rise over five years.

In related developments, foreign companies were permitted to build wholly owned factories, operated by Chinese workers, in the special economic zones; a state investment corporation planned a ten to fifteen billion yen (£24–36 million) debenture issue in Japan, the first time the communist government had entered a foreign capital market; and a rudimentary foreign exchange market was established within China itself, where authorised state enterprises could buy and sell foreign currency at rates determined solely by supply and demand.

But private enterprise was revived to greatest effect not in industry at all but in agriculture.

After the re-establishment of private plots and village trade fairs in 1978, and the decision to give greater autonomy to production teams in deciding which crops to grow, the key question was how to link the interests of the individual peasant with those of the collective. Mao's answer had been to distribute the team's profits equally among its members without paying too much attention to individual effort: in his view, this was a step beyond the Leninist principle, 'to each according to his work', towards the utopian communist ideal of 'from each according to his ability, to each according to his need'. Deng's answer was to make the individual peasant's earnings depend as closely as possible on the amount that he produced.

To this end a number of systems were tried out. The simplest was to divide the production team into work groups, numbering anywhere from three or four to thirty labourers. The team contracted out farm-work to each group, which was awarded a fixed number of workpoints for each task it completed. The more tasks a group carried out, the more workpoints and hence the more money it earned. In a slightly more refined version, the work group signed a long-term contract, to run a piggery for a year or to carry out all the farmwork from preparing the fields for seed to harvesting the final crop on a given part of the team's land. The group was then paid according to output, with a premium for production in excess of an agreed target.

In 1981, three-quarters of China's peasants were being paid by one or other of these methods. But by then, a much more radical reform was under way. Again, it was pioneered by Zhao Ziyang in Sichuan. Instead of the work group, the household was taken as the basic unit, either doing work on contract and being paid in accordance with output or, in a more controversial variant, leasing part of the team's land for a fixed annual rent, and keeping for itself whatever it produced beyond that.

As the land, draught animals and large agricultural implements continued to belong to the team and not the household, Zhao argued that the two conditions he had elaborated in November 1979 for distinguishing socialism from capitalism, that is, public ownership and remuneration according to labour, were both being fulfilled, and family farming was therefore an acceptable socialist method.[39] Others, including Chairman Hua, thought differently. In March 1980, *Hunan Ribao*, controlled by Hua's protégé, Mao Zhiyong, declared: 'This method is actually turning the collective economy into an individual economy . . . It is not permitted by Party policy and must be resolutely curbed.'[40] Many of Deng's own supporters also had reservations, and it was announced, in an oddly hypocritical gesture of conscience-salving, that remuneration on the basis of the household would be permitted only in poverty-stricken areas where the peasants had 'lost confidence in collective production' and 'needed a respite to get back their strength'.[41] Even when collective production proved economically inferior, its political superiority still had to be affirmed.

Nonetheless, by March 1981, twenty per cent of China's peasants were being paid on a household basis, and in the poorer regions the figure was higher: fifty per cent in Inner Mongolia and even more in Guizhou and Gansu.[42]

That month another major reform was announced. Production teams which did not apportion work by the household were allowed to increase the amount of land used for private plots from seven to fifteen per cent of the total. One member of each household could be exempted from collective production to raise private vegetables, poultry or livestock full-time. Banks were authorised to give loans for private farming in the same way as for individual businesses in the cities. And plots of mountainous or barren land were allocated to peasant families to plant trees for firewood.

Restrictions on the private ownership of livestock were lifted even earlier, and in another tacit admission of the failings of collective agriculture, pastoral areas began allotting collectively-owned kids and lambs to households to raise privately. 'In this way,' said one report from Xinjiang, 'hundreds of thousands of [head of] livestock [which would not have survived] will be saved.'[43]

By 1981, at least one-third of China's agriculture was being undertaken by what was essentially private farming. The household was beginning to replace the production team as the basic agricultural unit, amid clear signs that the leadership itself was losing confidence in the commune system. Oblique criticisms of 'excessive collectivisation' began appearing in the press, and discussion resumed within the Party of a proposal, first put forward in a poster at the Democracy Wall in 1978 and subsequently taken up by *Guangming Ribao*, calling for the restoration of the pre-1958 system of village, or *xiang*, government, so that the commune would lose its administrative role and become a purely economic unit.[44] In March 1981 it was disclosed that one production brigade near Peking had set up a *xiang* government to try out the system with a view eventually to applying it throughout the country. If carried through, the measure would spell the communes' final disintegration.

The reforms in agriculture, like those in other areas of the economy and in political life, were intended to decentralise decision-making, free individual initiative and, in the American phrase, 'get the government off the backs of the people'. The same principles were applied in other fields. Universities were given a bigger say in running their own affairs and scientists more discretion in carrying out research.

These developments were strongly emphasised by Hua and other leaders at the NPC in August and September 1980. What had been achieved so far, Hua said, was 'only a small first step' towards an overall reform. As individual units were given greater decision-making powers, the role of the bureaucracy would diminish and a 'large-scale simplification of administration' would become possible.[45] The role of state planning would also change: there would be fewer mandatory targets, and more which performed the function of guidance or forecasting.[46] '[The aim is] that the state will no longer intervene directly,' Zhao Ziyang told a Japanese delegation, 'instead it will guide the enterprises through pricing, taxation, credits, plan [guidelines] . . . and other means.'[47]

The prospect conjured up by such proposals was of an even more radical departure from the Soviet model than that undertaken by Yugoslavia and Hungary in the 1960s, and discussed in Czechoslovakia in 1968 and in Poland since 1980. *Le Monde* called it 'a categorical rejection of Maoist policy . . . China has left the era of mass exhortation and embarked on that of technocratic realism.'[48] The *New York Times* wrote of 'new policies . . . as sweeping in their implications as any since the communists' triumph in 1949', and noted that they took their inspiration not only from other communist states, but also from countries such as Taiwan and South Korea, which shared with China the legacy of Confucius, the sage who preached the virtue of ordered, benevolent rule.[49]

The Soviet Union in the 1950s faced very similar economic problems. Capital construction was over-extended, power was highly centralised, horizontal links between different departments and regions were virtually non-existent, and the economic structure was grossly unbalanced in favour of heavy industry. Indeed, it was precisely this system that China copied after 1949 and retained unchanged until Mao's death, the only difference being, according to Xue Muqiao, that its shortcomings became still worse when mechanically transplanted to Chinese conditions.

Khrushchev in 1956, like Deng two decades later, endeavoured to place more emphasis on the production of consumer goods; in the Soviet Union, as in China, defence plants started turning out motorcycles and radio sets. Like Deng, he made agriculture the first priority, and attempted a sweeping decentralisation. But the means he used to achieve these ends were fundamentally different from Deng's. Khrushchev's approach was that of Stalin, and of his own contemporary, Mao, rather than that of the next, more sophisticated generation of communist leaders.

Starting in 1957, he launched repeated political campaigns to promote the growing of maize, to plough up grassland, to popularise peat-compost, to 'catch up the United States in the production of meat and milk'. The method was the same, although not carried to the same extreme, as Mao used in the Great Leap Forward, and afterwards both men were criticised by their successors for the same error, 'subjectivism'. The Seven Year Plan inaugurated in 1959 called for impossible growth rates. Two years later, at the Twenty-Second Party Congress, Khrushchev unveiled a blueprint for the Soviet Union to surpass America in all major fields, and proposed providing some goods and services free by 1980: like Mao, he held that collective welfare was politically more advanced than personal consumption.

There were other parallels with the Chinese leader. Khrushchev insisted that university entrants must have worked for at least two years in industry or agriculture, but then had to abandon the scheme as impracticable – fifteen years before Mao unveiled the same proposal as one of the 'new-born things' of the Cultural Revolution. He closed many of the churches and synagogues which Stalin had allowed to reopen during and after the war. And, like Mao, to promote collective agriculture, he restricted the number of livestock each peasant household could own and reduced the size of private plots. All this was exactly

411

opposite to what Deng tried to do, and much of it was reversed after Khrushchev fell.

Khrushchev understood the need to encourage local initiative, and paid frequent lip-service to it. But in the end his basic instinct, that nothing would happen unless it were ordered from above, always reasserted itself.

This contradiction was reflected in his efforts to change the economic structure. In 1957, he abolished the central ministries, and created more than a hundred regional economic councils, or *sovnarkhozy*, whose activities were coordinated through the fifteen republics and the central planning agencies. To be effective, this would have required a real dispersion of central power through some form of market socialism. Since that was unacceptable, the system was constantly being patched up by the addition of new coordinating agencies. In 1962, to try to improve the Party's ability to supervise policy, most regional and district Party committees were divided into two parts, to take separate responsibility for industry and agriculture, and the number of *sovnarkhozy* was halved. This meant, however, that the borders of the *sovnarkhozy* no longer coincided with those of the political regions. At the same time new administrative boundaries for agricultural districts were drawn up. They did not coincide with political borders either. These 'hare-brained schemes', as they were later called, alienated the entire Party apparatus and paved the way for Khrushchev's fall.

But the more fundamental problem, of how to increase the efficiency of each individual factory and the output of each worker, which was the main preoccupation of the Chinese reformers, Khrushchev left completely untouched. During his last years in power, economists such as Libermann were already discussing ways of combining centralised planning with a market economy, of making factory managers responsive to consumer demand and of using computers to make planning more scientific. Their theories laid the groundwork for the later reforms in Hungary and Yugoslavia, and influenced Chinese economists such as Sun Yefang and Xue Muqiao. Yet, in the Soviet Union itself, it was not until Alexei Kosygin had succeeded Khrushchev as premier that their proposals were acted upon.

The reforms which Kosygin announced in September 1965 made profitability the primary index of economic efficiency. As in China, fifteen years later, enterprises were permitted to retain part of their profits for bonus schemes, and centralised controls on managers were relaxed. But the more radical ideas, such as the introduction of elements of a market economy, were never carried out, and the whole tenor of the new measures remained highly controversial. In the absence of corresponding political reforms, the conservatism of the regime ensured that even those economic reforms that were introduced were smothered by the rigidity and narrow-mindedness of those who had to administer them.

In July 1979, when falling growth rates convinced the Soviet leadership once more of the need for change, the Central Committee passed a resolution reaffirming the 1965 reforms and proposing that they should be implemented more thoroughly.

Few documents show more clearly the complete paralysis brought about by the consensus politics that have characterised the last years of Brezhnev's rule. It called for increased autonomy for industry, measures to make it harder for factories to claim plan-fulfilment by producing unsaleable goods, and larger bonuses for individual workers. But each proposal was so hemmed about with qualifications to satisfy those who held contrary views that no clear direction emerged, and it was plain from the start that the resolution had no hope of succeeding.

Even if larger bonuses were paid, they would serve no purpose unless there were more consumer goods to spend them on. However, the leadership's efforts to bring about a dramatic shift to consumer goods production failed. From 1968 to 1971, light industry in the Soviet Union did grow faster than heavy industry. But thereafter the traditional order of priorities reasserted itself. While the plan continued to call for light industry to come first, the heavy-industry bureaucrats and their clients, particularly the military – the 'metal-eaters', as Khrushchev used to call them – made sure that their own interests had priority. The share of heavy industry in total industrial output rose from 68.6 per cent under Stalin to 72.5 per cent under Khrushchev in 1960 and seventy-four per cent under Brezhnev in 1979.

Other indicators told the same story. The industrial growth rate fell from an average of eight per cent in the 1950s to 3.7 per cent in 1980, and the target for the 1981–85 Five Year Plan was the lowest since the Second World War. The proportion of investment tied up uselessly in unfinished capital construction works rose from sixty-nine per cent in 1965 to eighty-five per cent in 1979, the year in which China, with a similar proportion of non-productive investment, launched its readjustment policy.

Dr Andrei Sakharov commented in March 1980:

The basic necessity for economic reform, including, in part, the establishment of greater economic independence for state enterprises, decentralisation of planning and the introduction of elements of a mixed economy, appears incontrovertible. However, any such reforms, inevitably affecting the very foundations of the totalitarian economic and social structure, are very unlikely at the present time.[50]

A year later Nikolai Tikhonov, an elderly protégé of Brezhnev who took over as premier after Kosygin's death, spoke at the Twenty-Sixth Party Congress. He told the 5,000 delegates in the Kremlin that the days when the Soviet economy could expand by adding new workers and developing new resources were over: future growth would have to come from raising efficiency. This, he said, was a task as monumental as the industrialisation of the country under Stalin. But to accomplish it he could only suggest more of the mixture as before. No new move was made to substitute economic for administrative controls, nor any attempt to satisfy consumers by allowing more private trade, as was happening not only in China but all over Eastern Europe as well. The Central Committee resolution of July 1979 had sunk without trace.

Similar considerations applied to agriculture. Stalin wrecked Soviet farming by killing off the successful farmers, the kulaks, and driving the unsuccessful ones into collectives. Khrushchev ploughed up the Virgin Lands and launched endless political campaigns. Brezhnev tried to solve the problem with money: a third of all Soviet investment in the 1970s went into agriculture. But the one method that did bring a guaranteed increase in production – breaking collective farm brigades into smaller units called *zvena*, or 'links', so that the earnings of the individual farmworker were related more closely to his labour – was rejected, despite successful trials, because it was politically unacceptable.

Following a series of poor harvests, the Soviet government announced in 1977 that production on private plots was to be encouraged, and four years later restrictions on the ownership of livestock were lifted, banks were authorised to give loans of up to £2,000 for private farming, and the area of private plots was increased. On paper this could have been a significant reform. In practice it was promoted half-heartedly by the leaders at the top and stifled by the bureaucracy lower down; it became an attempt to avoid change by tinkering with the existing system and trying to muddle through.

Because of this overwhelming political aversion to reform, the Soviet Union, thirty years after Stalin's death, faces economic problems identical to those of China, five years after Mao's death. The missing decades, which could have been used to seek answers to those problems, had been frittered away. At the beginning of the 1980s, China, rather than Russia, was making progress towards their solution.

Confrontation

For Khrushchev, the economy was a battleground on which to wage the struggle for power. In 1955, he had championed the Stalinist doctrine of the primacy of heavy industry, in order to remove Malenkov from the premiership. At the Central Committee plenum in December 1956, the places were reversed: Malenkov attacked Khrushchev for putting too much stress on raising living standards, and by this device succeeded in regaining a good deal of his power.

In February 1957, Khrushchev responded by putting forward his proposal for the creation of the *sovnarkhozy*. His opponents, who on other questions had been divided, now had an issue on which they could unite against him. In June, Khrushchev was outvoted in the Politburo by seven votes to four.

Instead of accepting defeat, however, he exercised his right, under a little-used provision of the Party statutes, to take his case to the full Central Committee. For two days there was a full-scale political crisis, as Marshal Zhukov mobilised airforce planes to fly in Khrushchev's supporters. The committee, when it met, reversed the Politburo's decision, criticised Malenkov, Molotov and Kaganovich for acting as an 'Anti-Party Group' and dismissed them from all their posts, together with their supporters, Pervukhin and Saburov. Such was the tradition of monolithic unity that the resolution was passed unanimously, with one abstention: only Molotov refused to vote for his own demotion.

Malenkov was sent to run a power station in the Urals; Molotov to be ambassador to Outer Mongolia; Kaganovich to a minor managerial post. Later all three were expelled from the Party, and accused of criminal activities as well as political errors. But this was never followed up, and each enjoyed a comfortable retirement.

A year later, in August 1958, Khrushchev removed the other two who had voted against him – his long-time ally, Nikolai Bulganin, from whom he took over the premiership, and the aged Marshal Voroshilov. As both premier and Party leader, Khrushchev's power was complete. For the next six years, his position was not seriously challenged.

In China, disputes over economic policy were also a factor in the manoeuvring for power, and in June 1979, Hua made a mild self-criticism before the NPC for 'not taking full account' of the gravity of the economic problems caused by leftist policies, and adopting 'some measures [which] were not sufficiently prudent'.

However, the main vehicle for political struggle was the legacy of Mao and of the Cultural Revolution. The Mao question was crucial. Unless his policies were publicly discredited, officials would refuse to implement the new, un-Maoist policies which Deng was introducing, on the grounds that they would be 'chopping down Mao's banner', or could be accused of doing so if the political climate changed. Similarly, if Mao's aura of omniscience and infallibility were not completely destroyed, the risk remained that some future leftist group might raise his spectre to reverse course again. This was not abstract theorising. In 1981, the fear among Chinese officials of being accused of making 'rightist mistakes' was still the biggest single obstacle to getting the new policies put into effect.

Khrushchev worried away at the Stalin problem for similar reasons. Unless he was completely discredited, Stalinism might one day be revived and Khrushchev's vision of a more just and dynamic Soviet society would be lost. Later, in his memoirs, he cited the partial re-Stalinisation which took place under Brezhnev as showing his fears had been justified.

But Khrushchev had Lenin to put in Stalin's place. Mao *was* China's Lenin. 'To negate Chairman Mao,' said one provincial leader in 1979, 'is to negate People's China, the whole history of the Party and of an entire era.'[1] The speaker was a leftist, but not even Deng or Hu Yaobang would deny that Maoism was the ideological cement that held the country together. Given the importance of ideology to the Chinese, it could not lightly be discarded.

This dilemma was at the core of the struggle that now unfolded, more and more openly, between Deng and Hua.

The first major development came in the late summer of 1979, when the draft of a speech to mark the thirtieth anniversary of the People's Republic was circulated within the upper levels of the Party. After amendment, it was approved by the Central Committee at its Fourth Plenum in September.[2] To underline that it represented a consensus, the speech was delivered by Marshal Ye Jianying at a rally in the Great Hall of the People (though, perhaps significantly, the Marshal himself, ostensibly on the grounds of frailty, read only the first pages, praising Mao, leaving an aide to read the more critical portions of the text).

Mao's 'immortal contributions . . . without which there would be no new China today' were reaffirmed, as was his status as a 'great Marxist, great revolutionary and strategist', and 'the most outstanding representative' of the Chinese Party. But the definition of Maoist ideology was radically changed:

> Mao Zedong Thought is not the product of Mao Zedong's personal wisdom alone, it is also the product of his comrades-in-arms, the Party and the revolutionary people . . . It is the crystallisation of the experience accumulated over the past half century in China's revolutionary struggles and in her building of a new society, the crystallisation of the collective wisdom of the Chinese Party.

If Maoism were simply 'Marxism-Leninism as applied and developed in the Chinese revolution', it became possible to separate Mao's mistakes, and those of the Party, from the ideology which bore his name: the one could be criticised while the other was still affirmed.

Without spelling it out so clearly, this was what the speech did. Beginning with the anti-rightist campaign in 1957, it said, there had been a succession of ' "leftist" errors':

> [That year] the mistake was made of broadening the scope of the struggle. In 1958, we . . . made the mistakes of giving arbitrary directions, being boastful and stirring up a 'communist wind'. In 1959 . . . we ineptly carried out the struggle against so-called right opportunism . . . These errors . . . [helped to] bring about the serious economic reverses of the late 1950s and early 1960s.
>
> The Central Committee of the Party and Comrade Mao Zedong quickly perceived these errors in our rural and economic work and began to lead us in rectifying them . . . Early in 1962, an enlarged central work conference attended by 7,000 people was convened, at which . . . Comrade Mao Zedong criticised himself . . .
>
> Unfortunately, we were not always able to . . . bear in mind the lessons drawn from our errors. As a result we had to pay a very bitter price, and instead of avoiding errors which could have been avoided, we committed even more serious ones . . .
>
> In 1966 . . . the Cultural Revolution was launched with the aim of preventing and combating revisionism . . . But the point is that at the time when the Cultural Revolution was launched, the estimate made of the situation within the Party and the country ran counter to reality. No accurate definition was given of revisionism, and an erroneous policy and method of struggle were adopted, deviating from the principle of democratic centralism.
>
> Driven by counter-revolutionary motives, Lin Biao, the 'Gang of Four' and other conspirators and careerists exploited these errors [and] . . . attempted to . . . plunge our country once again into . . . bloodbaths and terror. The havoc . . . wrought for ten long years spelt calamity for our

417

people and constituted the most severe reversal to our socialist cause since the founding of the People's Republic . . . It was an appalling catastrophe suffered by all our people.

This went considerably further than anything that had been said in public before, and Marshal Ye, on behalf of the Party, made a public self-criticism. 'It is true,' he said, 'that the people's interests have sometimes been seriously harmed as a result of mistakes in our work . . . [But] we did eventually correct our mistakes, and have not let the people down.'

Nonetheless, it was much more cautious than Wang Ruoshui's secret speech, seven months earlier, and glossed over completely the question of Mao's responsibility. For more than a decade, the Chinese people had been taught that the Cultural Revolution was 'personally launched and led by Chairman Mao'. But now its authorship was camouflaged in evasions and its excesses blamed on others. Who made the wrong estimate of revisionism, who broadened the struggle in 1957, who stirred up a 'communist wind', was left discreetly unsaid.

Marshal Ye described the speech as a 'preliminary assessment', and said a formal summing up of Party history, including the Cultural Revolution, would be drafted later. However the same cautious approach was to be maintained. 'I am afraid that if it is written too meticulously, it will not be appropriate,' Deng Xiaoping explained.[3]

Meanwhile, the steady reversal of Mao's policies continued, accompanied by efforts to make his memory less obtrusive. In June 1979, the system of revolutionary committees was abandoned altogether, and the pre-Cultural Revolution nomenclature of mayors, provincial governors and people's governments was restored. The May 7th Schools were quietly transformed into agricultural training institutes. Mao's sayings, written up in white characters on huge red billboards at every other street corner, were painted over with advertisements or slogans promoting modernisation. Radio Peking stopped playing the Maoist anthem, 'The East is Red', at the start of its news bulletins, and articles appeared in the press ridiculing those who revered Mao blindly.

Parallel to these moves, Deng renewed his offensive against the leftists in the Politburo. The four 'Whateverists' – Vice-Chairman Wang Dongxing, Chen Xilian, Wu De and Ji Dengkui – were denounced as 'archcriminals instigating people to doubt and oppose the Third Plenum'. The *People's Daily* said 'these villains' had 'adopted despicable tactics' and 'wildly attempted to turn back the wheel of history and return us to the time when the "Gang of Four" ran amok', and demanded that the Party 'tear off their masks'.[4]

Wang Dongxing was accused by name, in officially inspired wall-posters at the Democracy Wall in June 1979, of having illegally diverted more than £2 million in government funds to build himself and his family a luxury villa in Zhongnanhai. Chen Xilian was also attacked in posters, and obliquely in the press, for his part in the killing of Zhang Zhixin, the woman brutally executed in Liaoning in 1975 for criticising the Cultural Revolution. The publicity given to this incident was carefully contrived. There were calls for her 'murderers' – meaning Chen and Mao's nephew, Mao Yuanxin – to be put on trial,[5] and when the affair was discussed at the NPC that month, passions ran so high that the session had to be suspended for a day. In the end it was announced that the case would not be pursued because it would bring demands for legal action in too many other similar cases of injustice. *Guangming Ribao* explained:

In handling unjust cases like Zhang Zhixin's, we usually do not advocate tracking down the murderer or investigating and affixing responsibility on a particular individual. Lin Biao, the 'Gang of Four' and the modern superstition they created, rather than the people engaged in the actual work, should be held responsible for the crime of creating so many unjust cases.[6]

However another of the deputies' demands was accepted: it was agreed that the 'Gang of Four' should stand trial, and the Director of the NPC's Legislative Affairs Commission, Peng Zhen, was charged with preparing the case against them. Shortly afterwards, the ashes of Hua's old patron, Kang Sheng, who had helped him become Public Security Minister in 1973, were unceremoniously removed from their resting place at Babaoshan cemetery for revolutionary leaders, desecrated and thrown into a storeroom.

This incident was described by Liu Binyan in a surrealistic short story called 'The Warning', written to warn China's leaders against suppressing dissent and so repeating the errors of the past. It recounts an exchange between Kang's ashes and those of three of his disgraced followers:

From outside the entrance came a weak and very familiar woman's voice. The voice broke the silence in this inhuman world. Then there were people's footsteps. Someone undid the lock and the door was opened . . .

'You will be held responsible for this,' the voice quavered. 'I shall lodge a complaint with the vice-chairman . . .'

At the same moment, the three souls knew: 'This is big sister C*.'

* Cao Yiou, Kang Sheng's widow.

A heavy thing, which was much heavier and bigger than their three sleeping caskets, was put on the ground in front of them. It was a big marble cinerary urn of hawksbill colour. The cinerary urns of the founders of the state were made of wood . . . and above them there were only small photographs like those used at memorial meetings. But the marble urn of this great person was surmounted by a bronze bust. The one blemish on its perfection was that it was now covered in human excrement and the bronze was scored and marked. Copper is too soft a metal. Had the maker known what would happen, he would have done better to use steel.

The three souls knew at once who this man was . . . In the last few years of his life, he had suffered from tormenting pain and hallucinations. Whenever he opened his eyes, he saw the spirits of those he had wronged, ghosts with dishevelled hair and blood and filth on their bodies; when he closed his eyes, the ghosts were still there. The sense of threat had smashed his mind. . . . All tranquillisers had lost their effectiveness. At the last, all the doctors could do was show him films all day long, so that the characters on the screen would drive away the hallucinations and give him some respite in his nervous exhaustion. In this way he could sleep two or three hours each day . . .

For several days the three souls kept silent. But from the big marble cinerary urn there came constant moans and groaning . . . Eventually the General, one of the three whose relations with the leader had been closer than the others, plucked up his courage to speak. But before two words had passed his lips a very angry voice came from the big marble sleeping casket:

'Be silent!'

A moment later they heard the familiar voice with its Shandong accent say, haltingly, moaning and shuddering between the words:

'It is necessary to put up with it. Let everyone forget, forget that we ever existed. Now there is only one hope. Let those persons [the present leaders] take the same road as we did [and they too will meet the same end]. That is the unique hope, and the unique hope lies there.'

The three souls understood what the leader had said, and the memory of his face appeared before them, a face with very thin cheeks and severe and menacing cold eyes looking over his spectacles.

Since then, there has been silence in the tomb-room. Will history develop as they hope? Will one day more urns be thrown there?

By September 1979, Deng was beginning to close in. At the Fourth Plenum, Peng Zhen and Zhao Ziyang were made full members of the Politburo, and another twelve of Deng's supporters were brought into the Central Committee. The 'Whateverists' were warned that the Party 'would not wait for them for ever' to change their stance, and for the first time were accused publicly of following the same line as the 'Gang of Four'.[7] In economic policy, Li Xiannian, the survivor of so many political twists and turns, was increasingly overshadowed by Chen Yun, who now headed a new super-ministry, the State Economic and Financial Commission, to oversee the readjustment programme. And Chen Yonggui, the model peasant from Dazhai, was attacked as an ultra-leftist.

All this was designed to increase the pressure on Hua, and a few days after the Fourth Plenum, the *People's Daily* published a full-page commentary, which for the first time hinted directly that he would have to go:[8]

> Naturally changes will take place in a collective leadership. The superseding of the old by the new is inevitable due to the laws of nature and to the development and change in individual people . . . So long as collective leadership . . . is upheld, *whether individuals stay or go will not affect the leadership's stability.* (Emphasis added.)

To make clear that it was Hua who was being referred to, the commentary questioned the legitimacy of the way Mao had appointed him his successor. This point had first been raised in a poster at the Democracy Wall nine months earlier, which had questioned Mao's reported statement to Hua in the summer of 1976, 'With you in charge, I am at ease.' 'Is this not treating China,' it asked, 'as though it were one man's property, to be bestowed as his personal gift, just like in feudal times?' In oblique fashion, the *People's Daily* repeated this criticism:

> According to the organisational principles of the Party, none of the secretaries or members of any Party organisation *at any level* has the right to hand over his office and power to another person, because this power belongs to the Party . . . *Talented people should emerge through practice, they should not be plucked high artificially.* (Emphasis added.)

Six weeks later, Deng gave a long interview to the editors of the *Encyclopaedia Britannica*, in which he spoke of the need to 'find good and reliable successors, so that once a succession takes place new turmoil will not break out again'.[9] The strange thing about this was that China was already supposed to have a 'good and reliable successor' – Hua. But Deng did not mention Hua's name.

Meanwhile the separation of Party and government posts in the provinces was speeded up. Before the year was out twenty-six out of twenty-nine provinces had their Party and government administrations headed by different men.

In December, the Politburo met and approved sweeping changes in both the composition and the structure of the leadership.[10] The 'Whateverists' – Wang Dongxing, Chen Xilian, Wu De and Ji Dengkui – were held to have committed 'grave errors' and dismissed from all leading posts,[11] though they remained members of the Central Committee and, like the 'Anti-Party Group' in the Soviet Union in 1957, were given appointments as minor functionaries before, in most cases, disappearing altogether. Chen Yonggui was not removed at the same time, apparently to make clear that his problem was of a different kind, and two years later he was still in name a member of the Politburo, though he had long since ceased to be one in fact.

The pre-Cultural Revolution Party secretariat was restored, and Hu Yaobang appointed General Secretary, the post which Deng himself had held until 1966.[12] Hu's other job as head of the Propaganda Department was taken over by Wang Renzhong, a cautious, rather pedestrian official who, like Li Xiannian, favoured orthodox middle-of-the-road policies. Wang's appointment was a setback for the reformers. But five of the other nine Party secretaries supported Deng's policies, thus ensuring him a narrow majority. They included Hu Qiaomu and two provincial leaders who were transferred to Peking, Peng Chong from Shanghai, and Wan Li from Anhui who was also appointed a vice-premier.

The purpose of re-establishing the secretariat was to 'deal with the day-to-day work of the Central Committee'.[13] In a parallel move, Zhao Ziyang was brought in from Sichuan and appointed standing vice-premier to deal with the day-to-day work of the government.[14] By this device Zhao and Hu between them took over much of the substance of power which Deng had wrested from Hua over the previous year. They were now firmly established as the team Deng wanted to assume the leadership if and when Hua could be dislodged altogether, and both were appointed members of the Politburo Standing Committee.

At sixty-one, Zhao was a year older than Hua, but still one of the youngest men in the top leadership. A landlord's son from Henan, he joined the Communist Youth League at the age of thirteen and became a full Party member six years later. His entire career had been spent as a professional Party functionary, first as a county secretary in his home province during the Sino-Japanese war in the 1940s, then in South China, where under the patronage of Tao Zhu he worked his way up to become first secretary of Guangdong province on the eve of the Cultural Revolution. In January 1967, Tao fell and Zhao fell with him. But four years later he was among the first of the purged former province chiefs to be rehabilitated, and by 1974 was back in his old job in Guangdong. The following year he went to Sichuan, where he established a reputation as a formidable administrator – a man concerned with devising practical policies to solve practical problems, and then making them work. Apart from the economic reforms he pioneered, Zhao was one of the few Chinese leaders with the confidence to depart from the standard text and set out his own views, clearly labelled as such. When he arrived in Peking at the beginning of 1980, it was with the determination to extend to the whole country the economic pragmatism that had already proved so successful among the 100 million people of Sichuan.

Progress was also made towards persuading some of the oldest Party leaders to retire, in line with Deng's campaign to appoint younger men to senior posts. In a big military reshuffle that winter, he himself stepped down as Chief of Staff, and several other elderly generals, including Xu Shiyou in Canton, retired from active commands. Deng had said as early as July 1979 that by the time he reached the age of eighty, in 1985, he hoped to give up all his posts, and at the next NPC session, in September 1980, he, Li Xiannian and Chen Yun all gave up their vice-premierships. But the traditional view that old leaders were wise leaders was not so easily overcome. Ye Jianying, at eighty-four, despite failing health, refused point-blank to give up the post of NPC Chairman,[15] and the demographer, Ma Yinchu, was appointed to the NPC Standing Committee at the age of ninety-nine. The new Chief of Staff, Yang Dezhi, was seventy. Even the Party secretariat, which was supposed to contain younger leaders who were being groomed to take over from the old guard, had an average age of sixty-six – a time of life at which politicians in the West are ending their careers.

The decisions of the December Politburo meeting were announced at the Central Committee's Fifth Plenum, held in February 1980, or in the weeks immediately before and after it. The same Plenum announced the long-awaited rehabilitation of Liu Shaoqi, the arch-demon of Maoist iconography against whom the Cultural Revolution had been launched.

This could have been an event as momentous as the rehabilitation of Trotsky would be in the Soviet Union – a symbolic overturning of an entire historical period.[16] And for some, who had built their careers on Liu's overthrow, it was. In Hainan, a nurse named Guan Minghua had been executed in 1971 for speaking out in Liu's defence. Now those who had denounced her asked: 'Guan Minghua has become a martyr. What are we, are we counter-revolutionaries?'[17] Ye Jianying and Xu Shiyou, who was increasingly at odds with Deng over the scope of de-

Maoisation, showed their disapproval by staying away from the state funeral held for Liu in May, and Hua presided with such ill grace that it was plain he had no wish to be there. But most of the impact had been dissipated by a deliberate campaign, going back over the previous six months, to accustom people to the idea gradually so that by the time it actually happened, it was almost a non-event. Deng had used the same technique to remove Mao from his pedestal, and he would use it again, in the coming year, for the final battle with Hua.

The decision to restore Liu to the pantheon of Chinese communist heroes was taken in the summer of 1979 and endorsed by the Fourth Plenum in September.[18] Within days, his photograph began reappearing at historical exhibitions and on television, and by December the press was once more referring to him as 'Comrade Liu Shaoqi'.

When the formal announcement came in February,[19] it described Liu's overthrow as 'the biggest frame-up in the history of our Party', and said it must be 'completely overturned . . . in order that the Party and the people will for ever remember this bitter lesson . . . so that frame-ups such as befell Comrade Liu Shaoqi and many other comrades inside and outside the Party shall never happen again'.

Liu himself was praised as 'a great Marxist and proletarian revolutionary [who] was loyal to the Party and people at all times over the past decades . . . and made indelible contributions', and for months afterwards the press was full of articles, building him back up to his former eminence as second only to Mao. But the question of Mao's responsibility for what the plenum called 'this grave and grievous mistake made by our Party' was once again avoided:

Because the appraisal on the eve of the Cultural Revolution of the situation in the Party and the country was contrary to fact, an entirely wrong and groundless inference was made, asserting that there was within the Party a counter-revolutionary, revisionist line, and then that there was a so-called 'bourgeois headquarters' headed by Comrade Liu Shaoqi.

Every Chinese knew that the 'entirely wrong and groundless inference' was made by Mao – but, in line with Deng's policy of 'not being too meticulous', the Party declined to say so. Indeed, two months later, on the eve of Liu's state funeral, the *People's Daily* published a long editorial asserting that Lin Biao and the 'Gang of Four' had concocted material against Liu 'to deceive the other members of the Central Committee, including its principal leaders', and that it was on this basis that the Party approved the 'absolutely erroneous decision' branding him a 'renegade, traitor and scab' in 1968. Mao, it implied, was not really to blame at all:

> During the Cultural Revolution Comrade Mao Zedong himself righted many wrongs . . . Although [he] nodded his approval in many cases, when he learned that they were false, that the evidence had been extorted and that the wronged comrades were persecuted in prison, he showed great indignation, used his authority to break through the obstacles created by Lin Biao and the Gang of Four and resolutely corrected the wrong handling of these comrades. [But] of course . . . it was impossible [for him] to carry through the work of rehabilitation to the end.[20]

This was sheer hypocrisy. Mao and no one else was responsible for Liu Shaoqi's death. But to minimise the potentially disruptive effects of Liu's rehabilitation, Deng was ready to shield Mao for as long as it took the Party to get used to it. 'In conducting any publicity campaign,' Hu Yaobang told the Fifth Plenum, 'we must guard against the trend towards total negation of Mao Zedong.'[21]

Even with all these precautions, however, Liu's comeback was a tremendous blow to what remained of Mao's prestige. To hundreds of millions of Chinese, Liu had been the personification of political evil throughout their adult lives. Now, no matter with what equivocations the Central Committee hedged it around, the message was that Liu had been right, and Mao had been wrong.

Liu's book, *How to be a Good Communist*, which Mao had condemned as anti-Marxist, was reprinted and described as 'a component part of Mao Zedong Thought', while the *People's Daily* derided Mao's 'Little Red Book' as 'a joke'.[22] Mao's insistence that the 'Four Clean-ups' campaign be directed against capitalist-roaders, which Liu Shaoqi had opposed, was acknowledged to be incorrect.[23] The claim that Mao had founded the Party was dropped: the founders, Chinese were told, were the long-discredited Chen Duxiu (the first General Secretary) and Li Dazhao; Mao had been merely one of the thirteen participants in the founding congress in 1921. His famous phrase, 'imperialism is just a paper tiger', was admitted to have been coined not by him but by Cai Hesen in 1922.[24]

Mao was portrayed as having been from the start a member of a collective leadership. Other veterans, such as Li Lisan and former General Secretary Qu Qiubai, were now rehabilitated. Visiting statesmen were taken to lay wreaths at the Monument to the People's Heroes, instead of Mao's mausoleum. 'The history of the Party,' the *People's Daily* declared, 'is not the history of one individual.'[25]

At the end of July 1980, the last portraits and statues of Mao came down – not always easily: one huge statue at Peking University resisted even dynamite. By August only a single image of the Great Helmsman remained on a public building out of all the millions put up earlier, and that was the benign-looking portrait that gazed out across Tian An Men Square from the Gate of Heavenly Peace. Even the 'four beards', as Chinese called them – the enormous paintings of Marx, Engels, Lenin and Stalin, which stood on the other side of the square – were dismantled, to be re-erected temporarily on National Day, once a year. There had been too many portraits of Mao and other leaders in public places, the Central Committee explained: it was 'lacking in political dignity'.[26]

From the beginning of 1980, the outlook for Hua was extremely bleak. The appointments of Zhao and Hu Yaobang, men of the same age as himself, wrecked his strategy of avoiding confrontations and hanging on to his posts at all costs in the hope of recovering his power when Deng and the other veterans died. Now the most he could hope for was to avoid being excluded altogether from the new collective leadership that was being formed. The standard phrase – the Central Committee 'led by Comrade Hua Guofeng' – was abandoned, exhibitions about his life were stopped, and it was stated that in future, the succession would be resolved by one collective leadership 'gradually and automatically' replacing another.[27]

The question of Zhao taking over as Premier was almost certainly discussed at the Politburo meeting in December 1979, but it seems no firm agreement was reached until the summer of 1980.[28]

The first public hint came from Deng in April, and, as usual, it was calculated to do Hua as much damage as possible. In an interview, published on the front page of the *People's Daily*, he said that whether or not Zhao would replace Hua was 'a question which cannot be answered by any one individual' – so, for the first time, telling the Chinese people explicitly that a question mark hung over Hua's career.[29]

'This is salami tactics,' a Yugoslav diplomat told me. 'They're chopping away at Hua's legs.' Hua evidently thought so too, and decided that if he were to make a stand, now was the time to do it. On April 21st, four days after Deng's interview, the *People's Daily* published a long speech by Zhao, setting out his proposals for economic reform, and accusing 'certain persons' of seizing on minor shortcomings in order to attack the reform programme as a whole.[30] A week later Hua struck back. Addressing an army conference, he criticised the reformers for putting too much emphasis on material incentives, and too little on politics:

China is a socialist country. The socialist system dictates that *primary attention should be paid to raising the ideological consciousness of the people* in solving economic problems and in doing work of all kinds . . .

No good results will be achieved if undue emphasis is placed on economic methods and material rewards while political work and efforts to raise the people's ideological awareness are relaxed . . .

Indifference to the weal and woe of the people is wrong, but *over-emphasis on improving the people's living standards* beyond the growth of production is unrealistic. *It is necessary to raise the people's political consciousness and encourage the revolutionary spirit* of building the country through diligence and thrift. (Emphasis added.)[31]

Hua had chosen his audience with care. In essence he was appealing for a return to Maoist values – to the belief that mind can triumph over matter, as one of his supporters put it later.[32] The PLA was more sympathetic to these views than any other group in China. Mao had been far more successful as a military leader before 1949 than as a civilian ruler afterwards, and the army had been almost untouched by the political storms which had shaken the rest of the country: the Cultural Revolution had actually benefited it, by increasing its political influence. Moreover Hua had been hinting for months that if he had real power, he would give more priority to military spending.[33]

He also used the conference to revive the Maoist slogan: 'Promote proletarian ideology and eliminate bourgeois ideology.' This had been the subject of an intense debate throughout 1979, with Hua's supporters saying that it was correct, and Deng's decrying it as 'ultra-leftist' and arguing that feudal, not bourgeois, ideas were China's biggest problem.[34]

For about a month the slogan was promoted at regional military conferences but then the campaign fizzled out. If Hua had seriously believed that he could rally the army behind him, as Mao had done on the eve of the Cultural Revolution, he was sadly mistaken. By late May he had been forced to agree to step down in Zhao's favour, and soon afterwards the press began alerting the Chinese people to the imminent change.[35] *Gongren Ribao* rebutted Hua's criticism of material incentives, declaring that 'ideological work must serve people's material interests, otherwise it has no point'. A big campaign was launched against feudalism, and in August, Deng told the Politburo that Hua's slogan was 'not complete enough, nor is it very accurate'.[36]

Support for Hua fell away very rapidly. All through the summer, he had been sniped at for the failure of the economic plans drawn up in his first two years in power. Now the Politburo members and ministers responsible for them also came under attack.

These were the so-called 'Petroleum Faction', headed by Li Xiannian.[37] Its adherents had all at one time or another been associated with the success of China's oil industry. In 1979, when the industry ran into problems and oil production stagnated, their star began to wane. Not only was Li himself overshadowed by Chen Yun, but the following year its next most powerful member, Yu Qiuli, was replaced by Yao Yilin, one of Deng's supporters, as head of the State Planning Commission. In August 1980 the Petroleum Minister, Song Zhenming, was sacked and the vice-premier in charge of the oil industry, Kang Shien, publicly reprimanded for trying to cover up an oil-rig disaster in which seventy-two men died. In a damaging innuendo, it was disclosed that investigation of the accident, which had occurred the previous winter, began only after the Fifth Plenum had appointed Zhao Ziyang to take over from Hua the day-to-day running of the government – implying that Hua also had been lax in carrying out his duty.[38]

Hua's old patron, Kang Sheng, was denounced by Hu Yaobang in a way deliberately calculated to humiliate him.[39] There were renewed attacks on Chen Yonggui, whose Dazhai production brigade Hua had supported. Even the authorities in Hua's home village were publicly censured for alleged wrongdoing.[40]

But the most menacing note was struck in a historical allegory, published in *Guangming Ribao* at the beginning of August, which described how a Tang dynasty eunuch had usurped power from the Emperor Xuan Zong. Hua, the article implied, was likewise a political eunuch who had usurped power from the dying Mao.[41]

A month later Hua stood before the NPC for the last time as premier and announced his resignation. 'The Central Committee,' he said, 'believes Zhao Ziyang is a suitable choice and worthy of trust.' However he conspicuously refrained from endorsing the appointment himself, and devoted much of his speech to a defence of his own record.[42] In vain. The biggest orderly transfer of power since Mao had resigned as head of state, two decades before, proved to be just one more stage in Hua's inexorable decline.

Although he remained Party Chairman the *People's Daily*, a few days later, published an immensely long article, once again questioning the legitimacy of his succession to that post. 'Whether a leader remains a leader is decided by the people,' it warned. 'It is natural that . . . some people will step down because they are unqualified.'[43]

At this point, several stands of political development come to fruition together. It was announced that the trial of the 'Gang of Four', which had been under preparation at secret pre-trial hearings throughout the summer, would open within the next few weeks.[44] The Party's Discipline

Inspection Committee completed its investigation into the careers of Kang Sheng and Hua's predecessor as Public Security Minister, Xie Fuzhi, and decided that both should be posthumously expelled from the Party.[45] Criticism of Hua increased, and for the first time veiled attacks were made on his one remaining ally of consequence, Marshal Ye Jianying.[46] The same week, a draft 'Resolution on Certain Questions of Party History' was circulated to members of the Politburo Standing Committee.[47]

It was the resolution that brought matters to a head. 60,000 words long, its purpose was to sum up the achievements and errors of the previous thirty years and establish a national consensus on Mao's merits and faults, so as to provide a firm basis for Deng's programme of reforms.

Drafting had begun in March and had already gone through nine revisions. Hua wanted a document that would affirm the essential correctness of Mao's line, while acknowledging that he had made mistakes.[48] Deng held that, after 1957, and in some cases even before, Mao's line had been wrong and it was necessary to say so. He set out his views in August in an extraordinarily frank interview with the Italian journalist Oriana Fallaci:[49]

> In the last part of his life Chairman Mao contradicted himself and the good principles he had formulated. Unhealthy thinking emerged, both in his actions and his style of work. The unhealthiest thinking of all [was] his ultra-leftist ideas. Well, maybe victory had made him less prudent, or maybe he had lost contact with reality . . .
>
> A patriarchal behaviour began to develop in him . . . I did not like his patriarchal behaviour . . . He never wanted to know the ideas of others, no matter how right they could be. He never wanted to hear opinions different from his. He really behaved in an unhealthy, feudal way. If you don't understand this, you cannot understand why there was the Cultural Revolution . . .
>
> When I say that Chairman Mao made mistakes, I also think of the mistake named Jiang Qing. She is a very, very evil woman . . . Yet Chairman Mao let her usurp power, form her own faction and use his name as her personal banner for her own personal interests, and use ignorant young people to build her private political base . . . Even after . . . he was living apart from her, he did not intervene to stop her and prevent her making use of his name.

To Hua, this was anathema, and he did not mince words. There was a furious exchange when the resolution was discussed at an enlarged Politburo meeting that month, and for the first time his competence as Party leader was openly questioned.[50] Two months later, when the

Politburo met in mid-October to discuss the new draft, he announced that he would not go along with it. Hu Yaobang accused him of threatening to split the Party by obstructing policies which the majority accepted. Hua had made historical errors, he said, and clung stubbornly to leftist views. He was not fit to remain Chairman. Deng spoke afterwards in similar vein.

No formal decision was taken, but by November 7th, when Deng received the Yugoslav Premier, Veselin Djuranovic, the first tantalising hints were emerging that Hua had been eased out of power.[51] Officially he submitted his resignation on November 13th, at the start of a nine-day Politburo meeting which considered the charges against him in detail. These covered four main areas.

Politically, he was accused of continuing the leftist workstyle of the 'Gang of Four', delaying Deng's reinstatement in 1977 and opposing the rehabilitation of Peng Dehuai and of the Tian An Men incident. Ideologically, he was said to have upheld the 'Two Whatevers' policy of uncritical adherence to Maoist orthodoxy, and to have obstructed the 'practice' debate which Deng launched in 1978. In the economic field, he was criticised for leftist adventurism, failing to control imports and attempting another 'Great Leap Forward'. And at a personal level, he was held to have promoted his own cult and, somewhat improbably for a man with so self-evidently modest a lifestyle, to have abused his position to obtain special privileges – a reference to his having lived in the 'No 8 Building', a very private and completely secure residence constructed for Mao in his last years, which was linked to the government offices at Zhongnanhai by several miles of underground tunnel.

The meeting continued intermittently until early December, but the dénouement came at least a week earlier. On November 26th, Deng told the Rumanian leader, Ilie Verdet, that Hu Yaobang was to have 'a big promotion'. The following day Hua made his last public appearance before dropping out of sight for the next two months.

On Deng's proposal, it was agreed that Hu should take over as Chairman while Deng himself would head the Military Commission 'because there is no other suitable candidate'. Hua was to be the junior vice-chairman. The changes would take effect at once, but would not be formalised until they had been approved by the full Central Committee at its next plenum, to be held early in the new year.

The Third Cold Wind

Hua's fall at the end of 1980 was the culmination of more than three years of unremitting political struggle. But even in Deng's moment of triumph, his offensive was beginning to falter.

One source of opposition was the PLA. The army, in their olive-green uniforms with no badges of rank, ostensibly the last defenders of egalitarian Maoism, were the most feudalistic of all Chinese social groups. It was their lack of enthusiasm for Hu Yaobang and the reforms he symbolised that prompted Deng to take over the Military Commission himself, in violation of the Party constitution, which stated that it should be headed by the Party Chairman. The other focus of resistance was the senior and middle-level bureaucrats, particularly in the provinces, who saw the reforms as a threat to their own vested interests and were at the receiving end of the practical problems which applying the new policies created. As winter approached, grumbling and discontent among both groups began to bubble over.

The army had no lack of grievances. The defence budget had been cut by thirteen per cent (and would be cut further within a few months). Military plants were being turned over to civilian production, which meant fewer new weapons. Defence was bottom of the list when it came to importing foreign technology, and as the political leadership began to re-examine the Leninist thesis of the inevitability of war, there was growing apprehension that the role of the military might be sharply reduced.

Even without that, the gradual repudiation of Mao, of the Cultural Revolution and the PLA's role in it, had greatly diminished its prestige. The privileges of the officer corps were constantly under attack, and among the civilian population conscription was no longer considered an honour: peasant recruits now complained that their families were being discriminated against, because under the new agricultural policy those whose menfolk were away from home earned less than they would have done before.

However, the final straw was the trial of the 'Gang of Four', which opened on November 20th. In the dock, beside Jiang Qing, Chen Boda and the other three civilian defendants, stood five military officers. A

431

decade earlier they had been among the most powerful men in China: Huang Yongsheng, formerly Chief of Staff; Li Zuopeng, Chief Naval Commissar; Wu Faxian, Commander of the Airforce; another deputy chief of staff and a senior airforce officer. Now, after nine years' imprisonment, they were human wrecks. On the opening day, Li collapsed (as did Chen Boda) and had to be given oxygen. Huang stammered, and Wu's mouth sagged open uncontrollably.

Ridicule is a cruel weapon, and the spectacle of the army's former leaders, arraigned with Mao's detested widow and abjectly confessing their 'crimes' in a caricature of impotence, was a terrible humiliation.

So it was intended to be. Although the military defendants were tried separately by military judges, the message that came through more and more clearly as the hearings progressed was that they had been reduced to this wretched state solely because they had become too closely involved in the scheming of politicians. It was an attempt to teach the army a lesson, part of a broader campaign to get it to abandon its political role and transform it into a professional force – undergoing the same sort of transition as was occurring in every sphere of civilian life. But the lesson was too harsh, and it was bitterly resented.

The principal accused, living and dead, at the trial of the 'Gang of Four': Left to right (back row): the four 'Great God Protectors' – Qiu Huizuo, Li Zuopeng, Wu Faxian and Huang Yongsheng; Jiang Tengjiao (in airforce uniform); Chen Boda; the 'Gang of Four' – Jiang Qing, Zhang Chunqiao, Yao Wenyuan and Wang Hongwen; (foreground): Lin Biao and his wife, Ye Qun; Xie Fuzhi and Kang Sheng.

The trial backfired in other ways too. All the panoply of justice was there: the sleek round-faced judges dressed in black, the procurators in grey, thirty-five of them altogether, sitting in serried ranks on crimson-upholstered benches; the accused, escorted to the dock by blue-garbed police bailiffs; the witnesses, weeping and gesticulating as they recited accusations from prepared scripts. Yet the substance of legality was missing. One of the defence lawyers said afterwards she had known all along there was no defence for such 'terrible, counter-revolutionary criminals' and had only taken part because the authorities had told her it would 'enhance China's international reputation' by showing that the legal forms were being observed.[1] What it actually showed was how primitive a concept of the rule of law China has – a grotesque, sad parody of a trial which, like the case against Wei Jingsheng a year earlier, belonged not in the courtroom but on the political stage.

Even at the political level, it was not a complete success. Zhang Chunqiao refused to recognise the court's authority to try him, and sat throughout the proceedings with half-closed eyes, slumped motionless in the dock, wearing an old black quilted peasant jacket, seeming to hear nothing that was said to him and uttering not a syllable in return. It was a strangely impressive performance, as was tacitly acknowledged in the campaign of vilification waged against him in the press.

Jiang Qing was equally intransigent. For the former actress, it was her last great starring role and she played it for all it was worth, by turns simpering and haughty, vicious and benign. At one point she was frog-marched from the court by two burly policewomen, to the applause of the invited audience, after a furious exchange with the judges which began when she interrupted an elderly writer, Liao Mosha, as he tearfully recounted how he had been tortured by prison guards in the Cultural Revolution.

'Stop pretending like this,' she said witheringly.

'You're not allowed to speak,' the old man raged back at her.

Her eyes glinting with suppressed fury, Jiang Qing snapped: 'I have the right to defend myself, and the right to expose you!'

When the judge ordered her to be silent, she retorted: 'I've already said it, and what are you going to do about it?' And she continued, almost spitting out the words: 'You call in these traitors, spies and bad elements here as witnesses. Actually, you make me glad . . .'

The court president sounded the bell for order, and as several voices began shouting at once, another judge roared at her that she was continuing to commit crimes. 'What do you mean – crimes?' she began mocking him, to be cut off by a bellow from the bench: 'Take the defendant away!'[2]

Such scenes were shown on Chinese television only after being vetted and approved by Deng Xiaoping himself, and for the first month of the hearings all statements implicating Mao were carefully edited out. The result was totally unreal, Watergate without Nixon, and in the end the pretence could not be sustained. On December 29th, Peking television broadcast excerpts from Jiang Qing's final defence statement which at last brought Mao's role into the open. It had been edited and agonised over by the Politburo for the previous five days, and was balanced by a prosecution statement which sought to blunt her charges and put them into perspective. Even so, it was political dynamite:

> After 1966, I and others . . . always and in all circumstances acted in accordance with the directives of Chairman Mao and the Party Central Committee. This was true up to Chairman Mao's death. I never had a programme of my own: I simply carried out and defended the directives of the Central Committee and Chairman Mao's revolutionary proletarian line . . .
>
> Don't forget, for thirty-eight years [I] was Mao's wife – and that's without counting the years we lived together before we were married! We shared the good and the bad together. In the war years, I was the only woman with Chairman Mao at the front. Where were you hiding then? . . .
>
> [Your] purpose is to make me stink, and through me to make Chairman Mao stink, so as to revise the development of Marxism-Leninism and the immense contributions Chairman Mao made. In vilifying me, you are vilifying him and the hundreds of millions of Chinese who took part in the Great Proletarian Cultural Revolution![3]

The hearing ended, once again, with Jiang Qing being forcibly removed. She told the judges that they were the real 'counter-revolutionaries', and greeted the possibility of execution with defiance: 'Let the monkey king come and bring me some replacement heads!'

The prosecution's response was that Mao's 'errors' were not the same as Jiang Qing's 'crimes', and the one could not justify the other:

> The people . . . are very clear that Chairman Mao was responsible, so far as his leadership was concerned, for their plight during the 'Cultural Revolution' and he was also responsible for failing to see through the Lin Biao and Jiang Qing counter-revolutionary cliques. However, the people . . . will never, for this reason, forget or obliterate Chairman Mao's great contributions.[4]

This was more than had been said in public before. (Deng's remarks on Mao's relationship with Jiang Qing, made to Oriana Fallaci in August, had not been published within China.) But it was not enough to counter Jiang Qing's claim that she and Mao had been acting together. As she had put it in another, unpublished part of her evidence: 'I was Chairman Mao's dog. Whom he told me to bite, I bit. Before you beat a dog, ask who is its master.'

Every thinking Chinese knew that this was no more than the truth. But it was a truth that the leadership could not admit without undermining still further the legitimacy of the Party's rule.

Already that month Hu Yaobang had gone on record as saying that the Cultural Revolution had no redeeming features whatever: 'nothing was correct or positive in those years'.[5] The *People's Daily* had recalled that it had been 'personally launched and led by Chairman Mao', a phrase which until then had been avoided.[6] And another newspaper for the first time came close to acknowledging that Mao had been personally responsible for the persecution of Liu Shaoqi.[7]

To the conservatives in the bureaucracy and the army, all this was playing with fire.

There were other problems, too. The Central Committee split over whether Jiang Qing and Zhang Chunqiao should be executed, and eventually put off a decision by sentencing them to death with a two-year reprieve. Jiang Qing, unrepentant as ever, was taken from the court in handcuffs, shouting, 'To rebel is justified! Making rebellion is no crime!'[8]

However, the trial failed most spectacularly as an attempt to start burying the past and establishing the national consensus on which Deng hoped to base future reform. Instead its revelations of torture and brutality, deceit and political intrigue, opened a can of worms which would have been better left closed. The bitterness it stirred up, coupled with uncertainties generated by Hua's removal, deepened the general malaise that had developed as the crisis of faith in the country became more acute and pervasive.

By the winter of 1980, this failure of popular confidence had become the regime's biggest problem. In part it was due to the unending changes of policy over the previous three decades, the constant alternation of repression and periods of relative licence. 'Change is necessary to bring order out of chaos,' observed the Heilongjiang leader, Yang Yichen. 'But changes may become so frequent that the confidence of the masses is eroded.'[9] The other main cause was the degeneration of the Party. This was frankly admitted by Hu Yaobang in a speech at the beginning of December:

> *The Party's prestige is not high now . . . Without improvement, the Party cannot go on leading.* Our Party . . . has been a ruling party over the last thirty-one years . . . What is the danger to a party after it has assumed power? *The danger is that it will degenerate, if it works carelessly.* (Emphasis added.)[10]

The workstyle of a ruling party, said Vice-Chairman Chen Yun, was 'a matter of life or death'.[11] This was not 'an exaggeration to scare people', added the *People's Daily*; it was a 'timely warning'.[12]

The crux of the problem was the pursuit of privilege and power by Party officials. Mao had tried to deal with it by sending them to 'learn from the masses' and do manual labour in the fields. But that only led to a new elite taking the place of the old.

Deng tried to attack the problem through the Discipline Inspection Commission and by publicly criticising offenders in the press. In theory, no one was exempt from the commission's investigations. But in practice important cases often had a political coloration. In November, three vice-premiers, Yu Qiuli, Gu Mu and Kang Shien, were reprimanded for abusing their positions to obtain more luxurious living quarters than the regulations allowed: all were members of the 'Petroleum Faction'. The previous spring two others who were not in Deng's group, Geng Biao and Chen Muhua, were rejected as prospective members of the Party Secretariat for nepotism and abuses of power.

At the end of 1979, new regulations were issued limiting the perquisites of high officials, and as a warning Peking television screened a film of officials' wives and children using government cars for private shopping expeditions. The press inveighed against 'unhealthy tendencies', and *Guangming Ribao* recalled that at the beginning of the Ming dynasty, 'the corpses of officials beheaded for taking bribes [were] skinned . . . [and] stuffed with straw, and placed beside the desk of the official in charge as a warning to others'. Now, once again, it said, 'such things as the concept of rank and the "special privilege" mentality have become ugly sores in our society.'[13]

One of the most telling incidents occurred in Shanghai, where a twenty-five-year-old peasant named Zhang Longquan pretended to be the son of a deputy chief of staff in order to get a complimentary seat at a play for which all the tickets had been sold. One deception led to another, and by the time he was arrested two months later he had been showered with gifts and money by officials who hoped for reciprocal favours from his supposedly powerful connections; the senior Party secretary at Fudan University had given him the use of his personal car and he had become engaged to the daughter of a wealthy former capitalist.[14] The case was far from unique. One of the great comic novels of this century, *The Twelve Chairs*, by Ilf and Petrov, describes the adventures of a similar confidence trickster in the Soviet Union in the 1920s. Another notorious trickster in China in the 1950s duped Party officials for four years. And in 1979, an elderly Soviet citizen named Zakhar Dvoiris was incarcerated in the psychiatric hospital at Kazan after acquiring a Moscow flat and two country houses by posing variously as a war hero and a Soviet government minister; according to the Soviet press, those who were fooled by him included 'statesmen whose faces are known to the whole nation'. But what made Zhang Longquan's case different was that he retorted to the police who interrogated him: 'If I really were the son of a deputy chief of staff, would any of the things I did be considered a crime?'

Zhang's story was widely reported and even turned into a play. In the words of *Guangming Ribao*, it 'picturesquely and vividly portrayed some of the "manners and mores" of our actual life'.[15]

Such exposés were a double-edged weapon, however. While they helped to keep abuses in check, they offended vast numbers of senior bureaucrats, who saw their own privileges under attack; yet these were the very people on whom Deng had to rely to implement his policies. Struggling against bureaucracy and the pursuit of privilege would be a long-term task, the *People's Daily* said, 'but there is a limit to this struggle; that is, it must not be allowed to hurt the Party's leadership, or interfere with the four modernisations'.[16] Moreover, the more the press exposed corruption and privilege, the more public opinion was sensitised to the subject, until, as *China Youth* reported, just the sight of a person sitting in a big limousine was enough to bring to people's faces a look of 'unspeakable aversion'. The crisis of faith, which the new candour was intended to cure, simply became more profound. Yet whenever the anti-privilege campaign was curbed, abuses flourished anew.

The relative openness of the press also brought other problems. To a largely uneducated population, who for years had been carefully sheltered from news of accidents and disasters, the descriptions of floods and typhoons, mining tragedies and explosions, modest though they were by the standards of the Western media, seemed like auguries of doom. And some reports had an even more direct impact: all through the autumn, the *People's Daily* carried detailed accounts of the unrest in Poland, where the calls for reform were in many respects similar to those being made within the Chinese Party. By November 1980, Chinese workers were also beginning to demand independent trade unions, and strikes and go-slows were being reported from various parts of the country.

Labour unrest never assumed serious proportions. But the collapse of the Polish Communist Party's authority and the emergence of Solidarity as an independent political force were viewed seriously in Peking. Moreover it coincided with a series of incidents which showed dramatically the tensions building up, particularly among Chinese youths.

On October 29th, a young demobilised soldier named Wang Zhigang, who had been made to settle in the provinces instead of returning to his home in the capital, set off four kilos of dynamite at rush hour in the Peking Railway Station, killing himself and ten others, and wounding seventy-nine more, in an act of despair that his demands had been ignored. Six weeks later another rusticated youth poured petrol over his clothes and burnt himself to death outside a park in the embassy quarter. In Xinjiang, starting in April 1980, a number of bloody clashes occurred between Uighurs and Hans.

Difficulties arose with the new election system. In Changsha, in October, 4,000 students marched through the streets and staged a three-day sit-in at the local Party headquarters after the authorities had disqualified one of their colleagues who was running as a non-Marxist candidate for the district people's congress. The next month several students, standing as candidates in the university district of Peking, campaigned for a reversal of the verdict on Wei Jingsheng, creating sufficient controversy for the *Peking Daily* to have to publish a detailed refutation of their arguments.

Crime got out of hand again. In the cities, groups of alienated young toughs hung around on street-corners, waiting for something to happen. In Peking a sixteen-year-old boy was sentenced to death and ten others given prison terms for murdering a bus conductor who had asked them to put out their cigarettes. The police were given greater powers to open fire on suspects, and in Shanghai, *Jiefang Ribao* reported that gangs were 'committing murder, arson, robbery, larceny, organising gambling parties, rape, gang-rape, forcing women into prostitution, organising call-girl clubs and peddling and smoking drugs'.[17]

There was talk of trying to restore Confucian precepts of morality. The Party Central Committee published a letter from a schoolmaster, who wrote: 'We criticised the "humanity, righteousness, courtesy, wisdom and trust" advocated by the Confucianists, but what can we put in their place?'[18] And Xinhua quoted a leading academic as saying that Confucius was 'a great philosopher, political thinker, moralist and educationalist', whose humanitarian doctrines were the 'cultural and spiritual treasures of the Chinese nation'.[19]

Significant numbers of young people turned to religion to find release. I met one former activist in the unofficial democracy movement who had become an acolyte at a Buddhist temple. Youths with greasy hair started turning up at church services, often to the dismay of the clergy who did not know what to make of them. The Bishop of Fuzhou, seventy-seven-year-old Moses Xie, who had once been a curate at Sheffield Cathedral, spoke of the young 'thirsting for something spiritual' which the regime could not give. And the *China Youth News* voiced official concern when it wrote:

> Because their desires and aspirations in work, study, marriage and cultural life cannot be met for the time being, some young people look to religion to lighten their sufferings. Others join religions because they like singing hymns, or because they find it interesting to pray to Buddha. In order to settle this problem, it is necessary to strengthen education and propaganda.[20]

In 1981, there was a craze for wearing crucifixes, and enterprising factory managers, benefiting from the liberal new economic policies, turned them out by the thousand. 'Selling religious objects in the marketplace is extremely injurious ideologically,' grumbled the Party Youth League, in terms almost identical to those used by *Moskovskaya Pravda* when a similar fad had swept the Soviet Komsomol, two years before.[21]

Other alien influences were also deeply controversial: the seemingly irresistible advance of pop music, which was held to 'corrupt young people's minds, sap their willpower and ruin their mental qualities'; and the glamorous image of life in the West, constantly reinforced by the showing of Western films on television and the increasing numbers of Western tourists. There were cases of foreign women seducing room-boys in hotels, and of Chinese girls approaching foreign men and asking to marry them as a means of leaving the country.[22]

The writers, whom at the beginning of 1980 Deng had effectively silenced, began to agitate again for more freedom from Party control. In October, the *People's Daily*, with support from Hu Yaobang and Hu Qiaomu, published a wrenching *cri-de-coeur* from China's most famous film actor, Zhao Dan, who lay dying in hospital of cancer. Written as a last testament, it starkly portrayed the frustration and rage of a creative intelligensia whose endeavours had been stifled for thirty years by the numbing grip of cultural commissars:

> People do not need the Party's leadership to know how to do farmwork, how to make furniture, how to cut a pair of trousers or how to fry vegetables. Nor do writers need the Party's leadership to know how to write or actors to know how to act. Writing is the business of writers, and art the business of artists. If the Party controls literature and art too tightly, there will be no hope. They will be finished . . .
>
> When did the Party ever bestow on a man the ability to write? Who told Karl Marx to write? . . . Why is it that our leaders only feel at ease when literature and art are administered by laymen who know nothing about them? . . .

Should any ideology . . . be rigidly stipulated as the sole guiding principle for literature and art? . . . History . . . shows that they do not prosper if only one stream is maintained while the rest are banned . . . Literature and art are highly individual and cannot be confined within the framework of a system . . .

For myself, I no longer have anything to lose by speaking openly . . . But will my words have any effect?[23]

It was the most uncompromising attack on the Party's interference in the arts since the mid-1950s, when Hu Feng was purged after similar demands for literary freedom – and, as though to underline the parallel, shortly after Zhao Dan died Hu was discreetly rehabilitated.

All these elements – the growing disaffection of the army and the bureaucracy, the widespread loss of confidence in the system, the collapse of the Party's prestige, the alienation and rising tensions among the young, the discontent of the intellectuals – 'factors of upheaval', as one newspaper called them, coincided with an abrupt deterioration in the state of the economy.

When the NPC met at the end of August 1980, the leadership seemed convinced that despite a budget deficit of seventeen billion yuan (£5.1 billion) in 1979 and a projected deficit of twelve billion yuan for the current year, and despite an admitted inflation rate of six per cent – and more than twice that much in the cities – no change of course would be necessary: the readjustment programme was on target. But within a month of the parliamentary session ending, that assessment was drastically revised. This was officially explained as a consequence of flooding in the Yangtse valley, which, coupled with drought further north, reduced the grain harvest by seventeen million tons, and left fourteen million people living on relief. As one leading Chinese economist wrote, the strains that resulted 'revealed more clearly the long-standing disproportions in the economy', and made people realise that unless they were tackled in earnest, 'all future economic growth would be jeopardised'.[24] Another factor, however, was the campaign against Hua: now that he no longer had power, the failure of economic policy, like the Party's failure to win popular trust, was a stick to beat him with.

Nonetheless, the problems exposed at the end of 1980 were real enough. The decision, announced eighteen months earlier, to cut down capital investment, had been successfully resisted by the local authorities charged with carrying it out. In 1979, 3,000 old factories had been closed or merged, but 9,000 new ones had opened. The following year, centrally allocated funds for capital construction were cut by a third, but funds raised by the local authorities more than doubled – with the result that in 1980 more new factories were being built than before the readjustment programme started, and the shortage of energy and raw materials, instead of diminishing, became still more acute.[25] The situation was exacerbated by moves to give the localities and individual enterprises greater autonomy. Because tobacco-growing provinces wanted more profit from their crop, they started building their own small factories producing low-grade cigarettes. As a result, in 1980 the big processing factories in Shanghai, making high-grade cigarettes, received only half the tobacco they needed. There were similar problems with silk and cotton. 'Small enterprises squeeze out large ones, the backward squeeze out the advanced,' one provincial radio station complained.[26]

In a capitalist country, price competition would eliminate the less efficient producers until supply and demand were back in balance. In China, price controls prevent that happening. 'Here the state will foot the bill for the losses,' the economist, Xue Muqiao, commented sourly, 'so we go on maintaining them all.'[27]

The bonus system was also in trouble. Managers schooled in Maoist egalitarianism rewarded all their workers indiscriminately. From being an incentive to work harder, a bonus became a precondition for doing any work at all. The trade union newspaper, *Gongren Ribao*, quoted one group of factory workers in Peking as saying: 'If there are more bonuses we shall work more, if there are less bonuses we shall work less; and if there are none we shall be idle.'[28] Not only did this create tremendous waste – some two billion yuan (£670 million) was estimated to have been paid out needlessly in 1979, and four billion yuan in 1980 – but bonuses ceased to have any effect on productivity.[29]

To maximise the amount of profit available for distribution to the workforce, some enterprises kept back money which should have been surrendered to the state, widening the budget deficit. Inflation cantered on alarmingly. In November 1979, to offset the higher prices paid to peasants for their produce, most food prices rose by twenty-five per cent. The increase was partly compensated by a five yuan (£1.50) a month cost of living allowance, but it was paid only to workers in state enterprises. 'We know this kind of thing happens in your country,' one disgruntled Chinese told me, 'but why should it happen here, under socialism?'

The rise in food prices was the signal for almost everything else to go up, usually without authorisation and often on the flimsiest pretext. A textile factory, producing towels with a design of a tiger going up a mountain, priced at six yuan (£1.80) each, reversed the image, so that the tiger was shown coming down the mountain, and marked the price up to nine yuan on the grounds that it was a new model. 'The masses are very annoyed,' reported the *People's Daily*. 'They say: "Whenever the tiger turns round, we have to pay three yuan more."' A month later the newspaper announced that its own price was to double.

Nothing and nobody were exempt. At country fairs, bicycles with well-known brand names were offered for sale, which on closer examination turned out to have frames made from bamboo and tyres stuffed with straw. Chinese television viewers suddenly found there were no new films to watch: despite the small number of sets and the paucity of entertainment material, the distributors insisted on a long run at the cinemas first in order to increase their revenue. Schools turned away children whose parents were too poor to pay the fees. Tourists, smarting from hidden surcharges, went home talking of 'the Great Chinese Rip-off', and at Peking's Friendship Store, Christmas trees for sale to foreign residents were priced at £60 each.

A booklet, entitled *Why there is no Inflation in China*, was discreetly withdrawn from the bookshops. 'Nowadays money is everything here,' a Chinese journalist sighed.

To the Chinese leaders, the common thread running through all these problems – the refusal to cut down capital construction, blind duplication of profitable enterprises, indiscriminate issuing of bonuses and arbitrary price rises – was indiscipline, and the putting of private interests before the overall interests of the country. It was a reflection in the economy of the same factors that were causing social unrest and the ideological crisis of faith. Nor was it limited to industry. Even in the countryside, where in general the new policies were succeeding, cases were coming to light of communes trying to reduce the area sown to grain in favour of more profitable crops.

One answer to these problems would have been to speed up the economic reform, allowing greater play to the remorseless discipline of supply and demand. Deng and Zhao Ziyang seemed to recognise that if the reforms were to succeed, that was the direction they must eventually take. But the late autumn of 1980, in the middle of a change of Party Chairman and with pressure growing from the army and the bureaucracy for tighter central controls, was not the moment for such a step.

Instead, Deng decided that the reforms must mark time while a rigorous programme was carried out to halt inflation, balance the budget and effect the retrenchment agreed the previous year but never implemented. The rationale, according to Deng's supporters, was that

only after the disproportions in the economy have been readjusted can the production units have the external conditions (such as supplies of energy and

442

raw materials) for enlarging their autonomy. And only then will the way be open for reforming the economic system as a whole.[30]

On December 16th, three weeks after the Politburo accepted Hua's resignation and designated Hu Yaobang to succeed him, the Central Committee gathered in Peking for a ten-day work conference, to hear a stark warning from Vice-Chairman Chen Yun that the country was once again on the brink of an economic precipice. It was necessary to retreat, he said, and this retreat must be 'sufficient to allow us to regain the initiative': development must be cut back to 'a level commensurate with our national financial and material strength'. 'It is better to suffer real pain for one year,' Chen told the conference, 'than to be sick for five.'[31]

The repercussions of this approach were dramatic. The 1981 capital construction budget was slashed from fifty to thirty billion yuan (£16.5 to £9 billion), and the responsible minister, Gu Mu of the 'Petroleum Faction', replaced. Up to 10 million workers were to be laid off, partly as a consequence of the cut-back, and partly because of closures of old, uneconomic plants. All new projects required the approval of a special commission, headed by Wan Li, the former Anhui Party leader, who was now appointed standing vice-premier in charge of the day-to-day work of the government. Instead of ending in 1982, readjustment was to continue at least until 1985, and was declared the 'main objective' of the sixth Five Year Plan, which was then under preparation. Efforts to restrain the growth of heavy industry were intensified, and in the first six months of 1981, output fell by 8.3 per cent, though steel production, and consequently the consumption of coal and electricity, remained obstinately higher than planned. For the second time, China announced it was unilaterally suspending 2.5 billion yuan (£750 million) of contracts with Japan and West Germany, but, unlike in 1979, this time it was in earnest and negotiations for compensation began. Local authorities and factories with surplus funds were required to subscribe to a 5 billion yuan (£1,500 million) treasury bond issue, the first since the 1950s, to reduce the currency in circulation and bring back to the national treasury some of the money scattered in the provinces as a result of greater financial autonomy. Credit and price controls were tightened, and price ceilings imposed on many goods sold at free markets.

1981, The Year of the Cock, should be a year of an iron cock – the traditional Chinese expression for a niggard – the *People's Daily* said, because 'from an iron cock, no feather can be plucked'.[32] The prospect was of hard grind, as the country tried to disencumber itself, in the words of Yao Yilin, the new head of the State Planning Commission, from 'the age-old malady of trying to get quick results'.[33]

Given the pressure to enforce austerity, a more repressive political climate was inevitable. To lay off millions of workers and cut back the bonuses of the rest in a country where fifteen per cent of the urban workforce was already unemployed, and inflation had just wiped out the benefits of the first sizeable wage rise most city dwellers had had for twenty years, was a risky undertaking, and Deng acknowledged the following summer that he had expected disorders – although in the event they did not come.[34] The situation was made more tense by the rifts in the political leadership, ideological uncertainty and existing social unrest, reflected in incidents such as the explosion at the Peking Railway Station and the racial clashes in Xinjiang.

All these elements combined to produce the most comprehensive and sustained political clampdown China had seen since Mao's death.

It was unveiled by Deng when he addressed the Central Committee on December 25th, 1980:[35]

The four basic principles [(of Party leadership, proletarian dictatorship, Mao Zedong Thought and the socialist road)] *have not been propagated actively, justly, forcefully and convincingly, and seriously mistaken ideas opposed to the four basic principles have not been effectively struggled against* . . . What is particularly serious is that in the Party press and also in Party life, very few people have boldly stepped out to wage serious ideological struggle . . . even against certain viewpoints *brazenly opposed to Party leadership and socialism. Certain figures connected with illegal organisations have been particularly active lately, publishing unbridled anti-Party and anti-socialist utterances under all kinds of pretexts. This danger signal should arouse the full vigilance of the whole Party and people* . . .

At the same time, *the tendency to worship capitalism and advocate bourgeois liberalisation, the rotten bourgeois ideology* of harming others to benefit oneself, being bent solely on profit and putting money above everything else, anarchism and out-and-out egoism, *must all be opposed and repudiated.* We should continue to associate with Western countries that are friendly to us . . . *but the above-mentioned struggles in the ideological and political fields must be carried through to the end* . . .

It has been found that in some places *a tiny handful of people who desire to see the world plunged into chaos are using the methods of the Cultural Revolution to instigate trouble. Some are even going so far as to clamour for a second 'Cultural Revolution'.* In some places, educated youths are making trouble. Illegal organisations and publications . . . are . . . *openly expressing anti-Party, anti-socialist views, distributing counter-revolutionary leaflets, spreading political rumours and so on.* The activities of the remnants of the 'Gang of Four', murder, arson, the planting of time-bombs, theft and robbery, rape, gang-rape, the abduction and sale of women, organised prostitution, smuggling and tax evasion, speculation, profiteering, bribery, graft and corruption, drug trafficking and other crimes are growing and running wild. Disclosing and selling state secrets, the reckless issuing of bonuses, the arbitrary raising of prices and other illegal activities are also occurring from time to time. *We must not treat these things lightly . . .*

The state machinery of the people's democratic dictatorship must be strengthened. All these forces sabotaging stability and unity must be resolutely smashed to disintegration. . . . *We must resolutely crack down and strike blows at all kinds of criminal activity.* . . . If these activities are not frustrated, they will threaten not only the economic readjustment but the people's democratic rights and *even their very existence* (Emphasis added.)

This was strong meat, even by the standards of Chinese political rhetoric. And though Deng emphasised that the crackdown should be carried out using 'the weapon of law' rather than 'the old [Maoist] method of launching political movements', he expressed himself in singularly uncompromising terms. New legislation must be enacted, he said, to control strikes and demonstrations, and if serious disturbances occurred, the local authorities could proclaim martial law.

In part, it was a scare tactic. At a time of grave social, political and economic uncertainty, Deng was warning the Party that unless it united behind him, the country risked sliding back into anarchy. 'Without Party leadership,' he said, 'China will go to pieces': but if Party leadership were to be maintained, it had to be improved – by cutting out the cancer of leftism and replacing the left-leaning Chairman Hua. On both issues, the Central Committee, most of whose members had been elected in 1977 when Hua's power was at its height, held more conservative views than the Politburo, where Deng's supporters were in the majority, and the work conference did not discuss Hua's position directly: the Committee was merely informed of the Politburo's decision. But Hua was attacked indirectly for failing to unify the thinking of the Party, and for continuing left-deviationist economic policies for the first two years after Mao died.

The economic failure was a two-edged weapon, however, and while Deng told the conference that Hua bore the main responsibility for it, he felt it necessary to acknowledge that 'part of the responsibility lies also with me'. For Deng was not beyond criticism himself. Much as he might insist that it was not his policies that were at fault, but shortcomings in carrying them out, his opponents could fairly reply that it was only since the Third Plenum in December 1978, when he emerged as the dominant figure in the leadership, that the problems had started coming to light.

For these reasons, as well as to buy support for the two measures he regarded as crucial – the repudiation of Hua and of the leftist policies he symbolised – Deng deliberately set out to appease the conservatives in the Central Committee by making concessions on almost everything else.

Here was the political retreat to match the economic retreat Chen Yun had demanded. Political reform would in future be carried out more cautiously, Deng said. Veteran officials would not be asked to retire until their successors had proved themselves in their new posts. More care would be exercised in exposing abuses of privilege in.the press 'to avoid giving the masses a false impression' that there was a 'bureaucratic class' within the Party. Hua's supporters were given assurances that they would not be victimised:[36]

> Historical problems should be dealt with in outline. *There is no need to go into details* . . . We must guide everyone to look ahead. *We must not rummage through all the old scores of the past in the revolutionary ranks.* If we do, it will cause confusion, and will not benefit stability and unity. (Emphasis added.)

Deng sympathised with the conservatives' outrage at the publication of Zhao Dan's testament – 'a counter-revolutionary document', some Central Committee members called it. He emphasised the need for a positive approach to Mao, and declared that old revolutionary slogans, such as 'Fear neither hardship nor death!', which to the fury of the orthodox had been criticised by followers of Hu Yaobang, were 'the chief pillar of our spiritual civilisation':[37]

> Instead of being effectively boycotted this ridiculous 'criticism' of solemn revolutionary slogans has even had some sympathy and support from people within our own ranks. Can any Party member who has a scrap of Party and revolutionary spirit tolerate this state of affairs any more?

Deng's campaign of blandishments to win round the hard-liners later became still more blatant. To appease the army, he reinstated his old opponent, Chen Xilian, the former Commander of the Peking Military Region, as a Standing Committee member of the Military Commission. In February 1981, Hu Yaobang bought off another long-time adversary, the Shandong leader, Bai Rubing, by publicly declaring that Bai's province was one of the best-run in the country.[38] And plans to purge the Party of dead wood by making all members re-apply for their Party cards were postponed as being too disruptive.[39]

However, the crackdown that began at the end of 1980 was not simply a matter of 'Deng putting on Hua's clothes to win over Hua's support- ers', as a Yugoslav diplomat put it. Even without conservative pressure, Deng had become convinced that strong measures were needed to overcome the crisis of morale, both within the Party and outside it. 'We must strengthen our own confidence first,' he said. 'Then we will be able to unite with the masses and strengthen their confidence.' Like the clampdown that ended the Peking Spring and the wave of repression that followed it, so, too, this 'third cold wind', as Chinese intellectuals called it, was fundamentally of Deng's own making.

Throughout 1981, economic austerity, a tightening of political controls and conciliation of the conservatives ran in parallel. One night in April, police went to the homes of Xu Wenli and Yang Jing, of the *April 5th Tribune*, and took them away in handcuffs. Ten days later, Wang Xizhe, of the group which had written the Li Yizhe poster in Canton in 1974, was arrested on his way to work. All three were accused of 'counter-revolutionary activities'. By August, at least thirty former members of the unofficial democracy movement had been detained, including Lu Lin of *Tansuo*.

Large numbers of criminals were executed. In one two-month period in the summer, eighty-seven men and women were shot for rape or murder, some within a week of arrest. Legal safeguards, introduced eighteen months earlier, requiring death sentences to be approved by the Supreme Court, were temporarily suspended until 1983, and a new law was passed banning repeat offenders from ever returning to their homes in the cities; instead, after serving their sentences, they had to remain at the camps as 'free workers' for the rest of their lives.

The trials of Mao's nephew, Mao Yuanxin, and others linked with the 'Gang of Four', which were to have begun in February 1981, were indefinitely postponed. Political study became obligatory again, and officials, up to and including the rank of minister, were required to spend several days a month doing manual labour, as had been the practice in Mao's day. Two of Jiang Qing's model operas were revived. The educational reforms in particular the streaming of classes and the setting-up of key schools for the academically gifted, were criticised and in some provinces reversed. The press was muzzled and became steadily duller, and a pro-communist newspaper in Hong Kong, which persisted in publishing embarrassingly well-informed accounts of the in-fighting in the leadership, was closed down altogether.

Contacts between Chinese and foreigners were once more actively discouraged, and it became so difficult for mixed couples to obtain permission to marry that one foreign student and his Chinese girlfriend committed suicide. In September 1981, the Chinese fiancée of a French diplomat was arrested and sent to a labour camp for two years *pour encourager les autres*, and Western correspondents were warned by Foreign Ministry officials that meetings with 'Chinese dissidents' were 'beyond the limits of normal news coverage'. The nude figures in the mural at Peking airport, ever a barometer of political change, were covered up again, this time with wooden panels nailed permanently into the wall.

The reform programme did not come to a complete halt: discussion continued over plans to abolish the communes, to improve the system of material incentives in industry by making more use of piecework rates, and to restore the post of Head of State.[40] But Deng's prime objective in 1981 – apart from completing the transfer of power from Hua to Hu Yaobang – was to bring about change in the army.

The Party's job was to make policy, he argued; the army's job was to carry it out. In January, the regional commands were warned that any questioning of Party policy would be treated as a breach of military discipline. Every soldier was required to take an oath to 'implement unswervingly the Party's policies, principles and line', and in March the Military Commission issued a directive for military parades to be revived, for the first time since the early 1960s, to 'strengthen military training . . . raise morale and improve discipline'.[41] Six months later the entire Politburo turned out to watch 100,000 troops, with armour and air support, carrying out the biggest peacetime military manoeuvres held in China since 1949.

If the criticism of leftism was Deng's stick in his dealings with the army, the war games and parades were the carrot. But the military were not so easily won over. When the ailing Marshal Xu Xiangqian retired as Defence Minister, they rejected Deng's candidate to replace him, the reformist vice-premier Zhang Aiping, and forced a compromise appointment in the person of Geng Biao. Later Deng was able to get a veteran supporter, Yang Shangkun, appointed Secretary-General of the Military Commission, but resistance to his policies continued. At the beginning of 1982, even so basic a proposal as the introduction of new uniforms and badges of rank, which had been under discussion for three years, remained firmly blocked.

The strained relations between Deng and the army conservatives, and his lack of success in winning them over, were thrown into relief by a simmering dispute over the film *Bitter Love*, made by the army poet, Bai Hua, which became a political *cause célèbre* lasting the entire year.

Bitter Love was not the most controversial of the works appearing at the end of 1980; that distinction belonged to an extraordinary, pacifist poem, entitled 'Generals and Soldiers', which by some freak of censorship was published in one of the army's own journals:[42]

> Generals wear medals,
> Tablets recording their merits are erected beside their tombs.
> The bloodstained bones of soldiers rot in the soil
> and have long since been forgotten . . .

Bai Hua's theme was more modest; indeed, when his script first came out it attracted no attention at all. It described the persecution of a Chinese painter who gave up a successful career in America to return home, only to starve to death, hiding in the countryside one winter after being attacked by Red Guards.

But Bai Hua had the backing of Hu Yaobang. To the military diehards, criticising *Bitter Love* was a way of criticising Hu and the liberal reformist policies he stood for – and after Deng had seen the film in December and commented that it 'had problems', they seized the opportunity with both hands. A group of senior generals demanded Bai's expulsion from the Party, and in April 1981 the *Liberation Army Daily* went for the film with a sledgehammer:

> The sentiment [the author] expresses is . . . resentment against our Party and socialist motherland . . . In America, there is brilliant sunshine throughout the land. In the socialist motherland, there is nothing but darkness. *Bitter Love* uses sharp contrasts to express clearly . . . [its] theme: New China is inferior to old China; the Communist Party is inferior to the Guomindang; socialism is inferior to capitalism; the socialist motherland not only has nothing worth loving, but is abominable and hateful . . .
>
> The eccentric sentiments permeating *Bitter Love* have harmed our Chinese people's spirit of patriotism and national self-confidence and are detrimental to stability and unity . . . [They] vilify the Party's leadership and the political power of the state.[43]

This was the first time since Mao's death, nearly five years earlier, that a writer had been publicly denounced, and many intellectuals feared it signalled a return to Maoist methods. Next day, however, Zhou Yang replied that writers who made mistakes 'should not be rashly and thoughtlessly labelled anti-Party or anti-socialist', and *Red Flag*, in a further rebuke to the army, said criticisms should be comradely and cautious and 'attention should be paid to their accuracy'.[44] Students in Peking and Shanghai held meetings to express support for Bai, and by June the controversy seemed over. No one need fear 'another anti-rightist campaign', Zhou Yang reassured the writers. 'The Party will not revert to the old practice.'

But the army was not reconciled to its defeat,[45] and later that month, during another Central Committee work conference on the eve of the Sixth Plenum, the Director of the PLA General Political Department, Wei Guoqing, publicly spelled out the conservatives' view:

> What we must negate are the ultra-leftist things of Lin Biao and the 'Gang of Four' which destroyed the correct principles of political work. *We are not*

trying to negate those correct principles themselves. Do not throw the baby out with the bathwater! (Emphasis added.)[46]

Not long after this, Deng decided that the campaign against Bai Hua should continue and that Hu Yaobang must be seen to support it. 'Hu is sincere, but he's a politician,' one of Bai's friends had told me months earlier. 'If he has to sacrifice Bai, he will.' In the event it did not come to that: Bai was able to continue writing. But Hu declared that *Bitter Love* represented 'a wrong tendency', and Deng, in a further concession to the conservatives, said the Party's ideological leadership had become so lax that 'erroneous tendencies cannot be criticised, and when they are it is called using a big stick'.[47] Throughout the autumn and winter of 1981, the press attacked 'bourgeois liberalism' and linked it to the crisis of faith.[48]

Decent Burial

The Sixth Plenum, at which Hu's appointment as Chairman was formally confirmed, was originally to have been held in February or March 1981. It was delayed, not because of differences over policy, nor even because of difficulties over Hua: by February his last real ally, Ye Jianying, had publicly acquiesced in his removal,[1] and though rumours continued to circulate that Hua was refusing to cooperate, he was in no position to resist.

The reason for the postponement was the same 'Resolution on Certain Questions of Party History' that had triggered Hua's downfall in the first place. At the work conference in December 1980, Deng reassured the conservatives that it would take a positive view of Mao and would draw a clear distinction between Mao Zedong Thought, which was affirmed as China's guiding ideology, and 'the ideas of Mao's later years'. He went on to explain the guidelines under which it was being drafted:

> The great achievements made in the past thirty-one years must be fully affirmed. Shortcomings and mistakes should be criticised seriously, but *it is not permitted to give an overall picture of utter failure*. Even serious mistakes, like the Cultural Revolution, are not to be considered as counter-revolutionary . . .
>
> Comrade Mao Zedong's merits come first, and his mistakes are secondary . . . His mistakes must not be attributed to his individual character . . . *If we are swayed by our emotions and exaggerate his mistakes, we will* only harm the image of the state, *jeopardise the prestige of the Party* and of socialism *and undermine the unity of the Party, the army and the people.* (Emphasis added.)[2]

By early April 1981 broad agreement had been reached on what the resolution should say, and articles began appearing in the press to prepare public opinion for it. The plenum finally took place from June 27th to 29th, timed to coincide with the Party's sixtieth anniversary to underline its importance as a watershed between one period and the next.

Not surprisingly for a document founded on a political compromise and elaborated through eighteen months of committees, the resolution turned out to be an odd mixture of criticism and exculpation, frequently inconsistent and highly defensive in tone.[3] Much of its scope and content had been anticipated by Wang Ruoshui's 'secret speech' in February 1979, and Deng's comments to Oriana Fallaci in August 1980 and to the Central Committee work conference in December. But it was one thing to have these views discussed within the Party and for a few phrases to be quoted selectively in the press, and quite another to present them publicly as a definitive assessment of the Party's achievements over thirty years – and thus its justification for continuing to rule.

The most striking sections dealt with the Cultural Revolution and with Mao's personal failings as a ruler:

The Cultural Revolution, which lasted from May 1966 to October 1976, was responsible for *the most severe setback and the heaviest losses suffered by the Party since the founding of the People's Republic.* It was initiated and led by Comrade Mao Zedong . . . The erroneous 'left' theses on which he based himself . . . conformed neither to Marxism-Leninism nor to Chinese reality. They represent an entirely erroneous appraisal of the prevailing class relations and political situation in the Party and state . . .

The Cultural Revolution did not in fact constitute a revolution or social progress in any sense, nor could it possibly have done so. [It] . . . brought catastrophe to the Party, the state and the whole people. (Emphasis added.)

Unlike the 'preliminary assessment', pronounced by Ye Jianying in September 1979, the resolution explicitly blamed Mao for launching the Great Leap Forward and the commune movement in 1958 'without careful investigation and study', and condemned his purge of Peng Dehuai in 1959 and the subsequent campaign against 'right opportunism' as being 'entirely wrong'. It accused him of 'widening and absolutising' class struggle in the early 1960s, and of becoming 'smug . . . and impatient for quick results':

Comrade Mao Zedong's prestige reached a peak, and he began to get arrogant . . . He gradually divorced himself from practice and from the masses, acted more and more arbitrarily and subjectively, and increasingly put himself above the Central Committee of the Party.

The resolution hinted at Mao's attacks on Zhou Enlai, and for the first time acknowledged that it had been Mao, not the 'Gang of Four', who had ousted Deng in 1976:

Comrade Mao Zedong could not bear to accept systematic correction of the errors of the Cultural Revolution by Comrade Deng Xiaoping, and triggered the movement to criticise [him] . . . once again plunging the nation into turmoil.

Yet the criticisms were more than offset by the omissions and excuses with which they were hedged about. Despite his errors, Mao was 'the great leader of the Party and the people', without whom China would have had 'to grope in the dark for much longer', and Mao Zedong Thought, now redefined as 'Marxism-Leninism applied and developed in China', was still to be upheld as 'the valuable spiritual asset of our Party [and] our guide to action for a long time to come'.

No reference at all was made to the purges of Mao's early career, or to the campaigns against the film, *The Life of Wu Xun*, in 1954,[4] and against Hu Feng a year later, even though they were already discredited, and it had been officially admitted that Hu Feng's supposed 'counter-revolutionary clique' never in fact existed.[5]

Mao's 'errors', according to the resolution, dated only from 1955. Thereafter his personal responsibility was acknowledged in principle, but in practice masked in euphemisms and evasions. The Cultural Revolution, in which one million people perished, was referred to as a 'blunder', committed by 'a leader labouring under a misapprehension'. The death of Liu Shaoqi, which was entirely of Mao's making, was dismissed blandly as 'nothing but a frame-up by Lin Biao, Jiang Qing and their followers'. The Great Leap Forward was acknowledged to have caused 'serious losses', but the fact that 20 million people had died was passed over in silence.

While the resolution accepted that Mao bore the 'chief responsibility' for all that had taken place under his leadership, it argued that 'we cannot lay the blame on him alone': his fellow leaders were also at fault, for acquiescing in what he did.[6] And, in what was clearly the central thought of the whole document, it declared that his error 'was, after all, the error of a great proletarian revolutionary', implying that it was therefore excusable. It continued:

> He imagined that his theory and practice were . . . essential for the consolidation of the dictatorship of the proletariat. *Herein lies his tragedy.* (Emphasis added.)

The formulation is almost identical to that used by Khrushchev, in the Secret Speech twenty-five years earlier, when after enumerating Stalin's crimes he said:

> Stalin was convinced that this was necessary for the defence of the interests of the working class . . . [and] the revolution's gains. *In this lies the whole tragedy.* (Emphasis added.)

Ever since 1978, Deng had gone out of his way to avoid any suggestion that he was treating Mao as Khrushchev had treated Stalin, and it is inconceivable that the resolution consciously echoed Khrushchev's words. Rather, the fact that the two countries' explanations of their former leaders' actions coincide so precisely on this point underlines the similarity of the historical processes each has undergone.

There were other parallels with the Soviet experience too. In an attempt to mitigate the indictment against Mao, the resolution said that during the Cultural Revolution, 'our Party was not destroyed . . . The State Council and the PLA were still able to do much of their essential work . . . The foundation of China's socialist system remained intact.' Analogous arguments were used in the Soviet Union about Stalin, and received a devastating answer from Roy Medvedev in his book, *Let History Judge*:[7]

> For thirty years, he was at the helm of the ship of state, clutching the wheel with a grip of death. Dozens of times he steered it on to reefs and shoals and far off course. Shall we be grateful to him that he did not sink it altogether?

In one respect, however, the Chinese resolution went well beyond anything the Russians had said. In 1980, *Guangming Ribao* had praised the view of the late President Tito, which Mao had always fiercely rejected, that it was not merely Stalin who was at fault but the system which had allowed him to act as he did.[8] The resolution took up this point and elaborated on it. As well as Mao's subjective errors, it said, the Cultural Revolution had 'complex social and historical causes':

> Feudalism in China has had a very long history . . . It remains difficult to eliminate the evil ideological and political influence of centuries of feudal autocracy. And for various historical reasons, we had failed to institutionalise and legalise inner-Party democracy and democracy in the political and social life of the country.

Nevertheless, taken as a whole, the resolution was not very convincing. On the one hand it proclaimed that the thirty-two years since 1949 were 'generally speaking' years in which the Party had 'very successfully led the people'. On the other, it described one of those decades as a catastrophe, and a second and part of a third as a period of 'serious faults and errors'. Where, then, were the successes?

The Chinese leaders themselves recognised this credibility problem. The Party journal, *Liaowang*, said the resolution had been expanded to include events before 1949 'in order to convince people that Mao Zedong's contributions are primary and his faults secondary'; the record after 1949, it implied, was so black that it could not stand on its own.[9] And this was so despite the fact that the resolution avoided altogether the issues which were most damaging to Mao's image, such as his relations with the 'Gang of Four'.

One reason for the resolution's inconsistencies was the need, as Deng put it, to avoid 'undermining the unity of the Party':[10] by the summer of 1981 it was clear that a majority of the Central Committee strongly opposed any further erosion of Mao's status.

The other was the fear of the void. 'Just imagine,' wrote the veteran General Huang Kecheng, two months before the resolution was passed, 'what would take the place of Mao Zedong Thought if it were abandoned?':

> We must have an ideological weapon to guide our great Party and our vast country . . . If Mao Zedong Thought were discarded, there would be ideological chaos in the Party and in people's minds. Our socialist state would probably change its nature and future generations would suffer . . . We Chinese communists have fostered our own noble ideas and beliefs in the course of long struggle . . . *We should not destroy our own beliefs*. (Emphasis added.)[11]

Mao's image had to be preserved, because there was nothing to fill the vacuum that repudiating him would leave. 'In a nutshell,' said the *People's Daily*,

> all we have been doing between the Third and the Sixth Plenums has been to carry out those things that Comrade Mao Zedong proposed but did not do; to do those things which he erroneously opposed; to correct what he did wrong; and to try to do well what he failed to do.[12]

While the resolution's primary task was said to be 'to uphold Mao Zedong Thought',[13] it also served other, in some ways no less important, purposes: it affirmed at the most authoritative level the leadership's continuing commitment to political and economic reform, and it wrote into Party history the end of the career of Chairman Hua:

> In his capacity as Chairman, Comrade Hua Guofeng continued to commit 'left' errors in guiding ideology. On the proposal of Comrade Mao Zedong, *he had become First Vice-Chairman of the Party and premier during the 'movement to criticise Deng Xiaoping' in 1976*. He contributed to the struggle to overthrow the counter-revolutionary Jiang Qing clique and did useful work after that. *But he promoted the erroneous 'Two Whatevers' policy . . . and took a long time to rectify the error*.
>
> He tried to suppress the discussions on the criterion of truth . . . He

procastinated and obstructed the work of reinstating veteran cadres . . . and redressing injustices left over from the past (including the case of the 'Tian An Men Incident' of 1976). He accepted and fostered a personality cult around himself while continuing the personality cult of the past . . .

The Eleventh Party Congress in August 1977 . . . owing to the limitations imposed by the historical conditions at that time and to the influence of Comrade Hua Guofeng's mistakes, reaffirmed the erroneous theories, policies and slogans of the Cultural Revolution instead of correcting them.

He also had his share of responsibility for impetuously seeking quick results in economic work, and for continuing certain other 'left' policies. *Obviously, under his leadership, it is impossible to correct 'left' errors within the Party, and all the more impossible to restore the Party's fine traditions.* (Emphasis added.)

For a man who, despite his uninspiring manner, had presided with considerable skill over a period of extraordinary change, it was a sorry epitaph. But politics has little place for fair play: no one was about to remind Deng that he, too, had paid lip-service to the Cultural Revolution in his day. In the weeks that followed Hua was likened to Lin Biao, and accused by innuendo of having tried to keep Deng out of office in 1977.[14] Like Wu De and Chen Yonggui before him, he continued to make token appearances in his new role as junior vice-chairman, but politically he was a broken man.

Besides formalising the appointments of Hu Yaobang as Chairman and Deng as head of the Military Commission, the Sixth Plenum promoted Zhao Ziyang to be a vice-chairman, ranking fourth in the hierarchy after Hu, Ye and Deng, and appointed Xi Zhongxun, a veteran official who had been close to Hu before the Cultural Revolution, to take over the routine work of the Secretariat.

If the Third Plenum and the suppression of the Peking Spring marked the end of the era of Mao, the Sixth Plenum was an attempt to give it decent burial; and for all the ambiguities of the resolution, it did so in strikingly symmetrical fashion. The policies Mao had promoted in the last twenty years of his life were condemned, and the man he had chosen to continue them after his death was deposed. Deng's policies were endorsed and the men he wanted to succeed him were placed in power.

On July 1st, the new leadership was symbolically presented to the country at a rally in the Great Hall of the People to mark the Party's sixtieth anniversary. Zhao Ziyang presided and Hu made his maiden speech as Chairman, while Deng, six weeks short of his seventy-seventh birthday, sat chain-smoking between them with the rest of the leadership, including a glum-looking Vice-Chairman Hua, ranged on either side.

The speech itself was non-controversial. While calling for more democracy and the appointment of younger men to senior posts, Hu praised Mao as 'the greatest national hero in Chinese history':[15] in this, as in much else during his first six months as Chairman, he was deliberately attempting to play down his liberal image and broaden his political base.

But what it lacked in content, it made up for in style. Chairman Hu exuded charisma and forcefulness, and a vigour that belied his sixty-six years. A tiny figure, sitting on a cushion to disguise his shortness, he harangued his audience for nearly two hours, gesturing and pounding the table with the explosive energy of a bundle of dynamite. Not everyone approved. A Hong Kong newspaper wrote afterwards that he had behaved 'like a thermo-nuclear power station'. But no one who watched was left in doubt that a new chapter in China was beginning.

Whoever rules in Peking, and whatever policies are followed, the problems to be faced are so vast as almost to defy solution.

China's 1,000 million people have an average age of twenty-six.[16] Even if population targets are met and one-child families become the norm, the Chinese government estimates that by the end of the century there will be 'more than 100 million surplus labourers in the countryside . . . and tens of millions of unemployed youths in the cities'.[17] The dangers inherent in those figures are well understood. 'Evil winds tend to spread easily when . . . the problem of unemployment cannot be solved,' wrote the *People's Daily* in 1979. 'This is an important factor leading to crime . . . and social unrest.'[18]

To the extent that population growth exceeds the target, unemployment and its attendant ills will be that much more severe. So will the problem of food.

Nine-tenths of China's land area is desert, mountain or grassland. It has to feed nearly a quarter of the world's people on seven per cent of the world's arable land. But the amount of land under cultivation is constantly decreasing as the villages and towns expand to house the extra population. Despite a vigorous land reclamation programme, the area under cultivation fell from 111 million hectares in 1957 to 99 million two decades later. The projected 100 million surplus agricultural labourers cannot be sent to open up new land, because there is none: in most areas, everything that can be reclaimed has been. The government talks of building more small towns to absorb the rural unemployed. But that will encroach still further on the meagre stock of cultivable land. 'Even if all the wasteland that is left is reclaimed,' said the journal, *Economic Management*, in 1980, 'it is doubtful that even the present level of per capita cultivated land can be maintained.'[19] Not is is just a matter of land. In Peking, the water-table has fallen sixty-five feet since 1957, and continues to fall at the rate of three feet a year because so much water is being drawn off for irrigation and industry.[20] Similar problems have occurred in other cities and in some rural areas.

The seriousness of these demographic factors cannot be overstated: in the short term, even assuming that large-scale unrest does not occur, they make economic development infinitely more difficult, and in the long term, the imbalance between population and resources can only be corrected if, for the next two generations, half of all Chinese parents abandon deeply-ingrained traditions and consent to raise families without sons.

Against this unpromising background, Chairman Hu and Premier Zhao have the task of leading China for the rest of this decade.

Hu, like Mao, is a man of broad vision, impatient of detail. Zhao is a finely-tuned administrator in the mould of Zhou Enlai. Hu represents the liberal element of the Party. Zhao, like Deng, is more cautious. Hu wants to promote political reform. Zhao puts economic reform first, and argues that political democratisation must be kept within manageable limits.

Between men of such different character, there is no lack of scope for discord. Yet, like Mao and Zhou, their abilities and ambitions are in many respects complementary and, provided their differences are kept in check, they will be a formidable combination. Certainly it is in their interests to cooperate, at least for the first few years. Although Deng is in good health, apart from slight deafness, he told an interviewer in August 1981 that he was beginning to tire easily, and in February 1982 it was disclosed that he was no longer actively participating in the daily work of the Party and government but, like Mao in the early 1960s, had withdrawn 'from the first to the second front'. As he nears eighty, his disengagement will become more complete. Hu and Zhao need to use this time to establish a national consensus in favour of their leadership before he leaves the stage.

The China that they are taking over is a vastly different place from the country Mao left behind. Driving out to the Great Wall one weekend in the autumn of 1981, as I was preparing to leave Peking, I passed a large, well-rounded woman in her sixties, sitting quite unabashed on the pavement outside her house, wearing only a voluminous pair of black silk trousers. Forty years ago that would have been a common hot-weather sight, but to encounter it again in the 1980s provides a striking illustration of how the obsessive puritanism of Mao's day is changing. A few weeks earlier, a British diplomat walking in the Summer Palace stumbled on a Chinese girl, sunbathing topless with her admiring boyfriend, hidden, as she thought, in a hollow by the lakeside. In Shanghai, a colleague of mine was accosted by an old man who asked him if he wanted a girl for the night. In Canton, venereal disease, which had been virtually wiped out, began to spread again, and regulations were re-promulgated banning brothels and opium parlours.

These are the outward signs of a society in flux. China is changing faster than its people or its leaders know, and the effort required just to absorb these changes is going to occupy its energies for many years to come.

The cities, particularly in the south, have taken on a veneer of Hong Kong; people have become materialistic and cynical, sickened by politics and the inconstancy of politicians. The technological miracle of Japan is a model to be aspired to. And the similarities with the Soviet Union are multiplying. China today bears a closer resemblance to Khrushchev's and Brezhnev's Russia than ever it did when Mao was alive.

Notwithstanding their uniquely Chinese context, events in Peking continue to parallel developments in Moscow in the late 1950s. When Deng wished to justify the clampdown in the winter of 1980, he told the Central Committee that although class struggle was no longer the main contradiction in society,

> owing to certain domestic factors and influences from abroad, class struggle will continue to exist within certain limits for a long time to come, and *may even grow acute under certain conditions* . . . It is imperative to maintain a high level of vigilance. (Emphasis added.)

In similar circumstances nineteen years earlier, the Soviet Central Committee declared:

> Changes in the domestic or external situation *may cause the class struggle to intensify in specific periods*. This calls for constant vigilance. (Emphasis added.)[21]

The Russian word for dissident is *inakomyslyashchiye*; the Chinese term is *chi bu tong zheng jiande ren*. Both mean 'a person who thinks differently'. In Deng Xiaoping's China, as in the Soviet Union under Brezhnev, those who think differently risk prison.

But above all China resembles the Soviet Union during the Khrushchev years in the alignment of internal forces struggling for and against change. The French sinologist, René Vienet, once described to me a television advertisement which showed a cow, standing behind a stove, making a *pot-au-feu*. She added vegetables, salt and pepper, but no matter how hard she stirred, the mixture did not taste right. Finally a voice was heard saying, 'To make a *pot-au-feu*, you need beef! – whereupon the wretched animal obediently plunged into the pot, creating a nourishing stew. The point of the story is that, if modernisation is to succeed, reform must be sufficiently thorough for the old system to be subsumed.

To this end, Chinese officialdom is being asked to abandon its privileges, vested interests and patronage, and corrupt, greedy ways, and to institute a meritocracy, so as to transform itself into a civil service capable of administering a modern country. To the majority of those in positions of power, aside from the top echelons of the leadership, that is tantamount to being asked to commit suicide. 'When some people hear the word "reform",' said *Red Flag* in November 1980, 'they are shocked and think disaster is imminent . . . They kick up a fuss and say this can't be done and that can't be done, and put up no-entry signs everywhere.'[22]

Khrushchev's attempts to reform the Soviet system failed not only because they were often ill-conceived, but because the bureaucracy charged with carrying them out obstructed them to protect its own interests. And eventually, in 1964, the disaffection of the powerholders in the *apparat* provided the crucial condition for his colleagues to strike him down.

Deng has likewise encountered growing resistance since his reform programme began in earnest in 1979. A rectification movement, the first major new political campaign for more than a year, was launched in January 1982, aimed at streamlining the administration, speeding up the retirement of veteran officials and purging leftists in the bureaucracy who were refusing to carry out the new policies. How China's future will develop depends in large measure on the success of Chairman Hu, Premier Zhao and Deng himself, in the years he has left, in carrying this movement through to completion.

The precedents are not altogether encouraging. Apart from the example of Khrushchev, the Chinese press itself has hinted at a possible parallel with the fate of the 1898 reform movement, when conservative military and civilian officials preferred the extinction of the dynasty to a reduction of their privilege and power.

If the situation in China does evolve on the Khrushchev model, the reforms will fail to bring the political and economic gains that would win round, or at least neutralise, their opponents, and argument over Mao's status will continue, despite the Sixth Plenum's 'definitive' assessment. Khrushchev had backtracked enough from the Secret Speech by 1960 for the *Great Soviet Encyclopedia* to write of Stalin: 'His name is inseparable from Marxism-Leninism. It would be a very gross distortion of historical truth to extend the mistakes Stalin made in the last years of his life to the entire period of his leadership.' That is identical to China's view of Mao in 1981. Yet, within a year of those words appearing, Stalin's embalmed remains had been removed from the mausoleum in Red Square and a new round of de-Stalinisation had begun, culminating in the publication of Solzhenitsyn's *One Day in the Life of Ivan Denisovich* in 1962. After another five years, however, Solzhenitsyn's book was withdrawn, and partial re-Stalinisation commenced. Sooner or later, Mao's remains must be removed from the mausoleum in Peking. But the result may be equally inconclusive.

The constant pressure of the reformists, trying to push through change, would then solidify the resistance of the bureaucracy, and either the reforms would have to be abandoned or the leadership would pass to more conservative men, committed, like Brezhnev, to maintaining the status quo.

Given the balance of political forces in China, that is the likeliest outcome. Yet the Chinese are not Russians; history repeats itself, but never in quite the same way. Although the odds are stacked against them, there is a chance that they will succeed in dragging their country from its feudal cocoon and turning it into a dynamic, economically vigorous modern state. Much depends on the way the economy performs: fundamental reform cannot be undertaken without sustained economic growth.

The only certainty is that China will not revert to the radical ultra-leftism of Mao's last decades, any more than the Soviet Union today could plunge back into the Stalinist terror of the 1930s; nor will it, any more than the Soviet Union, become a Western-style democracy; whatever else may occur, China's system will remain intrinsically Chinese, just as the Soviet system will remain Russian.

What will happen in Moscow after Brezhnev goes? A wry Soviet joke sums up his legacy. He, Khrushchev and Stalin were travelling by train, when it stopped, miles from any station. Stalin had the driver shot; but the train remained obstinately still. Khrushchev rehabilitated the corpse; still the train did not move. Brezhnev drew the curtains and said: 'Let's pretend we're moving.' Whoever eventually emerges as the Soviet Union's new leader will be confronted by the same problems that Khrushchev failed to solve in the 1950s and which Brezhnev has resolutely ignored.

Brezhnev himself has tried to designate a long-time associate, Konstantin Chernenko, seventy, as heir-apparent. But others in the Politburo also have ambitions, and there is almost certain to be an interregnum presided over by a collective leadership while the struggle for primacy is played out.

The steadily rising expectation of higher living standards, which a stagnant economy can no longer meet; the Soviet Union's own 'crisis of faith', held at bay since the 1960s by the visible evidence of progress, but now, once again, accentuated by the malaise and sense of drift that mark the dying years of the Brezhnev regime; the food shortages throughout the Soviet bloc that result from a blinkered agricultural policy; and the accumulation of external problems, from Poland and Afghanistan to the renewed arms race with the United States, all demand flexibility of vision and a willingness to accept basic change if they are to be tackled effectively.

Whether reforms are undertaken in the Soviet Union will be determined, however, as in China, not by internal factors alone: it also depends on continued peace. Unless the balance of power is maintained between Moscow, Washington and Peking, all guesses will be at risk.

Part V

The Politics of Power

Shortly before midnight on Christmas Eve, 1979, an airlift of Soviet troops in Central Asia set in motion a series of events that will go down in history as one of the political turning points of the last part of the twentieth century.

Within forty-eight hours, an estimated 5,000 men were set down in the Afghan capital, Kabul, ostensibly to help the radical pro-Soviet President, Hafizollah Amin, in his war against Moslem guerrillas. Instead, they stormed the presidential palace, Amin and his family were executed and the more pliable Babrak Karmal installed in his place. As the new year, 1980, began, the CIA estimated that the number of Soviet troops in Afghanistan had risen to 25,000. By mid-January, there were 100,000 and they were digging in to stay.

The occupation of Afghanistan did more to change Western perceptions of the Soviet Union's policies than any other Soviet action since the end of the Cold War, nearly two decades earlier. President Carter described it, somewhat misleadingly, as 'the greatest threat to peace since the Second World War'. In China, Deng Xiaoping commented, 'The 1980s will be a decade of troubles.' And by the autumn, East-West relations had become so envenomed that Brezhnev himself spoke of the 'growing danger of a slide into thermonuclear catastrophe'.[1]

Yet nothing the Soviets had done in Afghanistan was in itself enough to warrant the degradation of the international climate that such comments reflected. President Carter might fulminate against the Russians' 'blatant violation of internationally accepted rules of behaviour', but the fact was that both the Soviet Union and the United States had behaved in much the same way before. In 1963, America had engineered the assassination of a client ruler – President Diem of South Vietnam – in order to install a more effective leader in his place. In 1968, the Soviet Union had sent troops into Czechoslovakia to replace a leadership which had become disaffected. The so-called Brezhnev doctrine, that 'a socialist state that is in a system of other states constituting a socialist community cannot be free of the common interests of that community'[2] was never explicitly limited to Europe. Afghanistan, situated on the Soviet border and ruled since April 1978 by a pro-Soviet Communist Party, was also in the Soviet view part of the 'socialist community' and entitled to 'internationalist help' from other socialist countries. As for Western complaints that the Soviet Union had introduced its own troops into what was essentially a civil war, for that, too, there was a precedent: American troops had played the same role in Vietnam.

In this scheme of things, Soviet actions were in complete conformity with a code of conduct laid down over the years by the practice of the superpowers themselves. That is not to condone the Soviet occupation. But the problem is not one of morality – it is one of power. Expressions of outrage will not move a single soldier from Afghanistan. Self-interest determines the actions of nations, and it is a dangerous delusion to think otherwise; the best that can be hoped for is that the self-interest is enlightened. Morally both East and West operate a double standard: if your own side does a thing, it is considered legitimate, but if your opponent does that same thing, it is not. In the final analysis, to quote the journal *Novoye Vremya*, 'the main point is . . . the fundamental difference between the nature and goals of socialism and imperialism'.

The reluctance of the West, and particularly of the United States, to accept that its relations with the Soviet bloc are essentially a contest of equals is linked with a broader misconception about the nature of detente.

The former British Defence Minister, Francis Pym, told a NATO pressure group in 1981:

> Properly understood, the pursuit of detente means the attempt, without illusions, to identify and build on areas of common interest between East and West with the aim of establishing more understanding and more confidence between them . . . Arms control agreements which enhance security and trade which is of genuine benefit to both sides are examples . . . The strength of detente lies in the fact that neither side can do without trade. A genuine relaxation of tensions serves everybody's interests . . . But [it] . . . depends on the Soviet Union accepting that it must behave with restraint, and accepting that detente applies to all areas of international relations, not just to Europe.[3]

Part of this reasoning is specious: it is simply not true that neither side can do without trade. Western businessmen, and hence Western governments, may not wish to forgo Soviet-bloc trade, but that is a different problem.

However the main objection to such a definition of detente is that the Soviets have never agreed to it. The word, 'detente', in Russian as in English, means simply, 'relaxation of tension'; to the Kremlin, it is designed to ensure that the rivalry between the two antagonistic world systems of communism and capitalism can run its course without precipitating global war. Detente is intended to keep hostility within bounds so that competition can go on, not to stop hostility altogether. It follows that the core of detente is military, and that all the rest – trade, cultural and scientific exchanges, tourism and humanitarian contacts – on which the West has laid such emphasis, is marginal to Moscow, to be pursued as a matter of self-interest (imports of Western technology) or as part of a package deal desired for other reasons (the humanitarian provisions of the 1975 Helsinki Agreement, which the Soviet Union accepted because it wanted the West's endorsement of post-war European frontiers), but never as an end in itself. Conversely, in the Kremlin's view, any action to enhance Soviet influence, so long as it falls short of provoking a direct East-West conflict, is legitimate. That was the Soviet position in 1972, when President Nixon's visit to Moscow inaugurated detente, and it remains the Soviet position today.

In the 1950s and early 1960s, the West's military superiority was such that it could forcibly impose on Moscow its view of what was legitimate and what was not. In Korea, hints that the United States was preparing to use nuclear weapons brought the communists to the negotiating table. Over Cuba, ten years later, Kennedy outfaced Khrushchev. But when, in the 1970s, Nixon attempted a nuclear bluff to end the Vietnam war, the Soviet leaders ignored it. The Soviet military build-up after the Cuban debacle, spurred partly by a determination to avoid such weakness in the future, brought about a decisive change in the international balance of power. By the time the last Americans were evacuated from Saigon in 1975, with all the national humiliation which that withdrawal entailed, America was beginning dimly to perceive that the days when it could unilaterally enforce its will were past.

1975 was the year the Soviet Union began to flex its new muscles, and the gulf between Moscow's and Washington's perceptions of detente was brought into the open. No longer in awe of the American nuclear stockpile, the Kremlin sent Cuban troops to Angola, and then to Ethiopia; it promoted a coup in South Yemen to consolidate the local Marxist party's power; at the end of 1978, it underwrote Vietnam's invasion of Kampuchea; and finally, a year later, its own troops poured into Afghanistan. 'The determining feature of international relations at present,' said Brezhnev in 1980, 'is the shift in the correlation of forces in a direction favourable to peace, national independence and socialism.'

Far from being an isolated event that came out of the blue, the Soviet move into Afghanistan was the straw that broke the camel's back, the last of an accumulation of incidents which finally forced Western governments to confront truths that, for the previous five years, they had obstinately tried to ignore.

The lesson of Afghanistan was that Western policy towards the Soviet Union for much of the 1970s had been based on a false premise: in the new era of nuclear parity, Moscow would not 'exercise restraint' and pass up opportunities for expansion in order to safeguard detente. If the West wanted to stop future 'Angolas' and 'Afghanistans', it would have to be prepared to stop them on the ground. Nixon, under whose leadership detente flourished, understood this very well: his first summit in Moscow took place only a month after America mined Haiphong harbour and bombed into the ground a Soviet-armed Vietnamese offensive. After Afghanistan, the West began to think again about Nixon's original concept of arms control and armed resistance in tandem. As the *Economist* put it, a few days after the occupation began:

> Who invited 40,000 Russian soldiers . . . into Afghanistan? Answer: President Carter, the American Congress and American opinion – and those American allies who have . . . done little to remedy or reverse the crumbling of American willingness to exercise its power.[4]

Western leaders were understandably loath to admit that their own myopia was to blame. Britain acknowledged that there had been a 'misunderstanding' about the nature of detente, but qualified it by accusing the Soviets of having cheated by 'taking advantage of the misunderstanding'.[5] West Germany, vulnerable to the pressures of a divided nation, and France under President Giscard d'Estaing, still cherishing outdated notions of a special relationship with Moscow, clung desperately to the hope that the Kremlin might somehow yet be induced to espouse detente as they construed it. Even the United States did not wholly renounce the old doomed vision of a detente which could effectively control Soviet behaviour, and it resurfaced in the guise of 'linkage' when President Reagan took office a year later.

Linkage, whereby each side makes its actions conditional on corresponding actions by the other, is an attractive theory, but in practice successive US administrations have found it to be a mirage.

In the early 1970s, the Soviet Union was induced by a carefully orchestrated campaign of American encouragement to permit large-scale Jewish emigration. But when Senator Henry Jackson pressed for a public Soviet commitment to formalise this practice, in return for trade concessions, he was angrily rebuffed. Likewise in 1975 the Soviet Union was prevailed upon to accept the humanitarian provisions of the Helsinki Agreement. But it has never carried them out.

Linkage can only be applied where there is a *quid pro quo*. Henry Kissinger was unable to influence Soviet conduct in Angola by threatening dire consequences for the strategic arms negotiations because the Russians knew that arms control was as important to the Americans as to themselves. It is sometimes argued that since the Soviet gross national product is only half that of the United States, the Soviet economy is less able to withstand a renewed arms race and accordingly arms control is more in Moscow's interest than in Washington's. But that is to ignore the political constraints, largely absent in the Soviet Union, that limit defence spending in the West. Even so determined a hawk as President Reagan has been obliged to make some cuts in his proposals for defence spending, and the pressure on him to make more is bound to increase as his term of office elapses. So long as that remains the case, it is not in the West's interest to make disarmament measures hostage to progress on unrelated political issues. If arms control is worth having, it is an end in itself. Only if the West were to decide that reducing tension is not an attainable goal would it be logical to abandon disarmament talks in favour of a policy of confrontation.

In the United States, though not in Europe, the Soviet occupation of Afghanistan meant that detente was no longer treated as a sacred cow. It brought a belated awareness that detente was a means, not an end, and that if it did not contribute to America's peace and security it should be rejected. As one American newspaper wrote on January 2nd, 1980:

> If the Soviet Union continues to probe and find mush, it will continue to probe . . . Tough action is needed this time. It will surely damage, if not destroy, detente – but what price detente?[6]

Among a people increasingly frustrated by a perceived decline in American power, dramatised by America's impotence to free its hostages in Iran, Soviet adventures in Africa and the failure of the Helsinki Agreement to make the Soviet regime more tolerant, Afghanistan crystallised a national consensus that America's concrete strategic interests must be defended, and should no longer be subordinate to an abstract concept of 'relaxing tension'.

The change in national mood was dramatic. By May 1980, American public opinion was already outrunning the views of even the most hawkish members of the Carter administration. Zbigniew Brzezinski, President Carter's National Security Assistant, told a dinner-gathering in Los Angeles that month:

> We, as a people, must avoid swinging from euphoria about detente to hysteria about the Cold War. The problem we confront is not one of a head-on confrontation with the Soviet Union, but rather the danger that in some vital part of the world there will be a progressive disintegration of existing political structures resulting in an expansion of direct Soviet influence.[7]

Wise words, but in vain. The slogan of the time was 'Nuke the Ayatollah!', and by the end of the year Ronald Reagan was on his way to the White House with 'supply-side economics' and a combative, unyielding policy towards Moscow that matched the new assertiveness in the country.

After a decade when nuclear warfare was simply not discussed, Reagan's simplistic yet ultimately unarguable view that 'you shoot yours and we'll shoot ours' dismayed Europeans.[8] For the first time since the

Pravda 1980

1960s, the movement for unilateral nuclear disarmament became a force to be reckoned with, fuelled by truthful but insensitive American remarks about the possibility of a war limited to Europe.

In Moscow, the Soviets dug in for a season of wintry negotiation. Yet much as they disliked Reagan's rhetoric, they understood the kind of America he presided over more clearly than that of the weak but well-meaning Carter. America's continuing inability to accept that the scope of detente cannot be dictated by one side alone but is determined by the common aspirations of East and West together remained an obstacle to progress. However the opening in Geneva in November 1981 of Soviet-American talks on limiting long-range theatre nuclear forces in Europe, without any prior undertaking of political restraint by Moscow, marked a partial abandonment of linkage, which seemed to be confirmed two weeks later when the declaration of a State of Emergency in Poland did not cause the Americans to interrupt the meetings. Brezhnev offered 'very substantial reductions' in Soviet intermediate-range missiles if the West would renounce the deployment of 572 Pershing II and cruise missiles. And while this was not a realistic basis for negotiation – any more than was NATO's 'zero option' proposal, under which both superpowers would dismantle all their long-range theatre force systems – it did mark a retreat from previous Soviet claims of approximate parity (Western figures show a three to one Soviet advantage). To Washington, it was a sign that Reagan's tough line was beginning to bring results.

If, in the long term, the Soviet occupation of Afghanistan inaugurated a process of change in the Western approach to the Soviet Union, it did not happen at once: the initial Western reaction was a shambles. Lack of American leadership, President Carter's preoccupation (often, it seemed, to the exclusion of all else) with the plight of the American hostages in Iran, and the refusal of most of the European allies to face up to the reality of the occupation for months after the event, caused the most serious split in the Atlantic Alliance in the thirty years of its existence.

The failure of the West's response in the winter of 1979 is worth considering in some detail, for it shows with particular clarity the problems frustrating the development of a coherent Western strategy.

Its one redeeming feature was that the disunity was so glaring that Western leaders were forced to re-examine the mechanisms for policy cooperation, so that by the time the next crisis began, in Poland in August 1980, they were able to speak, if not with one voice, at least in harmony. A year later the European Community agreed on a formal crisis procedure, under which any three member countries could summon a ministerial meeting at forty-eight hours' notice, in order, as Lord Carrington put it, 'to prevent any repetitions of . . . the disarray we had over the invasion of Afghanistan'.[9] The limitations of these measures became only too obvious in the spring of 1982, after the military takeover in Poland; but at least the failures of coordination were slightly less conspicuous than had been the case two years earlier.

As serious as the discords within the Western camp, which were recognised if not really corrected, was the futility – amply demonstrated by Afghanistan – of trying to respond to Soviet actions by inapposite means.

The counter-measures announced by President Carter included a boycott of the Moscow Olympics; restrictions on Soviet cultural and consular activities in the United States and on air links with the Soviet Union; a partial embargo on American grain sales, a sharp reduction in the Soviet fishing quota in American waters and the suspension of American credits and sales of high-technology items; a partial suspension of political contacts with the Soviets, and postponement of consideration by the American senate of the Strategic Arms Limitation Treaty (SALT II) – an empty gesture if ever there was one since it stood no chance of ratification. Australia, Canada, the Europeans and New Zealand offered varying degrees of support through corresponding measures on their own account.

Even at the time, Western officials acknowledged that none of this would be sufficient to get Soviet troops out of Afghanistan. The purpose was rather to punish the Kremlin – to show that a price would have to be paid, and it would not get off scot-free: in other words, baldly stated, it was preferable to doing nothing. That much it certainly was, and those American politicians, from Edward Kennedy to George Bush, who, for partisan reasons, opposed measures such as the grain embargo without suggesting anything else in their place, did no credit to their integrity. Yet the form of the Western reprisals was not without disadvantages. It can be argued that it was never in the West's interests to let the Kremlin bridge its food deficit by buying Western grain, but having decided to do so, cutting off the supply – a measure directed at the Soviet people rather than their government – risked reinforcing Russian nationalism, strengthening the siege mentality and rallying support for the leadership, which was precisely what happened. Restricting cultural contacts and boycotting the Olympic games had a similar effect.

Moreover in one respect the Western package was totally counterproductive, for it gave Western leaders the illusion that they were tackling the Afghanistan problem in earnest, when in fact they were evading it.

Boycotting a sports meeting, however exalted, is not an appropriate response to a military invasion. This is not because sport and politics are separate: in the Soviet Union the two are inextricable, and no amount of blindness by Western Olympic committees will do anything to alter the fact. But if Moscow's fitness to host the Olympics was to be questioned, it should have been on the basis of its human rights record, and objections should have been raised in 1976, when the games were awarded, not in 1980. (The 1936 Olympics in Nazi Germany, with which the Moscow Olympics have been compared, are remembered with shame today not so much because of Hitler's invasion of the Rhineland but because of the persecution of German Jews.) To make sport the centrepiece of an orchestrated reprisal by one superpower for a strategic advance by the other – as happened in the summer of 1980 – was so ill-matched that it asked not to be taken seriously. Even if the Olympic boycott had been adhered to – which it was not – and if the West's economic sanctions had bitten harder, a Soviet military intervention could not be answered credibly without Western military counter-measures; throughout 1980, they were conspicuously missing.

True, Carter announced an increase in US military spending and urged the allies to follow suit; he set up a rapid deployment force, looked for bases in East Africa and the Gulf, and restored registration for the draft. But not until Reagan took office at the beginning of 1981 and convinced the Kremlin that he would not only expand America's military capability but was prepared to use it did the Soviet attitude start to change.

It was Reagan who reinstated plans to manufacture the neutron bomb and the B-1 bomber, which Carter had cancelled; Reagan who promised to increase defence spending from twenty-seven per cent of the budget in 1982 to thirty-seven per cent four years later; and Reagan who ordered regular arms supplies (though still not as much as were needed) for Afghan guerrillas fighting the Soviet occupation force.

By then the Olympics had come and gone, the grain embargo had been lifted and Poland had displaced Afghanistan at the forefront of the West's attention. As 1982 began, America was reverting to the same mixture of military toughness and willingness to recommence the strategic dialogue as had characterised Nixon's first term a decade earlier.

President Carter's economic sanctions against the Soviet Union were not a complete failure: although some American grain reached Russia under false papers, and Argentina made up part of the shortfall, the grain embargo cost the Kremlin at least five million tons of badly needed animal feed and several billion pounds worth of Soviet technology imports were cancelled or delayed.

Nevertheless, economically as well as politically, Afghanistan high-lighted the West's inability to enforce a rational, collective approach to its relations with the East. A total grain embargo by the West, even allowing for Argentinian supplies, would have cost the Kremlin 25 million tons, and after three years of successive Soviet crop failures the Soviet economy would have felt real pain. But no Western country, not even the United States, which continued to sell eight million tons a year, was prepared to make the sacrifices a total embargo would have required. And the partial embargo was undermined by corporate and national greed, and the absence of a rigorous policing mechanism to control what was being exported.

The same factors obstructed efforts to restrict sales of high technology. When the Aluminum Company of America withdrew from a 300 million dollar contract to build an aluminium plant in Siberia, the West German Kloeckner group stepped in to take its place – despite an undertaking by all the allies to ensure that none of their countries took up contracts which others cancelled as part of the embargo. The French company, Creusot-Loire, was awarded a 300 million dollar contract for a steel mill, previously to have been built by an American firm. In 1980, Soviet trade with America fell by almost half, compared with increases of fifty-eight per cent with France, thirty-two per cent with Italy, eleven per cent with West Germany and six per cent with Japan.

The problem of individual countries and companies breaking ranks is not new. In 1979, France sold the Soviet Union a computer for use at the Moscow Olympics after America had banned the sale in protest against arrests of Soviet dissidents. And throughout the 1970s, Western companies sold the Soviets equipment with direct military application, undeterred by the Western regulatory agency, COCOM, which proved as full of holes as a colander when jobs for Western workers were at stake. The German firm, Gildemeister, supplied Moscow with machine-tools for making high-quality artillery tubes, with the result that the Soviet Union, according to American estimates, now has 'the greatest gun-barrel manufacturing capacity in the world'. Precision grinding machines producing miniature ball bearings, sold to the Soviet Union by an American company in 1974, enabled the Soviets to develop the guidance system for the largest and most destructive Soviet missile, the SS 18. IBM 360 and 370 computers, diverted illegally to the Soviet Union two years earlier, provide the technical basis for the command system of Warsaw Pact air defence. Millions of dollars worth of sophisticated electronic equipment, from microprocessors for use in missiles to laser mirrors for killer satellites, has been exported clandestinely from California via European middlemen. American and West German firms helped to equip the Soviet Kama River lorry plant, whose products include troop transports used in the invasion of Afghanistan.

No one can seriously dispute that selling the Soviet Union machinery to make artillery tubes or laser mirrors for satellites is against the Western interest. But when it comes to equipping a lorry plant, the case is less clear-cut, and it raises much wider questions about the entire relationship between the military and non-military aspects of detente.

There are two diametrically opposed arguments on how this subject should be approached.

One view is that all trade with the Soviet Union strengthens the Soviet economy and therefore its military capacity: sales of American grain and European Community butter help feed Soviet troops in Afghanistan; they may help the West economically, but they are not in our interests strategically. Cutting trade, by this argument, would actually be a positive step, because it would expose more starkly the strains in the Soviet economy and hasten the day when the Soviet leadership is forced to undertake reforms to make it more efficient – which in turn would entail political reform and thus gradual movement to a less monolithic, more democratic system. Similarly, cultural and scientific exchanges should be cut, because they are of more benefit to the Soviet Union than the West: they relieve the frustration and sense of isolation of the intelligentsia, and enhance the regime's standing in the eyes of its people.

The other view, propounded by Henry Kissinger in the early 1970s, is that while arms control and the prevention of war form the core of detente, they do not in themselves provide a sufficient basis for stable relations between East and West: trade, cultural and scientific exchanges are needed to give the relationship solidity, build up mutual trust and create a web of interdependence. By promoting Soviet economic development, this would help to raise living standards – which in turn would foster a revolution of rising expectations among the Soviet people and thus generate pressure for reform and gradual democratisation. Cultural exchanges assist the process, since by giving the Soviet people a glimpse of life abroad they fuel the demand for change.

Reality is more complex. Interdependence works both ways: the risk of Poland defaulting on 20 billion dollars of Western loans in 1982 was at least as much a threat to Western bankers as it was to the creditworthiness of the Soviet bloc. The planned natural gas pipeline from Siberia to Western Europe will provide business for Western contractors, help tie the Soviet economy more closely to Western markets and make Western Europe dangerously dependent on Soviet energy supplies: by the 1990s, France may be obtaining thirty-three per cent of its natural gas from Russia and West Germany twenty-nine per cent. In 1980, Soviet-bloc trade with West Germany amounted to 200 dollars per head of population, far more than for any other Western country, and this, coupled with the human element of *Ostpolitik*, whereby West Germans were permitted to visit relatives in the East and hundreds of thousands of people of German descent in the bloc were allowed to emigrate, was undoubtedly the main reason for the feebleness of Bonn's response to the occupation of Afghanistan and, even more clearly, to the military takeover in Poland. When a Western country refrains from acting as it would wish for fear of attracting Soviet pressure, that is as good a definition as any of Finlandisation.

Similar considerations apply to cultural exchanges: the Soviet leadership wanted to host the Olympic Games because it would enhance Soviet prestige, but it also recognised that the presence of huge numbers of Western visitors risked 'ideologically contaminating' Soviet youth. (It solved the problem by sending hundreds of thousands of young Muscovites to summer camps in the countryside and restricting access to the city from the provinces while the games lasted.)

Nonetheless, there is a fundamental political choice to be made. Either the West should aim to exacerbate, or at least to maintain, the strains in the Soviet economy, on the basis that this will increase the pressure on the Soviet defence budget and will force the Kremlin to make reforms which will very gradually change the nature of the regime; or, to its own commercial advantage, it should seek to alleviate those strains so as to encourage the development of internal forces which will work to moderate the regime's behaviour.

Between these alternatives there is no logical middle path: you cannot both maintain and alleviate strains; you have to do one or the other.

However, for the last decade the choice has gone by default. Afghanistan partially disabused Western leaders of the notion that detente could prevent the Kremlin using force to expand its influence abroad, but it has not led to any fundamental rethinking of how Western policy might use economic and cultural levers to weaken Soviet expansionism from within. The Kissinger policy of virtually unrestricted trade and cultural cooperation has been discredited, but not ended, because, as the failure of the grain embargo showed, the West has not the will to end it. The result is that Western policy since 1980 has been a self-contradictory muddling through from one day to the next, without any directing idea to give it continuity and coherence. The criticism to be made of Western leaders, from Reagan to Schmidt, is not that they have failed to find the right answers, but that they have not yet asked the right questions; they have failed to go back to first principles and think rigorously about the purpose of the policies they are carrying out.

This is not abstract theorising: it relates to real problems. Should Western governments ban technology transfers to help expand Soviet oil production, as the Reagan administration believes, or should they ask, like Warren Christopher, Deputy Secretary of State under President Carter:

Is it prudent to seek to thwart the Soviets' development of their own energy resources? Is it prudent to squeeze them to the point that the enticement of the Gulf becomes a necessary gamble? Short of that, are they wanted on the world energy market, where their needs would cause the price to be raised for everyone?

Should Cuban troops be encouraged, or at least tolerated, in Africa, on the grounds that they 'stabilise the situation', as Carter's UN Ambassador, Andrew Young, argued in 1980? Should the West seek to bring about an 'organic relationship' between the Soviet Union and its East European allies in the belief that the strains between them, exemplified by the crisis in Poland, are a potential source of European war – as Helmut Sonnenfeldt, one of Kissinger's closest aides, proposed in 1975 – or should the West take the view that the uncertain loyalty of the East Europeans is a key factor restraining the Soviet Union from contemplating military action in Western Europe?

The arguments in favour of prudence are beguiling, but in the end they come down to a choice between competition and appeasement, confrontation and pacifism. Feeding a bear satisfies it for a while, but the result is a stronger bear. The lesson of more than a thousand years of Russian history is that the appetite of this bear grows with eating. As Professor Louis Halle wrote, shortly after the Soviet move into Afghanistan:

> Since the foundation of the Kiev state in the ninth century, Russia has been expanding, despite temporary setbacks, until it has become the immense empire that is still expanding today . . . It has been a defensive expansion, based on the insecurity of a nation . . . invaded from one side or another for a thousand years [and] suffering massacre and devastation in almost every generation – [a] nation [which] has had no other recourse than to push the hostile and encircling foreigners ever farther back. So the empire has grown, and so the Russian state has come to regard the outside world as made up of deadly enemies who must be foiled by guile, by deceit, and ultimately by as much military force as the state can generate. It is not too much to say that the outlook of the Russian state . . . has become paranoiac. This is not something the rest of the world can change by its own behaviour except over historical time.[10]

So pervasive is the sense of being threatened that, in the words of George Kennan, American Ambassador in Moscow in the immediate post-war years and the man who formulated the policy of containment, 'The price of Russia feeling secure is that everyone else must feel absolutely insecure.' To that historical fear has now been added a Leninist gloss. The empire no longer expands geographically; it expands by installing or promoting the accession of regimes which share its ideology and accept its suzerainty. The Soviet Politburo member in charge of relations with foreign parties, Boris Ponomarev, said in December 1978: 'We are heading towards an epoch in which socialism, in different concrete forms conditioned by the history of each country, will be the dominant social system on earth.' To what extent the drive to spread the communist faith is evangelical, a matter of ideology and doctrine, and to what extent it represents the old fear appearing in new clothes – as a fear that the Soviet system will remain liable to attack until all other powers subscribe to the same political goals – is unknowable and also irrelevant. What matters is that the drive exists and its well-springs run very deep.

Appeasement, no matter how attractively packaged, is not an effective defence against an expansionist power: the policy followed by France and Britain before the Second World War speaks for itself. In the 1980s, as in the 1960s, it has taken the form of a campaign for unilateral nuclear disarmament, which – without impugning the undoubted sincerity of its adherents – exemplifies the confusion that continues to pervade Western thinking about the Soviet bloc at all levels.

Unilateral nuclear disarmament would destroy the balance of power under which peace has been maintained in Europe since 1945, yet would leave the West's conventional defences intact: conventional weapons killed 50 million people in the Second World War and they are far more destructive now than they were then. A conventionally armed West, espousing an ideology with which, as the Soviet leaders never tire of repeating, communism is locked in implacable struggle, would be as much an adversary for Moscow as the West is with nuclear arms today.

Sooner or later a conflict with the Soviet Union would arise – over oil supplies from the Gulf, for instance, or a fourth Arab-Israeli war – and Western leaders would be faced with a choice between submission and making a stand with conventional forces against a nuclear-armed adversary.

Mao's dictum that 'political power grows from the barrel of a gun' is not limited to China. To believe that the Soviet Union, given preponderant military strength, would exercise political restraint towards its ideological foes, goes against both Russian history and common sense. Those who claim to do so are either naive or dishonest.

Not only do unilateralists refuse to face up to the political consequences of what they advocate, but the premise on which they base their arguments is flawed: as Japan learnt to its cost in 1945, not possessing nuclear weapons is no guarantee against nuclear attack. The only remotely reliable way of removing the threat of war would be outright pacifism and the complete dismantling of Western defences: no country goes to war to take what it can get without fighting. In an age when miniaturisation is producing artillery shells with neutron warheads whose destructive power is considerably less than conventional bombs used in the last war, it is meaningless to draw a distinction between nuclear and conventional weapons. Nor is there any moral justification for doing so. Death in war is no less obscene whether caused by mustard gas or radiation sickness, by an all-obliterating nuclear blast or a sniper's bullet: to the individual who dies, the fact of death and the suffering which precedes it are important, not their cause. Indeed, it can be argued that the neutron bomb, far from being the 'capitalist weapon which destroys people and spares property' that Soviet propaganda paints it, is a more humane means of waging war than most of the other weapons in the world's arsenals. The purpose of war has always been to kill or immobilise the enemy; in this the neutron bomb is no different from any other weapon. The fact that in doing so it causes less devastation than other explosives, nuclear and conventional, is a good thing, both practically and morally, for it means less suffering for the survivors, the families and friends of the dead, who have to pick up the pieces and carry on living after the war ends.

The argument adduced to counter such views, which is that deployment of neutron weapons would reduce the threshhold between non-nuclear and nuclear exchanges and therefore make nuclear war more likely, was lost ten years ago. Miniaturised nuclear weapons, and the knowledge to make them, exist: they cannot be disinvented.

For all these reasons, pacifism is a more logical response to the risk of war in a nuclear age than is unilateral nuclear disarmament – but it, too, would have political consequences which must be squarely faced. If West European defences were dismantled, America would retreat into isolation; the Soviet Union would have a free hand to win control of the resources of the Third World; the capitalist world would become Finlandised, and eventually reduced to a status similar to Eastern Europe. War would be avoided – but at the price of defeat.

Politicians do not win elections on a platform of national surrender: left-wing European parties which dangle before the electorate the half-truths of unilateralism are not so ingenuous as to call openly for pacifism.

Yet so long as the West retains any will to defend its system, the only logical alternative to pacifism is deterrence: you are either ready to fight for your beliefs or you are not. For deterrence to be effective, each side must be convinced that war is an unacceptably costly means of pursuing its political aims. And that in turn depends not only on the relative arsenals of the contending powers, but on their political perceptions and on the unity and cohesion of the forces each can array against the other.

China's emergence as a third force in this essentially bipolar world dates from the autumn of 1968, when the Soviet-led invasion of Czechoslovakia and the formulation of the 'Brezhnev doctrine' convinced Mao that Moscow, rather than Washington, was China's principal adversary. Six months later, on March 2nd, 1969, Chinese and Soviet troops clashed on the frozen wastes of the Ussuri River – leaving, by Moscow's account, twenty-three Soviets and an unknown number of Chinese dead – and the obsessiveness of Russian efforts to enlist American sympathy convinced President Nixon that the time had come to draw China into the strategic equation.

'From then on,' Henry Kissinger recounted, 'ambiguity vanished, and we moved without further hesitation toward a momentous change in global diplomacy.'[11]

For Mao, the decision to make common cause with China's old enemy, the United States, against the new and more terrible enemy in Moscow was a repetition of the communists' strategy during the Second World War, when they joined forces with Chaing Kai-shek's nationalists against Japan. Nonetheless, it took another four years before Peking publicly identified Moscow as 'the main enemy', at the Tenth Party Congress in 1973, and even that was diluted by the enunciation, a few months earlier, of Mao's 'Three Worlds' theory, in which the United States and the Soviet Union were treated alike as imperialistic superpowers, occupying the First World, while other industrialised countries, both capitalist and communist, made up the Second World, and developing nations, including China, formed the Third World. Six more years later, after the 'Brezhnev doctrine' had been revived in Afghanistan, the community of interest in resisting Soviet expansion began to develop into a tacit alliance. On January 9th, 1980, just two weeks after Soviet troops started landing in Kabul, President Carter's Defence Secretary, Harold Brown, announced in Peking that the United States was willing to supply China with 'dual-use' technology, having both civilian and military applications. It was made clear shortly afterwards that this would include military support equipment such as radar and transport aircraft. Under a secret agreement the United States was allowed to set up an electronic listening post, manned by Chinese technicians, near Aksu in Xinjiang, to monitor Soviet rocket tests following the loss of similar facilities in Iran after the downfall of the Shah. And in June 1981, President Reagan's Secretary of State,

Alexander Haig, disclosed that the US prohibition on selling lethal weaponry to China had also been lifted.

In theory the coming together of China and the United States could have occurred even earlier. Mao was already profoundly disenchanted with Khrushchev by the end of 1956, and by 1959, if not before, the Sino-Soviet split had become irreparable. However the notion of real enmity between the two main communist powers was so at variance with the accepted wisdom of that time that Western policymakers did not begin to grasp the implications of the schism until the mid-1960s.

Only after Brezhnev had increased the Soviet troop strength along the Chinese border from twelve divisions to forty between 1965 and 1969 did Nixon, alone among Western leaders – with what Kissinger called his 'instinct for the jugular' – perceive that this was a key area of Soviet strategic weakness, and start wondering how to exploit it.

Common opposition to the Soviet Union has been from the start the core of the relationship between the United States and China. This is understood, if not accepted, in Moscow, and the Chinese, for their part, make no secret of it: throughout the 1970s, the central theme of China's foreign policy, stated more and more openly as the years went by, was the need to create a united front embracing the United States, Canada, Japan and Western Europe, to contain the spread of Soviet influence. However, successive American administrations have maintained the fiction that Chinese-American relations are not aimed at any third country. This has been intended partly as a signal to the Kremlin of the United States' continued interest in East-West detente, but it also reflects the position of those in the State Department and in Western Europe who urge caution in strengthening cooperation with China on the grounds that it will exacerbate Soviet fears of encirclement and complicate the task, already difficult enough, of maintaining a stable balance between the Soviet Union and the West.

This argument against using 'the China card' was first heard in 1971 after it had been announced that Nixon was to visit Peking, and it has been revived at intervals ever since. It is not an argument that can be dismissed out of hand because Russians are viscerally, irrationally fearful of what they see as a 'yellow peril', a tide of humanity from the East which threatens to engulf the Soviet Union as completely as the Mongol horde subjugated Russia in the thirteenth century. This is something more than the siege mentality that has made Russians through the ages fear powerful neighbours; it is a mindless, atavistic fear which ignores reason, yet whose influence on the Russian psyche must not be underestimated. Solzhenitsyn has excoriated the Chinese as vigorously as any commentary in *Pravda*; political prisoners in a labour camp with the writer, Andrei Sinyavsky, in the 1960s, who said they would side with the West against Russia in any future war, also insisted they would fight for Russia against China. In the small towns of Siberia, Russians say, most people believe that war with China is inevitable.

The Soviet leadership has tried to manipulate this sense of threat to its own purposes, only itself to become entrapped by it. In Kissinger's phrase, the Soviet state is 'neuralgic about China'; and it is well for the West that it is, for otherwise there would be no 'China card' to play. By any objective criteria, China is so poor and its army so ill-equipped relative to Soviet forces that the idea of a Chinese attack on the Soviet Union is laughable. The threat exists only to the extent that the Soviet Union perceives it.

Far from complicating Western efforts to reduce tension with Moscow, the evidence is that the emerging entente with China in the 1970s actively promoted the development of East-West detente. There are many reasons why tension between Moscow and Washington began to ease when it did, and no one factor encompasses the whole explanation. Nonetheless, the improvement occurred at a time when hostility between the Soviet Union and China was at its most intense and when Moscow became aware that an understanding was developing between China and the United States. Detente, for the Kremlin, was designed at least in part to counter the risk of encirclement that this incipient Sino-American entente portended.

Fears that American-Chinese strategic cooperation may drive the Soviet Union into a pre-emptive strike against China are misplaced: that was an option in the 1960s, when China was isolated and internally convulsed, but in the 1980s it would only make sense if the Soviet Union were prepared to risk triggering a global war. The closer American-Chinese cooperation becomes, the greater that risk would be. The experience of recent years has been that the Soviet Union takes a very cautious attitude towards military conflict with China. In February 1979, when China attacked Vietnam, the Kremlin could well have staged a diversionary raid into Chinese Xinjiang: indeed the Chinese rated the chances of such an attack sufficiently highly that they secretly evacuated 300,000 people from Kashgar, which they regarded as the likeliest target for a Soviet punitive expedition, several weeks beforehand. But no Soviet attack came.

In theory, there is no limit to the extent to which the concentration of Chinese and American opposition to the Soviet Union can be developed. In practice, it depends on how much each country wants such cooperation.

China is no client state. Just as the scope of East-West detente is determined by both East and West, so the reach of Chinese-American relations is decided in Peking no less than in Washington. In this sense, there is no question of the West 'playing the China card', any more than there is of China playing the 'American card'. Although China calls for a united front against the Soviet Union, it is as anxious as the United States to avoid giving the impression of a formal alliance: both countries are independent centres of power in their own right. The question is to what extent they want to make their policies mutually reinforcing so as to extract concessions in the form of political restraint from a common adversary.

The matter of concessions is crucial. If increased Chinese-American cooperation to contain Soviet expansion is not to raise tension and lead to an eventual confrontation – as the Soviet leaders, for obvious reasons, are trying to persuade the West that it will – it must be accompanied by a willingness to negotiate: the stick of encirclement must be attached to the carrot of compromise and co-existence.

In principle, if not always in practice, the West has accepted the need to combine pressure and negotiation in dealing with Moscow ever since Nixon launched the policy of detente. But Mao saw no purpose in easing tension with the Soviet Union. To him, a new world war was inevitable and, indeed, necessary to push the wheel of history forward: China's alignment with America, like Stalin's alliances with Nazi Germany and subsequently with the Western powers, was a practical measure to ensure that it would survive.

Mao's attitude to detente, coupled with the improvement in Soviet-American relations in the first half of the 1970s, limited the United States' collaboration with China while Mao was alive. But in the years after his death, the political changes taking place within the country were gradually reflected in a fundamental reshaping of its view of the outside world. The Soviet Union went through an analogous process, in foreign as well as domestic policy, in the years after Stalin died: Khrushchev's rejection in 1956 of the doctrine of the inevitability of war led to peaceful co-existence with the West, the Soviet Union's first disarmament measures (the Partial Test Ban Treaty of 1963) and eventually, detente. In China, in 1977, leaders began to speak of the country's need for 'a long period of peace', and of the possibility of 'delaying' the outbreak of war if not avoiding it altogether; the following year, for the first time, China took part in an international disarmament conference; and in 1980 Hu Yaobang finally stated that war was not inevitable but could be prevented if all states joined together to resist Soviet hegemonism.

The rejection of the Maoist view of war was, for internal political reasons, highly controversial, and more than a year later it was still being treated with reserve. But the implications for Deng's China are the same as for Khrushchev's Russia: if war is avoidable, co-existence requires coming to terms with one's neighbours, which in turn implies, in some shape or form, detente.

However detente between China and the Soviet Union, like detente between the West and the Soviet Union, does not depend on one side alone, and events since Mao's death suggest that the main obstacles to a reduction of tension lie not with the Chinese but with the Soviet leaders.

With a heavy-handedness unusual even for the Kremlin, the Soviet message of condolences after Mao died was sent by the Soviet Party, with which the Chinese Party has no relations, thereby ensuring that it would be rejected. Then, for six months, the Soviet press halted polemics against China – and again there was no response, as the Russians should have known there would not be, for no Chinese leader could risk appearing soft on Moscow so soon after Mao's death and at a time when the struggle for the succession was still in full swing. Three years later, in September 1979, a Chinese delegation travelled to Moscow to discuss 'outstanding differences' after China had announced that it would not extend its friendship treaty with the Soviet Union, which dated from 1950, when it expired the following April. But again the talks foundered on the rock of Soviet insensitivity. The New China News Agency, Xinhua, reported from Moscow:

> It seems the Soviet Union still regards itself as the instructor of the Chinese people [with the right to] . . . teach them how to think, live and what way to choose . . . The adoption of such an attitude will lead nowhere. Consultation on an equal footing is the only correct way for two sovereign states to conduct negotiations.[12]

The Soviet Union wants China to return to the Soviet fold on Soviet terms: it must be all or nothing. China's position is that, in any future relationship, the Kremlin must accept Peking's complete independence from the Soviet system and abandon any hope that it will ever again be able to dominate China.

The talks were suspended after the occupation of Afghanistan in December, and it is unlikely that any real progress will be made until Brezhnev dies and a new leadership, less hidebound by the past, comes to power. That, at least, is what historical precedent suggests. In Stalin's last years, Moscow's relations with Yugoslavia were no less vitriolic than its relations with China today; yet two years after he died,

Khrushchev was able to paper over the rift. In China, since Mao died, the conditions for an eventual normalisation of Sino-Soviet ties have been steadily developing. As Chinese domestic policies have converged with, and in some cases gone beyond, Soviet internal policies, the ideological element of the schism has fallen away. By 1980, the 'Nine Comments', in which Mao set out his ideological grievances against Soviet (and, by inference, Chinese) revisionism in 1963–64, had been repudiated within the Party, though not in public, as part of the reassessment of the Cultural Revolution. The very term, revisionism, has been dropped. Polemics in the Chinese press on Soviet internal affairs were halted in 1978, and a year later some Chinese intellectuals suggested that the Soviet Union, despite its imperialistic foreign policy, was still essentially a socialist state. That view was quickly rejected by the authorities; however, Xinhua, for the first time since the early 1960s, acknowledged the existence of the Soviet Party, and occasional articles began to appear describing Soviet achievements.[13] Trade, while still a fraction of its level before the schism, increased from $40 million in 1971 to $500 million in 1980, and until the occupation of Afghanistan there were faint hints that China might resume cultural contacts with Russia.

These changes in the Chinese attitude have been largely masked by unabated vituperation against Soviet activities abroad, from Kampuchea to Poland. But given corresponding flexibility on the Soviet side, and barring a further marked degradation of the international climate, the internal logic of developments in China demands that a Sino-Soviet detente of some sort be under way by the end of the decade.

A detente between Peking and Moscow – that is, a reduction of tension between two of the world's three main adversary powers – is plainly in the West's interest. It would mean that China and NATO were pursuing parallel policies, and, by combining resistance with negotiation, would offer a real chance of achieving lasting stability.

Such a detente, however, has nothing in common with a Sino-Soviet *rapprochement*, in the sense of the two countries agreeing to bury their differences and returning to the outwardly friendly relations of the early 1950s.

That will not happen for a number of reasons. Taking a long view of the history of Chinese-Russian relations, the brief entente after 1949 appears not as the norm but as a short-lived anomaly. From the seventeenth century, when the eastward expansion of tsarist rule reached the Chinese frontier, the Russians imposed on the decaying Chinese empire a series of territorial treaties as humiliating as any of the foreign concessions exacted by the Western powers along the coast. After the Bolshevik Revolution in 1917, Lenin denounced the treaties, but they were never rescinded, and ten years later Chiang Kai-shek was complaining that Soviet Russia followed the same policy as the tsars. Relations between the Soviet and Chinese communists were hardly less difficult. Stalin's advice, conveyed through the Comintern, was often unsuited to Chinese conditions and more than once led the Party to the brink of disaster; had Mao not ignored his urging that the Chinese Party maintain a united front with the nationalists after the Second World War, the Communists would not have come to power in 1949.

Indeed, Stalin appears to have been ambivalent all along about the wisdom of fostering a powerful Chinese communist state on the Soviet border, perhaps foreseeing that the force of nationalism risked making it a rival which would one day revive all the old discords that had divided Russia and previous Chinese regimes.

Mao admired Stalin, and respected him as the leader of the world communist movement. But Khrushchev has recalled that even in the honeymoon period of Sino-Soviet relations, Mao resented the way that Stalin expected China to serve Soviet interests. That remains the core of the problem today. In the words of the *People's Daily*:

> The military threats and hegemonistic policy the Soviet Union carries out *against China* are the fundamental hindrance to the . . . normalisation of Sino-Soviet state relations. (Emphasis added.)[14]

It is not the border dispute or other bilateral issues, nor Soviet aggressiveness in expanding its power that prevents Sino-Soviet understanding; it is the urge to dominate.

This is why Chinese attempts to play the 'Soviet card' at moments of particular frustration with the West have been unsuccessful. In one such gesture, in December 1975, China released three Soviet airmen detained after their helicopter had strayed across the border; it followed a visit to Peking by President Ford which had failed to make any progress on the normalisation of Sino-American relations. In June 1981, Peking similarly signalled displeasure by publishing a long review of the Sino-Soviet border negotiations, after unproductive talks with Secretary of State Alexander Haig.

But warnings of this kind cannot be taken seriously so long as the Chinese feel that the price of a *rapprochement* with Moscow would be a return to subservience. The only circumstances in which China would put its head back into that noose would be as an act of desperation if it decided that the West had lost the will to resist Soviet domination. President Reagan's arms control adviser, Eugene Rostow, described one possible scenario in a speech in London:[15]

Europe is the ultimate target in terms of Soviet strategic theory, the geo-political key to world power. *If the Soviet Union achieves control of Western Europe, China . . . would draw the necessary conclusions.* (Emphasis added.)

Barring such a collapse of Western resolve, a Sino-Soviet *rapprochement* is not a realistic possibility. Nor is there any risk for the foreseeable future of China becoming so powerful as itself to constitute a threat to the West. Its main military resource is its people, and geography has placed them along the Soviet border, far from Western Europe and from the United States. Even if China wants to develop an offensive military capability to challenge more distant powers (and there is no evidence that it does), it will be well into the twenty-first century before it is able to do so. So remote and debatable a prospect is no basis on which to shape present Western policy.

The one problem that does jeopardise strategic cooperation between China and the West, or at least the United States, is the ambiguous status of the island of Taiwan. For thirty years, this has been the chief obstacle to normal relations between China and the non-communist world. Since China displaced Taiwan at the United Nations in 1971, and subsequently in the World Bank and the International Olympic Committee, and since all the Western countries now have diplomatic relations with Peking rather than Taibei, it is easy to conclude that the question has lost its force – and for most Western countries it has; for the United States, however, it has not.

The Shanghai Communiqué, approved by President Nixon and Zhou Enlai in February 1972, which is still the basic text for Sino-American relations, rests on an evasion:

The United States acknowledges that all Chinese on either side of the Taiwan Strait maintain there is but one China and that Taiwan is a part of China. The United States government does not challenge that position. It reaffirms its interest in a peaceful settlement of the Taiwan question by the Chinese themselves.[16]

America did not challenge the view that Taiwan was part of China, under Chinese sovereignty, but neither did it accept it. This was still so seven years later when the two countries established diplomatic relations. The United States recognised the Peking government as 'the sole legal government of China' and 'acknowledged' but did not endorse 'the Chinese position that . . . Taiwan is part of China'. That position was reiterated in a separate Chinese statement, which added: 'As for the way of bringing Taiwan back to the embrace of the motherland and reunifying the country, it is entirely China's internal affair.'

This device enabled President Carter to override the objections of right-wing Republicans, but by leaving uncertainty over whether America recognised Peking's sovereignty over Taiwan, it stored up trouble for the future.

Once America has accepted Peking as 'the sole legal government of China', any American arms sales to the island violated the United States' undertaking in the Shanghai Communiqué not to challenge the view that Taiwan 'is part of China'. Such sales amounted to arming a provincial authority with which the lawful government was technically in a state of civil war. Were the positions reversed, and China were arming a government set up by Confederate remnants in, say, Puerto Rico, following the American Civil War, it is not hard to guess what Washington's reaction would be.

From the day diplomatic relations were announced, China's public position had been that it 'absolutely cannot agree' to arms sales continuing, though in practice there was a tacit understanding that it would tolerate limited sales of defensive weaponry for a transitional period, so long as they did not exceed previous levels.

The problem thus buried, but never solved, resurfaced with a vengeance when Ronald Reagan was elected President after calling, among other things, for the restoration of 'official' ties with Taiwan. To the Chinese, the whole artfully contrived edifice of Sino-American relations seemed about to unravel before their eyes. Once in the White House, Mr Reagan relinquished, with some reluctance, the idea of an official relationship with Taibei, but discussion of a sizeable arms package continued. Throughout the first year of his administration, relations with Peking cooled, and there were clear signs of China distancing itself from the United States in case the arms sale should go through.

The risk inherent in America's refusal to get off the fence over Taiwan is not so much that China will downgrade relations to legation or even liaison office level; strategic cooperation against the Soviet Union could continue without a full diplomatic framework. The real danger is that if America disregards Chinese sensitivities over what Peking regards as a vital issue of national sovereignty, China may conclude that America is not a reliable partner: that will not lead to a *rapprochement* with the Soviet Union, but it could well turn the country back towards isolation. Deng Xiaoping told an interviewer in July 1981:

The United States thinks that China is seeking its favour. In fact . . . China is basically self-sufficient . . . Even if . . . relations retrogress to those prior to 1972, China will not collapse . . .

The Chinese people . . . will never bow and beg and scrape for help. Have the Chinese people not learned enough lessons since the Opium War? When US Secretary of State Haig came to China I told him the same thing . . . If the United States tries to force China to act in accordance with its own will, China will not agree . . .[17]

Western policy in the Middle East and Africa is open to criticism for failing to strike a correct balance between the strategic importance of Israel on the one hand and the Arab oil-producers on the other, and between South Africa and the black African states. But at least Israel and South Africa have intrinsic strategic value in their own right. In the case of Taiwan, for the United States to continue publicly supporting a regime of dubious democratic credentials, under no imminent threat, occupying an island of no strategic worth, against a vast totalitarian power playing a role of crucial geopolitical importance to the West – a power, moreover, whose sovereignty over that island America has already said it 'does not challenge' – is sheer folly.

Those Americans who favour closer ties between the United States and Taiwan point to the backwardness of China's army, and argue that 'stiffening China in order to offset the Russians would be as effective as lending a crutch to a cripple to scare a giant'.[18]

In terms of firepower, they may be technically correct. Yet that backward army is tying down forty-five Soviet divisions, comprising 750,000 troops (and will continue to do so, whatever limited detente develops between the two countries; a decade of detente in Europe has not led to the withdrawal of one Soviet soldier from the Western front). The monitoring station at Aksu plays a vital part in verifying Soviet compliance with arms control accords. And the broader geopolitical implications of China's emergence, alongside the West, in a more active world role, are beginning to shape a new balance of power.

Ultimately, the future of the West depends on its will to resist Soviet expansion. Yet the rivalry between the two great hostile power blocs, confronting each other across a divided Europe, is inherently unstable. To the extent that it evolves into a triangular balance in which the Soviet bloc, the West and China independently pursue policies of detente backed by military strength, a new and more stable world order will emerge. It may be a frail hope for peace, but in the long term it is the best hope the world has.

Notes

Part I: The Chinese and the Russians

1 'Avoir 20 Ans en Chine ... à la Campagne', Jean-Jacques Michel/Huang He, *Seuil*, Paris, 1978, pp. 56–7.
2 Ibid.
3 *People's Daily*, 5.7.79.
4 *People's Daily*, 15.11.79.
5 *China Youth News*, 12.1.80, see also *People's Daily*, 15.11.79.
6 *Beijing Ribao*, 5.7.80.
7 Moscow Radio World Service, 5.1.80.
8 Xinhua, 18.3.80.
9 *People's Daily*, 25.2.80.
10 Xinhua, 29.6.79.
11 Radio Shenyang, 20.7.79.
12 Canton Provincial Radio, 24.8.79.
13 Canton City Radio, 10.11.79.
14 *Nanfang Ribao*, 13.2.80.
15 *People's Daily*, 11.8.79.
16 *People's Daily*, 13.7.79.
17 *Red Flag*, No 2, January 1980.
18 *Guangming Ribao*, 17.6.79.
19 Yuri Zhukov on Moscow Television, 5.1.75.
20 *Zheng Ming*, Hong Kong, 1.3.80.

ANARCHY AND CONFORMISM:
SOVIET AND CHINESE MINDS – AND BODIES

1 Vladimir Pozner on Moscow Radio in English for North America, 21.11.79.
2 Radio Riga in Latvian, 22.1.80.
3 Quoted in *Twilight of the Kings*, by Daniel Vare, John Murray, London, 1948.
4 Quoted by David Shipler, in the *International Herald Tribune*, 16.6.79.
5 *The Death of Woman Wang* by Jonathan D. Spence, Weidenfeld and Nicolson, London, 1978, pp. 19–20.
6 *China Youth News*, 4.12.79.
7 'The Emancipation of Women' by V. I. Lenin, *Collected Works*, New York, 1966.
8 Radio Riga in Latvian, 17.1.80.
9 *Jiefang Ribao* (Quoted in *International Herald Tribune*, 2.9.80).
10 *Nanfang Ribao*, 13.2.80.
11 *China Youth*, March 1980.
12 *People's Daily*, 29.9.78.

13 *Wen Hui Bao*, 9.2.79.
14 *People's Daily*, 22.5.80, and see Peng Zhen, Speech to NPC, Xinhua, 2.9.80.
15 *People's Daily*, 11.12.79.

IMPERIAL SHADOWS

1 *Asiaweek*, 12.8.77.
2 *Bangkok Post*, 30.1.80.
3 *People's Daily*, 21.7.79.
4 *Guangming Ribao*, 2.10.79.
5 *People's Daily*, 9.12.77.
6 *Zhexue Yanjiu*, No 2, 1979, pp. 29–33.
7 *Hailanghua*, No 1, August 1979.
8 *Wen Hui Bao*, 16.9.79.
9 *People's Daily*, 1.7.80.
10 Xiao Sianfa, quoted by Xinhua, 20.9.79.
11 Xinhua in Chinese, 30.5.80.
12 *People's Daily*, 1.7.80.
13 *Guangming Ribao*, 11.12.79.
14 *The Real Tripitaka*, by Arthur Waley, Allen and Unwin, London, 1952.
15 *Complete Works of Zeng Guofan* (in Chinese), memorial section, Vol 15, p. 14, quoted in *Lishi Yanjiu*, 15.2.79.
16 *Old Buddha*, by Princess Der Ling, Dodd, Mead and Co., New York, 1928, pp. 225–33.
17 Radio Shanghai, City Service, 28.4.79.
18 *Kuang Chiao Ching*, Hong Kong, 16.5.80.
19 *Lishi Yanjiu*, 15.2.79.
20 Radio Shanghai, City Service, 28.4.79.
21 Xinhua, 8.9.89.
22 *Tainy Front (The Secret Front)*, by Semyon Tsvigun, Deputy Chairman of the KGB, Moscow, 1974.
23 *People's Daily*, 7.8.80.
24 *Beijing Ribao*, 18.3.79.
25 *People's Daily*, 21.11.79, and 27.11.79.
26 *People's Daily*, 9.9.80 and 10.9.80 (Ma Dayou).
27 *People's Daily*, 11.9.80.
28 *People's Daily*, 10.9.80 (Ma Dayou).
29 *International Herald Tribune*, 25.4.80.
30 Tass in Russian for abroad, 24.10.79.
31 *International Herald Tribune*, 16.17.79.
32 *Pravda*, 2.8.79.
33 Xinhua, 28.8.80.

34 Daniel Vernet in *Le Monde*, 14.10.79.
35 *China Reconstructs*, September 1980, pp. 8–10.
36 *Tianjin Ribao*, 7.10.79.
37 *Gongren Ribao*, 12.10.79.
38 *Beijing Ribao*, 12.12.79.
39 *People's Daily*, 15.11.79.
40 *People's Daily*, 4.1.80.
41 *People's Daily*, 14.1.80.
42 Xinhua, 20.9.80.

HALF STALINIST, HALF VICTORIAN

1 *Asahi Shimbun*, Tokyo, 19.10.79.
2 *People's Daily*, 12.9.80.
3 *Guangming Ribao*, 5.4.78.
4 *Gongren Ribao*, 14.5.80, Radio Nanning, 31.8.78, and Xinhua, 19.12.79; Radio Hefei, 10.3.80.
5 *Beijing Ribao*, 16.1.80.
6 Xinhua, 19.3.80.
7 *Gongren Ribao*, 20.6.80.
8 *People's Daily*, 9.9.80.
9 *Economic Research*, Peking, quoted in *Far Eastern Economic Review*, Hong Kong, 7.3.80.
10 *Red Flag*, No 2, January 1980.
11 *Guangming Ribao*, 17.11.79.
12 *Beijing Zhichun*, No 6, 17.6.79.
13 *People's Daily*, 16.11.79 and 24.1.80.
14 Quoted in *Des Femmes, hebdo*, Paris, 11–18.1.80, p. 19.
15 *People's Daily*, 28.2.80; Xinhua 17.11.79 and 7.7.80.
16 Xinhua in Chinese, 11.10.80.
17 *Zheng Ming*, Hong Kong, 1.3.80.
18 Xinhua, 28.5.80; 20.6.80 and 11.10.80
19 Xinhua in Chinese, 30.10.79.
20 Xinhua, 28.6.80; *People's Daily*, 24.6.78.
21 Xinhua, 19.12.79.
22 Ibid, 25.7.80; 28.6.80 and 5.3.80.
23 Ibid, 1.7.80 and 6.8.79.
24 Radio Moscow, Home Service, 19.3.80.
25 *People's Daily*, 16.6.78 and Daniel Vernet, *Le Monde*, 9.3.80.
26 *The Times*, 14.3.80.
27 Xinhua, 22.9.80.
28 Radio Canton, Provincial Service, 26.2.79.

THE IDIOCY OF RURAL LIFE

1 *Guizhou Ribao*, 22.4.80 (Reuter, 24.4.80), and 8.7.80 (Reuter, 10.7.80); *People's Daily*, 14.1.81.

2 Radio Hefei, 6.2.80.
3 Ibid, and Radio Jinan, 24.7.78; Radio Shenyang, 17.6.80; *China Youth News*, 7.6.79.
4 *International Herald Tribune*, 2.1.81; *Banyuetan*, December, 1980.
5 *China Youth News*, 16.9.80.
6 Xinhua in Chinese, 24.7.78.
7 *People's Daily*, 14.1.80; Radio Peking, 17.2.80; Radio Peking, City Service, 26.1.80.
8 *People's Daily*, 23.9.80.
9 Radio Jinan, 23.4.78.
10 *Xinhua Ribao*, 23.3.79.
11 *People's Daily*, 13.8.80.
12 Xinhua, 12.12.79; Radio Peking, City Service, 4.10.79; *China Youth News*, 29.11.79.
13 Radio Kiev in Ukrainian, 31.12.79; *People's Daily*, 5.12.79; *Guangming Ribao*, 18.7.79; *Beijing Ribao*, 14.10.79.
14 *People's Daily*, 1.6.79; Xinhua, 28.6.79; Radio Wuhan, 23.2.80.
15 Xinhua, 4.1.78; Ibid, 9.6.80; Radio Kunming, 10.1.80; Xinhua in Chinese, 22.7.80; Ibid, and Xinhua, 23.9.78.
16 *Overcoming Religious Survivals in the USSR*, quoted in *Khrushchev's Russia*, by Edward Crankshaw, Penguin, London, 1959, pp. 131–2.
17 *The Times*, 20.11.79.
18 Xinhua, 11.1.79.
19 *People's Daily*, 17.1.80; Xinhua in Chinese, 5.10.79; *People's Daily*, 5.11.80, 14.5.80 and 1.11.80; 'Economic Research', quoted in *Far Eastern Economic Review*, Hong Kong, 7.3.80; Radio Peking, 24.1.78; *Social Sciences in China*, No 2, 1980, p. 193.
20 Ibid
21 Xinhua in Chinese, 20.1.79 and 22.7.80; see also Xinhua, 24.10.80.
22 *Red Flag*, March 1978; *Le Monde*, 28.9.78.
23 Xinhua in Chinese, 20.11.78.
24 *People's Daily*, 15.6.80.
25 *Guangming Ribao*, 9.11.79.
26 *People's Daily*, 24.11.79; Radio Canton, 26.10.80; Xinhua in Chinese, 1.10.80.
27 *Red Flag*, No 1, January 1979; Radio Shanghai, City Service, 30.7.79.
28 Radio Canton, 26.10.80.
29 *People's Daily*, 26.8.79 and 22.9.79.
30 *Un bol de Nids d'Hirondelles ne fait pas le Printemps de Pekin*, Christian Bourgois, Paris, 1980, p. 107.

INSIDE THE SYSTEM

1 *The White House Years*, by Henry Kissinger, Michael Joseph, London, 1979.
2 Xinhua in Chinese, 29.9.80; 30.9.80.
3 Xinhua in Chinese, 27.2.80; *Le Monde*, 22.2.79.
4 Radio Changchun, 21.10.80.
5 *Tansuo* No 3, 11.3.79.
6 *Beijing Zhichun*, No 2, 27.1.79.
7 *People's Daily*, 20.10.79.
8 Radio Nanchang, 4.12.79; Radio Shenyang, 29.8.79.
9 *People's Daily*, 15.8.79; see also Radio Jinan, 26.8.79; *Hainan Ribao*, 18.9.80.
10 *People's Daily*, 1.2.79.
11 Abridged from *Beijing Zhichun*, No 1, 9.1.79.
12 Hua, Speech to Third Session Fifth NPC, 7.9.80.
13 *People's Daily*, 12.4.78; *Jiefang Ribao*, 22.7.79.
14 *People's Daily*, 14.11.80; *China Youth*, November 1979.
15 *People's Daily*, 29.2.80.
16 Xinhua in Chinese, 14.11.79.
17 Xinhua, 23.10.80.
18 *Beijing Ribao*, 10.1.80.
19 *The Times*, 22.8.80.
20 Ibid.
21 *Jilin Ribao*, 31.5.78; Radio Hangzhou, 31.3.78; Radio Changchun, 22.5.78.
22 Radio Haikou, 18.5.78; Xinhua in Chinese, 13.3.78.
23 *People's Daily*, 30.10.80.
24 *Renmin Wenxue*, No 9, 1979; translation excerpted from *Monsoon*, Hong Kong, March and April 1980.
25 *Guangming Ribao*, 17.10.79.
26 *People's Daily*, 31.3.80; Radio Peking, 23.10.80.
27 *People's Daily*, 22.6.80.
28 *Qishi Niandai*, Hong Kong, September 1979.
29 Radio Lhasa, 3.11.80.
30 Xinhua in Chinese, 27.9.79; *Gongren Ribao*, 19.3.80; *People's Daily*, 22.4.79; *Qishi Niandai*, Hong Kong, September 1979; *People's Daily*, 21.7.79.
31 *Red Flag*, No 4, 1978; Radio Harbin, 31.3.78.
32 *Privilege in the Soviet Union*, by Mervyn Mathews, Allen and Unwin, London, 1978, pp. 33–5.
33 *People's Daily*, 21.7.79.
34 *Gongren Ribao*, 8.10.79; *People's Daily*, 5.2.79.
35 *People's Daily*, 17.9.80.
36 Xinhua, 22.11.78.
37 Crankshaw, op. cit., p. 68.
38 Indictment of the Special Procuratorate under the Supreme People's Procuratorate Court of the PRC, 2.11.80, p. 33; Radio Changsha, 19.11.79.
39 *Guangming Ribao*, 17.10.80.
40 *People's Daily*, 21.9.79.
41 *China Youth News*, 12.10.78; *People's Daily*, 16.9.80.
42 *Gongren Ribao*, 18.6.80.
43 Radio Wuhan, 6.12.79; *China Youth News*, 21.6.80; Xinhua in Chinese, 7.8.79.
44 *China Youth News*, 21.6.80.
45 *Wen Hui Bao*, 9.11.79.
46 *Guangming Ribao*, 17.10.80.

Part II: Stalin and Mao

1 Peking Television, and Xinhua, 6.12.80; Radio Peking, 7.12.80.
2 *Encounter*, London, December 1979, p. 11.
3 Quoted by Erik de Mauny in *From Our Own Correspondent*, London, 1980, p. 12.
4 *Pravda*, 17.2.50.
5 *People's Daily*, 2.2.79; *Beijing Ribao*, 29.11.80.
6 *People's Daily*, 2.10.78; *Wen Hui Bao*, 16.9.79; *Guangming Ribao*, 26.10.78.
7 *Wen Hui Bao*, 16.9.79.
8 *Guangming Ribao*, 26.10.78; *Asian Wall Street Journal*, 17.5.79; *Wen Hui Bao*, 16.9.79; Xinhua, 11.1.79; *People's Daily*, 14.10.78.
9 *Wen Hui Bao*, 3.1.81.
10 *People's Daily*, 2.10.78.
11 Ibid; and *People's Daily*, 15.2.78, quoting Chief Justice Jiang Hua.
12 Xinhua, 13.7.78.
13 *People's Daily*, 13.11.79.
14 *Guangming Ribao*, 26.10.78.
15 *Wen Hui Bao*, 16.9.79.
16 *China Youth*, May 1979.

17 Bao Ruowang (Jean Pasqualini), *Prisoner of Mao*, Penguin, London, 1976, pp. 59–62.
18 Crankshaw, op. cit., p. 101; Willliam Campbell, in *The Listener*, 12.7.79, p. 46.
19 Quoted in *Ming Bao Yuekan*, Hong Kong, 1.2.80.

THE ABUSE OF TERROR

1 Xinhua, 11.12.80.
2 *The Revenge of Heaven* by Ken Ling, quoted in the *International Herald Tribune*, 14.4.80.
3 Radio Huhehot, 13.11.79.
4 Indictment, op. cit.
5 Ibid; Xinhua, 22.12.80; Radio Kunming, 10.9.78.
6 *People's Daily*, 22.12.80; Xinhua in Chinese, 14.7.78.
7 Indictment, op. cit; Radio Peking, 29.11.80; Xinhua, 30.11.80.
8 Radio Jinan, November 1978.
9 *Beijing Ribao*, 15.1.79.
10 Radio Hefei, 16.12.77.
11 Xinhua in Chinese, 10.4.78.
12 Radio Changchun, 11.6.78.
13 Radio Shanghai, City Service, 20.11.77.
14 Xinhua, 4.12.80.
15 Xinhua in Chinese, 4.12.80; Xinhua, 5.12.80; *People's Daily*, 5.12.80.
16 *People's Daily*, 18.4.78.
17 *China Reconstructs*, June 1980, p. 15; *Beijing Review*, No 13, 31.3.80, p. 26; Peking University Wallposter, April 1978; Xinhua in Chinese 23.2.78.
18 Ibid, 23.4.78; Indictment, op. cit., p. 47.
19 *People's Daily*, 14.5.78.
20 *People's Daily*, 20.12.80; Xinhua 23.12.80.
21 *China Reconstructs*, April 1980, pp. 44–5.
22 *Far Eastern Economic Review*, Hong Kong, 16.3.79.
23 Xinhua, 3.11.79; *People's Daily*, 14.5.78.
24 *Chinese Literature*, August 1980, pp. 76–7.
25 Xinhua, 23.12.80; *People's Daily*, 20.12.80.
26 Radio Lanzhou, 8.12.79.
27 Radio Harbin, 30.11.77.
28 Radio Guiyang, 5.12.77.
29 Radio Hefei, 8.12.77.
30 Xinhua, 1.9.80.
31 Radio Shanghai, City Service, 15.8.79; 21.12.79; Radio Nanchang, 5.9.79.
32 Central Committee Document No 73, 1980; *Zheng Ming*; Hong Kong, 1.11.80.
33 *Zheng Ming*, Hong Kong, 1.9.79; also Mao's *Selected Works*, Vol 5, pp. 176–9.

34 Central Committee Document No 73, 1980; Robert Guillain *Six Hundred Million Chinese*, New York, 1957, p. 176.
35 Guangzhou: Radio Canton, City Service, 29.1.80; Shandong: Radio Jinan, 15.12.79; Anhui: Radio Hefei, 17.2.79.
36 *No Jail for Thought* by Lev Kopelev, Penguin, London, 1979, pp. 32–3.
37 Sun Yefang, in *Economic Management*, February 1981. Quoted in Wallposters signed Zhang Lie, Peking, 4.2.79.
38 Quoted in Wallposters signed Zhang Lie, Peking, 4.2.79; *Prisoner of Mao*, op. cit., pp. 241–2.
39 Quoted in *Mao and China*, by Stanley Karnow, London, 1973, p. 102.
40 *Zheng Ming*, Hong Kong, 1.3.80.
41 Radio Lanzhou, 15.10.80.

THE GREAT PURGE AND THE CULTURAL REVOLUTION

1 Mao speeches on 24 and 25.10.66, quoted in *The Origins of the Cultural Revolution* vol. 1. *Contradictions Among the People 1956–1957* by Roderick MacFarquhar, Oxford University Press, London, 1974, p. 152.
2 *CCP Documents of the Great Proletarian Cultural Revolution*, Union Research Institute, Hong Kong, pp. 175–7; Xinhua, 17.7.79.
3 *The Great Terror* by Robert Conquest, Penguin, London, 1971, p. 703.
4 *People's Daily*, 3.7.79.
5 Indictment, op. cit., pp. 8–10.
6 *Guangming Ribao*, 22.8.79.
7 *People's Daily*, 12.12.80.
8 Quoted in Jean Esmein, *The Chinese Cultural Revolution*, Deutsch, London, 1975, p. 63.
9 *Gongren Ribao*, 5.12.80.
10 *Red Flag*, No 19, 1.10.80; *Beijing Zhichun*, No 8. 28.9.79.
11 *Red Flag*, No 19, 1.10.80; *Gongren Ribao*, 5.12.80.
12 Quoted in *Mao Papers* by Jerome Chen, Oxford University Press, London, 1970, p. 24.
13 *Beijing Review*, No 33, 11.8.67, p. 5.
14 *Gongren Ribao*, 5.12.80.
15 Xinhua in Chinese, 5.12.80.
16 Xinhua, 6.12.80; Xinhua in Chinese, 5.12.80 and 21.3.80.
17 *Gongren Ribao*, 8.12.80.

18 Xinhua, 4.6.80 and 3.12.80; *Beijing Ribao*, 6.12.80; Xinhua in Chinese, 7.3.80; Xinhua, 23.12.80.
19 *Gongren Ribao*, 8.12.80; *Wen Hui Bao*, 8.3.80.
20 *People's Daily*, 20.5.80.
21 *Gongren Ribao*, 6.12.80.
22 Ibid, 2.3.80; 8.12.80. Xinhua, 29.8.79.
23 Xinhua in Chinese, 13.9.78.
24 *Gongren Ribao*, 6.12.80 and 8.12.80; *China Sports*, No 2, 1980.
25 *People's Daily*. 10.12.78.
26 Xinhua, 23.12.80; *People's Daily*, 26.2.79.
27 Xinhua, 2.5.79; *People's Daily*, 13.12.80.
28 *Beijing Ribao*, 29.11.80; Xinhua, 22.11.79; *China Youth*, December 1980.
29 *People's Daily*, 12.1.79; Xinhua in Chinese, 12.12.80.
30 Peking Television, 9.12.80.
31 Ibid, 12.12.80.
32 Xinhua in Chinese, 12.12.80.
33 Radio Peking, 8.12.80.
34 *People's Daily*, 31.8.78 and 12.2.79.
35 Ibid, 9.1.80.
36 *Guangming Ribao*, 20.12.78.
37 Xinhua in Chinese, 9.12.80.
38 Xinhua, 5.12.80; Ibid, 9.12.80; *Da Gong Bao*, Hong Kong, 14.7.80; Xinhua in Chinese, 9.12.80.
39 Radio Huhehot, 4.12.78; Xinhua in Chinese, 6.10.79.
40 *Tansuo*, No 4, March 1979.
41 *Dongxiang*, No 20, Hong Kong, 16.5.80.
42 Quoted in *Far Eastern Economic Review*, Hong Kong, 15.9.78; see *People's Daily*, 18.3.79, and *Women in China*, January 1981; *People's Daily*, 19.4.80.
43 *People's Daily*, 25.5.79; *Beijung Zhichun*, No. 8, 28.9.79; *Zheng Ming*, Hong Kong, 1.9.79.
44 *Zhixin*, 1979, quoted in *Un Bol de Nids d'Hirondelles ne fait pas le Printemps de Pekin*, op. cit. p. 105.

45 Radio Shenyang, 2.7.79.
46 *People's Daily*, 27.1.81 and 14.3.78.
47 Xinhua, 20.11.80.
48 *Guangming Ribao*, 21.10.79.
49 Ibid.
50 Radio Shanghai, City Service, 13.2.80.
51 Xinhua in Chinese, 26.1.81.
52 Xinhua, 10.11.79; see *Inside Peking*, by Beverley Hooper, Macdonald, London, 1979, p. 163.
53 Xinhua, 3.3.79, and 21.1.79.
54 Xinhua, 14.12.79.
55 *People's Daily*, 22.2.80; *Zheng Ming*, Hong Kong, 1.1.80.
56 Xinhua in Chinese, 28.4.78, and 23.2.78.
57 *Guangming Ribao*, 11.12.79.
58 Xinhua in Chinese, 7.12.80; Radio Canton, 18.5.78.
59 Radio Canton, 6.4.78; *People's Daily*, 4.1.78; *Le Monde*, 11.4.80.

DYING YEARS

1 *Daily Telegraph*, 17.1.55.
2 *Le Monde*, 10.8.71.
3 *People's Daily*, 24.11.80 and Xinhua in Chinese, 29.11.80.
4 Xinhua in Chinese, 29.11.80; *People's Daily*, 24.11.80.
5 Indictment, op. cit., pp. 54–5.
6 *People's Daily*, 24.11.80.
7 Radio Zhengzhou, 5.3.80.
8 Evans Fordyce Carlson, *Twin Stars of China*, New York, 1940, pp. 249–52.
9 *Mao Papers*, Chen, op. cit., p. 40.
10 Quoted in Wallposter, 18.12.78.
11 *Jiefang Junbao*, 8.11.76; Xinhua in Chinese, 5.11.77.
12 *People's Daily*, 21–22.11.78.
13 *Guangming Ribao*, 22.12.78.
14 *Pravda*, 10.7.53.
15 *Nanfang Ribao*, 25.11.80.

Part III: The Peking Spring

THE SECOND COMING OF DENG XIAOPING

1 *Ming Bao*, Hong Kong, 26.5.77.
2 Xinhua, 23.8.77.
3 *People's Daily*, 14.7.77.
4 *Ming Bao*, Hong Kong, 26.5.77.

5 *People's Daily*, 17.2.77; *Wen Hui Bao*, 27.10.79.
6 Xinhua, 24.10.76.
7 Xinhua, 21.11.76.
8 Xinhua, 23.11.76; *People's Daily*, 29.11.76; Radio Changsha, 7.1.77.

9 Xinhua, 22.7.77; Communique of the Third Plenum of the Tenth Central Committee.
10 Ibid; and *Ming Bao*, Hong Kong, 26.5.77.
11 *Ming Bao*, Hong Kong, 16–17.8.77.
12 *People's Daily*, 23.7.77.
13 *People's Daily*, 27.4.77.
14 *Guangming Ribao*, 20.10.79.
15 Hua, speech to the Eleventh Party Congress, Xinhua, 22.8.77.
16 Ibid.
17 Xinhua, 9.9.77.
18 *Ming Bao*, Hong Kong, 16–17.8.77.
19 Xinhua, 22.8.77 and 9.9.77; *People's Daily*, 9.9.77.
20 *Guangming Ribao*, 20.10.79.
21 Hua, speech to Eleventh Party Congress, op. cit.
22 *Red Flag*, January 1978.
23 *People's Daily*, 18.1.77.
24 Xinhua, 22.8.77 and 21.3.78.
25 *People's Daily*, 22.11.77.
26 *People's Daily*, 27.8.77.
27 Ibid, 3.9.77, 18.12.77 and 15.2.78.
28 Hua, speech to Fifth NPC, Xinhua, 6.3.78.
29 *People's Daily*, 5.8.77.
30 Radio Peking, 20.1.78; *People's Daily*, 25.1.78.
31 Radio Peking, 22.2.78.
32 *People's Daily*, 26.2.78.
33 Xinhua, 12.9.77.
34 Hua, Speech to Fifth NPC, op. cit.
35 'A Miracle which is not a Miracle', by Yong Cun, *Peking Spring*, 9 and 27.1.79, 1 and 5.3.79 (Abridged).
36 Hua, Speech to Eleventh Party Congress, op. cit.

POLITBURO INTRIGUES: THE WIND FACTION, THE SLIPPERY FACTION, THE EARTHQUAKE FACTION AND THE COVER-UP FACTION

1 *Ming Bao*, Hong Kong, 16–17.8.77.
2 Deng, Speech to Eleventh Party Congress, Xinhua, 24.8.77; *Red Flag*, No 9, September 77; Xinhua in Chinese, 4.9.77.
3 *People's Daily*, 6.8.77, 6.10.77 and 7.10.77.
4 Hua, Speech to Eleventh Party Congress, op. cit.
5 *People's Daily*, 9.10.77 and 14.10.77.
6 Xinhua, 24.10.77, and *People's Daily*, 28.10.77.
7 Kunming Radio, 26.6.77.
8 Shenyang Radio, 23.11.77.
9 *Far Eastern Economic Review*, Hong Kong, 19.8.77.
10 Xinhua in Chinese, 14.7.78.
11 Changchun Radio, 10.5.78.
12 *People's Daily*, 13.2.78.
13 *People's Daily*, 14.1.78; *Red Flag*, No 2, February 1978, and *Tanjug*, 4.4.78.
14 *People's Daily*, 27.11.77.
15 Ibid, 6.1.78.
16 Ibid, 10.1.78.
17 Ye, Speech to Eleventh Party Congress, Xinhua, 23.8.77.
18 Xinhua in Chinese, 29.12.77.
19 *People's Daily*, 6.1.78, 10.1.78 and 22.2.78.
20 Xinhua, 21.3.78.
21 Xinhua, 25.3.78.
22 *People's Daily*, 22.2.78.
23 Ibid, 28.3.78.
24 Hua, speech to Eleventh Party Congress, op. cit.
25 Xinhua in Chinese, 15.3.78 and 2.5.78; Radio Hefei, 13.5.78; Radio Guiyang, 15.5.78.
26 Radio Peking, 5.4.78.
27 *People's Daily*, 13.5.78.
28 Ibid, 22.2.78.

MAO DETHRONED: SEEKING TRUTH FROM FACTS

1 *Red Flag*, September 1977.
2 *China's New Democracy*, by Qi Xin and others, Cosmos Books, Hong Kong, 1979, p. 147; *People's Daily*, 8.5.78.
3 Xinhua, 5.6.78.
4 Xinhua, 3.6.78.
5 Xinhua, 5.6.78.
6 *Jiefang Junbao*, 24.6.78.
7 Xinhua, 30.6.78.
8 *People's Daily*, 2.7.78.
9 Ren Zhongyi, *People's Daily*, 20.9.78.
10 *People's Daily*, 30.6.78 and 2.7.78.
11 *Red Flag*, No 7, July 1978.
12 *People's Daily*, 24.9.78 and 18.10.78; *Beijing Ribao*, 13.9.78.
13 *Guangming Ribao*, 5.9.78.
14 Ibid, 19.9.78.
15 *People's Daily*, 22.6.79.
16 *People's Daily*, 25.9.78.
17 *Guangming Ribao*, 26.9.78.
18 *Guangming Ribao*, 21.9.78.
19 *China Youth News*, 7.10.78.
20 *People's Daily*, 29.9.78 and 2.10.78; Shenyang CPC Committee, Radio Shenyang, 27.10.78; PLA Kunming Units, Radio Kunming, 16.10.78.

21 *People's Daily*, 4.5.78 and 27.10.78.
22 *Gongren Ribao*, 24.11.78.
23 *Gongren Ribao*, 17.11.78.
24 Xinhua, 18.11.78.
25 Xinhua, 20.11.78.
26 *Guangming Ribao*, 15.11.78.
27 *People's Daily*, 15.11.78.

THE DEMOCRACY WALL

1 Ye, speech to Eleventh Party Congress, op. cit.
2 *Red Flag*, No 7, 1.7.78.
3 *People's Daily*, 21.12.78.
4 *Gongren Ribao*, 24.11.78.
5 Quoted in Xinhua, 27.11.78.
6 *People's Daily*, 28.11.78.
7 *China Youth News*, 2.12.78.

THE THIRD PLENUM AND THE SECRET SPEECH

1 Alec Nove, *Stalinism and After*, Allen and Unwin, London, 1975, p. 124.
2 *Khrushchev Remembers*, Sphere Books, London, 1971, p. 309.
3 *Pravda*, 15.2.56.
4 *Pravda*, 18.2.56.
5 *Observer*, 19.2.56.
6 *Economist*, 25.2.56.
7 US State Department, 4.6.56.
8 *People's Daily*, 24.11.78.
9 Xinhua, 23.12.78.
10 *Mingbao Yuekan*, Hong Kong, 1.2.80.
11 Xinhua, 7.6.80.
12 Xinhua, 25.1.79 and 29.1.79.
13 *People's Daily*, 16.1.79; *Red Flag*, 1.7.79.

THE SECOND '100 FLOWERS'

1 René Goldman, *China Quarterly*, October–December 1962, p. 141.
2 Quoted in *Khrushchev's Russia*, op. cit., p. 115.
3 *Observer*, 20.10.57.
4 *Qimeng*, No. 3, 1.1.79.
5 *Jiedong*, 8.3.79.
6 *Beijing Zhichun*, No 2, 27.1.79.
7 *Observer*, 20.10.57.
8 *Reference News for the Masses*, No 4, 24.2.79.
9 *Siwu Luntan*, No 4, 22.1.79.
10 'The 19-point China Human Rights Declaration' in *Zhongguo Renquan*, February 1979.
11 Ibid.
12 *Tansuo*, No 5, 1.10.79.
13 *Qimeng*, No 3, 1.1.79.
14 *People's Daily*, 3.1.79 and 21.12.78.
15 Xinhua, 8.2.79.
16 *People's Daily*, 1.1.79 and 3.11.78.
17 *People's Daily*, 3.3.79, 15.12.78 and 26.2.79.
18 Radio Peking, 24.1.79; Xinhua, in Chinese, 23.1.79.
19 *People's Daily*, 8.3.79.
20 *People's Daily*, 14.12.78, 24.12.78, 29.12.78 and 16.1.79.
21 *Qimeng*, 1.3.79.
22 *Tansuo*, No 2, 29.1.79.
23 *Tansuo*, No 3, 11.3.79.
24 *People's Daily*, 8.11.78.
25 *Sihua Luntan*, 15.9.79.
26 *Gongren Ribao*, 27.5.80.
27 Radio Shenyang, 30.4.79; *Wen Wei Po*, Hong Kong, 8.6.80; *China Youth News*, 19.6.80.
28 *Beijing Ribao*, 24.5.80; *China Youth News*, 13.3.80.
29 *People's Daily*, 23.5.80.
30 *Beijing Ribao*, 12.6.80.
31 MacFarquhar, op. cit., pp. 37–8.
32 *Kommunist*, Moscow, January 1956.
33 Xinhua in Chinese, 2.3.79; Zhou Yang, Xinhua, 23.2.80.
34 *China Youth News*, 20.2.79; *Wen Hui Bao*, 11.2.80 and 13.5.80.
35 *The Times*, 11.4.57.
36 *Tiyu Bao*, 3.12.79.
37 See Xinhua in Chinese, 23.9.79.
38 Frank Ching, in *Asian Wall Street Journal*, June 1979.
39 *China Youth News*, 23.11.79.
40 Xinhua in Chinese, 10.2.80.
41 *Jiefang Ribao*, 16.2.79. See also Xinhua in Chinese, 9.2.78.
42 *People's Daily*, 9.2.79.
43 *People's Daily*, 27.1.79 and 18.1.79.
44 *Beijing Ribao*, 15.2.79.
45 *China Youth News*, 13.2.79; *People's Daily*, 12.2.79; *Wen Hui Bao*, 8.2.79.

CLAMPDOWN

1 *People's Daily*, 8.6.57.
2 *People's Daily*, 17.7.57.
3 *People's Daily*, 11.4.79.
4 Hua, speech to NPC, 18.6.79; *People's Daily*, 31.10.79.

5 Crankshaw, op. cit., p. 116; *Manchester Guardian*, 8.12.56.
6 *Tansuo*, No 2, 29.1.79.
7 Xinhua in Chinese, 13.8.79.
8 *Wen Hui Bao*, 17.7.79; *Le Monde*, 2.8.79; *Tianjin Ribao*, 2.8.79.
9 MacFarquhar, op. cit., pp. 221–2.
10 Xinhua in Chinese, 10.2.79; Radio Shanghai, 17.2.79; *Jiefang Ribao*, 14.2.79.
11 *People's Daily*, 24.2.79, 9.3.79 and 13.3.79.
12 *People's Daily*, 10.3.79, and Xinhua in Chinese, 27.2.79.
13 Radio Hefei, 19.3.79; Xinhua in Chinese, 12.3.79; Central Committee Document No 24, March 1979.
14 *Gongren Ribao*, 23.3.79, and Nanchang Radio, 13.4.79.
15 *Beijing Ribao*, 2.4.79.
16 *China Youth News*, 17.3.79.
17 Radio Peking, 31.3.79.
18 *Beijing Ribao*, 18.3.79; Radio Hunan, 22.3.79.
19 Radio Changsha, 12.4.79. See also Peking, City Service, 7.4.79.
20 Radio Xining, 2.6.79; *Gongren Ribao*, 19.4.79.
21 *Asian Wall Street Journal*, 3.5.79.
22 *Jiefang Ribao*, 2.1.79.
23 *Tansuo*, Special Issue, 25.3.79.
24 *Wen Hui Bao*, 2.5.81.
25 *Gongren Ribao*, 22.2.79.
26 *People's Daily*, 5.4.79 and 21.12.78.
27 *People's Daily*, 10.3.79; *Far Eastern Economic Review*, Hong Kong, 6.4.79; *Beijing Ribao*, 5.4.79.
28 *People's Daily*, 21.12.78.
29 *Beijing Ribao*, 31.3.79.
30 *People's Daily*, 21.2.79.
31 *People's Daily*, 26.9.79.
32 *Nanfang Ribao*, 26.10.79 and 5.8.79; Radio Lanzhou, 11.10.79.
33 Abridged from *Chinese Literature*, No 12, 1979, pp. 113–17.
34 *Zheng Ming*, Hong Kong, No 21, 1.7.79.
35 *Jiefang Ribao*, 22.4.79; *Ming Bao*, Hong Kong, 14.6.79; Inferred from *Guangming Ribao*, 6.4.79, and *Jiangxi Ribao*, 26.4.79.
36 Radio Peking, 3.5.79.
37 *Jiangxi Ribao*, 26.4.79; *People's Daily*, 9.5.79.
38 *People's Daily*, 9.5.79, 3.6.79 and 7.9.79; *Gongren Ribao*, 6.6.79; *Beijing Ribao*, 4.6.79.
39 Radio Shanghai, 31.8.79; *People's Daily*, 3.7.79; *Jiefang Junbao*, 13.7.79; *Wen Hui Bao*, 4.8.79; *Beijing Ribao*, 21.10.79.
40 Xinhua in Chinese, 10.9.79 and 13.6.79.
41 *Red Flag*, July 1979; *Wen Hui Bao*, 17.7.79; also Radio Canton, 16.6.79 and *Wen Hui Bao*, 4.8.79. *Tianjin Ribao*, 13.8.79.
42 Radio Shenyang, 15.10.79.
43 *Hainan Ribao*, 20.9.79.
44 *People's Daily*, 5.5.79 and 20.7.79; *Guangming Ribao*, 17.7.79.
45 Duan Junyi, Radio Zhengzhou, 6.9.79; *Gongren Ribao*, 22.5.79; Xinhua in Chinese, 27.6.79; *People's Daily*, 8.9.79; *Jiefang Ribao*, 16.10.79.
46 Xinhua, 23.5.79.
47 *People's Daily*, 5.5.79 and 6.5.79; Xinhua in Chinese, 22.4.79.
48 *People's Daily*, 9.5.79.
49 Xinhua in Chinese, 21.5.79; *Guangming Ribao*, quoted in *Asian Wall Street Journal*, 4.5.79.
50 *China Youth*, May 1978; *Guangming Ribao*, 22.8.79.
51 *Red Flag*, May 1979; *Beijing Ribao*, 22.3.79; *Wen Hui Bao*, 8.4.79.
52 *Guangming Ribao*, 19.6.79 and 26.10.79.
53 *People's Daily*, 3.7.79.
54 See *Xinhua*, 7.9.79.
55 *People's Daily*, 17.9.79.
56 *Wen Hui Bao*, 11.2.80.
57 *Chung Pao*, 2.3.80.
58 Interview with *Encyclopaedia Britannica*, 26.11.79.
59 See *Beijing Ribao*, 19.10.79.
60 *Asahi Shimbun*, Tokyo, 19.10.79.
61 *People's Daily*, 17.10.79.
62 *Beijing Ribao*, 19.10.79; *China Youth News*, 3.11.79.
63 Ibid, and *Guangming Ribao*, 26.10.79; Radio Peking, 28.10.79; Xinhua in Chinese, 19.10.79 and 18.10.79; *Beijing Ribao*, 17.10.79; *China Reconstructs*, 19.10.79.
64 Xinhua in Chinese, 9.11.79.
65 *Guangming Ribao*, 24.10.79.
66 Xinhua, 9.11.79.
67 *People's Daily*, 14.11.79.
68 Xinhua in Chinese, 30.10.79.
69 *People's Daily*, 13.11.79.
70 Meeting with US Governors, 17.10.79; and *Bangkok Post*, 10.2.80.
71 *Jiefang Ribao*, 9.11.79.
72 *People's Daily*, 16.11.79.
73 *Beijing Ribao*, 18.11.79; Xinhua in Chinese, 8.11.79; *People's Daily*, 8.11.79.
74 Xinhua in Chinese, 6.1.80; *Zheng Ming*, Hong Kong, 1.5.80.
75 *People's Daily*, 22.11.79; see also *Gongren Ribao*, 5.11.79.

76 *People's Daily*, 27.11.79; *Wen Hui Bao*, 5.11.79; *Tianjin Ribao*, 14.11.79; *Jiefang Junbao*, 23.11.79; *Gongren Ribao*, 5.11.79; *Chengdu Ribao*, 1.11.79; *Shenyang Ribao*, 26.11.79.

77 Xinhua, 29.11.79; *Beijing Ribao*, 29.8.79; *Jiefang Ribao*, 9.11.79; *Gongren Ribao*, 21.1.80.

78 *Beijing Ribao*, 1.12.79.

79 Xinhua, 27.12.79; Radio Hefei, 2.12.79; *People's Daily*, 9.12.79; *Gongren Ribao*, 10.12.79.

80 Radio Peking, 26.12.79.

81 Radio Tianjin, 24.12.79.

82 Radio Zhengzhou, 18.12.79.

83 *People's Daily*, 12.1.80.

84 Crankshaw, op. cit., pp. 118–19.

85 *Zheng Ming*, Hong Kong, 1.3.80.

Part IV: Crisis of Faith

1 *People's Daily*, 19.1.80.

2 Radio Changsha, 22.4.79; *People's Daily*, 25.6.80.

3 *Beijing Ribao*, 24.3.80; Xinhua in Chinese, 12.1.80.

4 *Zheng Ming*, Hong Kong, No 29, 1.3.80.

5 *People's Daily*, 24.2.81.

6 *Jiefang Ribao*, 13.9.79.

7 *Sunday Times*, 23.12.56; *Listener*, 12.7.79, p. 46.

8 *New York Times*, 30.9.56; *Observer*, 18.3.56 and 26.2.56.

9 *Wen Hui Bao*, 13.1.80.

10 *People's Daily*, 5.6.79; *Asian Wall Street Journal*, 22.4.81; Xinhua, 2.3.81 and 14.3.81; see also 6.10.79.

11 *Observer*, 26.2.56; Xinhua, 22.4.81.

12 *People's Daily*, 8.6.80 and 5.2.80. *China Youth News*, 13.12.79; Xinhua, 19.9.79.

13 *People's Daily*, 25.6.80.

14 Xinhua, 10.7.80 and 22.4.81; Radio Jinan, 6.7.80.

15 *Beijing Ribao*, 12.1.79.

16 Radio Canton, 12.1.81.

17 Simon Leys, *Ombres Chinoises*, Bibliothèque Asiatique, Paris, 1974, pp. 123–4.

18 *Red Flag*, No 7, 1.4.81.

19 *China Youth News*, 12.5.81.

20 *Gongren Ribao*, 14.3.81.

21 *Guangming Ribao*, 18.2.81.

THOUGHT CRIME AND REFORM

1 Xinhua, 23.12.78; *People's Daily*, 5.7.79; *Red Flag*, 1.5.78.

2 Criminal Code of the RSFSR, Art. 58(i), Moscow, 1949.

3 Criminal Law of the People's Republic of China, Art. 90, (*People's Daily*, 7.7.79).

4 *Beijing Ribao*, 4.8.79.

5 Xinhua, 30.6.79; *People's Daily*, 20.6.79;

see also Ren Zhongyi in *Gongren Ribao*, 29.6.79.

6 *Beijing Ribao*, 25.5.81.

7 Radio Shanghai, 19.11.79; *Beijing Review*, No 40, 6.10.80, p. 27.

8 *Red Flag*, No 11, 1.11.79.

9 *Guangming Ribao*, 16.10.80.

10 Xinhua, 24.8.80.

11 *Beijing Ribao*, 23.1.81.

12 *Jiefang Ribao*, 7.10.80.

13 *Asian Wall Street Journal*, 13.6.80.

14 *People's Daily*, 10.1.80.

15 *Gongren Ribao*, 11.12.80.

16 Xinhua in Chinese, 30.7.79.

17 Radio Peking, 9.1.80; *People's Daily*, 5.8.79.

18 Xinhua, 30.6.79.

19 *Beijing Zhichun*, No. 2, 27.1.79.

20 Xinhua in Chinese, 31.7.79; see also Ibid, 26.7.79; *Shaanxi Ribao*, 14.7.80; Radio Hangzhou, 3.12.80; Radio Shenyang, 4.10.80.

21 *People's Daily*, 30.8.80.

22 Xinhua in Chinese, 26.11.79; Radio Canton, 10.1.80; *Guangming Ribao*, 9.12.79.

23 *Guardian*, 26.6.56; *Pravda*, 6.7.56.

24 *Pravda*, 8.7.56.

25 Radio Kiev in English, 19.2.80.

26 *Chan Wang*, Hong Kong, No 461, 16.4.81.

27 *Chung Pao*, Hong Kong, 2.3.80.

28 *Wen Hui Bao*, 11.2.80; *China Youth News*, 12.2.80.

29 *Guangming Ribao*, 6.9.80; *People's Daily*, 7.9.80 and 11.9.80.

30 *People's Daily*, 9.6.79 (also Radio Peking, 24.10.79).

31 Xinhua in Chinese, 9.11.79; *Chung Pao*, Hong Kong, 2.3.80.

32 *Guangming Ribao*, 10.9.80; Xinhua, 8.9.80; *People's Daily*, 5.9.80.

33 Xinhua, 8.9.80.

34 *Guangming Ribao*, 30.10.80.
35 Radio Tianjin, 23.8.79; Radio Zhengzhou, 6.9.79.
36 *Zheng Ming*, Hong Kong, No 29, 1.3.80.
37 Xinhua, 29.9.79.
38 *Chan Wang*, Hong Kong, No 461, 16.4.81.
39 *Chan Wang*, Hong Kong, No 449, 16.10.80.
40 *Guangming Ribao*, 16.10.80; *Chan Wang*, Hong Kong, No 461, 16.4.81.

EXPLORING THE CAPITALIST ROAD

1 *Economic Research*, 20.3.79; *People's Daily*, 20.10.79.
2 *Guangming Ribao*, 27.10.79; see *People's Daily*, 16.6.80 and 28.11.80; Xinhua in Chinese, 22.3.79; Wang Bingqian, Speech to NPC, 30.8.80.
3 *People's Daily*, 16.6.80.
4 Ibid, 2.6.81.
5 *People's Daily*, 31.1.80.
6 *People's Daily*, 30.3.79 and 17.4.79.
7 Wang Bingqian, Speech to NPC, op. cit.
8 *People's Daily*, 9.6.80 and 2.6.80.
9 *People's Daily*, 23.1.81.
10 *People's Daily*, 3.12.79 and *Gongren Ribao*, 15.10.79.
11 Xinhua in Chinese 23.4.81; Radio Chengdu, 5.6.81; Yao Yilin, Speech to NPC, 30.8.80.
12 Reuter, 23.8.79; *People's Daily*, 9.4.81.
13 *People's Daily*, 29.3.79, 25.6.79, 17.7.79 and 20.10.79.
14 *Asian Wall Street Journal*, 31.1.81.
15 *People's Daily*, 2.11.80.
16 Xinhua, 13.2.79; *People's Daily*, 7.2.80 and 8.2.80.
17 *People's Daily*, 19.2.79; see also *Gongren Ribao*, 24.5.80.
18 Jay Mathews in *International Herald Tribune*, 28.10.80.
19 Xinhua in Chinese, 20.11.79.
20 Wang Bingqian, Speech to NPC, op. cit. Xinhua in Chinese, 12.3.81.
21 *Gongren Ribao*, 3.2.79.
22 Xinhua, 6.11.80.
23 *Yangcheng Wanbao*, 5.10.80.
24 Xinhua in Chinese, 1.11.80; *China Reconstructs*, March 1981, p. 10.
25 Xinhua in Chinese, 9.11.79.
26 Xinhua in Chinese, 4.5.80; *Economic Management*, 15.8.80.
27 *People's Daily*, 13.10.80.
28 *People's Daily*, 2.6.81.
29 *Gongren Ribao*, 17.7.80 and 5.9.80; *People's Daily*, 4.7.79; Xinhua, 3.2.80 and 20.11.80.

30 Xinhua in Chinese, 9.6.81, and *Gongren Ribao*, 6.10.80 and 21.10.80; Xinhua, 19.7.81.
31 *Beijing Review*, No 21, 25.5.81.
32 Xinhua in Chinese, 19.8.80.
33 *People's Daily*, 19.6.80, Xinhua in Chinese, 6.6.81.
34 *Beijing Ribao*, 7.11.80.
35 *People's Daily*, 24.3.79, 3.10.80 and 9.4.81; Ibid, 11.2.81, 26.6.80, 11.8.80 and 19.4.81.
36 *People's Daily*, 15.12.80.
37 *Asian Wall Street Journal*, 12.12.80.
38 Ibid and *People's Daily*, 30.9.80.
39 See *Gongren Ribao*, 15.1.80.
40 Radio Changsha, 9.3.80.
41 Radio Guiyang, 20.7.80; *Red Flag*, No 20, October 1980.
42 Xinhua, 31.3.81, and *People's Daily*, 22.3.81.
43 Xinhua in Chinese, 27.1.81; *People's Daily*, 5.6.80.
44 Xinhua, 16.3.81; Radio Huhehot, 10.8.80; *Guangming Ribao*, 6.11.79.
45 Hua, Speech to NPC, 7.9.80.
46 Yao Yilin, Speech to NPC, op. cit.
47 Xinhua, 11.9.80.
48 *Le Monde*, 5.9.80.
49 Fox Butterfield, in *New York Times*, 5.9.80.
50 *International Herald Tribune*, 10.3.80.

CONFRONTATION

1 Radio Changsha, 18.4.79.
2 Xinhua, 29.9.79.
3 *Zheng Ming*, Hong Kong, No 29, 1.3.80.
4 *People's Daily*, 3.7.79.
5 Xinhua, 25.6.79.
6 *Guangming Ribao*, 12.9.79.
7 *People's Daily*, 14.9.79; Xinhua in Chinese, 26.10.79.
8 *People's Daily*, 5.10.79.
9 *Bangkok Post*, 10.2.80.
10 *Dongxiang*, No 17, Hong Kong, 16.2.80.
11 Xinhua, 1.3.80.
12 *Dongxiang*, No 17, Hong Kong, 16.2.80; and see Radio Nanjing, 21.12.79.
13 Xinhua, 1.3.80.
14 Dongxiang, No 17, Hong Kong, 16.2.80.
15 *People's Daily*, 10.3.80; *Ching Pao*, Hong Kong, No 3, 10.3.80.
16 See *Economist*, 7.7.56.
17 *Nanfang Ribao*, 28.3.80.
18 See *Lishi Yanjiu*, Nos 4 and 7, 1979, and *People's Daily*, 6.7.79; *Zheng Ming*, Hong Kong, No 28, 1.2.80.
19 Xinhua, 29.2.80.

20 *People's Daily*, 16.5.80.
21 *Dongxiang*, 16.5.80.
22 *Guangming Ribao*, 10.3.80; Xinhua, 14.3.80; *People's Daily*, 7.1.80.
23 *Guangming Ribao*, 7.3.80.
24 *Jiefang Junbao*, 6.12.79; *People's Daily*, 27.6.80.
25 Ibid, 27.11.79.
26 Xinhua, 11.8.80.
27 *People's Daily*, 10.3.80; Xinhua, 29.2.80 and 11.8.80; *Guangming Ribao*, 5.4.80.
28 *Da Gong Bao*, Hong Kong, 17.3.80 and 30.5.80.
29 *People's Daily*, 18.4.80.
30 Ibid, 21.4.80.
31 Ibid, 8.5.80.
32 *Guangming Ribao*, 11.5.80.
33 Xinhua, 16.2.80.
34 *People's Daily*, 5.6.79 and 3.8.79; Xinhua, 15.9.79.
35 *People's Daily*, 14.7.80.
36 *Gongren Ribao*, 17.6.80; *People's Daily*, 1.7.80; and *Chan Wang*, Hong Kong, No 461, 16.4.81.
37 *Zheng Ming*, Hong Kong, No 34, 1.8.80.
38 *People's Daily*, 27.8.80.
39 Xinhua, 12.7.80.
40 *People's Daily*, 8.7.80, 9.7.80 and 9.8.80.
41 *Guangming Ribao*, 5.8.80.
42 Xinhua, 7.9.80.
43 *People's Daily*, 18–19.9.80.
44 Xinhua, 29.9.80.
45 Ibid, 31.10.80.
46 See Xinhua, 18 and 19.9.80; *Guangming Ribao*, 20.9.80.
47 *Zheng Ming*, Hong Kong, No 37, 1.11.80.
48 See *Vjesnik*, Zagreb, 10.8.80.
49 *Washington Post*, August 1980.
50 *Zheng Ming*, Hong Kong, No 40, 1.2.81 and Xinhua, 29.6.81.
51 See Zhao Ziyang, Speech at Banquet for Djuranovic.

THE THIRD COLD WIND

1 *Democracy and Law*, Shanghai, May 1981.
2 Radio Peking and Peking Television, 12.12.80.
3 Peking Television, 29.12.80.
4 Xinhua, 29.12.80.
5 *People's Daily*, 15.12.80.
6 Ibid, 22.12.80.
7 *Gongren Ribao*, 5–6.12.80.
8 *Guangming Ribao*, 26.1.81.
9 *Red Flag*, July 1979.
10 Ibid, No 24, 16.12.80.
11 Xinhua in Chinese, 10.12.80.
12 *People's Daily*, 11.12.80.
13 *Guangming Radio*, 16.10.79 and 9.11.79.
14 *Wen Hui Bao*, 11.9.79.
15 *Guangming Ribao*, 9.11.79.
16 *People's Daily*, 22.11.79; see also Radio Chengdu, 1.11.79.
17 *Beijing Ribao*, 26.5.81; *People's Daily*, 15.7.80; and *Jiefang Ribao*, 10.1.81.
18 *Banyuetan*, 10.5.80.
19 Xinhua, 18.11.80.
20 *China Youth News*, 11.3.80.
21 Ibid, 6.8.81; and *Le Monde*, 13.10.79.
22 *Beijing Ribao*, 26.5.81.
23 *People's Daily*, 8.10.81.
24 *Jingji Yanjiu*, 20.1.81.
25 *Gongren Ribao*, 16.1.81; Xinhua in Chinese, 29.1.81.
26 Radio Canton, 26.12.80; see also *People's Daily*, 20.5.80 and Xinhua in Chinese, 22.11.80.
27 *People's Daily*, 2.6.81.
28 Quoted in *Asian Wall Street Journal*, 28.4.81; see also Xinhua, 25.4.81.
29 *Zheng Ming*, 1.3.80; *Jingji Yanjiu*, 20.1.81; *People's Daily*, 15.5.81.
30 *Jinghi Yanjiu*, 20.1.81.
31 *Zheng Ming*, Hong Kong, No 40, 1.2.81; *People's Daily*, 30.12.80, and *Da Gong Bao*, Hong Kong, 28.12.80.
32 Quoted by Radio Peking, 6.1.81.
33 Xinhua, 28.2.81.
34 Deng, Conversation with Yugoslav Foreign Minister, Josip Vrhovec, 31.5.81.
35 Central Committee Circular, 5.1.81.
36 Radio Canton, 22.11.80; *People's Daily*, 25.11.80. See also Radio Nanchang, 28.11.80.
37 Central Committee Circular, 5.1.81.
38 Radio Jinan, 30.4.81.
39 *Zheng Ming*, Hong Kong, No 37, 1.11.80.
40 *People's Daily*, 15.5.81; Xinhua in Chinese, 21.9.81 and 25.8.81.
41 Radio Kunming, 5.2.81; Xinhua in Chinese, 2.3.81; and *Da Gong Bao*, Hong Kong, 1.8.81.
42 *Bianjiang Wenyi*, No 12, December 1980; *Chanwang*, Hong Kong, 1.3.81.
43 *Jiefang Junbao*, 20.4.81.
44 *People's Daily*, 21.4.81; *Red Flag*, No 9, 1.5.81.
45 *Jiefang Junbao*, 15.5.81.
46 *People's Daily*, 22.6.81.
47 Radio Peking, 30.8.81.
48 *People's Daily*, 18.9.81.

DECENT BURIAL

1 Xinhua in Chinese, 4.2.81.
2 Central Committee Circular, 5.1.81.
3 'Resolution on Certain Questions in the History of Our Party since the Founding of the People's Republic of China', 30.6.81.
4 Guangming Ribao, 6.8.80; Beijing Wanbao, 27.8.80.
5 Chinese Foreign Ministry Spokesman, 22.4.81.
6 See also Huang Kecheng, Xinhua in Chinese, 10.4.81, and Hu Yaobang, Xinhua, 1.7.81.
7 Let History Judge, by Roy Medvedev, Macmillan, London, 1972, p. 564.
8 Guangming Ribao, 17.10.80.
9 Xinhua, 15.7.81.
10 Central Committee Circular, 5.1.81.
11 Xinhua in Chinese, 10.4.81.
12 People's Daily, 6.7.81.
13 Xinhua in Chinese, 15.7.81.
14 People's Daily, 20.7.81 and 21.7.81.
15 Xinhua, 1.7.81.
16 Xinhua, 3.5.81.
17 People's Daily, 3.2.81.
18 Ibid, 8.6.79.
19 Economic Management, Peking, 15.7.80.
20 Xinhua, 1.4.81.
21 Quoted in Robert Conquest, Russia after Khrushchev, Pall Mall, London, 1965, p. 49.
22 Red Flag, 1.11.80.

Part V: The Politics of Power

1 Zheng Ming, Hong Kong, 1.3.80, and Tass, 23.9.80.
2 Pravda, September 1968.
3 Francis Pym, Speech to Atlantic Treaty Association, London, 30.9.81.
4 Economist, 5.1.80.
5 Pym, op. cit.
6 International Herald Tribune, 2.1.80.
7 Speech to Los Angeles World Affairs Council, 9.5.80.
8 International Herald Tribune, 21.10.81.
9 Press Conference, 13.10.81.
10 The Times, April 1980.
11 Henry Kissinger, The White House Years, op. cit., p. 171.
12 Xinhua in English, 7.10.79.
13 Ibid, 16.5.79, 21.10.80; and 1.6.79.
14 People's Daily, 17.6.81.
15 Eugene Rostow, Speech to the Atlantic Treaty Association, London, 30.9.81.
16 Beijing Review, No 9, 3.3.72, pp. 4–5.
17 Ming Bao, Hong Kong, 25.8.81.
18 New York Times, 6.1.81, and International Herald Tribune, 5.5.81.

Index

Abakumov, Viktor, 205
advertisements, 309–11
Afghanistan: Soviet invasion of, 10, 112, 465–9, 472–7, 480, 484
agriculture: productivity levels, 26, 222; in USSR, 267, 411, 414; in China, 397, 408–10; *see also* peasants
Akhmadulina, Bella A., 66
Akhmatova, Anna, 5
alcoholism, 28–9, 40, 67–8, 70, 102
Aleksanyants, Kirill, 20
Alexandra, Tsarina, 37
Aliger, Margaret, 365
Aluminum Company of America, 474
Amalrik, Andrei, 305
Amin, Hafizollah, 465
Amnesty International, 113, 354, 363
Andropov, Yuri, 34, 113
Angola, 467–8
animals, treatment of, 102
anti-Semitism, 59, 266; *see also* Jews
April 5th Tribune (magazine), 259–61, 291–2, 330, 338, 357
Armenia, 60
art and artists: in USSR, 66–7, 346; in China, 67, 218–19, 345–7, 440
Ashraf, Princess, of Iran, 138
Azerbaijan, 127

Ba Jin, 160, 222
Baader-Meinhof gang, 265
Bagirov, Mikhail, 205
Bai Hua, 149, 163, 359–60, 373, 448–50
Bai Rubing, 446
Bai Yun, 156–7
banks, 404, 409
bao-jia, 71
Bao Wenli, 369
Baoshan steelworks, 406
Baryshnikov, Mikhail, 66
Beijing Ribao, see *Peking Daily*

Beijing Zhichun, 222
Belhomme, Albert, 166
Belov, Vasily, 66
Beria, Lavrenti, 5, 191–2, 203–5, 265–6, 269
bicycles, 93–4, 105
Bierut, Boleslaw, 136, 326
Binyon, Michael, 128
birth control, 23–4, 38, 41
birthrates, 92
Bitter Love (film), 448–50
black market, 126–8, 311
blacks (Negroes), 57–8; *see also* racialism
blat, 126–8
Blok, Alexander, 34
Bo Yibo, 182–3
Boxer Rebellion, 50, 189
Brecht, Bertolt, 150
Brezhnev, Leonid: successors, 2, 9, 13, 461, 464; printed speeches, 29; regime, 30, 34, 289, 413, 461; imports Western technology, 51; and Russian nationalism, 60; and housing, 81; earnings, 85; and Nixon's visit, 109; meets Gerald Ford, 116; rise to power, 117; nepotism, 119; and scandals, 133; motor cars, 136; *dacha*, 137; stops confidential documents, 139; in Politburo, 203, 283; and law, 380, 385; agricultural policy, 414; satirised, 461; on nuclear danger, 465, 471; and foreign relations, 467; doctrine, 480; and clash with China, 481
bribery *see* corruption
British Broadcasting Corporation, 301
Brokans, Emiljans, 29
Brown, Harold, 480
Brzezinsky, Zbigniew, 293, 469
Buddhism, 46–7
Bukharin, Nikolai I., 146, 162, 167, 278
Bulganin, Nikolai, Marshal, 268, 415

503

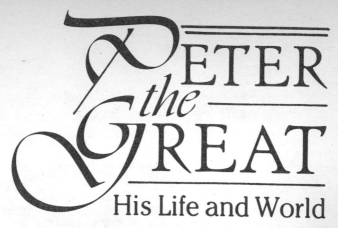

PETER the GREAT

His Life and World

The Pulitzer Prize-winning Biography by

ROBERT K. MASSIE

Peter the Great combined the advanced skills
and learning of seventeenth century Europe
with the raw material of the largest nation on
earth to forge an empire that dominated both
East and West. Despite his progressive and
enlightened attitudes towards science and the
state, Peter was a barbarous feudal tsar with a
personal love of torture. His character –
volatile, restless, far-sighted and cruel –
embodied the greatest strengths and weaknesses
of Russia. This long-awaited biography is a
superb full-length portrait of the man
in his time.

BIOGRAPHY   0 349 12281 4   £5.95

PATRICK MARNHAM

DISPATCHES FROM AFRICA

'We fear Africa because when we leave it alone, it works,'
says the author of this provocative book. Patrick
Marnham shows how outsiders – British, Russian,
American, French and Chinese – have repeatedly tried to
alter a land they do not understand. The relief workers,
scientists, businessmen, tourists and conservationists all
roam through Africa wreaking havoc as they go,
attempting to mould the continent into their numerous
images and ideals. Here are the elephants of Kenya and
their predators, the game wardens; the West African
outposts and their swollen populations of refugees; the
tourists of Africa, who come to enjoy the 'primitive life'
by observing a tribe which is desperately trying to flee
from them; the citizens of Bamako, building their houses
at night only to watch them being bulldozed the next
morning; and Gambia, a country of eight barristers and
no psychiatrists, where the British Ambassador's grant
ignored the inadequate hospitals and instead equipped a
new cricket team.

DISPATCHES FROM AFRICA reveals a country
beset by illogical boundaries, horribly mismanaged
financial aid and comically incompetent government
structures. But the true brilliance of the book is its ability
to allow still another Africa to seep through. The Africa of
powerful ideas and raw energy which, for reasons of
politics and ignorance, have gone awry. This Africa is a
land of Northern ineptitude superimposed on an inherent
native harmony.

'This shrewd, acrid book is an excellent antidote to the usual
guff written on Africa' *Sunday Telegraph*

WORLD AFFAIRS   0 349 12280 6   £1.95

IRELAND
a history
ROBERT KEE

the book of the major
BBC/RTE Television series

'A careful, well-balanced, sensitive book, the fruit of
long, fascinated reflection over its subject matter; it
is warmly to be recommended, not only to those who
know little or nothing about Irish history, but also,
and especially to those who think they know a lot
about it . . . an excellent book.'
Conor Cruise O'Brien, OBSERVER.

'His achievement is to explain, lucidly and vividly,
the bloodiness of the conflict . . . he is twice the man
in print.' SUNDAY TIMES.

In the book of the successful, and often controversial, television series, Robert Kee examines the
'prison of Irish history', going back to its very
beginnings to identify the principal groups involved
in modern Ireland. He traces the emergence of each
group and their links over the ages, establishing how
past facts have bred present myths.

HISTORY   0 349 12081 1   £5.95

RULE BRITANNIA

JAMES BELLINI

In 1086 the Domesday Survey charted Britain's power structure. It found the rich man in his castle and the poor man at his gate. Nine centuries later only the cast has changed.

After a two-hundred-year stint as the workshop of the world, industrial Britain is finished. As the once solid manufacturing base shatters into permanent unemployment and street war, two strong areas of stability and profit remain – land and the new information technologies.

In this scathingly controversial survey, economist and broadcaster James Bellini argues that Britain is splitting into two nations: one for lords in computer castles and one for rack-rent serfs.

The division has already begun. In the new feudal state Britons *can* be slaves.

CURRENT AFFAIRS   0 349 10299 6   £2.75

JAROSLAV HAŠEK

THE RED COMMISSAR

Truant, rebel, vagabond, play-actor, anarchist, practical joker, bohemian (and Bohemian), alcoholic, traitor, bigamist and Red Commissar, Jaroslav Hasek is best known as the creator of the Idiot of the Company, the Good Soldier Svejk. THE RED COMMISSAR shows that Svejk was not Hasek's only great comic achievement.

As well as the earliest Svejk stories, this collection contains Hasek's riotous account of the troubled life of a Red Commissar in Russia and numerous other stories satirising bureaucratic idiocy and pomposity which ring as true now as when they were written. Whether slapstick or political parody Hasek's comedy is sharp, humane and very funny.

FICTION   0 349 11645 8   £2.95

Other titles available from ABACUS

All Abacus books are available at your local bookshop or newsagent, or can be ordered direct from the publisher. Just tick the titles you want and fill in the form below.

Name _____

Address _____

_____

Write to Abacus Books, Cash Sales Department, P.O. Box 11, Falmouth, Cornwall TR10 9EN

Please enclose cheque or postal order to the value of the cover price plus:

UK: 45p for the first book plus 20p for the second book and 14p for each additional book ordered to a maximum charge of £1.63.

OVERSEAS: 75p for the first book plus 21p per copy for each additional book.

BFPO & EIRE: 45p for the first book, 20p for the second book plus 14p per copy for the next 7 books, thereafter 8p per book.

Abacus Books reserve the right to show new retail prices on covers which may differ from those previously advertised in the text or elsewhere, and to increase postal rates in accordance with the PO.

113
239411